Das Beste aus dem Vogtland

Band II

Leistung trifft auf Leidenschaft

The Very Best of Vogtland

Volume II

Performance meets Passion

Verlag
Herausgeber/Published by

Von Mensch zu Mensch A Personal Word	Interview mit dem Landrat des Vogtlandkreises Dr. Tassilo Lenk (Marjon Thümmel) Interview with the chief administrative officer of the Vogtland District, Dr. Tassilo Lenk	6-9
	Dr. Rüdiger Kroll: Emanzipation, Innovation und Führung (André Zeidler) / Emancipation, Innovation and Leadership	10-11
	Ein Holzfäller und Intendant – Alexander Iljinskij besuchte für „SuperIllu" seine Heimat The Vogtland people are a plucky mountain people – Alexander Iljinskij Visited His Home District for the "SuperIllu"	12-13
	Peter Maffay und das Vogtland / Peter Maffay and the Vogtland Region	14-16
Wirtschaftstradition A Traditional Business Region	Ideen und Innovationen haben Tradition im Land der grünen Auen (Bert Walther) Ideas and Innovations Are a Tradition in the Land of Green Meadows	17-18
POLLER Unternehmensgruppe	Kompetenz und Leistung ohne Umwege / Direct Expertise and Service	19
HTR Reichenbach GmbH	Wir machen Leistung sichtbar / The Fruit of Our Labours is Visible	20
BSV Beteiligungsgesellschaft	Wir investieren in das Wachstum unserer Region / We Are Investing in the Growth of Our Region	21
Made in Vogtland Vogtland Economy	Stärken und Dynamik – die Wirtschaft im Vogtland (André Zeidler) The Vogtland Economy – Strong and Dynamic	22-24
ENKA in Elsterberg	100 Jahre Werk Elsterberg / Centenary at Elsterberg Factory	25
SGB in Neumark	Die Neumarker SGB GmbH sorgt weltweit für Power / SGB GmbH in Neumark Delivers Power World-wide	26
Nema AirFin in Netzschkau	Mit Wärmetauschern weltweit gutes Renommee / Excellent world-wide reputation for heat exchangers	27
J. Steiniger Metallwarenfabrik	Wer nicht kämpft, der hat schon verloren / Without a Fight You Lose Anyway	28-29
Ertex Jacquard Rodewisch	So fein webt niemand / There is No Finer Weave	30-31
GK SOFTWARE AG Schöneck	High Tech für den Handel / High Tech for international Retailers	32
IK Elektronik GmbH	Ohne Kabel aber mit viel Energie / Wireless but with Plenty of Energy	34-35
NARVA Speziallampen in Plauen	NARVA Speziallampen GmbH in Plauen / Tradition meets Innovation	36
Theumaer Fruchtschiefer	Naturstein mit Charakter / "Theuma Slate" – Natural Stone with Character	37
Meiser Gitterroste KG	MEISER – weltweit in 25 Ländern aktiv und auch engagiert im Vogtland / MEISER – worldwide in 25 countries and is also engaged in the Vogtland	38-39
ALSTOM in Neumark	In Neumark hat der Kesselbau Tradition / Neumark has a tradition of boiler manufacture	40-41
Kunststofftechnik Schedel	Kunststofftechnik Schedel – ein Unternehmen auf dem Vormarsch / Schedel Plastics – a Company Forging Ahead	42-43
TUBETECH GmbH	Eine Erfolgsgeschichte mit klarem Bekenntnis zur Region / A Success Story with a Clear Commitment to the Region	44-47
Kunststofftechnik Kainath	Kompetenz in punkto Schweißtechnik / Expertise in Welding Engineering	48
BANG Kransysteme	Dem Himmel ein Stück näher / A Little Closer to the Sky	49
Maschinenbau / Engineering	Der Wirtschaftsfaktor Maschinenbau / Engineering as an Economic Factor	50-55
AUERBACH Maschinenfabrik	Tradition und Innovation, Kompetenz und Flexibilität / Tradition and Innovation, Competence and Flexibility	56-57
WEMA VOGTLAND GmbH	Wema Vogtland GmbH startet durch! / Wema Vogtland Turns the Corner!	58-59
Modellbau Roth in Theuma	Eine Sache der Form / A Question of Shape	60
LEHMANN-UMT GmbH	Innovation für die Zukunft – Maschinenbau auf höchstem Niveau / Innovation for the future – mechanical engineering at the highest level	61
Automobile Kompetenz Automobile Expertise	Im Spannungsfeld des Automobils (Christian Suhr) At the Centre of the Automobile Industry	62-75
Magnetto Automotive Deutschland GmbH	Mit italienischem Charme ein Presswerk zum Erfolg gebracht Italian Charm Brings Success to a Press Shop	76-77

HAL Automotive Plauen	Know-how-Teile ... präzise und pünktlich /	Skilfully Produced Parts ... Precise and on Time	78-79
AIW	Der Fortschritt braucht Bewegung /	Flexibility is Needed to Move Ahead	80
Weidmann in Treuen	Vom Vogtland aus den Markt erobert /	To capture the market from the Vogtland	81
Stol f ig GmbH Pausa	Wir machen alles was kommt /	We Do Anything That Comes	82
C. H. Mül ler	Bewährtes und Know-how verbinden /	Combining Proven Methods and Expertise	83
Autohaus Meinhold	Tradition und Fortschritt kennzeichnen unser Unternehmen. /	Tradition and Progress Are the Hallmarks of Our Company.	84
Autohaus OPPEL	Marken versprechen! Aber sie verpflichten auch. /	Brands Promise Much – But Have to Deliver the Goods.	85
Autohaus Strauß	Das Plus an Leistung macht den Unterschied /	The Extra Service Makes the Difference	86-87
Seidenweberei PONGS	Der Stoff, aus dem Faszination gemacht wird /	The Material that Creates a Sense of Fascination	88
Innovation Textil	Technischen Textilien gehört die Zukunft /	Technical Textiles Have a Great Future	89
Westsächsische Hochschule	Textil- und Ledertechnik – eine Tradition mit Zukunft /	Textiles and Leather Engineering – a Tradition with a Future	90
(FH) HT Reichenbach	Fundierte Ausbildung – Visionen erlaubt /	Well-Founded Training – and Visions Are Allowed	91
DIPLOMA Studienzentrum PL	Studienzentrum Plauen der DIPLOMA Fachhochschule Nordhessen – Zukunftssicherung für Unternehmen		92-93
	The Plauen College of the North Hessen DIPLOMA Vogtland University of Applied Sciences – Ensuring Companies have a Future		
bsw Regionalzentrum	Partner der Unternehmen /	A Partner for Companies	94
Fachkräfteausbildung	Unser wertvollstes Kapital /	OUR MOST VALUABLE RESOURCE	95
Training Ski l led Personnel			
Bildungsnetzwerk	Stärken verbinden /	Linking up Strong Points	96
bsw Bildungszentrum Rb.	Beste Chancen im Beruf /	The Best Professional Opportunities	97
MedFachschule Bad Elster	Stärke durch Vorsprung /	Strength through Being One Step Ahead	98
IWB Plauen	Erfolg bedeutet: Mehr zu tun als notwendig! /	Success Means: Doing More Than the Minimum!	99
e.o.plauen	Kompetent in Technik und Design /	Vocational School Centre e.o.plauen – Competence in Technology and Design	100
Fördergesellschaft	Erfolgreich auf das Berufsleben vorbereiten /	Successfully Preparing People for Their Professional Careers	101
Bildungslandschaft im Vogt-	In die Bildung investieren – das heißt Zukunft gestalten.		102/104
land/ Education in Vogtland	INVESTING IN EDUCATION – SHAPING THE FUTURE		
Mittelschule und Gymnasium	Oelsnitz/Vogtl. Das macht Schule /	Off to School	103
Futurum Gymnasium	Freiraum für Persönlichkeit (Petra Steps)/	Scope for Personalities to Develop	105-106
Familie und Soziales	Kindertagesstätten der AWO Fähigkeiten sind nichts ohne Möglichkeiten.		107
The Family and Social Af fairs	Abilities Are Nothing without Opportunities.		
Kita-Projekte	Vom Kopf bis zum Herzen – ganzheitliche Bildung /	FROM HEAD TO HEART – INTEGRATED CHILDCARED	108-109
ARGE-Projekte	„Vital ab 50" und „VOR JU ALL" /	LABOUR AGENCY WORKING GROUP PROJECTS	110-111
	IN THE VOGTLAND DISTRICT FOR OLD AND YOUNG		
Gesundheitsregion Vogtland	Gesundheitsregion Vogtland / Vogtland Health Region /	Vogtland Health Region	112-115
Vogtland Health Region			
Klinikum Obergöltzsch	Rundum gut versorgt /	In Very Good Hands	116-117
SKH Rodewisch	Im Mittelpunkt steht der Mensch /	People are the Focus of Attention	118-119
Kur & Rehabilitation			
Spa Facilities and Rehabilitation			
BGK Falkenstein	Nachhaltige Gesundung in der grünen Lunge des Vogtlandes /	Long-term Recovery in the Natural Vogtland Air	120-121
Klinik Bad Brambach	Klinik Bad Brambach: Mit Radon gegen Rheuma /	Bad Brambach Clinic – Fighting Rheumatism with Radon	122
Klinik am Brunnenberg Bad Elster	Gesundheit gewinnen - Vitalität erleben - Erholung genießen /	Gaining Health - Experiencing Vitality - Enjoying Relaxation	123

	Wir setzen alles in Bewegung **We Get Everything Moving**	Immer nah für Sie da / Always Available Locally	124
	DB Regio	Zukunft braucht Bewegung / Mobility is Essential for the Future	125
	Die Vogtlandbahn	Beste Verbindungen durch Engagement und Leidenschaft für die Schiene / THE BEST CONNECTIONS FOR RAIL TRAVEL ACHIEVED THROUGH COMMITMENT AND ENTHUSIASM	126-127
	Plauen – eine Reise wert **Plauen - Worth a Visit**	Einkaufen im Plauener Zentrum / Shopping in the City of Plauen	128
	Stadtgalerie Plauen	Einkaufsmagnet für das Vogtland / Shopping Magnet for the Vogtland Region	129
	In Plauen gut unterwegs **In good hands in Plauen**	Plauen - die Stadt in der „Klingenden Ferienregion Vogtland" / Plauen – the City in the "Vogtland Musical Holiday Region"	130-132
		PSB und SBG Ihre kommunalen Partner für Mobilität in und um Plauen / Your Local Mobility Partners in and around Plauen	133
	Oelsnitz/Vogtland	Altes Bewahren – Neues wagen / Cherishing the Old – Daring the New	134-136
		SWOE Kompetenz in Sachen Energie / Competence in Energy	137
		Elstergarten: Freizeit, Sport und Erholung / Leisure, Sport and Relaxation	138
		Katharinenkirche: Eine Gabe für nachfolgende Generationen / A Gift to Future Generations	139
		9,5 Kilometer Akten ziehen um in das Schloss Voigtsberg / 9.5 Kilometres of Files Move into Voigtsberg Castle	140-141
	Klingenthal	Musik- und Wintersportstadt / Music and Winter Sports Town	142-143
	Treuen	Internationaler Wirtschaftsstandort / International Business Centre in the Centre of the Vogtland Region	144-145
	Auerbach	Mehr als drei Türme / More than Three Towers	146-147
	Rodewisch	Lebendig, dynamisch, fortschrittlich und traditionell zugleich / Living, Dynamic, Progressive and Yet Still Traditional	148-149
	Falkenstein	Die Kleinstadt mit dem großstädtischen Flair / The Small Town with the Flair of a City	150
	ERFAL Falkenstein	An die Spitze durch Innovationen und besten Service / At the Top because of Innovations and the Best Service	151
	VOBA Hammerbrücke	Im Mittelpunkt der Mensch / People are the Main Focus	152
	Schweiker Grünbach	Arbeiten wo andere Urlaub machen / Working Where Others Go on Holiday	153
	Grünbach	Natürlich, fröhlich und traditionell / Natural, pleasant and traditional	154-155
	Erlbach	Familienfreundlich, grün, erholsam und beständig / Family-friendly, Green, Relaxing and Stable	156-157
		Das Beste aus Erlbach / The Best of Erlbach	158-160
		Vogtländisches Freilichtmuseum Eubabrunn: Lebendige Traditionen / Living Traditions	161
	Elsterberg	Elsterberg – im grünen Tal der Weißen Elster / Elsterberg – in the Green Valley of the "Weisse Elster"	162-163
	Mylau	Geschichte bewahren, Zukunft gestalten / Enshrine History, Design Future	164-165
	Gutes für Leib und Seele **Good for Body and Soul**	Was gut schmeckt im Vogtland	166-167
	Adler-Tropfen	Der Tradition im Vogtland verbunden / Keeping up Traditions in the Vogtland Region	168
	Wernesgrüner Pils Legende	Über 570 Jahre Brautradition / More than 570 Years of Brewing Tradition	169
	Unilver Werk Auerbach	Die beste Instantsuppen-Fabrik in Europa / The Best Instant Soup Factory in Europe	170
	Agro-Dienst-Marktfrucht	Sensibel, modern, verantwortungsbewusst - Landwirtschaft im Vogtland / Sensitive, Modern, Responsible – Agriculture in the Vogtland Region	171
	Jacob's Bauernmarkt	Vom Bauern direkt - das schmeckt / Direct from the Farm – with a Great Taste	172
	Gläserner Bauernhof	Ein Ort der Bildung, Begegnung & Entspannung / A place of Education, Encounters & Recreation	173
	Landwirtschaft/Farming	Landwirtschaft ist unser Leben. / FARMING IS OUR LIFE	174-175
	Klopfermühle	Guter Geschmack aus Tradition (Petra Steps) / A Great Traditional Taste	176-177
	Erneuerbare Energien **Renewable Energies**	Auf dem Weg zur energieautarken Region / On the Way to Becoming a Self-Sufficient Region in Energy	178-179
	BRUNNER Holzsolarhaus	Sicher – das Haus der Zukunft / A Good Investment – the House of the Future	180
	J. Chemnitz Pausa	Regionaler Marktführer für Solartechnik und alternative Energien / Regional Market Leader for Solar Technology and Alternative Energy Sources	181

🟩	Natur und Umwelt / Nature and the Environment	EVV: Wir machen Ihren Abfall zu unserer Sache. / We Make Your Waste Our Business.	182-183
		ZWAV: Wasser und Abwasser – alles aus einer Hand / Water and Sewage – Everything from One Source	184-185
⬛	Natürliche Ressourcen / Natural Resources	Talsperren im Vogtland (B. Kempe-Winkelmann) / Reservoirs in the Vogtland District	186-193
		Der Naturpark Erzgebirge/Vogtland / The Ore Mountains/Vogtland National	194-196
		Schützenswert / Worth Protecting	197-199
		NUZ: Von der Natur lernen / Learning from Nature	200-203
		Orgelpfeifen für Putin (Petra Steps) / Organ Pipes for President Putin	204
🟥	Gelebte Traditionen / Traditions Perpetuated	Kunst kommt von Können (Petra Steps) / Ability Gives Birth to Art	205
		Echte Handarbeit spricht sich rum (Petra Steps) / Word Gets Around about Real Craftsmanship	206
		Kompetenz lässt Leistung reifen / Expertise Allows Performances to Mature	207
		Expertise Allows Performances to Mature (Ekkehard Glass) / Tradition Means Passing Things	208-211
	Fohlenhof Schöniger	Mekka des Sports (Marjon Thümmel) / The Mecca for Sports Lies in the Vogtland Region	212-213
		Da liegt Musik im Blut (Petra Steps) / When Music Runs in the Blood	214
		Musikschule hat eine lange Tradition im Vogtland / Music Schools have a Long Tradition in the Vogtland	215
		Ein Dorf im SR2-Fieber (B. Kempe-Winkelmann) / A Village in SR2 Fever	216
	Horchmuseum	Die Erinnerung an August Horch in Reichenbach wird gewahrt. / The Memory of August Horch Is Being Kept Alive in Reichenbach.	217
	„De Gockesche"	Vogtländischer Volksmusikverein pflegt Traditionen (B. Kempe-Winkelmann) / Vogtland Traditional Music Club Fosters Traditions	218
	Landfrauen	Schönes bewahren und Leidenschaften pflegen (Petra Steps) / Preserving Beauty and Cultivating Passion	219
	Spitzenmuseum Plauen	Das Plauener Spitzenmuseum / The Plauen Lace Museum	220
	Prinzessinnen	Adel verpflichtet - Schönheit ist nicht genug (Petra Steps) / High Class Brings Responsibilities – Beauty Is Not Enough	221
🟥	Menschen mit Format / People of Calibre	Ein edles Beispiel macht die schweren Taten leicht (Marjon Thümmel) / A GOOD EXAMPLE MAKES DIFFICULT TASKS EASY.	222
		Wolfgang Mattheuer: Gesicht zeigen (Petra Steps) / Show Your True Colours	223-224
		Thomas Kropff - Weltenbummler mit vogtländischen Wurzeln (Petra Steps) / Globe Trotter with Vogtland Roots	225
	Schicki-Micki	Der „weltgrößte Zuckertütenshop" (Petra Steps) / The "Largest Cone-Shaped Sweet Package Shop in the World"	226
	Annemarie Schramm	Leuchtturm e. V. (Petra Steps) / "Lighthouse" Association	227
	Beate Schad	Erfahrungen und Leidenschaft weitergeben (B. Kempe-Winkelmann) / Passing on Experience and Enthusiasm	228
	Raum für Kunst / Room for Art	Kulturraum – Raum für Kultur (Ekkehard Glaß) / Room for Art	229-234
		Landwirtschaft küsst Muse (Petra Steps) / FARMING INSPIRED BY LIGHT ENTERTAINMENT	235
	Christoph Krumbiegel	Ideen werden phantastische Wirklichkeit (Petra Steps) / When Ideas become Fantastic Reality	236
	Maren Schwarz	Täterin im Geiste (Petra Steps) / Täterin im Geiste	237
	Malerin Söllner-Burr	Malerin Susanne Söllner-Burr (B. Kermpe-Winkelmann) / Painter Susanne Söllner-Burr	238
	Mario Urlaß	– Kunst, die begeistert (Petra Steps) / – Art that Delights Others	238
	Jörg Halsema	Ideen werden phantastische Wirklichkeit (Petra Steps) / Von einem, der seine Ideen zu bewegten Bildern macht	240
	Familie Seidel / Orgelvesper	Ein ganzes Leben mit der Musik (B. Kermpe-Winkelmann) / A WHOLE LIFE WITH MUSIC	241
	Vogtland-Philharmonie	Gute Musik ist der kürzeste Weg in die Herzen (Ekkehard Glaß) / Good Music is the Quickest Way to People's Hearts	242-245
🟥	Kunst und Kultur	Vogtland Kultur GmbH: Kultur erleben im Vogtland / Culture to experience in the Vogtland	246-249
🟦	Touristische Höhepunkte / Tourist Highlights	Das Vogtland – die klingende Ferienregion (Tourismusverband) / The Vogtland Region – the Musical Holiday Area	250-252
		Bad Elster und Bad Brambach – Wellness, Kuren, Kultur & Sport / – Wellness, Spas, Culture & Sports	253
	Chursächsische	Chursächsische Veranstaltungs GmbH: Kultur- und Festspielstadt Bad Elster / The Cultural and Festival Town of Bad Elster	254-255
	IFA-Schöneck Hotel & Ferienpark	So machen Ferien Spaß / How to Enjoy your Holiday!	256-257
	Schöneck	So schön ist Schöneck – und das zu jeder Jahreszeit / Schöneck is Beautiful – at Any Time of the Year	258-259
	Deutsche Raumfahrtausstellung	Der Himmel auf Erden (Ekkehard Glaß) / Heaven on Earth – The German Space Travel Exhibition	260-262
	Unter Tage	Blick in die Unterwelt (Petra Steps) / Glimpse into the Underworld	263-264
	Musikinstrumentenmuseum	Marknechkirchen: Ein besonderes Handwerk hautnah erleben / Experiencing Special Skills Close Up	265
	Goldmuseum	Goldmuseum (Petra Steps) / The Vogtland Gold Museum in Buchwald – A True El Dorado	266
	Bergbaumuseum	Bergbau hautnah (Petra Steps) / Mining Museum – Mining from Close Up	267
	Schloss Schönberg	Ein Besuch lohnt sich (Petra Steps) / Schönberg Castle – Worth a Visit	268
	Ausflugtipps	Musikinstrumentenmuseum: Das kleinste der Welt, Schloss Leubnitz, Müllerburschenweg (B. Kermpe-Winkelmann)	269-271

Interview mit dem Landrat des Vogtlandkreises Dr. Tassilo Lenk
Interview with the chief administrative officer of the Vogtland District, Dr. Tassilo Lenk

Jede Region „buhlt" angesichts fehlender Arbeitsplätze um die Ansiedlung neuer Unternehmen. Was hat das Vogtland, was andere nicht haben?

Landrat: Hervorragende infrastrukturelle Bedingungen in einem Vierländereck, das in dieser Wettbewerbsform einmalig ist in Europa. Hier gibt es top Fachkräfte und eine Bildungslandschaft, die ständig für qualifizierten Nachschub auch im mittleren und oberen Management sorgen kann. Ansiedlung heißt auch Zuzug von Familien, die sich hier wohlfühlen sollen. Und dafür haben wir im Vogtland eine Menge zu bieten.

Wie viele Unternehmen haben sich in den vergangen fünf Jahren im Vogtlandkreis angesiedelt?

Landrat: Rund 15 mit perspektivisch 2.000 bis 3.000 Arbeitsplätzen.

Every region is seeking to attract new companies to the area to compensate for the lack of jobs available. What does the Vogtland region have, which sets it apart from other regions?

Lenk: Excellent infrastructure at a location where four states meet; this is a unique situation in Europe in this battle to impress companies. There are top specialists here and training facilities, which can constantly provide qualified young workers – at middle and senior management level too. Attracting companies also means that families move in and they should feel at home here. We have plenty to offer them here in the Vogtland region.

How many companies have set up in business in the Vogtland district over the past five years?

Lenk: About 15 with the prospect of creating 2,000-3,000 jobs.

(Fotos/Photos by Igor Pastierovic, Text/Text by Marjon Thümmel, Übersetzung/Translated by David Strauss)

Braucht es noch die Wirtschaftsförderung oder reicht die Mundpropaganda der Unternehmen?

Landrat: Das Unternehmer-Wort hat ein großes Gewicht. Unstrittig wichtig ist aber die Wirtschaftsförderung, weil sie die Rahmenbedingungen schaffen muss. Für mich ist die Schaffung neuer Arbeitsplätze weiterhin Chefsache. Wenn Familien Arbeit haben, dann gibt es sozialen Frieden und auch einen positiven Blick in die Zukunft.

Legen Sie auch das gleiche Augenmerk auf den Mittelstand?

Landrat: Der Mittelstand ist der Schatz der Region. Ich fühle mich gar nicht so richtig wohl, wenn wir große Ansiedlungen besonders feiern, weil auch das Engagement der regionalen mittleren und kleinen Unternehmen riesig ist, sie fleißig ihr Tagwerk tun und unbemerkt erweitert haben. Da fallen mir sofort 42 Betriebe ein.

Gibt es einen Wandel im Vogtlandkreis von Landwirtschaft hin zum Industriestandort?

Landrat: Es gilt beides gut abzuwägen. Die Landwirtschaft beklagt sich bereits über den Flächenverzehr. Wo möglich, sollten alte Industriebrachen abgerissen, versiegelte Flächen wieder nutzbar gemacht werden als Ausgleich für neuen Flächenverzehr. Auch muss nicht ständig mehr Aufforstung als Ausgleichsmaßnahme geschehen, sondern diese Fläche weiter für landwirtschaftliche Nutzungen bereit stehen.

Die Neuansiedlungen konzentrieren sich also vorwiegend an der Autobahn, andere gehen leer aus ...

Landrat: Wir bieten Investoren zuallererst dezentrale Flächen an. Doch unumstritten ist die Autobahnnähe für Unternehmen ein Ko-Argument, dem wir uns nicht verschließen können. Fakt ist aber auch, dass ein etwa 30 Kilometer langer Arbeitsweg heute nichts Ungewöhnliches ist. In einem solchen Radius sind die Unternehmen in den Gewerbegebieten von nahezu allen Orten des Vogtlandes aus zu erreichen.

Bald öffnen sich die Grenzen zu Tschechien ...

Landrat: Verwaltungsgrenzen müssen weg. Sie beschreiben den Integrationsgrad einer Region, Tradition und Brauchtum, aber sie sind unwichtig für zusammenwachsende Arbeits- und Wirtschaftsmärkte. Und in diesen liegt unser Entwicklungspotenzial. Wir müssen mehr lernen, über die starren Verwaltungsgrenzen hinaus zu denken, Planungen und Raumdenken auf die Herausforderung der Zukunft zu richten und nicht mit Instrumentarien des klassischen Industriezeitalters antworten. Hier ist noch viel zu tun.

Do we still need business development schemes or is word of mouth from the companies enough?

Lenk: Recommendations from companies are enormously important. But without any doubt, business development schemes continue to be important because they create the general conditions. My top priority is still creating jobs. If families are in work, there is no conflict in society and people can view the future positively.

Are you paying the same attention to medium-sized companies?

Lenk: Medium-sized enterprises are the gem of this region. I do not feel all that comfortable if we particularly celebrate the arrival of a large company, because the commitment of medium-sized and small enterprises in the region is enormous – they go about their daily work efficiently and have grown without anybody noticing. I can immediately think of 42 such companies.

Are we witnessing a change in the Vogtland district from agriculture to an industrial location?

Lenk: Both need to be considered carefully. Agriculture is already complaining about the loss of land. Wherever possible, old industrial plant should be demolished and what was developed land should be made available for use again to compensate for any destruction of agricultural land. Reforestation must not immediately take place, but this land should be made available for agricultural use.

Most new companies are setting up in business near the motorway – does this mean that other regions have no chance?

Lenk: We initially offer investors more remote areas. But there is no doubt that proximity to the motorway is an element for companies and we cannot close our eyes to this fact. But it is also true that it is not unusual for people to travel about 30 kilometres to work nowadays. So the companies on the business parks can be reached from any part of the Vogtland region.

The border with the Czech Republic will soon be open...

Lenk: Administrative restrictions must be dismantled. They describe the degree of integration in any region, traditions and customs, but they are not important for jobs and business markets that are growing together. And this is where our development potential lies. We have to learn how to think beyond rigid administrative restrictions, direct our planning and spatial concepts towards the challenges of the future and not respond with tools that were part of the classical industrial period. We still have a lot to do here.

» *Hier gibt es top Fachkräfte und eine Bildungslandschaft, die ständig für qualifizierten Nachschub auch im mittleren und oberen Management sorgen kann.* «

» *There are top specialists here and training facilities, which can constantly provide qualified young workers – at middle and senior management level too.* «

Welche Industriezweige werden in Zukunft im Vogtland vorherrschen?

Landrat: Zunächst die traditionellen, wie Maschinenbau, Textil-, Elektro-, Musikinstrumente- und Lebensmittelindustrie. Schneller als erwartet fasst auch die Automobilindustrie als völlig neue Branche immer stärker Fuß. Als Aufbruchsmarkt wird künftig der Sektor alternative Energien, Umwelttechnologien neue Arbeitsplätze schaffen. Zuwachs verspricht auch der Gesundheitsmarkt, wie Medical Wellness in unserer Kurregion.

Was ist mit der IT-Branche?

Landrat: Zwar haben wir mit der GK Gläss GmbH in Schöneck einen Weltmarktführer in der Branche, aber dennoch sind wir nicht dort, wo wir hinwollen. Obwohl wir mit dem Berufsschulzentrum Rodewisch in Deutschland einmalig ein IT-Abitur anbieten.

Gibt es künftig mit der Stadt Plauen eine gemeinsame Wirtschaftsagentur?

Landrat: Ich bin einer der intensivsten Verfechter einer Wirtschaftsagentur. Es gibt nichts Wichtigeres, als auf dem Wirtschafts- und Bildungssektor in der Region, die sich bis nach Tschechien erstreckt, zusammenzuarbeiten. Wir könnten so als Europaregion für das Vogtland viel besser werben und nationale und internationale Aufmerksamkeit und Bekanntheit erfahren.

Which industrial sectors will dominate the Vogtland region in future?

Lenk: First of all, the traditional ones like engineering, textiles, electrical engineering, musical instruments and the food industry. The automobile industry is also gaining a foothold as a completely new sector faster than had been expected. The new markets of the alternative energy sector and environmental technologies will create new jobs in future. The health market is also promising – for example, medical wellness in our spa region.

What about the IT sector?

Lenk: We do have a world leader in this sector in the shape of GK SOFTWARE AG in Schöneck, but we have not arrived at the point where we should be. Although we are the only place in Germany that can provide IT school finishing exams at the Rodewisch Vocational Training College.

Will there be a joint business agency with the city of Plauen in future?

Lenk: I am one of the most ardent defenders of a business agency. There is nothing more important than working in the business and training sector in the region, which stretches into the Czech Republic. We could provide much better advertising for the Vogtland district as a European region, attract much more domestic and international attention and create a higher profile.

» *Wenn Familien Arbeit haben, dann gibt es sozialen Frieden und auch einen positiven Blick in die Zukunft.* «

» *If families are in work, there is no conflict in society and people can view the future positively.* «

Emanzipation, Innovation und Führung
Emancipation, Innovation and Leadership

Emanzipation, Innovation und Führung als Zukunftsaufgaben des vogtländischen Mittelstandes

Dr. Rüdiger Kroll ist ein profunder Kenner der wirtschaftlichen Situation im Vogtland. Als früherer Geschäftsführer der Goldbeck GmbH am Standort Treuen und nunmehr Beauftragter des Wirtschaftssenat Sachsens für den BVMW (Bundesverband mittelständischer Wirtschaft) liegt ihm besonders die Zukunftsfähigkeit der mittelständischen Unternehmen am Herzen. „Wenn es dem Mittelstand gut geht, profitieren auch die kleineren Unternehmen und Dienstleister davon", weiß Dr. Kroll aus Erfahrung.

Momentan stellt sich für den Wirtschaftsexperten die Situation des vogtländischen Mittelstandes aussichtsreich dar: „In der Region hat sich eine Vielzahl namhafter Firmen mit exzellenten Marktpositionen angesiedelt. Diese partizipieren stark an der guten Konjunktur und den guten Rahmenbedingungen." Doch trotz oder gerade wegen der positiven Auftragslage ist die Zukunftssicherung der mittelständischen Unternehmen im Vogtland eine Kernaufgabe, mahnt Dr. Kroll und nennt die drei wichtigsten Anforderungen für die Zukunft.

Zum einen müssen sich demnach die Unternehmen lösen vom Image und durchaus auch vom Status quo der verlängerten Werkbank und sich von den Firmenzentralen stärker emanzipieren. Forschung und Entwicklung, erweiterte Kompetenzen und Leitungseigenständigkeit an den eigenen Standort zu holen ist die zentrale Aufgabe der Firmenleitung.

Aufbauend auf diese Forderung sollten Unternehmensführungen mehr und mehr den Nachwuchs in das Top-Management eingliedern. Durch die Einbindung in wichtige Entscheidungen und die Übertragung von Verantwortung an den Führungskräftenachwuchs wird dessen Motivation und die Bereitschaft im Vogtland zu arbeiten entscheidend geprägt. Oft sind alteingesessene Geschäftsführungen noch nicht dazu bereit, diesen entscheidenden Schritt nach vorn zu wagen.

The future responsibilities of small and medium-sized enterprises in the Vogtland region

Dr. Rüdiger Kroll knows all about the economic situation in the Vogtland region. He was formerly managing director at the Treuen branch of Goldbeck GmbH and he is now a representative of the Association of Small and Medium-sized Businesses (BVMW) on Saxony's Business Committee. So he is particularly interested in the future success of small and medium-sized businesses.

Dr. Kroll speaks from experience: "If medium-sized companies are doing well, smaller businesses and service providers benefit."

The business expert believes that the situation for the Vogtland region's medium-sized enterprises is promising: "A variety of well-known companies with excellent market positions have settled in the region. They are playing an important role in improving the economy and the excellent general conditions." Nevertheless Dr. Kroll believes that guaranteeing the future of medium-sized enterprises in the Vogtland region should be a primary focus despite or perhaps because of the full order books. He names the three most important requirements for the future.

Firstly, companies must shed the image and the very present idea of dependence on parent companies and exert more efforts to break free of group headquarters. The central task of company managers is to pursue research and development, expand areas of expertise and ensure that companies are self-reliant in their work.

On top of this demand, business managers should increasingly integrate junior staff into top management positions. Their motivation and readiness to work in the Vogtland region will be sharpened by involving them in important decisions and delegating responsibility to them. Well-established company managers are still often reluctant to take this crucial step.

(Fotos/Photos by Hartmut Briese, Text/Text by André Zeidler, Übersetzung/Translated by David Strauss)

» *Wenn es dem Mittelstand gut geht, profitieren auch die kleineren Unternehmen und Dienstleister davon.* «

» *If medium-sized companies are doing well, smaller businesses and service providers benefit.* «

Die dritte und wichtigste Voraussetzung, die die ersten beiden Punkte maßgeblich bedingt, ist laut Dr. Kroll die spezifische Ausbildung des Führungsnachwuchses aus der Region. Denn neben der fachlichen Qualifikation nimmt die Sozial- und Methodenkompetenz einen immer höheren Stellenwert ein bei der Leitung eines Unternehmens.

Eines weiß Dr. Kroll dabei sicher: Viele talentierte Hochschulabsolventen aus dem Vogtland mit Anstellung in einem großen Konzern an einem renommierten Standort wie München oder Stuttgart kämen trotz deutlicher Lohneinbußen gern zurück in die Heimatregion, um nach und nach die Geschicke der ansässigen Firmen in die Hand zu nehmen. Und genau diesen Prozess forciert Dr. Kroll. Die Organisation spezieller Führungsseminare, intensive Verbandsarbeit und der Dialog mit den Unternehmen sind nur einige seiner Projekte, die allesamt ein Ziel haben: Den wichtigen wirtschaftlichen Faktor Mittelstand für das Vogtland zu sichern und in eine erfolgreiche Zukunft zu führen.

According to Dr. Kroll, the third and most important requirement also forms the basis for the previous ones: the need for specific training for junior management staff in the region. Social expertise and a knowledge of methodology are becoming more and more important in managing a company, so purely technical qualifications are no longer enough.

Dr. Kroll is certain about one thing: many talented university graduates from the Vogtland region, who are currently employed at major corporations at well-known locations like Munich or Stuttgart, would love to return to their home area despite a significant drop in salary. They would gradually like to shape the destiny of local businesses. Dr. Kroll would like to accelerate this process. Organising special management seminars, working intensively with the members of the Association of Small and Medium-sized Enterprises and a constant dialogue with the enterprises are just some of his projects, which all have one purpose: to ensure that small and medium-sized companies remain the dominant economic factor in the Vogtland region; he wants to steer them towards a successful future.

Ein Holzfäller und Intendant
The Vogtland people are a plucky mountain people

Alexander Iljinskij besuchte für die Zeitschrift „SuperIllu" seine Heimat

Die Vogtländer, sie sind ein beherztes Bergvölkchen, dem Reichtum nicht in die Wiege gelegt wurde. Die vom 30jährigen Krieg genauso gebeutelt wurden wie später von den Diktaturen und denen auch die Wende manch einen wirtschaftlichen Tiefschlag verpasst hat.
Der Vogtländer ist kein Sachse. Auch wenn das Vogtland natürlich zum Freistaat zählt.
„Mir sprechen vogtländisch!" Meine Auswahl kreist um den Teil des Vogtlandes, in dem ich Kindheit, Schulzeit und Lehre erlebte.

Musikinstrumentenbau, die heimische Holzwirtschaft und der sich entwickelnde Tourismus sind die wirtschaftlichen Standbeine für diesen Teil meiner Heimat.

Da wäre Klingenthal zu nennen – der Musikwinkel. Die Gründung reicht bis 1600 zurück. Der Ortsname soll vom Klang eines Hammerwerkes im waldigen Tal stammen. Böhmische Handwerker brachten den Musikinstrumentenbau ins Vogtland. Hier bin ich aufgewachsen. Habe brav mein Akkordeon gespielt, mit Begeisterung die Theaterfahrten nach Plauen erlebt und parallel mit dem Abitur den Beruf des Forstfacharbeiters erlernt. Das war in meinem Jahrgang üblich und später haben sich meine Theaterkollegen nicht selten über die Mischung aus Intendant und Holzfäller gewundert.
Wanderungen in die nähere Umgebung zählten zur sonntäglichen Pflicht und die Geschichten und Sagen, die die Mutter dabei erzählte, haben manchen Kilometer leichter werden lassen.

Hieß das Wanderziel Muldenberg, beeindruckte die gewaltige Trinkwassertalsperre und es wartete ein Bad im Sauteich oder im Floßgraben auf uns. Die Flößerei war in der Vergangenheit ein wichtiger Erwerbszweig für die Region. Holz und Wald gehören zu den natürlichen Reichtümern des Vogtlandes. Und Unmengen von Brennholz wurden bis in die Mitte des 19. Jahrhunderts von den vogtländischen Flößern bis nach Halle und Leipzig auf dem Wasserwege geflößt. Ein Flößerverein mit Sitz in Muldenberg, der auch schon Flößer aus aller Welt zu Gast hatte, erinnert an diese schwere Zunft mit ihren Traditionen.

Landschaft pur – das ist meine Heimat. Und wenn ich am Aschberg stehe, genieße ich an besonders klaren Tagen den Fernblick nach Franken oder in die Leipziger Ebene.

Ein Schritt vom Wege in das Grenzland der damaligen ČSSR gehörte zu den Mutproben meiner Kindheit. Heute kann man den kleinen Grenzverkehr nutzen und sieht etwas wehmütig auf die noch geschlossenen Ausflugslokale und findet viele ortsübliche Familiennamen der Gegend auf den zugewachsenen Grabstätten des Flecken Schwaderbach an der deutsch/tschechischen Grenze. Den 1938 errichteten Gedenkstein an den Heimatdichter Anton Günther sucht man vergebens. Wie viele Erinnerungen wurde er 1945 zerstört. Aber langsam beginnt die Ortschaft (Bublova) wieder zu leben, wohl auch wegen der einmaligen Landschaft, in die sie eingebettet ist.

Alexander Iljinskij Visited His Home District for the "SuperIllu" Magazine

They have never been blessed with much wealth and were shaken as much by the 30 Years War as by dictatorships and the economic downside of the fall of the Berlin Wall.
Vogtland people are not Saxons, even though the Vogtland district is part of the Free State of Saxony. "We speak the Vogtland dialect!" I have chosen to talk about that part of the Vogtland region where I spent my childhood, my school days and learned my trade.

Musical instrument making, the local timber industry and growing tourism are the economic pillars of this part of my home region.

Klingenthal – in Musicon Valley - is worth mentioning here. Its origins go back as far as 1600. The town's name comes from the German word for the sound (klingen) of a hammer mill in a wooded valley (Tal). Bohemian craftsmen brought musical instrument making to the Vogtland region. I grew up here. I learned to play the accordion like a good boy, enjoyed theatre trips to Plauen and learned my trade as a certified forestry worker while completing my school studies. This was nothing unusual at the time, but later my theatre colleagues were often surprised by this strange choice of occupations: theatre director and lumberjack.

We always went for a walk in the surrounding area on Sundays and the stories and legends recounted by my mother made it easier for me to cover the huge distances. If our destination was Muldenberg, I was struck by the huge reservoir and we either went for a swim in the "pigs pond" or the log rafting canal. Log rafting was an important business in our region in the past. Timber and forests are one of the Vogtland region's natural resources. Vogtland rafters sent huge amounts of firewood down the rivers as far as Halle and Leipzig until the mid-19th century. There is a rafters' club in Muldenberg, which has welcomed rafters from all round the world, and it ensures that we do not forget this tough trade and its traditions.

My home region is full of unspoilt countryside. When I stand on Aschberg hill, I can enjoy the view that stretches as far as Franconia or the plains near Leipzig on a clear day.

Taking a step across the border into the former Czechoslovak Republic was one of the things we dared to do as children. Today the border is open for non-commercial traffic and people can nostalgically gaze at the closed restaurants and find many names that are common to the region on the overgrown gravestones in the village of Schwaderbach on the German/Czech border. You will have to look hard for the memorial stone set up for the local poet Anton Günther in 1938. It was destroyed in 1945 along with many memories. But the little town, now called Bublava, is beginning to come to life again, probably because of the beautiful countryside that surrounds it.

(Mit freundlicher Genehmigung der SUPERillu/ With kind approval of SUPERillu magazine, Fotos/Photos by B. Trenkel/SUPERillu (1), Text/Text by Alexander Iljinskij, Übersetzung/Translated by David Strauss)

Unbedingt muß ich den Schneckenstein erwähnen, ein Topasfelsen, der die Schatztruhen der Wettiner mit den Halbedelsteinen füllte, die heute noch in Dresdener Grünen Gewölbe zu besichtigen sind.

Im wahrsten Sinne des Wortes eine Wiedergeburt erlebte der Wintersport mit dem Bau der Vogtlandarena. Als die „Asch", die Aschbergschanze 1990/91 abgerissen wurde, schien es das Aus zu sein für die Wintersportträume, die so erfolgreich mit der Bronzemedaille des Klingenthalers Harry Glaß bei den olympischen Winterspielen 1956 begannen. Jetzt strahlen die Lichter wieder und setzen eine der weltmodernsten Sprungschanzen im Mittelpunkt der Vogtlandarena ins gebührende Licht.

Hausmusik, Brauchtum, die vogtländische Küche, Trachten, Moosmänner und die vielen Erinnerungen an die Heimat gehören auch heute noch zu meinen gern gelebten Traditionen. Etwas unbescheiden meine ich, eine Weihnachtsrevue am Friedrichstadtpalast in Berlin hätte es wahrscheinlich ohne die Wurzeln seines Intendanten nicht gegeben. Denn Beharrung und Stehvermögen, Naturverbundenheit und Heimatliebe zeichnen uns Vogtländer aus.

I definitely need to mention Schneckenstein, a topaz rock, which filled the treasure chests of the Wettin rulers with semi-precious stones. They can now be seen in the Green Vault in Dresden.

Winter sports have experienced a real revival here in the truest sense of the word with the construction of the Vogtland Arena. When the old Aschberg ski jump was demolished in 1990-91, it looked as if that was the end of any winter sports dreams, which had begun so successfully when Harry Glass from Klingenthal won a bronze medal at the 1956 Winter Olympics.
Today the floodlights are back on and they fittingly illuminate one of the world's most modern ski jumps right in the middle of the Vogtland Arena.

It may sound immodest, but I doubt whether there would ever have been a Christmas revue at the Friedrichstadtpalast Theatre in Berlin if its director not had his roots in the Vogtland region. For Vogtland people are characterised by perseverance and stamina, a love of nature and their home region. Alexander Iljinskij (with kind permission from SuperIllu Magazine)

Peter Maffay und das Vogtland

Peter Maffay and the Vogtland Region

Peter Maffay und Udo Lindenberg im Dezember 2004 bei der Benefiz-Gala zu Gunsten der „Peter- Maffay-Stiftung im Wernesgrüner Brauereigutshof./Peter Maffay and Udo Lindenberg at the benefit gala for the Peter Maffay Foundation at the Wernesgrüner brewery estate in December 2004.

Es ist schon eine besondere, intensive Beziehung, die den wohl erfolgreichsten deutschen Rockmusiker Peter Maffay und das Vogtland miteinander verbindet. Diese führte den Künstler sowohl zu mehreren Konzerten in die Region, aber auch seine persönlichen Kontakte sowohl zur Wernesgrüner Brauerei als auch zum Automobilzulieferer Magnetto Automotive Deutschland in Treuen sind ein Beweis dafür.

Gerade vom Markneukirchener Musikwinkel, den Maffay im November 1998 besuchte und er für seine Stiftung eine wertvolle Violine von Ekkard Seidl erhielt, spricht der Künstler noch heute mit voller Hochachtung. „Ich hatte echt keine Ahnung, was das Vogtland für eine schöne Region ist und was mich hier erwartete ... ich bin sprachlos." Eine Doppelbodengitarre von Eberhard Kreul gehört heute zum Fundus seiner umfangreichen Gitarrensammlung. Diese Gitarre von einem vogtländischen Meisterbetrieb ist sogar auf seiner CD „Bis ans Ende der Welt" zu hören.

The relationship that connects the person who is probably the most successful German rock star, Peter Maffay, with the Vogtland region is a special and intense one. This has brought the artist to the region to hold several concerts, but his personal contacts with the Wernesgrüner brewery and the automobile parts supplier Magnetto Automotive Deutschland in Treuen are also evidence of this.

The artist still speaks of the Markneukirchen Musicon Valley with a great deal of respect; he visited the area in November 1998 and received a prized violin from Ekkard Seidl for his foundation. "I really had no idea how beautiful the Vogtland region is and what was awaiting me here ... I am speechless." A double-backed guitar from Eberhard Kreul is just one of the guitars in his collection. This guitar made by a Vogtland master craftsman can even be heard on his CD entitled "To the End of the World".

Im Jahr 2003 holte die Wernesgrüner Brauerei den Rockmusiker zu zwei exklusiven Open-Air-Konzerten an einem Wochenende in das Vogtland. „Die schönsten Sommernächte 2003" schrieben die Medien nach den vor jeweils über 4.500 begeisterten Fans im exklusiven Rahmen des ausverkauften Wernesgrüner Brauereigutshofes durchgeführten Konzerten. „Musik kann dabei helfen, die Mauern in den Köpfen einzureißen", war es Maffay ein besonderes Anliegen bei der Vorbereitung des Konzertevents. So kamen sie, nicht nur aus dem Vogtland, sondern aus ganz Deutschland, Alt und Jung, zu einem Konzert durch 30 Jahre Musikgeschichte Peter Maffay.

The Wernesgrüner brewery brought the rock musician to the Vogtland region for two exclusive open-air concerts over a weekend in 2003. "The most beautiful summer nights in 2003" was the headline in the media after the concerts that were a full house and were held in the presence of 4,500 enthusiastic fans in the exclusive atmosphere of the Wernesgrüner brewery estate. "Music can help to break down the walls in our thinking," Maffay said in the run-up to the concerts. People of all ages did not just come from the Vogtland region, but from all over Germany for a concert that reflected 30 years of musical history with Peter Maffay.

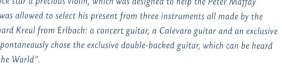

Peter Maffay besuchte im November 1998 den vogtländischen Musikwinkel. In der Musikhalle Markneukirchen wurde dem Künstler ein rauschender Empfang bereitet. Zwei wertvolle Instrumente durfte der Musiker aus dem Traditionsstandort des Musikinstrumentenbaus mitnehmen .
Ekkard Seidl überreichte dem Rockstar eine kostbare Violine, die sollte der Peter-Maffay-Stiftung zugute kommen.. Aus drei Fabrikaten, einer Konzertgitarre, einer Calevaro-Gitarre und einer exklusiven Doppelbodengitarre, allesamt hergestellt von Gitarrenbaumeister Erberhard Kreul aus Erlbach, konnte Peter Maffay sein Geschenk auswählen.. Er entschied sich ganz spontan für die exklusive Doppelbodengitarre, die auf der CD „Bis ans Ende der Welt" zu hören ist.

Peter Maffay visited Musicon Valley in the Vogtland region in November 1998. The artist received a rapturous welcome at the Markneukirchen Music Hall. The musician was able to take with him two valuable instruments from the traditional musical instrument making centre. .
Ekkard Seidl handed the rock star a precious violin, which was designed to help the Peter Maffay Foundation. Peter Maffay was allowed to select his present from three instruments all made by the master guitar maker Eberhard Kreul from Erlbach: a concert guitar, a Calevaro guitar and an exclusive double-backed guitar. He spontaneously chose the exclusive double-backed guitar, which can be heard on the CD "To the End of the World".

(Fotos/Photos by Igor Pastierovic, Eberhard Kreul, Übersetzung/Translated by David Strauss)

Nur fünf Konzerte gab Peter Maffay 2006. Das einzige Konzert in den neuen Bundesländern war im Vogtland. Zur Pressekonferenz am 31.05.2006 im Waldhotel in Klingenthal sagte er, dass er sich auf den Auftritt an der neuen Großschanze in der Vogtland Arena freut. Längst ist Maffay der Region durch seine Besuche und Auftritte nicht nur musikalisch verbunden. Im Hinblick auf die Schanze überreichte der Landrat Dr. Tassilo Lenk dem Vollblutmusiker eine Fanfare mit der Aufschrift „Zieeeh …". Das neue Musikinstrument nahm Maffay mit scherzenden Worten auf: „Kann man daraus auch trinken?".

Peter Maffay only gave five concerts in 2006. The only concert in Eastern Germany was in the Vogtland region. At the press conference on 31 May 2006 in the Waldhotel in Klingenthal he said that he was looking forward to his appearance at the new ski-jump facility in the Vogtland Arena. Maffay not only has links with the region through his visits and musical appearances. Chief administrative officer Dr. Tassilo Lenk handed the full-blooded musician a fanfare with the inscription "Zieeeh…" looking forward to his appearance at the ski-jump facility. Maffay received the new musical instrument with a sense of humour: "Can you drink out of it too?"

Die Begeisterung und auch die Erfahrungen der ersten beiden Konzerte führten dazu, dass auf der Open-Air-Tournee 2005, genau am 17. Juni des Jahres, Wernesgrün das bis dahin größte Konzertereignis in seiner Geschichte erlebte. Mehr als 12.000 enthusiastische Musikfans kamen zum „Laut und Leise"-Konzert in den kleinen vogtländischen Ort. Aber damit noch nicht genug.

Am 16. Juli 2006 kam Peter Maffay erneut ins Vogtland und gab in der Vogtland-Arena zu Füßen der neuen Großschanze vor einer imponierenden Kulisse ein fast 3-stündiges umjubeltes Konzert. Die Premiere in Klingenthal war zugleich das einzige Konzert in diesem Jahr in den neuen Bundesländern und damit der richtige Auftakt für zukünftige Events in der Vogtland Arena. Rund 10.000 Menschen verfolgten in der Arena, zahlreiche Gäste auch außerhalb des Ovals ein bis heute einmaliges Konzert. Maffay, der mit diesem Event den Auftakt in der Vogtland Arena gab, meinte: „Ich freue mich immer, wenn ich einem Vogtländer begegne. Es ist einfach ein prima Menschenschlag." Recht hat er.

(Fotos/Photos by Igor Pastierovic)

The excitement and the experience of the first two concerts created a situation where Wernesgrün lived through what was the biggest concert in its history on 17 June during the 2005 open-air tour. More than 12,000 enthusiastic music fans came to the "Loud and Soft" concert in the small Vogtland town. But that was not all.

Peter Maffay came back to the Vogtland region on 16 July 2006 and gave a concert lasting almost three hours in the Vogtland Arena at the foot of the new ski-jump facility to the cheers of the crowd – an imposing setting. The premiere in Klingenthal was also the only concert that Maffay gave in Eastern Germany during the whole year and it was the right prelude for future events at the Vogtland Arena. About 10,000 people watched a unique concert in the arena and many guests were outside the perimeter. Maffay, who opened the Vogtland Arena with this concert, said: "I am always happy to meet a person from the Vogtland region. They are simply great people." And he is right.

Freie Presse, Tageszeitung im Vogtland, berichtete wie folgt: „Klingenthal. Ein langer Blick ins weite Rund, zwei, drei sportive Hüpfer und ein lockeres Winken – so betrat Peter Maffay am Sonntagabend die Bühne der neuen Vogtlandarena in Klingenthal. Das Publikum dort hatte er vom ersten Moment an im Griff und ließ es für zweieinhalb Stunden nicht wieder los. … Als sich die Nacht über die Vogtland-Arena neigte, war ihre Verbindung mit der Bühne auch von optischem Reiz: Oben der beleuchtete Schanzentisch, unten das Flirren der Lichtshow. Ein Wiedersehen mit Maffay an der Vogtland-Arena? Aber gern!

The Freie Presse, the daily paper in the Vogtland region, carried the following report: "Klingenthal. A long look at the broad arena, two or three sporty steps and a relaxed wave – this was how Peter Maffay appeared on the stage at the new Vogtland Arena on Sunday evening. He had the crowd in his hand right from the outset and did not let them go for two-and-a-half hours. … As night fell over the Vogtland Arena, its link to the stage was also a wonderful sight: the illuminated jump-off platform up above and the flickering of the light show down below. Would we like to see Maffay back at the Vogtland Arena? Yes, please!

Bei der Benefizveranstaltung für die Peter-Maffay-Stiftung im Neuberinhaus in Reichenbach am 16.07.2006 überreichte Dieter Pfortner, Geschäftsführers der Magnetto Automotive Deutschland GmbH, stellvertretend für zahlreiche Vogtländer an Peter Maffay einen Spendenscheck. Der Rockstar war sichtlich gerührt. /At the benefit event for the Peter Maffay Foundation in the Neuberin Theatre in Reichenbach on 16 July 2006, Dieter Pfortner, managing director of Magnetto Automotive Deutschland GmbH representing many people from the Vogtland region, handed over a gift cheque to Peter Maffay. The rock star was visibly moved.

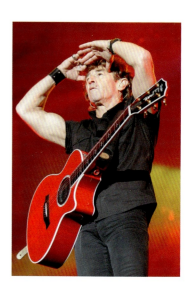

Aber nicht nur die Musik, sondern auch sein soziales Engagement sind für Peter Maffay ein besonderes Anliegen. Er gründete die Tabaluga Kinder- und Jugendhilfe und die Peter-Maffay-Stiftung, um sich für junge Menschen einzusetzen, die auf ihrem Lebensweg bisher viel Leid, Not und Elend erfahren haben. Die Tabaluga Kinder- und Jugendhilfe ist dabei eine heilpädagogisch-therapeutische Einrichtung mit bereits langjähriger Erfahrung. Im Tabaluga-Haus, in den Tabaluga-Wohngruppen, dem Tabaluga-Hof, dem Montessori-Kindergarten, der Tabaluga-Familienberatungsstelle und dem Sternstundenhaus, einem überregionalen Therapiezentrum, werden traumatisierte Kinder betreut, die im familiären Umfeld missbraucht, geschlagen und benutzt wurden.

Der Schwerpunkt der Peter-Maffay-Stiftung wiederum liegt in Pollença, einem Ort im Norden der Urlaubsinsel Mallorca. Auf einer Finca mit Ökogarten, hofeigener Schaf- und Ziegenhaltung mit Molkerei und Käserei, dem Stadthaus mit Bioladen, Café und Restaurant und einem Tagungsraum abseits vom Massentourismus im idyllischen Hinterland der Insel gibt es Unterkünfte, Betreuung, Spaß und Lebensfreude für 20 Kinder und Jugendliche. Diese Gruppen werden aus den unterschiedlichsten Ländern zusammengeführt und können somit im wahrsten Sinne des Wortes Grenzen erweitern. Das Mallorca-Projekt bietet für Kinder und Jugendliche somit eine ideale Ergänzung zu professionellen pädagogischen Alltagsbetreuung ihrer Herkunftsprojekte.

Zahlreiche Ehrungen erhielt Peter Maffay für dieses eher unübliche Engagement eines Künstlers. Erst jüngst erhielt er dafür vom Presseclub Dresden den Erich-Kästner-Preis als Anerkennung für sein unermüdliches Wirken zu Gunsten leiderfahrener, junger Menschen. Aber auch hier gibt es eine Verbindung in das Vogtland. Vertreter aus Industrie, Handwerk, Gewerbe, Vereinen, Verbänden, Institutionen aber auch Privatpersonen unterstützten einen Aufruf des Geschäftsführers der Magnetto Automotive Deutschland GmbH in Treuen, genau diese Peter-Maffay-Stiftung nachhaltig zu unterstützen. Im Rahmen einer Benefizveranstaltung im Juli 2006 konnte der Initiator, Dieter Pfortner, mehr als 56.000 Euro an den Künstler überreichen. Diese Aktion soll keine Einmaligkeit sein, versprach der Geschäftsführer und plant gemeinsam mit Geschäftspartnern bereits ein neues Event.

Wo auch immer Maffay auf Tournee ist, sind vogtländische Fans mit Plakaten zugegen. „Grüße zurück ins Vogtland", ruft er dann mit den verbindenden Worten: „Es ist wunderbar euch zu sehen und zu fühlen!" Dieses Verbindende wünschen wir uns auch für die Zukunft.

But Peter Maffay is not only interested in his music, but also his social commitment. He founded the Tabaluga Children's and Young People's Support and the Peter Maffay Foundation to help young people who have experienced a lot of suffering, need and misery during their lives. The Tabaluga Children's and Young People's Support is a therapeutic centre with many years of experience. Traumatised children, who have been abused, beaten or misused in their family environment, are cared for at Tabaluga House, in Tabaluga residential groups, the Tabaluga farm, the Montessori nursery school, the Tabaluga family advice centre and the Magic Moment House, a national treatment centre.

The major focus of the Peter Maffay Foundation is in the town of Pollença, situated in the north of the holiday island of Majorca. There is accommodation, care, fun and a zest for life for 20 children and young people on a farm with an organic garden, its own sheep and goats with a dairy and cheese dairy, the town house with an organic shop, a café and restaurant and a day room well away from mass tourism in the idyllic interior of the island. The groups of youngsters come from a wide variety of different countries and can therefore expand their horizons in the real sense of the word. The Majorca project provides children and young people with the ideal complement to professional care in their home regions.

Peter Maffay has received many distinctions for what can only be described as a rather unusual commitment for an artist. Only recently he received the Erich Kästner Prize from the Dresden Press Club in recognition of his tireless work on behalf of young people who have suffered a great deal. But this also links him to the Vogtland region. Representatives from industry, trades, commerce, clubs, associations, institutions and private individuals are all backing a plea from the managing director of Magnetto Automotive Deutschland GmbH in Treuen to provide long-term support for the Peter Maffay Foundation. The man behind this call, Dieter Pfortner, was able to hand over more than € 56,000 to the artist at a benefit event in July 2006. "This campaign is not going to be a one-off," the manager promised and he is already planning a new event with other business partners.

Wherever Maffay's tours take him, fans from the Vogtland region are present with their placards. "Send my greetings to the Vogtland region," he says and adds: "It is wonderful to see and feel you!" We hope that this link will continue in future.

(Fotos/Photos by Igor Pastierovic)

Ideen und Innovationen haben Tradition im Land der grünen Auen

Ideas and Innovations Are a Tradition in the Land of Green Meadows

Was haben der Entdecker der Kometenbahn, der Erfinder des Vierzylinder-Motors, der Baumeister gewaltiger Brückenbauwerke, eine Theaterreformerin oder auch die beiden ersten deutschen Männer im Weltall gemeinsam? Alle sind sie im Vogtland geboren oder haben hier ihre beruflichen Spuren hinterlassen.

Der Nicht-Vogtländer wird sich wundern, dass diese Region hier solch interessante Zeitgenossen zu bieten hat und das Buch wird belegen, dass es solche hellen Köpfe und kreativen Menschen auch heut noch in dieser südwestsächsischen Region angrenzend an Bayern, Thüringen und Tschechien gibt. Normalerweise ist mit dem Vogtland vor allem die schöne Landschaft verbunden, wie es im Lied: „Vogtlandheimat, traut und schön, Land der frischen grünen Auen", heißt. Doch Ideenreichtum, Innovationskraft, wirtschaftliches Denken, der Mut, Visionen zu haben in einem großen Teil der Bevölkerung sind ein essenzieller Standortvorteil im Land der frischen grünen Auen.

Der in Plauen geborene Georg Samuel Dörffel führte vor 350 Jahren den Nachweis, dass die Kometen sich auf parabolischen Bahnen bewegen, in deren Brennpunkt die Sonne steht. Brennpunkt im Vogtland ist die Schaffung neuer, moderner Arbeitsplätze und deren Sicherung in der Zukunft. Doch den Vogtländern muss dabei nicht bange sein, wie die vergangenen Jahre beweisen. Nicht zuletzt auch deshalb stellt Landrat Dr. Tassilo Lenk klar: „Hier weiß jeder, wo sein Platz ist, und was er auf diesem zu leisten hat, zum Wohle aller!"

Das dürfte vermutlich auch den Maschinenbauingenieur und Autopionier August Horch 1902 dazu bewogen haben, in Reichenbach eine Fabrik zu eröffnen. Dort entwickelte er mit seinen Fachleuten aus der Region den Vierzylindermotor.

Motor der heutigen wirtschaftlichen Entwicklung sind gut ausgebildete Menschen. In den unterschiedlichen Bildungsstätten ist das Vogtland darauf eingestellt. Ob im Hochschulteil der Westsächsischen Hochschule Zwickau (FH) in Reichenbach, in der Plauener Außenstelle der Universität Pilsen, in der BA Plauen (Berufsakademie), in den engagierten privaten Bildungsträgern oder in den auf den neuesten Stand gebrachten Berufsschulzentren – hier erhalten die Vogtländer das nötige Rüstzeug. Ausgezeichnete Vorarbeit für die berufliche Bildung leisten die modern gestalteten Grund- und Mittelschulen, Gymnasien sowie die zahlreichen Kindertagestätten.

Als Universalingenieur gilt der Konstrukteur und Hochschullehrer Johann Andreas Schubert, der 1808 im vogtländischen Wernesgrün geboren wurde. Mit 29 Jahren entwickelte er das erste Dampfschiff auf der Oberelbe. Doch auch in seiner Heimat hinterließ er eine unübersehbare Spur, mit der von ihm konstruierten Göltzschtalbrücke. Das Mammutbauwerk auch noch aus heutiger Sicht, und das nach über 150 Jahren, ist mit über 26 Millionen Ziegelsteinen die größte Ziegelbrücke der Welt. Sie ist 574 Meter lang und 78 Meter hoch und hat 81 Bögen. Ein Superlativ – und das im Land der frischen grünen Auen!

What do the following people have in common: the man who discovered how to plot the path of comets, the inventor of the four-cylinder internal combustion engine, a builder of huge bridges, a theatre reformer or the two first Germans to travel into space? All of them were either born in the Vogtland region or have left behind traces of their life and work here. People who are unfamiliar with the Vogtland region may be surprised to find that it has given birth to so many interesting personalities. This book will prove that such bright and creative people can still be found in the southwest Saxon region that borders on Bavaria, Thuringia and the Czech Republic. Normally, the Vogtland region is known for its beautiful scenery. One folk song speaks of "its homely beauty and its lush green meadows". But large numbers of the population have a wealth of ideas, innovative power, business acumen, the courage to have visions and these are major positive elements in this business location set in the countryside with its green meadows.

Georg Samuel Dörffel, who was born in Plauen, proved 350 years ago that comets follow parabolic paths and use the sun as their focal point. The focus in the Vogtland region is on creating new, modern jobs and securing them for the future. However, the people of the Vogtland region should not be fearful, as the last few years have shown. For this reason, the chief administrative officer, Dr. Tassilo Lenk, is happy to point out: "Everybody knows their place here, and what they should do for the good of all!"

This may also have motivated the mechanical engineer and automobile pioneer August Horch to open a factory in Reichenbach in 1902. He and his skilled team of workers from the region developed the four-cylinder internal combustion engine.

The force driving today's business developments is that of well trained people.

The Vogtland region is well prepared for this with its various training centres: the Reichenbach branch of the West Saxon University of Applied Sciences in Zwickau, the Plauen branch of the University of Pilsen, the Plauen University of Cooperative Education, the committed private educational institutions or the training centres, which have been thoroughly modernised – this is where Vogtland people gain the ammunition that they need. The modernised primary and middle schools, grammar schools and the many nursery schools provide excellent preparatory work for local people's professional training.

The designer and university professor Andreas Schubert was born in the Vogtland town of Wernesgrün in 1808 and is considered to be an all-round engineer. He developed the first steamer for the Upper Elbe river at the age of just 29. But he also left a highly visible mark on his home region by building the Göltzsch Valley Bridge. This mammoth construction is – even in today's world more than 150 years later – the largest brick bridge in the world with more than 26 million bricks. It is 574 metres long, 78 metres high and has 81 arches. It is a masterpiece – and yet is located in the land of lush, green meadows!

(Fotos/Photos by Hartmut Briese, Text/Text by Bert Walther, Übersetzung/Translated by David Strauss)

Eine Brückenfunktion besitzt das Vogtland zwischen Nord und Süd sowie zwischen Ost und West nicht zuletzt dank der gut ausgebauten Verkehrsinfrastruktur. Neben einigen Bundesstraßen, die durch das Vogtland verlaufen, ist die Autobahn A72 von Hof nach Chemnitz (weiter im Bau bis Leipzig) eine wichtige Verkehrsachse. Außerdem befindet sich das Hermsdorfer Kreuz (Autobahnen A4 und A9) in der Nähe von Gera, sowie die Autobahndreiecke Bayrisches Vogtland (Autobahnen A9 und A72) und Hochfranken (Autobahnen A93 und A72) in der Nähe von Hof (Bayrisches Vogtland). Für den Grenzverkehr nach Tschechien stehen Übergänge in Klingenthal (nur PKW) und Bad Brambach zur Verfügung, sowie nahe gelegene Übergänge im Erzgebirge und Franken. Dabei ist aber das Vogtland nicht nur ein Transitland. Die Unternehmen der Region haben mit einer Exportquote von über 30 Prozent einen Spitzenwert innerhalb Sachsens und der jungen Länder inne.

Wenn auch die Theaterreformerin Friederike Caroline Neuber auf den ersten Blick nichts mit der Wirtschaft des Vogtlandes zu tun hat, so verkörpert doch die vor über 200 Jahren lebende streitbare Vogtländerin Charaktereigenschaften, die bei den anderen Respekt hervorriefen: Scharfsinnig, ausdauernd, gewandt und kühn. Und genau das sind Charakterzüge und Eigenschaften, die den Vogtländer seit jeher ausmachen, die ihm zahlreiche geschichtliche Wendepunkte erfolgreich überwinden ließen und ihm letztlich zum wirtschaftlichen Erfolg geführt haben. Mögen das einst der Spitzenfabrikant Fedor Schnorr sein oder die nach der politischen Wende in Deutschland loslegenden Unternehmer Dr. Rüdiger Kroll, der frühere Chef von Goldbeck-Bau oder Erich Süßdorf von der Oelsnitzer Firma TUL-Tec. Die Liste ließe sich problemlos verlängern. Wären wir abschließend bei den beiden deutschen Himmelsstürmern Sigmund Jähn aus Morgenröthe-Rautenkranz und Ulf Merbold, der im thüringisch-vogtländischen Greiz aufwuchs. Damit kann sich keine andere Region schmücken, dass im Vogtland der erste Kosmonaut der DDR und der erste Astronaut der Bundesrepublik Deutschland aufwuchsen.

The Vogtland region also acts as a bridge between north and south and east and west – not least because of its well developed infrastructure. The A72 motorway from Hof to Chemnitz (which is being extended as far as Leipzig) is an important transport route in addition to the main roads that pass through the Vogtland region. The Hermsdorf junction (on the A4 and A9 motorways) is situated near Gera and the Bavarian Vogtland interchange (A9 and A72 motorways) and the Upper Franconia interchange (A72 and A93 motorways) are located near Hof (in the Bavarian Vogtland region). There are border crossings into the Czech Republic at Klingenthal (cars only) and Bad Brambach and other crossings nearby in the Ore Mountains and Franconia. But the Vogtland area is not only a transit region. The export quota of companies in the region exceeds 30 percent, which is the top figure in Saxony and Eastern Germany as a whole.

Even if the theatre reformer Friederike Caroline Neuber had nothing to do with the economy of the Vogtland region at first sight, this pugnacious Vogtland lady, who lived more than 200 years ago, possessed character traits that earned her respect in the eyes of others: she was sharp-witted, persevering, versatile and bold.

These are exactly the character traits and qualities of people in the Vogtland region, which have helped them deal with many defining moments in the past and have given them a taste of economic success at the end of the day. We could mention lace factory owner Fedor Schnorr or the entrepreneurs Dr. Rüdiger Kroll, former director of the construction company Goldbeckbau or Erich Süßdorf from the Oelsnitz company TUL-Tec, who seized the opportunities available after the fall of the Berlin Wall. It would not be difficult to extend this list.

And so we come to the last two high-flyers, Sigmund Jähn from Morgenröthe-Rautenkranz and Ulf Merbold, who was raised in Greiz in the Thuringian Vogtland region. No other part of Germany can proudly declare that the first cosmonaut in East Germany and the first astronaut from the Federal Republic of Germany both grew up in its home region.

Kompetenz und Leistung ohne Umwege
Direct Expertise and Service

Die Poller Systemlogistik GmbH und die Poller Spedition GmbH sind die vogtländischen Spezialisten für europaweite Ladungs- und Stückgutlogistik.

Als Richard Poller mit einem Pferdefuhrwerk die ersten Transporte in und um Ellefeld ausführte, konnte sich der Firmengründer ganz sicher auch in seinen kühnsten Träumen nicht vorstellen, dass das von ihm 1925 gegründete Unternehmen im 21. Jahrhundert europaweit agieren wird. Wie vor fast 100 Jahren gehören auch heute noch Flexibilität, Ideenreichtum und Engagement zu den besonderen Stärken der über 230 Mitarbeiter, die im Vogtland täglich eine Vielzahl von Sendungen auf den Weg zu den verschiedenen Empfängern im In- und Ausland bringen. Seit Jahren bildet POLLER Lehrlinge aus, um systematisch gut ausgebildeten eigenen Nachwuchs an zukünftige Aufgaben heranzuführen. Kontinuierliche Investitionen in moderne Fahrzeug- und Lagertechnik sichern der POLLER Unternehmensgruppe auch weiterhin ein kontinuierliches Wachstum. Mit Umweltbewusstsein, effizient gestalteten Prozessabläufen und innovativen Produkten sorgt POLLER am vogtländischen Logistikmarkt ständig für wirtschaftliche Leistungsfähigkeit. In jüngster Zeit wurde das Leistungsspektrum in Plauen durch ein neues Hochregallager mit einer Kapazität von 5.000 Palettenplätzen und der Eröffnung einer Niederlassung mit 2.000 Quadratmeter Umschlagfläche in Klipphausen bei Dresden nochmals erweitert.

Um die Stärke ihrer Unternehmen noch weiter zu steigern, und ihren Kunden ein noch weiteres Leistungsspektrum anbieten zu können, haben sich die Zwickauer Unternehmensgruppe WECK und die POLLER Unternehmensgruppe zur WECK+POLLER Holding GmbH zusammengeschlossen. Auch weiterhin zählen Qualität und Kundennähe, für diesen mit über 500 Mitarbeitern und mehr als 300 Fahrzeugen gut aufgestellten mittelständischen Firmenverbund, zu den wichtigsten Erfolgsfaktoren.

Poller Systemlogistik GmbH and Poller Spedition GmbH are the specialists in the Vogtland region for pan-European full load and bulk materials logistics.

When Richard Poller provided the first haulage services in and around Ellefeld with a horse and cart, the founder of the firm could probably not imagine in his wildest dreams that the company that he set up in 1925 would be working across Europe in the 21st century. Just as was the case almost a century ago, flexibility, a wealth of ideas and commitment are just some of the special strengths of the more than 230 members of staff in the Vogtland region, who transport a variety of shipments to various recipients in Germany and abroad. POLLER has been training apprentices for years in order to have a supply of well-trained personnel to tackle future tasks. Continual investments in modern vehicles and storage technology have ensured that the POLLER company group has grown continually. Using its ecological awareness, efficiently planned process sequences and innovative products, POLLER ensures that the Vogtland logistics market has an efficient business partner. The range of services has recently been expanded in Plauen by installing a new high-shelf storage facility with space for 5,000 pallets and by opening a branch with 2,000 square metres of handling space in Klipphausen near Dresden.

The WECK company group in Zwickau and the POLLER company group have now merged to become WECK+POLLER Holding GmbH to further increase the strength of the companies and provide their customers with an even greater range of services. Quality and proximity to customers continue to be the most important success factors for this well-placed medium-sized network of firms that employs more than 500 members of staff and has more than 300 vehicles..

Kernkompetenz:
- internationale Spedition
- Projektlogistik
- Lagerhaltung
- Kommissionierung
- Distribution
- Logistikberatung
- Systempartner der S.T.a.R und E.L.V.I.S. Kooperationen

Core areas of competence:
- International haulage
- Project logistics
- Storage
- Warehouse logistics
- Distribution
- Logistics advice
- System partner in the S.T.a.R and E.L.V.I.S. cooperation arrangements

Poller Systemlogistik GmbH
Zum Plom 23
08541 Neuensalz
Telefon +49 (0) 3741 4157-0
Telefax +49 (0) 3741 4157-37
www.poller-syslog.de

Spedition Poller GmbH
Reumtengrüner Weg 19
08236 Ellefeld
Telefon +49 (0) 3745 75142-0
Telefax +49 (0) 3745 75142-22
www.spedition-poller.de

(Fotos/Photos by Poller Systemlogistik GmbH, Übersetzung/Translated by David Strauss)

Wir machen Leistung sichtbar

The Fruit of Our Labours is Visible

Wenn ein Unternehmen der Baubranche stetig wächst, obwohl die äußeren Bedingungen, sprich beispielsweise die enorm gestiegenen Diesel- und Rohstoffpreise, ruinöser Preiskampf, schlechte Zahlungsmoral und ausufernde Schwarzarbeit, immer ungünstiger werden, dann sollte man mal genauer hinschauen.

Die Hoch- und Tiefbau Reichenbach GmbH (HTR) gibt es seit 1992. Gegründet als Tochter der Wayss & Freytag AG, erwarben Rolf und Ingolf Nöbel sämtliche Gesellschafteranteile und lösten sich 1999 einvernehmlich von der Mutterfirma. „Es war eine fruchtbringende Zeit mit Wayss & Freytag, die erfahrenen Leute aus dem Westen haben uns fit für die Marktwirtschaft gemacht", so das Resümee Rolf Nöbels. Doch die Nöbels wären keine echten Vogtländer, wenn sie nicht die Zeichen der Zeit erkannt hätten und sich nicht neuen Herausforderungen stellen wollten. Und so starteten Vater und Sohn als alleinige Gesellschafter voll durch: Die Zahl der Beschäftigten stieg von 79 auf 100, der Umsatz wuchs von fünf auf fast 13 Mio. im Jahr 2006 und fast 5 Mio. reinvestierte das Unternehmen in neues Gerät. Dadurch kann jeder Bauarbeiter der Firma jeweils drei Maschinen bewirtschaften und es kann parallel an mehreren Baustellen gearbeitet werden.

Doch wie geht das? Die Firmenchefs jedenfalls machen daraus kein Geheimnis. Qualität, Termineinhaltung, Spezialisierung und Verlässlichkeit – so die Eckpfeiler des Erfolgs. Die Firmenphilosophie läßt sich so ganz einfach umschreiben: „Wir müssen astreine Arbeit abliefern und überdurchschnittlich produktiv sein!" Beschaffung von Arbeit, straffe Planung, verantwortungsvolle Einschätzung der Auftragslage, das Abwägen von Kosten und Nutzen mit dem steten Blick auf die Sicherung der Arbeits- und Ausbildungsplätze und den Prinzipien treu bleiben – das ist Tagesgeschäft dieses erfolgreichen vogtländischen Bauunternehmens. Und überall im Dreiländereck sieht man was von den fleißigen Bauleuten aus Reichenbach. In den letzten Jahren von der HTR fertig gestellte Großprojekte sind zum Beispiel: B 283 Morgenröthe-Rautenkranz, Kreisverkehr in Plauen-Schöpsdrehe, die Kreisel Reichenbach, Goldene Höhe Treuen und Netzschkau, die Kreuzung in Lengenfeld, der Reichenbacher Kirchplatz, der Parkplatz an der Göltzschtalbrücke, 35 km Kanalbau an der A 72 Chemnitz-Leipzig und Arbeiten im Zuge der Weststraße zwischen A 72, Anschlussstelle Reichenbach und der A 4.

If a company in the construction industry is growing continually, even though the ambient conditions are worsening due to enormous increases in the price of fuel and raw materials, a cut-throat price war, reluctance to settle invoices or the black market that has got out of hand, it is well worth taking a closer look.

Hoch- und Tiefbau Reichenbach GmbH (HTR) has existed since 1992. Founded as a subsidiary of Wayss & Freytag AG, it split from the parent company amicably in 1999 when Rolf and Ingolf Nöbels acquired all the partner shares. "It was a fruitful time with Wayss & Freytag", summarizes Rolf Nöbels. "Coming from western Germany, they helped us get in shape for the free market economy." Yet the Nöbels would not be real Vogtland people if they had they not recognised the signs of the time and wanted to face new challenges. So father and son started their own business, the two of them being the sole partners. The number of employees increased from 79 to 100, turnover grew from € 5 to almost € 13 million in 2006; and the company reinvested almost € 5 million in new equipment. This means that every construction worker at the company can now operate three machines so that work can proceed at various constructions sites at the same time.

But how did they accomplish this? The company managers are happy to reveal their secret. Quality, meeting deadlines, specialisation and reliability are the key pillars of their success. The company philosophy is easy to summarise: "We need to provide first-class work and our productivity must be above average!" Acquiring work, tight planning, appraising the order book situation in a responsible manner, assessing the costs and benefits, guaranteeing jobs and apprenticeship positions and remaining true to principles – that is the day-to-day business at this successful Vogtland construction company. The busy construction workers from Reichenbach can be seen all over the Vogtland region. Some of the major projects completed by HTR over the past few years include the B283 main road in Morgenröthe-Rautenkranz, the roundabout at Plauen-Schöpsdrehe, the roundabouts in Reichenbach, Goldene Höhe Treuen and Netzschkau, the cross roads in Lengenfeld, the church square in Reichenbach, the car park at the Göltzsch Valley Bridge, 35 km of drains along the A72 motorway between Chemnitz and Leipzig and work that forms part of the Western Road project between the A72 motorway junction at Reichenbach and the A4 motorway.

Hoch- und Tiefbau Reichenbach GmbH
Friedensstraße 43
D-08468 Reichenbach
Telefon +49 (0) 3765 7888-0
Telefax +49 (0) 3765 7888-39
www.ht-reichenbach.de
HTR_RC@t-online.de

Übersetzung/Translated by David Strauss

Wir investieren in das Wachstum unserer Region
We Are Investing in the Growth of Our Region

Ob Investition, Wachstum oder Unternehmensnachfolge – die BSV-Beteiligungsgesellschaft der Sparkasse Vogtland mbH begründet mit einer offenen oder stillen Beteiligung eine langfristige Partnerschaft mit Ihnen und Ihrem Unternehmen. Bei der Zusammenarbeit legen wir Wert darauf, das operative Geschäft und die unternehmerische Verantwortung in den Händen des Managements zu belassen. Bei strategischen Fragestellungen sind wir ein anerkannter Sparringspartner, der auf Erfahrungen aus über 40 Beteiligungen in den unterschiedlichsten Branchen zurückgreifen kann. Unternehmen schätzen vor allem unsere Zuverlässigkeit, Geschwindigkeit und Flexibilität. Aber auch langfristige Orientierung und Berechenbarkeit zählen zu unseren Stärken.

Die BSV-Beteiligungsgesellschaft der Sparkasse Vogtland mbH ist eine Tochtergesellschaft der Sparkasse Vogtland und stellt Beteiligungskapital für kleine und mittelständische Unternehmen im Wirtschaftsraum Vogtland zur Verfügung. Seit 1997 investieren wir in das Wachstum unserer Region. Mit einer Investitionssumme von mehr als 20 Mio. Euro ist die BSV eine der größten Sparkassenbeteiligungsgesellschaften.

Das Team der BSV besteht aus den Geschäftsführern Thomas Bleier und Maik Immel sowie 3 weiteren Mitarbeitern.

Im Rahmen von branchenübergreifenden Engagements stellen wir Risikokapital ohne Sicherheiten für Investitionen, die Erschließung neuer Märkte, Forschung und Entwicklung sowie die Unternehmensnachfolge zur Verfügung.

Die BSV wendet sich insbesondere an Unternehmen, die eine Eigenkapitalstärkung benötigen, um damit eine schnellere und bessere Verwirklichung von Unternehmenszielen zu erreichen.

Langjährige Erfahrungen in Finanzierungsfragen und eine schlanke Unternehmensstruktur garantieren Ihnen eine flexible und zeitnahe Entscheidungsfindung zu Ihrer Beteiligungsanfrage. Vertrauen Sie auf das gewachsene Know-how unserer Beteiligungsmanager. Profitieren Sie von unseren speziellen Dienstleistungen zur Steuerung und Unterstützung von Planungs- und Controllingprozessen, unserem umfangreichen Netzwerk sowie unseren Angeboten zum Wissenstransfer.

Regardless of whether investments, growth or corporate succession is at stake – the BSV Investment Company at the Vogtland Savings Bank will set up a long-term partnership with your company by taking an open or dormant partner's holding. During the partnership we place great important on leaving the operational business and the responsibility for the company firmly in the hands of the managers. We are a recognised sparring partner when it comes to strategic issues and we can resort to experience from more than 40 holdings in a wide variety of sectors. Companies primarily appreciate our reliability, speed and flexibility. But our strengths also include long-term orientation and predictability.

The BSV Investment Company at the Vogtland Savings Bank is a subsidiary of the Vogtland Savings Bank and makes investment capital available for small and medium-sized companies in the Vogtland business region. We have been investing in the growth of our region since 1997. The BSV is one of the largest savings bank holding companies with total investments of more than € 20 million.

The BSV team consists of the managers Thomas Bleier and Maik Immel and 3 other members of staff.

As part of our commitment that spans various types of business, we make venture capital available without any securities for investments so that companies can open up new markets, carry out research and development and arrange corporate succession issues.

The BSV particularly approaches companies, which need to reinforce their equity capital to achieve their company goals more quickly and in a better way.

Many years of experience in funding matters and a slim company structure guarantee that the decision making process related to your enquiry on holdings will be flexible and fast. Trust the mature expertise of our investment managers. Benefit from our special services for managing and supporting planning and controlling processes, our comprehensive network and our proposals for transferring knowledge.

Zuverlässiger und fairer Partner mittelständischer Unternehmen:
- gemeinsam unternehmerische Chancen realisieren
- innovative, maßgeschneiderte Finanzierungen durch Bereitstellung von Eigenkapital
- Netzwerk und umfangreiche Geschäftskontakte
- Kompetent in Fragen der Finanzierung und Fördermittelberatung

Geschäftsführer von links Thomas Bleier und Maik Immel

BSV Beteiligungsgesellschaft der Sparkasse Vogtland mbH

Dr.- Friedrichs-Straße 37
D-08606 Oelsnitz/Vogtl.
Telefon +49 (0) 37421 729 66
Telefax +49 (0) 37421 729 67
bsv-beteiligungsgesellschaft@t-online.de
www.sparkasse-vogtland.de

(Fotos/Photos by Igor Pastierovic, Text/Text by BSV, Übersetzung/Translated by David Strauss)

Stärken und Dynamik – die Wirtschaft im Vogtland
The Vogtland Economy – Strong and Dynamic

Die Geschichte der Wirtschaft im Vogtland ist ähnlich gekennzeichnet wie dessen Topografie – Berge wechseln sich ab mit Tälern, Tiefen mit Höhen, kahle, windumtoste Pöhle mit dichten, lauschigen Tannenwäldern ... Nachdem das gesamte Vogtland Jahrhunderte geprägt war von einer subsitenzlastigen Agrarwirtschaft und bescheidenem Kleingewerbetum, setzte Ende des 19. Jahrhunderts ein enormer wirtschaftlicher Boom ein. Zwar war das Vogtland schon immer durchzogen von Transitstraßen und –wegen, doch ein Ausbau dieser Trassen und insbesondere das Hinzukommen verschiedener Eisenbahnstrecken gaben der regionalen Wirtschaft entscheidende Impulse. Natürlich konnte zu dieser Zeit die Effizienz wachsender Wirtschaften hervorragend an den damals auch schon internationalen Märkten in Anschlag gebracht werden. So entwickelten sich im Vogtland hochmoderne, innovationsstarke und markendominierende Branchen und Produkte. Vornehmlich die Textilindustrie (Plauener Spitze) und der Maschinenbau (s. Seiten 52 bis 53 und Seiten 62 bis 75) waren hier die treibenden Kräfte. Die Stadt Markneukirchen errang 1910 gar den ersten Platz der Städte mit den reichsten Einwohnern in Bezug auf die Einwohnerzahl.

Kurzum: Die hervorragende internationale Konjunktur dieser Zeit (nicht zu vergessen ist hierbei auch die gestärkte Kaufkraft und Zuversicht der Menschen durch die Gründung bzw. Zusammenfassung des Deutschen Reiches 1871), die Folgen der technisch-industriellen Revolution und die verkehrgünstige Lage des Vogtlandes erwiesen sich als die wesentlichen Erfolgsfaktoren. Nach nunmehr gut 100 Jahren des Blühens, des Vergehens, des Wiederaufbaus, der Stagnation und zunächst schleppend verlaufender Restaurationsversuchen der wirtschaftlichen Kraft nach der Wende scheint sich der Kreis zu schließen. Auch wenn die Thematik „Parallelen zur Geschichte" polarisiert – die gegenwärtige Lage der vogtländischen Wirtschaft lässt durchaus Vergleiche auf die Zeit kurz nach der Jahrhundertwende vor 100 Jahren zu. Aufbruchstimmung, Zukunftsvertrauen, Investitionsfreude und eine Vielzahl neuer gewerblicher Ansiedlungen gaben damals Aufschluss über wachsende Prosperität.

Sowohl die Rahmenbedingungen als auch die harten und weichen Indikatoren zeigen deutliche Gleichnisse zur heutigen Situation der vogtländischen Wirtschaft. Eine positive globale Konjunkturentwicklung, die Autobahn A72 als infrastrukturelle Lebensader und die explosionsartige Entwicklung von Innovationen sowie die Erschließung neuer Märkte bilden dabei den Handlungsrahmen.

Ein markantes Merkmal dieser Entwicklung sind die bestehenden und neu hinzukommenden Gewerbegebiete. Ob das Gewerbegebiet Neuensalz in Plauen, Johannisberg in Oelsnitz, die Goldene Höhe in Treuen, das Gewerbegebiet Reichenbach und viele andere – Unternehmen jeder Couleur haben sich bereits im Vogtland niedergelassen. Zudem ist eine verstärkte Neuan-

The history of the economy in the Vogtland region is similar to its topography – hills alternate with valleys, troughs with high points, bare, windy peaks with dense, snug pine forests. After life in the whole Vogtland region had been dominated by subsistence farming and small businesses for centuries, an enormous economic boom started at the end of the 19th century. It is true that the Vogtland region was always criss-crossed by transit routes and paths, but the upgrading of these routes and particularly the arrival of various railway lines provided the regional economy with a powerful boost. Of course it was possible to tune expanding businesses efficiently to the markets that were already operating in an international manner at the time. So the Vogtland region developed extremely modern, innovative sectors and products with brand names that dominated the market. The driving forces here were primarily the textile industry (Plauen lace) and engineering (see pages 52-53 and pages 62-75). The town of Markneukirchen was even top of the list of towns with the richest residents related to the size of its population in 1910.

In short, the excellent international economic situation at this time (the increase in purchasing power and people's confidence caused by the founding of the German Empire and integration into it in 1871 should not be forgotten at this point), the results of the industrial revolution and the favourable location of the Vogtland region in transport terms were all major success factors. Now after a good 100 years of prosperity, decay, reconstruction, stagnation and what were initially sluggish attempts to revitalise the economy after the fall of the Berlin Wall, it appears that the process has turned full circle. Even if the subject of "parallels with history" tends to polarise opinions – the current situation in the Vogtland economy definitely allows comparisons to be drawn with the time shortly after the turn of the century 100 years ago. A sense of optimism, confidence in the future, a readiness to invest and a number of firms moving to the area to set up in business were the marks of growing prosperity at that time.

Both the general conditions and the hard and soft indicators reflect clear parallels with the current situation in the Vogtland economy. The trading environment is marked by positive global economic developments, the A72 motorway as the infrastructure lifeline, the explosive development of innovative products and the ability to tap into new markets.

The business parks that already exist and those that will join them are one of the striking features of this development. Whichever business park it is – Neuensalz in Plauen, Johannisberg in Oelsnitz, Goldene Höhe in Treuen, the Reichenbach commercial park or many others – companies of every shade have already set up factories in the Vogtland region. Other companies, some of them well-known, are setting up in business in the area. In addition, traditional sites and factory buildings – like the production facilities of Philips or MAN – have been retained or even expanded.

(Fotos/Photos by Hartmut Briese, Text/Text by André Zeidler, Übersetzung/Translated by David Strauss)

siedlung zum Teil renommierter Unternehmen zu verzeichnen. Aber auch traditionelle Standorte und Werksanlagen wie die heutigen Produktionsstätten von Philips oder MAN konnten aufrechterhalten und sogar ausgebaut werden.

Dabei ist die Balance zwischen Unternehmen, die ihren Sitz im Vogtland haben und denen mit auswärtiger Firmenzentrale relativ ausgeglichen. Ein Grund dafür ist die erfolgreiche Förderpolitik der Verantwortlichen. Ein unternehmerfreundliches Umfeld, eine schnelle Abwicklung bürokratischer Prozesse, hervorragend ausgebildete Fachkräfte und die exzellente Verkehrsanbindung machen das Vogtland zu einem zukunftsweisenden Standort.

Ein besonderes Wachstum zeigt sich im Bereich der Industrie und der gewerblichen Fertigung. Firmen wie Magnetto, Weidmann Plastics, CarTrim oder Optiplan sind Zulieferer für die Automobildindustrie; Neoplan oder die WEMA sind gar im Bereich der Automobilfertigung tätig. Daneben gibt es eine Reihe weiterer Firmen, die in ihrer jeweiligen Branche führende Positionen und sogar Markt entscheidende Einflüsse haben.

Auf einer Augenhöhe mit den Niederlassungen großer Unternehmen und Konzerne im Vogtland befinden sich durchaus auch regional ansässige, junge und dynamische Firmen. Engagierte und couragierte Vogtländer haben hier Beachtliches zu Wege gebracht. Oft war der Weg zu einer erfolgreichen Marktteilnahme von bescheidensten Mitteln und äußerst vagen Zukunftsaussichten flankiert. Doch genau diese Firmen sind es in der Regel auch, die mit Innovationen international Akzente setzen und der Region neue Impulse verleihen. Sei es die IK Elektronik GmbH, die elektronische Wireless-Komponenten entwickelt, sei es die GETT Gerätetechnik GmbH, die neue Lösungen in der industriellen Dateneingabe erfindet, oder die Lengenfelder Kobra, die einzigartige Bauelemente vermarktet – das Vogtland ist nicht nur günstiger Standort für produzierende Niederlassungen, sondern ein Innovationsstandort, der national und international Achtungszeichen setzt.

Neben der Ansiedlung neuer Branchen, Firmen und Technologien werden traditionelle Wirtschaftszweige erfolgreich, wenn auch zum Teil in kleinerem Umfang als in den jeweiligen Epochen der Massenproduktion, weitergeführt. Dies betrifft insbesondere den Exportschlager „Plauener Spitze" oder den Bau von Musikinstrumenten im „Musicon Valley", der bereits seit über 350 Jahren im Raum Klingenthal-Markneukirchen währt.

Alles in allem befindet sich das Vogtland auf dem Weg zu einem exzellenten Wirtschaftsstandort, der von mittelständischen Firmen dominiert wird und der zunehmend innovative Kräfte entwickelt. Ein mehr als geeigneter Standort also für Unternehmen, die auf Synergien setzen und die ein gesundes, nachhaltiges Wachstum im Blickfeld haben.

The balance between companies, which have their headquarters in the Vogtland region and those with company headquarters at a distance, is relatively good. One reason for this is the successful subsidies policy pursued by the authorities. The Vogtland region is a forward-looking area – it has a business friendly environment, bureaucratic processes are handled quickly and specialists with outstandingly good training and excellent transport links are available.

Industry and the manufacturing sector have shown particularly strong growth. Companies like Magnetto, Weidmann Plastics, CarTrim or Optiplan are suppliers to the automobile industry; Neoplan or WEMA are actually involved in making vehicles. Then there are a number of other companies, which occupy a leading position in their sector or are even dictating the market.

There are also young, dynamic, regionally based firms, which are well able to hold their own against the branch offices of large companies or groups. Committed and bold Vogtland individuals have achieved a great deal. Often their pathway to a successful market position was accompanied by a lack of funds and extremely vague prospects for the future. But these companies are exactly the ones that are setting the tone internationally and are providing the region with new incentives – companies like IK Elektronik GmbH, which is developing electronic wireless components, or GETT Gerätetechnik GmbH, which is providing new solutions for industrial data input, or Kobra in Lengenfeld, which is marketing unique components – the Vogtland region is not only a good location for manufacturing companies, but also an innovative area, which is setting the tone at home and abroad.

As well as attracting new sectors, companies and technologies, traditional business sectors are also being continued successfully – even if some of them are much smaller than in the periods of mass production. This particularly relates to the export hit "Plauen lace" or the making of musical instruments in "Musicon Valley", which has been continuing in the Klingenthal-Markneukirchen area for more than 350 years.

All in all, the Vogtland region is on the way to becoming a business centre of excellence, which is dominated by medium-sized enterprises, and it is increasingly showing that its innovations are a force to be reckoned with. So it is a more than ideal location for companies on the look-out for synergies and healthy, sustained growth.

Made in Vogtland / Vogtland Economy

» *Engagierte und couragierte Vogtländer haben hier Beachtliches zu Wege gebracht. Oft war der Weg zu einer erfolgreichen Marktteilnahme von bescheidensten Mitteln und äußerst vagen Zukunftsaussichten flankiert. Doch genau diese Firmen sind es in der Regel auch, die mit Innovationen international Akzente setzen und der Region neue Impulse verleihen.* «

» *Committed and bold Vogtland individuals have achieved a great deal. Often their pathway to a successful market position was accompanied by a lack of funds and extremely vague prospects for the future. But these companies are exactly the ones that are setting the tone internationally and are providing the region with new incentives.* «

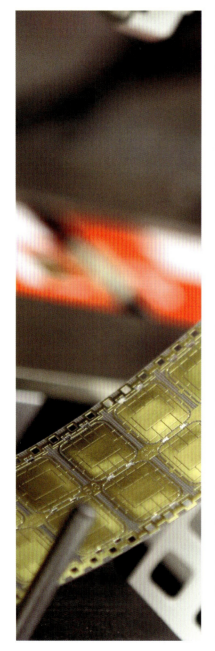

(Fotos/Photos by Igor Pastierovic)

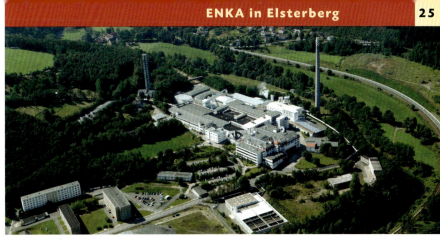

100 Jahre Werk Elsterberg
Centenary at Elsterberg Factory

Im Jahr 1909 wurde der Grundstein für ein Werk gelegt, das noch heute, nach rund 100 Jahren, den wirtschaftlichen Mittelpunkt der vogtländischen Kleinstadt Elsterberg bildet.
In der Region, die von der Textilindustrie gekennzeichnet war, wurde 1909 erstmals eine Krimmerfabrik aufgebaut. Der mangelnde Absatz ließ dieses Unternehmen recht bald wieder schließen, aber die Voraussetzungen für eine Ansiedlung weiterer Industrie war durch die örtliche Erschließung gegeben.
Die Geburtsstunde der heutigen „ENKA" schlug im Dezember 1918: die „Spinnfaser Aktiengesellschaft Elsterberg" wurde gegründet. Künftig sollte hier ein Viskosefilamentgarn gesponnen und so weiter behandelt werden, dass es direkt zur weiterverarbeitenden Textilindustrie verkauft werden kann.
Von mancher Schließung bedroht, stabilisierte sich das Werk besonders in den 30er und 60er Jahren, in denen die Produktionsanlagen und auch die Verfahrenstechnik geändert und automatisiert wurden.
Anfang der 90er Jahre begann die grundhafte Sanierung des Werkes. Anlagen des chemischen und textilen Bereiches, Roh- und Hilfsstoffläger wurden modernisiert bzw. neu gebaut. Kraftwerk, Abluftreinigungsanlage und eine Kläranlage entstanden nach den neuesten Umweltnormen. Seitdem gehen in Elsterberg, dem größten Chemiebetrieb des Regierungsbezirkes Chemnitz, Chemie und Umwelt miteinander konform.
Seit nunmehr fast 90 Jahren wird hier Viskosefilamentgarn hergestellt. Die einst körperliche Schwerstarbeit wurde durch modernste rechnergesteuerte Maschinen wesentlich erleichtert. Mit dem Wissen und Können der Mitarbeiter wird heute in Elsterberg Viskoseseide in höchster Qualität für Kunden in aller Welt hergestellt.
Aus der ehemaligen „Spinn", die hier gut bekannt war, wurde die „ENKA", die weit über Deutschlands Grenzen einen Namen hat und deren Viskosefilamentgarn von den Kunden der Textilindustrie begehrt und bevorzugt gekauft wird.

The foundations for a factory were laid in 1909 – and it still accounts for the lion's share of the economy in the small Vogtland town of Elsterberg almost 100 years later.
A krimmer factory was established here in 1909 in a region that was dominated by the textile industry. However a lack of sales led to the closure of this company very soon afterwards. But the conditions for attracting other industries had been created by the development of this site.
The beginnings of today's "ENKA" works go back to December 1918: the "Spinnfaser Aktiengesellschaft Elsterberg" was set up. It was designed to spin viscose filament yarn and then treat it in such a way that it could be sold directly to the textile industry for further processing.
Threatened by closure on many occasions, the factory's fate settled down in the 1930s and 1960s when the production equipment and the process engineering were changed and automated.
A fundamental upgrading of the factory began in the early 1990s. The equipment in the chemical and textile areas, raw and ancillary materials stores was modernised or reconstructed. The power station, waste air purification plant and a sewage works were installed to meet the latest environmental standards. Since that time, the chemicals industry and the environment have gone hand in hand at Elsterberg – which also happens to be the largest chemicals plant in the Chemnitz administrative district.
Viscose filament yarn has been produced here for almost 90 years now. What was once hard physical labour has now been made much easier by the installation of the latest computer-controlled machinery. Top-quality viscose silk is manufactured here in Elsterberg for customers all round the globe using the workers' expertise and skills. What used to be called the "Spinn" is now known as "ENKA" and its reputation has spread far beyond Germany's borders. Customers in the textile industry are keen to purchase its viscose filament yarn, which is much in demand.

ENKA®
THE ART OF VISCOSE

EP Elsterberg GmbH & Co. KG
Walter-Suchanek-Str. 29
D-07985 Elsterberg
Telefon +49 (0) 36621 84-0
Telefax +49 (0) 36621 84-201
info@enka.de
www.enka.de

(Fotos/Photos by ENKA, Übersetzung/Translated by David Strauss)

SGB Sächsisch-Bayerische Starkstrom-Gerätebau GmbH

Die Neumarker SGB GmbH sorgt weltweit für Power
SGB GmbH in Neumark Delivers Power World-wide

Ein Unternehmen mit Power ist die SGB in Neumark – und das im wahrsten Sinne des Wortes. Seit vielen Jahren ist das 320 Mann starke Unternehmen Marktführer im Bereich von Ortsnetzverteilungstrafos. Diese Geräte bilden die finale Stufe der Energieumspannung vom Kraftwerk bis zu den Endabnehmern. Die Kunden für solche Trafos sind große Energiekonzerne, mittlere Energieversorger wie Stadtwerke, die Industrie mit eigenen Netzen oder Elektroanlagenbauer. Mit etwa einem Drittel Marktanteil ist die SGB seit Jahren Marktführer in Deutschland. Rund 10 000 Trafos setzte das Unternehmen im letzten Jahr ab, davon 4 500 im Export, 5 500 in Deutschland. Insgesamt betrug der Umsatz im vergangenen Jahr 120 Millionen Euro.

Eine Besonderheit ist, dass das Unternehmen seit Jahren der einzig verbliebene Großproduzent von Verteiltransformatoren am Standort Deutschland ist. Während multinationale Konzerne ihre Produktion längst in das benachbarte osteuropäische Ausland verlegt haben, ist die SGB im Vogtland überaus erfolgreich. Wolfgang Kessler, technischer Geschäftsführer des Unternehmens, kennt die Werttreiber seines Unternehmens sehr genau: „Unsere konsequente Ausrichtung auf die Kundenbedürfnisse, präzise Just-in-Time-Prozesse und unbedingte Termintreue bei Lieferungen sind unsere Erfolgsgaranten. Hier im Vogtland haben wir dabei ideale infrastrukturelle Bedingungen und können uns auf unser qualifiziertes Personal verlassen."

Das offizielle Gründungsjahr der SGB GmbH, die zur SGB Gruppe mit Sitz in Regensburg gehört, ist 1990. Doch die Historie geht weiter zurück, denn das Unternehmen firmierte früher unter dem weithin bekannten Namen Transformatorenwerk Reichenbach, welches 1947 gegründet wurde. Nach Joint-venture, Firmenverlegung und Sanierung befindet sich der Neumarker Trafospezialist in einem stetigen Aufwärtstrend. „Durch die wachsende Inhomogenität des Strommarktes und die immer spezifischeren Anforderungen sehen wir für uns ein hohes Wachstumspotenzial", prognostiziert Wolfgang Kessler die Entwicklung der nächsten Jahre.

The SGB in Neumark is a company with power – in the truest sense of the word. The company with its 320 employees has been the market leader in the field of local network distribution transformers for many years. These units form the final stage where energy from power stations is transformed for use by the final consumer. The main customers for these transformers are major energy conglomerates, medium-size electric supply companies like municipal suppliers, industries with their own supply networks or electrical installation manufacturers. SGB has been market leader in Germany for years with a market share of about a third. The company sold about 10,000 transformers last year, 4,500 of them abroad and 5,500 in Germany. Last year overall turnover was € 120 million.

There is something very special about this company: it has been the only remaining large-scale producer of distribution transformers in Germany for years. While multinational corporations shifted production to neighbouring countries in Eastern Europe a long time ago, SGB in the Vogtland region is extremely successful. Wolfgang Kessler, technical manager at the company, knows very well what the value drivers for the company are: "Our consistent focus on customer needs, precise just-in-time processes and absolute adherence to delivery dates are the things that guarantee our success. Here in the Vogtland region we have ideal infrastructure and we can rely on our qualified staff."

SGB GmbH, which is part of the SGB Group with its headquarters in Regensburg, was officially set up in 1990. But its history goes back even further. It used to trade under the well-known "Transformatorenwerk Reichenbach" name and that company was founded in 1947. After a joint venture, the relocation of the company and restructuring, the Neumark transformer specialist has shown continual growth. "Due to the increased disparity of the electricity market and more and more specific requirements, we believe we have huge growth potential," Wolfgang Kessler predicts as he looks forward to developments over the next few years.

Partners in Power

SGB Sächsisch-Bayerische Starkstrom-Gerätebau GmbH
Ohmstraße 1
D - 08496 Neumark
Telefon +49 (0) 37600 83-0
Telefax +49 (0) 37600 3414
info@sgb-neumark.de
www.sgb-trafo.de

(Fotos/Photos by Igor Pastierovic, Text/Text by André Zeidler, Übersetzung/Translated by David Strauss)

Mit Wärmetauschern weltweit gutes Renommee

Excellent world-wide reputation for heat exchangers

Mit 180 Mitarbeitern, viele davon sind Ingenieure, zählt die NEMA AirFin GmbH aus Netzschkau zu den stabilen Unternehmen des Vogtlandes. Die zum amerikanischen SPX-Konzern gehörende Firma fertigt so genannte luftbeaufschlagte Wärmetauscher. Dabei strömen vom Prinzip her in Rohren flüssige oder gasförmige Medien, wie zum Beispiel Wasser oder Öle, Gase oder Dämpfe, die mittels Luft gekühlt werden. An der Außenseite der Rohre befindet sich Luft, deshalb luftbeaufschlagt. Dabei ist der Betrieb in der Lage, vom Wärmetauscher als Komponente bis hin zur vollständigen Kühlanlage alles zu montieren. Konstruktion, Fertigung, Montage und Service wird von den Vogtländern offeriert.

Gegenwärtig fertigen die Netzschkauer für Siemens Power Generation den zweiten Satz Kühlsysteme, sieben an der Zahl, für Kraftwerke in Südafrika. Ebenso sind zwei große Luftkühler für die Bayern-Oil-Raffinerie in Ingolstadt in Arbeit. Jüngst konnte ein größeres Projekt mit BP in Gelsenkirchen abgeschlossen werden. Ebenfalls renommierte Kunden waren und sind weltweit Dow Chemical oder Royal Dutch Shell.

Seit 2002 gehört die NEMA AirFin GmbH zu dem amerikanischen Konzern aus Charlotte und ist dort Teil des Konzernbereichs Flow Technology.

Zu den 180 Beschäftigten gehören auch insgesamt zehn Auszubildende im kaufmännischen und gewerblichen Bereich. Die Mitarbeiterzahl konnte in den vergangenen Jahren gesteigert werden, noch vor vier Jahren zählte die Firma 150 Frauen und Männer als Arbeitnehmer.

Das Unternehmen ist stolz auf die positive Entwicklung in den vergangenen Jahren, betont der Vertriebsleiter Stefan Fiedler. Ebenso fühlt man sich der Region verbunden, indem beispielsweise der TSV Nema Netzschkau unterstützt wird.

With 180 employees, a lot of them engineers, the limited corporation Nema AirFin GmbH from Netzschkau is among the most stable companies of the Vogtland. The company that is part of the American SPX group produces so called air cooled heat exchangers. According to this principle liquid or gaseous mediums such as water or oil, gases or vapours, are flowing inside the tubes that are cooled down by use of air, which is on the outside of the tubes; hence the term air cooled. On top of that the company is able to assemble everything from a heat exchanger as a simple component to a complete cooling plant. Design, manufacturing, erection and service are all offered by this Vogtland company.

At the moment the Netzschkau based company is supplying a second set of cooling systems, precisely 7 of them, for the Siemens Power Generation which will be operated in power plants in South Africa. At the same time the company is also working on two large air condensers for the Bayern-Oil-Refinery in Ingolstadt. In addition, a larger-scale project for BP in Gelsenkirchen was completed a short while ago. Further well-known worldwide clients have been and are Dow Chemical or Royal Dutch Shell.

The Nema AirFin GmbH has been a society of the American SPX group from Charlotte since 2002 and is part of the group's Flow Technology division.

Ten of the 180 employees of the company are apprentices for the commercial department or the workshop. In the past years the number of employees could be increased. Four years ago there were only 150 men and women working for the company.

The Nema AirFin GmbH is proud of its positive development in the past years, emphasizes sales manager Stefan Fiedler. Similarly, there is a close connection to the region, which results in the company being the proud sponsor for the TSV Nema Netzschkau sports club.

NEMA AirFin GmbH
Reinsdorfer Weg 4
D-08491 Netzschkau
Telefon +49 (0) 3765 492-0
Telefax +49 (0) 3765 492-567
nema@balcke-duerr.de
www.nema-airfin.de

(Fotos/Photos by Igor Pastierovic ,Text/Text by Bert Walther)

Johannes Steiniger Metallwarenfabrik

Wer nicht kämpft, der hat schon verloren
Without a Fight You Lose Anyway

Im Jahre 1934 gründete Johannes Steiniger die Firma Johannes Steiniger & Co., die sich bis zum 2. Weltkrieg mit der Herstellung von Bauklempnerartikeln befasste. Der Krieg hatte dem Unternehmen schwer zugesetzt, Fachkräfte und Rohstoffe fehlten. Mit geringstem Materialaufwand wurden in enger Zusammenarbeit mit der Firma Seidel & Eckert Plauen aus alten Munitionskästen Kohleherde gefertigt.

In der sozialistischen Planwirtschaft waren die Möglichkeiten für erfolgreiches wirtschaftliches Handeln als Privatunternehmen stark reglementiert. Doch das besondere Geschick der Hammerbrücker Firma hatte sich wohl herumgesprochen, denn sie sollte für die Leuna-Werke Blechverpackungsmittel herstellen. „Das war ein verlockendes Angebot, Artikel fertigen zu können, die gebraucht werden", erinnert sich die Firmenchefin. Für ein Weiterkommen in der damaligen DDR musste das Familienunternehmen allerdings „Staatliche Beteiligung" aufnehmen, es entstand 1959 die „Johannes Steiniger KG". Zur tatkräftigen Unterstützung für den mittlerweile 60-jährigen Firmengründer nahmen im gleichen Jahr Tochter Renate und deren Mann Ulrich Albert ihre Tätigkeit im Betrieb auf. Die Beschäftigtenzahl stieg rasch an und von Seiten der staatlichen Organe wurde die Forderung erhoben, die gesamte Erzeugnispalette zu vervollkommnen. So wurden neben den 200- und 100-Liter-Sickenfässern noch Hobbocks der Größen 25 bis 50 Liter, Enghalskannen, Kanister und Blechstreifenkörbe gefertigt. Den laufenden Forderungen nach mehr Quantität bei entsprechender Qualität nachkommen zu können und rentabel produzieren zu können, entschloss sich der Komplementär Steiniger im Einvernehmen mit seiner Familie eine für die derzeitige Größe des Betriebes erhebliche Investition durchzuführen. Selbst als Hauptauftraggeber fungierend und bei laufender Produktion erfolgten ab Frühjahr 1969 die Baumaßnahmen und die Produktionsumstellung. Nach Realisierung aller Vorhaben im Februar 1972 dauerte die Freude nicht lange an, denn der Betrieb wurde im April enteignet, den Besitzern innerhalb von 14 Tagen entrissen. Unter Leitung der Tochter des Alteigentümers war der VEB (Volkseigener Betrieb) Blechpackung Hammerbrücke bis zum Zusammenbruch der sozialistischen Staatsmacht Alleinhersteller von Blechemballagen der Größen 25 - 100 Liter für die gesamte chemische Industrie der damaligen DDR.

Kein Stillstand, kein Zögern: Die Geschicke des Betriebs nahm Renate Albert nach der Wende wieder in die eigenen Hände und leitete die Reprivatisierung ein. Die Gebäude und Ausrüstungen waren in einem desolaten Zustand, Altschulden in erheblicher Höhe mussten übernommen werden und die Hälfte des Absatzmarktes war weg gebrochen. „Wie können wir unser Unternehmen retten, welche Ersatzproduktion könnten unsere erfahrenen Mitarbeiter aufnehmen?" Getragen von dem Gedanken des Überlebens und der leidenschaftlichen Begeisterung der Belegschaft wurde mit den vorhandenen Maschinen und Einrichtungen eine Edelstahlproduktion, Schornsteinsysteme ein- und doppelwandig aufgebaut. Mit primitivsten Mitteln und erfinderischem Improvisationsgeist hielt man sich anfangs über Wasser, um sich ein finanzielles Polster für Kredite und den Kauf neuer Maschinen zu schaffen. Und wieder wurde ein neues Kapitel „Steiniger" aufgeschlagen!

Johannes Steiniger founded his company Johannes Steiniger & Co. in 1934; it specialised in the production of plumbing articles until the Second World War. The war affected the company badly, for there was a shortage of qualified labour and raw materials. Coal stoves were manufactured out of old ammunition boxes with minimum material expenditure in close cooperation with the Seidel & Ecker company in Plauen.

The chances of trading successfully as a private company under the socialist planned economy were very limited. However, word of the special skills available at the company in Hammerbrücke had spread: the company was asked to produce sheet metal packaging for the Leuna refineries. "That was a tempting offer – to actually produce something that was needed", the company boss recalls. But in order to be able to make further progress in former East Germany, the family business had to accept some degree of state intervention and this gave birth to the "Johannes Steiniger KG" company in 1959. At the same time daughter Renate and her husband Ulrich Albert started working at the business to support the company's founder, who was now 60 years old. The number of employees increased rapidly and soon the state authorities were demanding that the complete product range should be manufactured. So the production of 200 and 100 litre steel drums was soon expanded to include 25 - 50 litre canisters, narrow-necked jugs, jerry cans and sheet metal cages. In order to be able to meet the demand for greater quantities of goods while maintaining the high quality and cost-effective production methods, the general partner and his family agreed to make what was a significant investment considering the size of the company at that time. Acting as the main customer, the company started construction work in the spring of 1969 and switched the manufacturing procedures without interrupting production. After completing all these measures in February 1972, the sense of satisfaction did not last long. The company was nationalised and taken out of its owners' hands within two weeks in April. Under the management of the daughter of the former owner, the state-owned "Blechpackung Hammerbrücke" combine was the only company producing metal packaging and tin containers in 25 – 100 litre sizes for the whole of the chemicals industry in former East Germany until the socialist state collapsed.

But this was not followed by stagnation or hesitation: after German reunification Renate Albert immediately took control of the company again and started the process of re-privatisation. The buildings and the equipment were in a sorry state, huge previous debts had to be taken over and half of the former sales market had disappeared. "How can we save our business and what new products could our qualified staff make to replace the old ones?" Driven by the will to survive and the passionate dedication of its workers, the company began manufacturing stainless steel to make single and double-skinned chimney stack systems using the existing machinery and equipment. The company survived initially by using the most primitive equipment and plenty of innovative talent. This was needed to create a financial cushion for loans and the purchase of new machinery. The Steinigers opened a new chapter in the history of the company!

(Fotos/Photos by Igor Pastierovic, Übersetzung/Translated by David Strauss)

Johannes Steiniger Metallwarenfabrik

„Wer kämpft, der kann verlieren. Wer nicht kämpft, der hat schon verloren." Für die Firma Johannes Steiniger Metallwarenfabrik GmbH, allen voran Geschäftsführerin Renate Albert, die Tochter des Firmengründers, scheint das Lebensphilosophie zu sein. Immer wieder wurde etwas Neuartiges auf die Beine gestellt, damit es im Betrieb weitergeht. „Es war ein einziger harter Kampf", so beschreibt die Firmenchefin den Neubeginn. „Wir haben 1990 praktisch wieder bei Null angefangen."

Heute werden Umsätze in Millionenhöhe realisiert und gute schwarze Zahlen geschrieben. Systematisch hat sich das Unternehmen einen hochmodernen Maschinenpark zugelegt und rund 15 Mio. Euro investiert. Inzwischen stehen beispielsweise ein Laserschneidzentrum, Stanznippelmaschine, hydraulische Abkantpressen, Tafelscheren und Bandverarbeitungsmaschinen in den modernisierten Produktionshallen. Das Unternehmen hat seinen Platz auf dem Markt gefunden und sich auf die Herstellung von Edelstahlschornsteinen spezialisiert. Gefragt sind auch verschiedene Heizungskomponenten, Kamintüren und Ofeneinsätze aus Metall. Speziell nach Kundenwunsch werden Lagersysteme wie Regale und komplette Werkstattausrüstungen aus Metall gefertigt. Als Dienstleister für andere Firmen bieten die Hammerbrücker Metallarbeiter verschiedene Stanz-, Schneide- und Biegearbeiten bis 100 Tonnen Presskraft an. Und ganz nebenbei hat man noch den „Vogtlandgrill" erfunden. In robuster langlebiger Edelstahlausführung ist er ideal zum Grillen mit Holzkohle.

Der Belegschaft ist es immer wieder gelungen, sich an neue Techniken und Produkte zu wagen. Gezielte Qualifizierungsmaßnahmen und eine bewusste Lehrlingsausbildung sichern die fachliche Zukunft des Betriebes. Die Firma Steiniger ist zertifiziert nach DIN EN ISO 9001:2000. Dass die Fertigung in hoher handwerklicher Qualität, einem attraktiven Preisniveau und bei Bedarf individuell und nach Kundenwunsch erfolgt, hat sich in der Welt herumgesprochen. „Wir haben Kunden in 10 Ländern und 30 % der Produktion gehen ins Ausland", sagt die Firmenchefin. „Mit dem Kunden gemeinsam an den Produkten arbeiten, das ist unsere Stärke. Egal wo die Kunden ihren Sitz haben, wir besuchen sie persönlich vor Ort."

Mit Stolz und mit Blick auf das 75-jährige Firmenjubiläum verweist die Firmenchefin auf die lange Firmentradition, die zugleich auch ein Stück weit Familiengeschichte ist. „Tradition schafft Vertrauen", weiß sie vor allem aus ihren Erfahrungen mit den Kunden im Ausland. „Der Prozess darf nie stillstehen. Wir müssen Vorhandenes verfeinern und Neues entwickeln. Vision ist unser Motor für die Zukunft und Innovation die Brücke beides miteinander zu verbinden, so ihre Zusammenfassung.

"Those who fight may lose, but without a fight you lose anyway." This seems to be the philosophy of the Johannes Steiniger Metallwarenfabrik GmbH company and especially its managing director Renate Albert, the daughter of the company's founder. They repeatedly started up something new in order to keep the business running. "It was a never-ending fight", says company boss Albert. "We virtually started from scratch again in 1990."

The company now has turnover running into millions and is making a profit. The business gradually acquired the latest machinery and has invested more than € 15 million. The modernised production facilities are now home to a laser cutting centre, a metal punching machine, hydraulic press brakes, plate shears and machines for processing strip metal. The company has found its niche in the market and specialises in manufacturing stainless steel chimneys. Various heating components, fireplace doors or furnace elements made of metal complete the product range. Storage systems such as shelves and all the fittings for workshops are made to meet customer requirements. The metalworkers at Hammerbrücke also act as service providers and can handle special punching, cutting or bending tasks with a pressing force of up to 100 tonnes. And they also invented what is known as the "Vogtlandgrill" almost as an afterthought. It is ideal for barbequing with charcoal with its sturdy, durable stainless steel design.

The employees at the company have always been able to come up with new techniques and new products. Specific qualification standards and a deliberate policy of training apprentices ensure that the company will have a future. The Steiniger company is certified according to DIN EN ISO 9001:2000. Word has spread around the world that this company produces quality craftsmanship at attractive prices and, if necessary, is able to produce items to meet individual customer requests. "We have customers in 10 different countries and 30% of our production goes abroad", says the company director. "Our strength is being able to work on products with our customers. Wherever customers are located, we will visit them personally on site."

In view of the 75th anniversary of the company, its director proudly points to the long tradition of the business, which is also a part of her own family history. "Tradition creates trust", especially with customers abroad, she emphasises. "This process must never stop. We have to refine what we have and develop new items. Vision is the engine for the future and innovation is the bridge that connects both," Albert concludes.

Johannes Steiniger GmbH
Falkensteiner Str. 3
D-08269 Hammerbrücke
Telefon +49 (0) 37465/454-0
Telefax +49 (0) 37465/454-25
metall@steiniger-gmbh.de

So fein webt niemand

There is No Finer Weave

Wenn der Präsident von Mali Amadou Toumani Touré hohen Staatsbesuch empfängt oder zu seinem Volk spricht, dann trägt er einen Boubou aus feinstem Afrika-Damast, hergestellt in der ERTEX Jacquard Rodewisch, einem Unternehmensbereich der PEPPERMINT Holding GmbH.

Seit 1995 ist das Unternehmen ERTEX Jacquard auf besonders feine Damaststoffe spezialisiert. Mittlerweile sind es 70 Prozent der Gesamtproduktion, das sind fünf Millionen Quadratmeter, die jährlich in Rodewisch das Haus in Richtung Afrika verlassen. Besondere Webfertigkeiten und technisches Know How haben das Unternehmen zum Marktführer in diesem Bereich werden lassen. Kunden dieses hochwertigen feinstfädigen Gewebes sind aus islamisch geprägten afrikanischen Ländern nördlich des Äquators, wo Männer und Frauen den Boubou als traditionelles Gewand tragen. Für diese Bekleidung werden feinste Baumwollsorten verwendet und es müssen besonders dünne Fäden verarbeitet werden. Zum Beispiel wiegen 135 Meter gerade mal 1 Gramm. Das heißt, es gibt Webmaschinen, die mit über 20.000 Kettfäden produzieren.

Die Qualität des Gewebes prüft der Abnehmer weder mit Lupe noch mit Waage, er erfühlt die Beschaffenheit und Güteklasse des Stoffes.

Die Produktpalette umfasst neben feinfädigem Bekleidungsdamast auch hochwertige Tisch- und Bettwäsche, Dekorationsstoffe, Hemden- und Blusenstoffe, Möbelbezugsstoffe sowie technische Textilien für die Automobilzulieferindustrie. Die Produktionstiefe bei ERTEX Jacquard besteht aus Zettelei, Schlichterei, Weberei und Rohwarenschau. In der Rohwarenschau werden alle Gewebe vor Auslieferung vollständig und gewissenhaft auf Fehler geprüft, auf Länge vermessen und je nach Verwendung zur Weiterverarbeitung vorbereitet.

Die Maschinenbedienung, aber auch die Webvorbereitung erfordern von den Mitarbeitern ein spezielles Geschick, welches nur im Unternehmen selbst ausgebildet werden kann. Deshalb müssen angehende Mitarbeiter ihre Ausbildung erweitern. Wenn zum Beispiel ein bereits im Beruf tätiger ausgebildeter Weber eines anderen Unternehmens in die ERTEX kommt, dann braucht dieser ca. 3 Monate, um sich in die speziellen Anforderungen einzuarbeiten, bei Wirkern sind das sogar bis zu 12 Monate.

When the president of Mali, Amadou Toumani Touré welcomes state visitors or speaks to his people, he wears a boubou made of the finest African damask made by ERTEX Jacquard Rodewisch, a division of PEPPERMINT Holding GmbH.

The ERTEX Jacquard company has been specialising in particularly fine damask materials since 1995. This business now accounts for 70 percent of total production – that is to say, five million square metres, which leave the factory in Rodewisch bound for Africa every year. Particular weaving skills and technical expertise have made the company the market leader in this field. Customers of this high-quality fabric with its finest threats mainly come from Islamic African countries north of the Equator, where men and women wear the boubou as traditional dress. The finest kinds of cotton are used for this clothing and the threads that are processed have to be particularly thin. 135 metres of the material, for example, weigh just 1 gram. This means that there are weaving machines, which work with more than 20,000 warp threads.

Customers do not have to check the quality of the fabric with a magnifying glass or scales – they can feel the consistency and high quality of the material. The company's range of products includes fine filament damask for clothing, high-quality table covers and bedding, decorative materials, fabrics for shirts and blouses, furniture covers and technical textiles for suppliers to the automobile industry. ERTEX Jacquard covers the following production stages: warping, sizing, weaving and inspecting untreated materials. The latter involves checking all the fabrics completely and scrupulously for any errors before supplying them to customers, measuring their length and preparing them for further processing, depending on what they are going to be used for.

Members of staff have to have particular skill to operate the machines and prepare the materials for weaving and this skill can only be acquired through training at the company. This is why prospective staff members have to go through further training. If, for example, a weaver joins ERTEX from another company, he or she needs approx. 3 months to become acquainted with the special demands – and this period may be as long as 12 months in the case of hosiery workers.

(Fotos/Photos by Igor Pastierovic, Hartmut Briese [1], Übersetzung/Translated by David Strauss)

Die Belegschaft mit 125 Festangestellten und derzeit 10 Lehrlingen allein in Rodewisch produziert die begehrten Stoffe auf 74 modernen Webautomaten. In dem im Jahre 2006 eröffneten neuen Werk in Siebenbürgen in Rumänien, welches für die ERTEX als Lohnweberei dient, stehen 32 Webstühle. Kett- und Schussmaterial werden dorthin geliefert, die Rohware kommt zur Qualitätskontrolle und zum Verkauf zurück nach Rodewisch. Das Werk ist derzeit an seiner Kapazitätsgrenze angelangt. Um die zahlreichen Aufträge zu erfüllen, plant die Unternemensführung den Kauf weiterer Webautomaten und damit die Schaffung neuer Arbeitsplätze.

Es war richtig für das Unternehmen sich auf dem Markt der Premiumprodukte zu etablieren. Qualität, eine große Webbreite und die Spezialisierung auf die Verarbeitung feinster Fäden – das sind die Stärken der ERTEX-Produkte und zugleich die Standards, die Billiganbieter nicht liefern können. Im Bereich technischer Textilien ergeben sich für die Jacquard-Weber ebenfalls neue Märkte. Die modernen und sehr flexiblen Jacquard-Technologien erfüllen hervorragend die zunehmenden Anforderungen an die Komplexität der Gewerbekonstruktionen.

Der Grundsatz der Unternehmensphilosophie lässt sich kurz und treffend auf den Punkt bringen: Die drei M – das sind Mensch, Maschine und Material – müssen stimmen, um am Markt erfolgreich zu sein.

The workforce consisting of 125 permanent staff and 10 apprentices at the moment produces the much sought-after materials on 74 modern automatic weaving machines in Rodewisch. There are 32 looms available at the new factory in Transylvania in Romania, which was opened in 2006; it carried out weaving work for ERTEX on a commission basis. Warp and weft material is delivered there; the raw material is subjected to quality checks and is delivered back to Rodewisch ready for sale. The factory has already reached the limits of its capacity. The company managers are planning to purchase more automatic weaving machines to cope with the many orders and thereby create new jobs.

The company made the right decision to start its business in the premium products market. The strengths of ERTEX products and the standards, which cheap suppliers cannot meet, are quality, a huge range of weaving products and specialisation in processing the finest threads. New markets are also opening up for the Jacquard weavers in the field of technical textiles. The modern and highly flexible Jacquard technologies ideally match the growing demand for complex fabric designs.

The company philosophy can be summed up very briefly and aptly: the three Ms – man, machine and material – have to be just right to be a success on the market.

ERTEX
JACQUARD

ERTEX Jacquard
ein Unternehmensbereich der
PEPPERMINT. Holding GmbH
Kohlenstraße 1
D-08228 Rodewisch
Telefon +49 (0) 3744 363-0
Telefax +49 (0) 3744 363-205
info@ertex.de
www.ertex.de

High Tech für den Handel
High Tech for international Retailers

Was haben führende europäische Handelsketten wie dm-drogerie markt, Douglas, EDEKA, Kaufhof, Lidl, Netto, Tchibo oder die Telekom-Shops gemeinsam? Sie alle arbeiten mit Software aus Schöneck im Vogtland.

Die GK SOFTWARE AG ist führender europäischer Hersteller von Softwarelösungen für den Einzelhandel. Mit Software aus Schöneck arbeiten modernste Kassen in Supermärkten und Discountern, Parfümerien und Warenhäusern, werden Inventuren durchgeführt oder Waren bestellt.

Als die Firma 1990 als Zwei-Mann-Firma gegründet wurde, war an eine solche Perspektive noch nicht zu denken. Doch von Anfang an setzten die beiden Unternehmensgründer konsequent auf die Entwicklung eigener Softwareprodukte. Dabei begann schon früh die Spezialisierung auf den Einzelhandel.

Spitzentechnologie verbunden mit hoher Qualität ist seit vielen Jahren das Markenzeichen der Softwarelösungen aus dem Vogtland. Damit wurde die GK SOFTWARE AG weit über die Grenzen unseres Landes hinaus bekannt. Die Software aus Schöneck ist mittlerweile über 50.000 mal und in mehr als 20 Ländern auf vier Kontinenten im Einsatz.

Die GK SOFTWARE AG beschäftigt mehr als 180 Mitarbeiter an mehreren Standorten. Der 2001 eingeweihte und 2007 stark erweiterte moderne Firmensitz in Schöneck bietet ausgezeichnete Arbeitsbedingungen. Inmitten intakter Natur in einem Ort mit hohem Freizeitwert können die Mitarbeiter vielfältige sportliche Aktivitäten mit kreativer Arbeit verbinden.

What do leading European trade chains such as dm-drogerie markt, Douglas, EDEKA, Kauhof, Lidl, Netto, Tchibo or Telekom-Shops have in common? They all work with software from Schöneck in the Vogtland.

The GK SOFTWARE AG is leading European producer of software solutions for the retail trade. With software from Schöneck, up-to-date cash registers are working in supermarkets and discount markets, perfume shops and department stores, inventories are carried out, or goods are ordered.

When the company was founded as two-man company in 1990, such a perspective could not be expected. However, from the first beginning, the two enterprise founders consistently focused on the development of own software products. At that, the specialization in the retail trade early began.

For many years, top technology connected with high quality is the brand mark of the software solutions from the Vogtland. With that, the GK SOFTWARE AG became known far beyond the borders of our country. In the meantime, the software from Schöneck is used 50,000 times in more than 20 countries on four continents.

The GK SOFTWARE AG has more than 180 employees at several locations. The modern headquarters in Schöneck inaugurated in 2001 and strongly extended in 2007 offer excellent working conditions. Embedded in an intact nature, in a small town with high recreational value, the employees can cause manifold sporting activities to be combined with creative work.

GK SOFTWARE AG
Waldstraße 7
08261 Schöneck
Telefon +49 (0) 37464 84-0
Telefax +49 (0) 37464 84-15
info@gk-software.com
www.gk-software.com

Mit Sicherheit die besten Karten

Definitely the Best Cards

Wir alle benutzen sie täglich und ohne groß darüber nachzudenken. Sie verbinden uns mit dem modernen Leben: mit unserem Bankkonto, unserer Krankenversicherung, weisen uns als treue Kunden aus, gewähren Zutritt oder bestätigen unsere Identität. Die Rede ist von Chipkarten.
Eine nicht unerhebliche Menge, etwa 25 Millionen Stück pro Jahr, kommen aus dem Vogtland, von der ComCard GmbH aus Falkenstein.

Als Anbieter von Smartcard-Systemen für Gesundheitswesen, Zahlungsverkehr, Identifikation und Kundenbindung, betreut die Firma seit 1991 Banken, Kreditkartenherausgeber, Krankenversicherungen und Handelsorganisationen.

Als mittelständisches, inhabergeführtes Unternehmen versteht sich ComCard als Partner an der Seite seiner Kunden. Deshalb werden nicht nur die Karten selbst von Falkenstein aus deutschland- und weltweit verschickt. Das Unternehmen bietet alle Leistungen rund um die Karte aus einer Hand. Soll heißen: Von einer individuellen Beratung bis hin zur passenden Systemlösung inklusive Mailing, Versand und Responsemanagement wird alles bestens durchdacht und realisiert.

Basis für den Erfolg sind Qualität, modernste Technik und, in dieser Branche ganz wichtig, eine hohe Sicherheit. So berechtigt die Zertifizierung durch Visa und Mastercard sowie ein Qualitätsmanagement nach DIN EN ISO 9001:2000 zur Herstellung von Geld- und Kreditkarten.

Neben aller Technik steht bei ComCard vor allem der Mensch im Mittelpunkt. Seit über 15 Jahren ist die Firma einer der großen Arbeitgeber im Vogtland. So wuchs die Zahl der Beschäftigten allein im Jahre 2007 um 18 auf insgesamt 116. Jährlich werden 3 – 4 Lehrlinge ausgebildet. Aktiv unterstützt die ComCard GmbH u.a. den Kinder- und Jugendsport in Falkenstein und übernimmt somit auch ganz bewusst soziale Verantwortung in der Region.

We all use them every day without paying much attention to them. They are our link with modern life: with our bank account or health insurance scheme, they prove that we are a loyal customer, they open doors for us or even prove our identity. We are talking about chip cards.
A significant number, some 25 million per annum, come from a company based in the Vogtland region: ComCard GmbH in Falkenstein.
The company has served banks, credit card firms, health insurance schemes and commercial organizations since 1991 by supplying smart card systems for health care, monetary transactions, identification and customer loyalty schemes.
ComCard, a medium-sized company, which is managed by its owner, sees itself as a partner providing support for its customers. So cards are sent out from Falkenstein to destinations across Germany and countries all over the world. The company provides all sorts of services related to cards from one source. This means that everything is thought through and carried out from the individual consultations at the outset to providing proper system solutions that include mailing, dispatch and response management.
Quality, the latest technology and high security – which is particularly important in this sector – form the basis of the company's success. Certification from Visa and Mastercard and a quality management system, which meets the standards in DIN EN ISO 9001:2000, entitle the company to produce bank and credit cards.

But despite all the technology, individual people are the primary focus at ComCard. The company has been one of the large employers in the Vogtland region for more than 15 years. The number of employees grew by 18 to 116 in 2007 alone. 3-4 apprentices undergo training every year. ComCard GmbH also actively supports children's and young people's sports in Falkenstein, so fulfilling its social responsibilities in the region.

ComCard GmbH
Hammerbrücker Str. 3
D-08223 Falkenstein
Telefon +49 (0) 3745 769-0
Telefax +49 (0) 3745 769-335
info@comcard.de
www.comcard.de

(Fotos/Photos by Igor Pastierovic, Übersetzung/Translated by David Strauss)

IK Elektronik GmbH

Ohne Kabel aber mit viel Energie

Wireless but with Plenty of Energy –

Die IK Elektronik GmbH als echte Made-in-Vogtland-Erfolgsgeschichte

Nicht nur „Made in Vogtland" sondern „Tailor made in Vogtland" sind die Produkte der IK Elektronik GmbH. Dabei handelt es sich nicht um klassische Endprodukte, sondern vielmehr um verschiedenste Einzelprojekte. Denn seit mehr als 10 Jahren ist das Hammerbrücker Unternehmen der professionelle Partner für spezifische Entwicklungen im Bereich der Hochfrequenz-Technik. Baugruppen der kabellosen Datenübertragung bilden dabei das Leistungsprogramm für die Kunden aus dem Bereich der Industrie- und Haustechnik. Der Claim des Unternehmens lautet daher folgerichtig Make it wireless. „Standardprodukte gibt es bei uns nicht, alles wird jeweils nach Kundenanforderung gefertigt. Diese Anforderungen sind so speziell, dass sie in der Regel in einmalige und abgeschlossene Projekte münden" gibt der Firmengründer und Geschäftsführer Jan-Erik Kunze Auskunft.

Die IK Elektronik GmbH bietet dem Kunden von der Beratung, der Entwicklung über die Konstruktion bis hin zur Produktion alle Leistungen. Ob RFID-Projekte oder Lösungen für die Industrieautomation, ob kabellose Steuerungen für Geräte der Haustechnik oder energieautarke Schaltelemente: Auf der Kundenliste des Technologie-Unternehmens finden sich prominente Namen. SIEMENS, BMW, Blaupunkt oder MINOL sind nur einige wenige.

>> *Standardprodukte gibt es bei uns nicht, alles wird jeweils nach Kundenanforderung gefertigt. Diese Anforderungen sind so speziell, dass sie in der Regel in einmalige und abgeschlossene Projekte münden.* <<

IK Elektronik GmbH is a real "Made in Vogtland" success story

The products at IK Elektronik GmbH are not only "made in Vogtland" but also "tailor made in Vogtland". The company does not provide final products in the normal sense of the word, but a wide variety of individual project components. The company in Hammerbrücke has been a professional partner for specific developments within the high frequency technology sector for more than 10 years. Electronic devices for wireless data transmission are central to the product range, which the company offers customers in industry or domestic machinery. So it is no accident that the company's motto is: "Make it wireless". "We do not offer standard products," explains company founder and director Jan-Erik Kunze, "everything is tailor-made to meet special customer requirements. They are usually so specific that they are normally unique and self-contained projects."

IK Elektronik GmbH can provide customers with a full range of services including professional advice, development and design and even production. The company handles RFID projects or industrial automation solutions, wireless controls for devices in domestic machinery or switching elements that are self-sufficient in terms of energy: the customer list of this technology enterprise includes well-known names like SIEMENS, BMW, Blaupunkt or MINOL, to name just a few.

(Fotos/Photos by Igor Pastierovic, Text/Text by André Zeidler, Übersetzung/Translated by David Strauss)

> *We do not offer standard products, everything is tailor-made to meet special customer requirements. They are usually so specific that they are normally unique and self-contained projects.*

1996 gegründet, hat das Unternehmen einen dynamischen aber stabilen Aufstieg genommen. „Der relativ schnelle Erfolg des Unternehmens war – trotz unseres bereits vorhandenen Know-Hows – durchaus zufallsgetrieben", bekennt Jan-Erik Kunze freimütig, „ohne die notwendige Fortune geht es nun mal nicht. Die Voraussetzung für den Erfolg sind aus meiner Sicht vor allem Aufgeschlossenheit und Ehrlichkeit." Von Anfang an konnte der Diplom-Ingenieur eine Vielzahl komplexer Entwicklungsaufträge gewinnen. Daran an schloss sich die Ausweitung der Leistungspalette auf die Produktion der entwickelten Baugruppen bis hin zur Eigenbestückung von Leiterplatten. Heute beschäftigt das Unternehmen 41 Mitarbeiter, darunter 10 Entwicklungsingenieure.

Für den gebürtigen Hammerbrücker Jan-Erik Kunze, der zunächst eine erfolgreiche berufliche Karriere in Dresden und Leipzig startete und schließlich nahezu symbolträchtig im Haus seiner Eltern und Großeltern ein erfolgreiches Technologieunternehmen gründete, ist Nachhaltigkeit das entscheidende Prinzip. Konsolidierung, Festigung und Stabilität stehen dabei im Mittelpunkt für die nächsten Jahre, was irgendwie an urvogtländische Tugenden erinnern mag.

Founded in 1996, the business has made both dynamic and steady progress. "The relatively rapid success of the company - despite our expertise – did include a measure of good fortune," Jan-Erik Kunze admits generously. "It is not possible without having some luck. To my mind, the foundations of success are open-mindedness and honesty." Right from the outset the certified engineer was able to win a number of complex development orders. Following this success, he expanded his range of services to produce the units that had been designed and even assemble printed circuit boards. The company now employs 41 people, 10 of them design engineers.

Jan-Erik Kunze was born in Hammerbrücke and initially launched his successful professional career in Dresden and Leipzig. He finally set up a successful technology business at his parents' and grandparents' home in an almost symbolic act. Sustainability is the most important principle in his eyes. Consolidation, perseverance and stability will be his main focus for the next few years - which seems rather reminiscent of the traditional values found in Vogtland people.

IK Elektronik GmbH
Friedrichsgrüner Str. 11-13
D - 08269 Hammerbrücke
Telefon +49 (0) 37465 4092-0
Telefax +49 (0) 37465 4092-10
info@ikhf.de
www.ikhf.de

NARVA Speziallampen GmbH in Plauen

Tradition meets Innovation

Das seit fast 60 Jahren in Plauen ansässige Traditionsunternehmen NARVA Speziallampen GmbH, Plauen entwickelt, produziert und vertreibt mit 480 Mitarbeitern Automobil-Frontbeleuchtungs-Halogenlampen, Halogenminiaturlampen sowie eine Reihe von Speziallampen für z.B. Eisenbahn-, Flugfeld- und Applikationen im medizinisch-wissenschaftlichen Bereich.

Seit fast 18 Jahren gehört das Unternehmen als 100%ige Tochter zum weltweit agierenden niederländischen Philipskonzern. Royal Philips Electronics mit Hauptsitz in den Niederlanden ist das weltweit führende Unternehmen für Healthcare, Lifestyle und Technology. Philips beschäftigt 128.100 Mitarbeiter in über 60 Ländern und erzielte 2006 einen Umsatz von 27 Milliarden Euro. Das Unternehmen ist weltweit marktführend bei diagnostischer Bildgebung, Patientenüberwachungssystemen, energieeffizienten Beleuchtungslösungen, Elektro-Hausgeräten sowie Unterhaltungselektronik.

Umfangreiche Investitionen in den zurückliegenden Jahren am Standort Plauen in modernste Produktionstechnologie sichern ein kontinuierliches Wachstum und die fortlaufende Ausweitung des Marktanteils von Lampen-Produkten aus dem NARVA- und Philips-Portfolio. Dies führte auch dazu, dass der Plauener Betrieb das weltweite Hartglas-Kompetenzzentrum des Philipskonzerns ist und außerdem für das globale Ersatzteilmarkt-Geschäftsfeld von Philips zuständig ist.

Die NARVA ist seit Ihrer Gründung Ausbildungsbetrieb, vornehmlich in den Fachrichtungen Industriemechaniker/in und Industriekaufmann/-frau. So führt das Unternehmen seit Jahrzehnten systematisch gut ausgebildeten eigenen Nachwuchs an zukünftige Aufgaben heran und wird seiner sozialen Verantwortung für die Region gerecht. Seit Jahren besteht des Weiteren eine erfolgreiche Kooperation mit einer Behindertenwerkstatt, wodurch zahlreiche behinderte Menschen für das Unternehmen beschäftigt werden.

NARVA Speziallampen GmbH has been based in Plauen for almost 60 years and develops, manufactures and sells halogen front lamps for motor vehicles, miniature halogen lamps and a number of special lamps for railways, airports and other applications, e.g. in the medical science field. It employs 480 members of staff.

The company has been a wholly owned subsidiary of the global Dutch Philips Group for nearly 18 years. Royal Philips Electronics has its headquarters in the Netherlands and is the world's market leader for health care, lifestyle and technology. Philips employs 128,100 people in more than 60 countries and its turnover was € 27 billion in 2006. The company is the global leader in diagnostic imaging, patient monitoring systems, energy-efficient lighting solutions, electrical household appliances and entertainment electronics.

Extensive capital investments in the latest manufacturing technology in Plauen over the past few years have ensured continual growth and the steady expansion of the global market share of lamp products from the NARVA and Philips ranges. As a result, the Plauen site has become the Philips Group's centre of excellence for hard glass production and it is also responsible for Philips' global spare parts business division.

NARVA has been a training company since it was set up, primarily for industrial mechanic apprentices and industrial business management assistants. So for decades the company has been bringing up its own young workers, who have undergone thorough training, to cope with future tasks. The company also fulfils its social obligations to the region. NARVA has worked closely with a workshop for handicapped people for years; as a result, many handicapped persons are working for the company.

NARVA Speziallampen GmbH, Plauen
L.-F.-Schönherr-Straße 15
D-08523 Plauen
Telefon +49 (0) 3741 396-0
Telefax +49 (0) 3741 396-396
info@narva-plauen.de

(Fotos/Photos by Igor Pastierovic [2], Übersetzung/Translated by David Strauss)

Made in Vogtland – Theumaer Fruchtschiefer

Naturstein mit Charakter
"Theuma Slate" – Natural Stone with Character

Hier links: Kirche von Theuma
In der Bildleiste unten von links sind die Referenz-Objekte Japanischer Garten in Erfurt, Volksbank in Lech/Österreich und die Paracelsiusklinik in Bad Elster zu sehen.

Der „Theumaer Fruchtschiefer" ist Naturstein mit Charakter

Vor mehr als 300 Millionen Jahren entstand ein wertvoller Rohstoff: der „Theumaer Fruchtschiefer", ein Quarzschiefer. Seit über 100 Jahren wird der „Daamische Staa", wie er liebevoll im Vogtland genannt wird, abgebaut und verarbeitet.
Seinen Namen verdankt der „Theumaer Fruchtschiefer" den markanten dunklen, länglichen Einlagerungen, den sogenannten Cordieriten – man fühlte sich an „Feldfrüchte" erinnert und gab ihm deshalb die alte noch heute gebräuchliche Bezeichnung „Fruchtschiefer".
Typische Gesteinseigenschaften, die dieses Natursteinvorkommen weltweit einmalig machen, sind:
- einzigartige blaugraue Färbung,
- hohe Witterungs- und Frostbeständigkeit,
- vielfältige Verwendungs- und Bearbeitungsmöglichkeiten.

Bereits die 1456 geweihte Kirche von Theuma wurde mit Natursteinen aus der unmittelbaren Umgebung erbaut und ist heute wohl der beste Beweis für die jahrhundertealte Tradition des Steinebrechens sowie die hervorragende Verwitterungsbeständigkeit dieses Gesteins.

Unser Sortiment umfasst neben Bodenplatten, Fassadenplatten, Fensterbänken, Abdeckplatten auch Mauerwerke, Massivstücke und Schüttgüter. Weiterhin finden Sie bei uns Produkte für den Garten- und Landschaftsbau (Quarzschiefersteine, Stelen, Spaltfelsen usw.).
Profiliert hat sich unser Werk vor allem durch individuelle Steinbearbeitungen. Dies belegen eine Vielzahl von Referenzobjekten, die auch europa- und weltweit errichtet wurden.

Die verschiedenen Oberflächenbearbeitungen wie diamantgeschliffen, feingeschliffen, geflammt, gebürstet, gesandelt und gespalten lassen den Stein in unterschiedlichen Farbnuancen erscheinen. Durch Innovation und Weiterentwicklung kamen seit kurzem die neuen Bearbeitungsmöglichkeiten getrommelt und sclypiert dazu.
Gerne steht Ihnen unser Verkaufsteam bei der Planung und Umsetzung Ihrer Bauvorhaben zur Verfügung.
Für die Verlegung und Ausführung am Bau steht Ihnen unsere Bauabteilung fachmännisch zur Seite.

A valuable raw material was created more than 300 million years ago: "Theuma slate", which is a quartz slate.

The "Daamische Staa", as it is affectionately known in the Vogtland region, has been extracted and machined for more than 100 years.

"Theuma slate" owes its name to the prominent, dark interstratifications that run lengthwise, what are known as cordierites – people were reminded of "fruits of the field" and therefore gave the slate its common name "fruit slate"(in German).
The stone has typical features, which make this natural stone unique around the world:
- its unique blue/grey colour,
- a high degree of resistance to weather and frost,
- a wide variety of opportunities to use and machine the material.

The church in Theuma, which was dedicated as early as 1456, was built using natural stone from the immediate vicinity and is the best evidence of the centuries-old tradition of breaking stone – and the stone's outstanding resistance to the elements.

Our range of products includes floor slabs, façade slabs, window ledges, cover panels, brick work, solid slabs and bulk solids. Our products are also used in gardens and for landscaping (quartz slate, pillars or split rocks etc).
Individual stone machining work has given our factory its special reputation. A number of buildings, which have been constructed in Europe and around the world, are included on our list of references.

The various surface finishes – diamond grinding, precision grinding, mottled, brushed, sand blasted and split – mean that the stone appears in various shades of colour. New processes like tumbling and milling grooves in the stone have been added recently.
Our sales team will be happy to help you plan and realise your building project.
Our specialist building department will be happy to help you lay the stone and complete the building work.
Thanks to the creative work with our customers and the outstanding properties of Theuma slate, new applications and opportunities of using the stone are constantly opening up.

Natursteinwerk Theuma AG
Zum Plattenbruch 6 - 8
D - 08541 Theuma
Telefon +49 (0) 37463 224-30
Telefax +49 (0) 37463 224-70
info@nwtag.de
www.natursteinwerk-theuma.de

(Fotos/Photos by Natursterinwerk Theuma AG, Übersetzung/Translated by David Strauss)

MEISER – weltweit in 25 Ländern aktiv und auch engagiert im Vogtland

Als Edmund Meiser 1956 sein Unternehmen im Saarland gründete, ahnte noch niemand, dass gerade einmal 51 Jahre später MEISER der führende Hersteller von Gitterrosten in Europa sein wird. Gelingen konnte das durch eine ebenso naheliegende wie selten geübte Strategie: Man tut das, was man am besten kann und versucht, das jeden Tag noch besser zu machen.

Auch mit der Gründung 1991 von MEISER in Plauen und den darauf folgenden Gründungen der uwM Stahlbearbeitung im Jahre 1996 und der uwM Stanztechnik im Jahre 1998 zeigt das Unternehmen ein klares Bekenntnis zum Standort Deutschland. So arbeiten heute 1.400 Mitarbeiter für das Familienunternehmen, davon ca. 1.000 in Deutschland und davon wiederum 550 in Oelsnitz, Vogtland.

Diese Mitarbeiter zeigen jeden Tag, dass „Made in Germany" keine Worthülse, sondern ein echtes Qualitätsversprechen ist. Auf 19 Fertigungsstraßen werden Gitterroste jeglicher Form und Abmessung produziert. Eine große Produktpalette von Treppenanlagen, Blechprofilrosten und kompletter Bauteillieferung ergänzen das Programm.

When Edmund Meiser set up his business in the Saarland in 1956, nobody anticipated that MEISER would go on to be the leading manufacturer of gratings in Europe just 51 years later.

The key to the success of the company lay in its strategy – one which was both obvious but rarely pursued: Doing what one does best and endeavouring to improve upon these skills every day.
Even with the founding 1991 from MEISER in Plauen, and the subsequent creation of uwM Stahlbearbeitung in the year 1996 and the uwM Stanztechnik in the year 1998, the company is showing a clear commitment to Germany.

Today, the family-owned enterprise employs a total of 1,400 members of staff, 1,000 of whom work in Germany, with 550 of these in Oelsnitz, Vogtland.

Every day these employees demonstrate that "Made in Germany" is not an empty phrase, but rather a genuine assurance of quality. Gratings of all shapes and sizes are made on 19 production lines.

The portfolio of products also comprises a large range of stair systems, rofile plankings and the supply of complete components.

MEISER – worldwide in 25 countries and is also engaged in the Vogtland

Eine herausragende Qualität kann nur dann gewährleistet werden, wenn man alle wichtigen Prozesse selbst in der Hand behält. Deshalb gehören zu MEISER heute eigene Verzinkereien, Stahlbearbeitungsbetriebe und Kaltwalzwerke.

Eine weitere Betriebsstätte, die MEISER Bandverzinkung befindet sich auf dem Gelände der ehemaligen Drahtwerke St. Ingbert.

Hauptaufgabe der Meiser Bandverzinkung ist die Herstellung von verzinktem Bandstahl. Einsatzgebiete sind u. a. die Elektroindustrie – für Erdungsbänder als Blitzschutz, Faßbänder und fertige Faßringe für die Weinindustrie (Barriquefässer), Formteile für Rohrschellen, Scharniere für Möbelindustrie sowie Befestigungsteile für den Hausbau.

Mit Niederlassungen und Vertretungen in 25 Ländern betreut MEISER seine Kunden persönlich vor Ort.

Outstanding quality can only be ensured if all major processes are carried out by the company itself. For this reason, MEISER today maintains its own galvanising and steel achining plants (slitting plants) as well as cold rolling centres.

A further production plant, MEISER Bandverzinkung (strip galvanising), is located on the premises of the former Drahtwerke St. Ingbert. The core area of business of Meiser Bandverzinkung concerns the manufacture of galvanised strip steel. Areas of application for these products include the electrical industry – for earthing strips as lightning protection, strips for barrels and finished barrel rings for the wine industry (barrique barrels), shaped parts for pipe clips, hinges for the furniture industry as well as mounting parts for house construction.

MEISER has subsidiaries and agencies in 25 countries to provide its clients with personal, on-site service.

Meiser Gitterroste KG
Am Lehmteich 3
D-08606 Oelsnitz
Telefon: +49 (0)3 74 21/50-0
Fax: +49 (0)3 74 21/50-21 20
E-Mail: info@meiser.de
Internet: www.meiser.de

ALSTOM in Neumark

Fertigung um 1900/*Photo top middle Manufacture around 1900*

In Neumark hat der Kesselbau Tradition
Neumark has a tradition of boiler manufacture

Mit Neumark untrennbar verbunden ist der Kesselbau. Generationen von Menschen haben bereits in diesem Geschäft gearbeitet. Heute führt die ALSTOM Power Service GmbH diese über 110-jährige Tradition fort. Neumark – der moderne Standort mit langer Geschichte ist heute ein entscheidender Teil einer weltweiten Service-Organisation. Mit Sachkompetenz in allen Produktions- und Planungsverfahren, mit außergewöhnlicher Einsatzbereitschaft und hoher Zuverlässigkeit haben sich die Neumarker Kesselbauer einen besonderen Stellenwert innerhalb des ALSTOM-Konzerns erarbeitet und bestätigen dieses mit jedem Projekt neu.

Am 29. Juni 1890 gründeten Oskar Wackwitz und Moritz Weichelt unter dem Namen Weichelt & Wackwitz Maschinen- und Dampfkesselfabrik Neumark/Sachsen eine damals noch recht bescheidene Kesselschmiede. Beide Firmengründer verfügten über weitgehende fachliche und kommerzielle Voraussetzungen, waren sie doch zuvor als leitende Ingenieure in bekannten sächsischen Maschinenfabriken tätig. Die aus der Freiberger Gegend stammenden Gründer wählten Neumark nicht zuletzt wegen der Nähe zur Bahnstrecke. Denn so konnten sie die tonnenschweren Kessel auf kürzestem Weg zum Bahnversand bringen, welcher damals das einzige Schwerlast-Transportmittel war.

Nach einer bewegten Firmengeschichte kaufte 1991 die damalige EVT Energie- und Verfahrenstechnik GmbH in Stuttgart den ehemals volkseigenen Betrieb. Inzwischen gehört der Kesselbau in Neumarkt zum weltweit operierenden ALSTOM-Konzern. Rund 245 Mitarbeiterinnen und Mitarbeiter sind heute bei der ALSTOM Power Service GmbH in Neumark beschäftigt, davon sind mehr als ein Drittel weltweit auf Montage. Seit 1. April 2002 gehört Neumark zum Service-Segment im Power Sektor. Geschäftsführung und Mitarbeiter fühlen sich heute, nach der Eingliederung des Betriebs in die Service-Organisation, mehr denn je der Tradition verpflichtet. Man will die positiven Erfahrungen der Firmengeschichte in die neuen Aufgaben einbringen.

Während früher in Neumark neben Industriekesseln sogar Druckkörper und Flutkästen für U-Boote der Kriegsmarine gebaut wurden, fertigen heute mehr als 50 qualifizierte Mitarbeiter moderne Komponenten für Großdampferzeuger und für die chemische Industrie. Dazu gehören unter anderem Rohrschlangen, Dampftrommeln, Brennkammerwände, Sammler, Wärmetauscher und Hochdruckvorwärmer. Nach Herstellung transportabler Größen in der Werkstatt folgen der Zusammenbau und die Komplettierung der Dampferzeuger auf der Baustelle durch das Montagepersonal. Besonderen Wert legen die Verantwortlichen in Neumark auf die Qualität ihrer Produkte.

Boiler manufacturing is inextricably linked with Neumark and generations of people have worked in this sector. Today ALSTOM Power Service GmbH is continuing this over 110 year tradition as Neumark – the modern location with a long history is today a crucial part of a worldwide service organisation. With technical expertise in all production and planning procedures and with its extraordinary commitment and dedication and a high level of reliability, the Neumark boiler manufacturers have developed a specific value within the ALSTOM Group and they reconfirm this with every project.

On 29 June 1890 Oskar Wackwitz and Moritz Weichelt founded Weichelt & Wackwitz Machine and Steam Boiler Factory Neumark/Saxony and at the time it was a very modest boiler making operation. Both company founders had extensive technical and commercial qualifications as they had both previously worked as leading engineers in well-known Saxon engineering factories. The founders who originated from the Freiberg area selected Neumark not least due to the proximity of the railway. This enabled them to despatch the boilers which weighed tonnes using the quickest and then only means of transport for heavy loads, namely rail.

In 1991 after an animated company history the then EVT Energie- und Verfahrenstechnik GmbH in Stuttgart purchased the former state-owned company. Now the boiler manufacturing company in Neumark is part of the worldwide ALSTOM Group. ALSTOM Power Service GmbH in Neumark now employs about 245 people of whom more than a third work on assembly worldwide. Since 1st April 2002 Neumark is part of the service segment in the power sector. Today after the integration of the company into the service organisation, the management and staff feel more than ever that they have an obligation to uphold the traditions. They want to introduce the positive experiences of the company history into the new tasks.

Whereas in the past in addition to the industrial boilers, pressure cylinders and flood crates for U-Boats were built in Neumark, today more than 50 qualified employees produce modern components for large steam generators and for the chemical industry. These include pipe coils, steam drums, combustion chamber walls, collectors, heat exchangers and high-pressure preheaters. After the production of transportable sizes in the workshop, the assembly and the completion of the steam generator is carried out on the factory site by the assembly staff. Those with positions of responsibility in Neumark place particular emphasis on the quality of their products and ALSTOM Neumark has a lot of reasons to be proud as now boiler components are delivered to China, Russia,

Fotos v. l. n. r. aus dem Bereich Fertigung: Schweißarbeiten am Brenner für Wai Gao Qiao China, Aufrichten des Brenners Wai Gao Qiao China/*Photos from left to right: The manufacturing operation Welding work on the burner for Wai Gao Qiao China, Raising the burner Wai Gao Qiao China*

(Fotos/Photos by ALSTOM ,Text/Text by ALSTOM)

ALSTOM in Neumark

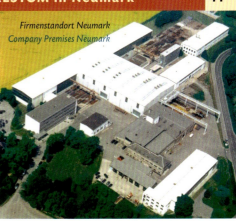

Firmenstandort Neumark
Company Premises Neumark

Fotos v. l. n. r. Montagebaustellen:
Vorbereitung der Hubmontage für den Ecoblock,
Aufrichten der Hubmontage für den Ecoblock
Photos from left to right: Assembly sites.
Preparation of the lift assembly for the Ecoblock
Raising of the lift assembly for the Ecoblock

Und ALSTOM Neumark hat allen Grund stolz zu sein, werden doch Kesselkomponenten mittlerweile zum Beispiel nach China, Russland, Polen und Österreich geliefert. Für den chemischen Apparatebau sind die Vogtländer unter anderem in Laos, Südamerika, Trinidad, Holland und China tätig. Das größte Projekt, welches die erfahrenen und erfolgreichen Kesselbauer der Region bisher umsetzten, war das „Autoklave"-Projekt 2004 für die laotische Bergbaugesellschaft „Sepon Copper". Der in Neumark entwickelte und gebaute Kessel wird im Bergland von Laos zur Aufbereitung von Kupfererz genutzt. Die Reise des 157 Tonnen schweren Riesen aus dem Herzen Mitteleuropas in den Dschungel Südostasiens war nicht minder aufregend.

ALSTOM Neumark verfügt über modernste Prüf- und Fertigungseinrichtungen, wobei die Geschäftsführung der Meinung ist, dass die Produktqualität natürlich in erster Linie von den Mitarbeitern erbracht wird. Besonders gern investiert man deshalb in die Qualifikation der Mitarbeiter sowie in ein gutes Arbeitsklima. Das Bürogebäude erhielt in den letzten Jahren eine neue Außenfassade, die Büros selbst wurden gründlich renoviert. Als Firmenphilosophie haben sich die ALSTOM-Kesselbauer den Leitspruch des französischen Politikers und Philosophen Jean Jaures auf ihre Fahnen geschrieben: „Tradition ist nicht die Bewahrung der Asche, sondern das Schüren des Feuers."

Poland and Austria. Chemical apparatus construction is also being carried out by the Vogtland company in Laos, South America, Trinidad, Holland and China amongst others. The largest project which the region's experienced and successful boiler makers have installed to date is the "Autoclave" Project 2004 for the Laotian mining company "Sepon Copper". The boiler that was developed and built in Neumark is used in the mountainous country of Laos to process copper ore. The journey of the giant weighing 157 tonnes from the heart of central Europe to the jungle of south-east Asia was no less exciting.

ALSTOM Neumark has the most modern testing and production facilities and the management is of the opinion that product quality is of course first and foremost delivered by the employees. Therefore the company is very keen to invest in qualifications for the employees and in a good working environment so the office building was given a new exterior façade over the last few years and the offices themselves have been thoroughly renovated. The ALSTOM boiler manufacturers have adopted the motto of the French politician and philosopher, Jean Jaures: "Tradition is not the preservation of the ashes but the stoking of the fire".

- Servicepartner mit der Kompetenz des Anlagenbauers für Kunden aus den Bereichen:
  - Energieversorgung
  - Industrie
  - Müllverbrennung

- Service partners with expertise in building plants for customers in the following sectors:
  - Energy supply
  - Industry
  - Refuse incineration

Fotos v. l. n. r.
Montagebaustellen:
Kesselmontage Wandzug;
Kesselmontage; Kohlemühle
Photos from left to right
Assembly sites:
Boiler Manufacture;
works at the façades;
Boiler Manufacture;
coal pulverising mill

ALSTOM Power Service GmbH
Standort Neumark
Am Bahnhof 11 · D-08496 Neumark
Telefon +49 (0) 37600 81-01
Telefax +49 (0) 37600 81-863
www.alstom.com

Kunststofftechnik Schedel GmbH

Kunststofftechnik Schedel – ein Unternehmen auf dem Vormarsch

Schedel Plastics – a Company Forging Ahead

Südafrikanische, schwäbische und vogtländische Wurzeln sind vereint in der Kunststofftechnik Schedel und der Vertriebstochter Schedel BAD + DESIGN in Falkenstein. Firmenchef Markus Schedel ist ein gebürtiger Südafrikaner. Dessen Vater aus Schwaben ging vor über 40 Jahren nach Südafrika und baute dort ein styroporverarbeitendes Unternehmen in Johannesburg und Kapstadt auf. Er brachte es damit zum Marktführer. Mit dem Ende der Apartheid und dem Wandel zur jungen Demokratie in den frühen 1990er Jahren, drohten die neuen Machthaber mit einer Zwangsverstaatlichung der Firmen. Beinahe zur gleichen Zeit zeichnete sich mit der politischen Wende im Osten Deutschlands gerade ein anderer Trend ab. Die Familie Schedel stand nun vor der Entscheidung, was sie machen sollte. 1991 erwarb die Familie den Falkensteiner Betriebsteil der Jenoptik, die so genannten „Elaste" und gründete die Kunststofftechnik Schedel GmbH. Wäre der Schwabe nicht gekommen, hätte die Firma aus dem Vogtland vor dem Aus gestanden, weiß Markus Schedel.

Mit dem ersten Firmenstandbein bezog er die südafrikanischen beruflichen Wurzeln ein. Er legte mit Styropor los. Dabei ging es um die Fertigung von technischen Formteilen und Verpackungen jeglicher Art sowie Perlmaterial. Dahinter verbirgt sich ein Zulieferprodukt für die Putzindustrie.

Aber schon ein Jahre später kam das nächste Firmenstandbein hinzu, die eigene Produktlinie „Schedel-MULTISTAR*-Wannenträger". Basis dessen ist Styropor. Einher ging das Ganze mit der Schaffung einer neuen Vertriebsstrategie sowie der Entwicklung eigener Patente.

„Ein eigenes Produkt ist für uns wichtig, als Markenzeichen unserer Produktion und natürlich unserer Existenz, sonst ist ein Überleben nicht möglich!", begründet der Firmenchef diesen Schritt mit der Produktlinie. Die Angebotspalette von Schedel-MULTISTAR*-Wannenträgern umfasst derzeit rund 5300 verschiedene Modelle. Um die kundennahen Vertriebsaktivitäten noch zu verbessern, entschied sich die Familie Schedel im Jahr 2006 die Schedel BAD+DESIGN GmbH als neue Vertriebsgesellschaft zu gründen.

South African, Swabian and Vogtland roots all meet at Schedel Plastics and its sales subsidiary Schedel Bad + Design in Falkenstein. Company manager Markus Schedel was born in South Africa. His father, who came from Swabia, moved to South Africa more than 40 years ago and set up a company that processed polystyrene in Johannesburg and Cape Town. He managed to turn it into the market leader. But when apartheid ended and the country switched to a young democracy in the early 1990s, the new government was threatening to impose nationalisation on companies. Things were moving in the very opposite direction in East Germany at almost the same time when the Berlin Wall fell. The Schedel family now had to make a decision about what they were going to do. The family purchased the Falkenstein part of the Jenoptik company in 1991, what was known as "Elaste", and founded Schedel Plastics (Kunststofftechnik Schedel GmbH). Markus Schedel now knows that the Vogtland company would have faced ruin if he had not arrived on the scene.

He used his South African professional roots in the company's first main business. He started working with polystyrene. The company manufactured all kinds of moulded parts, packaging materials and pearl material. This is a product that is supplied to the plaster industry.

The second string to the company's bow followed one year later – the company's own "Schedel MULTISTAR* bath support" product line. The main element is polystyrene. In addition, a new sales strategy was developed and the company's own patents were registered.

"It's important for us to have our own product as a trade mark for our manufacturing skills and our source of livelihood, otherwise it is not possible to survive," the company manager says, justifying the decision to set up the company's own product line. The range of products in the Schedel MULTISTAR* bath support line currently comprises about 5,300 different models. The Schedel family decided to set up Schedel BAD+DESIGN GmbH as the new sales company in 2006 in order to improve customer-oriented sales activities even more.

(Fotos/Photos by Igor Pastierovic (5), Kunststofftechnik Schedel, Text/Text by Bert Walther, Übersetzung/Translated by David Strauss)

Der Name BAD+DESIGN steht für vielseitige Gestaltungsmöglichkeiten voller Ästhetik und Funktionalität. Hier umfasst das Sortiment, neben den kreativen Gestaltungselementen wie Säulen oder Ablagen, auch Liegen- und Sitzelemente, Wasch- und Regaleinheiten, innovative Dampfkabinen, Duschplatzlösungen sowie bodenebene Duschelemente mit Rinnensystem.

Dies spiegelt sich auch im Schedel Projektmanagement wider. Dabei werden gezielt Produkte für größere Vorhaben entwickelt. Partner sind in diesem Angebotssegment beispielsweise Villeroy & Boch. Aber auch mit der internationalen Kette Kempinski gibt es gemeinsame Projekte wie für einen renommierten Hotelbau in Indien, gegenüber vom Taj-Mahal oder auch in Dubai. Ebenfalls eine gute Zusammenarbeit haben die Falkensteiner mit der Steigenberger-Unternehmensgruppe.

2004 investierte Schedel 1,5 Millionen Euro in eine Lager- und Fertigungsstätte im Gewerbegebiet Neuensalz, direkt an der Autobahn. Kunststofftechnik Schedel fertigen in diesem Jahr Produkte mit einem angepeilten Umsatz zwischen 11,5 und 12 Millionen Euro. Des Weiteren bildet der Betrieb fünf Lehrlinge aus. 1991 war der heutige Firmenchef der jüngste Mitarbeiter und blickt mit Interesse auf das Engagement des künftigen Firmennachwuchses, ohne dabei den hohen Einsatzwillen seiner 105 Mitarbeiter zu vergessen.

Wichtige Voraussetzungen im Schedel Team sind Engagement, Flexibilität und Leistungsbereitschaft. Dass diese Anforderungen erfüllt werden, zeigt die TÜV-Zertifizierung nach DIN EN ISO seit 1998.

The name BAD+DESIGN represents a huge variety of design options that fully combine aesthetics and functionality. The range here not only covers creative design elements like pillars or racks, but also couch and seat elements, washing and shelf units, innovative steam cubicles, shower solutions and shower elements with a system of channels at floor level.

These principles are also reflected in Schedel's project management department. It deliberately designs products for fairly large schemes. Other partners involved in this range of products include Villeroy & Boch, for example. But Schedel is also involved in joint projects with the international Kempinski hotel chain, a renowned hotel building in India opposite the Taj Mahal and even in Dubai. The Falkenstein company also works closely with the Steigenberger company group.

Schedel invested € 1.5 million in a storage and manufacturing facility at the Neuensalz business park right next to the motorway in 2004. Schedel Plastics is aiming to manufacture products worth an estimated € 11.5 – 12 million this year. The company is also training five apprentices. The man who is company manager today was the youngest member of staff in 1991 and he pays a great deal of attention to the commitment of the next generation of employees, without forgetting the outstanding willingness to work on the part of his 105 employees.

Members of the Schedel team have to be committed, flexible and prepared to work hard. The fact that the company has had DIN EN ISO certification from the German Technical Inspection Agency since 1998 is evidence that these requirements are being met.

Kunststofftechnik Schedel GmbH
Oelsnitzer Straße 55
D - 08223 Falkenstein
Telefon +49 (0) 3745 745-0
Telefax +49 (0) 3745 5351
info@schedel-gmbh.de
www.schedel-gmbh.de

Eine Erfolgsgeschichte mit klarem Bekenntnis zur Region
A Success Story with a Clear Commitment to the Region

Die TUBETECH GmbH – als eigenständige Gesellschaft innerhalb einer mittelständischen, inhabergeführten Unternehmensgruppe, der Gesellschaft für Oeltechnik mit Sitz in Waghäusel (Karlsruhe), ist das Unternehmen im Spezial-Anlagen- und Apparatebau für die internationale Kraftwerksindustrie als auch für die chemische und petrochemische Industrie tätig und gilt hier als zuverlässiger Partner für so namhafte und klangvolle Namen wie Siemens Power Generation, Siemens PGI, MAN-Turbo, Bayer-Werke, Holborn, Sasol, als auch die Raffinerien internationaler Konzerne wie Shell, Esso, BP, OMV, Total, Mobil und Miro.

Das im Jahre 2001 gegründete Unternehmen ist seit dem Jahre 2004 auf einem stabilen Wachstumskurs. Mit insgesamt 85 engagierten Mitarbeiter und einer der Auftragslage angepassten zusätzlicher Anzahl von Fachkräfte von Partnerunternehmen produziert die TUBETECH GmbH in 3 völlig unterschiedlichen Produktgruppen: Anlagenbau, Rippenrohrfertigung und Apparatebau.
Im Anlagenbau werden Komponenten als auch komplette Skids, wie Schmierölsysteme für Turbinen geplant und hergestellt. Die Rippenrohre werden in allen gängigen Materialkombinationen hergestellt, so auch beispielsweise in so hochwertigen Werkstoffen wie Titan. Kunden hierbei sind neben namhaften Wettbewerbern im Wärmetauschergeschäft vor allen Dingen die internationalen Tochtergesellschaften der Unternehmensgruppe. Im Apparatebau werden kundenspezifische Druckbehälter als auch Wärmetauscher und Luftkühler konzipiert und hergestellt. Etwa 70% aller Produkte gehen in den Export. Mit der erfolgreichen Abwicklung einer ganzen Reihe größerer Projekte konnte sich das Unternehmen im Markt eine wesentliche Vollreferenz erarbeiten. So wurde im Jahre 2006 eine ganze Serie neuer Kraftwerke in Südafrika mit Lube Oil Skids ausgestattet und im Spätsommer 2007 ein technisch sehr anspruchsvolles Raffinerieprojekt in Bayern mit Erfolg umgesetzt. Derzeit wird ein Großauftrag, 8 Lube-Oil-Skids für eine Serie von Turbomaschinensträngen zur Energiegewinnung, die mit Abstand weltweit größten ihrer Art, mit dem Auslieferziel Katar hergestellt.

TUBETECH GmbH – an autonomous company within a medium-sized group of companies managed by the owner, the Gesellschaft für Oeltechnik with its headquarters in Waghäusel (Karlsruhe) – is the company operating in the special equipment and apparatus construction sector for the international power generation business and also the chemical and petrochemical industry and is a reliable partner for well-known and illustrious names like Siemens Power Generation, Siemens PGI, MAN-Turbo, Bayer, Holborn, Sasol, and refineries belonging to international groups like Shell, Esso, BP, OMV, Total, Mobil und Miro.

The company was founded in 2001 and has been on a steady path of growth since 2004. TUBETECH GmbH manufactures goods in 3 completely different product groups: plant construction, finned tubes and apparatus construction with 85 committed members of staff in all and an additional number of specialists from partner companies, which is adjusted to meet the volume of orders.
In the plant construction sector, components are designed and manufactured as complete skids like greasing systems for turbines. The finned tubes are manufacturing using all the standard combinations of materials and also in high-quality substances like titanium. Customers in this sector include not only well-known competitors in the heat exchanger business, but also international subsidiaries of the company group. In the apparatus construction sector, pressurised containers, heat exchangers and air coolers are designed and produced to meet customer requirements. About 70% of all the products are exported. Now that it has successfully completed a series of fairly large projects, the company has been able to draw up an impressive list of references. A whole series of new power stations in South Africa were equipped with lube oil skids in 2006 and what was technically a very challenging refinery project was successfully completed in Bavaria in the late summer of 2007. The company is currently manufacturing a major order for 8 lube oil skids for a series of turbo machinery trains for generating energy, easily the largest of its kind in the world and due to be delivered to Qatar.

Luftaufnahme der TUBETCH GmbH in der Hammerstraße in Plauen
Aerial photo of TUBETECH GmbH in Hammer Street in Plauen

(Fotos/Photos by TUBETECH GmbH, Hartmut Briese ,Text/Text by TUBETECH GmbH, Übersetzung/Translated by David Strauss)

TUBETECH GmbH

In einer modernen Unternehmensorganisation und sehr erfolgreichen Marktstrategie entwickelt sich die TUBETECH GmbH zu einer wahren Erfolgsgeschichte. Das Geschäftsvolumen verdoppelte sich seit 2004. Garant hierfür sind die Mitarbeiter, die sich durch ihre hohe Eigenmotivation und Kundenorientierung besonders auszeichnen. Mittels eingeführter Werkereigenkontrolle, gepaart mit einem hohen Ausbildungsgrad wird ein überdurchschnittlich hoher Qualitätsstand erreicht und Terminhaltungsgrad sichergestellt.

TUBETECH GmbH has developed into a real success story with modern company organisation and a very successful marketing strategy. The volume of business has doubled since 2004. The members of staff are the reason for this success – they have shown a high degree of initiative and customer orientation. As a result of internal checks introduced by them and a high degree of training, high quality standards far above average are met and deadlines are guaranteed.

Fotos oben von links: Plugschraubendichtungen, Rohrboden für Wärmetauscher, Herstellung Rippenrohre
Foto darunter: Vorbereitung TÜV-Prüfung Luftkühler-Raffinerie
Fotos hier links: hochwertige Schweißarbeiten

Photos above from left: plug screw gaskets, tube plate for heat exchangers; manufacturing fin tubes
Photo below: preparation for TÜV checks on air cooler for refinery
Photos on left here: high-quality welding work

TUBETECH GmbH

 Bei der Auswahl der Mitarbeiter und der Zulieferer eindeutig auf die Region vertrauen.

 When selecting employees and suppliers, putting the faith in the local region.

Im Rahmen seiner Unternehmensphilosophie vertraut die TUBETETECH GmbH bei der Auswahl der Mitarbeiter und Zulieferanten eindeutig auf die Region.

Bei der Suche und spezifischer Ausbildung der geeigneten Fachkräften ist die Zusammenarbeit mit der zuständigen Arbeitsagentur und dem Bildungswerk der Sächsischen Wirtschaft (bsw) besonders hervorzuheben. Dabei wird in Bezug auf das Alter bei fachlicher Eignung kein Unterschied gemacht.
Auch wird der Ausbildung junger Menschen große Bedeutung beigemessen. In den gewerblichen Ausbildungsberufen Konstruktionsmechaniker, Mechatroniker und Anlagentechniker und als Industriekaufmann im kaufmännischen Bereich wird mit derzeit 8 Auszubildenden nicht nur das Ziel eines guten Ausbildungsabschlusses angestrebt, sondern mittelfristig auch die Sicherstellung der eigenen Mitarbeitermannschaft erfolgen. Um diese ehrgeizigen Ziele zu erreichen, werden die Ausbildungen als Verbundausbildung durchgeführt – Ausbildungspunkte, die das Unternehmen aus seiner spezifischen Ausrichtung heraus nicht optimal anbieten kann, werden beim Bildungswerk der Sächsischen Wirtschaft (bsw) oder Partnerunternehmen vermittelt.

Bei der Lieferantenauswahl hat sich die Zusammenarbeit mit in der Region ansässigen Unternehmen als weiteren Erfolgsfaktor stabilisiert. Im Rahmen der strategischen Ausrichtung des Unternehmens werden neben allgemeinen Materialien auch ganze Baugruppen und Dienstleistungen an kleinere Fachunternehmen der Region vergeben, die sich durch Wirtschaftlichkeit, Flexibilität, Qualität und Zuverlässigkeit einen sicheren Stand bei der TUBETECH GmbH erarbeiten konnten. Dieses gesamte gelungene Zusammenspiel geeigneter Fachunternehmen hat sich unter dem Begriff „Integrierte Teamarbeit" in Sachsen bereits einen Namen gemacht.

As part of its company philosophy, TUBETECH GmbH puts its faith in the local region when selecting employees and suppliers.

When looking for suitable staff and giving them specific training, special mention should be made of the cooperation with the local Labour Agency and the Saxon Business Education Centre (bsw). No distinction is made regarding a person's age, provided that they have the right qualifications.
Great importance is attached to training young people. 8 apprentices are currently being trained in the business professions of design mechanic, mechatronics experts and systems engineers and as a business management assistant in the commercial sector and the goal is not only to provide them with good training qualifications, but also guarantee a supply of new qualified workers for the medium term. In order to achieve these ambitious goals, training is carried out in a combined arrangement – training issues, which the company cannot ideally provide because of its specialities, are taught at the Saxon Business Education Centre (bsw) or associated companies.

Another success factor has been the decision to cooperate with supplier companies based in the region. Orders for general materials and complete components and services are placed with smaller specialist companies in the region as part of the company's strategic orientation – and they have been able to gain a good reputation with TUBETECH GmbH as a result of their efficiency, flexibility, quality and reliability. This successful combination of suitable specialist companies has already made a name for itself in Saxony under the heading "Integrated Teamwork".

Schmierölanlage Kraftwerksgruppe ATLANTIS in Südafrika
Lubricating unit for the ATLANTIS group of power stations in South Africa

Schmierölanlage für industrielles Kraftwerk
Lubricating unit for industrial power station

Doppelrohrwärmetauscher für Raffinerie an der Nordsee
Double pipe heat exchanger for refinery on the North Sea

Luftkühler für Raffinerie
Air cooler for refinery

Kühlanlagen für Gasverdichterstation in Sibirien
Refrigerating unit for gas compression station in Siberia

TUBETECH GmbH

Kernkompetenzen
Core areas of competence

Extrudierte Rippenrohre
Extruded fin tubes

Gewickelte Rippenrohre
Coiled fin tubes

Druckbehälter
Pressurised containers

Wärmetauscher
Heat exchangers

Luftkühler
Air coolers

Komplette Kühlanlagen
Complete refrigeration units

Schmierölanlagen
Lubricating units

Anlagenkomponenten (große Schweißkonstruktionen und große Tanks)
Plant components (large welded units and big tanks)

Luftkühleranlage für die petrolchemische Industrie
Air cooler unit for the petrochemical industry

Luftkühleranlage für Projekt in Ägypten
Air cooler unit for project in Egypt

Luftkühleranlage für Großprojekt in Katar
Air cooler unit for major project in Qater

Verladung Rohrreaktor für die chemische Industrie
Loading pipe reactor for the chemical industry

Die Geschäftsaussichten für die kommenden Jahre sind auch aufgrund der internationalen Grundausrichtung des Unternehmens sehr positiv und so sehen die Planungen für die kommenden Jahre einen weiteren Ausbau der Produktpalette und demnach des Geschäftsvolumens vor. Um diesen ehrgeizigen Zielen gerecht zu werden, ist das Unternehmen ständig auf der Suche nach qualifizierten Mitarbeitern. So werden Ingenieure für den Anlagen- als auch für den Wärmetauscherbau, für das Projektmanagement und für den Vertrieb gesucht. Im gewerblichen Bereich werden TÜV - geprüfte Schweißer im Bereich MAG, WIG+E (C und CrNi-Stähle) und Orbital (Rohreinschweißung) als auch Konstruktionsmechaniker gesucht.

The business outlook for the next few years is very positive because of the company's fundamental international orientation. So plans for the coming years envisage an expansion of the range of products and therefore business volumes. The company is constantly searching for qualified staff in order to meet these ambitious challenges. Engineers are needed for plant construction and heat exchanger work, project management and sales. Construction technicians are needed and qualified welders in the MAG, WIG+E (C and CrNi-steel work) and orbital (pipe welding) fields.

TUBETECH GmbH

Hammerstraße 68
D - 08529 Plauen
Telefon +49 (0) 3741 2806-0
Telefax +49 (0) 3741 2806-40
zentrale@tubetech.de
www.tubetech-gmbh.de

Kompetenz in punkto Schweißtechnik

Expertise in Welding Engineering

Dass Plastik nicht rostet, haben alle in der Schule gelernt. Dass die Firma Kunststoff-Schweißtechnik Kainath nicht rastet, belegen die vielen Baustellen und Einsätze deutschlandweit. Immer geht es dabei um Kunststoff und meistens auch um Flexibilität.
Und sogar in Vietnam hat man sich das Know-how der Firma zu Nutze gemacht. "In Hanoi haben wir als erste Firma überhaupt eine Gasrohrleitung aus Polyethylen für die Erschließung eines Neubauwohngebietes verlegt", so der Firmenchef.
Mit modernster Schweißtechnik und allen Spezialgeräten und Werkzeugen für die Kunststoffverarbeitung ausgestattet, realisieren die mittlerweile 20 Mitarbeiter Aufträge in den Bereichen Erd-Rohrleitungsbau, Anlagenbau, Apparate- und Behälterbau und bei Behälterauskleidungen z.B. mit thermoplastischen Bahnen.
3 Millionen Euro wurden im letzten Jahr erwirtschaftet und einem weiteren Wachstum steht nichts im Wege, denn die Hausaufgaben sind und werden gemacht. Lehrlingsausbildung, Zertifizierungen und Weiterbildung nehmen dabei obere Plätze der Prioritätenliste ein.
In der 500 Quadratmeter großen, hellen und freundlich eingerichteten Werkstatt strahlen die unzähligen Grünpflanzen echte Geborgenheit aus.
Qualität und Zuverlässigkeit sind das Markenzeichen der Firma. Kein Wunder also, dass neue Aufträge vorhandener Kunden auch wieder vergeben werden an die Kunststoff-Schweißtechnik Kainath – garantiert rostfrei.

Schoolchildren learn that plastic does not rust. The many building sites and assignments across Germany are proof that the Kainath Plastics Welding Engineering company is not resting on its laurels. The company concentrates on plastics applications and usually needs to be very flexible.
The company's expertise has even been put to use in Vietnam. "We were the first company to lay a gas pipeline made of polyethylene to provide a link with a new residential area in Hanoi," says the company manager.
Equipped with the latest welding technology and every special unit and tool needed to process plastics, the 20 members of staff process orders in the fields of laying underground pipes, plant construction, apparatus engineering and tank construction and container linings, e.g. with thermoplastic strips.
Turnover last year was € 3 million and there are no obstacles to further growth, for the company has done and continues to do its homework.
The training of apprentices, certification and further training are top of the list of priorities.
The many plants decorating the workshops, which measure 500 square metres and are large, bright and arranged in a friendly manner, provide a real homely atmosphere.
Quality and reliability are the hallmarks of the company. So it is no wonder that new orders are placed by existing customers with Kainath Plastics Welding Engineering company, which guarantees that no rust will develop.

Der Kunststoff-Spezialist
Fachbetrieb nach DVS · DVGW · TÜV

**Kunststoff-Schweißtechnik
Kainath & Kaden GmbH**
Buchenstraße 14
Gewerbegebiet Ost
D-08468 Reichenbach
Telefon + 49 (0) 3765 12 990
Telefax + 49 (0) 3765 718344
HOK.Reichenbach@t-online.de

(Fotos/Photos by Igor Pastierovic [3], Übersetzung/Translated by David Strauss)

Dem Himmel ein Stück näher

A Little Closer to the Sky

Über die Jahrhunderte wären viele herausragende Leistungen der Menschheit ohne den Einsatz von Kranen nicht denkbar gewesen. Krane und Hebezeuge sind heute mehr denn je essentieller Bestandteil von Produktionssystemen in einer von Hochtechnologie geprägten Industrielandschaft. Spezialist für optimale Lösungen von fördertechnischen Aufgaben ist BANG Kransysteme GmbH & Co. KG.

Gegründet 1989 mit Firmensitz im vogtländischen Oelsnitz liefert die Bang Kranssysteme GmbH & Co. KG hochwertige Krananlagen an renommierte Unternehmen in Deutschland und den Nachbarländern sowie an Unternehmen in Skandinavien und im osteuropäischen Raum.

Das Geschäftsfeld des erfolgreichen Unternehmens ist die Planung, Fertigung, Montage und Wartung von Krananlagen für die Stahl- und Automobilindustrie sowie für kerntechnische Einrichtungen mit Traglasten bis 500 Tonnen. Die Fertigung innovativer Krananlagen beginnt am Firmenhauptsitz in Oelsnitz. Hier werden die Anforderungen des Kunden durch ein hochmotiviertes Team umgesetzt. An modernen CAD-Arbeitsplätzen entwickeln und konzipieren erfahrene Konstrukteure hochwertige Krananlagen. Ist ein Projekt technisch mit dem Kunden abgestimmt, beginnt nach der Fertigungsfreigabe die Herstellung der tragenden Teile des Krans am Standort Falkenstein. Der „Große Eignungsnachweis Klasse E" in Verbindung mit einem zertifizierten Qualitätsmanagementsystem nach DIN EN 9001 garantieren höchste Qualität. In den Werkhallen mit 20.000 m² Produktionsfläche können Kranbrücken mit einer Länge von mehr als 35 Metern und über 30 Tonnen Einzelstückgewicht hergestellt werden.

Bevor die Spezialtransporte – die meist nachts oft mehrere tausend Kilometer quer durch Europa unterwegs sind – das Firmengelände verlassen, wird durch die Spezialisten von BANG Kransysteme GmbH & Co. KG alles sicher verladen und verzurrt, damit die Systeme die zum Teil sehr weiten Reisen unbeschadet überstehen. Erfahrene Monteure errichten die Anlage beim Auftraggeber schnell und kompetent. Durch die vormontieren Baugruppen ist der Kran meist schon nach einem Tag auf der Schiene.

In vielen Industriezweigen in Deutschland aber auch bei internationalen Kunden haben die Spezialisten der BANG Kransysteme GmbH & Co. KG bereits mehr als 5000 Kransysteme ausgeliefert, die höchsten Qualitätsansprüchen gerecht werden.

Ob Stahl- und Papierindustrie, Krananlagen für die Nukleartechnik, Sonderkonstruktionen oder auch Standardkrane – BANG Kransysteme GmbH & Co. KG hat die maßgeschneiderte, hochwertige Lösung zu einem fairen Preis.

Outstanding achievements by people down through the centuries are simply inconceivable without the use of cranes. Cranes and lifting gear are more than ever an essential part of production systems today in an industrial world dominated by high technology. BANG Kransysteme GmbH & Co. KG specialises in providing ideal solutions for tasks where objects have to be hoisted and conveyed.

BANG Kransysteme GmbH & Co. KG, which is based in Oelsnitz in the Vogtland district, was founded in 1989 and supplies high-quality crane equipment to well-known companies in Germany and its neighbours, Scandinavia and Eastern Europe.

The successful company deals with planning, manufacturing, assembling and servicing crane equipment for the steel and automobile industries and for nuclear power facilities needing to handle loads of up to 500 tonnes. The manufacturing process for innovative crane equipment starts at the company's headquarters in Oelsnitz. A highly motivated team processes the customer's requirements. Experienced design engineers develop and plan high-quality crane equipment at modern CAD workplaces. Once a project has been agreed with the customer and the green light has been given to go ahead with the manufacturing processes, production of the load-bearing parts starts at the Falkenstein works. The "Class E Verification of Suitability" scheme coupled with a certified quality management system in line with DIN EN 9001 guarantees the highest levels of quality. Crane bridges with a length of more than 35 metres and each weighing more than 30 tonnes can be manufactured in the workshops, which have 20,000 m² of production space.

Before the special haulage companies leave the company premises – and they often have to cover several thousand kilometres across Europe at night – they specialists at BANG Kransysteme GmbH & Co. KG securely load and clamp everything to ensure that the goods survive what may be a very long journey. Experienced assembly workers erect the crane at the customer's premises quickly and safely – the crane is usually standing on its rails within one day as a result of the pre-assembled components. The specialists at BANG Kransysteme GmbH & Co. KG have already supplied more than 5,000 crane systems to many industrial sectors in Germany and international customers. All the machines meet the highest quality standards.

Whether you operate in the steel or paper industry, need crane equipment for nuclear technology or even standard cranes – BANG Kransysteme GmbH & Co. KG has a tailor-made, high-quality solution at a fair price.

Ein Spezialgebiet von BANG Kransysteme GmbH & Co. KG sind Brückenkrane für den Großwerkzeugtransport in der Automobilindustrie. Im modernsten Presswerk der Welt – bei der Audi AG in Ingolstadt - sorgen leistungsfähige Krananlagen von BANG für zuverlässiges und schnelles Werkzeughandling was zu minimalen Stillstandszeiten der Umformpressen beiträgt. / Bridge cranes for transporting huge tools in the automobile industry are one specialist area for BANG Kransysteme GmbH & Co. KG. Powerful cranes from BANG ensure that tools can be handled reliably and quickly in the most modern press shop in the world – at Audi AG in Ingolstadt. This helps reduce downtimes on the machine presses to a minimum.

BANG Kransysteme GmbH & Co. KG
Hohe Straße 3
D-08606 Oelsnitz/Vogtl.
Telefon +49 (0) 37421 485-0
Telefax +49 (0) 37421 485-22
info@bang-kransysteme.de
www.bang-kransysteme.de

(Fotos/Photos by BANG Kransysteme, Hartmut Briese, Text/Text by BANG Kransysteme, Übersetzung/Translated by David Strauss)

Der Wirtschaftsfaktor Maschinenbau
Engineering as an Economic Factor

Der mit Abstand führende Standort im europäischen Maschinenbau ist Deutschland. In Deutschland ist der Maschinenbau nach dem Fahrzeugbau der bedeutendste Industriezweig. (www.destatis.de)
In der Gesamtbetrachtung des deutschen Maschinenbaus befinden sich 85 Prozent aller Maschinenbauunternehmen in den alten Bundesländern und diese Firmen erwirtschaften mehr als 90 Prozent des Umsatzes. Diese Situation ist sehr stark historisch bedingt.

In den neuen Bundesländern ist der Freistaat Sachsen Maschinenbau-Standort Nummer 1 – ca. die Hälfte der Beschäftigten des ostdeutschen Maschinenbau arbeiten in Sachsen. (www.otto-brenner-stiftung.de/publikationen/publikationen/ostdeutschland.html)

Sachsen
Der Maschinenbau bildet eine der vier Kernbranchen Sachsens neben dem Fahrzeugbau, der Biotechnologie und der Mikrotechnik.
Der Umsatzanteil des Maschinenbau am verarbeitenden Gewerbe Sachsens betrug durchschnittlich in den letzten fünf Jahren ca. 7 Prozent und konnte sich kontinuierlich steigern. Im Jahr 2006 erwirtschaftete der Maschinenbau etwa 12 Prozent des kompletten Jahresumsatzes im verarbeitenden Gewerbe 2006.
Die exportstarke Branche erbringt etwa 16 Prozent des Auslandsumsatzes des verarbeitenden Gewerbes im Bundesland. Die höchste Exportquote weist dabei der Fahrzeugbau (53 Prozent) auf, gefolgt vom Maschinenbau (42,5 Prozent). Diese Zahlen belegen die starke Exportorientierung.

Die Branche Maschinenbau (442 Unternehmen) weist nach der Metallerzeugung und -bearbeitung (473 Firmen) die höchste Anzahl von Betrieben im verarbeitenden Gewerbe im Jahr 2006 auf. In Sachsen ist die Branche Maschinenbau vorrangig durch kleine und mittelständische Unternehmen (KMU) geprägt, wobei der Großteil der Unternehmen weniger als 100 Beschäftigte hat. (Statistisch erfasst: Betriebe mit mehr als 20 Mitarbeitern)

Vergleicht man die Regierungsbezirke Dresden, Leipzig und Chemnitz miteinander, findet man Firmen der Branche Maschinenbau vorrangig in den Regionen Dresden und Chemnitz. Der Regierungsbezirk Chemnitz verfügt über die meisten Betriebe und Mitarbeiter. Der Großraum Dresden ist führend hinsichtlich Umsatz und Exportquote, es wird die höchste sächsische Wertschöpfung in diesem Industriesektor erreicht.

Germany is easily the European centre for engineering. Engineering is the most important industrial sector in Germany after the automobile industry. (www.destatis.de).
If the German engineering sector is viewed as a whole, 85 percent of all engineering companies are located in Western Germany and these firms account for more than 90 percent of turnover. This situation is due to major historical factors.

The Free State of Saxony is the engineering location number 1 in Eastern Germany – approx. half of the employees in the Eastern German engineering sector work in Saxony.
(www.otto-brenner-stiftung.de/publikationen/publikationen/ostdeutschland.html)

Saxony
Engineering forms one of the four key sectors in Saxony alongside the automobile sector, biotechnology and microtechnology.
The share of turnover in engineering in terms of Saxony's manufacturing industry accounted for approx. 7 percent on average over the past five years and has increased continually. Engineering accounted for approx. 12 percent of the complete annual turnover in manufacturing industry in 2006.
This sector, which supplies so many goods for export, generates about 16 percent of foreign business in manufacturing industry in the federal state. The highest export quota is in the automobile industry (53 percent) followed by engineering (42.5 percent). These figures show how these sectors are strongly oriented towards export markets.

The engineering sector (442 companies) had the largest number of companies in the manufacturing sector in 2006 after metal production and processing (473 companies). The engineering sector in Saxony is primarily made up of small and medium enterprises (SMEs) and the majority of these companies have less than 100 employees. (Figures compiled statistically: companies with more than 20 employees).

If we compare the administrative districts of Dresden, Leipzig and Chemnitz, engineering companies are mainly found in the Dresden and Chemnitz regions. The Chemnitz administrative district has the highest number of companies and employees. The Dresden area is foremost in terms of turnover and export quotas and the highest Economic Value Added in Saxony is achieved in this industrial sector.

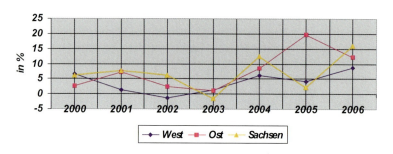

Wachstumsmarkt Sachsen
Umsatzveränderungen gegenüber Vorjahr

(Text/Text by VEMAS, Übersetzung/Translated by David Strauss)

Maschinenbau / Engineering

>> *Das Vogtland als Brücke zwischen Mittel- und Osteuropa bietet generell gute Bedingungen für Industrie und Gewerbe.* <<

>> *The Vogtland region acts as a bridge between Central and Eastern Europe and provides good conditions for industry and business in general terms.* <<

Die Wiege des Maschinenbaus im Vogtland

Der Ursprung des Maschinenbaus in Plauen geht zurück auf die ortsansässige Maschinenstickerei und nicht zuletzt auf die Entwicklung der weltberühmten „Plauener Spitze" im Jahre 1880. Als Vorgänger der heutigen WEMA VOGTLAND GmbH kann man die 1881 gegründete Firma „J. C. & H. Dietrich" betrachten, die 1895 in die „Vogtländische Maschinenfabrik AG" (VOMAG) umgewandelt wurde. Eine der Sternstunden schlug 1910, als es dem in Plauen lebenden Erfinder Robert Zahn bei der VOMAG gelang, den ersten Stickautomaten der Welt zu erfinden. Doch nicht nur Stickautomaten rollten von Plauen aus in alle Welt. Ab 1896 wurden auch Rotationsdruckmaschinen produziert. (Heute: MAN Roland Druckmaschinen AG ist der weltweit zweitgrößte Hersteller von Drucksystemen und dabei Weltmarktführer im Rollendruck. Das Unternehmen hat seine Hauptstandorte in Offenbach, Augsburg und Plauen.) Die cleveren vogtländischen Unternehmer spezialisierten sich aber auch – wie heute wieder – zunehmend auf den Sonder- und Spezialmaschinenbau sowie den Fahrzeugbau. (Bitte lesen Sie auch Seiten 62 bis 75 hier im Buch.).

Offizielles Gründungsdatum der Werkzeugmaschinenfabrik VOGTLAND, in der Region kurz WEMA genannt, ist der 12. Oktober 1948. In der Stresemannstraße startete damals die Produktion der Maschinenfabrik Vogtland mit 22 Personen auf notdürftig reparierten Maschinen. Ab 1953 begann unter dem heutigen Firmennamen die Herstellung von Sondermaschinen und Taktstraßen – eine Anknüpfung an die Maschinenbautradition der alten VOMAG. Zur Kapazitätserweiterung erfolgte 1958 der Umzug auf das neue Betriebsgelände an der Schenkendorfstraße. Mit 10 Hektar Fläche und einer Hallenkapazität von 20.700 Quadratmetern ist hier auch heute noch der Sitz des Unternehmens.

Bis 1989 belieferte WEMA VOGTLAND vor allem die osteuropäischen Staaten – insbesondere die Sowjetunion – mit Anlagen zum Beispiel für die Fertigung von Elektromotorengehäusen, Mähfingern für Erntemaschinen oder auch Kurbelwellen für Verdichter. Nach dem Zusammenbruch dieses Marktes ist es gelungen, einen komplett neuen Kundenstamm aufzubauen. (Quelle WEMA, MAN Band I dieses Buches)

The cradle of engineering in the Vogtland region

The origins of engineering in Plauen go back to the local mechanical embroidery works and not least to the development of world-famous "Plauen lace" in 1880. The "J. C. & H. Dietrich" company, which was founded in 1881 and became the "Vogtländische Maschinenfabrik AG" (VOMAG) in 1895, can be viewed as the forerunner of today's WEMA VOGTLAND GmbH. One of those magic hours occurred in 1910 when the inventor Robert Zahn, who was living in Plauen and working at VOMAG, managed to invent the first automatic embroidery machine in the world. But automatic embroidery machines were not the only ones being shipped around the globe from Plauen. Rotation printing machines were also produced from 1896 onwards (today's company, MAN Roland Druckmaschinen AG, is the world's second largest manufacturer of printing systems and is the world market leader in web printing. The company has its main production sites in Offenbach, Augsburg and Plauen). But the clever Vogtland entrepreneurs also increasingly concentrated on special engineering sectors and the automobile industry – as they are doing today. (Please read pages 62 – 75 in this book).

The official date of the founding of the Werkzeugmaschinenfabrik VOGTLAND, known in the region simply as WEMA, was 12 October 1948. The production at the Vogtland engineering factory started in Stresemannstrasse with just 22 people. The production of special machines and assembly lines – linking up with the engineering tradition at the former VOMAG company – began in 1953 when the company began operating under its current name. The company moved to a new site in Schenkendorfstrasse in order to expand its capacity. This is still the headquarters of the company – the site measures 10 hectares and production facilities cover 20,700 square metres.

WEMA VOGTLAND mainly supplied Eastern European countries until 1989 – especially the Soviet Union – with plant for manufacturing electrical motor housings or cutters for harvesting machines and even crankshafts for compressors. After this market collapsed, the company managed to build up a completely new customer base. (Source: WEMA, MAN, Volume I of this book)

Quadratmetern ist hier auch heute noch der Sitz des Unternehmens.
Bis 1989 belieferte VOGTLAND vor allem die osteuropäischen Staaten – insbesondere die Sowjetunion – mit Anlagen zum Beispiel für die Fertigung von Elektromotorengehäusen, Mähfingern für Erntemaschinen oder auch Kurbelwellen für Verdichter. Nach dem Zusammenbruch dieses Marktes ist es gelungen, einen komplett neuen Kundenstamm aufzubauen. (Quelle WEMA, MAN Band I dieses Buches)

(Fotos/Photos by Igor Pastierovic/Der Stickautomat von Robert Zahn ist zu sehen im Spitzenmuseum in Plauen)

Maschinenbau / Engineering

» *Der Auslandsumsatz im Maschinen- und Anlagenbau liegt im Vogtland mit ca. 30 Prozent doppelt so hoch wie der sächsische Durchschnitt.* «

Vogtland

Die Region Vogtland im „Dreiländereck" Sachsen, Bayern, Thüringen gelegen und mit Angrenzung an die Tschechische Republik nimmt zunehmend eine Schlüsselrolle in der Branche ein. Der Maschinenbau spielt in der Tschechischen Republik eine bedeutende Rolle. Das Vogtland ist durch seine zentrale Lage in Europa und traditionelle Verbindungen zu osteuropäischen Nachbarländern gekennzeichnet. Daraus ergeben sich entscheidende Standortvorteile wie kurze Wege durch günstige Verkehrsanbindungen nach Osteuropa, Erleichterung des grenzüberschreitenden Handels durch den EU-Beitritt der Tschechischen Republik und kostengünstige Produktionsmöglichkeiten praktisch vor der Haustür. Das Vogtland als Brücke zwischen Mittel- und Osteuropa bietet generell gute Bedingungen für Industrie und Gewerbe.

Betrachtet man die Umsatzanteile des Maschinenbau mit dem verarbeitenden Gewerbe im Vogtland (Vogtlandkreis und Plauen), ist der Maschinenbau mit 15 Prozent Umsatzanteil ein sehr bedeutender Wirtschaftszweig der Region (in Sachsen durchschnittlich 7 Prozent). Der Auslandsumsatz im Maschinen- und Anlagenbau liegt mit ca. 30 Prozent doppelt so hoch wie im sächsischen Durchschnitt. Der Maschinen- und Anlagenbau ist im vogtländischen Gebiet fest verankert und nimmt einen wichtigen Stellenwert in der regionalen Wirtschaft und dem Außenhandel ein. Der erreichte Umsatz von Maschinen und Anlagen in Plauen ist doppelt so hoch wie im Vogtlandkreis, obwohl es dort nur halb so viele Betriebe gibt. In Plauen sind mehr Menschen im Maschinenbau tätig und es wird eine höhere Auslandsumsatz verzeichnet. (www.statistik.sachsen.de)
Man kann schlussfolgern, dass es im ländlichen Gebiet des Vogtlandkreises viele kleinere Betriebe unterschiedlichster Branchen gibt, wie es auch für Sachsen typisch ist.

Tendenzen, Visionen, Marktchancen für das Vogtland

Deutlich erkennbar ist das Wachstumspotenzial des Maschinenbau im sächsischen Raum anhand der Entwicklung der vergangenen Jahren. Die Unternehmensgründungen, der Absatz der Maschinen und der Außenhandel steigerten sich deutschlandweit, in Ostdeutschland gedieh der Maschinenbau hinsichtlich der prozentualen Umsatzveränderungen zum Vorjahresergebnis besser als im alten Bundesgebiet.
An Hand der Grafik auf der vorangegangenen Seite wird ersichtlich, dass sich die im Maschinenbau erwirtschafteten Umsätze in Sachsen besonders stark steigern konnten. Vergleicht man die prozentuale Veränderung des Umsatzes mit dem Vorjahr von Ost- und Westdeutschland, konnte Sachsen einen mehr als doppelt so starken Zuwachs wie Westdeutschland verzeichnen. Darin zeigt sich das beträchtliche sächsische Potenzial im Maschinenbausektor.
Diese Entwicklung ist auch im Vogtland ersichtlich. Der Umsatz im verarbeitenden Gewerbe des Vogtlandes stieg generell an, wobei der Auslandsumsatz sich besonders stark steigern konnte. Die Exportquoten stiegen in den letzten 3 Jahren um 30 Prozent an. Diese

» *Sales of exports in the engineering and plant construction sector are approx. 30 percent, i.e. twice as high as the Saxon average figure.* «

Vogtland

The Vogtland region, where the states of Saxony, Bavaria and Thuringia meet and encounter the border with the Czech Republic, is increasingly assuming a key role in this sector. Engineering plays an important role in the Czech Republic. The Vogtland region is located in a central position in Europe and has traditional links with neighbouring countries in Eastern Europe. This provides crucial advantages for businesses setting up factories here: it is only a short distance to Eastern Europe as a result of convenient transport links, trade has been made much easier by the Czech Republic's entry into the EU and there are cheap production facilities virtually on the doorstep. The Vogtland region acts as a bridge between Central and Eastern Europe and provides good conditions for industry and business in general terms.
If we compare the share of turnover in engineering with manufacturing industry in the Vogtland region (the Vogtland district and Plauen), engineering is a very important business factor in the region with a 15 percent share of business (in Saxony the average figure is 7 percent). Sales of exports in the engineering and plant construction sector are approx. 30 percent, i.e. twice as high as the Saxon average figure. Engineering and plant construction are firmly rooted in the Vogtland area and are very important in the regional economy and foreign trade. Turnover in engineering and plant construction is twice as high in Plauen as in the Vogtland district, although the former only has half the number of companies. More people are employed in the engineering sector in Plauen and higher export figures are achieved.
(www.statistik.sachsen.de)
So it is possible to conclude that there are many fairly small companies in a wide variety of sectors in the rural area of the Vogtland district, which is typical of Saxony.

Trends, Visions, Market Opportunities for the Vogtland Region

The growth potential for engineering in Saxony can be clearly seen in developments over the past few years. The number of companies being set up, sales of machines and foreign trade have risen across Germany, but the engineering sector in Eastern Germany has performed even better than its counterpart in Western Germany in terms of percentage gains in turnover over the previous year's results.
Based on the graphics on the preceding page, it is clear that turnover in Saxony in the engineering sector has been able to increase in a particularly strong way. If we compare the percentage change in turnover with the previous year in Eastern and Western Germany, Saxony has been able to record growth that is more than double that of Western Germany. This demonstrates the considerable potential in Saxony in the engineering sector.
This development is also clearly visible in the Vogtland region. Turnover in manufacturing industry in the Vogtland region increased in general terms, while turnover abroad has risen par-

Maschinenbau / Engineering

„Wir wollen Hochschulen und Institute mit den Unternehmen zusammenbringen, um Innovationen in neue, wettbewerbsfähige Produkte zu überführen", erklärt VEMAS-Projektmanager Dr.-Ing. Ralf Lang. „Kooperationen anregen, moderieren und koordinieren, das ist unsere Aufgabe." Durch zielgerichtete produkt- bzw. technologieorientierte Kooperationen werden etwa die Vorzüge der klein- und mittelständischen Betriebe, wie schnelle Reaktionsfähigkeit und Flexibilität, gestärkt. Die gemeinsam mit der Birmingham Chamber of Commerce neu geschaffene dreisprachige virtuelle Plattform www.technologymall.de dient dagegen der weltweiten Vermarktung von Produkten, Technologien und Dienstleistungen.
Kontakt: www.vemas-sachsen.de
VEMAS, Reichenhainer Str. 88, 09126 Chemnitz

VEMAS VERBUNDINITIATIVE MASCHINENBAU SACHSEN

"We want to bring together universities and institutes with companies in order to transfer innovations into new, competitive products," explains VEMAS project manager Dr.-Ing. Ralf Lang. "It is our job to stimulate cooperation arrangements, act as an impartial referee and coordinate them." The advantages of small and medium-sized enterprises – e.g. rapid reaction times and flexibility – are reinforced by deliberate cooperation arrangements related to products or technologies. The newly created trilingual virtual platform with Birmingham Chamber of Commerce – www.technologymall.de – helps support the global marketing of products, technologies and services.

Region profitiert von der unmittelbaren Nähe zum osteuropäischen Ausland und kann die Stärke im Maschinenbau weiter ausbauen. (www.statistik.sachsen.de)
Um wettbewerbsfähig zu sein und sich als Unternehmen nachhaltig am Markt zu behaupten, ist die Entwicklung von Innovationen in kurzer Zeit ausschlaggebend.
Der Freistaat Sachsen bietet gute Forschungs- und Entwicklungseinrichtungen als Grundlage dafür. Der Technologietransfer zu den kleinen und mittelständischen Maschinen- und Anlagenbauern bietet noch sehr großes Potenzial zur Wissensvermittlung und sollte zukünftig verstärkt genutzt werden, um innovative Produkte zu schaffen und sich zu etablieren.

Netzwerke

Die Erfolgsfaktoren der sächsischen Maschinen- und Anlagenbauer sind eine Neuprofilierung des Produktprogramms, gepaart mit einer wirksameren Innovationstätigkeit. Gerade diese Faktoren haben die Wettbewerbsfähigkeit der Maschinenhersteller im Osten deutlich erhöht. Nach wie vor bestehende Produktivitätsrückstände gegenüber Westdeutschland – auf die Gesamtbranche bezogen – rührten vor allem aus Unterschieden in der Produktstruktur und den Betriebsgrößen. Zur Überwindung dieser Hürden ist ein aktives Zusammenarbeiten zwischen den sächsischen Firmen und FuE-Einrichtungen noch stärker in den Mittelpunkt zu rücken. Dies ist nicht zuletzt auch das Anliegen von Netzwerken wie z.B. der Verbundinitiative Maschinenbau Sachsen (VEMAS) und dem Verband deutscher Maschinen- und Anlagenbauer (VDMA), welche ebenfalls einen wesentlichen Anteil an der kontinuierlich positiven Entwicklung dieser Branche im Freistaat haben.
Diese bündeln die Interessen von Maschinen- und Anlagenbauern, Zulieferern, Kunden, Verbänden sowie von Forschungs- und Entwicklungseinrichtungen, um die Wettbewerbsfähigkeit des sächsischen Maschinenbau weiter zu verbessern.

Der wiedererstarkte Maschinenbau

Wie schon an der historischen Entwicklung ersichtlich, wird Sachsen als „Wiege des Maschinenbau" bezeichnet. Durch diese gewachsene Tradition gehört der Maschinenbau zu den Hauptbranchen im Verarbeitenden Gewerbe und spielte auch in der Politik der DDR auf Grund der großen Fertigungstiefe eine wichtige Rolle. Nach 1990 war diese Branche starken Veränderungsprozessen ausgesetzt, welcher mit einem gravierenden Abbau der Kapazitäten einherging. Die Umsätze und der Personalbestand sanken drastisch auf nur noch ca. ein Zehntel des Vorwendevolumens. In den darauf folgenden Jahren der Neuorientierung am Markt konnten sich die Betriebe konsolidieren und von einem niedrigen Niveau ausgehend langsam aber stetig wachsen.

Beeindruckende Beispiele engagierter und erfolgreicher Firmenentwicklungen im Vogtland lesen Sie in unserem Büchern „Das Beste aus dem Vogtland" Band I und hier im Band II.

---

ticularly strongly. Export quotas have risen by 30 percent over the past 3 years. This region is benefiting from its direct proximity to Eastern European countries and will be able to further expand its strong position in the engineering sector. (www.statistik.sachsen.de)
In order to remain competitive and maintain a long-term presence in the market, it is vital for companies to develop innovative products within a very short time.
The Free State of Saxony provides good research and development centres as the basis for this. The transfer of technology to small and medium-sized engineering and plant construction businesses provides huge potential for transmitting knowledge and this could be used more effectively in future to create innovative products and enable companies to establish their presence in the market place.

Networks

If Saxon engineering and plant construction manufacturers are going to be successful, they have to adjust their range of products and engage in more effective innovation work. These factors have increased the competitiveness of engineering manufacturers in Eastern Germany markedly. Shortfalls in productivity, which still exist in comparison with Western Germany – in terms of the whole sector – stem mainly from differences in the product structure and the size of companies. Active cooperation between the Saxony companies and R&D centres needs to become an even greater focus of attention if these obstacles are to be overcome. This is not least the task of networks, e.g. the Engineering Network Initiative in Saxony (VEMAS) or the German Engineering Federation (VDMA), which are also playing a major role in ensuring that this sector continues to develop positively in the Free State.
They pool the interests of engineering and plant construction manufacturers, suppliers, customers, associations and research and development centres in order to further improve the competitiveness of the Saxon engineering sector.

Engineering a Force Again

As is clear from historical developments, Saxony is sometimes called the "cradle of the engineering industry". Engineering is one of the main areas of manufacturing industry as a result of this deeply rooted tradition. It also played an important role in the policies pursued by East Germany because of the depth of manufacturing facilities here. This sector was exposed to huge changes in procedures after 1990 and this led to a serious dismantling of production capacity. Turnover and the number of personnel plunged drastically to approx. one tenth of the figures before the fall of the Berlin Wall. During the next few years of reorientation in the market, companies were able to consolidate and, starting from a low level, grow slowly but surely.

You can read impressive examples of how committed and successful companies have developed in our books "The Very Best of Vogtland" volume I and here in volume II.

Maschinenbau / Engineering

» *Starke Leistungen unter höchster Belastung und ohne Umwege.* «

» *Excellent Work under Great Pressure and without any Fuss.* «

Exzellenter Maschinenbau am Traditionsstandort lebt wieder

Beispielhaft für 60 Jahre Industriegeschichte im Vogtland. steht die heutige AUERBACH Maschinenfabrik. Vom einstigen Werkzeughersteller hat sich AUERBACH zum leistungsfähigen Produzenten von Fräsmaschinen und kombinierten Tiefbohr-Fräsmaschinen entwickelt.

Im Ursprung wegen Kriegswichtigkeit bestehender Zerstörungsgefahr durch Bombenangriffe im Jahre 1943 als kleiner Privatbetrieb aus dem Rheinland in Auerbach Schutz suchend angesiedelt, entwickelte sich das Unternehmen bis zur Wende zu einem Großbetrieb mit über 1200 Beschäftigten, mit enormer Bedeutung für Stadt und Region, in einer für das ländliche Vogtland eher untypischen Branche.

Mehrfach wechselnde Eigentumsformen und Zugehörigkeiten ebenso wie die immobile und bauliche Basis bestimmten den Werdegang des Unternehmens. Markant für die Entwicklung des 1957 in die VEB Werkzeugmaschinen Auerbach umstrukturierten volkseigenen Betriebes war auch die Zusammenführung mit dem Ellefelder Maschinenbaubetrieb (Ellma) im Jahre 1970, welche sich bis heute als äußerst vorteilhaft für die Erweiterung erweißt.

Für die personelle und räumliche Vergrößerung zeichneten sich die steile Produktentwicklung von einfachsten Gegenständen des täglichen Gebrauchs im Nachkriegsbeginn bis zu flexibel automatisierten Fertigungssystemen und automatischen Bearbeitungsstationen verantwortlich, unterstützt von enormer Bedeutung für die DDR-Wirtschaft hinsichtlich der Ausrüstung der Metall verarbeitenden Industrie und durch eine hohe Exportquote, insbesondere in die damalige Sowjetunion.

Dies sollte sich nach deren und dem Zusammenbruch der DDR im Jahre 1989/90 als besonders folgenschwer erweisen. Im Zusammenhang mit der Währungsreform entzog sich der inzwischen zu einer GmbH umgewandelten, in Treuhandbesitz befindlichen WEMA Auerbach, der Absatzmarkt. Diese verursachte innerhalb kürzester Zeit einen drastischen Arbeitskräfteabbau. Darüber hinaus dominierte Kurzarbeit. Die Produktion entwickelte sich so rückläufig, dass in der Talsohle des Tiefs Ende 1991/Anfang 1992 der Monatsumsatz sich auf nur noch eine Maschine beschränkte. Der Betrieb galt als nicht sanierungsfähig und wurde von der für die Privatisierung der volkseigenen DDR-Wirtschaft zuständigen Treuhandanstalt zur Liquidation vorgesehen. Nachdem mehrere Kaufinteressenten wieder absprangen und auch eigene Teillösungen sich nicht verwirklichen ließen, vollzog sich Anfang 1992 die einstweilige Rettung durch die Übernahme in die Wagner-Gruppe, einem Unternehmen aus Baden/Würtemberg.

Diese Lösung zum Erhalt in letzter Minute begünstigte die starke Position der WEMA Auerbach GmbH mit seiner Top-Ausrüstung, guter Gebäudesubstanz, einem starken Potential an Fachkräften und einem enormen Know-how, gesammelt im Bau von über 20 000 Werkzeugmaschinen. Zunächst zeigte sich eine positive Entwicklung mit begrenzten

Excellent Engineering Resurrected at a Traditional Site

The AUERBACH Engineering Company serves as an example of 60 years of industrial history in the Vogtland region. It was once a tool-making company, but AUERBACH has now developed into a powerful manufacturer of milling machines and combined deep drilling/milling machines.

Originally set up as a small company moved from the Rhineland to Auerbach in 1943 because of the danger of destruction from Allied bomb attacks in 1943 and the need to preserve it for the war effort, the company developed into a huge business with more than 1200 employees by the time the Berlin Wall fell and it was enormously important for the town and region in a sector, which was not exactly typical of the rural Vogtland region.

The company's development has been marked by changing forms of ownership and affiliation as well as the buildings housing it. The nationalised company was restructured in 1957 to form the Auerbach machine tool combine and a significant development took place in 1970 when it merged with the Ellefeld Engineering company (Ellma) – and this has proved to be extremely advantageous for its further development to this day.

The expansion in personnel and company property was due to the rapid development in production from the simplest objects in daily use at the start of the postwar period to automated manufacturing systems and automatic processing stations with a high degree of flexibility; this was backed by its enormous importance for the East German economy in equipping the metal processing industry and because of its high export quotas, particularly to the Soviet Union at that time.

The collapse of the Soviet Union and East Germany in 1989/90 had particularly serious consequences for the company. WEMA Auerbach had now been converted into a limited company and was owned by the trust overseeing the privatisation of East German companies when it was hit by two crucial factors: the currency reform and the loss of its sales markets. This triggered a dramatic reduction in staff numbers within a very short time. Short-time work then became the norm. Production figures fell to such a degree that during the blackest period at the end of 1991/beginning of 1992 monthly turnover was earned on just one machine. The trust overseeing the privatisation of former East German companies believed that the company was not worth saving and was planning to wind it up. After several parties interested in purchasing the company pulled out and some partial solutions did not materialise, a temporary reprieve was granted when it was taken over by the Wagner Group, a company from Baden-Württemberg, at the beginning of 1992.

This solution to save the company at the last minute benefited the strong market position of WEMA Auerbach GmbH, which had top equipment, buildings that were in good shape, strong potential with specialist staff and an enormous level of expertise that had been gained from manufacturing more than 20,000 machine tools. Positive developments ensued at a low level initially, but this was followed by another, even more serious crisis in the mid-1990s. The company slid into liqui-

(Fotos/Photos by Silke Keller-Thoß, Text/Text by Ulrich Franz, Übersetzung/Translated by David Strauss)

Maschinenbau / Engineering

Niveau, die jedoch Mitte der neunziger Jahre in eine weitere, noch krassere Krise umschlug. Hervorgerufen durch eine weltweite Rezession im Maschinenbau und schlechter Zahlungsmoral wichtiger Kunden und Zwischenhändler schlitterte der Betrieb in die Insolvenz.

Es halfen weder weiterer Personalabbau noch der Abstoß von Immobilien einschließlich der Auflösung der Standorte in Auerbach und Morgenröthe-Rautenkranz. Die Jahre 1996/97 prägte der Versuch der Insolvenzverwaltung das Unternehmen vor der Liquidation zu retten. Weitaus bedrohlicher als vor der ersten Privatisierung zeigte sich nunmehr der Ernst der Lage. Nachdem einige dieser Schnellmaßnahmen nicht mehr fruchteten, schien für die Treuhand-Nachfolgegesellschaft (BVS) und das sächsische Wirtschaftsministerium das Schicksal des Betriebes besiegelt. Mit Leidenschaft und Kampfbereitschaft leistete die Belegschaft, mit ihrem Betriebsratsvorsitzenden Friedrich Fuchs an der Spitze, noch Widerstand. Eine Zeit zwischen Hoffen und Bangen brach an. In Solidarität, wie sie bereits zu DDR-Zeiten entstand, als mehrfach der Betrieb seine Eigenständigkeit verlieren und zu einem Zulieferer degradiert werden sollte und im Wissen wie gut man sich vor der ersten Privatisierung entwickelte, stand man zusammen und demonstrierte in Berlin und Dresden. Derweil lief die Produktion, unterstützt von der damaligen Kreissparkasse, erstmal weiter. Die Beschäftigtenzahl fiel jedoch auf den absoluten Tiefstand. Nach hartem Kampf gelang zum zweiten Mal die Rettung in letzter Minute. In Person der IXION-Gruppe aus Hamburg, die bereits erfolgreiches Engagement im Osten nachweisen konnte, der man jedoch zunächst seitens der Treuhand nicht traute, erschien die Lösung. Die Presse titelte: „Ein Wunder ist geschehen". Es ist jedoch kein Wunder geschehen. Mit Leistung und Leidenschaft hatten engagierte Vogtländer, bauend auf geschaffene Grundlagen in Form von Immobilien, Ausrüstungen und Fähigkeiten, den Erhalt einer traditionsreichen Branche erkämpft. Stolz konnte man zur 725-Jahr-Feier der Stadt Auerbach im August 2007 auf 50 Jahre Werkzeugmaschinenbau verweisen (siehe Bild oben links).

Doch vorher musste in den bisherigen 10 Jahren des IXION-Engagements ein mühsamer Weg der Konsolidierung begangen werden. Nachdem die Beschäftigtenzahl auf unter 100 gesunken war, stehen derzeit 115 Mitarbeiter und 20 Auszubildende in Lohn und Brot. Der Umsatz steigt wieder kontinuierlich. Das Produktionssortiment galt es umzubilden, nicht mehr wirtschaftlich zu fertigendes wegzulassen und einen Platz mit Anspruch und Niveau auf dem Sektor Fräsen und Tiefbohren zu finden. Lesen Sie dazu die nachfolgenden Seiten. IXION Auerbach – Tradition und Innovation, Kompetenz und Flexibilität.

dation as a result of a global recession in the engineering sector and poor payment practices by important customers and distributors.
Further reductions in personnel and the sale of property, including the closure of the works at Auerbach and Morgenröthe-Rautenkranz, were unable to do the trick. The company receiver used the years 1996-97 to try to save the company from bankruptcy. The situation was now even more precarious than at the time of initial privatisation. After some of the rapid measures proved ineffective, the company's fate seemed doomed in the eyes of the successor to the trust responsible for privatising former East German companies (BVS) and the Saxon Ministry of Economics. The staff resisted this development with a high degree of fervour and a readiness to fight, with works council chairman, Friedrich Fuchs, leading the way. The mood swung back and forth between hope and fear. But the workers stood together and demonstrated in Berlin and Dresden with the same sense of solidarity that had been fashioned in East German days – when the company was supposed to lose its independence on several occasions and be downgraded to a supplier – and in the knowledge of how well the company had developed before initial privatisation. For the moment production continued, supported by the district savings bank. The number of employees, however, plunged to an all-time low.

Following a tough battle, the company was saved at the very last minute for a second time. On this occasion the solution came from the IXION Group in Hamburg, which had already demonstrated its commitment to Eastern Germany; but the trust overseeing the privatisation of East German companies was not impressed initially. The headline in the press was: "A Miracle Has Taken Place". But it was not a miracle. Committed people from the Vogtland region, building on the foundations that had already been laid in the form of property, equipment and expertise, had successfully fought to save a traditional company with fervour and all their might. During the 725th anniversary of the town of Auerbach in August 2007, the company was able to proudly highlight its 50 years of machine tool manufacturing (see photo on the left at the top).

But prior to this, the company has had to tread a painful path of consolidation during the 10 years that IXION has been involved. After the number of employees sank to below 100, 115 employees and 20 trainees now have a job at the company. Turnover is increasing continually. The range of products was revamped to ensure that nothing that could be produced economically was omitted and the company had to find a new market position with high standards and quality in the milling and deep drilling sector. Please read the following pages to find out more about this. IXION Auerbach – tradition and innovation, expertise and flexibility.

Tradition und Innovation, Kompetenz und Flexibilität
Tradition and Innovation, Competence and Flexibility

Die heutige AUERBACH Maschinenfabrik steht beispielhaft für 60 Jahre Industriegeschichte im Vogtland. Vom einstigen Werkzeughersteller hat sich AUERBACH zum leistungsfähigen Produzenten von Fräsmaschinen und kombinierten Tiefbohr-Fräsmaschinen entwickelt.

Der Grundstein wurde 1943 gelegt, als die Firma Alfred Berghaus Spezial-, Fräs- und Senkwerkzeugfabrik ihre Produktion verlagerte. Mit 71 Mitarbeitern begann die Produktion für die Panzer- und Flugzeugfertigung. Nach Kriegsende wurde zunächst mit der Herstellung von einfachen Gebrauchsgegenständen begonnen. Bis 1956 waren Werkzeuge die Hauptproduktion des Betriebes. Der sinkende Bedarf führte 1957 zur Umstrukturierung des Unternehmens. Mit wenigen erfahrenen Fachkräften begann man mit der Produktion einer kleinen 4t-Exenterpresse sowie einer Handhebel-Fräsmaschine mit einer Tischgröße von 125 x 400 mm.

Im Laufe der nächsten Jahrzehnte passte das Unternehmen sich und seine Produktpalette immer wieder den jeweiligen Gegebenheiten an.

Neben der Übernahme und Produktion von bestehenden Produktprogrammen der damaligen DDR wie z.B. Nutenfräsmaschinen, Universalfräsmaschinen, Holzbearbeitungsmaschinen, hat AUERBACH immer in Neu- und Weiterentwicklungen investiert und mit starken Partnern aus Wissenschaft und Forschung zusammengearbeitet.

So wurden hier die ersten eigenen Entwicklungen von handgesteuerten und teilautomatischen Konsolfräsmaschinen realisiert, die erste Nockenprogrammsteuerung und später auch eine erste eigene NC-Steuerung entwickelt.

Parallel zur Maschinenentwicklung leistete AUERBACH in Zusammenarbeit mit Hochschulen und Forschungszentren umfangreiche Entwicklungsarbeit auf dem Gebiet der Verfahrenstechnik, insbesondere zur Kurven- und Gewindeherstellung. Vielfältige technologische Lösungen flossen in die Maschinenentwicklungen ein. Dieser Tradition bleibt das Unternehmen bis heute treu.

AUERBACH machine company in its current form represents 60 years of outstanding industrial history in the Vogtland region. AUERBACH was once a tool-making company, but has now developed into a highly efficient manufacturer of milling machines and combined deep drilling and milling machines.

It all started in 1943 when the Alfred Berghaus company for special tools, milling and countersinking tools changed its production. Its 71 employees started to manufacture products for the tank and aircraft construction industries. After the Second World War, the company started producing simple articles for daily use again. The company mainly manufactured tools until 1956. But a fall in demand led to a restructuring of the company in 1957. Production of a small four-ton eccentric press and a hand-lever milling machine with table dimensions of 125 x 400 mm started with just a few experienced, skilled workers.

Over the next few decades the company was able to adapt itself and its product range to continually changing circumstances.

The company not only took over the production of existing, current product programmes in East Germany – such as groove milling machines, universal milling machines and wood processing machines – but AUERBACH always invested in research and development and worked with strong partners in science and research too.
The company designed the first manually controlled and semi-automatic console milling machines; and the first camshaft control system and later the first NC controls were developed.

Parallel to machines, AUERBACH also carried out development work in the field of process engineering in collaboration with universities and research centres. The main focus was on manufacturing cams and threads. A variety of technical solutions were integrated in machine developments. The company still maintains this tradition today.

IXION AUERBACH

AUERBACH Maschinenfabrik GmbH
Gewerbering 10 · D-08236 Ellefeld
Telefon   +49 (0) 3745 31-0
Telefax   +49 (0) 3745 5160
www.auerbach-gmbh.de
info@auerbach-gmbh.de

(Fotos/Photos by IXION, Text/Text by IXION, Übersetzung/Translated by David Strauss)

AUERBACH Maschinenfabrik

Bis zum Jahr 1996 produzierte AUERBACH Bearbeitungszentren und Revolverkopf-Fräsmaschinen sowie NC-Konsolfräsmaschinen, Fertigungszellen, komplexe, verkettete Maschinensysteme, Universalfräsmaschinen, Bettfräsmaschinen, Elektronenstrahl-Bearbeitungsmaschinen).

Heute gehört das Unternehmen zur IXION-AUERBACH-Firmenguppe.

AUERBACH hat sich auf seine Kernkompetenzen auf dem Gebiet des Fräsens konzentriert und produziert Bettfräsmaschinen und Fahrständerfräsmaschinen (FBE-Baureihe, IA5B-Baureihe, IA5F-Baureihe). Da diese Maschinenkonzepte auf einem Baukastensystem basieren und vielfältige Optionen zur Verfügung stehen, können die AUERBACH-Maschinen optimal den Kundenwünschen angepasst werden kann.

IXION ist ein traditionelles Hamburger Unternehmen, dessen Kernkompetenz in Bohrmaschinen, speziell Tiefbohrmaschinen liegen. Diese Kompetenz gepaart mit AUERBACH's Fräserfahrungen führten zu gemeinsamen Produktentwicklungen. So produziert AUERBACH heute auch kombinierte Tiefbohr-Fräsmaschinen mit einer oder 2 Spindeln (IA 7 M / IA –TLF-Baureihe) in verschiedenen Baugrößen und mit vielfältigen Optionen. Es können verschiedene Bohrtechnologien eingesetzt werden – ELB oder BTA-Bohren, auch kombinierbar an einer Maschine.

Damit gehören neben den traditionellen Maschinenbauunternehmen und Fertigungsdienstleistern vor allem auch Werkzeug- und Formenbauer zum AUERBACH-Kundenkreis.

Die Tieflochbohr-Lohnfertigung der TiXBo GmbH, ein weiteres Unternehmen der IXION-AUERBACH-Gruppe sowohl am Standort Ellefeld als auch in Hamburg, rundet das Leistungsangebot der Unternehmensgruppe ab. Leistungsfähige Fertigungszentren für die Eigen- und Lohnfertigung stehen an beiden Standorten zur Verfügung. Natürlich bietet AUERBACH auch Fräskapazitäten auf eigenen Maschinen an.

Insgesamt arbeiten 240 Mitarbeiter im Firmenverbund, davon etwa 115 bei AUERBACH. Zusätzlich werden 20 Lehrlinge im Ellefelder Unternehmen ausgebildet.

Niederlassungen der Unternehmensgruppe in den USA, Italien und China sowie zahlreiche in- und ausländische Vertretungen sichern eine gute Marktbearbeitung sowie ein gutes Serviceangebot.

Die Marktreaktionen auf die neuen AUERRBACH-Produkte ist gut. Entsprechend der Unternehmenstradition wird es auch in Zukunft weitere Entwicklungen und Marktanpassungen geben.

Kernkompetenzen:
- Bettfräsmaschinen
- Fahrständerfräsmaschinen
- kombinierte Tiefbohr-Fräsmaschinen
- Lohnfertigung (Tiefbohren, Fräsen)

AUERBACH produced machining centres, turret head milling machines, as well as NC console milling machines, manufacturing cells, complex linked machine systems, universal milling machines, bed-type millers and electron beam processing machines until 1996.

Today the company is part of the IXION-AUERBACH group.

AUERBACH now focuses on its core competence in the field of milling and produces bed-type milling machines and travelling column milling machines (FBE, IA5B and IA5F series). Since these machines are based on a modular construction concept, a variety of options are available to customize AUERBACH machines to meet customers' requirements.

IXION is a traditional Hamburg-based enterprise. Its core competence is in the field of drilling machines, especially deep drilling machines. This know-how, in combination with AUERBACH's experience with milling machines, has led to the development of joint products.

So AUERBACH now manufactures combined deep drilling and milling machines with one or two spindles (IA 7 M and IA-TLF series) with different dimensions and a variety of options. Various drilling technologies can be used: STS or gun drilling or they can be combined on one machine.

This means that tool and moulded parts manufacturers are numbered among AUERBACH's customers alongside traditional mechanical engineering and manufacturing companies.

Contract deep-drilling work carried out by TiXBo GmbH, another company in the IXION-AUERBACH group operating at Ellefeld and Hamburg, rounds off the range of services provided. Efficient production centres at both sites are available for the company's own production and contract deep-drilling work. Of course AUERBACH also offers milling capacity on its own machines.

240 employees work for the group, 115 of them at AUERBACH. The Ellefeld company is also training 20 apprentices.

Group branches in the USA, Italy and China and many domestic and international authorized dealers ensure that the market is covered and excellent services are provided.

The market reaction to AUERBACH products is good and, in line with the company's traditions, further developments and adjustments to the market situation will follow.

Core areas of competence:
- bed-type milling machines
- travelling column milling machines
- combined deep drilling and milling machines
- contract production (deep drilling, milling)

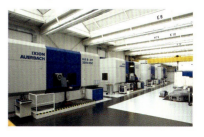

WEMA VOGTLAND GmbH startet durch!
WEMA VOGTLAND Turns the Corner!

Sich neu erfinden, um am Markt bestehen zu können, diesem Ziel hat sich die traditionsreiche WEMA VOGTLAND GmbH in Plauen verschrieben, deren Wurzeln bis ins Jahr 1881 reichen. Nach einem Eigentümerwechsel wurde das Unternehmen im Dezember 2006 neu gegründet. Aus einem reinen Hersteller von Sondermaschinen und Taktstraßen wird eine Firma, die vor allem ein- und zweispindlige Bearbeitungszentren und Sonderlösungen anfertigt.

Den mit der Firmengründung einhergehenden Strategiewechsel begründet der Geschäftsführende Gesellschafter Franz Margraf mit den Kundenwünschen insbesondere aus der Automobil- und Zulieferbranche. Umrüstfreundlich und rekonfigurierbar lauten die Stichworte, für die die Produkte aus Plauen stehen. Nach einer fast 16-jährigen Übergangsphase sind die Vogtländer in ruhiges Fahrwasser vorgedrungen, ja sogar auf den Wachstumspfad eingebogen. Der Firmenchef bezeichnet das Jahr 2007 als Wachstumsjahr. Startete man mit 12 Mio. Euro Jahresumsatz, werden für heuer 25 Mio. angepeilt - und die WEMA VOGTLAND GmbH schreibt schwarze Zahlen. 2008 sei auftragsmäßig so gut wie gelaufen, zeigt sich Margraf zuversichtlich.

Gerade diese positive Entwicklung schafft auch wieder Zuversicht in der Belegschaft. Sank in den vergangenen Jahren die Mitarbeiterzahl erheblich, stabilisiert sich der Wert bei 180 Arbeitern und Angestellten, darunter sind auch zehn Lehrlinge.

Gegenwärtig ist die Firma erstmalig wieder auf der Suche nach Fachkräften. In den kommenden Jahren wird sich in der WEMA VOGTLAND GmbH die Zahl der Auszubildenden auf 15 junge Menschen erhöhen, um der Überalterung der Belegschaft entgegen zu wirken.

Mit 35 bis 36 Prozent Exportquote liegt der Wert des vogtländischen Traditionsunternehmens über dem Landesschnitt in Sachsen. Gerade der chinesische Markt, in dem man mit einer Firma kooperiert, aber kein Joint-Venture betreibt, ist ein Markt der Zukunft. Die Exportquote soll im kommenden Jahr sogar noch weiter steigen. Ein aufstrebender Markt ist der osteuropäische. Trotzdem ist der deutschsprachige Markt das A und O für die Spitzenstädter.

Renommierte Kunden sind die großen Autohersteller VW, BMW, Daimler oder auch Opel, aber ebenso gehören renommierte Zulieferfirmen wie Continental Teves, FTE, Krupp Hoesch ins Kundenportfolio.

Innovationen und Investitionen sind das Essential, um am Markt bestehen zu können. So investiert der Werkzeugmaschinenmacher rund 1,5 Mio. Euro in die Modernisierung. Auf der Branchenleitmesse EMO 2007 stellte WEMA VOGTLAND ein modular aufgebautes Maschinenkonzept vor, das für spanende Fertigungsaufgaben in mittleren und großen Serien geeignet ist.

Firmenchef Margraf will mit der WEMA VOGTLAND GmbH weiter auf dem Wachstumspfad vorankommen.

WEMA VOGTLAND GmbH in Plauen, a company with a long history and roots going back to 1881, has taken the bold step of relaunching itself to survive in the market place. Following a change of ownership, the company was refounded in December 2006. The company used to make special machines and transfer lines, but it now primarily manufactures single and double spindle machining centres and special solutions.

The managing director, Franz Margraf, justifies the change in strategy associated with the relaunch of the company by pointing to customer demand, particularly from the automobile and supplier sectors. The catch phrases describing the products made in Plauen are: "easy to retool" and "reconfigurable". After a transitional period lasting almost 16 years, the Vogtland company has now moved into calmer waters and has turned the corner in terms of growth. The company director is calling 2007 the year of growth. The company started with an annual turnover of € 12 million – but this year it is expecting that figure to rise to € 25 million – and WEMA VOGTLAND GmbH is back in the black. Margraf says that he is confident that orders for 2008 are almost "in the bag" even at this stage.

This positive development has also given the workforce a new sense of confidence. The number of staff fell dramatically over the past few years, but has now stabilised at 180, including ten trainees. For the first time the company is now looking for specialist staff again.

(Fotos/Photos by WEMA VOGTLAND GmbH, Text/Text by Bert Walther, Übersetzung/Translated by David Strauss)

> *Das Vogtland ist bekannt für Spitzenqualität. Diesen Ruf haben wir mit geprägt.*

Franz Margraf,
geschäftsführender Gesellschafter
der WEMA VOGTLAND GmbH

WEMA VOGTLAND GmbH will increase the number of trainees to 15 young people over the coming years to counter the ageing process among its staff.

With an export quota of 35-36 percent, the traditional Vogtland company is well above the average for the state of Saxony. The Chinese market, where the company has a cooperation arrangement with a local firm, but not a joint venture, is a market with a clear future. The export quota is expected to rise still further in the coming year. The Eastern European market is also expanding. But most of the lace city company's orders still come from the German-speaking market. The major car manufacturers VW, BMW, Daimler and even Opel are customers of note, but the company's portfolio of customers also includes renowned suppliers like Continental Teves, FTE and Krupp Hoesch.

Innovations and investments are essential for survival in the market place. So the machine tool manufacturer is investing some € 1.5 million in modernisation. WEMA VOGTLAND presented a modular machine design at the leading fair for this sector, the EMO, in 2007; it can be used for machining tasks for medium-sized and large-scale production runs.

Company director Margraf wants to ensure that WEMA VOGTLAND GmbH continues to move forward in terms of growth.

WEMA VOGTLAND GmbH
Schenkendorfstr. 14
D-08525 Plauen
Telefon   +49 (0) 3741 592-0
Telefax   +49 (0) 3741 592-485
www.wema-vogtland.de
info@wema-vogtland.de

Modellbau Roth GmbH in Theuma

Eine Sache der Form
A Question of Shape

Geschäftsführer und Firmengründer Bernd Roth mit seiner Frau Dagmar, die seit 1991 ihren Mann im Unternehmen tatkräftig unterstützt.

Managing director and company founder Bernd Roth with his wife Dagmar, who has been a real support to her husband at the company since 1991

Wer den Weg der Besten gehen will, darf sich nicht damit begnügen, es heute nur so gut zu machen wie gestern. Es sind ständig neue Herausforderungen, denen sich das vogtländische Unternehmen Modellbau Roth GmbH in dem beschaulichen Ort Theuma stellt.

Den Schritt in die Selbständigkeit wagte Bernd Roth 1991. Zunächst stellte der Betrieb Gießereimodelle aus Holz, später hochwertige Modelle auch aus Kunstharz und Aluminium her. Die vom Kunden gebrachten Skizzen und Zeichnungen mußten modelltechnisch aufbereitet werden und anschließend baute man von Hand das maßstabsgetreue Modell. Der steile Werdegang des Unternehmens beschreibt sich so: 1993 erste bauliche Erweiterung – ein Zuschnittbereich und Sozialräume entstanden. Dem folgten 1999 die Investition in den Bau einer neuen Fertigungshalle. Es wurde die erste 5-Achs-HSC-Fräsmaschine angeschafft und 3D-CAD/CAM-Arbeitsplätze entstanden. Im Jahre 2004 folgte die zweite 5-Achs-HSC-Fräsmaschine und mit dem Bau der zweiten Fertigungshalle wurde begonnen. Der Neubau konnte im August 2005 feierlich eingeweiht werden.

Der Begriff Modellbau ist für das heutige Wirken des mittlerweile zu einem stattlichen mittelständischen Betrieb herangewachsenen Unternehmens nicht mehr ganz zutreffend. Zur Produktionspalette gehören nach wie vor Gießereimodelle, aber auch die Fertigung von Modellen und Prototypen, Formen und Werkzeugen, Datenkontrollmodellen und Lehren für die Fahrzeugindustrie sind Bestandteil der Leistungen. In der neuen Fertigungshalle stellt das Unternehmen Zulieferteile für die Luftfahrt- und Automobilindustrie her. So fliegen beispielsweise im Airbus A380 Teile aus Theuma mit. Die Außenhaut aus Spezialblech für die Türen der meisten Airbusse wird bei Modellbau Roth bearbeitet. Im Prototypenbau reicht das Spektrum vom Rasenmähergehäuse bis hin zu kompletten Auto-, Schiebe- und Klimadächern oder Heckklappen aus Magnesium für Kraftfahrzeuge aus der Premiumklasse.

Besondere handwerkliche Fertigkeiten, hohes technisches Verständnis, innovatives und flexibles Denken und die Liebe zum Detail sind die Eigenschaften, die den Modellbauern noch heute zugute kommen. Aber der wirtschaftliche Erfolg und die Stabilität des Unternehmens mit mittlerweile 18 Angestellten und einer firmeneigenen Lehrlingsausbildung begründen sich auch auf die Investitionen in modernste Technik und hochqualifizierte Fachkräfte. Zuverlässigkeit, Kundenzufriedenheit, ein positives Betriebsklima und unternehmerischer Mut sind die von Bernd Roth geprägten Grundpfeiler der Firmenphilosophie.

Those who set out to be the best cannot afford to be satisfied with just performing as well today as they did yesterday. The Vogtland company called Modellbau Roth GmbH, with its headquarters in the tranquil village of Theuma, constantly faces new challenges.

Berndt Roth took the plunge and set up his own business in 1991. The company initially manufactured casting moulds made of wood and later high-quality moulds made of synthetic resin and aluminium. The sketches and drawings supplied by customers had to be processed technically and then the scale model was made by hand. The company's rapid development can be described as follows: the first new buildings were added in 1993 – consisting of a blanking area and recreations rooms. This was followed by investing in the construction of new production workshops in 1999. The first 5-axis HSC milling machine was purchased and 3D-CAD/CAM workplaces were set up. The second 5-axis HSC milling machine was bought in 2004 and work was started on the construction of a second production centre. The new building was inaugurated with a celebration in August 2005.

The term mould making no longer completely describes the work now carried out by a company that has become an impressive medium-sized enterprise. Casting moulds are still part of the range of products, but the company also makes models and prototypes, moulds and tools, data control models and templates for the automobile industry. Parts made in Theuma can even be found on board Airbus A380 planes. The outer skin made of special sheet metal for the doors on most of the Airbus planes is made at Modellbau Roth. The company's prototype work includes making housings for lawn mowers or complete car roofs, sun roofs, air-conditioning roof sections or boot lids made of magnesium for luxury vehicles.

The model makers here are able to make full use of their skilled craftsmanship, a high degree of technical expertise, innovative and flexible thinking and a love for detail. But the business success and the stability of the company, which now employs 18 people and has its own apprenticeship training programme, are based on investments in the latest technology and highly qualified specialist personnel. Reliability, customer satisfaction, a positive working environment and the capacity to venture into new areas are the foundation stones of the company philosophy drawn up by Bernd Roth.

MODELLBAU ROTH GmbH

Lottengüner Straße 57
D-0854 Theuma
Telefon +49 (0) 37463 88285
Telefax +49 (0) 37463 88275
info@modellbauroth.de
www.modellbauroth.de

(Fotos/Photos by Igor Pastierovic, Übersetzung/Translated by David Strauss)

Innovation für die Zukunft – Maschinenbau auf höchstem Niveau

Innovation for the future – mechanical engineering at the highest level

Die LEHMANN - UMT GmbH, ansässig im reizvollen Naherholungsgebiet der Talsperre Pöhl, ist ein mittelständiges Unternehmen, das in 3. Generation wächst. Feste Bestandteile des Firmenprofils sind Engineering, 3D–Konstruktion, Fördertechnik, Blechbearbeitung und Sondermaschinenbau. Mit dem 32–köpfigen kompetenten Mitarbeiterteam und der umfassenden Produktpalette realisiert die Firma Aufgabenstellungen nach Kundenwunsch – von der Standardanlage bis zur individuellen Komplettlösung, termingerecht und anschlussfertig montiert, alles aus einer Hand.

Vor über 9 Jahren trat die LEHMANN - UMT aus der LEHMANN - Maschinenbau GmbH heraus und entwickelte eine Menge an Know how in der metallverarbeiteten Branche. Investitionen in neueste Fertigungstechnologien sichern Arbeitsplätze, sorgen für jährlich steigende Umsätze und sind maßgebend für hervorragende Qualität. Dazu zählen leistungsstarke 3D Laser- , Plasma- und Brennschneidanlagen sowie moderne CNC - Bearbeitungszentren. Besonders hervorzuheben ist die 3D Fräsmaschine Pentapod. Für den Eigenbedarf gebaut, ermöglicht sie komplizierte und übergroße Bauteile, in einer Aufspannung präzise zu fertigen.

Des weiteren gehören Produktion und Vertrieb individueller Förder- und Filteranlagen zum Geschäftsfeld der LEHMANN-UMT. Für den Abtransport verschiedener Späne, Abfälle und zur Aufbereitung von Kühlschmierstoffen eingesetzt, erleichtern sie das Recycling in Industrie und umwelttechnischen Bereichen.

Im Gebiet Sondermaschinenbau wird mit komplexer Handling– und Automatisierungstechnik zur Beseitigung von Rationalisierungsreserven beigetragen. Nennenswerte Beispiele für Entwicklung und Realisierung von kundenspezifischen Lösungen sind Projekte, wie eine vollautomatische Filteranlage zum Aufbereiten von Kühlschmierstoffen und Prozesswässern oder die automatisierte Vlieslegelinie zur Verarbeitung von Naturfaserstoffen.

Keinesfalls ungenannt sollen die „Lehmann – Edelstahlgrills" bleiben. Zeigen sie nicht nur die Liebe der Vogtländer zum Grillen, sondern repräsentieren hochwertige Erzeugnisse „Made in Germany", die in viele europäische Länder exportiert werden. Das Sortiment ist weit gefächert: von Feuerstellen über Räucheröfen bis zum praktischen Campinggrill kann alles erworben werden. Ein kleiner Tipp für das nächste Werbegeschenk - wie wäre es mit einem „ Lehmann – Edelstahlgrill"?.

Die Kooperation mit regionalen Firmen und der wirtschaftlich interessante Standort Vogtland bieten für weitere Expansionen eine zuverlässige Basis. Durch Innovationskraft, Flexibilität und unser Qualitätsbewusstsein kann die Wettbewerbsfähigkeit der LEHMANN – UMT permanent erhalten und erweitert werden. Dabei streben wir eine hohe Kundenzufriedenheit an, die es auch in Zukunft erlaubt, eigene Produkte erfolgreich am Markt zu etablieren.

Having its seat in the attractive recreation area of the Pöhl storage dam, LEHMANN – UMT GmbH is a medium-sized enterprise in its third generation. The company profile comprises engineering, 3D design, materials-handling technology, sheet metal working and special purpose machine building as its integral parts. An experienced team of 32 employees and an extensive range of products enable our company to meet special customer requirements fulfilling orders in time and in a working order, no matter whether it is a standard plant or an individual complete unit.

Over 9 years ago, LEHMANN - UMT emerged from LEHMANN - Maschinenbau GmbH developing an extensive know-how in the metal working industry. Investments in the latest manufacturing technologies secure jobs, ensure annual turnover increases and are decisive for an outstanding quality. This is achieved by using high-performance 3D laser, plasma jet and gas cutting installations as well as modern CNC working centres. We should like to make particular mention of our Pentapod 3D milling machine. Built for corporate use, it enables us to precisely manufacture complicated and oversized components held in a clamping.

Furthermore, LEHMANN-UMT's business activities include the production and sale of individual transporting equipment and filtering installations. Being used for transporting different kinds of chips, cuttings and waste, and for treating cooling lubricants, they facilitate recycling works in industrial and environmental technology fields.

In the field of special purpose machine building, complex handling and automation systems help utilize rationalization reserves. Projects such as the automatic filtering installation for the treatment of cooling lubricants and process waters or the automated fleece folding machine for processing natural fibrous materials are appreciable examples of the development and realization of special custom-made solutions.

Not to forget the „Lehmann – Edelstahlgrills" (stainless steel grills) showing the Vogtland people's love of barbecues and, moreover, representing superior products „Made in Germany" which are exported to numerous European countries. There is a wide range of types: you have a choice of different fireplaces, smoking ovens and handy camping grills. Just a tip for your next advertising gift – why not give a „Lehmann – Edelstahlgrill"?.

A reliable basis for further expansions is provided by the cooperation with regional firms and the economically interesting location of the Vogtland region. Innovative power, flexibility and quality awareness enable LEHMANN – UMT to permanently maintain and improve its competitiveness. This is combined with our striving for high customer satisfaction making it possible for us to continue placing products on the market successfully.

LEHMANN - UMT GmbH
Engineering · Fördertechnik · Blechbearbeitung · Sondermaschinenbau

Jocketa - Kurze Straße 3
D-08543 Pöhl
Telefon +49 (0) 37439 744-70
Telefax +49 (0) 37439 744-75
info@lehmann-umt.de
www.lehmann-umt.de

(Fotos/Photos by Lehmann UMT , Text/Text by Lehmann UMT, Übersetzung/Translated by Lehmann UMT)

Im Spannungsfeld des Automobils
At the Centre of the Automobile Industry

Als es den Automobilpionier August Horch auf seiner Suche nach Geldgebern zu Beginn des letzten Jahrhunderts ins Vogtland verschlug, gab es im Königreich Sachsen bereits einen ersten Automobilbauer. Der Fabrikant Emil Hermann Nacke aus Coswig, bis dato erfolgreich in der Fertigung von Maschinen für die Strohstoff- und Papierfertigung, hatte schon im Jahr 1900 in seiner Fabrik eine Abteilung für Automobilbau eingerichtet. Im gestandenen Alter von 57 Jahren widmete sich Nacke noch einmal einem neuen Feld, dem noch jungen Automobil, das seit einiger Zeit große Begeisterung bei ihm hervorgerufen hatte. Obwohl die Aufnahme jener Fertigung wohl überlegt und von langer Hand vorbereitet war, ist sein Name und die seiner Automobile heute längst vergessen. Zunächst unter der Bezeichnung „Coswiga" angeboten, fehlte es den später nach seinem Schöpfer benannten „Nacke"-Wagen an den durchschlagenden Neuerungen und der passenden Kapitaldecke, um eine größere Fertigung wie auch florierenden Vertrieb zuzulassen. Die Nacke-Automobile waren von solider Ausführung, erfreuten sich einer treuen Kundschaft aber blieben weitgehend einem kleinen Interessentenkreis vorbehalten. Seit 1903 kamen aus Coswig auch Lastwagen und Omnibusse, die nach dem Ersten Weltkrieg vor allem durch ihren ungewöhnlichen Schneckenrad-Antrieb der Hinterachse als Außenseiter bekannt wurden. Doch eine führende Rolle im Automobilbau blieb Nacke versagt, so dass der Personenwagenbau frühzeitig einschlief und selbst der Nutzfahrzeugbau in den zwanziger Jahren ein Schattendasein fristete. Mit dem Ableben des Initiators im Mai 1933 hatte sich längst auch sein Automobilbau vollendet.

Gänzlich anders verhielt es sich mit August Horch, dem findigen Konstrukteur, der nach Erfahrungen bei „Papa" Benz in Mannheim nicht nur den Automobilbau ins Vogtland brachte sondern auch nachhaltige Impulse für die technische Entwicklung einleitete. 1899 in Köln begonnen, lobte ihn ein Geldgeber, den er dringend für den Aufbau einer rentablen Automobilfertigung suchte, zunächst in dessen Heimatstadt Plauen. Auf Umwegen hatte Horch den Plauener Kaufmann Moritz Bauer gefunden, der bereit war, in die ehrgeizigen Pläne des Tüftlers zu investieren. Gleichzeitig schlug dieser aber auch den Umzug ins Vogtland vor. Voller Hoffnung entstieg August Horch am 11. März 1902 einem Zug auf dem Plauener Bahnhof, musste aber voller Enttäuschung hinnehmen, dass sich bis dahin keine leerstehende Fabrikhalle in Plauen hatte finden lassen. Seine Maschinen waren aus Köln kommend bereits unterwegs und guter Rat nun teuer. So erfuhr er von einer leerstehenden Textilfabrik in Reichenbach, sah sich diese an und schloss ohne Zögern einen Pachtvertrag ab. Die Maschinen konnten somit nach Reichenbach umgeleitet werden und am 22. März 1902 der Arbeitsbetrieb aufgenommen werden. Der älteste erhaltene Automobilprospekt von Horch aus dem Jahre 1902 tituliert daher noch: „A. Horch & Cie., Plauen i.V. – Reichenbach i.V."

When the automobile pioneer August Horch landed up in the Vogtland region in his search for investors at the beginning of the last century, there was already an automobile builder in the Kingdom of Saxony. The manufacturer Emil Hermann Nacke from Coswig – who had successfully made machines for producing straw pulp and paper up to that time – had already set up a department for building cars in his factory as early as 1900. At the fine age of 57, Nacke opened up a new area of business, the manufacture of motor cars, which was just in its infancy; this had generated real excitement in him for some time. Although he had considered this new step carefully and he had thought through the manufacturing process for a long time, his name and that of his cars has long since been forgotten. Initially sold under the "Coswiga" brand, the cars, which were later marketed using their creator's name "Nacke", failed to introduce resounding innovations and did not have the necessary financial backing to allow large-scale manufacturing operations or flourishing sales. The Nacke cars were solidly designed, had a faithful customer base, but were largely restricted to a small circle of interested parties. Lorries and buses were also built in Coswig from 1903 onwards – but they were overtaken by the rest of the market after the First World War largely due to their unusual worm gear drive system on the real axle. Nacke failed to play a leading role in manufacturing vehicles with the result that the car operations came to a halt at an early stage and even commercial vehicle operations were overshadowed by others in the 1920s. His automobile operations had long since finished by the time the inventor died in May 1933.

Things were very different for August Horch, the resourceful designer, who not only introduced the automobile industry to the Vogtland region after gaining experience with "Papa" Benz in Mannheim, but also introduced long-term ideas for technical developments. Horch began operations in Cologne in 1899, then an investor, whom he was desperately looking for in order to set up a profitable car manufacturing business, invited him to come to his home town of Plauen. By various roundabout routes, Horch had got to know the Plauen trader, Moritz Bauer, who was prepared to invest in the inventor's ambitious plans. At the same time he suggested that Horch should move to the Vogtland region. Full of hopes, August Horch got off a train at Plauen station on 11 March 1902, but was very disappointed that he had so far not been able to locate any empty factory in Plauen. His machines were already on their way from Cologne so what should he do? So he heard about an empty textile factory in Reichenbach, inspected it and signed a tenancy agreement without any hesitation. He was able to divert the machines to Reichenbach and working operations started on 22 March 1902. Horch's oldest car brochure dating from the year 1902 is entitled "A. Horch & Cie., Plauen i.V. – Reichenbach i.V."

(Fotos/Photos by Christian Suhr, Text/Text by Christian Suhr, Übersetzung/Translated by David Strauss)

August Horch am Steuer seines 10 bis 12 PS leistenden Tonneau vor der Fabrik in Reichenbach 1902./ August Horch at the steering wheel of his 10-12 bhp tonneau in front of the factory in Reichenbach in 1902.

In Reichenbach hegte Horch große Pläne. Der noch in Köln entwickelte Wagen mit Zweizylindermotor und modernem Kardanantrieb sollte hier nicht nur effizient gebaut werden, vielmehr sollte er Grundlage eines umfassenden Modellprogramms werden. Horch träumte von Ein-, Zwei-, Drei- und Vierzylindermotoren, wobei der Vierzylinder paarweise gegossene und alle Typen mit Wassermantel umschlossene Brennräume haben sollte. Wie aus erwähntem Prospekt zu entnehmen ist, sollte das Programm ferner durch eine Vielfalt von Aufbauvarianten glänzen, die vom Sportwagen bis zum Hotelbus und Lastwagen reichten. Verwirklicht wurden hingegen weder Ein- und Dreizylindermotore, noch die meisten der Aufbauten, die erst viel später umgesetzt werden konnten. Richtungsweisend aber waren Neuerungen, die schon in Reichenbach auf den Weg gebracht wurden. Das betraf beispielsweise die erstmalige Verwendung von Leichtmetall für Motoren-, Getriebe- und Differentialgehäuse. Modern war weiterhin die Kraftübertragung mittels Kardanwelle, die schräg stehende Lenksäule und der Bienenwabenkühler.

Horch had great plans for Reichenbach. But the car with a two cylinder engine and modern fully suspended drive, which had been developed in Cologne, was not only supposed to be built here in an efficient manner, but it was also to form the basis for a comprehensive range of models. Horch dreamed of one, two, three and four cylinder engines, where the four-cylinder was to have pairs of cast combustion chambers and all the models would be surrounded by a water-cooling jacket. As can be seen in the brochure already mentioned, the range of models was also supposed to impress people with various bodywork shapes ranging from a sports car to a hotel bus and lorry. However, the one cylinder or three cylinder engines were not built nor were most of the bodywork designs – many of them were only produced much later. But innovations introduced in Reichenbach proved to set a new trend. This particularly applied to the first use of light metal for engines, gear boxes and rear axle housings. The use of a fully suspended drive system to transmit power, having the steering column rising diagonally and the honeycomb radiator were also modern ideas.

Brachte den Automobilbau ins Vogtland: August Horch (1868-1951)/ He introduced motor vehicle production to the Vogtland region: August Horch (1868-1951)

Auf Probefahrt an der berühmten Göltzschtalbrücke: Das in Reichenbach gebaute Horch-Zweizylinder-Modell im Jahre 1903./ On a test drive by the famous Göltzsch Valley Bridge: the Horch two-cylinder model built in Reichenbach in 1903.

Die Reichenbacher Verhältnisse waren für Horchs Pläne in mehrerlei Hinsicht zu eng. Zu wenig Ausbreitungsmöglichkeiten, mangelnde Arbeitskräfte und zu dünne Kapitaldecke ließen bald das nur wenig entfernt liegende aber größere Zwickau als neuen Standort ins Visier gelangen. So kehrte der Automobilpionier 1904, schon zwei Jahre nach seiner Ankunft im Vogtland, Reichenbach den Rücken und siedelte nach Zwickau über. Zudem in eine Aktiengesellschaft als „August Horch & Cie. Motorwagen-Werke AG" umgewandelt, war man nunmehr besser aufgestellt und der Siegeszug von Horch-Wagen begann seinen Lauf zu nehmen. Mit dem Rausschmiss Horchs aus der Firma, die weiterhin seinen Namen trug, war im Jahre 1909 der Erfolg jener Marke keineswegs beendet. Im Gegenteil: Die Neugründung der Audi-Werke (audi = lateinisierte Form von Horch) in unmittelbarer Nachbarschaft sorgte für belebende Konkurrenz und etablierte Zwickau endgültig zur Autostadt.

Von der allgemeinen Euphorie des Automobilbaus getrieben, keimten inzwischen im Vogtland neue Automobilbauer heran. Zum einen war es das Automobilwerk Reißig in Plauen-Reißig. Etwa 1907 hatten deren Gründer Mädler und Köhl-Krügel unter dem Namen „Siegfriedwerke" begonnen, ein Automobil zu bauen, das unter den Initialen der Inhaber als M & K beziehungsweise MuK vertrieben wurde. Einziges Modell war ein konventioneller Personenwagen der Leistungsformel 6/26 PS (Angabe der Steuer-PS / tatsächlichen Leistung). Leider ist nur wenig über diesen Wagen bekannt, es blieb aber bei einem kurzem Intermezzo, das schon im Herbst 1918 ein Ende fand. Arno Kohl-Krügel, seit 1912 Alleininhaber des Automobilwerkes Reißig gewesen, setzte seine Laufbahn im Automobilgeschäft dann später als Teilhaber einer Mercedes-Benz-Vertriebsstelle in Plauen fort. Erfolgreiche und jede Menge weniger erfolgreiche Automobilpioniere gehörten zum Alltag jener Kindertage des Automobils. Gerade jedoch in Ballungszentren, die wie Sachsen zur Wiege des Automobils gehörten, war man reich an „Nachahmungstätern". Zu der Vielzahl heute längst vergessener Vertreter gehört unter anderem die Plauener Maschinenfabrik Endesfelder & Weiß, 1895 gegründet, die laut Pressemitteilungen 1909 den Automobilbau aufnahm, jedoch schon 1912 im Zwangsvergleich endete. Was sich hinter deren Aktivitäten im Automobilbau wirklich verbarg, bleibt leider im Dunkeln. Aber auch solche Zeugnisse belegen den Enthusiasmus damaliger Vogtländer, ihren Beitrag zum aufstrebenden Automobilbau leisten zu wollen.

Schon zu ihrer Zeit eine Rarität: Von den in Plauen-Reißig um 1910 gebauten MuK-Wagen mit 6/26 PS ist heute kaum noch etwas bekannt./ A rarity even in its heyday: hardly anything is known now about the MuK car with 6/26 bhp built in Plauen-Reissig in about 1910.

The facilities in Reichenbach were far too cramped for Horch's plans in many respects. Too few opportunities to expand, a lack of workers and a too shaky capital base soon led the inventor to cast his eye on Zwickau as a new base – it was only a short distance away, but was larger. So the automobile pioneer turned his back on Reichenbach and the Vogtland region in 1904, just two years after his arrival here, and moved the business to Zwickau. Having changed his business into a public corporation – "August Horch & Cie. Motorwagen-Werke AG" – he was now in a better position and the success of Horch cars began. The success of the brand did not end when Horch was thrown out of the company in 1909, which continued to bear his name. On the contrary: the establishment of the Audi works (audi = Latin form of Horch) in the immediate vicinity provided lively competition and finally established Zwickau as a car-making city.

Driven on by the general euphoria in the automobile sector, new car manufacturers shot up in the Vogtland region. There was the Reissig automobile works in Plauen-Reissig. Their founders Mädler and Köhl-Krügel had started building cars in about 1907 at the "Siegfriedwerke" works. They were sold using the initials of the owners M & K or MuK. The only model was a conventional car with a 6/26 power output (taxable horse power/actual performance). Unfortunately very little is known about this car; production continued for a short period and was shut down in the autumn of 1918. Arno Kohl-Krügel, who had been the sole owner of the Reissig car works since 1912, later continued his career in the automobile business as a shareholder in a Mercedes-Benz sales office in Plauen. Successful automobile pioneers and a number of less successful ones were common during the early days of motor cars. But in major centres, which were the cradle of the motor car like Saxony, there were plenty of "imitators". One of the many, who has long since been forgotten, was the Plauen engineering factor called Endesfelder & Weiss, which was set up in 1895, started car production in 1909 according to press releases, but ended production in bankruptcy as early as 1912. Unfortunately we do not have any details of their activities in the automobile business. But even reports like these are evidence of the enthusiasm of Vogtland people of the time, who clearly wanted to play their part in the fast growing automobile sector.

Automobile Kompetenz Automobile Expertise

Die skurrile Cyklonette war, wenngleich man das sich heute kaum noch vorstellen kann, ein Verkaufserfolg. Zum großen Teil im vogtländischen Mylau gefertigt, wurde sie über 20 Jahre lang gebaut!/
The odd Cyklonette was a sales hit, even though it is hard to imagine it today. It was produced for 20 years and most of the vehicles were made in Mylau in the Vogtland region!

Zunächst galt das Auto als ein Luxusspielzeug betuchter Kreise. Im Vogtland, zum beginnenden 20. Jahrhundert reich an etabliertem Mittelstand, sorgte der Aufschwung in Textilindustrie und Maschinenbau für gute Absätze dieser neuen Fortbewegungsmittel. Aber schon damals zeigte sich, dass nur mit innovativer Technik die Konkurrenz gegen eine ständig wachsende Zahl von Anbietern zu bezwingen sei. Kleine und völlig unzureichend finanziell wie auch technologisch aufgestellte Firmen schossen aus dem Boden wie Pilze und verschwanden ebenso schnell wieder. Erfolg stellte sich hingegen ein, wenn man neue Wege beschritt und damit Marktlücken auszufüllen vermochte.

Eine solche Marktlücke füllte die Cyklonette aus dem vogtländischen Mylau. Für ihre Konstruktion zeichnete Ing. Franz Hüttel aus Erlau in Sachsen verantwortlich. Er hatte um 1900 begonnen, in seiner kleinen Fahrradfabrik Krafträder zu bauen. Ungewöhnlich war der Frontantrieb, mit denen er seine Motorräder auszustatten pflegte. Ein über dem Vorderrad angeordnetes Triebwerk wurde so auch Kernstück eines von ihm aus den „Cyklon"-Motorrädern hervorgebrachten Dreirades. Als „Cyklonette" war jenes primitive aber dem Motorrad überlegene Fortbewegungsmittel für größere Kundenkreise erschwinglich, die sich sonst hätten kein Automobil leisten können. Für lange Zeit strahlte die Cyklonette eine Vorbildwirkung aus und wurde von anderen Firmen kopiert. Bekannteste Kopie ist wohl das Pendant der Phänomen-Werke Gustav Hiller A.-G. aus Zittau, den späteren Robur-Werken. Doch jene Kopie ist genau genommen eine Weiterentwicklung, denn 1907 hatte Hüttel die einstmals eigene Firma verlassen und bei der Zittauer Konkurrenz das „Phänomobil" geschaffen.

Die skurril-primitiven Dreiräder aus Mylau mit anfangs Ein-, später auch Zweizylinder-Motoren, bescheidenen 3,5 oder 6 PS waren ein frühes Mittel der schon frühzeitig angestrebten aber erst in den dreißiger Jahren tatsächlich beginnenden Volksmotorisierung. 1903 hatte man die Fertigung von Erlau in die Reichshauptstadt Berlin verlegt und 1919 zusätzlich eine Fabrik in Mylau gekauft. Durch den Standortvorteil Berlin erhoffte man sich neben dem gut gehenden Geschäft mit Gewerbetreibenden und Kleinbürgertum auch den Einstieg in das Taxigeschäft zu finden. Das häufige Umkippen der Dreiräder bei zu forscher Kurvenfahrt verängstigte jedoch viele Fahrgäste und vereitelte große Absätze bei den Droschkenbesitzern. Immerhin wurde die Cyklonette nahezu unverändert zwei Jahrzehnte lang gebaut. 1923 musste man sich der Erkenntnis beugen, dass in zunehmenden Maß vollwertige Kleinautomobile den Dreirädern den Rang abliefen. Durch

Initially cars were a luxury toy for the well-to-do classes. The Vogtland region had plenty of middle-class people at the beginning of the 20th century and the boom in the textile industry and mechanical engineering ensured good sales of this new means of transport. But even at that time it became clear that the competition from a growing number of manufacturers could only be beaten off by introducing innovative technology. Small companies with hopelessly inadequate funding or technology shot up like mushrooms and disappeared again just as quickly. Companies were successful, if they branched off in new directions and were able to fill gaps in the market.

The Cyklonette built in Mylau in the Vogtland region was just one of those. Engineer Franz Hüttel from Erlau in Saxony was responsible for its design. He had begun to build motorcycles in his small bicycle factory in about 1900. The front-wheel drive system, which he fitted to his motorbikes, was unusual. An engine located above the front wheel also formed the basis for a three-wheeler manufactured by "Cyklon" motorbikes. This primitive means of transport, which was superior to the motorbike, was affordable for large numbers of customers, who would not have been able to afford a motor car. The Cyklonette set an example for other companies for a long time and was copied by them. The most famous copy is probably the Pendant from the Gustav Hiller A.-G. Phänomen works in Zittau, later to become the Robur factory. But this copy was actually a further development, for Hüttel left the factory that he formerly owned in 1907 and created the "Phänomobil" at the rival factory in Zittau.

The ludicrously primitive three-wheeler from Mylau, with a one-cylinder engine at first and a two-cylinder later and a modest 3.5 or 6 bhp, was an early attempt to get people on the move – but motorisation did not really catch on among the masses until the 1930s. In 1903 the Erlau manufacturing factory was switched to the imperial capital Berlin and in 1919 a factory was also bought in Mylau. By being based in Berlin, the company hoped to see business grow with trades people and individual persons – and there was a desire to get into the taxi business. But the fact that the three-wheelers often turned over if the driver took a corner too fast worried many passengers and prevented huge sales with cab owners. Nevertheless, the Cyklonette was manufactured for almost twenty years without any changes being made. In 1923 the company had to face the fact that high-quality small cars outstripped three-wheelers. As a result of inflation, the Cyklon works, which were now a public corporation, had fallen into the

Auch die Netzschkauer Maschinenfabrik Franz Stark & Söhne versuchte sich 1925 mit einem Kleinautomobil, der „Nemalette"./The Franz Stark & Söhne engineering factory in Netzschkau also tried its luck with a small car called the "Nemalette" in 1925.

die Inflation waren die Cyklon-Werke, inzwischen in eine Aktiengesellschaft umgewandelt, zudem in die Hände des Börsenspekulanten Jacob Schapiro geraten, der große Teile der deutschen Automobilindustrie an sich riss. Unter seiner Regie wurde der Bau gehobener Vier- und Sechszylinder-Automobile forciert.

Im allgemeinen Fusionsstrudel gingen die Cyklon-Automobilwerke AG, Mylau i.V. und Berlin (man beachte die Reihenfolge!) jedoch schnell zu Grunde. Der Schapiro-Konzern, zu dem schon die Dixi-Werke in Eisenach, die Gothaer Waggonfabrik, die NSU-Werke in Neckarsulm und die Berliner Karosseriefabrik Schebera gehörten, verkaufte das Berliner Werk und ließ mit etwa 320 Beschäftigten in Mylau Fahrgestelle für einen 5/20 PS-Wagen montieren, die bei Schebera in Berlin ihre Karosserien erhielten. 1926 brachten die Cyklon-Werke ein eigenes 9/40 PS-Modell heraus, den billigsten Sechszylinderwagen Deutschlands. Dennoch geriet er zum Flop. 1931 war die Firma endgültig erloschen.

hands of the stock market speculator, Jacob Schapiro, who had seized huge chunks of the German automobile industry. He pressed ahead with making up-market four-cylinder and six-cylinder cars. But in the general confusion caused by mergers, the Cyklon-Automobilwerke AG, Mylau i.V. and Berlin (note the order!) was soon bankrupt. The Schapiro company, which also owned the Dixi works in Eisenach, the Gotha railway carriage works, the NSU works in Neckarsulm and the Berlin bodywork factory Schebera, sold the Berlin factory and used about 320 employees in Mylau to manufacture chassis for a 5/20 bhp car, which was provided with bodywork at Schebera in Berlin. The Cyklon works brought out their own 9/40 bhp model in 1926, the cheapest six-cylinder car in Germany. But it was a flop. The company finally closed down in 1931.

Anzeige der Cyklon-Werke aus dem Jahr 1922. Mit dem Ende der dreirädrigen Cyklonette blieben dem Hersteller trotz vollwertiger Nachfolgemodell weitere Erfolge versagt. Er ging wie viele andere in der Weltwirtschaftskrise sang und klanglos unter./An advertisement by the Cyklon works dating from 1922. The company did not manage any other success despite high-quality successor models once the three-wheel Cyklonette went out of production. The company collapsed without a whimper like so many others in the global economic crisis.

Das Thema Volksmotorisierung war schon kurz nach dem Ersten Weltkrieg immer wieder Thema im Automobilbau. Hersteller wie Cyklon praktizierten dies frühzeitig, lange noch bevor die nationalsozialistische Propaganda jenes Thema für sich entdeckt hatte. Vielerorts in Deutschland gab es Klein- und Kleinstautohersteller, deren Namen heute nur noch Schall und Rauch sind. Natürlich verleitete der Erfolg der Cyklonette und die Aussicht auf eine rentable Fertigung primitiver Kleinwagen auch weitere regionale Betriebe, sich im Autobau zu versuchen. So auch die benachbarte Netzschkauer Maschinenfabrik Franz Stark & Söhne, die ihr Kernsegment im Bau von Textilmaschinen hatte aber auch landwirtschaftliche Geräte und Apparate für die Heizungs- und Lüftungstechnik baute. Ihr Versuch, 1925 mit der Nemalette auf den Markt zu kommen, scheiterte. Konstruktive Mängel des kleinen Zweisitzers auf drei Rädern, angetrieben mit einem 4 PS starken Zweitakt-Motor, vereitelten im Frühstadium große Pläne im Automobilbau. Ähnlich erging es der Plauener Ari Motorfahrzeugbau GmbH, die mit ihrem Arimofa-Kleinwagen 1923 von sich Reden gemacht hatte. Auch das Z.-Kleinauto aus der Plauener Z.-Werkstatt des Ingenieurs Zimmermann blieb ein Gespenst, von dem mehr in der Zeitung zu lesen war als wirklich auf die Straße fand.

The subject of cars for the masses was a major issue in car production shortly after the First World War. Manufacturers like Cyklon practised this at an early stage, long before the Nazis discovered the subject for their own propaganda. There were manufacturers of small and tiny cars all over Germany, whose names have disappeared in thin air. Of course the success of the Cyklonette and the prospect of being able to manufacture primitive cars and make a profit tempted other regional companies to try their luck manufacturing vehicles. These included the Franz Stark & Söhne mechanical engineering factory in neighbouring Netzschkau, which mainly focused on manufacturing textile machines, but also built agricultural appliances and units for the heating and ventilation sectors. Its attempt to penetrate the market with the Nemalette in 1925 failed. Design faults in the small two-seater on three wheels driven by a two-stroke engine with 4 bhp disappointed large-scale plans for manufacturing vehicles at an early stage. Ari Motorfahrzeugbau GmbH in Plauen, which aroused attention with its Arimofa small car in 1923, suffered a similar fate. The Z small car produced by the Z. workshops in Plauen belonging to the engineer Zimmermann remained a phantom – and the articles in the newspapers on the car were more numerous than the vehicles actually on the road!

Dennoch sind dies alles Zeugen eines Potentials, dass sich im Vogtland frühzeitig herausbildete. Ob im Einzelfall erfolgreich oder nicht, machten sich viele findige Köpfe immer wieder auf, dem Automobilbau neue Impulse zu geben. Warum gerade dem Automobilbau? - wird man sich fragen. Neben der vorherrschenden Textilindustrie und dem allgemeinen Maschinenbau galt der Automobilbau jeher als eine Spitzenform des Maschinenbaus, in dem die kompliziertesten Techniken auf ein Produkt zusammenliefen. Und noch etwas banales trägt dazu bei: Automobile sind im öffentlichen Leben allgegenwärtig. Ihre Erscheinung und ihre Leistungen sind offenkundiger als noch so spektakuläre Technologien, die hinter verschlossenen Werkstoren praktiziert werden. Ein anschauliches Beispiel für diese These ist zweifelsohne der erfolgreichste vogtländische Automobilbauer, die VOMAG.

1881 als Stickmaschinen-Fabrik von Johann Conrad Dietrich und seinem Namensvetter Paul Hermann Dietrich gegründet, lagen die wirklich epochemachenden Verdienste des 1895 in die Vogtländische Maschinenfabrik A.-G. (kurz: VOMAG) umgewandelten Unternehmens auf ganz anderen Gebieten. Mitten im Zentrum der Stickereiindustrie hatte die VOMAG großen Anteil am Reichtum und der Blüte Plauener und vogtländischer Textilfabrikanten. Erst die Aufnahme einer Maschinenfertigung versetzte die Region wieder in die Lage, gegen andere Stickereizentren konkurrenzfähig zu sein. Die Erfindung des Stickautomaten durch den späteren VOMAG-Direktor Zahn war bahnbrechend und schaffte den internationalen Durchbruch. Der Stickautomat setzte Maßstäbe bezüglich Fertigungskosten und -zeit. Neben dem explodierenden Reichtum der vogtländischen Stickereiindustrie stieg die VOMAG zum weltweit führenden Lieferanten für derartige Fabrikausrüstungen auf und galt kurz vor Ausbruch des Ersten Weltkriegs als weltgrößte Stickmaschinenfabrik. Parallel dazu nutzte man den Aufwärtstrend im Unternehmen erfolgreich zur Diversifikation. 1899 lieferte man die erste Druckmaschine aus und konnte sich binnen weniger Jahre auch in diesem Segment an die Spitze setzen. Europas größte Druckmaschinenfabrik saß in Plauen!

Gemessen an diesen Leistungen fiel das dritte Standbein, dem sich die VOMAG zu widmen begann, zurück und blieb doch über dreißig Jahre lang der bekannteste und noch heute faszinierendste Geschäftszweig, ohne die erheblichen Verdienste im Automobilbau zu schmälern. Auf Veranlassung der Heeresleitung nahm die Vogtländische Maschinenfabrik 1915 den Bau des sogenannten Regel-Dreitonners auf. Wenngleich es sich – wie der Name schon sagt – um eine Lastwagen-Konstruktion handelte, die durch Heeresvorgaben reglementiert war, galt es diese dennoch eigenständig zu schaffen. Zwar war die VOMAG mit Präzisionsbau bestens vertraut und durch eigene Gießerei hervorragend gerüstet. Dennoch musste das Know-how eingekauft werden. Nach guter Sitte verpflichtete man einen Fachmann ersten Ranges, den von der Berliner NAG (Nationale Automobilgesellschaft)

But this is all evidence of the potential, which was emerging at an early stage in the Vogtland region. Whether they were successful or not with their individual projects, many resourceful minds set out to provide new ideas for manufacturing cars. Why cars of all things? – people might ask. Alongside the predominant textile industry and general mechanical engineering, manufacturing motor cars was regarded as a superior form of mechanical engineering, where the most complicated technologies were combined in one product. And there was also a mundane reason: automobiles are omnipresent in public life. Their appearance and performance are more evident that spectacular technologies, which are used behind closed factory doors. Without any doubt, one vivid example of this theory is the most successful Vogtland vehicle builder, VOMAG.

Johann Conrad Dietrich and his namesake Paul Hermann Dietrich founded a knitting machine factory in 1881. But its epoch-making success lay in quite different fields. The name of the company was changed to the Vogtländische Maschinenfabrik A.-G. (abbreviated to VOMAG) in 1895. Located at the heart of the embroidery industry, VOMAG shared in the wealth and success of the Plauen and Vogtland textile manufacturers. But only when the region had started manufacturing machines was it in a position to compete with other embroidery regions. The invention of the automatic knitting machine by the later VOMAG director Zahn blazed a trail and ensured an international breakthrough. The automatic knitting machine set standards with regard to manufacturing costs and time. Alongside the exploding wealth of the Vogtland embroidery industry, VOMAG rose to become one of the world's leading suppliers of factory equipment for this sector and had the world's largest knitting machine factory shortly before the outbreak of the First World War. The boom in the company was also used to diversify its products. It supplied the first printing machine in 1899 and was able to capture the top spot in this sector too within just a few years. Europe's largest printing machine factory was based in Plauen!

Viewed in the light of this performance, the third line of business, which VOMAG began to pursue, fell behind the others, but still remained the best known and most fascinating business sector for more than thirty years, without belittling the major advances made in the vehicle building business. At the instigation of the German army, the Vogtländische Maschinenfabrik began building what was known as the standard three tonne vehicle in 1915. Even if it was a lorry design – as its name betrays – which was governed by input from the army, the company had to build these vehicles on its own. It is true that VOMAG was very familiar with precision manufacturing work and had outstanding equipment in the shape of its own foundry. But the company had to buy in expertise. In good tradition, they employed a top expert, Peter Teigland, poached from the Berlin company NAG (Nationale Automobilgesellschaft) – in its day one of the

Automobile Kompetenz Automobile Expertise

Die Plauener VOMAG: Nicht nur weltgrößte Stickmaschinen- und Europas größte Druckmaschinenfabrik. Als eine der größten sächsischen Industriebetriebe nahm man hier 1915 auch den Lastwagenbau auf./ VOMAG in Plauen: not only the world's largest knitting machine factory and Europe's largest printing machine factory. One of Saxony's largest industrial companies began manufacturing lorries here in 1915.

Mit dem sogenannten Regel-Dreitonner für die Heeresverwaltung begann die erfolgreiche Periode Plauener Nutzfahrzeugbaus./The successful period of commercial vehicle building in Plauen began with the so-called standard three tonne model for the German army.

1927 führte die VOMAG zusammen mit der Sächsischen Waggonfabrik Werdau erstmals den Ganzstahl-Omnibus serienmäßig ein./In 1927 VOMAG introduced a bus made of nothing but steel in conjunction with Sächsische Waggonfabrik Werdau.

– zu jener Zeit eine der führenden deutschen Automobilfabriken – abgeworbenen Peter Teigland. Er schuf den ersten VOMAG-Lastwagen und sorgte nach Ablieferung von über 1000 Stück bis Kriegsende für den weiteren Ausbau zu einem umfassenden Programm. Unmittelbar nach Kriegsende konnte die VOMAG ein Spektrum von Lastwagen über Zwei-, Drei- und Vier- bis Fünftonner abdecken. Dabei stattete man die leichtesten mit dem fortschrittlichen Kardan-Antrieb aus. Beim Dreitonner hatte man die Wahl zwischen Kardan- und dem damals noch verlässlicher angesehenen Kettenantrieb. Die schweren Kaliber verfügten zunächst ohnehin nur über Kettenantrieb. Schon damals erarbeiteten sich die VOMAG-Lastwagen einen überregionalen Ruf als solide, robust und zweckmäßig. Wiederholte Erfolge bei den russischen Zuverlässigkeitsfahrten bestätigten dies und ließen sich nutzbringend in der Werbung vermarkten.

Die Absatzeinbrüche während der schweren Inflationsjahre konnte die VOMAG vor allem dadurch meistern, dass sie sich frühzeitig um enge Zusammenarbeit mit Aufbauherstellern bemühte und so Varianten anbot, die schon damals vom hydraulischen Kipper über Kommunalfahrzeuge bis hin zu Omnibussen reichte. Zudem galt die VOMAG als eine der innovativsten Lastwagenhersteller der Branche. Die Einführung des Niederrahmens bei Omnibussen 1924, eine erste, wenngleich nicht durchschlagende Dreiachs-Konstruktion im gleichen Jahr und die Einführung des ersten Ganzstahl-Omnibusses in Zusammenarbeit mit der

leading Germany vehicle manufacturers. He created the first VOMAG lorry and arranged for this product range to be expanded after more than 1,000 vehicles had been supplied by the end of the war. Immediately after the end of the war, VOMAG was able to supply a range of lorries: two, three and four-five tonne models. They equipped the lightest vehicles with the advanced fully suspended drive system. Customers could choose whether to order the three tonne model with a fully suspended drive system or what was regarded at the time as the more reliable chain drive. The heavy models initially only had the chain drive system. At the time VOMAG lorries gained a national reputation as solid, robust and functional. Repeated successes in Russian reliability tests confirmed this and were used in the company's advertising materials.

VOMAG was able to survive the fall in sales during the difficult years of inflation mainly because it made efforts to work closely with bodywork manufacturers at an early stage and was therefore able to provide models, which ranged from hydraulic tippers to vehicles for local authorities and even buses. VOMAG also had a reputation as one of the most innovative of all lorry manufacturers. Key data in this successful development are the introduction of a low frame on buses in 1924, the first three-axle design in the same year, even if it was not a resounding success immediately, and the introduction of the first bus made solely of steel in conjunction with the Sächsische Waggonfabrik company in Werdau. The

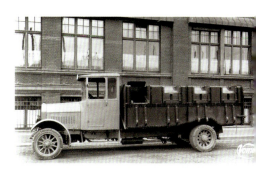

In den zwanziger Jahren glänzte die VOMAG durch solide Technik und einfallsreiche Verbindungen zu verschiedensten Aufbauherstellern, um spezielle Lösungen wie diesen Müllwagen offerieren zu können. / VOMAG's strong points were solid technology and imaginative connections to a wide variety of bodywork manufacturers in the 1920s so as to be able to provide special solutions like this dust cart.

Nach dem Ende der Ersten Weltkriegs stieg die VOMAG auch erfolgreich in den Omnibusbau ein. Es gelangen umfangreiche Lieferungen an den staatlichen sächsischen Kraftomnibusverkehr und die Deutsche Reichspost. / VOMAG successfully started manufacturing buses after the end of the First World War. It managed to sell many vehicles to the Saxon state bus company and the German Reich postal

sächsischen Waggonfabrik Werdau sind Eckdaten dieses Erfolges. Weiter machte die kleine aber feine Lastwagenschmiede in Plauen durch ehrgeizige Projekte wie einem Omnibus mit Frontantrieb und abkuppelbarem Fahrgastteil im Jahre 1928 von sich Reden. Mit Reduzierung des Typenprogramms auf einen Standardlastwagen im Fünftonnen-Segment stellte die VOMAG Mitte der zwanziger Jahre konsequent die Weichen Richtung Schwerlastwagenbau und effizienter Fertigung.

Dennoch geriet der Nutzfahrzeugbau des mit in besten Zeiten über 6500 Mann Belegschaft zählenden sächsischen Industriegiganten langsam ins Hintertreffen. Büssing in Braunschweig hatte sich 1926 mit der Präsentation seines patentierten Dreiachsers mit zwei getriebenen Hinterachsen einen Wettbewerbsvorteil vor der gesamten Branche verschafft. Obwohl VOMAG in der „Königsklasse" der Dreiachser mit acht bis neun Tonnen Nutzlast schon 1928 nachzog, war die Büssing-Übermacht nicht mehr zu brechen. Zudem geriet die Abteilung Autobau mit weiter praktizierter Reihenfertigung statt modernem Fließbandsystem in die Kostenfalle. Nach Zeiten innovativer Projekte wandelte sich der Ruf des VOMAG-Lastwagens hin zu einem qualitativ hochwertigen, konventionellen aber teuren Spitzenprodukt, deren Absatz entsprechend hinter anderen Marken zurückfiel.

small, but high-quality lorry manufacturer in Plauen also created a stir in 1928 with ambitious projects like a bus with front-wheel drive and a vehicle section that could be uncoupled. By reducing the model range to a standard lorry in the five tonne segment, VOMAG consistently prepared the way for manufacturing heavy goods lorries and efficient manufacturing processes in the mid-1920s.

Despite this, commercial vehicle manufacturing at the Saxon industrial giant, which employed more than 6,500 people in its heyday, slowly fell behind its competitors. Büssing in Braunschweig had acquired a competitive advantage in the whole sector when it presented its patented three-axle vehicle with two rear axles that were driven. Although VOMAG managed to make good the ground in the "top class" of three axle vehicles capable of carrying a load of eight or nine tonnes, it was no longer able to beat the superior products from Büssing. In addition, the vehicle building department fell into a cost trap by continuing to use series production instead of modern conveyor belt systems. After periods when it was able to introduce innovative projects, the reputation of VOMAG lorries had developed into a high-quality, conventional, but expensive top product – and sales fell behind those of other brands.

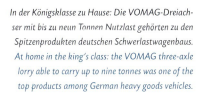

Erfolgstyp: Der VOMAG-Fünftonnen-Standardlastwagen, Modell 5 Cz, aus den zwanziger Jahren. / A success: the VOMAG five tonne standard lorry, the 5 Cz model, from the 1920s.

In der Königsklasse zu Hause: Die VOMAG-Dreiachser mit bis zu neun Tonnen Nutzlast gehörten zu den Spitzenprodukten deutschen Schwerlastwagenbaus. At home in the king's class: the VOMAG three-axle lorry able to carry up to nine tonnes was one of the top products among German heavy goods vehicles.

Moderne Schnell-Lastwagen der Dreitonnenklasse rundeten Anfang der dreißiger Jahre das Plauener Lastwagenprogramm nach unten ab. / Modern fast lorries in the three tonne class rounded off the range of vehicles available from Plauen in the 1930s in the lower weight class.

Der legendäre VOMAG-Lastwagen schlechthin: Als Fernverkehrszug waren die Sechseinhalbtonner-Modelle 6 LR Mitte der dreißiger Jahre der Traum eines jeden Kapitäns der Landstraße./The legendary VOMAG lorry: the six-and-a-half tonne model 6 LR was a dream fulfilled for any lorry driver in the mid-1930s.

Durch die Weltwirtschaftskrise gebeutelt, geriet die VOMAG Anfang der dreißiger Jahre insgesamt in Schieflage und musste 1932 Konkurs anmelden. Das gerade in den Kinderschuhen steckende, vierte Standbein trug wesentlich dazu bei, durch einen Schulterschluss mehrerer Banken dem größten Arbeitgeber Plauens wieder auf die Füße zu helfen. Die Entwicklung modernster Feinstbohrwerke vorwiegend für die Automobil- und Motorenbauer sowie der Druckmaschinenbau wurden aufgebaut beziehungsweise fortgeführt, der unrentable Stickmaschinenbau ruhen gelassen. Auch dem Autobau gab man erneut die Chance, wenngleich durch fehlende Mittel der Wandel zum Dieselmotor, den Konkurrenzmarken inzwischen vollzogen hatten, unterblieben war. Für eine eigene Entwicklung war es zu spät. So half nur eine Lizenznahme des Wirbelkammer-Dieselmotors der Schweizer Firma Oberhänsli. Glücklicherweise hatte man aufs richtige Pferd gesetzt und mit dem allgemeinen Aufschwung der Automobilbranche unter den Nationalsozialisten die Absätze wieder aus dem Tiefstand von monatlich zwei bis drei Neuzulassungen geholt. Dennoch blieb VOMAG die kleine aber feine Lastwagenmarke für Kenner und die, die bereit waren, für Qualität ein paar Reichsmark mehr zu bezahlen.

Zusätzliche Belebung der Absätze brachte in Plauen nach dem Neuanfang als VOMAG-Betriebs-A.-G. ab 1932 eine neue, sogenannte Schnell-Lastwagen-Baureihe. Von diesem Dreitonnen-Segment reichte das Programm bis zum dreiachsigen Spitzenmodell mit neun Tonnen Nutzlast, wahlweise auch als Reichspost-Omnibus mit einem Fassungsvermögen von über einhundert Personen lieferbar. Kontinuierlich vervollständigte man das Programm, so 1935 noch durch eine Straßenzugmaschine, den sogenannten Eilschlepper, wie auch durch einen speziellen Fernlastwagen der Sechseinhalbtonnen-Klasse. Mit ihren langen Hauben, der kantigen Erscheinung und ihren 160 PS leistenden Sechszylinder-Dieselmotoren gehörten sie zu den „Königen der Landstraße" und prägten sich nachhaltig in den Köpfen einer ganzen Generation ein.

Seit 1938 wieder als VOMAG Maschinenfabrik A.-G. firmierend, überraschte man ein Jahr später die Kundschaft mit einer neuen, nunmehr gänzlich moderner als die Konkurrenz auffallenden Linienführung. In Plauen begann die Zeit der sogenannten „Rundhauber", fliesend schön und modern gestalteter Hauben, unter denen sich weiter die erwartet robuste und starke Technik verbarg. Auch im Omnibusbau knüpfte man wieder an alte Bestzeiten an. Die Kraftverkehr Freistaat Sachsen A.-G. (kurz: KVG Sachsen), einst Deutschlands größter und modernster Omnibusbetrieb, kaufte wie schon zehn Jahre zuvor wieder verstärkt in Plauen ein. Glanzstücke des Staatsbetriebes waren 15 Exemplare aus Plauen mit 300 PS starken Maybach-Panzermotoren. Die seinerzeit stärksten Omnibusse in Deutschland hatte man vorwiegend für die steigungsreichsten Strecken des Erzgebirges, so hinauf zum Fichtelberg, beschafft. In Zusammenarbeit mit dem Berliner Karosseriebauer Gaubschat entstanden zudem einige der ersten deutschen Gelenkomnibus-Züge auf VOMAG.

Shaken by the world economic crisis, VOMAG as a whole was in a precarious situation at the start of the 1930s and applied for bankruptcy in 1932. The fourth line of business, which had just been started, was the main reason why several banks were able to help Plauen's largest employer get back on its feet. The development of the latest super finish drills mainly for the automobile and engine building sectors and the manufacture of printing machines were built up and continued, while the unprofitable knitting machine sector was abandoned. The company was also given a fresh opportunity in the automobile sector, even if, as a result of a lack of resources, it failed to switch to the diesel engine as its competitors had already done. It was too late for the company to produce its own design. So it was only able to enter a licensing arrangement with the swirl chamber diesel engine produced by the Swiss company Oberhänsli. Fortunately they had backed the right horse and sales in the automobile sector under the Nazis recovered from the all-time low of two or three new vehicles a month. But VOMAG remained the small, high-quality lorry brand for those familiar with the vehicles and those who were prepared to spend a few more Reich marks for quality.

Sales were further boosted in Plauen after VOMAG-Betriebs-A.-G made a fresh start in 1932 when a new, so-called fast lorry was introduced. In this three tonne sector, the models ranged up to a three-axle lorry able to carry a load weighing nine tonnes – and it could also be supplied as a Reich postal bus able to carry more than one hundred people. The model range was continually expanded so that by 1935 a trailer towing vehicle, the so-called speedy tractor, and a special long-distance lorry in the six-and-a-half tonne class had been introduced. With their long bonnets, their angular appearance and their six-cylinder diesel engines developing 160 bhp, they were known as the "kings of the road" and left a lasting mark on a whole generation.

Trading under the name of VOMAG Maschinenfabrik A.-G. again from 1938 onwards, a new range of models, which appeared to be much more modern than those of its rivals, surprised customers. The time of what were known as the "round bonnets" began in Plauen, bonnets that were smooth and beautiful with a modern design, which continued to conceal the robust and powerful engines as expected. There was also a revival of the good old days in bus manufacturing. Kraftverkehr Freistaat Sachsen A.-G. (abbreviated to KVG Sachsen), once Germany's largest and most modern bus company, once again purchased its vehicles from Plauen as it had done ten years earlier. The top models at the state company were 15 buses from Plauen with 300 bhp Maybach tank engines. These were the most powerful buses in Germany at the time and they were mainly used on the hilly routes in the Erzgebirge mountains, up to the Fichtelberg. Some of the first articulated buses were also built in conjunction with the Gaubschat bodywork company in Berlin on VOMAG chassis.

Die neue Linie: Ab 1938 führte die VOMAG auffallend moderne Erscheinungen durch die neue „Rundhauber"-Generation ein./The new range: VOMAG introduced a striking modern appearance with the new "round bonnet" generation in 1938.

In die Jahre des Zweiten Weltkriegs ging die VOMAG gewissermaßen mit einer Sonderstellung. Kapazitätsmäßig nicht für große Stückzahlen geeignet, fertigte man in Plauen mehr schlecht als recht den sogenannten Einheitsdiesel, einen speziellen Wehrmachts-Lastwagen nach MAN- und Henschel-Lizenz. Die eigenen Modelle hatten sich schon frühzeitig bei der durch die Nazis propagierten Umstellung auf heimische Treibstoffe hervorgetan. Schon ab 1934 hatte die VOMAG erfolgreich bei Testfahrten mit Holzgasantrieben teilgenommen und wertvolle Erfahrungen gesammelt. Serienmäßig mit Imbert-Holzgas-Generatoren ausgestattet, verwendete man ab 1940 zunächst die ausschließlich als Dreitonner, ein Jahr später als Viereinhalbtonner zugelassenen Modelle für die Verteilung an die Versorgung rückwärtiger Dienste. Auf Bezugsschein blieb ein großer Teil von VOMAG-Lastwagen in der Heimat unterwegs, nur wenige Einheiten der Wehrmacht wurden mit dem Plauener Fabrikat bestückt. Zudem lieferten die Plauener in Zusammenarbeit mit dem Aufbauhersteller Harmening aus Bückeburg große Zahlen erstmals selbsttragender Omnibusse, im Heck mit einer integrierten Holzgasanlage bestückt.

Das Streben, endlich auf eine moderne Fließbandproduktion umzustellen und darauf einen neuen, dann 200 PS leistenden Sechseinhalbtonner zu bauen, wurde für die VOMAG zum Verhängnis. Man errichtete noch im Krieg eines der modernsten Lastwagenwerke Europas auf dem gegenüberliegenden Ufer des an der Elster gelegenen Hauptwerkes. Statt Lastwagen sollten jedoch Panzer der Gattung IV vom Band rollen. Trotz vernichtender Bombardements auf das Plauener Stadtzentrum gegen Kriegsende und wiederholter Angriffe auf die im Tal gelegene VOMAG sahen die Chancen für einen Wiederanlauf der Lastwagenfertigung für Februar 1946 vielversprechend aus. Anders als bei den namhaften Fahrzeugbauzentren in Chemnitz, Zwickau, Eisenach, Zittau oder Zschopau wurden in Plauen die Festlegungen des Potsdamer Abkommens konsequent durchgezogen. Es blieb nicht bei der vollständigen Demontage. In Plauen wurden auch sämtliche, der immerhin zu 60 % noch intakten Gebäude gesprengt, die VOMAG damit vollständig ausgelöscht.

During the Second World War, VOMAG had a special task. It did not have the capacity to handle large-scale production runs, so Plauen somehow manufactured what was known as the standard diesel, a special German army lorry in line with a MAN and Henschel licensing arrangement. The company's own models had excelled at an early stage in the switch to home fuels as propagated by the Nazis. VOMAG had successfully participated in tests with wood gas drive systems and had gathered valuable experience. With Imbert wood gas generators as standard equipment, the models licensed initially as three tonne models in 1940 and as four-and-a-half tonne models one year later were used to distribute supplies to services behind the lines. Most of the VOMAG lorries were kept in Germany and went to customers who were authorised to purchase them; very few units in the German army were supplied with lorries from Plauen. The Plauen factory also supplied large numbers of self-supporting buses with the bodywork constructor Harmening from Bückeburg and they had a wood gas burner in the rear.

Efforts to finally switch to modern conveyor belt production and manufacture a new six-and-a-half tonne model with 200 bhp proved fatal for VOMAG. During the war one of the most modern lorry production sites in Europe was built on the opposite bank from the main factory situated on the river Elster. But instead of lorries, mark IV tanks were supposed to roll off the conveyor belt. Despite the devastating bombardment of the city centre
in Plauen at the end of the war and repeated attacks on VOMAG, which was located in the valley, the chances of restarting lorry production in February 1946 looked very promising. In contrast to well-known vehicle centres in Chemnitz, Zwickau, Eisenach, Zittau or Zschopau, the decisions adopted by the Potsdam Conference was put into practice to the letter. But stripping the factory was not all that happened. All the buildings in Plauen, which were still intact, 60% of them, were blown up and VOMAG was completely wiped out as a result.

Automobile Kompetenz Automobile Expertise

Ein typischer Vertreter für den handwerklichen Karosseriebau war die Vogtländische Fahrzeugfabrik Oscar Schneider & Söhne in Reichenbach. Hier ein hochwertig ausgestatteter Omnibus auf MAN-Chassis von etwa 1936./Vogtländische Fahrzeugfabrik Oscar Schneider & Söhne in Reichenbach was a typical example of hand-crafted bodywork. This is a bus built on a MAN chassis with high-quality fittings in about 1936.

Zwischen den zahlreichen Versuchen kleiner und kleinster Autobauer der zehner und zwanziger Jahre bis zum Ende des Zweiten Weltkrieges hatte sich in der deutschen Automobilindustrie viel verändert. Die meisten der einstigen Pioniere und deren Automarken waren vergangen. Die Flut von Anbietern, Inflation, Scheinblüte und Weltwirtschaftskrise hatten einerseits ihre Reihen gelichtet, andererseits hatten Fusionen zu schlagkräftigeren Werken geführt. Das Bild der sächsischen Automobilindustrie in den dreißiger Jahren war vor allem durch die aus den vier Marken Audi, DKW, Horch und Wanderer gestärkt hervorgegangenen Auto Union geprägt. Das Vogtland, im wesentlichen mit der VOMAG repräsentiert, saß inmitten eines Umlandes, dass von der Automobilindustrie wie kaum ein anderer Landstrich bestimmt wurde. Unmittelbar im benachbarten Westsachsen erstreckte sich die Auto Union mit ihren Fertigungsstätten im Dreieck Zwickau, Chemnitz, Zschopau, umlagert von einer Vielzahl von kleinen Zulieferbetrieben aber auch Spezialfirmen, die mit dem Aufbau beziehungsweise Karossierung von Fahrgestellen betraut waren. So hatte sich die einstige Sächsische Waggonfabrik in Werdau inzwischen zu einer der ersten Adressen für Nutzfahrzeugaufbauten in Form der Fahrzeugbau Schumann gewandelt. Im Personenwagen-Bereich zählte man Hornig in Meerane und Dietzsch in Glauchau zu den bedeutenden Karosseriefabriken der Region.

Überhaupt trennte sich seit Herausbildung des Automobils das Endprodukt in zwei wichtige Fertigungsbereiche: das Fahrgestell und der Aufbau. Während die Fahrgestellfertigung, also die technische Basis, sich frühzeitig auf größere Hersteller konzentrierte, gab es neben wenigen großen Karosserielieferanten, die durch Verträge an die Autohersteller gebunden waren, quasi auf jedem besseren Dorf Stellmacher, die sich auch mehr oder weniger gut darauf verstanden, individuell und handwerklich gefertigte Aufbauten zu fertigen. Mit zunehmend komplizierteren Formen und Ausstattungen schwand dieser Teil, einige davon vermochten sich jedoch lange zu halten und auf Spezialgebieten zu glänzen. Ein vogtländisches Beispiel für einen solchen typischen mittelständischen Karosseriebauer ist die „Luxuswagenfabrik von Oscar Schneider". Aus einem 1858 vom Vater in Netzschkau gegründeten Wagenbau mit Stellmacherei entwachsen, erkannte Oscar Schneider 1919 das Potential, dass Automobilkarosserien versprachen und gründete in Reichenbach die Vogtländische Fahrzeugfabrik Oscar Schneider & Söhne. Zweck der dafür am neuen Standort reich bemessenen Räume war die fabrikmäßige Herstellung von Karosserien. Nur zum Teil ließ sich dies mit Aufträgen der Zwickauer Audi-Werke oder von MAN-Lastwagen auch letztlich umsetzen. Man fiel weitgehend auf die damals übliche Individualkundschaft zurück, die zumeist spezielle Nutzaufbauten, selten auch einmal Luxuskarosserien für ihre Personenwagen in Auftrag gab. In den dreißiger Jahren stützte man sich vorwiegend auf drei Standbeine: Omnibuskarosserien, Lastwagenaufbauten und Lastanhänger. Daneben betrieb man na-türlich, wie vergleichsweise üblich, eine Tankstelle und eine Automobilvertretung. Nach dem Krieg gab es jede Menge Arbeit mit Karosseriereparaturen, es folgten erste Neuaufbauten als Ersatz für verbrauchte oder zerstörte Wagenkästen älterer Chassis. Mit endgültigem Verschleiß alter Vorkriegstechnik und fehlenden Nachschüben stand auch der seit 1942 in Schneider KG umgewandelte Mittelständler vor einer Trendwende. Durch staatlichen Zugriff unterwandert und in den „sozialistischen Wirtschaftskreislauf" eingebunden, wurde der Betrieb 1972 komplett verstaatlicht und als VEB Karosseriewerk Reichenbach zur Serienfertigung von Kofferaufbauten, zunächst für den Lastwagen S 4000-1, später auch für Barkas-Kleinlaster und seit Mitte der siebziger Jahre hauptsächlich für Robur-Lastwagen umgestaltet.

Die Nachkriegsentwicklung brachte, ohne an dieser Stelle darauf in Einzelheiten eingehen zu müssen, durch den kommunistisch-diktatorischen Einfluss der Besatzer große administrative Einschnitte. Im Vergleich zu Westdeutschland barg die Ausgangssituation in der Sowjetischen Besatzungszone und späteren DDR durch die politischen Verhältnisse erhebliche Unterschiede. Während in der Bundesrepublik der Aufbau im „Wirtschaftswunder" gipfelte, hinterließen die russischen Besatzer in der Ostzone „verbrannte Erde". Die einstmals leistungsfähige VOMAG, der einzige Schwerlastwagenbauer auf dem Gebiet der späteren DDR, war nicht nur leergeräumt und vernichtet worden, auch das Know-how war in alle Winde zerschlagen. Viele Fachleute waren zu den verschiedensten Firmen nach Westdeutschland geflüchtet, darunter auch der ehemalige Chefkonstrukteur Keilhack, der mit zwei getreuen Mitarbeitern bei Krupp neuen Lastwagenkonstruktionen das Laufen lernte. Zuvor hatte er noch für Horch in Zwickau und das Kraftfahrzeugwerk Werdau Dienste geleistet, wo man quasi bei Null anfing, eine neue Lastwagenfertigung für der DDR aufzuziehen.

Wie allgemein in Sachsen, der früher blühenden Automobilbauregion, an sich, so düster sah es auch im Vogtland aus. Lediglich durch eine während des Krieges von Fichtel & Sachs aus Schweinfurt in die Reichenbacher Großdruckerei Carl Werner ausgelagerte Fertigungslinie bestand eine Basis, den schwierigen Aufbau einer Automobilproduktion in der DDR als Zulieferer zu begleiten. Die Reichenbacher Naben- und Kupplungswerke, kurz Renak genannt, fertigten nicht nur Fahrradnaben und Tretkurbeln sondern auch Kupplungen für die gesamte DDR-Automobilfertigung. Für den Kleinwagen Trabant bis zum Traktor kamen die Kraftübertragungen aus Reichenbach. Im nahegelegenen VEB Einspritzpumpenteilewerk Wolfspfütz fertigte man überdies Einspritzdüsen und Pumpenelemente. Beide Betriebe gehörten nach der Kombinatsbildung in den achtziger Jahren zum VEB IFA-Kombinat Personenkraftwagen Karl-Marx-Stadt und waren dem Barkas-Werk zugeordnet.

Das VEB Karosseriewerk Reichenbach war in den siebziger und achtziger Jahren vor allem durch seine Kofferaufbauten auf Robur-Lkw bekannt./The VEB Karosseriewerk Reichenbach was well-known for its van bodies on Robur lorries in the 1970s and 1980s.

A great deal had changed in the German automobile industry between the many attempts by small and tiny motor car manufacturers in the 1910s and 1920s until the end of the Second World War. Most of the early pioneers and their brands had passed away. The flood of manufacturers, inflation, apparent prosperity and the global economic crisis had sorted out the men from the boys and had led to mergers to form more effective companies. The scene in the Saxon automobile industry was dominated by the Auto Union name, which had emerged stronger from the four brands of Audi, DKW, Horch and Wanderer. The Vogtland region, primarily represented by VOMAG, was located in the middle of a surrounding area, which was dominated by the automobile industry to a unique extent. On its doorstep in West Saxony, Auto Union had its manufacturing facilities in the Zwickau, Chemnitz and Zschopau triangle, surrounded by a variety of small suppliers and special companies, which were entrusted to look after the bodywork or coachwork on the chassis. The former Sächsische Waggonfabrik works in Werdau had become one of the top addresses for commercial vehicle bodywork in the shape of Fahrzeugbau Schumann. As far as cars were concerned, Hornig in Meerane and Dietzsch in Glauchau were major bodywork factories in the region.

Since the early development of the motor car, the final product had required two important manufacturing stages: for the chassis and the bodywork. While the manufacture of the chassis, i.e. the technical base, was concentrated on fairly large manufactures from an early stage, there were a few large bodywork suppliers, who were bound to car manufacturers by means of contracts, but also cart-wrights in almost any largish village, who knew how to make bodywork that was shaped individually and by hand. These people involved in the production process disappeared as shapes and equipment became more and more complicated, but some of them were able to survive for a long time and were experts in special fields. One Vogtland example of a typical medium-sized bodywork builder was the "Luxuswagenfabrik von Oscar Schneider". Having grown out of a carriage works set up in Netzschkau by his father in 1858, Oscar Schneider recognised the potential of car bodywork in 1919 and he set up the Vogtländische Fahrzeugfabrik Oscar Schneider & Söhne in Reichenbach. The purpose of the workshops with their huge dimensions was to manufacture mass-produced bodywork. But in the end orders from the Zwickau Audi works or from MAN lorries only kept part of the works busy. The works were largely dependent on individual customers, who usually ordered special commercial bodywork, but rarely luxury bodywork for their cars. In the 1930s, the company mainly specialised in three fields: bus bodywork, lorry bodywork and goods trailers. Of course, the works also operated a petrol station and a motor car sales branch. After the war there was plenty of body repair work available and new bodywork was designed to replace spent or destroyed car bodies on older chassis. Once the pre-war technology had worn out and due to a lack of fresh supplies, the medium-sized company, which had been known as Schneider KG since 1942, faced a complete turnaround. Undermined by state intrusion and caught up in the "socialist economic cycle", the company was completely nationalised in 1972 and had been reorganised as the VEB Karosserie Reichenbach (state combine) to mass-produce van bodies for the S 4000-1 lorry, then for the Barkas minibus and mainly for Robur lorries since the mid-1970s.

Developments after the war brought huge administrative changes as a result of the dictatorial communist influence of the occupiers, without going into details at this juncture. In contrast to West Germany, the starting point in the Soviet Occupation Zone and later East Germany was hugely different as a result of the political circumstances. While the developments in West German peaked in the "economic miracle", the Russian occupiers left behind a "scorched earth" in the eastern part of the country. VOMAG, the former heavy goods lorry manufacturer in what later became East Germany, a company which was once so efficient, was not only devoid of any machinery and destroyed, but its expertise was scattered in every direction too. Many experts had fled to various companies in West Germany, including the former chief designer, Keilhack, who together with two faithful colleagues enabled Krupp to roll out heavy goods vehicles. He had earlier worked for Horch in Zwickau and the vehicle works in Werdau, which were starting from scratch again to manufacture lorries for East Germany.

As elsewhere in Saxony, what used to be the flourishing automobile region, things looked pretty bleak in the Vogtland region too. But a production line moved to the Carl Werner major printing works in Reichenbach by Fichtel & Sachs from Schweinfurt during the war provided the basis for setting up a supplier business to the automobile production industry in East Germany. The Reichenbacher Naben- und Kupplungswerke, known as Renak, not only manufactured bicycle hubs and foot pedals, but also clutches for all the vehicle production sites in East Germany. The transmission systems ranging from small Trabant car to tractors all came from Reichenbach. The VEB Einspritzpumpenteilewerk Wolfspfütz works nearby manufactured fuel injectors and pump elements. After the formation of state combines in the 1980s, both companies were part of the VEB IFA-Kombinat Personenkraftwagen Karl-Marx-Stadt and were attached to the Barkas works.

Die Reichenbacher Renak-Werke lieferten Kupplungen für alle Fahrzeuge des gesamten DDR-Fahrzeugbaus sowie Fahrradteile./The Renak works in Reichenbach supplied clutches for all the vehicles made in East Germany and bicycle parts.

Automobile Kompetenz Automobile Expertise

Neben einer Vielzahl im Vogtland ansässiger Zulieferer der Automobilindustrie werden bei Neoplan in Plauen nach modernsten Gesichtspunkten Omnibusse von Grund auf gebaut./Buses are built from scratch at the Neoplan works in Plauen using the latest processes; there are also a number of suppliers to the automobile industry that are based in the Vogtland region.

Als sich zur Wende 1989 die ganze Breite des maroden DDR-Automobilbaues offenbarte, glaubte keiner mehr, dass in Sachsen noch einmal der Kraftfahrzeugbau eine neue Blüte erleben sollte. Doch der Grundstein dafür war schon Ende August 1988 gelegt worden, als VW-Vorstandsvorsitzender Dr. Carl Hahn zusammen mit dem IFA-Kombinatsleiter Personenkraftwagen das Gemeinschaftsprojekt Viertakt-Motor besiegelte. Eigentlich als Lieferant für Viertaktmotoren der DDR-Modelle Trabant und Wartburg gedacht, bildete das Barkas-Motorenwerk in Karl-Marx-Stadt den Ausgangspunkt für neue Engagements des Volkswagen-Konzerns nach der Wende in Sachsen. Bekanntlich errichtete VW in Mosel nahe Zwickau ein neues Montagewerk und investierte in das Chemnitzer Motorenwerk. Diese Initialzündung, die bereits im Laufe der neunziger Jahre fruchtbaren Boden für zahlreiche Zulieferbetriebe in der Region bereitete, zog mit BMW und Porsche vor wenigen Jahren noch zwei weitere namhafte deutsche Automobilhersteller nach Sachsen. Inzwischen zählt das Vogtland knapp vierzig Betriebe, die in der Kraftfahrzeugbranche tätig sind, etwa ein Dutzend allein in der Vogtlandmetropole Plauen. Das Spektrum reicht von traditioneller Textilherstellung in Form von Vliesstoffen für die Innenausstattung über neue Ansiedlungen der Umformtechnik bis hin zum einzigen Komplettanbieter, der Neoplan Omnibus GmbH Plauen. In den einzig aus dem VOMAG-Erbe erhalten gebliebenen Hallen des Werksteiles Leuchtsmühle zog nach der Wende neues Leben ein.

Zu DDR-Zeiten als Instandsetzungsbetrieb für Omnibusse dahinvegetierend und allenfalls noch symbolisch mit dem Glanz einstigen Omnibusbaus in Plauen verbunden, investierte nach der Wende der Stuttgarter Omnibusbauer Gottlob Auwärter kräftig. Er baute das kleine Werk zu einem seiner wichtigsten Standorte aus. Inzwischen ist Auwärter und seine Omnibusmarke Neoplan vom MAN-Konzern übernommen worden. Im Gegensatz zu anderen Fertigungsstätten wie auch dem vormaligen Stuttgarter Neoplan-Hauptwerk, die größtenteils geschlossen wurden, erfuhr der Standort Plauen in den letzten Jahren weiteren Ausbau. Ziel war, dass nunmehr alle Rohgerippe für Neoplan-Busse aus Plauen kommen. In geringem Maße werden sie in der ehemaligen VOMAG-Halle auch weiterhin auslieferungsfähig komplettiert.

Der Automobilbau ist stärker denn je im Vogtland ansässig und verwurzelt. Dass dies so bleibt, dafür geben täglich motivierte Fachleute ihr Bestes, genauso wie es ihre Vorfahren schon taten. Gingen unsere Altvorderen noch daran komplette Automobile zu bauen, ist das Augenmerk durch fortschreitende Komplexität der Technik heute auf sehr spezielle Einzelbaugruppen gerichtet. Die Erinnerung an das, was unsere Vorfahren hervorbrachten, wach zu halten, ist Christian Suhr aus Reichenbach/V. und Ralf Weinreich aus Halle/Saale ein Bedürfnis. Sie gründeten im März 2004 den Verlag Kraftakt, den einzigen Fachverlag für Automobilliteratur in den fünf neuen Bundesländern. Anders als branchenüblich, geben bei der Auswahl der Themen nicht ausschließlich kommerzielle Aspekte den Ausschlag. Man versteht sich als Plattform auch für fachspezifische Randthemen wie auch regionale Bezüge. Bevorzugt werden Publikationen über Nutzfahrzeuggeschichte aber auch vergessene Automobilmarken auf den Weg gebracht. Dass dieses Konzept zusammen mit einem hohen Anspruch an die Qualität der Publikationen aufgeht, beweist ein wachsender Leserkreis und das zunehmend umfangreicher dargebotene Verlagsprogramm. Denn so viel steht fest: Zukunft braucht Herkunft!

Seit der Wende verlassen moderne Neoplan Omnibusse die einzig aus dem VOMAG-Erbe verbliebene Halle am Plauener Leuchtsmühlenweg. Im Juni 2005 konnten die Besucher anlässlich der Festivitäten zum 90-jährigen Jubiläum Plauener Nutzfahrzeugbaus im Neoplan-Werksgelände neben den aktuellen Omnibusmodellen auch vielerlei über die VOMAG-Geschichte erfahren./ Modern Neoplan buses have been leaving the only works remaining from the VOMAG past on Leuchtsmühlenweg since the fall of the Berlin Wall. Visitors to the festivities linked to the 90th anniversary of commercial vehicle production in Plauen in June 2005 were able to discover plenty about current coach models and a great deal about the history of VOMAG at the Neoplan works site.

(Fotos/Photos by Christian Suhr, Text/Text by Christian Suhr, Übersetzung/Translated by David Strauss)

» Zukunft braucht Herkunft! «

» The future needs the past! «

When the full extent of the ailing East Germany automobile industry was revealed when the Berlin Wall fell in 1989, nobody believed that vehicle construction would experience a new boom again in Saxony. But the foundation stone for this was laid at the end of August 1988, when VW chairman Dr. Carl Hahn sealed a joint project for four stroke engines with the IFA combine manager for cars. Conceived as a supplier of four-stroke engines for the East German Trabant and Wartburg models, the Barkas engine works in Karl-Marx-Stadt formed the starting point for new commitments made by the Volkswagen company in Saxony after the fall of the Berlin Wall. As is generally known, VW built a new assembly plant in Mosel near Zwickau and invested in the Chemnitz engine works. This initial spark, which prepared fruitful ground for many supplier companies in the region during the 1990s, attracted two other well-known German automobile manufacturers to Saxony in the shape of BMW and Porsche just a few years ago. The Vogtland region now has almost forty companies operating in the vehicle sector, about a dozen of them in the Vogtland capital, Plauen, alone. They range from traditional textile manufacturing in the shape of non-woven materials for interior fittings to new factories set up in the metal forming sector and there is even a complete provider, Neoplan Omnibus GmbH Plauen. New life was breathed into the only remaining factories that had been preserved from the VOMAG heritage at Leuchtsmühle after the fall of the Berlin Wall. Vegetating as a maintenance company for buses in East German times, but still symbolically linked to the glory days of former bus construction in Plauen, the Stuttgart bus manufacturer Gottlob Auwärter made considerable investments after the fall of the Berlin Wall. He expanded the small works into one of his most important business sites. Auwärter and its Neoplan bus brand have since been taken over by the MAN group. In contrast to other manufacturing bases and the former Neoplan main works in Stuttgart, most of which have been closed, the Plauen works have continued to be expanded over the past few years. The aim was to ensure that all the base frames for Neoplan buses should come from Plauen. On a small scale some of them continue to be completed in the former VOMAG works to make them ready for delivery to customers.

Motor car manufacturing is at home and rooted in the Vogtland region to a greater degree then ever before. Motivated specialist workers are doing their best to ensure that this remains the case, just as their ancestors did. If they went about producing complete cars, the focus today is on highly specialised individual components as a result of advancing technology. Christian Suhr from Reichenbach/V and Ralf Weinreich from Halle/Saale are determined to keep alive the memory of what our forbears achieved. They set up the Krafttakt publishing house in March 2004, the only specialist publishing house for automobile literature in Eastern Germany. In contrast to what is normal in this sector, they do not focus exclusively on commercial matters when selecting subject matter. They see themselves as a platform for specialist side issues and regional specialities. They give preference to publications on the history of commercial vehicles, but they also cover long forgotten car brands. A growing circle of readers and the increasingly comprehensive publishing house programme are proof that this concept along with high quality products is being well received. For one thing is certain: the future needs the past!

Christian Suhr aus Reichenbach publiziert und bewahrt neben seiner einmaligen Sammlung zur Geschichte deutschen Automobilbaus wie auch über die Plauener VOMAG im speziellen nicht nur jede Menge Dokumente, sondern restauriert auch selbst. Im Bild sein VOMAG 5 LR von 1940 in jenem Stadium, wie er seinerzeit vor dem Aufbau eingefahren wurde./Christian Suhr from Reichenbach not only publishes and preserves a huge number of documents alongside his unique collection on the history of the German automobile industry and VOMAG in Plauen in particular, but he also restores vehicles himself. This photo shows his VOMAG 5 LR dating from 1940 as it was before the bodywork was added.

Im Vogtland zu Hause: Von einst über 10.000 gebauten VOMAG-Lastwagen sind heute weltweit keine zwei Dutzend Komplettfahrzeuge mehr bekannt. Einige der Raritäten werden in ihrer Heimat liebevoll gepflegt./At home in the Vogtland region: of the 10,000 VOMAG lorries built, there are probably no more than two dozen complete vehicles left today. Some of these rare vehicles are lovingly cared for at their home base.

Magnetto Automotive Deutschland GmbH

Mit italienischem Charme ein Presswerk zum Erfolg gebracht
Italian Charm Brings Success to a Press Shop

Eine italienische Erfolgsgeschichte mitten im Vogtland ist der Automobilzulieferer Magnetto Automotive Deutschland GmbH in Treuen. In einer Rekordbauzeit von nur elf Monaten wurde das Werk auf einem neuen Industriegebiet errichtet. Zu verdanken ist diese erfolgreiche Ansiedlung einem von BMW im Jahre 2001 ausgeschriebenen Konzeptwettbewerb für die Herstellung von Karosseriebauteilen. Den konnte die italienische Muttergesellschaft mit Hauptsitz in Turin für sich entscheiden. Voraussetzung für die folgenden Aufträge war jedoch der Bau eines Werkes in Deutschland. Und im Ergebnis einer bundesweiten Suche fiel die Wahl auf das Vogtland mit dem Industriestandort Treuen – Goldene Höhe, auf dem das Unternehmen bisher nahezu 55 Millionen Euro investierte.

Mit zwei großen vollautomatisierten, hydraulischen Pressenlinien und mittlerweile acht komplett roboterisierten Karosseriebaulinien gehören die Vogtländer inzwischen zu einer festen Größe in der deutschen Automobilzulieferbranche, unterstreicht Geschäftsführer Dieter Pfortner, was er anhand beeindruckender Zahlen belegen kann. Berücksichtigt man, dass der Serienbetrieb erst im Jahr 2004 begann und mit knapp 300 Mitarbeitern im Jahr 2007 einen Umsatz von 82 Millionen Euro erreicht wurde, so steckt dahinter die Arbeit eines hoch motivierten, kompetenten und jederzeit einsatzbereiten Teams der Magnetto-Mitarbeiter. Optimistisch blickt deshalb das Unternehmen auch in die Zukunft. Neben den Zulieferungen an die BMW-Group für die 1er- und 3er-Baureihe zählen Volkswagen, Skoda, Opel und ebenso die französischen Autobauer Renault und Peugeot zum Kundenkreis. Mit seinem Business und Technology Center in Frankfurt/Main arbeitet das Unternehmen intensiv daran, die Geschäftsbeziehungen zur deutschen als auch zur internationalen Automobilindustrie zu erweitern. Selbstverständlich erfüllt das Unternehmen die mehrfach geprüften Anforderungen für ein erfolgreiches Qualitätsmanagement- als auch Umweltmanagement-Zertifikat. Komplettiert wird dieser Status durch Kundenzertifikate, die Magnetto als einen erstrangigen, qualifizierten Zulieferer einstuft.

The automobile supplier Magnetto Automotive Deutschland GmbH in Treuen is an Italian success story at the heart of the Vogtland region. The factory was constructed on a new business park in record time – just eleven months. The company was encouraged to build the factory here as the result of a design competition for the production of car body components that BMW had advertised in 2001. The Italian parent company with its headquarters in Turin won this contest. The condition for receiving further orders was that they should build the factory in Germany. After an extensive search throughout Germany, the factory was built on the Goldene Höhe industrial park in Treuen in the Vogtland district, where the company has now invested almost € 55 million.

Managing director Dieter Pfortner points out that the factory has now become firmly established among German automotive suppliers. The Treuen site has two large fully-automated, hydraulic press lines and eight entirely robot-controlled bodywork production lines. The director underlines the company's success with some impressive figures: having started series production in 2004, the company now has about 300 employees and turnover of € 82 million. These figures are the result of the highly-motivated and competent work carried out by the members of staff at Magnetto. Consequently, the company can face the future with a sense of optimism. Besides supplying the BMW group's 1 and 3 series models, Magnetto's customers also include Volkswagen, Skoda, Opel and the French automakers Renault and Peugeot. The company is also working hard to expand its business relations with the German and international automobile industries at its Business and Technology Center in Frankfurt/Main. It goes without saying that the company successfully fulfils the requirements for several quality management and environmental management certificates. This is backed up by customer certificates that rate Magnetto as a first-rate, qualified supplier.

(Fotos/Photos by Igor Pastierovic, Text/Text by Bert Walther, Übersetzung/Translated by David Strauss)

Magnetto Automotive Deutschland GmbH

Das Unternehmen investiert auch in die Heranbildung des eigenen Nachwuchses. Derzeit werden hier 16 Lehrlinge sowie eine Werksstudentin ausgebildet. Beim Ingenieur- und Managementnachwuchs schaut Magnetto insbesondere auf die in Sachsen ansässigen Universitäten, Fachhochschulen und Berufsakademien, aus denen im Herbst 2007 neun Studenten im Werk ihr Praktikum durchführen oder ihre Diplomarbeit erstellen. Doch ebenso im Vogtland selbst, bei der Diploma-Fachhochschule in Plauen, wurden die Treuener fündig. Pfortner lobt insbesondere diese Bildungseinrichtung für ihre Effizienz bei der Ausbildung junger Fachkräfte, verbunden mit guten Fremdsprachenkenntnissen.

Aber auch seiner regionalen und sozialen Verantwortung kommt Magnetto nach. Nicht nur die Unterstützung von Kindergärten, Sportvereinen, des Natur- und Umweltzentrums oder regionaler Höhepunkte sind dem Unternehmen ein Anliegen. Es unterstützt auch nachhaltig regionale als auch überregionale Stiftungen, deren Inhalte sich auf konkrete Projekte der Betreuung, ärztlichen Behandlung und Gesundheitsförderung von Kindern und Jugendlichen konzentrieren.

The business is also investing in the next generation of staff. 16 apprentices and one student are currently being trained at the company. Magnetto is particularly keen on working with students from Saxon universities, colleges or vocational colleges when it comes to finding engineering and management trainees. In the autumn of 2007 nine students from these institutions were involved in a placement or were carrying out research for their final degree dissertation at the Treuen factory. The Vogtland company has even found a competent training partner in the shape of the Diploma University of Applied Sciences in Plauen. Dieter Pfortner praises this educational institution for its efficiency in training young specialists and providing excellent training in foreign languages.

However, Magnetto is also meeting its regional and social responsibilities. The company is not only keen to support nursery schools, sports clubs, the Nature and Environment Centre or regional events. It also backs regional and national charities, which focus on specific projects that provide support, medical care and health promotion for children and young people.

Magnetto Automotive Deutschland GmbH
Treuener Höhe 1 · D - 08233 Treuen
Telefon +49 (0) 37468 68-0
Telefax +49 (0) 37468 68-122
info@de.ma.mmagnetto.com
www.mmagnetto.com

HAL Automotive Plauen

Know-how-Teile ... präzise und pünktlich
Skilfully Produced Parts ... Precise and on Time

Um zu fliegen, muss man nicht nur Flügel haben, sondern sie auch bewegen. Der strenge Konsolidierungsprozess der HAL Automotive Plauen GmbH trägt Früchte. Mittlerweile schreibt der Automobilzulieferer schwarze Zahlen. Die Auftragsbücher haben sich gefüllt, die Produktpalette wird sukzessive erweitert.

Im Jahre 2001 als Tochterunternehmen der Plauener Werkzeugmaschinenfabrik Vogtland GmbH (Wema) gegründet, nabelte sich das Werk 2005 von der Mutter ab. Seither spezialisierten sich die Plauener auf die Entwicklung und den Bau von Komponenten für die Automobilindustrie und etablierten sich nicht nur am deutschen sondern auch am internationalen Markt. Kernsegment der Produktion sind Zylinderkopfhauben für Drei- und Vierzylinder-Motoren, sowie Getriebe-, Fahrwerk- und Bremsteile für die Automobil- und Motorradindustrie. Dabei setzt die HAL Automotive Plauen nicht nur auf eine hohe Qualifikation des 52-köpfigen Mitarbeiterstamms. Auch der Einsatz modernster Technologien erlaubt es, rasch und flexibel auf aktuelle Erfordernisse zu reagieren und gegebenenfalls komplette Fertigungsanlagen umzurüsten. „Wir sind nicht nur Lieferant von Gussteilen. Wir liefern auch komplette Systeme, machen Dichtprüfungen und Restschmutzbestimmungen", so Geschäftsführer Manfred Hünger.

Seit 2005 ist in den Plauener Betrieb auch eine Produktionsstätte in Leipzig mit 15 Beschäftigten integriert. Dort wird vorwiegend Großguss bearbeitet, unter anderem bis zu drei Meter lange Gehäuse und Ölwannen für die Elektroindustrie oder den Maschinenbau. „Beide Standorte ermöglichen uns, Synergien zu nutzen", so Hünger. Zudem habe Plauen Bearbeitungs-Know-how einbringen können. Mit rund 80 Prozent generiert HAL Automotive den Großteil seines gesamten Geschäftsvolumens in der Automobilindustrie. Einer der Hauptkunden ist das VW Motorenwerk in Chemnitz. Ein weiterer Großkunde der Plauener ist WABCO, ein international anerkannter Automobilzulieferer für Bremssysteme. Verträge bestehen auch zu Skoda in Tschechien.

In order to fly you not only need wings, but you also have to move them. The strict consolidation process at HAL Automotive Plauen GmbH is bearing fruit. The automobile supplier is now back in the black. The order books are full and the range of products is gradually being expanded.

Set up in 2001 as a subsidiary of the WEMA Vogtland company based in Plauen, HAL gained independence from its parent company in 2005. Since then the Plauen enterprise has specialised in developing and manufacturing components for the automobile industry and has established itself not only on the German market, but also internationally. Production focuses on cylinder-head covers for three and four cylinder engines, as well as gearbox, chassis and brake parts for the automobile and motorcycle industry. HAL Automotive Plauen not only has 52 highly qualified members of staff, but it also uses the latest technologies to react to current requirements in a rapid and flexible way and can also retool complete manufacturing units, if this is required. "We not only supply cast parts, but can also deliver entire systems, carry out leak-proof tests and assess residual dirt levels," says manager Manfred Hünger.

A production facility in Leipzig with 15 employees has been part of the company since 2005. Large castings are mainly processed there, including housings measuring up to three metres and oil pans for the electrical or engineering industries. "Both sites enable us to use synergies," says Hünger. Plauen has also been able to introduce machining expertise. HAL Automotive generates nearly 80 percent of its entire business in the automobile industry. One of the main customers is the VW engine works in Chemnitz. Another major customer of the Plauen company is WABCO, an internationally recognized automobile supplier for brake systems. The company also has contracts with Skoda in the Czech Republic.

The HAL group of companies not only includes HAL Automotive Plauen GmbH, but also HAL Aluminiumguss Leipzig GmbH (parent company) and HAL Aluminiumguss Bitterfeld GmbH. This means that expertise in the fields of metal machining and aluminium castings is brought together in one company.

The company invested € 13 million in modern plant in 2001/2002, which was supplied by WEMA Vogtland. Another 3-D coordinate measuring machine was acquired in 2006 and the company has been able to provide evidence of its ability to work accurately down to thousandths of a millimetre.

(Fotos/Photos by Igor Pastierovic, Text/Text by Martina Meier, Übersetzung/Translated by David Strauss)

HAL Automotive Plauen

Zur HAL Unternehmensgruppe gehören neben der HAL Automotive Plauen GmbH noch die HAL Aluminiumguss Leipzig GmbH (Mutterunternehmen) und die HAL Aluminiumguss Bitterfeld GmbH. Damit sind Kompetenz in den Bereichen Metallbearbeitung und Aluminiumguss unter einem Haus vereinigt. Bereits 2001/2002 investierte das Unternehmen 13 Millionen Euro in moderne Anlagen, welche von der Plauener Wema geliefert wurden. 2006 gehörte zu den Neuanschaffungen eine weitere 3-D-Koordinatenmessmaschine, mit der das Unternehmen den Nachweis der Qualitätsfähigkeit im Tausendstel-Bereich weiter verbessern konnte.

Um die internationale Marktpräsenz weiter auszubauen, präsentiert sich das Unternehmen jährlich auf der Leipziger Zuliefermesse. Im Vorjahr war das Unternehmen auch Aussteller auf der IAA Nutzfahrzeuge in Hannover. Es gelang, das Portfolio auch auf andere Branchensegmente im Bereich Elektroantriebe und Getriebeherstellung auszuweiten. Damit soll u. a. auch die relative Abhängigkeit von der Automobilindustrie reduziert werden.

Das Management der HAL Automotive Plauen ist auf vier Säulen aufgebaut. „Damit sind wir in der Lage, uns ausschließlich auf unsere Kernkompetenz zu konzentrieren und für unsere Kunden optimale Ergebnisse zu erzielen", sagt Hünger. Im Bereich des Fluid-Managements kooperiert das Unternehmen mit kompetenten externen Partnern, die sowohl für die fachgerechte Bereitstellung als auch Entsorgung von Materialien wie Kühlschmierstoffe verantwortlich zeichnen. Im Tool-Management arbeitet HAL Automotive Plauen mit Partnern aus dem Werkzeugbau zusammen. Das Logistik-Management wird über zuverlässige externe Unternehmen gesteuert. Das Personal-Management übernimmt sämtliche personelle Abläufe. Zukünftig sollen auch Lehrlinge ausgebildet werden. „Wir bauen auf Fachkräfte aus den eigenen Reihen", so der Geschäftsführer. Nicht zuletzt stellen die bisherigen Mitarbeiter - vorwiegend bodenständige Vogtländer – einen wichtigen Erfolgsfaktor des Unternehmens dar. „Unser Team ist hoch motiviert, gut ausgebildet, engagiert und auch unter extremen Bedingungen des Drei-Schicht-Betriebs belastbar und zuverlässig", erklärt Hünger.

The company has a stand at the Leipzig suppliers' trade fair every year in order to expand its international market presence. Last year the company was an exhibitor at the Commercial Vehicles Motor Show in Hanover. The company also managed to expand its portfolio to other branch sectors in the field of electric drive systems and gearbox manufacturing. This is designed to reduce any relative dependence on the automobile industry.

The management system at HAL Automotive Plauen is built on four pillars. "This means we are able to concentrate exclusively on our core competence and achieve the best results for our customers," Hünger explains. The company cooperates with competent external partners in the field of fluid management; they are responsible for the correct supplies and disposal of materials like cooling lubricants. In the tool management sector, HAL Automotive Plauen works with tool manufacturing partners. The logistics management processes are handled by reliable outside firms. The personnel management department handles all personnel matters. The company aims to train apprentices in future. "We are relying on qualified personnel from within our own ranks," says the manager. Last but not least, current employees – predominantly down-to-earth Vogtland people – form an important part of the success of the company. "Our team is highly motivated, well trained, committed, resilient and reliable, even in the extreme conditions created by a three shift system," Hünger explains.

HAL Automotive Plauen GmbH
Schenkendorfstraße 14
D-08525 Plauen
Telefon +49 (0) 3741 554-639
Telefax +49 (0) 3741 554-645
www.hal-gruppe.de
info@hal-automotive.de

Automotive Interior World Production GmbH

- Automobilinnenausstatter / Vehicle interior specialist
- Logistikdienstleister / Logistics provider

Der Fortschritt braucht Bewegung.
Flexibility is Needed to Move Ahead

Der Unternehmer Peter Meinel ist gebürtiger Klingenthaler, ein waschechter Vogtländer. Mit 47 Jahren hat der gelernte Werkzeugmacher und Meister der Landwirtschaft Erstaunliches geleistet. Beim Aufbau einer Reihe von Firmen, die nicht nur eng zusammenarbeiten, sondern auch international aktiv sind, schrieb er Wirtschaftsgeschichte am Standort Vogtland.

Nach der Wende machte sich Meinel selbstständig. Mit seinem Fuhrunternehmen verzeichnete er ständiges Wachstum. Das bekannte Logistikunternehmen mit Sitz in Neuensalz, dessen Alleininhaber Meinel seit 1992 ist, firmierte bis vor zwei Jahren unter dem Namen M+H. Schon 1991 hatte Meinel den Kfz-Ausstatter TUP in Markneukirchen gegründet. Die Firma hat 400 Beschäftigte, 1993/1994 schied Meinel aus dem aktuellen Geschäft aus, blieb aber Gesellschafter. Durch seine cleveren Transport-Logistikleistungen wird ein großer Automobilproduzent auf Meinel aufmerksam. Der Vogtländer hatte unter anderem Lkw-Doppelstockzüge entwickelt. Heute tut es ihm leid, dass er die Innovation nicht patentieren ließ. Meinel erhielt ein Angebot von einem führenden Systemlieferanten für die Ausstattung von Fahrzeugen. Innerhalb von sechs Wochen stellte er die Produktion von Mittelarmlehnen und Kopfstützen für einen großen Konzern auf die Beine. Der Unternehmer erwarb einen alten Hühnerstall, welchen er in kürzester Zeit für die Produktion ausbaute. Es hat mittlerweile Betriebsstätten in Tschechien, der Slowakei, Russland und mehrere in Deutschland und produziert für fast alle führenden europäischen und sowie für asiatische Automobilhersteller Teile der Innenausstattung.

Die Firmengruppe beschäftigt derzeit ca. 700 Mitarbeiter und wird im Jahr 2008 1100 Beschäftigte haben. Lehrlingsausbildung wird groß geschrieben im kaufmännischen und handwerklichen Bereich mit dem Ziel, Know-how im Betrieb zu halten. Der Firmenchef ist selbst Lehrausbilder. Zur Zeit werden mehrere Lehrlinge im Unternehmen ausgebildet. 2006 wurde Automotive ausgezeichnet von der Bundesagentur für Arbeit für vorbildliche Ausbildung. Zweieinhalb bis drei Jahre dauert die Lehrzeit. Voraussetzung sind „Elan und Fleiß". Die Chancen übernommen zu werden sind gut, das Know-how soll dem eigenen Betrieb erhalten bleiben. Auch die eigene Ausbildung hat Meinel im Auge behalten und berufsbegleitend Betriebswirtschaft studiert.

Ultraschallverschweißung für Leder, Plaste, Kunstleder mit Plaste sind neue Technologien bei der Produktion von Autoausstattung, die der innovative Unternehmer eingeführt und serienreif gemacht hat. Motto: „energiesparend und umweltschonend". Der Umsatz des Unternehmens liegt im zweistelligen Millionenbereich. Doch Peter Meinel hat sich ein ehrgeiziges Ziel gesetzt und peilt eine Steigerung auf dreistelligen Millionenbereich mittelfristig an. Die Weichen dafür sind gestellt mit der Übernahme eines Textilbetriebs in Regnitzlosau. Dort baut der Unternehmer eine hochmoderne Produktion von technischen Textilien auf, die unter anderem Verwendung bei der Herstellung von Reifen, Drucktüchern und Förderbändern finden. Der Clou dabei, auch hier wird Umweltschutz groß geschrieben. Verwendung finden erneuerbare Stoffe, die sich natürlich abbauen.

Bei aller beruflichen Inanspruchnahme findet der Unternehmer noch Zeit für familiäres und ehrenamtliches Engagement. Der Vater von vier Kindern ist in seiner Heimatstadt Markneukirchen Präsident des renommierten Bundesligaclubs der Ringer AV Germania 06.

The entrepreneur Peter Meinel was born in Klingenthal and is a genuine native of the Vogtland region. The trained toolmaker and farmer has achieved a huge amount by the age of 47. He has set up a number of companies, which not only work closely together, but also operate on the international market. In this sense he has written business history in the Vogtland region.

After the fall of the Berlin Wall, Meinel went self-employed. He achieved constant growth with his haulage company. The well-known logistics company based in Neuensalz operated under the company name M+H until two years ago – Meinel, by the way, has been the sole owner since 1992. He had founded the vehicle supplier TUP in Markneukirchen back in 1991. The company employs 400 people; Meinel withdrew from the everyday business in 1993/94, but has remained a partner. His clever transport logistics services attracted the attention of a major car manufacturer. One of the things that the native of the Vogtland region developed was double-decker trains for lorries. He is now sorry that he did not arrange for the invention to be patented. Meinel received an offer from a leading systems supplier to provide equipment for vehicles. Within six weeks he had started to manufacture arm rests and headrests for a major company. The entrepreneur acquired an old chicken house and converted it into a production site in a very short time. The company now has factories in the Czech Republic, Slovakia, Russia and at several sites in Germany and produces interior fittings for almost all the leading European and Asian car manufacturers.

The company group currently employs approx. 700 staff and this figure will rise to 1100 in 2008. The company attaches great importance to training apprentices in the commercial and technical areas with the aim of keeping the expertise within the company. The firm's boss is a trainer too. Several apprentices are currently being trained at the company. Automotive was commended by the German Labour Agency for its excellent training work in 2006. The apprenticeship period lasts from two-and-a-half to three years. The young people have to demonstrate "enthusiasm and industriousness". The chances of being taken on as permanent staff are good – after all, the expertise is designed to remain within the company. Meinel himself has not neglected his own training either and has studied business management part-time while continuing to work.

Ultra-sound welding for leather, plastics and artificial leather with plastic are the new technologies that are used to manufacture equipment for vehicles; the innovative entrepreneur has introduced this and now uses it in series production. His motto is: "saving energy and the environment". The company has turnover running into double digits in millions of euros annually. But Peter Meinel has set himself an ambitious target to achieve turnover running into triple digits in millions of euros in the medium term. He has paved the way for this by taking over a textile company in Regnitzlosau. The entrepreneur is setting up a facility for producing technical textiles in a very modern way – they are used in manufacturing tyres, printing blankets and conveyor belts. The trick is to ensure that as little damage is caused to the environment. Renewable materials are used and they break down naturally.

Despite all his professional demands, the businessman still finds time for his family and voluntary work. The father of four children is president of the renowned top-flight wrestling club AV Germania 06 in his home town of Markneukirchen.

Automotive Interior World Production GmbH
Gewerbepark 11 · 08258 Markneukirchen
Telefon +49 (0) 37422 42-0
Telefax +49 (0) 37422 42-10
www.interior-world.com

(Fotos/Photos by Automotive Interior World Production GmbH, Text by Renate Wöllner, Übersetzung/Translated by David Strauss)

Vom Vogtland aus den Markt erobert

To capture the market from the Vogtland

Die Autozulieferregion hat mit der Weidmann Plastics Technology Deutschland AG in Treuen einen weiteren renommierten Branchenvertreter gewonnen. Das Unternehmen gehört zur Schweizer WICOR-Gruppe (Weidmann International Corporation) mit Sitz in Rapperswil am Zürichsee.
Mit dem Unternehmensbereich Plastics Technology ist die WICOR Gruppe ein führender Entwickler und Hersteller von Kunststoffkomponenten im Bereich von Frischluftmanagement und Folienhinterspritzen.

Die Kernkompetenzen liegen in der Beherrschung state-of-the-art-Technologien rund um das Spritzgießen in allen seinen Varianten unter Einschluss der Mehrkomponenten-Technik in den Branchen Fahrzeugbau, Sanitär-, Sensor- und Medizintechnik.

Am Standort in Treuen fertigt Weidmann mit rund 200 Mitarbeitern im 3- und 4-Schichtbetrieb technisch anspruchsvolle Kunststoffkomponenten im Bereich Frischluftmanagement und Türelemente für Schlüsselkunden in der Automobilindustrie. Ausgerüstet werden damit die neuen Modellreihen des 1er und 3er von BMW, der Peugeot 207 und die neue C-Klasse der Daimler AG. Jüngster Produktionsanlauf sind Lieferumfänge für den neuen Audi A4. Inzwischen verlassen mehr als 4 Millionen Teile pro Jahr das Werk im Vogtland.
Weiteres Wachstum mit neuen Aufträgen ist Ziel von Weidmann. Genügend Fläche steht dafür zur Verfügung.

Das Weidmann-Werk mit seiner technisch hoch modernen Ausrüstung an Spritzgiessmaschinen, Handhabungs- und Automatisierungstechnik, Montage, Werkzeuginstandhaltung und Logistik braucht zum

störungsfreien Betrieb und zur Sicherung höchster Lieferqualität gegenüber den Kunden natürlich gute Fachkräfte. Diesen Bedarf versucht man, gezielt aus der Region abzudecken. Auch der Ausbildung eigener Lehrlinge kommt deshalb große Bedeutung zu. Zwei Auszubildende pro Ausbildungsjahr sind in der Firma integriert. Zu den Hochschulen in der näheren Umgebung bestehen aus gleichem Grund gute Kontakte; Weidmann bietet Studenten eine Plattform für Studien- und Diplomarbeiten – Übernahme in ein Anstellungsverhältnis nach Ende des Studiums nicht ausgeschlossen.

The car supplier region has gained a new renowned branch representative with Weidmann Plastics Technology Deutschland AG in Treuen. The company belongs to the Swiss WICOR-Group (Weidmann International Corporation) with its domicile in Rapperswil at the Zürich lake.
With the sector Plastics Technology, the WICOR Group is a leading developer and producer of synthetic components in the field of fresh air management and in-mould decoration.

The core competences are the mastery of state-of-the-art-technologies relating to injection moulding in all its variations, including the multi-component-technique in the sectors vehicle construction, sanitary-, sensor- and medicine technology.

At the site in Treuen and with around 200 employees in the 3- and 4-shifts-system, Weidmann produces exacting synthetic components in the field of fresh air management and door elements for major customers in the automobile industry. The new model ranges of the 1series and 3series by BMW, the Peugeot 207 and the new C-class by Daimler AG are equipped with those components. The recent commencement in production is scopes of supply for the new Audi A4. Since then, more than 4 million parts per year have left the plant in Vogtland. Weidmann's purpose is further growth through new orders. There is enough room for this aim to be achieved.

The Weidmann-plant with its technically highly modern equipment of injection moulding machines, operation- and automation technology, assembly, tool maintenance and logistics of course needs skilled employees for trouble-free handling and for securing of the highest delivery quality for the customers. We try to cover this need directly from the region. Therefore, great importance is attached to the training of our own apprentices. Two apprentices are integrated in the company each year. By the same token, we have made good contact with universities in the vicinity; Weidmann offers students a platform for student research projects and diploma theses – being taken on as an employee with a work contract after termination of studies is absolutely possible.

WEIDMANN
PLASTICS TECHNOLOGY

Weidmann Plastics Technology Deutschland AG
Treuener Höhe 3 · D - 08233 Treuen
Telefon +49 (0) 37468 681-0
Telefax +49 (0) 37468 681-186
info.plastics@weidmann-plastics.com
www.weidmann-plastics.com

(Fotos/Photos by Igor Pastierovic, Text/Text by Weidmann)

Wir machen alles was kommt.
We Do Anything That Comes

Stolfig® gibt es in Deutschland, in Tschechien und China, insgesamt vier Niederlassungen in drei verschiedenen Ländern. Darüber hinaus hat das Unternehmen mehrere Vertriebsbüros an strategisch wichtigen Standorten. Ursprünglich wollte Peter Stolfig nur eine Maschine in Pausa kaufen, entschied sich dann für den gesamten Betrieb und gründete 1999 die STOLFIG GmbH Pausa. Heute sind an diesem Standort 40 Mitarbeiter beschäftigt. Die Lehrlinge haben beste Chancen als Facharbeiter übernommen zu werden.

Die Besonderheit des Unternehmens besteht darin, dass Teile und Systeme entwickelt, konstruiert und produziert werden können. Ein hohes Potential an Kreativität und Ingenieurwissen verbunden mit hochqualifizierten anpassungsfähigen Mitarbeitern und der moderne Maschinenpark ermöglichen dem Betrieb, sich rasch auf die sich stetig ändernden Anforderungen, speziell im Automobilbau, einzustellen. Für die besondere Flexibilität sorgt außerdem, dass das benötigte Werkzeug in der Firma selbst hergestellt werden. Als Partner der Industrie produziert, fertigt und vertreibt die Stolfig® Group seit mehr als 15 Jahren Vorserien-, Serienteile, Serienwerkzeuge und Modelle aus Stahl, Aluminium, Magnesium oder Kunststoff. Porsche, VW, Mercedes-Benz, Webasto, Audi, Skoda, Continental Bugatti, um nur einige Auftraggeber zu nennen, vertrauen auf die Leistungen von Stolfig®. Das Leistungsspektrum reicht von CAD-Technologien mit CATIA-Software über CNC-Fräsen, Kanten und Umformen, dreidimensionaler Lasertechnik, der patentierten Schweißtechnologie, Erodieren (Drahtschneiden), genauester Messtechnik bis hin zu verschiedenen Fügetechniken. Der technische Geschäftsführer der STOLFIG GmbH in Pausa bringt es auf den Punkt:. „Wir machen alles was kommt und machen alles möglichst möglich."

Der Leichtbau aus Stahl, Aluminium und Magnesium ist der zentrale Schwerpunkt der Stolfig® Group. Hier forscht und entwickelt das Unternehmen zusammen mit renommierten Hochschulen und Forschungseinrichtungen. Eine patentierte Magnesiumlegierung (MnE21) aus eigener Entwicklung zeichnet sich durch hohe Druck-, Hitze- und Korrosionsbeständigkeit aus und wird mit einem eigens dafür entwickelten Verfahren verarbeitet. Außerdem hat das Unternehmen ein neues Verfahren zur Serienherstellung von Magnesium-Blechteilen entwickelt, um die derzeitigen Prototypenpreise für Magnesium-Blechteile drastisch zu senken. In den neuen Fertigungs- und Produktionshallen wird man mit diesen innovativen Verfahren in Serienfertigung gehen.

Stolfig® operates in Germany, the Czech Republic and China, with four branches in three different countries. The company also has several sales offices at strategically important locations.

At the outset Peter Stolfig just wanted to buy a machine in Pausa, but then he decided to buy up the whole company and he founded STOLFIG GmbH Pausa in 1999. The company now employs 40 members of staff at this site. Apprentices have a very good chance of being employed as specialists after completing their training.

The special thing about the company is that it develops, designs and produces parts and systems. A high degree of creativity and engineering expertise coupled with highly qualified and adaptable staff and a modern range of machinery allows the company to adapt quickly to demands that are constantly changing, particularly in the automobile sector. The company is particularly flexible because the tools required are manufactured by the firm.

The Stolfig® Group is a partner to industrial companies and has been making pre-series and series production parts, series production tools and design models made of steel, aluminium, magnesium or plastic for more than 15 years. Porsche, VW, Mercedes-Benz, Webasto, Audi, Skoda, Continental Bugatti – to name just a few customers – trust the work carried out by Stolfig®. The spectrum of products ranges from CAD technologies using CATIA software to CNC milling, chamfering and shaping, three-dimensional laser engineering, a patented welding technique, erosion (wire-cutting), high-precision testing methods and even includes various joint techniques. The technical manager at STOLFIG GmbH in Pausa summarises things succinctly: "We do anything that comes and make anything possible to the greatest possible degree."

The Stolfig® Group mainly focuses on lightweight construction using steel, aluminium or magnesium. The company is carrying out research and development in conjunction with well-known universities and research institutions. A patented magnesium alloy (MnE21), which the company has developed, has a high degree of resistance to pressure, heat and corrosion and it is made using a process specially developed for this purpose. The company has also developed a new process for the series production of magnesium sheet metal parts in order to drastically reduce the current price of prototypes made from this kind of metal. The company will start series production using these innovative processes in the new production workshops.

ALUMINIUM MAGNESIUM STAHL KUNSTSTOFF

STOLFIG GmbH Pausa
Neukirchener Straße 12
D-07952 Pausa
Telefon +49 (0) 37432 602-0
Telefax +49 (0) 37432 602-12
pausa@stolfig.com
www.stolfig.com

(Fotos/Photos by Igor Pastierovic, Übersetzung/Translated by David Strauss)

C. H. Müller GmbH

Bewährtes und Know-how verbinden
Combining Proven Methods and Expertise

Innovation, Reaktionsfähigkeit und Flexibilität, Termintreue sowie ein hoch entwickeltes Qualitäts- und Umweltbewusstsein – das sind unsere Stärken. Am 09.09.1868 legte Carl Heinrich Müller den Grundstein für über 135 Jahre bewegte Firmengeschichte. Zu allen Zeiten setzte die Firmenleitung auf die Verbindung von Bewährtem mit hochmodernem Know-how und Technik.

In den letzten Jahren hat sich unser Unternehmen zu einem der Marktführer im Bereich Kaschierungen und Beschichtungen in Europa entwickelt. Neben den traditionellen Techniken, wie der Verarbeitung von Dispersionsklebstoffen und der Flammkaschierung, haben wir schon frühzeitig in Technologien, die mit Hotmelts arbeiten, investiert und können heute ein sehr breites Spektrum an Kaschiertechnik und Weiterverarbeitung anbieten.

Zur optischen Kontrolle des Materials stehen fünf modernst ausgerüstete Warenschau-Maschinen und zwei kombinierte Zuschnitt- und Warenschausysteme mit computergestützter Fehlererfassung zur Verfügung. Sie werden selbst den strengsten Anforderungen der Automobilzulieferindustrie gerecht. C. H. Müller verfügt zusätzlich über zwei Maschinen zur Herstellung von rechteckigen Zuschnitten sowie Längsschnitt von Rollenware und einen vollautomatischen Zuschnittautomaten. Die Herstellung von Stanz- und Zuschnittteilen aller Art und Form aus kaschierten und beschichteten Materialien komplettiert das umfangreiche Dienstleistungsangebot.

C. H. Müller definiert sich durch Innovation in Verbindung mit modernster Technik durch alle Fertigungsstufen. Aus diesem Grund setzen wir auch zukünftig auf modernste Lasertechnologie – vielseitig einsetzbar für die Herstellung von Zuschnitten aus Rollware und die individuelle Gestaltung von Dekormaterialien aus Textil bis hin zu Echt- und Kunstledern.

Wichtige Instrumente, um diese hohen Anforderungen durchzusetzen, sind die Qualitätssicherung, der Einsatz umweltfreundlicher Materialien und Prozesse und eine optimale Arbeits- und Brand-Sicherheit in allen Bereichen des Unternehmens. Ein gut geschultes und sich permanent weiter bildendes Team mit langjähriger Berufserfahrung überwacht alle Prozesse und unterzieht im werkseigenen Labor die verarbeiteten Materialien den mit unseren Kunden vereinbarten Prüfungen. Ein speziell für uns entwickeltes PPS-System und die qualifizierte Arbeit mit dem IMDS unterstützen unser integriertes Q.U.S.-Managementsystem.

Innovation, the ability to react and flexibility, adherence to delivery dates and a highly developed awareness of quality and environmental issues are our strengths. Carl Heinrich Mueller laid the foundation stone for more than 135 years of eventful company history on 9 September 1868. The company managers have succeeded in combining proven methods and the latest expertise and technology at all times.

Our company has become a market leader in the field of lamination work and coatings in Europe over the past few years. We have continued to use traditional technologies like processing dispersion glues and flame lamination, but we also invested in technologies that work with hot melts at an early stage and so we are able to provide a very wide range of lamination and finishing technologies.

Five of the latest highly sophisticated inspection machines and two combined cut and inspection systems with computer-aided error detection are available to check the materials optically. They even meet the most stringent demands made by the automotive supply industry. C. H. Müller also has two machines to make rectangular and longitudinal blanks on rolled materials and a fully automated blanking machine. The comprehensive range of services is rounded off by the capability to manufacture all kinds of stamped and blanked parts from laminated and coated materials.

Innovation combined with the latest technology is the hallmark of C. H. Müller at every stage of the production processes. This is the reason why we are putting our faith in the latest laser technology for the future – it can be used in many ways to cut blanks from rolled materials and provide individual designs for decorative materials made of different textiles, even including real and imitation leather.

The company uses important tools to meet these high demands; they include quality assurance, the use of eco-friendly materials and processes and the best possible occupational health and safety and fire protection in all areas of the business. A well-trained team, which is constantly gaining further training and has many years of experience, monitors all the processes; it also uses the company laboratory to subject the processed materials to the tests that have been agreed with our customers. Our integrated QES management system is backed up by a production planning and monitoring system developed by ourselves and skilful use of the International Materials Data System.

C. H. Müller GmbH
Gewerbering 1
D-08468 Heinsdorfergrund
Telefon +49 (0) 3765 3939 42
Telefax +49 (0) 3765 3827 82
info@chmueller.de · www.chmueller.de

(Fotos/Photos by Igor Pastierovic, Übersetzung/Translated by David Strauss)

Autohaus Meinhold GmbH

Tradition und Fortschritt kennzeichnen unser Unternehmen.
Tradition and Progress Are the Hallmarks of Our Company.

Das Autohaus Meinhold wurde am 16. Januar 1978 als Kfz-Werkstatt von Jürgen Meinhold in Jägersgrün innerhalb des elterlichen Fuhrbetriebes gegründet. Daraus entwickelte sich in dreißig Jahren Firmengeschichte ein mittelständisches Unternehmen mit zwei Standorten, 60 Mitarbeitern und derzeit 8 Auszubildenden. In der zurückliegenden Firmengeschichte wurde das Service- und Dienstleistungsangebot ständig und kontinuierlich erweitert und konsequent auf die Kundenbedürfnisse ausgerichtet. Automobile Begeisterung und hohes fachliches Können sind die Eckpfeiler des Autohauses.

Die unternehmerischen Erfolge zeigten sich rasch und sind ganz konkret in Jahreszahlen zu belegen: Im Jahr 1980 erhielt der Kfz-Meister einen Vertrag mit dem VEB Sachsenring Automobilwerk in Zwickau. Die Mitarbeiterzahl wuchs bis 1989 auf zehn Mitarbeiter. Bereits im Mai 1990 schloss VW mit dem Handwerksmeister aus dem Vogtland einen Händlervertrag ab. Im Juni 1992 wurde am heutigen Standort in Auerbach-Rebesgrün der Grundstein für einen Firmenneubau gelegt. Die Einweihung des VW- und Audi-Autohauses auf dem 8,5 Hektar großen Grundstück erfolgte am 04. Dezember 1992.

Im Zuge der Markenseparierung wurde am 01. Mai 2000 das Audi-Autohaus Meinhold in Rodewisch (Gewerbepark Göltzschtal) eröffnet. Im März 2006 wurde das VW Autohaus (Werkstraße 6) umgebaut. Ein neues „Outfit" soll allen Kunden und Besuchern einen optimalen Eindruck von Harmonie und Sachlichkeit vermitteln.

Das alles verdeutlicht, dass das Traditionsunternehmen Autohaus Meinhold den Wechsel vom klassischen Reparaturbetrieb hin zum modernen Mobilitätsdienstleister vollzogen hat.

Die Qualifikationen der Mitarbeiter in Verbindung mit modernster Technik hat sich mit den Ansprüchen der Kunden entwickelt, so dass das volle Leistungsspektrum in beiden Betriebsstätten abgedeckt werden kann. Es umfasst nicht nur den Handel mit Neu- und Gebrauchtfahrzeugen, sondern auch alle vielfältigen Serviceleistungen rund ums Auto im eigenen Haus. Dazu gehören die Bereiche der Autoelektrik und Karosserieklempnerei genauso wie die spezialisierte Fahrzeuglackierung.

Besuchen Sie uns auf der Internetseite **www.autohaus-meinhold.de.** Hier finden Sie nähere Informationen zu den beiden Standorten. Oder am besten Sie kommen gleich bei uns vorbei!

The Meinhold Car Dealership was founded by Jürgen Meinhold in Jägersgrün on 16 January 1978 as a garage within his parents' haulage company. In the thirty years of company history it has developed into a medium-sized enterprise with two branches, 60 employees and 8 trainees at the moment. The company's history has been marked by the constant and ongoing expansion of the range of services on offer in order to meet customer demand. The pillars of the dealership are an enthusiasm for motor cars and a high degree of specialist skills.

The company successes can be quickly documented quite specifically by looking at the year dates: the master mechanic obtained a contract to work with the Sachsenring Automobile Combine in Zwickau in 1980. The number of employees had risen to ten by 1989. VW signed a dealership agreement with the master craftsman from the Vogtland region as early as May 1990. The foundation stone for a new company building was laid in June 1992 at the current premises in Auerbach-Rebesgrün. The inauguration of the VW and Audi dealership took place at the 8.5 hectare site on 4 December 1992.

As part of the separation of the brands, the Meinhold Audi dealership opened in Rodewisch (Göltzsch Valley business park) on 1 May 2000. The VW garage (Werkstraße 6) was rebuilt in March 2006. A new outfit was designed to give customers and visitors an ideal impression of harmony and practicality.

All this makes clear that the traditional Meinhold car dealership has completed the switch from a classical repair shop to a modern mobility service company.

The qualifications of the employees and the latest technology have kept pace with customer requirements so that the full package of services can be provided at both places of business. This not only covers doing business with new and used vehicles, but also a variety of services related to cars on company premises. These include car electrics, bodywork repairs and special vehicle paintwork.

Visit us at our Internet website: www.autohaus-meinhold.de

Here you will find more detailed information on the two business sites. Or why not call in? That is an even better idea!

Autohaus Meinhold GmbH
Werkst. 6 · 08209 Auerbach/Rebesgrün
Tel. 03744 2507-0 · Fax 03744 2507-20
Göltzschtalblick 2a · 08228 Rodewisch
Tel. 03744 188-0 · Fax 03744 188-120
info@autohaus-meinhold.de
www.autohaus-meinhold.de

(Fotos/Photos by Autohaus Meinhold GmbH, Hartmut Briese, Übersetzung/Translated by David Strauss)

Marken versprechen! Aber sie verpflichten auch.

Brands Promise Much – But Have to Deliver the Goods.

Wer eine Marke erfolgreich führen will, ist verpflichtet, ihr Versprechen konsequent einzulösen. Und damit nichts Geringeres zu tun, als die daran geknüpften Erwartungen des Kunden uneingeschränkt zu erfüllen.

Das Autohaus OPPEL mit Betriebsstätten in Plauen, Ellefeld und Aue hat sich seit 80 Jahren der Premiummarke Mercedes-Benz erfolgreich verschrieben. Das 160-köpfige Mitarbeiterteam um Geschäftsführer Gerhard Nadolny weiß sehr genau um die hohen Qualitätsstandards in jedem einzeln Geschäftsbereich. „Nicht nur der Name allein, sondern die spürbare Leistung, die dahinter steht, macht eine Marke erst zu einem wertigen Symbol", weiß man im Hause Oppel.

Die Kompetenz des Autohauses OPPEL findet sich in den Sparten: PERSONENWAGEN, TRANSPORTER und LASTKRAFTWAGEN. Dies nicht nur allein im Verkauf sondern natürlich auch im Kundendienst Damit gehört das Unternehmen in der Automobilbrache zu den wenigen Anbietern, die Gewerbe-, Geschäfts- und Privatkunden gleichermaßen umfassend bedienen und betreuen können. Höchste Priorität genießt dabei ein sehr hoher Ausbildungsstand der Mitarbeiter im fachlichen aber auch persönlichen Bereich. „Ständige Fortbildung und Entwicklung unserer Mitarbeiter ist die Basis einer nachhaltigen Kundenzufriedenheit und eines letztlich langfristig erfolgreichen Unternehmens" berichtet Gerhard Nadolny und führt weiter an: „ Unser Geschäft ist überwiegend lokal fokussiert und so bemühen wir uns stets, unseren Personalbedarf aus unserer Wirtschaftsregion zu decken um so auch unsere Verbundenheit zu beweisen. Höchstmögliche Integration in das wirtschaftliche, gesellschaftliche und soziale Umfeld ist uns einfach ein besonderes Bedürfnis". Die große Akzeptanz, die das Unternehmen bei den hochwertigen Präsentationen, Veranstaltungen und Events erfährt, beweist die Richtigkeit dieser Philosophie!

Im Vogtland leisten die Verkaufs- und Serviceteams der Oppel-Gruppe einen wertvollen Beitrag, die Premiummarke Mercedes-Benz mit Leidenschaft, Sachverstand und absoluter Kundenorientierung erstklassigt zu positionieren.

Anybody who wants to successfully market a brand has to make sure that the goods live up to their promises. This means nothing less than ensuring that you meet customer expectations to the full.

OPPEL car dealership with its branches in Plauen, Ellefeld and Aue has been committed to the Mercedes-Benz premium brand for 80 years. The 160 members of staff along and managing director Gerhard Nadolny are very aware that high quality standards have to pervade each business division. "The name alone does not make a brand a quality symbol, but the tangible service that goes along with it," is the motto at the OPPEL dealership.

The expertise at OPPEL is spread over three lines of business: CARS, VANS and LORRIES – and not just in sales, but also in customer services. The company is one of the few in the motor vehicle business, which serves and looks after commercial, business and private customers at the same time. This means that the staff have to be trained to a very high degree in how to handle the technical details and people. "Providing ongoing further training and development for our members of staff is the foundation for customer satisfaction and in the end for a company that is going to be a success in the long term," says Gerhard Nadolny and continues: "Our business largely focuses on the local area and so we are always seeking to cover our personnel needs from the business region to demonstrate our commitment to this area. We really sense the need to be fully integrated in the business and social environment." The truth of this philosophy is demonstrated by the degree of acceptance, which the company enjoys at high-quality presentations and events!

The sales and services teams in the OPPEL Group with their enthusiasm, expert knowledge and clear customer focus are playing a major role in ensuring that the Mercedes-Benz premium brand enjoys a high reputation in the Vogtland region.

Oppel GmbH
Autorisierter Mercedes-Benz
Verkauf & Service
Dresdener Str. 14 · D-08529 Plauen
Telefon   +49 (0) 3741 456-0
Telefax   +49 (0) 3741 456 - 282
info@Oppel-Automobile.de
www.Oppel-Automobile.de

(Fotos/Photos by Igor Pastierovic, Text/Text by André Zeidler, Übersetzung/Translated by David Strauss)

Autohaus Strauß GmbH

Das Plus an Leistung macht den Unterschied

The Extra Service Makes the Difference

Unter dem Motto: „Wir beraten wie ein Freund", kümmern sich die Mitarbeiter der vier Filialen der Autohaus Strauß GmbH um ihre Kunden und solche, die es werden sollten. Besonders stolz ist das Unternehmen auf die Verleihung des Titels „Erfolgspartner der BMW Group" im Jahre 2002 und die erfolgreiche Titelverteidigung im Februar 2005, denn nur wenige BMW Händler in Deutschland erreichen diesen hohen Standard innerhalb der BMW Group.

Vertreten durch die Geschäftsführer Sören Strauß und Andreas Scholz ist die Autohaus Strauß GmbH ein erfolgreiches vogtländisches Unternehmen der Automobilbranche, welches den kompletten Service der Produkte von BMW und MINI bearbeitet, durchgängig kompetente Beratungen durchführt und exklusiv die Kunden betreut.

Mit 5 Mitarbeitern begann alles 1992 in einer ehemaligen LPG in der Nähe von Oelsnitz. Enthusiasmus und der konsequente Wille, den Ansprüchen der Kunden stets gerecht zu werden, machte es erforderlich, 1994 das Autohaus Oelsnitz, Willy-Brandt-Ring 17, auf einem über 5.000 m² großen Firmengelände zu eröffnen. Ein weiterer Meilenstein in der Firmenentwicklung war im Jahr 2001 die Eröffnung der ersten Filiale in Plauen. Auf einem über 15.000 m² großen Gelände bietet der Neubau an der Pausaer Straße den Kunden auch hier Service vom Feinsten. Ende 2002 arbeiteten bereits 54 Mitarbeiter in den bis dahin zwei modernen Autohäusern.

Under the slogan "We advise you like a friend", the staff at the four branches of Autohaus Strauss GmbH are very careful about the way they look after their customers and those about to join their number. The company is particularly proud of having been awarded the title "Successful Partner in the BMW Group" in 2002 – and having successfully defended this title in February 2005 – as only very few BMW dealers in Germany have achieved this high standard within the BMW Group.

Represented by the managers Sören Strauss and Andreas Scholz, Autohaus Strauss GmbH is a successful Vogtland company in the automobile sector. The firm provides complete services for the BMW and MINI brands, consistent expert advice and looks after its customers in an exclusive manner.

It all began in 1992 with 5 members of staff in a former agricultural combine building near Oelsnitz. Enthusiasm and the consistent desire to always meet customer requirements made it necessary to open the Oelsnitz dealership on Willy-Brandt-Ring 17 in 1994 on premises measuring more than 5,000 m². The opening of the second branch in Plauen in 2001 marked a further milestone in the company's development. The new building on Pausaer Street provides customers with the very best in service on a site measuring more than 15,000 m². By the end of 2002 those working at the two modern car dealerships already numbered 54.

(Fotos/Photos by Igor Pastierovic [6] Autohaus Strauß GmbH, Hartmut Briese, Übersetzung/Translated by David Strauss)

Autohaus Strauß GmbH

Der gute Ruf, das Vertrauen der Kunden und vor allem der bekannte Service der Mitarbeiter der Autohaus Strauß GmbH eilten dem Unternehmen voraus und so wurde nach umfangreichen Renovierungs- und Modernisierungsarbeiten im Februar 2003 die zweite Filiale eröffnet. Mit der Eröffnung der Auerbacher Filiale entstand ein weiterer kompetenter BMW und MINI Service- und Verkaufsstandort im Vogtland und 75 Mitarbeiter kümmern sich vogtlandweit um die Belange der Kunden.

Doch damit nicht genug – im Herbst 2007 verschlägt es die geschäftstüchtigen Vogtländer in die Stadt Zwickau auf den Windberg. Entstanden ist eine automobile Erlebniswelt. Und wie das bei Strauß so üblich ist, erwartet auch dort ein hoch motiviertes und qualifiziertes Team interessierte BMW und MINI Fahrer und solche, die es werden wollen. Die bewährte erfolgreiche Firmen- und Markenphilosophie zum Nutzen der Kunden umzusetzen – das haben sich die Mitarbeiter der neuen Filiale auf die Fahnen geschrieben. Neben BMW ist in der neuen MINI Lounge der Auftritt dieser Lifestylemarke mit unverwechselbarem Fahrerlebnis, welches das Autohaus Strauß als Markenhändler in Südwestsachsen exklusiv vertritt, zu erleben.

Mit großer Freude und ausgerüstet mit modernster Technik arbeiten mittlerweile rund 90 Mitarbeiter in vier Filialen. Durch fachkundige Beratung in den Bereichen Neue und Gebrauchte Automobile vermitteln die Verkaufsberater den Kunden die ganze Faszination der Marken BMW und MINI. Und da in die Autolandschaft von heute keine Autohäuser von gestern passen, dürfen wir gespannt sein, was das Autohaus Strauß in Zukunft noch für die Liebhaber der Marken BMW und MINI im Petto hat.

The good reputation, the confidence of customers and, above all, the renowned service provided by the staff at Autohaus Strauss GmbH spread rapidly and after a great deal of redevelopment and modernisation work, the company opened its third branch in February 2003. The opening of the Auerbach branch provided the Vogtland region with another competent BMW and MINI sales and service centre; by now 75 members of staff were looking after customer needs around the Vogtland region.

But that was not the end of the story. The enterprising Vogtland company also landed in the city of Zwickau on the Windberg in the autumn of 2007. The company has created a world of adventure for car lovers. And as it quite normal with Strauss, a highly motivated and qualified team awaits interested BMW and MINI drivers and those wishing to join their number. The staff at the new branch are taking up the cause of upholding the tried and tested company and brand philosophy for the benefit of customers. The two lifestyle brands can be enjoyed in the new MINI Lounge with the unmistakeable driving experience of these cars, for which Autohaus Strauss is the sole official dealer in South-West Saxony.

About 90 members of staff now work at the four branches and combine a great deal of enthusiasm with the latest technology. The sales staff provide customers with expert advice on both new and used vehicles in the fascinating world of the BMW and MINI brands. And as yesterday's car dealers do not fit into today's car world, we can only wait with bated breath to see what Autohaus Strauss has in store for lovers of the BMW and MINI brands in future.

Autohaus Strauß GmbH
Willy-Brandt-Ring 17
08606 Oelsnitz/V.
Telefon 037421/465-0

Filiale Plauen
Pausaer Straße 190
08525 Plauen
Telefon 03741/5574-0

Filiale Auerbach
Willy-Brandt-Straße 11
08209 Auerbach/V.
Telefon 03744/8359-0

Filiale Zwickau
Werdauer Straße 164
Telefon 0375/440066-0

Hotline 0180/55 74 000
www.bmw-strauss.de

Seidenweberei PONGS GmbH

Der Stoff, aus dem Faszination gemacht wird
The Material that Creates a Sense of Fascination

Die Seidenweberei **PONGS** in Mühltroff hat mit reiner technischer Weberei erfolgreich eine Marktnische am deutschen und internationalen Markt besetzt. Eine vollstufige Produktion technischer Gewebe im Bereich von fünf Metern Breite sowie Digitaldruck in Großformaten machte das Unternehmen zum Marktführer. Damit beweist **PONGS** mit heute ca. 120 Beschäftigten, darunter 18 Auszubildenden, dass die Textilbranche keinesfalls so angekratzt ist wie ihr Image. Im Jahre 1992 übernahm die **PONGS** Unternehmensgruppe Stadtlohn die Mühltroffer Weberei mit ca. 30 Mitarbeitern, die ausschließlich Futterstoffe herstellte. Über 35 Mio. Euro wurden in die Erweiterung der Produktionsanlagen und in den Bau von neuen Produktions- und Fertigungshallen investiert. Noch einmal neun Mio. Euro Investitionen sieht der aktuelle Investplan für bauliche und ausrüstungstechnische Ausgaben bis 2010 vor.

Mit eigener Produktionsvorbereitung, Schärerei, Färberei, Web- und Digitaldruckmaschinen im 5-Meter-Bereich ist **PONGS** heute in der Lage, den gesamten Produktionsablauf vom Entwurf bis zum fertigen Produkt vor Ort zu steuern. Dieses Know How ist weltweit einzigartig. Damit ist das Unternehmen aufgestellt, auf Marktentwicklungen und Kundenwünsche aktuell, kompetent und zuverlässig zu reagieren. Die beschichteten oder unbeschichteten Gewebe und Gewirke für den Digital- und Transferdruck kommen unter anderem als Akustik- oder Spanndecken in der Altbausanierung sowie Sonnenschutz zum Einsatz. Aber auch der Messe-, Bühnen oder Theaterbau sind Abnehmer. Nicht zuletzt stammt so mancher Dekostoff für die Schauwerbung aus Mühltroff. Nach Europa, Osteuropa und den USA gehören zunehmend auch Nationen weltweit zu den Abnehmern. Dies nicht zuletzt, da sich die **PONGS** Gruppe auf nahezu allen namhaften Textilmessen präsentiert. Sowohl Umsatz- als auch Auftragslage stellt die Geschäftsführung zufrieden. Großes Augenmerk liegt derzeit darauf, das Produktionssortiment weiter auszubauen, nach neuen Märkten zu suchen und dabei den Service für die Kunden weiter zu optimieren.

The PONGS silk weaving mill in Mühltroff has filled a niche in the German and international market – it produces nothing but technical textiles. The complete production of these technical textiles measuring up to 5m wide and large format digital printing have made the company a market leader in this field. PONGS has approximately 120 employees, including 18 apprentices, and proves that the textile industry is not as tarnished as its image. The PONGS group from Stadtlohn took over the weaving mill in Mühltroff In 1992; it had about 30 employees and only produced lining materials at that time. More than € 35 million have been invested in the expansion of the production plants and the construction of new production and processing sites since then. The company's current investment plan envisages that a further € 9 million will be spent on construction work and machinery by 2010.

PONGS is able to handle the complete production process from the design to the final product at its site, as it has its own departments for production preparation, warping and dying and web or digital printing machines that are up to 5m wide. This expertise is unique in the world. It allows the company to react to market developments and customer requests in an immediate, competent and reliable manner. The coated or plain fabrics and woven fabrics for digital and transfer printing are used for sound insulation or suspended ceilings when upgrading buildings or as sunshade fabrics. But their products are also used for construction work at trade fairs, on stages or in theatres. And some of the decorative fabrics used in advertisements may even come from Mühltroff. Europe, Eastern Europe and the USA are not the only destinations for its products: more and more of their customers come from nations scattered around the world - not least because the PONGS Group attends almost all the well-known textile trade fairs around the globe. The company's managers are delighted by the order books and turnover. The focus at the moment is on further expanding the product range, looking for new markets and improving services for customers.

PONGS SEIDENWEBEREI

Seidenweberei PONGS GmbH
Werk Mühltroff
Bahnhofstraße 21 · 07979 Mühltroff
Telefon +49 (0) 36645 350-0
Telefax +49 (0) 36645 350-99
www.pongs.de

(Fotos/Photos by Igor Pastierovic, Text/Text by Martina Meier, Übersetzung/Translated by David Strauss)

Technischen Textilien gehört die Zukunft
Technical Textiles Have a Great Future

Der traditionsreiche Studiengang Textil- und Ledertechnik der Westsächsischen Hochschule (FH) am Hochschulteil Reichenbach ist gefragter denn je. Absolventen der Hochschule verfügen über das notwendige Know-How, um den bedeutenden Anforderungen in diesem Wachstumsmarkt gerecht zu werden. Diplomingenieure für Textil- und Ledertechnik (FH) werden deutschlandweit nur in der Fachgruppe Textil- und Ledertechnik (TLT) am Hochschulteil Reichenbach der Westsächsischen Hochschule Zwickau (WHZ) ausgebildet.

Seit 1994 gehört die einstige traditionsreiche „Höhere Textilfachschule" und spätere Ingenieurschule für Textiltechnik zur WHZ. Das Einmaleins für Ingenieure wird während der ersten beiden Semester überwiegend in Zwickau gelehrt. Nach dem ingenieurtechnischen Grundlagenstudium werden im Fachstudium zunächst alle technologischen Schritte für die Herstellung von Textilien und Leder beginnend beim Rohstoff bis zum fertig konfektionierten Produkt gelehrt. Das Fachstudium am Reichenbacher Hochschulteil ist nach den wirtschaftlichen Anforderungen der deutschen und internationalen Textilindustrie konzipiert.

Reichenbach kennen die Lehrkräfte ihre Studenten noch namentlich, obwohl seit 2003 stets mehr als 30 „Neue" immatrikuliert wurden. „Die geringen Matrikelstärken sind von Vorteil. Die Ausbildung ist praxisorientiert, so wie es an einer Fachhochschule sein soll. Wir haben hier alle möglichen Maschinen und bekommen jedes Zahnrad erklärt. Wir dürfen nähen, drucken und kreativ sein", lobt die Studentin Marleen Ahnert (Matrikel 2001) die Bedingungen.

In den zum Teil hoch modern ausgerüsteten Technika wird sowohl praxisrelevant gelehrt als auch innovativ geforscht. Die Fachgruppe arbeitet in der Textilforschung mit anderen Bereichen der WHZ zusammen, zum Beispiel mit der Kraftfahrzeugtechnik auf dem Gebiet der Faserverbundwerkstoffe.

Ein weiterer Forschungsschwerpunkt ist das Sticken, welches traditionell in der Region beheimatet ist. Hier werden sowohl künstlerische als auch rein technische Themen bearbeitet.

The traditional textile and leather engineering course at Zwickau University of Applied Sciences in Reichenbach is more in demand than ever before. Graduates from this university have the necessary expertise to meet the challenging demands of this growth market. The Reichenbach branch of Zwickau University of Applied Sciences is the only place in Germany where graduate engineers in textile and leather technology (TLT) are trained.

The former "Higher Textile College", which later became the Engineering School for Textile Technology, has been part of Zwickau University of Applied Sciences since 1994. The fundamentals are mainly taught during the first two semesters in Zwickau. After the basic engineering course, all the technological stages for producing textiles and leather are taught, starting from the raw materials and progressing to the finished product. The specialist studies at the university department in Reichenbach are designed to meet the business requirements of the German and international textile industry.

In Reichenbach, the teaching staff still know all their students by name although there have always been more than 30 "new" entrants every year since 2003. "The low numbers of students starting are an advantage. The training is practically oriented, as it should be at a university of applied sciences. We have all kinds of machines here and every single cogwheel is explained. We are allowed to sew, print and be creative", says student Marleen Ahnert (who started in 2001), praising the conditions.

The technical centre, parts of which have been modernised, is used both for highly practical teaching and as an innovative research centre. This specialist group is working on textile research with other departments at the university – for example on fibre composites with the motor vehicle technology department.

Embroidery, which has its roots in this area, is another area of research; work in this field covers artistic and also purely technical themes.

(Fotos/Photos by Kersten Mahler (4), Text/Text by Fachbereiche, Übersetzung/Translated by David Strauss)

Textil- und Ledertechnik – eine Tradition mit Zukunft

Textiles and Leather Engineering – a Tradition with a Future

Die WHZ hat es sich zum Ziel gesetzt, als Hochschule „Rund um das Auto" zu gelten. In diesem Zusammenhang läuft ab dem Wintersemester 2006 der Diplomstudiengang (8 Semester) Textil- und Ledertechnik mit den Schwerpunkten Technische Textilien/Leder und Textilbasiertes automobiles Interieur.
„Gegenwärtig ist die Nachfrage nach jungen Textilingenieuren etwa fünfmal größer als die Absolventenzahl", meint die Fachgruppenleiterin Prof. Dr.-Ing. Silke Heßberg. Kontakte zur Wirtschaft gehören genau so zum Ausbildungsprogramm wie das Ausprobieren im Rahmen verschiedener Projekte. Bei Kontaktbörsen oder zu den jährlichen Symposien „Technische Textilien" kommen Vertreter von Textilfirmen aus ganz Europa nach Reichenbach. Sie halten Vorträge, knüpfen Kontakte oder bieten Praktikums- und Diplomthemen an. Zu bekannten vogtländischen Firmen wie Vowalon Treuen, C. H. Müller in Netzschkau/Reichenbach oder der Car Trim Gruppe Plauen gibt es enge Beziehungen. Die Textilforschungsinstitute in Greiz und Chemnitz betreuten mehrfach Diplomanden, von denen einige auf Grund ihrer sehr guten Kenntnisse als Mitarbeiter von den Instituten übernommen wurden. Gute Verbindungen existieren in Richtung Oberfranken. Von dort erhalten die Studenten häufig Einladungen zu Fachvorträgen und Kolloquien. In der Liste der Firmen für Diplomarbeiten finden sich auch BMW, Hugo Boss, die Modemission GmbH Berlin, Johnson Controls, die Volkswagen AG, das Fraunhofer Institut oder die Firma Südleder GmbH & Co. KG Rehau.
Die Studenten der Fachgruppe TLT beteiligen sich auch an Wettbewerben. So waren sie 2006 beim Digital Textile Design Award der Messe Textilveredlung & Promotion in Stuttgart vertreten. Weiterhin wurde zur Einweihung der Vogtlandschanze 2006 ein spezieller „Vogtlandpaletot" vorgestellt, der großen Anklang fand.
In den letzten drei Jahren wurden die Absolventinnen Katja Claus, Berit Winkler und Stefanie Ring durch den Verein Deutscher Textilveredlungsfachleute für die jeweils beste Diplomarbeit des Jahrganges ausgezeichnet. Die Mehrzahl der Absolventen bleibt übrigens gleich in ihrer „Diplom"-Firma. Weiterhin erhielten zwei Absolventinnen des Studienganges TLT (Constanze Simmerer und Martina Kögler) in den letzten beiden Jahren den vom Rotary-Club Plauen ausgelobten Innovationspreis für ihre Abschlussarbeiten.
Aus dem Leben der Stadt Reichenbach sind die Studenten kaum wegzudenken. An Veranstaltungen wie dem Kornblumenfest oder dem Mode-Event im Neuberinhaus nahmen sie mehrmals mit selbst gestalteten Modellen teil. Außerdem beteiligen sich die Studenten aktiv an der Vorbereitung und Durchführung solcher regionaler Höhepunkte wie dem „Tag der Sachsen" 2007 und der „Landesgartenschau" 2009. Zur internationalen Messe „Techtextil/Avantex" 2007 in Frankfurt/Main präsentierte sich die Fachgruppe TLT ebenfalls erfolgreich.

The university has set itself the goal of being viewed as the centre for "anything related to cars". As a result, a degree course in textile and leather (lasting 8 semesters) focussing on technical textiles/leather and textile-based car interiors started in the winter semester in 2006.
"Currently the demand for young textile engineers is about five times higher than the number of graduates," says department head, Professor Silke Hessberg. Contacts with business are just as much part of the training programme as experimenting on different projects. Representatives from textile companies from all over Europe come to Reichenbach as a result of networking services or to the annual "Technical Textiles" symposiums. They give lectures, make contacts or offer training placements or dissertation subject areas. There are close contacts with well-known Vogtland companies such as Vowalon Treuen, C. H. Müller in Netzschkau/Reichenbach and the Car Trim Group in Plauen. The textile research institutes in Greiz and Chemnitz have supported many students while they were writing their degree dissertation and some of the former students have started work at these centres on account of their excellent knowledge. Contacts with Upper Franconia are also good. Students often receive invitations to attend specialist lectures and conferences there. The list of companies helping with final year degree dissertations includes BMW, Hugo Boss, Modemission GmbH Berlin, Johnson Controls, Volkswagen AG, the Fraunhofer Institute and Südleder GmbH & Co. KG Rehau.
Students from the TLT department also take part in competitions. In February 2004, for example, they won the second prize at the 2nd Digital Textile Design Award at the Textile Finishing & Promotion Fair in Stuttgart. A special "Vogtland paletot" was presented at the inauguration of the Vogtland Arena in 2006 and met with high approval.
In the last three years, the graduates Katja Claus, Berit Winkler and Stefanie Ring were all highly commended by the Association of German Textile Finishing Experts for the best degree dissertation in their year. Most of the graduates stay on to work at the company where they have completed their dissertation. Two graduates from the TLT course (Constanze Simmerer and Martina Kögler) also received the Innovation Prize presented by the Rotary Club in Plauen for their final examination work.
Life in Reichenbach is hard to imagine without its students now. They have often presented their own designs at events like the Cornflower Festival or the Fashion Event in the Neuberin Theatre. The students also participated in the preparations for the 2007 "Saxon Festival" and they are working hard for the 2009 National Horticultural Show. The TLT department also successfully participated in the 2007 "Techtextil/Avantex" Fair in Frankfurt/Main.

Westsächsische Hochschule Zwickau (FH)
Hochschulteil Reichenbach
Fachbereich Textil- und Ledertechnik
www.fh-zwickau.de/textil

Fundierte Ausbildung – Visionen erlaubt

Well-Founded Training – and Visions Are Allowed

Der Fachbereich Architektur der Westsächsischen Hochschule Zwickau (WHZ) wurde 1996 an der Außenstelle in Reichenbach gegründet. Seit 2006 wird das Studium auf die an den europäischen Hochschulraum angepassten und EU-weit anerkannten Bachelor- und Master-Studiengänge umgestellt. Mit den aufeinander aufbauenden, konsekutiven Studiengängen bereiten diese umfassend auf die vielseitige Tätigkeit eines/einer Architekten/-in vor. Dabei lernen die künftigen Architektinnen und Architekten all das, was mit der Planung und dem Entwurf von Räumen, Bauwerken oder städtebaulichen Anlagen zusammenhängt. Im Fachbereich Architektur werden pro Studienjahr bis zu 40 Studierende im Bachelor-Studiengang und ab 2008 bis zu 30 Studierende im Master-Studiengang immatrikuliert. Der Bachelor-Studiengang führt zu einem ersten berufsqualifizierenden Abschluss mit der Verleihung des Grades „Bachelor of Arts". Er bereitet auf einen Berufseinstieg vor. Nach einer Praxisphase und dem erfolgreichen Abschluss des Master-Studienganges als „Master of Arts" steht ein weites Berufsfeld offen, egal ob im freien Beruf, als Mitarbeiter/'in eines Architekturbüros oder in der Verwaltung. Nach derzeit zweijähriger Berufstätigkeit ermöglicht der Masterabschluss die Eintragung in die Architektenliste der Architektenkammern und die Führung der geschützten Berufsbezeichnung „Architekt" bzw. „Architektin". Neben entwurfsmethodischen, technischen und gestalterischen Grundlagen beeinflussen auch historische, soziale, ästhetische, rechtliche, ökonomische und ökologische Aspekte die Projekte. In allen Bereichen sind deshalb Grundkenntnisse notwendig.

In Reichenbach verfügt jede/-r Student/-in über einen eigenen Arbeitsplatz mit modernster technischer Ausstattung. Im Ausbildungskonzept des Fachbereiches wird Wert auf den engen Bezug zur Praxis gelegt. In den fachübergreifend angelegten Semesterprojekten lernen die künftigen Architekten/-innen ihre Entwürfe vor Fachleuten über Pläne, Modelle und digitale Medien zu präsentieren. Dabei wurden in den vergangenen Jahren anspruchsvolle Themen bearbeitet, die sich auch in der Region verorten. Beispielsweise entwickelten die Studenten/-innen Konzepte für den „Ort der Stille" der Landesgartenschau 2009 in Reichenbach. Eines der Projekte wurde von den Verfasserinnen Andrea Böhm und Katja Henschel bis zur Ausführungsreife entwickelt und wird ab Herbst 2007 realisiert. Es wird ein introvertierter Pavillon aus 20.000 PET-Wasserflaschen entstehen. Reichenbacher Studierende beteiligten sich auch erfolgreich an regionalen und bundesweiten Wettbewerben und Preisen. Ihre Praktika absolvieren sie in renommierten Architekturbüros in Europa und darüber hinaus. Der Falkensteiner Ingo Glätsch wurde während seiner Studienzeit auf den Architekten Pius Pahl aufmerksam. Der 1909 Geborene war der letzte Student beim weltbekannten Bauhausarchitekten Ludwig Mies van der Rohe. Als Ingo Glätsch erfuhr, dass Pius Pahl in Südafrika lebt und sein Architekturbüro bei Kapstadt erst mit 90 Jahren aufgegeben hat, bemühte er sich um ein Praktikum in einem Architekturbüro bei Kapstadt. Mehrmals traf er sich mit dem bekannten Architekten und erstellte eine Foto-Recherche über dessen Bauten. An Projekten wie dem Rugby-Ausbildungszentrum Pretoria oder dem Überwachungstower im Durbaner Hafen durfte er mitwirken.

The architecture department at the West Saxon University of Applied Sciences in Zwickau (WHZ) was set up at a university facility in Reichenbach in 1996. By 2006 the course was switched to bachelor and master degrees, which have been adapted to the European university standards and are recognised throughout the EU. The programmes of study, which progress logically in a consecutive fashion, prepare students comprehensively for the all-round business of working as an architect. The future experts learn everything connected to planning and designing rooms, structures or urban facilities. As many as 40 students are studying the bachelor's course in any year and from 2008 up to 30 students will be registered for the master's course. The bachelor's course leads to the first professional qualification exams and gives students a Bachelor of Arts degree. It prepares students to start working in their career. After a practical phase and the successful completion of a further course leading to a Master of Arts degree, graduates can choose whether they wish to work on a free-lance basis, as a member of an architectural office or in administration. After two years' professional experience, the master's degree allows people to be placed on the list of architects at chambers of architects and use the legally protected title of "architect". Projects are often not only influenced by design, technical and creative principles, but also historical, social, aesthetic, legal, economic and ecological issues. So a fundamental knowledge of all these fields is essential. Each student in Reichenbach has their own workplace with the latest technical equipment. The educational concept of this specialist department places great importance on relating issues closely to everyday practice. The future architects learn how to present their designs to experts using plans, models and digital media during the semester projects, which are designed to be multidisciplinary. Challenging subjects have been tackled over the past few years, which are also rooted in the local region. For example, the students drew up concepts for a "place of quiet" for the 2009 National Horticultural Show in Reichenbach. One of the projects was developed until completion by the authors Andrea Böhm and Katja Henschel and it is being built from the autumn of 2007 onwards. It will be an inward-looking pavilion made of 20,000 PET water bottles. Students from Reichenbach have also successfully taken part in regional and national competitions and prizes. They complete their placements at renowned architectural offices in Europe and beyond. Ingo Glätsch from Falkenstein became interested in the architect Pius Pahl during his university days. The man, who was born in 1909, was the last student to learn from the world-famous Bauhaus architect Ludwig Mies van der Rohe. When Ingo Glätsch discovered that Pius Pahl was living in South Africa and had given up his architect's office near Cape Town at the age of 90, he tried to obtain a placement in an architect's office in the city. He met the famous architect on several occasions and prepared a photographic record of his buildings. He was allowed to get involved in projects like the rugby training centre in Pretoria or the control tower in Durban Harbour.

Westsächsische Hochschule Zwickau (FH)
Hochschulteil Reichenbach
Fachbereich Architektur
www.fh-zwickau.de/architektur

Studienzentrum Plauen der DIPLOMA Fachhochschule Nordhessen – Zukunftssicherung für Unternehmen

The Plauen College of the North Hessen DIPLOMA Vogtland University of Applied Sciences – Ensuring Companies have a Future

Hoch qualifizierte Fachkräfte aus der Region, für die Region, das ist das Motto der privaten, staatlich anerkannten DIPLOMA Fachhochschule Nordhessen mit ihrem Studienzentrum in Plauen.

Dieter Pfortner, Geschäftsführer von Magnetto in Treuen, ist begeistert, von dem, was dort geboten wird: „Ich kenne die Diploma nicht nur wie viele andere Geschäftsführer des Vogtlandes in ihrer Außendarstellung, sondern meine Tochter zählte zu den ersten Studenten 1998. Es wird dort insbesondere Wert auf ausschlaggebende Schwerpunkte gelegt: ökonomische Grundkenntnisse, praktische Informatik, Fremdsprachen, Teamfähigkeit, Engagement und Verantwortungsbereitschaft." Und Pfortner hat sich auch gleich einen Diploma-Absolventen, Jan Pohl, nach Abschluss des Studiums abgeholt. Pohl, noch jung an Jahren, ist heute bereits Magnetto-Personalchef und Assistent der Geschäftsführung. Doch nicht nur im Vogtland, sondern in ganz Deutschland greifen Unternehmen gern auf Diploma-Absolventen zurück, so unter anderem bei Porsche und Siemens in Leipzig, bei Mercedes sowie der MAN Druckmaschinen AG und Wincor Nixdorf.

Auf welche Fachkräfte kann ein Investor im Vogtland bei der Diploma setzen? Geboten werden gegenwärtig sowohl das Direkt- als auch das Fernstudium zum Bachelor für Betriebswirt, Wirtschaftsjuristen, Computerdesigner, Mechatroniker, Event- und Tourismusmanager sowie Fernstudiengänge für Physio- und Ergotherapeuten. Des weiteren sollen die entsprechenden Studiengänge im Fernstudium alle auch für den Master angeboten werden. Was aufhorchen lässt: Der Studiengang zum Betriebswirt ist in fünf Spezialbereichen möglich – Europäische Betriebswirtschaft, Versicherungen und Finanzdienstleistungen, Steuern und Revision, Eventmanagement sowie Hotelmanagement und Tourismus. Das Direktstudium kann durch eine straffe Organisation sogar auf drei Jahre verkürzt wer-

Highly qualified specialists from the region for the region – that is the motto of the state recognized North Hessen DIPLOMA University of Applied Sciences with a college in Plauen.

Dieter Pfortner, the managing director of Magnetto in Treuen, is thrilled by what the college has to offer. "I don't just know DIPLOMA from the outside, as many other managers in the Vogtland region do, but my daughter was one of the first students there in 1998. The college particularly focuses on crucial main themes: the fundamentals of economics, practical IT training, foreign languages, teamwork, commitment and the readiness to assume responsibility". And Mr Pfortner also immediately employed a DIPLOMA graduate, Jan Pohl, after he had completed his studies. Despite his young age, Pohl is already personnel manager at Magnetto and assistant to the management. DIPLOMA graduates are not only in demand in the Vogtland region, but all over Germany, e.g. at the Porsche and Siemens works in Leipzig, MAN Druckmaschinen AG and Wincor Nixdorf.

What kind of specialist staff from DIPLOMA can an investor in the Vogtland region expect to find? Currently there is a direct course and a correspondence course leading to bachelor degrees in business studies, business law, computer design, mechatronics, event and tourism management and a correspondence course for physiotherapy and occupational therapy. On top of this, the correspondence courses can all lead to a master's degree. What is interesting is that the course in business management covers five possible specialist areas: European business studies, insurance and financial services, tax and auditing, setting up in business and taking over a business, international accounting systems, event management, and tourism. If students are really organised, the direct course can even be completed in

(Fotos/Photos by Hartmut Briese, Text/Text by Diploma, Übersetzung/Translated by David Strauss)

DIPLOMA Studienzentrum Plauen

den. Viele Studenten arbeiten im vierten Jahr bereits bei Firmen, die sie sozusagen direkt von der Fachhochschule weg "eingekauft" haben. Damit ist die Diploma, in der es zudem kleine Seminargruppen gibt, eine persönliche Atmosphäre vorherrscht und immer ein unmittelbarer Kontakt zu den Dozenten – etwa 30 an der Zahl – gewährleistet ist, staatlichen Fachhochschulen weit voraus.

Vor allem die Praxisnähe überzeugt, die bei der Diploma sowohl von den Kommunalpolitikern als auch von Unternehmern immer wieder gelobt wird. So hat die Diploma zusammen mit dem BVMW ein Curriculum entwickelt, welches dafür sorgt, dass die Studenten so oft wie möglich in der Praxis, in den Firmen vor Ort, mit Geschäftsführern, Unternehmensgründern, Rechtsanwälten, Steuerberatern und vielen mehr zusammentreffen.

Einen in der Region völlig neuen Weg beschritt die Diploma, als sie sich 60 Studenten aus der Volksrepublik China ins Haus holte. Angestrebt werden ein Doppelabschluss mit der Universität Pilsen sowie eine Partnerschaft mit einer der Diploma vergleichbaren chinesischen Fachhochschule, so dass ein reger Studenten- und Ideenaustausch möglich wird. Einige der jungen Leute aus Asien wollen im Vogtland bleiben, und unter anderem im Bäderwesen in Bad Elster und Bad Brambach sowie in den Bereichen Wellness und Kosmetik tätig werden. Überhaupt wird an der Diploma Kreativität groß geschrieben. Ständig ist man hier auf der Suche nach neuen Studiengängen, um so den Anforderungen in der Wirtschaft noch besser gerecht zu werden. Der Prorektor Prof. Dr. Dr. Johannes Soukup: „Wir wollen auf Dauer einen wichtigen Beitrag für die Region leisten und hoffen, auch über deren Grenzen hinaus zu wirken. Geschäftsführer, Unternehmer, Verbände und Institutionen, denen wir mit unseren Angeboten möglicherweise helfen können, bitten wir, Kontakt mit uns aufzunehmen. Umgedreht sind wir dankbar für Vorschläge, Ideen und eine fruchtbare Zusammenarbeit."

three years. In their fourth year many students are already working at companies, which have "bought them up", so to speak, directly from the college. DIPLOMA is far ahead of state universities of applied science – DIPLOMA has small seminar groups, there is a personal atmosphere and direct contact with the lecturers – there are 30 of them in all – is always guaranteed.

Above all, it is DIPLOMA's emphasis on practical experience, which has drawn praise from both local politicians and companies. DIPLOMA has drawn up a curriculum in conjunction with the German Confederation of Small and Medium-Sized Businesses, which ensures that students see managers, company pioneers, lawyers, accountants and many others at work as often as possible at local companies.

DIPLOMA branched out into completely new territory for the region, when it recently accepted 60 students from the People's Republic of China. The college is seeking to establish dual qualifications with the University of Pilsen and a partnership with a Chinese University of Applied Sciences similar to DIPLOMA, so that there can be a lively exchange of students and ideas. Some of the young people from Asia want to stay in the Vogtland region and work, at the spas at Bad Elster and Bad Brambach or in the cosmetics and wellness sectors, for example. Creativity is extremely important at DIPLOMA. The staff are constantly looking for new courses in order to meet the demands of the business world even more effectively. The course section focussing on event and conference economics (event, incentive, conference and exhibition management) is probably unique in Germany. The prorector in Plauen, Prof. Dr. Dr. Johannes Soukup, says: "We want to play an important role in the region in the long term and hope to exert some influence in regions beyond. We would ask managers, entrepreneurs, associations and institutions, which we may be able to help with our courses, to get in touch with us. And in turn, we are grateful for any suggestions, ideas and fruitful cooperation."

DIPLOMA Europäische Hochschulen

DIPLOMA HOCHSCHULE
Fachhochschule Nordhessen
Studienzentrum Plauen
Rückertstraße 35 · D-08525 Plauen
Telefon +49 (0) 3741-550730
Telefax +49 (0) 3741-550733
soukup@diploma.de
www.diploma.de

Partner der Unternehmen

Die Bildungswerk der Sächsischen Wirtschaft gGmbH ist im Auftrag der sächsischen Unternehmen für Arbeitgeber und Wirtschaftsverbände tätig.

Bereits seit 1990 unterstützt das bsw mit seiner Bildungsarbeit die unternehmerischen, wirtschaftlichen und fachlichen Kompetenzen von Fachkräften und Mitarbeitern der Unternehmen, sowie von Jugendlichen und Arbeitssuchenden der Region des Vogtlandes und des Freistaates Sachsen. Dabei stehen für die Mitarbeiterinnen und Mitarbeiter die Erfüllung der Bedürfnisse der Kunden durch kompetente Beratung, zuverlässige Dienstleistung und bestmöglichen Transfer in die Praxis an erster Stelle. Die marktnahen und kundenspezifischen Bildungsprogramme steigern die Wettbewerbsfähigkeit der Kunden. Bildungserfahrung und konstruktive Zusammenarbeit sind Kompetenzgrundlagen für eine vertrauensvolle Kooperation und sichern dem Kunden größten Nutzen.

In unseren drei regionalen Bildungszentren im Vogtland in Auerbach, Plauen und Mylau bietet das bsw eine breitgefächerte Palette von Qualifizierungs- und Fortbildungsangeboten in modern ausgestatteten Werkstätten und Unterrichtsräumen.

Erstausbildung – Verbundausbildung und geförderte Ausbildung
In Kooperation mit Unternehmen der Region bieten wir Ausbildungsmöglichkeiten in den Berufsfeldern Metalltechnik, Mechatronik, Bautechnik, Holztechnik, Farbtechnik, Textiltechnik, Wirtschaft und Verwaltung, Garten- und Landschaftsbau sowie Lager und Logistik.

Aus- und Weiterbildung
- Fachkräfteaus- und weiterbildung
- Umschulungen
- Metalltechnik: CNC-Steuerungen (Heidenhain, Sinumerik, Fanuc), SPS, CAD SolidWorks, Schweißtechnik (DVS- oder TÜV-Richtlinien), Qualitätsmanagement mit 3D-Koordinatenmesstechnik von Carl Zeiss
- Wirtschaft und Verwaltung, ECDL, Handel und IT
- Textiltechnik, GRAFIS Grafische Schnittgestaltung
- Baumaschinenführer- und Gabelstaplerausbildung

Fachschule für Technik
Ausbildung zur Staatlich geprüften Technikerin/zum Staatlich geprüften Techniker in den Fachrichtungen:
- Maschinentechnik, Schwerpunkt Fertigung
- Elektrotechnik, Schwerpunkt Automatisierung

Zum Leistungsspektrum des Service- und Dienstleistungszentrums Mylau gehören Personalakquise, Personalentwicklung, Fachkräftevermittlung, Ausbildungsmanagement, Projektentwicklung, industrielle Fertigungsleistungen.

A Partner for Companies

The Saxon Business Education Centre (bsw) works for employers and business associations on behalf of Saxon companies.

The "bsw" has been providing training to back up entrepreneurial, business and specialist expertise among specialists and staff members at enterprises since 1990 and has been supporting young people and those seeking work in the Vogtland region and the Free State of Saxony. The major focus for members of staff at the centre is to meet customers' needs by providing competent advice, reliable services and the best possible transfer of skills into practice. The training programmes, which are market-related and are designed to meet specific customer needs, increase customers' competitiveness. Experience in training and constructive cooperation are the fundamental principles for a reliable working relationship and they ensure the greatest possible usefulness for customers.

The "bsw" provides a wide selection of courses for qualifications and further training in well-equipped, modern workshops and teaching rooms at its three regional training centres in the Vogtland area in Auerbach, Plauen and Mylau.

Initial training – combined training and state-aided training
We provide training opportunities in conjunction with companies in the region for the following jobs: metalwork, mechatronics, building, woodwork, painting, textiles, business and administration, gardening and landscaping, stores and logistics.

Training and further training
- Training and further training for specialists
- Retraining
- Mechanical engineering: CNC controls (Heidenhain, Sinumerik, Fanuc), SPS, CAD SolidWorks, welding (German Welding Association or TÜV guidelines), quality management with 3D coordinate measuring technology from Carl Zeiss
- Business and administration, ECDL, commerce and IT
- Textile technology, GRAFIS graphical pattern design
- Driving instruction for construction equipment and forklift trucks

Technical college
Training to become a state certified technician in specialist fields:
- Machine technician, specialising in manufacturing
- Electrical engineering, specialising in automation

Personnel recruitment, personnel development, obtaining specialist staff, training management, project development, industrial manufacturing services are all part of the work carried out by the Mylau Service Centre.

Bildungswerk der Sächsischen Wirtschaft gGmbH
Regionalbereich Westsachsen
Bildungszentrum für Technik
Hans-Sachs-Str. 53 · D-08525 Plauen
Telefon   +49 (0) 3741 5715-0
Telefax   +49 (0) 3741 5715-40
rb-westsachsen@bsw-mail.de
www.bsw-ggmbh.de

(Übersetzung/Translated by David Strauss)

Unser wertvollstes Kapital
OUR MOST VALUABLE RESOURCE

Fachkräfte sind schon jetzt rar und werden in den nächsten Jahren noch weit mehr gefragt werden. Zum einen halbieren sich die Schülerzahlen der vergangenen Jahre, zum anderen sind fähige Leute aus dem Vogtland wegen fehlender Arbeit weggegangen. Was also tun? „An den sinkenden Schülerzahlen lässt sich so schnell nichts ändern. Aber daran, dass hochqualifizierte Fachkräfte außerhalb der Region arbeiten müssen", sagte Landrat Dr. Tassilo Lenk: „Wir müssen Vogtländer ansprechen wieder nach Hause zu kommen. Gerade bei den Pendlern, die jede Woche hunderte Kilometer weit fahren, sehe ich gute Chancen. Die Verbundenheit zu ihrer Heimat, zu Familie und Freunde ist ein gutes Argument, natürlich gepaart mit einer ansprechenden Entlohung in den hiesigen Unternehmen. Die Leuchttürme sind die Menschen, wenn sie ihre Impulse frei machen können. Der Übergang zur Wissens- und Kommunikationsgesellschaft ist eine große Herausforderung der Gegenwart. Das heißt aber heraus aus dem Denken des Industriezeitalters. Heute sind flexible Arbeitszeiten gefragter denn je. Und deshalb fängt das Umdenken schon bei der Kinderbetreuung an, will man hochmotivierten Frauen und Männern das nötige Umfeld bieten."

Um jungen Leuten schon frühzeitig zu zeigen, dass es auch im Vogtland eine gute berufliche Perspektive gibt, ist die Idee des Berufswahlpasses entstanden. Er öffnet den Schülern den Weg in die Betriebe, damit sie sich vor Ort ein Bild machen können. Gut angenommen werden die Projekte Schule und Wirtschaft. Und auch den Berufsinformationszentrum der Arbeitsagentur kommt eine immer stärkere Bedeutung zu.

„Zwar fehlt uns im Vogtland eine Hochschule und die damit verbundenen Studentenzahlen, doch im Umkreis von 50 Kilometern findet sich eine hochinteressante Angebotspalette von Berufsakademie bis Fachhochschulen", betonte Lenk weiter.

Umdenken ist auch in den Unternehmen gefragt. Wer junge Leute für sich begeistern will, muss sich in der Öffentlichkeit darstellen und somit Appetit auf mehr machen. Viele Betriebe laden schon jetzt zu Rundgängen ein. Aber auch der Weiterbildung der Mitarbeiter muss künftig forciert werden. Angebote gibt es viele, ob in Bildungseinrichtungen oder bei der Industrie- und Handelskammer sowie der Handwerkskammer direkt vor Ort.

Fachkräfte können aber auch aus dem Ausland kommen. Gerade die Nachbarschaft zu Tschechien bietet ein großes Potenzial vor dem sich niemand aus falscher Angst verschließen sollte.

Qualified employees are already a rarity and over the next few years will be increasingly in demand. Over the last few years, the number of school pupils has halved and another problem is that qualified people have left the Vogtland region in search of a job. So what can be done? "Little can be done quickly to increase the number of pupils; but we can do something about highly qualified people leaving the region to find work elsewhere," says the chief administrative officer, Dr Tassilo Lenk, "We have to talk to these people about returning to the Vogtland region. I think our chances are good with commuters, who travel hundreds of kilometres every week. The feeling of belonging to their home region, family and friends is a good argument, coupled of course with a suitable wage from a local firm. The lighthouses are people, who are enabled to follow their impulses. The change to a scientific and communication-based society is a big challenge at the present time. That means we have to abandon our industrial era thinking. More and more employees want flexi-time. That means that we have to start by thinking of ways to provide child-care facilities in order to provide the right environment for both men and women."

The idea of a professional passport was introduced in order to show young people that there are good job prospects in the Vogtland region as early as possible. It has opened the way for pupils to go into firms to see for themselves. The "School and Business" project has been well received. The centre for careers advice at the Labour Agency has become more and more important too.

"We may not have a university, and with it the students, but we do have a very interesting number of centres ranging from a vocational college to universities of applied sciences within a 50 mile radius," Lenk emphasizes.

Firms must also change their way of thinking. Companies who want to attract young people must advertise and make people want to work for them. Many firms are already inviting young people to visit them. But on-the-job training for current employees must also be promoted. There are plenty of opportunities, either at training centres or with the Chamber of Industry and Commerce or the Chamber of Trade locally.

Qualified employees could also come to the Vogtland region from abroad. Our closest neighbour, the Czech Republic, provides huge potential, which we ignore at our peril.

Bundesweit beste Textilveredler/in sind Lehrlinge bei C. H. Müller. Franziska Kirchner wurde 2006 als bundesweit beste Textilveredler/in ausgezeichnet und Manfred Lenzner konnte 2007 diese Ehrung entgegennehmen.

Trainees at C. H. Müller are the best textile finishers in Germany. Franziska Kirchner was crowned the best textile finisher in Germany in 2006 and Manfred Lenzner was able to win this title in 2007.

(Fotos/Photos by Igor Pastierovic , Text/Text by Marjon Thümmel, Übersetzung/Translated by David Strauss)

Stärken verbinden

Linking up Strong Points

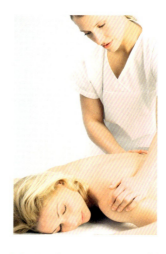

Vogtländer vernetzen Berufsausbildung im Gesundheitswesen

„Mit einer Hand lässt sich kein Knoten knüpfen", so sagt ein altes Sprichwort. Wie wichtig es ist, in einer Zeit des demographischen Wandels Hand in Hand zu gehen, beweist das im Jahr 2007 von drei beruflichen Schulzentren im Vogtland gegründete Bildungsnetzwerk für Gesundheitsfachberufe im Vogtland.

Anlass für dieses anspruchsvolle Projekt war der Umstand, dass es im Vogtland seit nahezu fünf Jahren keine öffentliche Medizinische Berufsfachschule mehr gibt: Konsequent zog sich der Freistaat Sachsen aus diesem Feld beruflicher Bildung zurück und überließ die Ausbildung in den Gesundheitsfachberufen den Privatschulen. Doch was hieß das für Schülerinnen und Schüler, die einen Beruf des Gesundheitswesens lernen wollten? Bedeutete „Privatschule" für ihre Eltern, künftig hohe Schulgelder zahlen zu müssen und sich deshalb diese (bei vielen Absolventen von Mittelschulen und Gymnasien beliebte) Berufsausbildung nicht mehr leisten zu können?

Hier sahen sich das Bildungszentrum für Soziales, Gesundheit und Wirtschaft aus Reichenbach, das IWB Plauen und die Medfachschule Bad Elster in der Verantwortung, als die drei großen beruflichen Schulzentren für Gesundheitsfachberufe im Vogtland den Eltern und Schülern Hilfestellung zu geben. Schließlich wird die Ausbildung nach wie vor in hohem Maße durch den Freistaat Sachsen gefördert; bei den Eltern und Schülern verbleibt lediglich ein symbolischer Beitrag, der als Schulgeld zu zahlen ist und auf den in sozialen Härtefällen auch verzichtet werden kann. Darauf hat auch der Sächsische Landtag in der Novellierung des Privatschulrechtes 2007 wieder hingewirkt.

Sekundärer Gedanke der im Bildungsnetzwerk vereinten Schulträger ist es weiterhin, auf die Stärken privater Schulen hinzuweisen. Die Vorteile der Ausbildung an einer Privatschule liegen auf der Hand: Diese Einrichtungen trumpfen nicht damit auf, ihr Angebot den Bedürfnissen und Wünschen der Schüler individuell anzupassen und hohe Ausbildungsqualität zu liefern. Sie leben diesen Anspruch! Wenig Ausfallstunden, modern ausgestattete Unterrichtsräume, Lehrmittel auf dem neuesten Stand, hoher Praxisbezug und ein umfangreiches Angebot an Fort- und Weiterbildungskursen sind weitere nennenswerte Vorteile privater Schulen.

Die drei größten Medizinischen Berufsfachschulen des Vogtlandkreises gehen als gutes Beispiel voran, die Ausbildung in den Gesundheitsfachberufen zu sichern und zu verbessern – die ersten Knoten sind geknüpft und dank zahlreicher Kooperationspartner werden weitere nennenswerte folgen. Damit junge Menschen auch morgen noch als Krankenschwester, Physiotherapeutin, Ergotherapeut, PTA/MTA, Logopädin oder Medizinischer Dokumentationsassistent ihre berufliche Zukunft im Vogtland haben!

(Übersetzung/Translated by David Strauss)

Vogtland institutions create network for professional training in the health sector

"You cannot tie a knot with one hand" is an old proverb. The training network for professions, which was set up in the health sector in the Vogtland region by three training centres in 2007, demonstrates how important it is to join forces in an age of demographic change.

This sophisticated project was triggered by the fact that the Vogtland region had been bereft of any public sector medical training facility for five years: the Free State of Saxony systematically withdrew from this area of professional training and left the training programmes for the health sector firmly in the hands of private institutions. But what were the consequences for students, who wished to train for a job in the health sector? Did "private college" mean that parents had to pay high school fees with the result that people could no longer afford to train for these jobs (which are popular with many young people who finish their schooling at 16 or 18)?

The Training Centre for Social Welfare, Health and Business in Reichenbach, the IWB Plauen and the Medical Vocational College in Bad Elster recognised their responsibility to provide assistance to parents and young people in their capacity as the three major vocational training colleges for health sector professions in the Vogtland region. After all, the training programmes continue to be largely sponsored by the Free State of Saxony; parents and students only have to pay a small fee and this can be waived if the families are suffering hardship. The Saxon Parliament is working towards this goal in the 2007 amendment to the Private Schools Act.

The secondary idea at the educational institutions that have joined forces in this training network is to underline the strengths of the private colleges. The advantages of training at a private college are very obvious: these institutions do not just state that they adapt their courses to meet the needs and wishes of students and provide high-quality training. They also live up to this reputation! The number of lectures cancelled is low, the training facilities are modern, the teaching materials are the very latest, the courses are geared to practical situations and the range of further training courses is very wide. These are all noteworthy advantages of private institutions.

The three largest medical training centres in the Vogtland Rural District are setting a good example when it comes to guaranteeing and improving training in the health professions – the first knots have been tied and others will follow, thanks to many cooperation partners. This will ensure that young people will continue to be able to gain the necessary training to work as nurses, physiotherapists, occupational therapists, pharmaceutical or medical assistants, speech therapists or medical filing clerks in the Vogtland region!

Beste Chancen im Beruf
The Best Professional Opportunities

Berufsausbildung im Gesundheitswesen am Bildungszentrum Reichenbach

Die Pflegebranche boomt und wird bis zum Jahr 2030 zum Wachstumsmotor der deutschen Volkswirtschaft! – Mit dieser Nachricht überraschte die Initiative Neue Soziale Marktwirtschaft im Sommer 2007 die Öffentlichkeit. Dabei wurden im Vogtland die Zusammenhänge zwischen demographischer Entwicklung und der deutschen Wirtschaft viel zeitiger erkannt: Bereits 1993 gründete das Bildungswerk der Sächsischen Wirtschaft (bsw) in Reichenbach eine Fachschule für Altenpflege und verschrieb sich der Ausbildung von Fachkräften in diesem Bereich.

Heute ist das schon Geschichte. Längst kamen weitere Bildungsgänge dazu, die sich im Bildungszentrum für Soziales, Gesundheit und Wirtschaft vereinen – einem beruflichen Schulzentrum, das einmalig ist im Vogtland und weit über seine Grenzen hinaus ausstrahlt. Hier lernen angehende

- Altenpflegerinnen und Altenpfleger
- Gesundheits- und Krankenpflegerinnen/-krankenpfleger
- Podologinnen und Podologen (Medizinische Fußpfleger)
- Logopädinnen und Logopäden
- Ergotherapeutinnen und Ergotherapeuten
- Physiotherapeutinnen und Physiotherapeuten

ihr berufliches Handwerk und starten in eine traumhafte Berufskarriere. Immerhin liegen die Vermittlungsquoten der Absolventinnen und Absolventen in Arbeit bei über 85 Prozent!

Die Gründe für diesen und weitere Erfolge sind vielfältig: Zum einen steht mit dem bsw als dem Arbeitgeberbildungswerk des Freistaates Sachsen ein starker Träger hinter dem beruflichen Schulzentrum. Zum anderen wird hier die Ausbildung zu den Gesundheitsfachberufen sowohl interdisziplinär wie auch praxisnah verknüpft. Seit dem Einzug in das neue Schulgebäude 2003 besitzt das Haus ein eigenes Therapiezentrum, in dem niedergelassene Therapeuten mit Patienten arbeiten und die Schüler und Studenten vom ersten Tag an in die Therapie mit einbezogen werden. Ein großer Fachbereich für medizinische Fort- und Weiterbildung flankiert mit seinen Kursangeboten für Schüler, Studenten und ausgebildete Fachkräfte das Portfolio des Hauses.

Nicht zuletzt bieten sich hier Möglichkeiten der akademischen Aufbauqualifizierung im Rahmen von Bachelor- und Masterstudiengängen. Kompetent, erfahren und leidenschaftlich bereitet das Bildungszentrum für Soziales, Gesundheit und Wirtschaft auf Berufe mit Zukunft vor. Genug Gründe für eine Aus- oder Weiterbildung im vogtländischen Reichenbach.

Vocational training for the health sector at Reichenbach Training Centre

The health care sector is booming and will become a major source of growth in the German economy by the end of 2030. The New Social Market Economy Initiative surprised the public with this piece of information during the summer of 2007. The links between demographic developments and the German economy were recognised at a much earlier stage in the Vogtland region. The Saxon Business Training Centre (bsw) in Reichenbach set up a vocational school for geriatric care as early as 1993 and has committed itself to training specialists in this field.

That is all history today. Further training courses have been added, which have been brought together under the umbrella of the Training Centre for Social Welfare, Health and Business – a vocational training centre, which is unique to the Vogtland area and is known far beyond the region's borders. There are courses for prospective

- geriatric nurses
- nursing staff (including public health nurses)
- chiropodists
- speech therapists
- occupational therapists and
- physiotherapists,

where they can learn their trade and start out on a dream career. The proportion of graduates from the college entering work is more than 85 percent!

There are many reasons for this success rate and others: the bsw vocational college has a powerful backer in the shape of the Free State of Saxony's employer association, for which it trains staff. Training for health professions here is also linked in an interdisciplinary and practical way. Since the college moved into its new premises in 2003, it has had its own therapy centre where therapists work with patients and the students are involved in treatments from the very first day. A large specialist department for further medical training rounds off the college's portfolio with special courses for pupils, students and trained specialists.

Last but not least, there are opportunities for students to upgrade their qualifications by taking bachelor or master degrees. The Training Centre for Social Welfare, Health and Business prepares people for professions with a future in a competent, skilful and enthusiastic manner. So there are plenty of reasons why people should come to Reichenbach for their initial or further training.

Bildungswerk der Sächsischen Wirtschaft e.V.
Bildungszentrum für Soziales, Gesundheit und Wirtschaft

Kirchplatz 7 · D-08468 Reichenbach
Telefon +49 (0) 3765 5540-0
Telefax +49 (0) 3765 5540-40
fs-reichenbach@bsw-mail.de
www.bsw-ev.de
www.bildungszentrum-reichenbach.de

(Übersetzung/Translated by David Strauss)

Stärke durch Vorsprung

Strength through Being One Step Ahead

Mit der Theorie der Praxis voraus sein, denn es gibt nichts Praktischeres als ein gute Theorie. Immer einen Schritt voraus sein – so lautete schon die Überschrift im ersten Band der Besten aus dem Vogtland und genau das hat sich neben der Lehrqualität an der staatlich anerkannte Medizinische Berufsfachschule Bad Elster auch nicht geändert.

Im Sinne des europäischen Gedankens ist die Medfachschule seit vielen Jahren bestrebt Kontakte zu ausländischen Partnereinrichtungen zu knüpfen und zu pflegen. Erste Beziehungen nahm die Schule schon Mitte der 90er Jahre mit der Hogeschool Arnhem en Nijmegen in den Niederlanden auf. Es folgten zahlreiche Studenten- und Dozentenaustauschprogramme und führten schließlich zur Entwicklung eines einjährigen Aufbaustudiums im Fachbereich Physiotherapie. Mitentscheidend für die Verbindungen mit dieser und anderen Fachhochschulen war die Aufnahme der Medfachschule als erste deutsche Einrichtung im COHEHRE, dem „Consortium of Institutes of Higher Education in Health and Rehabilitation in Europe" als assoziiertes Mitglied. Seit 2006 ist die Schule Vollmitglied in diesem Konsortium. Der Medfachschule Bad Elster ist es dabei als Mitglied der COHERE gelungen, ab 2008 ein Schüleraustauschprogramm mit der Kansas-University (USA) zu starten. Diese Zusammenarbeit soll den Schülern und Studenten die Möglichkeit geben, auf internationaler Ebene Erfahrungen in medizinischen Bereichen auszutauschen. Forschung und praktisches Training sollen dann in den Bereichen Physiotherapie und Ergotherapie zwischen den Auszubildenden thematisiert werden. „Unsere Absolventen können mit der Berufsfachschulausbildung der Medfachschule sofort weltweit als Ergotherapeut/in arbeiten", so die globale Zielsetzung der Ausbildung. „Dies ermöglicht unsere nach WFOT-Standards anerkannte Ergotherapieausbildung." WFOT bedeutet World Federation of Occupational Therapists/Weltverband der Ergotherapeuten.

Mit den Kerngedanken der Praxis immer einen Schritt voraus zu sein und die Ausbildung am zukünftigen Bedarf zu orientieren, hat die Medfachschule Bad Elster in den letzten Jahren umfangreiche Kooperationen mit Partnereinrichtungen des In- und Auslandes geschlossen. Nach Abschluss der jüngsten Kooperationsvereinbarung mit der Hamburger Fern-Hochschule ist es künftig möglich, ein ausbildungsintegriertes Studienprogramm direkt am Schulstandort Bad Elster anzubieten. Dadurch erhalten die Schüler der Medfachschule schon nach einem Jahr Ausbildung die Möglichkeit sich als Student am Studienzentrum Bad Elster einzuschreiben, um so ein weiterführendes Studium in ihrem Ausbildungsberuf aufnehmen zu können. Das ausbildungsintegrierende Studienprogramm wird die Ausbildungsberufe Physiotherapie, Ergotherapie, Logopädie, Gesundheits- und Krankenpflege umfassen und mit einem Bachelor-Abschluss enden.

It is always good for theory to be ahead of practice, because there is nothing more practical than good theory. Always being one step ahead – that was the heading in the first volume in the first volume of "The Best from the Vogtland" and this is exactly what has not changed at the Bad Elster state-approved Medical Vocational College along with the teaching quality.

In line with European thinking, the medical training school has been eager to make contact with foreign partner institutions and remain in touch for many years. The first contact with the "Hogeschool Arnhem en Nijmegen" in the Netherlands was made by the school in the mid-1990s. Various student and lecturer exchange programmes followed and finally led to the development of one-year postgraduate course in physiotherapy. One of the crucial factors for the relationship with this university of applied sciences and others was the fact that the Medical Vocational College was accepted as the first German institution to become an associated member of COHEHRE, the "Consortium of Institutes of Higher Education in Health and Rehabilitation in Europe". The school has been a full member of this consortium since 2006. As a member of COHERE, Bad Elster Medical Vocational College has managed to launch a student exchange programme with Kansas University (USA), due to start in 2008. This cooperation will give pupils and students the chance to talk about their experiences in the field of medicine at an international level. Research and practical training in the fields of physiotherapy and occupational therapy can be discussed by the trainees too. "Our graduates will now be able to work as an occupational therapist all over the world with the training they have received at our Medical Vocational College." – that is the global purpose of the training. "Our training as an occupational therapist, which is approved by WFOT-standards, makes this possible." WFOT means World Federation of Occupational Therapists.

The Bad Elster Medical Vocational College has entered into comprehensive agreements with partner organisations in Germany and abroad over the past few years, motivated by the central idea of being one step ahead of current practices and training people for future needs. After signing the most recent cooperation agreement with Hamburg Correspondence University, it will soon be possible to offer a graduate school course combined with training directly on site at the school in Bad Elster. The students at the Medical Vocational College are given the option of enrolling as a student at the Bad Elster Study Centre after one year's training, so as to be able to start a degree course in the job for which they are being trained. The course, which involves practical training, will include courses in physiotherapy, occupational therapy, speech therapy, healthcare and nursing and will lead to a bachelor's degree.

Bad Elster

Medizinische Berufsfachschule
Bad Elster GmbH
Alte Reuther Str. 38 · D-08645 Bad Elster
Telefon +49 (0) 37437 554-0
Telefax +49 (0) 37437 554-23
www.medfachschule.de
office@medfachschule.de

(Übersetzung/Translated by David Strauss)

IWB Institut für Wissen und Bildung

Erfolg bedeutet: Mehr zu tun als notwendig!
Success Means: Doing More Than the Minimum!

» *IWB – Ich will Bildung! Die Formel für Ihre berufliche Zukunft!* «
IWB – I Want to Be trained! The formula for your professional career!

Seit vielen Jahren ist das Institut für Wissen und Bildung (IWB) – Medizinische Berufsfachschulen GmbH eine ausgezeichnete Adresse in Sachen beruflicher Ausbildung im medizinischen Bereich. Die Kostenexplosion im Gesundheitswesen wird die Eigenverantwortung und –initiative für einen guten, gesunden Lebensstil jedes einzelnen Menschen fordern. Beratung, Information, sachkundige Hilfe und Unterstützung gewinnen dabei zunehmend an Bedeutung. So erhalten die Gesundheitsfachberufe einen neuen Stellenwert und die medizinischen Ausbildungsberufe bieten damit eine zukunftsorientierte Perspektive. Hochmotivierte Lehrkräfte erteilen im Zusammenwirken mit Kooperationspartnern aus Forschung und Praxis in allen Ausbildungsrichtungen einen modernen, innovativen und praxisnahen Unterricht. Ein hohes Maß an medizinischem Wissen, ein ausgeprägtes Verantwortungsbewusstsein, eigenverantwortliches Handeln und Teamgeist sind die Herausforderungen an die Schüler des IWB.
Aber das IWB bietet getreu seinem Motto noch mehr: In allen Ausbildungsrichtungen beinhaltet der Berufsabschluss eine zusätzliche Qualifikation in einem Spezialgebiet.

An den medizinischen Berufsfachschulen werden die Gesundheitsfachberufe
- Pharmazeutisch-techn. Assistent mit ZQ Wellness- und Kosmetikberater,
- Medizinisch-techn. Assistent mit ZQ Zellkulturtechnik oder Molekularbiologie,
- Veterinärmedizinisch-techn. Assistent mit ZQ Zellkulturtechnik oder Molekularbiologie,
- Medizinischer Dokumentationsassistent incl. Erwerb des Europäischen Computerführerscheins
- Diätassistent/-Ernährungstherapeut mit Zusatzqualifikation Übungsleiter Breitensport
- Podologe (berufsbegleitend) mit ZQ French pedicure ausgebildet.

An der Ergänzungsschule für Ganzheitskosmetik (einjährig) bieten wir die ZQ Naildesign.

Später studieren –aber erst Abitur? Kein Problem! Am IWB in Plauen befindet sich das erste private
- Berufliche Gymnasium mit Spezialisierung Biotechnologie in Sachsen.

Hier fördert das IWB die generelle Studierfähigkeit und führt zur Allgemeinen Hochschulreife. So werden Voraussetzungen für die Ausbildung in qualifizierten Berufen mit erhöhten Anforderungen und für die Ausübung von Leitungspositionen in allen Bereichen geschaffen.
Und noch etwas zeichnet das IWB aus: Seit dem Schuljahr 2007/08 wird am IWB ein Stipendium ausgeschrieben, welches sich auf die gesamte Dauer der Ausbildung an den Berufsfachschulen wie auch am Gymnasium bezieht.

The Institute for Knowledge and Training (IWB) – Specialist Medial Training College has been an excellent address for those wishing to train for a career in the health sector. Exploding costs in the health sector will make it vital for individuals to take responsibility for their health and seize the initiative by leading a healthy lifestyle. Advice, information, competent help and support will become increasingly important. As a result, health professions will become more significant and jobs in the medical sector will hold out good prospects for the future. Highly motivated teachers provide modern, innovative and practical tuition in all the training fields in tandem with cooperation partners from the world of research and practice. A high level of medical knowledge, a pronounced sense of responsibility, an ability to seize the initiative and team spirit are the challenges facing students at the IWB.
But in line with its motto, the IWB provides much more: the final professional qualifications in all the training fields include additional aptitude in a special subject area.

Training is provided at the specialist college for the following medical jobs:
- pharmaceutical technical assistant with special qualifications as a wellness and cosmetic advisor,
- medical technical assistant with special qualifications in cell culture technology or molecular biology,
- veterinary technical assistant with special qualifications in cell culture technology or molecular biology,
- medical records assistant including the European Computer Driving License
- dietician/nutrition therapist with additional qualifications as a trainer for amateur sports
- chiropodist (in-service) with additional qualification in French pedicure.

We also provide additional qualifications in nail design at the Complementary School for All-Round Cosmetics.

Do you want to go to university later – but first need to pass your final secondary school examinations?
No problem! The IWB in Plauen is the first private
- grammar school specialising in in biotechnology training in Saxony.

The IWB develops students' general abilities to study and coaches them through the final school exams. This paves the way for them to train in qualified professions with stringent demands and exercise management positions in all these fields.
And there is one other special thing about the IWB: a scholarship has been available since the 2007/08 college year and this covers the entire duration of the training period at the medical college or the grammar school.

Dobenaustraße 14-16
D-08523 Plauen
Telefon +49 (0) 3741 28028-0
Telefax +49 (0) 3741 2828-11
iwb.plauen@t-online.de
www.iwb-plauen.de

(Übersetzung/Translated by David Strauss)

Berufliches Schulzentrum e.o.plauen

Kompetent in Technik und Design
Vocational School Centre e.o.plauen — Competence in Technology and Design

"An der e.o. habe ich mich gut gefühlt, da stimmen Inhalt und Atmosphäre." So oder ähnlich ist es immer wieder im Gästebuch der Internetseite des Schulzentrums zu lesen.
Was zeichnet das berufliche Schulzentrum e.o.plauen aus? Das sind die über 175-jährige Tradition der gewerblich-technischen Aus- und Weiterbildung, die Größe und Vielfalt der Einrichtung, die weit über die Region ausstrahlt. Das ist die Symbiose aus Technik und Design, die seit der Schulgründung 1832 Unterrichtsinhalte und Lernatmosphäre bestimmt.
Innovation ist das beste Rezept – dieser Leitgedanke des Schulgründers prägt noch heute das berufliche Schulzentrum e.o.plauen. In 36 Berufen der Metall-, Elektro-, Holz-, Textil- und Ernährungsbranche werden begleitend zur praktischen Ausbildung Kenntnisse und Kompetenzen vermittelt. Die Schule ist in einigen Berufen – vor allem im Designbereich – auch selbst Ausbilder und folgt dabei denselben Qualitätsstandards wie das duale System.
Wichtige Säule ist die Hochschulvorbereitung. Jedes Jahr verlassen fast 200 Absolventen mit dem Abitur oder der Fachhochschulreife das Berufliche Schulzentrum e.o.plauen. Die vom Fördern und Fordern geprägte Lernatmosphäre ist Grundstock für eine überdurchschnittlich hohe Erfolgsquote in Sachsen. Absolventen der Schule sind erfolgreiche Unternehmer oder z. B. Professor.
Dritte Säule ist die berufliche Weiterbildung. Seit 1992 gibt es auf Fachschulniveau zweijährige Studiengänge für Textil- und Bekleidungstechnik, Produkt- und Kommunikationsdesign sowie Technische Informatik, die die Studenten auf ihre Aufgaben im mittleren Management vorbereiten.
Eine Besonderheit ist die Designausbildung, die sich wie ein roter Faden durch alle Schulformen zieht und die Tradition der Plauener Kunstschule weiterführt.
Die Vielfalt und Kombination der Ausbildung ist sicher einmalig in Deutschland. 120 Lehrkräfte, viele direkt aus der Wirtschaft, unterrichten mehr als 2.200 Schüler und Studenten oder bilden sie praktisch aus.
Enge Kooperation mit Wirtschaft und Hochschulen, moderne Ausrüstung und projektorientierter Unterricht sind einige der Erfolgsgaranten, die das Berufliche Schulzentrum e.o.plauen kompetent machen. Das Schulklima wird von der offenen und persönlichen Lern- und Arbeitsatmosphäre bestimmt, zu der ein attraktives außerschulisches Angebot gehört.
Ende Januar gibt es die Tage der offenen Tür, die Event und Leistungsschau zugleich sind. Die Internetseite (www.bsz-eoplauen.de) dokumentiert das Leistungsvermögen und die Atmosphäre des Beruflichen Schulzentrums e.o.plauen.

A 170-years lasting tradition in business-technological training and further education marks the Vocational School Centre e.o. plauen. The symbiosis of technology and design having been managing teaching and learning atmosphere since the foundation of the school in 1832, still determines this institution which is reflected far behind regional borders.
Knowledge and skills are taught theoretically and practically in 36 business and trade jobs in the fields of electro-technology, metal- , wood-, textile- and food. The school itself is trainer in some jobs, especially in the field of design obeying the same quality standards as education in the dual vocational system.
Another important column is the preparation of learners for their studies. Every year almost 200 students leave the vocational school centre having a certificate in their pocket that allows them to study at an institution of higher education. Promoting and demanding are the base for a quota of success above average in Saxony.
Vocational further education is the third column. The institution has been offering studies in textile processing and fashion design, product- and communication design as well as information technology on the level of further education since 1992 lasting two years. This has an objective to prepare students for basic management duties.
A speciality of e.o.plauen is definitely the training in design running like a thread through all types of school and by this following the tradition of the Plauen Art School. Certainly, this kind of training in its diversity and combination is unique in Germany.
120 trainers, many of them having worked in economy jobs, teach more than 2,200 pupils and students theoretically and practically.
Close cooperation with business and institutions of further education, modern equipment and project focused teaching methods are all successful guarantors making the vocational school centre e.o.plauen a competent partner.
School climate is determined by an open, personal learning and working atmosphere as well as by attractive after school offers.
At the end of January the house is open to everybody on two days which are both - event and presentation of strength. The school's homepage (www.bsz-eoplauen.de) reports this strength and atmosphere of the vocational school centre e.o.plauen.

Berufliches Schulzentrum e.o.plauen
Uferstraße 8 · D-08527 Plauen
Telefon +49 (0) 3741 291-2100
Telefax +49 (0) 3741 291-2109
info@bsz-eoplauen.de
www.bsz-eoplauen.de

Fachkräfteausbildung/Training Skilled Personnel

Erfolgreich auf das Berufsleben vorbereiten
Successfully Preparing People for Their Professional Careers

Berufspraktische Erstausbildung auf hohem Niveau hat im Vogtland einen Namen: Fördergesellschaft für berufliche Bildung Plauen-Vogtland e.V.

Unsere Kompetenzen liegen in der berufspraktischen Erstausbildung, in der Fortbildung von Fachkräften und Meistern sowie in der internatsmäßigen Unterbringung von Jugendlichen und in der Weiterbildung im Rahmen des Programms der VHS.

Wir sind an 4 Standorten in Plauen mit insgesamt 950 Teilnehmern, 90 festangestellten Mitarbeitern und 65 Honorarkräften präsent. Wir unterhalten 3 Berufsbildungszentren, 1 Berufsfachschule. Wir sind Träger der VHS Plauen und betreiben ein Lehrhotel, was immerhin im Jahr auf 35.000 Übernachtungen verweisen kann. Ca. 750 Jugendliche werden zu Zeit bei uns berufspraktisch ausgebildet und zum IHK-Abschluss bzw. Staatsexamen geführt.

Wir bilden in den Berufsfeldern Textil, Metall, Elektro, Informatik, Einzelhandel, Gastronomie, Lager und Diätetik aus. Unser berufliches Ausbildungsspektrum reicht bei 35 Berufen von B wie Bauzeichner bis Z wie Zerspanungsmechaniker. In all den genannten Berufsfeldern verfügen wir über gut ausgestattete Ausbildungsräume, d.h. wir haben Werkstätten, Ateliers, Lehrküchen und Lehrrestaurants, um unsere Auszubildenden erfolgreich zum Berufsabschluss zu führen.

Im Lehrhotel sind 200 Jugendliche internatsmäßig untergebracht, die in Plauen einen Beruf erlernen oder hier zur theoretischen Ausbildung in Berufsschulen gehen. Des Weiteren haben wir hier 12 Plätze im sozial-pädagogisch begleiteten Wohnen für besonders benachteiligte Jugendliche. An den Wochenenden und in den Ferien bieten wir zu günstigen Konditionen Jugend- und Sportgruppen sowie Vereinen unsere Übernachtungsmöglichkeiten mit gastronomischer Betreuung an. Es freut uns besonders, dass auch Partnerstädte von Plauen schon diese Angebote nutzten.

Das wir Qualität im gesamten Tätigkeitsfeld der Fördergesellschaft liefern, haben wir uns bescheinigen lassen, d.h. wir sind seit April 2005 zertifiziert nach DIN ISO 9001:2000.

Die Vielfalt und Breite der Fördergesellschaft ist das Ergebnis von 16 Jahren engagierter und fachkompetenter Arbeit. Heute sind wir ein regional und überregional anerkannter Bildungsträger, der eng mit der vogtländischen Wirtschaft zusammen arbeitet und junge Menschen erfolgreich auf das Berufsleben vorbereitet.

Training that is related to practices at a high level has a name in the Vogttland region: the Plauen-Vogtland Professional Training College.

Our expertise lies in providing initial training with plenty of practical experience, further training for experts and master craftsmen, providing boarding school-like accommodation for young people and providing further training as part of the national evening school programme.

We have 4 locations in Plauen with a total of 950 participants, 90 members of staff with a permanent contract and 65 freelance workers. We have 3 professional training centres and 1 training college. We support the Plauen evening school programme and operate a teaching hotel, where about 35,000 overnight stays are recorded each year. About 750 young people are currently being trained for professions and are being coached for Chamber of Industry and Commerce or state examinations.

We provide training for people training for jobs in the textile, metal, electrical, IT, retail, catering, stores and dietetics fields. Our professional training covers 35 different trades. We have well equipped training rooms for all the jobs mentioned here – i.e. we have workshops, studios, teaching kitchens and teaching restaurants to be able to successfully guide our trainees to obtain their professional qualifications.

200 young people are accommodated in the teaching hotel as if it were a boarding school. They are learning a profession in Plauen or are here for their theoretical training at training colleges. We also have 12 places in the accommodation designed to help particularly disadvantaged young people. We offer overnight accommodation with meals to young people's and sports groups and clubs at weekends and in the holidays at very reasonable prices. We are particularly pleased that Plauen's twin towns have also made use of our facilities.

We have obtained certification to guarantee that we provide quality in all the college activities – i.e. we have been certified in line with DIN ISO 9001:2000 since April 2005.

The variety and breadth of the professional training college is the result of 16 years of committed and competent work. We are now a recognised educational institution locally and nationally and we work closely with industry in the Vogtland region and successfully prepare young people for their professional careers.

 Fördergesellschaft für berufliche Bildung Plauen-Vogtland e.V.
Dobenaustr. 8 · D-08523 Plauen
Telefon +49 (0) 3741 126-0 · Telefax +49 (0) 3741 126-102
info@fg-bildung.de · www.fg-bildung.de

(Fotos/Photos by Igor Pastierovic, Übersetzung/Translated by David Strauss)

In die Bildung investieren – das heißt Zukunft gestalten.
INVESTING IN EDUCATION – SHAPING THE FUTURE

Bildungslandschaft Vogtland

Vielfalt ist Trumpf in der Bildungslandschaft Vogtland. Das verdeutlichen sowohl die verschiedenen Schultypen und Bildungsträger in der Region, als auch das überaus vielseitige Angebot an beruflichen Entwicklungswegen für junge Menschen.

42 Grundschulen, 16 Mittelschulen, sechs Gymnasien, vier Berufliche Schulzentren, ein Förderschulzentrum, vier Förderschulen, zwei Klinik- und Krankenhausschulen sowie eine Volkshochschule und zwei Kreismedienstellen prägen das Angebot im Vogtlandkreis, das durch die Bildungseinrichtungen in der Stadt Plauen komplettiert wird. Neben traditionellen handwerklich-gewerblichen Berufen wird in der Region eine möglichst breite Offerte so genannter Zukunftsberufe in den Bereichen Dienstleistung, Kommunikation und Information angestrebt. Zielgerichtet wurde dazu in den vergangenen Jahren die Ausstattung der Bildungseinrichtungen mit Lehr- und Unterrichtsmitteln auf den modernsten Stand gebracht, der sich im deutschlandweiten Vergleich durchaus sehen lassen kann. Darüber hinaus wurden mit Unterstützung von Fördermitteln des Freistaates Sachsen Schulen und Berufsschulzentren neu gebaut beziehungsweise umfassend modernisiert. Über die Medienoffensive des Freistaates und die daraus resultierende flächendeckende Ausstattung von Bildungseinrichtungen mit Computertechnik wurden wesentliche Fortschritte auf dem Informations- und Kommunikationssektor erreicht. „Im Vogtland besteht neben einem ausgeglichenen Schulnetz ein breitgefächertes Spektrum an Bildungsprofilen, das sich vom musischen bis zum technischen und sportlichen Profil erstreckt", erklärt Arndt Schubert, der Pressesprecher der Sächsischen Bildungsagentur, Regionalstelle Zwickau. Er verweist zudem auf ein ausgewogenes Verhältnis von Haupt- und Realschulbildungsgang sowie eine regionale Verbreitung von Ganztagesangeboten an den Schulen. Doch damit nicht genug: „Schulen in freier Trägerschaft mit alternativen Bildungsangeboten von der Grundschule bis zur Gymnasialstufe, wie beispielsweise Einrichtungen in Schöneck und Mylau, sowie die Förderschulen ergänzen in ihrer Spezifik die Bildungslandschaft des Vogtlandes", unterstreicht Arndt Schubert. „Beispielgebend ist in der Region die Kooperation von Bildungseinrichtungen mit Firmen, Vereinen und Verbänden bei unterrichtsergänzenden Projekten vielfältiger Art."

Ziel der Ausbildungsförderung des Landkreises ist es, jedem jungen Menschen unabhängig von seiner sozialen oder wirtschaftlichen Situation eine qualifizierte Ausbildung zu ermöglichen. Neben der Berufsschule und der Berufsfachschule bilden die Fachschule, die Fachoberschule und das Berufliche Gymnasium die fünf Säulen der Ausbildung an den Beruflichen Schulzentren. Die im Vogtland angebotenen Richtungen der Beruflichen Gymnasien sind Technik, Wirtschaft sowie Informations- und Kommunikationstechnologie.

EDUCATION IN VOGTLAND

The trump card of education in the Vogtland region is its variety. This is clear from the various types of schools and responsible bodies in the region and the wide variety of professional pathways that young people can pursue.

42 primary schools, 16 middle schools, six grammar schools, four training colleges, a special school centre, four special schools, two clinic and hospital training colleges, an adult education centre and two media training schools are all located in the Vogtland district and they are complemented by the educational facilities in the city of Plauen. The region is seeking to provide training in what are known as forward-looking sectors like services, communications and IT as well as traditional tradesmen's jobs. The equipment at educational centres has been deliberately modernised over the past few years with the latest teaching materials and they stand up to comparison across the country. In addition, schools and vocational colleges have been rebuilt or at least modernised with subsidies provided by the State of Saxony. Major progress has been made in the IT and communications sector through Saxony's media offensive and the equipping of educational centres with computers across the board. "In the Vogtland region there is not only a balanced network of schools, but also a broad spectrum of educational focuses, ranging from musical to technical and sports," says Arndt Schubert, press officer at the Saxon Education Agency in Zwickau. He also points to the balanced relationship between courses at different kinds of secondary modern schools and the increasing number of schools that stay open all day. But that is not all: "Privately run schools with different educational facilities ranging from primary to grammar school level, for example in Schöneck and Mylau, and special needs schools supplement the educational landscape in the Vogtland region," underlines Arndt Schubert. The co-operation arrangements in the region between educational institutions and firms, organisations and associations in all kinds of extra-curricular projects are also worth mentioning.

The aim of the training subsidies provided by the Vogtland district is to ensure that every young person, regardless of their social or economic situation, is given a chance to gain training qualifications. Training colleges and vocational schools, technical schools, specialised technical schools and career-oriented grammar schools form the five pillars for training programmes. The Vogtland region offers technical, business, information and communication technology courses at its career-oriented grammar schools.

(Text/Text by Jürgen Hübner/Translated by David Strauss)

Das macht Schule
Off to School

Oelsnitzer Nachwuchs hat gute Bildungschancen. Der Landkreis griff von 1995 bis 1997 tief in die Tasche, um das Julius-Mosen-Gymnasium in der Melanchthonstraße aufwändig zu rekonstruieren. Das rote Klinkersteingemäuer wurde 1900 eingeweiht. Den Namen des Vogtland-Poeten trägt es seit 1992. Für den Sportunterricht nutzt die Schule die neue Dreifeldturnhalle am Oelsnitzer Stadion. Mehrfach wurde ihr der Titel „Sportfreundliche Schule" verliehen. Großer Wert wird auf die musische Ausbildung in den Bläserklassen und mehreren Ensembles gelegt.

Schüler können sich für das naturwissenschaftliche oder sprachliche Profil entscheiden, seit der Angliederung des Sportgymnasiums Klingenthal auch für das vertiefte sportliche Profil. Neben der ersten Fremdsprache Englisch wird Unterricht in Französisch, Russisch und Latein angeboten. Die dritten Fremdsprache, Tschechisch, hat eine langjährige Tradition.

Seit 1967 unterhält die Schule eine Partnerschaft mit dem Gymnasium Cheb. Gepflegt werden regelmäßiger Schüleraustausch mit Unterrichtsbesuch und das gemeinsame Chorlager. Auch mit dem Gymnasium Sokolov und dem Lyzeum Charlieu gibt es fruchtbare Beziehungen. Für die nicht mehr genutzte Turnhalle im Schulhof entwickelt das Julius-Mosen-Gymnasium ein Konzept als Deutsch-Tschechisches Sprach- und Kommunikationszentrum. All diese Aktivitäten unterstützt der Förderverein.

Die Generalsanierung der Mittelschule Oelsnitz am Karl-Marx-Platz geht im November 2007 zu Ende. Rund 7,5 Millionen Euro investierte die Stadt Oelsnitz für den Umbau zur Ganztagsschule. Das rote, denkmalgeschützte Klinkerstein-Gebäude von 1887 bietet jetzt moderne Fachkabinette mit interaktiven Whiteboards. Fahrbare Computer- und komfortable Sprachlerntechnik stehen den Mittelschülern zur Verfügung. Mit Bläserklasse, Boxerklasse und Cheerleaderklasse gibt es spezielle Bildungsangebote.

Die Mittelschule Oelsnitz verbindet seit 1972 eine beständige Schulpartnerschaft mit der Oberschule im tschechischen Stríbro. Organisiert werden jährliche Sportwettkämpfe, Schüleraustausch und Treffen der Kollegien.

Children in Oelsnitz have great educational opportunities. Between 1995 and 1997, the district council dug deep into its pockets to finance the comprehensive redevelopment of the Julius Mosen Grammar School in Melanchthon Street. The red clinker brick building was inaugurated in 1900, and has been named after the Vogtland poet since 1992. The school now uses the new Dreifeld gymnasium by the stadium in Oelsnitz for its sports lessons and it has been awarded the title of "sport-friendly school" several times. Great emphasis is also put on musical education in the school's brass instrument classes and a number of ensembles.

Pupils can chose to follow either a natural sciences or language-based curriculum and since the sports grammar school in Klingenthal has been affiliated, it is now possible to offer a sports-based curriculum as well. In addition to English, which is taught as a first foreign language, lessons are also provided in French, Russian and Latin, and the teaching of Czech as a third language has a tradition going back many years.

The school has been partnered with the grammar school in Cheb since 1967: regular exchanges allow pupils to attend each other's lessons and their choirs take part in joint camps. The school also has fertile relations with grammar schools in Sokolov and Charlieu. The Julius Mosen Grammar School has also developed a concept for the now disused gym in the schoolyard: it is to be used as a German-Czech language and communications centre. All these activities are supported by the development association.

The general reconstruction of the Oelsnitz Middle School on Karl Marx Square was completed in November 2007. The town has invested some € 7.5 million in its conversion into an all-day school. The red clinker brick building was built in 1887 and is under a preservation order. It now offers modern specialist rooms with interactive white boards and pupils have access to both portable IT and comfortable language-learning technology. The school also offers tuition for special wind instruments, boxing and cheerleading classes.

Since 1972, Oelsnitz Middle School has had an ongoing partnership with the secondary school in Stríbro in what is now the Czech Republic and the two schools organize annual sports tournaments, pupil exchanges and meetings between their governing bodies.

(Fotos/Photos by Oelsnitzer Stadtmarketing und Tourismus GmbH, Harald Sulski, Text/Text by Renate Wöllner, Übersetzung/Translated by David Strauss)

Mittelschule Oelsnitz/Vogtl.
Pestalozzistraße 2
Telefon +49 (0) 37421 22347
www.ms1-oelsnitz.de

Julius-Mosen Gymnasium
Olsnitz/Vogtl.
Melanchthonstraße 11
Telefon +49 (0) 37421 22572
www.mosen-gymnasium.de

Bildungslandschaft in Vogtland / Education in Vogtland

Eine erstklassige Bildungseinrichtung mit überregionaler Bedeutung, vor allem für den Bereich der Informationstechnologie sowie bei fremdsprachenintensiven Ausbildungen, ist das Berufliche Schulzentrum für Wirtschaft Rodewisch. Nur wenige Fahrkilometer entfernt befindet sich das Schulzentrum für Technik und Hauswirtschaft Reichenbach, das eine Fülle von Ausbildungen in technischen Bereichen anbietet und sich zu einem Kompetenzzentrum für Kälte- und Klimatechnik entwickelt hat. Ausbildungen in den Branchen Kfz-, Metall- und Sanitär- sowie Heizungs- und Klimatechnik stehen im Beruflichen Schulzentrum Oelsnitz im Mittelpunkt. Im Schulzentrum für Ernährung- Haus-, und Agrarwirtschaft Falkenstein werden Fachleute für das Gastgewerbe, das Friseurhandwerk und hauswirtschaftliche Berufe ausgebildet, denen sich nach einer erfolgreichen Ausbildung Job-Chancen weit über Deutschland hinaus eröffnen. In der Außenstelle Morgenröthe-Rautenkranz erfolgt inmitten ausgedehnter Wälder quasi hautnah in der Natur die Ausbildung von Forstwirten in Landesfachklassen des Landes Sachsen.

Wenn von Besonderheiten der Bildungslandschaft im Vogtland die Rede ist, dürfen die Berufsfachschulen des Musikinstrumentenbaues in Klingenthal sowie die Stickereifachschule beziehungsweise die Medien- und Designer-Ausbildung am Beruflichen Schulzentrum e.o. plauen nicht unerwähnt bleiben, die in ihrer Art einmalig in Deutschland sind. Im Herzen des traditionsreichen Kurortes Bad Elster wird zum Beispiel der Nachwuchs in medizinischen Berufen, wie Physio- oder Ergotherapeut, Masseur und medizinischer Bademeister, für den Berufsalltag fit gemacht.

Last but not least hat das Vogtland mit der Außenstelle Reichenbach der Westsächsischen Hochschule Zwickau eine renommierte Textilfachschule zu bieten, die mit den Fachrichtungen Textil- und Ledertechnik sowie Architektur zu den ältesten höheren Textil-Ausbildungsstätten Deutschlands gehört.
Jüngster Mosaikstein in der Schullandschaft des Vogtlandes mit überregionaler Ausstrahlung ist das Schulzentrum „Amtsberg" in Klingenthal, das als Eliteschule des Sports hervorragende Ausbildungsmöglichkeiten und beste Trainingsbedingungen miteinander vereint. Gerade in Verbindung mit der Schanze in der „Vogtland-Arena" Klingenthal ist diese sportliche Talentschmiede ein bedeutsamer Fortschritt im Gesamtkonzept eines deutsch-tschechischen Wintersportzentrums im Oberen Vogtland, betont Landrat Dr. Tassilo Lenk. Fazit: In der Vogtland-Region ergänzen und verknüpfen sich traditionelle Ausbildungsrichtungen mit neuen, zukunftsweisenden Angeboten auf sinnvolle Weise.

The Rodewisch Vocational Business College is a first-class education institute that serves a wide area, particularly in the field of IT. The College of Technology and Housekeeping in Reichenbach is just a few kilometres away; it provides comprehensive training in technical fields and has developed into a specialist centre for refrigeration and air-conditioning. Oelsnitz Training College focuses on courses for car mechanics, metalworkers, plumbers and heating and air-conditioning technicians. The Falkenstein College for Nutrition, Housekeeping and Farming trains specialists for the tourism, hairdressing and housekeeping sectors, so that students have an opportunity to get a job throughout Germany or beyond. The Morgenröthe-Rautenkranz branch provides students with forestry courses where they can gain a State of Saxony qualification in the subject and spend time in extensive woodlands on the doorstep.

And talking of unique training opportunities in the Vogtland region, the vocational training college for making musical instruments in Klingenthal and the embroidery school and media and design training at the "e.o. plauen" Training College should be mentioned, because they are unique in Germany. The next generation of medical staff – physiotherapists, occupational therapists, masseurs and balneotherapists – are all equipped for their work at the heart of the traditional spa town of Bad Elster.
Last but not least, the Vogtland region houses a renowned college of textiles at the Reichenbach branch of Zwickau University of Applied Sciences. It provides specialist training in leather and textiles and architecture and is one of the oldest textile training colleges in Germany.

The newest piece of the mosaic in the Vogtland region's school landscape is the "Amtsberg" school complex in Klingenthal, which is an elite sports school serving an area greater than just the Vogtland region. It provides outstanding training opportunities and ideal training conditions. "This sporting training centre marks real progress in realising the idea of a German-Czech winter sports centre in the Upper Vogtland area, particularly with its links with the "Vogtland Arena" ski-jump facility," says chief administrative officer, Dr. Tassilo Lenk.
To sum up: traditional training centres are combined with and supplemented by new future-orientated courses in a new and forward looking manner in the Vogtland region.

(Fotos/Photos by BSZ für Technik Adam Friedrich Zürner Oelsnitz, Harald Sulski, Text/Text by Jürgen Hübner/Translated by David Strauss)

Freiraum für Persönlichkeit
Scope for Personalities to Develop

"Futurum Vogtland" startete am 1. September 2007 als Evangelisches Gymnasium in Mylau im Vogtland mit 44 Schülern in zwei fünften Klassen in Trägerschaft des Evangelischen Schulvereins Vogtland e.V. Sie ist die erste private Schule ab Sekundarstufe I im Kreis. In jedem Schuljahr sollen zwei weitere fünfte Klassen dazu kommen, sodass in sieben Jahren alle Klassenstufen belegt sind. Für die Schüler und Lehrer gilt wie für alle anderen Schüler in Sachsen die Orientierung am Lehrplan des Freistaates Sachsen. In der 10. beziehungsweise 12. Klasse werden Prüfungen abgelegt. Zensuren gibt es jedoch erst ab Klasse 9.

Der Eröffnung der Schule ging eine mehrjährige Vorbereitungsphase voraus. Der Schulverein ist Träger der Montessorigrundschule Limbach und hatte bereits einen Anlauf zur Eröffnung einer weiterführenden Schule unternommen. In der Stadtverwaltung Mylau stießen die Initiatoren auf offene Ohren und finanzielle Unterstützung. Die Verwaltung bemühte sich seit der Schließung der Mittelschule im Jahr 2003 um die Neubelebung der Schullandschaft in der Stadt.

Bei der Erarbeitung ihres Konzeptes ließen sich die Mitglieder des Schulvereins von der gesellschaftlichen Entwicklung und der Rolle der Bildung in diesem Prozess leiten. Mit der durchschnittlichen Lebenserwartung von etwa 80 Jahren haben die im Jahr 2000 geborenen Kinder in der Bundesrepublik Deutschland gute Chancen, das Jahr 2080 zu erleben. Ein Blick in die Geschichte macht deutlich, was für Veränderung ein derartiger Zeitraum beinhalten kann. Der Schule kommt eine bedeutende Rolle zu, da die Schülerinnen und Schüler von heute die Gestalter von morgen sind. Sie müssen Fähigkeiten entwickeln, mit denen sie ihr Leben selbst in die Hand nehmen können, denn die Herausforderungen der Zukunft werden nicht kleiner. Schlagwörter wie Demographie, Globalisierung, Rohstoffverknappung, Klimakatastrophe oder die Zunahme ethnischer Konflikte deuten darauf hin. Bildungsziel des Futurum Vogtland ist die ganzheitliche Entfaltung der Kinder und Jugendlichen. Dabei wird der individuellen Entwicklung, der Ausdrucksfähigkeit und der Begabung eines jeden einzelnen Kindes große Aufmerksamkeit geschenkt. Gleichzeitig ist die Förderung der sozialen Entwicklung, der Kommunikations-, Konflikt- und Kritikfähigkeit und der Fähigkeit zu Nächstenliebe und Toleranz Bestandteil des Lernkonzeptes.

The "Futurum Vogtland" grammar school was founded on 1 September 2007 as a Lutheran institution in Mylau. The school, which is backed by the Vogtland Lutheran School Association, opened with 44 students in two fifth grade classes. It is the first private school at secondary level in the region. Two new fifth grade classes will be added every school year so that all the classes will be present in seven years' time. The curriculum of the Free State will be compulsory for teachers and pupils, as at every other school in Saxony. Examinations will be taken at classes 10 and 12. But marks will only be awarded from class 9 onwards.

Several years' preparation work preceded the school's opening. The School Association is also the supporter of the Montessori Primary School in Limbach and had previously tried to establish a similar school at a secondary level. The initiators were received with open arms by the Mylau authorities and financial support has been made available. The municipal authorities were keen to re-establish a school in the town after the secondary school in Mylau was closed down in 2003.

While planning the concept for their school, the members of the School Association were guided by current social developments and the role that education plays in this process. With an average life expectancy of 80 years, children born in Germany in the year 2000 have a good chance of living until 2080. A glance at the past shows what changes can occur during such a long time period. Schools play an important role in this process as today's pupils shape tomorrow's world. They must develop the right skills to mould their own future, for life's challenges will not become any easier. Catchwords such as demography, globalisation, a scarcity of resources, climate change or an increase in ethnic conflicts indicate what kind of problems the future may bring.

The educational goal at the Futurum Vogtland is to enable children to develop every part of their being. Great attention is paid to each child's individual development, their ability to express themselves and their talents. This educational concept also promotes social development, the ability to communicate, the ability to handle criticism and conflict and the ability to love your neighbour and show tolerance.

(Fotos/Photos by Petra Steps, Text/Text by Petra Steps/Translated by David Strauss)

Bildungslandschaft in Vogtland / Education in Vogtland

Von anderen Schulen unterscheidet sich diese private Schule besonders durch die Lernstruktur und die Organisation. Sie ist eine Art „Selbstlernzentrum". An jedem Tag wird den Schülerinnen und Schülern Zeit für das selbstständige Lernen eingeräumt. Hierbei werden vor allem Projekte zu einem bestimmten Epochenthema realisiert und präsentiert. Die Lehrer helfen dabei als Berater und Betreuer.

Außerdem lernen die Kinder in Trainingseinheiten und Seminaren gemeinsam, wobei die Lehrer für die nötige Individualisierung des Lernens sorgen. Dabei helfen bedarfsorientierte Tages- oder Wochenpläne, die altersgemäße Gestaltung der Schulräume als Arbeits- und Lebensraum der Schüler und Lehrer, die Arbeit in Gruppen oder mit Partnern, ein sinnorientiertes, fächerübergreifendes Lernen, um ein ganzheitliches Arbeiten zu fördern und Zeit zum vertiefenden Lernen zu geben, aber auch selbständige Lernphasen zur individuellen Entfaltung der Schülerpersönlichkeit. Es gibt schülerorientierte und im Schulalltag integrierte Angebote zum Ausgleich geistiger Anstrengung mit Raum für Bewegung, Entspannung und Meditation. Die Schüler können darüber hinaus interessenorientierte Angebote der Schule wahrnehmen oder selbstständig und bei Bedarf auch mit Hilfe der Lehrer die Schule am Nachmittag als Lernraum nutzen. Auch Kontakte zu anderen Ländern, Religionen und Kulturen werden eine große Rolle spielen. Ein besonderes Merkmal von Futurum Vogtland dürfte die enge Zusammenarbeit von Lehrern, Schülern und Eltern sein.

The structure and organisation of the curriculum in particular sets this private school apart from ordinary schools. It is a kind of "self-teaching centre". Pupils have some time for private study every day. During this time pupils prepare and present special projects on a topic from a particular time in history. The teachers help with advice and supervision.

In addition, the children learn together in training units or seminars where the teachers also adapt the material to individual needs. A number of techniques are used to achieve this goal. Daily or weekly timetables are adjusted to the needs of the pupils, class rooms are designed according to the age requirements of the learners and are seen as a working and living environment for both pupils and teachers, work in groups or with partners, interdisciplinary learning orientated towards all the senses to promote all-round work and give pupils time to go deeper into subjects – and leaving pupils to learn on their own to allow their personalities to develop. Everyday school life also provides room for pupil-orientated, integrated programmes like sports, relaxation and meditation as a counter-balance to all the mental effort. In addition, pupils can make use of school facilities for various interests and use the school building on their own or with a teacher's assistance to learn more in the afternoons. Contacts with other countries, religions or cultures will play a major role. The Futurum Vogtland will also encourage close collaboration between teachers, pupils and parents.

(Fotos/Photos by Petra Steps, Text/Text by Petra Steps/Translated by David Strauss)

Familie und Soziales / The Family and Social Affairs

Fähigkeiten sind nichts ohne Möglichkeiten.
Abilities Are Nothing without Opportunities.

Aufbruch mit Null oder Lernlust erlaubt.

Unter diesem Motto werden derzeit in 17 Kindertagesstätten der AWO Vogtland Bereich Reichenbach e.V. im gesamten Vogtlandkreis 1104 Kinder im Alter von 10 Wochen bis 10/ 11 Jahren betreut. Dafür Sorge tragen 112 pädagogische Fachkräfte, die sich in den vergangenen drei Jahren, entsprechend der Vorgaben des sächsischen Bildungsplanes, in 176 Stunden auf die Spuren der professionellen Bildungsarbeit in den Kindertagesstätten begeben haben. Entdeckt haben sie dabei, das Kinder die Welt erkunden, egal ob mit einem oder mit zehn Jahren, wie Wissenschaftler – systematisch, konzentriert und unbeirrbar konsequent. Die Erzieherinnen haben gelernt, den Kinder dabei Begleiterinnen zu sein, sie zu unterstützen, ihnen Herausforderungen zu bieten und Räume für lustvolles Lernen zu schaffen. Dies tun sie auf der Grundlage vielfältiger Konzepte, wie zum Beispiel der Fröbel-, der Montessori- , der Kneipppädagogik oder dem Situationsansatz, die sich alle auf das Leitbild des Trägers beziehen.

Die Vielfalt der 17 Einrichtungskonzepte regt zu einem kontinuierlichen Austausch über die pädagogische Arbeit an, der durch die Fachberatung des Trägers gefördert wird. Besonders tiefgründig wird das im Qualitätszirkel der AWO Kitas praktiziert. Der Qualitätszirkel entstand mit der Einführung des Qualitätsmanagementsystems QM elementar im Jahr 2003 in allen AWO Kitas . Aus dieser Arbeit heraus und unter der aktuellen Thematik „ Gesund aufwachsen in Kindertagesstätten" entwickelt derzeit ein Gremium aus Leiterinnen, Erzieherinnen und Fachberatung ein Konzept zur Gesundheitsförderung in den AWO Kitas. Dazu gehören unter anderem die Schwerpunkte Ernährungserziehung, Bewegungsförderung, Sprachentwicklung und -förderung. Die Umsetzung hat bereits in einigen Bereichen begonnen. So können sich zwei Kindertageseinrichtungen am Projekt „Tiger Kids" der AOK beteiligen. In allen AWO Kitas wird ab Januar 2008 eine gesunde Vollverpflegung angeboten. Mehrere Einrichtungen nutzen Wasseranwendungen nach Kneipp oder besuchen mit den Kinder regelmäßig die Sauna. Einmal jährlich findet die AWO Kinderolympiade statt, bei der sich jeweils sechs Kinder pro Einrichtung in fünf unterschiedlichen Disziplinen messen können. Die Sieger des Gesamtwettkampfes werden mit dem AWO Wanderpokal geehrt. Künftig wird ein AWO Fitness Pass, der bestimmte sportliche Übungen für die unterschiedlichsten Altersgruppen beinhaltet, für alle Kinder, das Konzept der Bewegungsförderung ergänzen.

Damit kein Talent unentdeckt bleibt und jedes Kind entsprechend seiner Stärken Herausforderungen findet, bilden sich die pädagogischen Fachkräfte derzeit im Rahmen der Beobachtung und Dokumentation von Entwicklungs– und Bildungsprozessen von Kindern weiter. Bildung ist, wie beschrieben, ein lebenslanger Prozess, den die Kinder die wir betreuen, gerade erst beginnen und die Erzieherinnen in den Einrichtungen dürfen sie ein Stück auf diesem Weg begleiten – eine Aufgabe mit sehr hohem Anspruch, dem die AWO Vogtland sich mit ihren Mitarbeiterinnen gern stellt.

Starting at the age of zero or pleasure in learning is allowed.

This is the motto for 17 child-care centres run by the Vogtland Industrial Welfare Organisation (AWO) in Reichenbach in the whole Vogtland district for 1104 children aged from 10 weeks to 10/11 years old. 112 teachers set out to look at professional education work in the child-care centres for 176 hours over the past three years in line with the guidelines of the Saxon education plan. In the process they worked out that children discover the world – regardless of whether they are tiny babies or ten years old – in a systematic and concentrated manner without being distracted. The teachers have learned to accompany children and support them, provide them with challenges and create space for them to enjoy learning. They do so by following various concepts, e.g. Fröbel or Montessori or Kneipp theories or the approach favoured by the mission statement of the authority backing the school.

The variety found in the 17 concepts pursued stimulates ongoing discussions about the tuition work and this is supported by the specialist advice provided by the supporting body. This is practised in great detail in the quality assessment group at the AWO child-care centres. This group was created when the QM quality management system was introduced at all the AWO child-care centres in 2003. Based on this work and tackling the subject of "Growing up healthily in child-care centres", a committee consisting of leaders, teachers and specialist advisors is currently developing a concept to promote health at the AWO child-care centres. The main issues include nutrition education, promoting physical exercise, speech development and promotion. The theory has already begun to be implemented in some areas. Two child-care centres are taking part in the AOK health insurance scheme's "Tiger Kids" project. Full meals will be provided at all the AWO child-care centres from January 2008 onwards. Several centres are using Kneipp water facilities or are visiting a sauna regularly with the children. The AWO Children's Olympics take place once a year, where six children from each centre compete in five different disciplines. The winners of the overall competition are presented the AWO challenge cup. An AWO fitness passport, which contains particular sporting exercises for various age groups, will complement the concept of promoting physical exercise for all children in future.

The teachers are currently receiving more training by watching and documenting the development and educational processes in children to ensure that no talent remains hidden and each child faces challenges that match their strengths.

As has been outlined, education is as lifelong process, which the children being looked after are just starting. The teachers at the centres have the privilege of accompanying them on part of their journey – it is a job, which makes great demands, but the Vogtland branch of the AWO is happy to face the challenge.

(Übersetzung/Translated by David Strauss)

AWO *Vogtland - Bereich Reichenbach*

Albertistr. 38 b · 08468 Reichenbach
Telefon 03765 5550-0 · Fax 03765 555077

Vom Kopf bis zum Herzen – ganzheitliche Bildung
FROM HEAD TO HEART – INTEGRATED CHILDCARE

Der Vogtlandkreis hilft, Familie und Beruf unter einen Hut zu bringen

Familie und Beruf in Einklang bringen zu wollen, ist für die meisten Frauen in Ostdeutschland von jeher ein Bedürfnis. Ein großflächiges Angebot an Kindertagesstätten schafft dafür die Voraussetzungen. Auch im Vogtland wird man dem Anspruch eines jeden Kindes auf einen Krippen-, Kindergarten- oder Hortplatz gerecht. 139 Kindergärten und Horte gibt es in der Region, saniert und auf den modernsten Stand gebracht. Dass in Ellefeld und Pausa sogar neue Kindereinrichtungen gebaut worden sind, zeugt einmal mehr vom Interesse des Landes Sachsen, des Vogtlandkreises und der Kommunen, Kinder als höchstes Gut anzusehen, als Investition in die Zukunft.

Landrat Dr. Tassilo Lenk ist als Verfechter eines funktionierenden Wirtschaftsstandortes Vogtland der festen Auffassung, dass durch eine starke Wirtschaftskraft stabile und förderliche Bedingungen für ein gedeihliches Aufwachsen junger Menschen gestaltet werden können. Ein wichtiger Fakt, Familien in der Region zu halten. Der Grundgedanke der Vereinbarkeit von Familie und Beruf widerspiegelt sich im vogtlandweiten Bündnis für Familie. Jährlich fließen 78 000 Euro aus dem Kreishaushalt ins Netzwerk der Familienförderung. Und 2007 wurde im Beisein der Sozialministerin Helma Orosz die erste Kooperationsvereinbarung zur Mitarbeit im Netzwerk für Kinderschutz in Sachsen im Rahmen des Landesmodellprojektes „Pro Kind" durch den Landrat und den Geschäftsführer der Arbeiterwohlfahrt Auerbach, Wilfried Rink, unterzeichnet.

THE VOGTLAND DISTRICT IS HELPING PEOPLE TO COMBINE THEIR CAREER AND FAMILY

Most women in Eastern Germany want to combine a family and their job. A wide range of day care centres cater for this requirement. The Vogtland region also seeks to provide every child with a place in a nursery, kindergarten or after-school care centre. 139 nursery schools and after-school care centres exist in the region, all of which have been redeveloped and modernised to the latest standards. The fact that new child-care facilities have been built in Ellefeld and Pausa demonstrates how the State of Saxony, the Vogtland district and the local communities view children as their greatest asset and see such facilities as an investment in the future.

Chief administrative officer, Dr Tassilo Lenk wants to see the Vogtland economy flourish and he firmly believes that a strong economy will create stable and beneficial conditions to allow young people to thrive as they grow-up. One important means is to keep families in the area. The thinking behind the need to combine family and career is reflected in the Vogtland "Family Alliance". € 78,000 per annum flow from the district budget into this network designed to support families. The first cooperation agreement as part of the network to protect children in Saxony – part of the "Pro Child" state project – was signed by the chief administrative officer and the manager of the Auerbach branch of the Industrial Welfare Organisation (AWO), Wilfried Rink, in the presence of the Minister for Social Affairs, Helma Orosz, in 2007.

(Foto/Photo by Harald Sulski, Igor Pastierovic [1], Text/Text by B. Kempe-Winkelmann)

(Übersetzung/Translated by David Strauss)

Familie und Soziales / The Family and Social Affairs

„Kindertagesstätten sind Orte der Bildung", ist Landrat Lenk überzeugt. Spielen und Lernen sei kein Widerspruch, sondern sind zwei Seiten einer Medaille. So habe das kreisliche Projekt „Vorschulerziehung" spürbar dazu beigetragen, dass für die Kinder der Übergang in die Grundschule erleichtert wird. Bereits 2003 wurden Kooperationsvereinbarungen zwischen Kindertagesstätten und Grundschulen abgeschlossen. Eine Auswertung nach drei Jahren hat ergeben, dass 99 Prozent der bestehenden Kindertageseinrichtungen diese Zusammenarbeit mit Erfolg umsetzen.

Vorschulkinder und Grundschüler beteiligen sich an gemeinsamen Aktionen und Projekten – zum Beispiel am Projekt „Compukids" (Umgang mit dem Computer) oder an der Aktion „Lustiges aus Stroh". Eine Menge Spaß hatten beispielsweise die Mädchen und Jungen des Kindergartens „Zwergenland" in Neumark gemeinsam mit Kindern der Grund- und Mittelschule, als das Zirkusprojekt „Fantastico" über die Bühne ging. Regelmäßig kommen Kooperationsverantwortliche in die Kindergärten und schätzen in Abstimmung mit den Eltern den Entwicklungsstand der Vorschüler ein. Mit Begeisterung lernen die Kinder ihren künftigen Schulweg und das Schulhaus kennen.

„Gesund aufwachsen"

Gesunde Ernährung und Bewegung sind Inhalt des Kreisprojektes „Gesund aufwachsen im Vogtland". Die Programme in den Kindergärten sind so interessant und abwechslungsreich gestaltet, dass selbst größte Sport- oder Ess-Muffel Spaß dran haben. So jubeln zum Beispiel die Kinder der Tagesstätte „Am Park" in Lengenfeld, wenn ein Waldtag angesagt ist. Im Wald gibt es ja so viel zu entdecken. Und wer jetzt schon gut zuhört, kennt sich später in der Schule mit den Pflanzen um so besser aus. Aber auch der Storchenlauf barfuß im Garten ist beliebt. Das Schwitzen in der Sauna sowieso. Nicht nur der Lengenfelder Kindergarten verfügt über eine eigene Sauna.

Ob Kneipp-Anwendungen oder Kinder-Yoga, die Bewegungsbaustelle im Garten oder eine Fußfühlstrecke – der Phantasie in den Kindergärten sind keine Grenzen gesetzt. Paart sich dies noch mit gesunder Ernährung, können Eltern beruhigt ihrer Arbeit nachgehen.

In den meisten Tagesstätten bereiten die Kinder gern ihr gesundes Frühstück selbst zu. Obst und Gemüse stehen dabei im Mittelpunkt. Ernährungswochen werden organisiert und Besuche in Landwirtschaftsbetrieben. Die „Burgsteingeister" in Großzöbern beispielsweise führen das Projekt des Vogtlandkreises „Vom Bauernhof frisch auf den Tisch" weiter.

Standortfaktor

Im Rahmen der bundesweiten Aktionswoche „Kinder sind Zukunft" gab der Vogtlandkreis im Frühjahr 2007 den Startschuss für den Wettbewerb um die „Familienfreundlichste Gemeinde" im Vogtland. Zehn Kommunen haben dazu ihre Unterlagen eingereicht. Im lokalen Bündnis für Familie gehören neben dem Landrat als Schirmherr auch Vertreter des Jugendamtes, der DAK, der Stadt Oelsnitz, des Unternehmens Goldbeckbau Treuen sowie die Gleichstellungsbeauftragte der Jury an.

Die Vereinbarkeit von Beruf und Familie wird künftig immer deutlicher ein Standortfaktor für die Region. Wo dieser Teil der Infrastruktur stimmt, siedeln sich gern Unternehmen an.

The chief administrative officer, Tassilo Lenk is convinced that "child-care centres are places of learning". Playing and learning are not contrary to each other, but are two sides of the same coin. The district "Pre-School Education" project seeks to make it easier for children to switch from a nursery school to a primary school. Cooperation agreements were made between nursery schools and primary schools back in 2003. An assessment after three years showed that this degree of cooperation had been 99% successful.

Pre-school and primary school children take part in joint activities and projects – for example, "Compukids" (learning how to use computers) or "Fun with Straw". The boys and girls at the "Zwergenland" nursery school in Neumark had a lot of fun with school children from primary and middle schools when the "Fantastico" circus project took to the stage. Those responsible for the cooperation agreements make regular checks in the nursery schools to see how the pre-school children are developing – in consultation with their parents. The children are very eager to learn the way to school and get to know the school building itself.

GROWING-UP HEALTHILY.

Healthy food and exercise are the contents of the "Growing-up healthily in the Vogtland region" project. The programme in nursery schools is so interesting and varied that even the greatest haters of sports and food have a lot of fun. For example, the children in the "By the Park" daycare centre in Lengenfeld are very happy when they know they are going to have a day in the woods. There is so much to discover there and those who listen carefully know more about plants when they go to school. Walking barefoot like storks in the garden is very popular or sweating in the sauna. The Lengenfeld nursery is not the only one to have a sauna.

There are no limits placed on imagination in the nursery schools: whether it is a Kneipp spa facility or children's yoga, the exercise area in the garden or a foot sense path. This is coupled with healthy food – which means that parents can go off to work without worrying about their offspring.

Children prepare their healthy breakfast themselves at most of the day-care centres. Fruit and vegetables are a central part of the meal. "Nutrition weeks" are organised and the children visit farms. For example, the "Burgsteingeister" in Grosszöbern run a project called "Fresh from the farm to your table".

A FAMILY-FRIENDLY ENVIRONMENT AS A CRITICAL LOCAL FACTOR

The Vogtland district began a competition to find the most family-friendly community in the Vogtland region as part of the nationwide programme week called "Children are our Future" in the spring of 2007. Ten communities responded with details of their activities. The local "Family Alliance" jury includes the chief administrative officer as its patron, representatives from the youth office, the DAK health insurance scheme, the town of Oelsnitz and the "Goldbeckbau Treuen" company and the equal opportunities' commissioner.

Combining family and career will be increasingly important in future in determining the success of regions. Businesses are glad to set up in business if this element in the social infrastructure is working well.

(Foto/Photo by Harald Sulski, Hartmut Briese)

Familie und Soziales / The Family and Social Affairs

„Vital ab 50" und „VOR JU ALL"
LABOUR AGENCY WORKING GROUP PROJECTS IN THE VOGTLAND DISTRICT FOR OLD AND YOUNG

Projekte der ARGE Agentur für Arbeit – Vogtlandkreis für Ältere und Jugendliche

Über 50-Jährige, über lange Zeit arbeitslose Menschen haben oft kaum noch eine Chance, auf dem Arbeitsmarkt Fuß zu fassen. Dieser Situation wird seit 2005 mit neuen Ideen entgegengewirkt. Das Bundesministerium für Arbeit und Soziales fördert Projektideen zur Verbesserung der Beschäftigungschancen älterer Langzeitarbeitsloser. Der Initiative „Perspektive 50plus" schloss sich auch die ARGE Agentur für Arbeit – Vogtlandkreis mit einem klaren Konzept an. Der Pakt im Vogtland ist mittlerweile einer der erfolgreichsten. Bundesweit agieren 62 solcher regionalen Beschäftigungspakte.

„Vital ab 50"

Am Beispiel von Bernd Maciejok aus dem Vogtland wird deutlich, wie das Projekt „Vital ab 50 – Vogtländische Initiative für Training und Arbeit Lebensälterer" den Zugang zum Arbeitsmarkt erleichtern kann. Herr Maciejok, einst Baufacharbeiter und Lehrfacharbeiter, verlor durch eine Krankheit vor vier Jahren seinen Job. Nach seiner Genesung hat er über 350 Bewerbungen geschrieben. Immer wieder hoffte er und wurde doch enttäuscht. Mit „Vital ab 50" kam für ihn die Wende. Die ARGE Agentur für Arbeit – Vogtlandkreis mit ihrer Geschäftsführerin Martina Kober suchte sich Partner (Landrat, Agentur für Arbeit, Kammern etc.) in der Region und bildete einen Pool von über 1200 Bewerbern, die fit für einen Neuanfang sind. Kontakte zu aufgeschlossenen Arbeitgebern wurden geknüpft, die die besonderen Kompetenzen und Einstellungen Älterer erkannt haben und schätzen – Gelassenheit, Verantwortungsbewusstsein, Zuverlässigkeit, fachliches Know-how, Ruhe und Ausgeglichenheit. Mehr als 300 klein- und mittelständische Unternehmen nutzen diese Potenziale. Eines davon ist die Neue Lengenfelder Maschinen- und Stahlbau GmbH mit dem Geschäftsführer Stefan Ruoff. Dort wurde Bernd Maciejok als Hausmeister eingestellt. Er ist nicht nur für Sauberkeit, Reparaturen, Rasenpflege und Ordnung im Objekt zuständig, er hilft auch in der Produktion oder erledigt Kurierfahrten. Durch seinen Einsatz erwarb er sich Anerkennung und erhielt sein Selbstwertgefühl zurück.

Herr Maciejok ist einer von vielen im Vogtland. Insgesamt wurden über das Projekt 1288 ältere Bewerber aktiviert. 588 über 50jährige Alg II-Empfänger konnten seit Ende 2005 in eine sozialversicherungspflichtige Beschäftigung vermittelt werden. Darunter 197 Frauen. Für 852 Bewerber wurde eine Kompetenzbilanzierung erstellt. 215 Projektteilnehmer konnten eine Qualifizierung oder ein betriebliches Training absolvieren. Mehr als 350 wurden über individuelle Coachingmaßnahmen aktiviert. Ergebnisse, so Martina Kober, die nur durch enge Zusammenarbeit mit dem Bildungsinstitut Pscherer gGmbH erreicht werden konnten. Das Institut ist als Projektkoordinator tätig.

„Perspektive 50plus" soll weitere drei Jahre fortgeführt werden. Die ARGE im Vogtlandkreis reichte ihren Antrag auf Verlängerung von „Vital ab 50" beim Bundesministerium für Arbeit und Soziales ein.

"Fit after 50" or "VOR JU ALL"

The over-fifties, who have been out-of-work for a long time, seldom have a chance of getting back into work. Efforts have been made to counter this trend since 2005. The Federal Ministry for Labour and Social Affairs has been encouraging ways to improve the opportunities of finding work for older people, who have not had a job for a long time. The Vogtland District Labour Agency and the "50+ Perspective" have joined forces with a clear concept. This arrangement in the Vogtland region has now become highly successful. 62 of these regional employment agreements have been signed up and down the country.

"Fit after 50"

Bernd Maciejok from the Vogtland region clearly illustrates how the "Fit after 50" project, the Vogtland Initiative for Training and Work for Older People can make it easier for people to get back into work. Mr Maciejok, a construction worker, lost his job four years ago because of an illness. After recovering, he sent off more than 350 job applications. Each time, his optimism was dashed, but with "Fit after 50" things changed. The Labour Agency Working Group in the Vogtland district under the leadership of Martina Kober was looking for partners (such as the district administration office, labour agencies, professional chambers etc) in the area and built up a pool of more than 1200 applicants who were ready for a new start. Contacts with open-minded employers were forged – people who recognise and value the benefits of employing older people with their composure, conscientiousness, reliability, special expertise and ability to remain calm and balanced. More than 300 small and medium-sized firms are making use of this potential. One of them is the Neue Lengenfelder Maschinen- und Stahlbau GmbH, where Stefan Ruoff is the managing director. They gave Bernd Maciejok a job as a caretaker. He is not only responsible for cleaning the place, repairs, mowing the lawns and keeping things in order, but he helps out in the production work and transports materials. He has been praised for his work and has regained a sense of self-worth.

Mr Maciejok is one of many in the Vogtland region. In all, 1288 older applicants have found work as a result of the project. 588 over-fifties, who were receiving unemployment benefits, have been given employment involving the payment of national insurance contributions since the end of 2005, among them, 197 women.

A list of the abilities of 852 applicants has been drawn up. 215 participants in the project have gained further qualifications or received training at a company. More than 350 have received individual coaching. According to Martina Kober, all this has only been possible through a close working relationship with the Pscherer Vocational Training Institute. The Institute is coordinating the project. "50+ Perspective" should continue for the next three years. The Vogtland working group has sent an application to extend the "Fit after 50" project to the Federal Ministry of Labour and Social Affairs.

(Foto/Photo by Igor Pastierovic, Text/Text by B. Kempe-Winkelmann)

Familie und Soziales / The Family and Social Affairs

> » *Ein altes Sprichwort besagt: Es ist besser ein Licht anzuzünden, als über die Dunkelheit nachzudenken.* «

> » *There is an old saying: It is better to turn on a light than to think about the darkness.* «

„VOR JU ALL"

Schwierigkeiten, einen Job zu bekommen, haben nicht nur Menschen über 50. Jung, alleinerziehend und berufstätig ist mindestens ebenso problematisch zu bewerkstelligen. Und das, obwohl sich allerorten Fachkräftemangel abzeichnet. Zu den Gründen gehören die oftmals eingeschränkte Mobilität und Flexibilität Alleinerziehender, zu wenige flexible Arbeitszeitmodelle und unzureichende Kinderbetreuungsmöglichkeiten außerhalb der üblichen Arbeitszeiten.

Die ARGE im Vogtlandkreis hat mit „VOR JU ALL" (Vogtländische Strategie zur Reintegration jugendlicher Alleinerziehender) ein Konzept entwickelt, mit dem Jugendliche mit oder ohne Berufsabschluss trotzdem eine Beschäftigung oder einen Ausbildungsplatz finden. Dazu wurde ein umfangreiches Netzwerk mit Kammern und Jugendamt aufgebaut. Im Projekt werden 40 Alleinerziehende betreut. 13 von ihnen konnten bislang in Arbeit, Ausbildung oder Qualifizierung vermittelt werden.

Eine von ihnen ist Nicole Dietzsch. Die 27-Jährige aus Mylau hatte Hauswirtschafterin gelernt und war als Beiköchin rund zwei Jahre im Schützenhaus ihres Wohnortes tätig. Vor sechs Jahren wurde sie aus betrieblichen Gründen entlassen. Ein Jahr später bekam sie ihr Kind, war aber bald schon auf der Suche nach Arbeit. „Mir ist es wichtig arbeiten zu gehen", sagt sie. „Ich habe Bewerbungen geschrieben, mich um ABM-Stellen und Ein-Euro-Jobs gekümmert. Ich habe eigentlich immer mal wieder irgendwo gearbeitet, aber nie eine feste Anstellung bekommen."

Über das Projekt der ARGE wurden Nicole Dietzsch Wege geebnet. Ihre Stärken und Defizite wurden herausgearbeitet, Kontakte für sie geknüpft, viele Gespräche wurden geführt. Seit Jahresanfang 2007 ist sie bei der Arbeiterwohlfahrt (AWO) Reichenbach als Köchin angestellt. Zunächst arbeitete sie in der Küche eines Kindergartens, jetzt in der Großküche der AWO, die Kindergärten und ein Altersheim mit Mahlzeiten versorgt. 20 Stunden in der Woche hat Nicole nun eine Tätigkeit, die ihre Freude macht und ein festes Einkommen sichert.

Mit den Erfolgen über das Projekt „VOR JU ALL" wurde die ARGE Vogtlandkreis im Jahr 2006 Bundessieger im Wettbewerb „Jugend in Arbeit" in der Kategorie SGB II-Umsetzer.

"VOR JU ALL"

Difficulties in gaining employment are not restricted to people over 50. Young people and single parents find it just as difficult to find work – even though there is a shortage of skilled labour. Single parents are often restricted as regards mobility and flexibility, there are too few flexi-time jobs and inadequate child-minding facilities outside normal working hours.

The Vogtland district working group has developed a concept called "Vor Ju All" (the Vogtland strategy for reintegrating young single parents) to find these people a job or give them an opportunity to train with or without receiving final training qualifications. A network involving chambers of commerce and the youth office has been built up. 40 single parents are being helped through this project, 13 of them have already found jobs, are being trained or completing their qualifications.

One of them is Nicole Dietzsch. The 27year-old from Mylau studied home economics and worked for about two years as an assistant cook in a clubhouse in her home town. Six years ago she was fired for commercial reasons and a year later she had a child, but soon after the birth started seeking employment again. "It is important for me to work," she says. "I have sent off job applications and tried to get involved in job creation schemes and one euro jobs. I have always worked somehow, but have never got a permanent job."

The working group project opened up a door for Nicole Dietzsch. It helped recognise her strengths and weaknesses, contacts were made and a lot of talks were held. Since the beginning of 2007 she has been employed by the Industrial Welfare Organisation (AWO) in Reichenbach as a cook. First of all, she worked in a nursery school kitchen and she is now working in the large AWO kitchen, which provides meals for nursery schools and an old people's home. She works 20 hours a week and enjoys her job and the security of a regular income.

The Vogtland working group won the "Young people in employment" competition in the Social Security Code II category in 2006 with its "Vor Ju All" project.

(Übersetzung/Translated by David Strauss)

Die Gesundheitsregion Vogtland
Vogtland Health Region

Die Gesundheit der Menschen liegt sowohl dem Vogtlandkreis als auch der Stadt Plauen am Herzen. Davon zeugen die Investitionen, die zuerst die Altkreise, ab 1996 der Vogtlandkreis, sowie die Spitzenstadt Plauen für die technische und medizinische Ausstattung getätigt haben. Dazu kommen nach der Privatisierung der meisten Einrichtungen noch die Eigenmittel der Träger sowie durch sie in Anspruch genommene Fördermittel. Das Versorgungskonzept vom Haus- oder Facharzt über Therapeuten und Krankenhäuser bis zu Reha-Einrichtungen gehört zu den modernsten in Sachsen und darüber hinaus.

Die vogtländische Krankenhauslandschaft ist einer permanenten Veränderung unterworfen. Die Ursachen dafür sind vielfältig. Neue Untersuchungs- und Behandlungsmethoden werden übernommen, hochmoderne Geräte angeschafft, die Verweildauer der Patienten im stationären Bereich damit verkürzt. Andererseits muss auf Sparzwänge und politische Entscheidungen reagiert werden. Und auch Eigentümerwechsel waren im Vogtland in den letzten Jahren keine Seltenheit. Davon kündet zum Beispiel die Geschichte der Paracelsus- Klinik Reichenbach, die seit der Privatisierung 2001 vier Mal den Träger wechselte und sich jetzt endlich wieder in ruhigeres Fahrwasser begeben hat.

281 Mitarbeiter, davon 34 Ärzte und 132 Beschäftigte im Pflegedienst gehören zum Reichenbacher Krankenhaus. Die Bettenzahl hat sich seit 1990 von 415 auf 185 im Jahr 2007 verringert. In dem regionalen Akut-Krankenhaus der Regelversorgung werden jährlich mehr als 7.300 Patienten mit einer durchschnittlichen Verweildauer von 7,6 Tagen stationär behandelt und rund 11.000 Menschen ambulant versorgt. Mit den Fachabteilungen Anästhesie und Intensivmedizin, Chirurgie, Gynäkologie und Geburtshilfe, Innere Medizin, Urologie und Orthopädie wird eine große Breite der medizinischen Versorgung abgedeckt.

Wie in allen vogtländischen Einrichtungen werden modernste Behandlungs- und Diagnoseverfahren angeboten. Dazu gehören schonende laparoskopische Operationen, als „Schlüssellochtechnik" bekannt, sowie Untersuchungen mit dem Computertomografen und die Mammografiediagnostik. Fortschrittlichste Methode ist die Doppel-Ballon-Endoskopie, bei der der gesamte Dünndarm ohne Operation untersucht und behandelt werden kann. Für Schlagzeilen sorgte eine neue Behandlungsmethode für Männer mit Prostata-Krebs, bei der die erkrankten Zellen mit hochintensiviertem fokussiertem Ultraschall (Hifu) erhitzt und abgetötet werden. Sie ergänzt bisher angewandte Methoden. Die Reichenbacher Klinik bietet diese Therapie als einziges Krankenhaus in Westsachsen an. Seit 1992 entstanden ein neues Bettenhaus, ein Funktionsneubau, die neue zentrale Notaufnahme und die Rettungsstelle. Die Radiologische Abteilung wurde modernisiert. Das Krankenhaus nimmt an der externen Qualitätssicherung nach § 137 SGB V teil.

Das Reichenbacher Krankenhaus ist nicht das einzige in Trägerschaft der Paracelsus-Kette, was sich als günstig für den Erfahrungsaustausch und die Zusammenarbeit der Kliniken untereinander erweist. So gehören die Paracelsus-Kliniken in Reichenbach, Adorf und Schöneck genau wie das SKH Rodewisch dem Telematikverbund Vogtland an, der die digitale Radiografie auf- und ausbaut, die Bildkommunikation

People's health is the major focus of the Vogtland district and the city of Plauen. Investments made by the former districts and the Vogtland district from 1996 onwards and the lace city of Plauen in technical and medical equipment are ample evidence of this. And after most of the centres were privatised, the responsible bodies invested their own funds – and finances were made available by the public sector. The care concept ranging from general practitioners to specialists, treatment and hospitals and even rehabilitation clinics is one of the most modern in Saxony and beyond.

The Vogtland hospital landscape has been subjected to permanent change. There are many reasons for this. New methods of examining and treating people have been adopted, extremely modern equipment purchased, the time spent by patients on wards has been shortened. On the other hand, hospitals have had to respond to calls to make savings and political decisions. And changes of ownership have been commonplace in the Vogtland region too. The history of the Paracelsus Clinic in Reichenbach, which has changed hands four times since being privatised in 2001, is one good example of this – but it has now entered a period of greater stability.

281 members of staff, including 34 doctors and 132 nursing personnel, work at the Reichenbach hospital. The number of beds has been cut from 415 in 1990 to 185 in 2007. More than 7,300 patients, who on average spend 7.6 days on a ward, and some 11,000 outpatients are treated at the regional acute hospital for basic care every year. A wide range of medical care is provided in the anaesthetics, intensive care, surgery, gynaecology and obstetrics, internal medicine, urology and orthopaedics departments.

The latest treatment and diagnosis procedures are provided here, as at all the Vogtland health centres. These include laparascopic operations – known as "key-hole" – and examinations using computer tomography and mammography diagnostics. Double balloon enteroscopy is the most advanced method, where the whole of the small bowel can be examined and treated without the patient undergoing an operation. A new method of treatment for men with prostate cancer hit the headlines – where the diseased cells are heated with highly intensive, focussed ultrasound (Hifu) and killed off. It complements other methods that are being used. The Reichenbach clinic is the only hospital in West Saxony to offer this treatment. A new ward building, a new service building, the new central emergency reception area and the emergency centre have been built since 1992. The radiology department has been modernised. The hospital has submitted itself to external quality controls in line with Section 137 of the Social Welfare Code, Volume V.

The Reichenbach hospital is not the only one that is part of the Paracelsus Group – which is beneficial when it comes to exchanging experience and working together with other clinics. The Paracelsus clinics in Reichenbach, Adorf and Schöneck and the Rodewisch Saxon Hospital are involved in the Vogtland telematics network, which

(Foto/Photo by Igor Pastierovic, Text/Text by Petra Steps)

(Übersetzung/Translated by David Strauss)

Gesundheitsregion Vogtland / Vogtland Health Region

erweitert und die Kommunikation der Krankenhäuser untereinander und mit interessierten Partnern sowohl quantitativ als auch qualitativ verbessern möchte. Mit der Projektumsetzung soll die Qualität der Diagnosen weiter erhöht und die Zeit bis zur Freigabe der Befunde verkürzt werden.

Die Paracelsus-Klinik Schöneck befindet sich in Toplage mitten im „Balkon des Vogtlandes" genannten Urlauberort, der vor allem im Winter sportbegeisterte Touristen anzieht. In dem 135-Betten-Haus wird Wert auf individuelle Patientenbetreuung und familiäre Atmosphäre gelegt. Schwerpunkte sind die Abteilungen Innere Medizin, Chirurgie, Gynäkologie als Belegabteilung, die Anästhesie-Intensivmedizin sowie die Radiologie. Das relativ kleine Krankenhaus kooperiert eng mit externen Spezialkliniken. Um die Nachsorge kümmern sich Hausärzte und Pflegedienste in der Umgebung. Zum sanierten Altbau gehört ein 1998 in Betrieb genommener Neubau, der mit einem Gesamtinvestitionsvolumen von 23 Millionen Euro, davon 21,07 Millionen Euro Fördermitteln des Landes Sachsen entstand. In dem Gebäude sind zwei Pflegestationen, die komplette OP-Abteilung, die Sterilisation, die Physikalische Therapie sowie die Küche mit entsprechenden Personal- und Speiseräumen untergebracht. Die Paracelsus-Klinik Schöneck verfügt über ein Qualitätsmanagementsystem in der gesamten Einrichtung. Im August 2002 erhielt sie das Zertifikat für die Erfüllung der ISO-Norm nach DIN ISO 9001:2000.

Gar nicht weit entfernt finden wir die Paracelsus-Klinik Adorf, die das ehemalige Waldkrankenhaus Obervogtland mit dem 1996 durch den Vogtlandkreis finanzierten Ersatzneubau für die geschlossenen Krankenhäuser in Oelsnitz und Bad Elster vereint. In fünf chefärztlich geleiteten Fachabteilungen und weiteren Abteilungen für Diagnostik und Therapie stehen 172 Betten zur Verfügung. Die Klinik verfügt über eine im Kreißsaal integrierte Geburtswanne, die die Entscheidung für eine Wassergeburt wesentlich erleichtert, da die werdenden Mütter nicht den Raum wechseln müssen. Das Klinikum ist zugelassen als Weiterbildungsstätte für Ärzte, zum Beispiel auf dem Gebiet der Anästhesiologie und der Inneren Medizin.

Das landkreiseigene Klinikum Obergöltzsch Rodewisch ist das einzige Krankenhaus in Trägerschaft des Vogtlandkreises. Es verfügt über 310 Betten, sieben Kliniken (Innere Medizin, Chirurgie, Gelenk- und Unfallchirurgie, Gynäkologie/Geburtshilfe, Kinderheilkunde, Intensiv- und Schmerztherapie und HNO-Belegabteilung) sowie eine Notfallambulanz, die 365 Tage im Jahr durchgängig geöffnet ist. Als erstes vogtländisches Krankenhaus wurde das Klinikum nach dem krankenhausspezifischen Qualitätsverfahren KTQ (Kooperation für Transparenz und Qualität) zertifiziert und im September 2007 rezertifiziert. Durch das Verfahren nach KTQ wird die Qualität der Krankenhausbehandlung, die Leistung und Leistungsfähigkeit des Klinikums mittels eines sogenannten Qualitätsberichtes für alle Patienten, aber auch für niedergelassene Ärzte, die Krankenkassen und alle Interessierten transparent gemacht. Das durch die Deutsche Krebsgesellschaft e.V. und die Deutsche Gesellschaft für Senologie zertifizierte Brustzentrum Vogtland des Rodewischer Klinikums stellt ein ausgeprägtes Netzwerk aller an der Behandlung von Brustkrebspatienten beteiligten Fachgebiete dar. Dafür wurde eine Koope-

sets up and enlarges the exchange of digital radiography data, expands image communications and thereby improves communications between the hospitals and with interested parties in terms of quantity and quality. This project is designed to improve the quality of diagnosis and reduce the time needed to release diagnostic reports.

The Paracelsus Clinic in Schöneck right up on the "balcony of the Vogtland region", as the resort is known, attracts a large number of sports enthusiasts, especially in winter. Great importance is attached to individual patient care and a family atmosphere in the building that has 135 beds. The main focuses are internal medicine, surgery, gynaecology as an affiliated department, anaesthetics/intensive care and radiology. The relatively small hospital cooperates closely with external specialist clinics. General practitioners and nursing staff in the vicinity provide patients with after-care. The redeveloped old building includes a new building, which was opened in 1998 and was built with investments totalling € 23 million, € 21.7 million of which were subsidies from the state of Saxony. Two nursing wards, the complete operating theatre, the sterilisation unit, the physical therapy and the kitchen with the appropriate staff and dining rooms are housed in the building. The Paracelsus Clinic in Schöneck uses a quality management system in the whole facility. It was awarded the certificate for fulfilling the ISO standards in line with DIN EN 9001:2000 in August 2002.

The Paracelsus Clinic in Adorf is not situated that far away. It was the former Upper Vogtland Forest Hospital with the new building financed in 1996 by the Vogtland district to replace the hospitals in Oelsnitz and Bad Elster, which were closed. There are 172 beds available in five specialist departments led by a head physician for diagnosis and treatment. The clinic has a birth pool, which makes it easier for people to opt for a birth underwater as the expectant mother does not have to leave the room. The clinic is certified as a further training institute for doctors, e.g. in the field of anaesthetics and internal medicine.

The Obergöltzsch Hospital in Rodewisch is the only hospital which belongs to the Vogtland rural district. It has 310 beds, seven clinics (internal medicine, surgery, joint and accident surgery, gynaecology/obstetrics, paediatrics, intensive and pain care and an affiliated ENT department). It also has an outpatients' emergency department, which is open 365 days a year. It was the first hospital in the Vogtland region to be certified in line with the specific hospital quality procedure known as KTQ (Cooperation for Transparency and Quality) and was recertified in September 2007. The quality of the hospital treatment, the performance and efficiency of the hospital is revealed using a so-called quality report for all the patients, the doctors, health insurance schemes and all those interested as a result of the KTQ. The Vogtland Breast Centre, which has been certified by the German Cancer Society and the German Society for Senology, at the Rodewisch hospital provides a clear network for all the specialist departments involved in treating breast cancer patients. A cooperation arrangement involving

(Fotos/Photos by Franko Klinikum Obergöltzsch, Hartmut Briese)

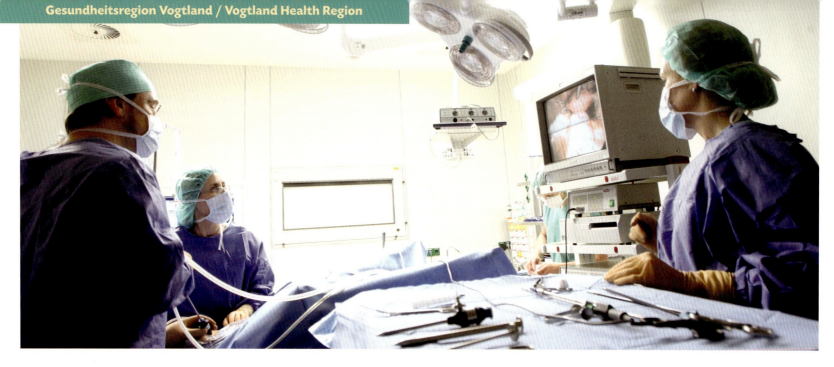

ration verschiedener Spezialisten gebildet. Den Patientinnen stehen in jeder Phase der Erkrankung, in Diagnostik, Therapie und Nachsorge die notwendigen Fachkompetenzen für die bestmögliche Versorgung zur Verfügung. Über 80 Millionen Euro flossen in den Bettenhaus- und Funktionsdiagnostik-Neubau, in die Sanierung sämtlicher Pflegestationen sowie in hochwertige Medizintechnik.

Das HELIOS Vogtland-Klinikum Plauen mit 610 Betten ist ein Krankenhaus der Schwerpunktversorgung mit überregionaler medizinischer Aufgabenstellung. Jährlich werden etwa 22.000 Patienten stationär und 37.000 ambulant behandelt. Damit gehört das Klinikum zu den großen Gesundheitseinrichtungen des Freistaates Sachsen. Als Akademisches Lehrkrankenhaus der Universität Leipzig übernimmt die Einrichtung wesentliche Aufgaben bei der Ausbildung von Fachpersonal. Einen Grund zur Freude hatten Mitarbeiter und Patienten im Juli 2007, als der neue Zentralbau in Betrieb genommen wurde. Damit fand eine zweijährige Baumaßnahme ihren Abschluss, in die rund 32 Millionen Euro flossen. Der neue Klinikkomplex umfasst ein Bettenhaus für 200 Betten mit Pflegestationen sowie zentralen Untersuchungs- und Behandlungsbereichen. Die modernen Räume und Geräte zur Diagnostik und Behandlung in allen Fachbereichen befinden sich in einem Gebäude und sorgen für kurze Wege. Für die Patienten verkürzen sich dadurch die Klinikaufenthalte und die Wartezeiten auf Operationen. Ein weiteres neues Bettenhaus mit 200 Plätzen befindet sich bereits in Planung.

Genau wie das Vogtland-Klinikum Plauen hat auch das Sächsische Krankenhaus für Psychiatrie und Neurologie (SKH Rodewisch) einen überregionalen Versorgungsauftrag. Es wurde 1893 als „Königlich Sächsische Landes-Heil-und Pflegeanstalt für Geisteskranke zu Untergöltzsch" eröffnet. Bis 1914 entstanden 41 Gebäude. Die Einrichtung entsprach damals den modernsten Vorstellungen für die Unterbringung psychisch Kranker. Heute verfügt die Klinik über 144 Betten und 20 Tagesklinikplätze in der Erwachsenenpsychiatrie, 76 Erwachsenen- und 18 Jugendplätze in der Forensischen Psychiatrie, 50 Betten und 20 Tagesklinikplätze für Kinder und Jugendpsychiatrie und 32 Betten in der Neurologie. Außerdem gibt es eine Institutsambulanz.

Weit über die Region hinaus bekannt ist die Rehabilitationseinrichtung für Suchtkranke mit 30 Therapieplätzen. Im Krankenhaus sind über 500 Mitarbeiter in allen Berufsgruppen beschäftigt.

Mit dem Bethanien-Krankenhaus Plauen steht dem Vogtland auch eine kirchlich-diakonische Gesundheitseinrichtung zur Verfügung. Das Krankenhaus ist ebenfalls nach den KTQ-Verfahren zertifiziert.

Zur Gesundheitsregion Vogtland gehört ein einzigartiges Ärztekonzept, das ge-

various specialists has been established. Patients have the necessary specialists available to provide them with the best possible care during each phase of the illness, diagnosis, treatment and aftercare. More than € 80 million were invested in the new ward and diagnostic centre, redeveloping old wards and high-quality medical technology.

The HELIOS Vogtland Hospital in Plauen with its 610 beds focuses on providing medical care to a wider region. About 22,000 inpatients and 37,000 outpatients are treated every year. This means that the hospital is one of the largest health centres in the Free State of Saxony. The centre assumes responsibility for important tasks in training specialist personnel in its role as an academic teaching hospital affiliated to the University of Leipzig. Staff and patients were delighted when the new central building was opened in July 2007. This concluded building work, which had continued for two years and cost approx. € 32 million. The new clinic complex comprises a building for 200 beds with nursing wards and central examination and treatment areas. The modern rooms and equipment for diagnosis and treatment in all the departments are in one building, so no long walks are involved. Patients' stay in hospital is reduced as a result – as are the waiting times for operations. A new building for a further 200 beds is already being planned.

The Saxon Hospital for Neurology and Psychiatry also cares for patients coming from a wide area, like the Vogtland Hospital in Plauen. It was opened in 1893 as the "Royal Saxon State Hospital and Care Centre for the Mentally Ill in Untergöltzsch". 41 buildings had been put up by 1914. The centre met the latest standards for dealing with mentally ill patients at the time. The hospital now has 144 beds and 20 day clinic places for adult psychiatry, 76 adult and 18 young people's places in the forensic psychiatry department, 50 beds and 20 day clinic places in the children's and young people's psychiatry department and 32 beds in the neurological department. There is also an outpatient department.

The rehabilitation centre for addicts with its 30 places is well known beyond the region. More than 500 members of staff are employed at the hospital in all the professional groups.

The Vogtland region also has a church/social care health centre at the Bethanian Hospital in Plauen. It is also certified in line with the KTQ process.

The Vogtland region also has a unique concept for its doctors, which was jointly drawn up by members of the district administrative office and the district medical association and was adopted in 2003. The Internet web-

(Fotos/Photos by Igor Pastierovic, Petra Steps)

Gesundheitsregion Vogtland / Vogtland Health Region

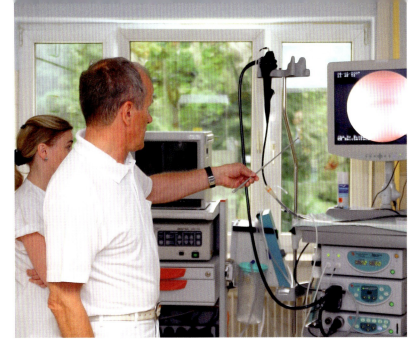

meinsam von Mitarbeitern der Kreisverwaltung und der Kreisärztekammer erarbeitet und 2003 beschlossen wurde. Auf der Internetseite www.vogtlandkreis.de unter dem Stichwort „Ärztekonzept" wird aktuell über Praktikumsplätze für Gymnasiasten und Studenten berichtet, es gibt eine Übersicht über offene Stellen sowie über das Angebot an Krankenhäusern und Rehakliniken, mit denen der Vogtlandkreis Vereinbarungen abgeschlossen hat und in denen man sich für eine Aus- und Weiterbildung bewerben kann. Bereits frühzeitig steuerte der Kreis dem drohenden Fachärztemangel entgegen und informiert über freiwerdende Arztpraxen, für die Nachfolger gesucht werden. Das Konzept soll junge Ärzte an die Region binden. Dabei beginnt die Zusammenarbeit zwischen den Gesundheitseinrichtungen und den künftigen Fachkräften bereits in der Schule. Regelmäßig bietet zum Beispiel das Klinikum „Obergöltzsch" Tage der offenen Tür für Gymnasiasten an, die später einen medizinischen Beruf erlernen wollen. Bis auf das Medizinstudium können alle Berufe in verschiedenen Einrichtungen des Vogtlandes gelernt werden. Die Krankenhäuser pflegen dafür sehr enge Beziehungen zu den Bildungseinrichtungen. Nach dem Medizinstudium kann die Facharztausbildung in einheimischen Krankenhäusern absolviert werden. Teilweise existieren schon Betreuungsverträge zwischen Studenten und ihrer künftigen Arbeitsstätte. Einmalig dürfte der finanzielle Zuschuss für Praktikanten und Famulatoren sowie für Schüler bei der Ferienarbeit sein. Mit all diesen Maßnahmen soll Schülern, Studenten und jungen Ärzten eine Perspektive in der Region geboten werden.

Zur lückenlosen Versorgung der Patienten gehört auch die Rehabilitation. In Falkenstein entstand aus dem ehemaligen DDR-Regierungssanatorium die Berufsgenossenschaftliche Klinik für Berufskrankheiten, die vor allem die Träger der gesetzlichen Unfallversicherung für ihre Versicherten nutzen. Dort wird nicht nur diagnostiziert und behandelt, sondern auch gutachterlich beurteilt. In der Bäderregion Bad Elster/Bad Brambach im Oberen Vogtland existieren modernste Kurkliniken. Die Kurkliniken mit ihren verschiedenen Eigentümern bieten eine breite Palette an. Es gibt nur wenige allgemein anerkannte Therapieformen, für die Patienten weite Reisen in Kauf nehmen müssen. Dabei verlassen sich Patienten und Ärzte nicht mehr nur auf schulmedizinische Verfahren, sondern nutzen zunehmend die integrative Medizin nach neusten Erkenntnissen. In den Kurorten existiert eine „weiße Industrie", die sich zu einem nicht zu unterschätzenden Wirtschaftsfaktor entwickelt hat und viele Arbeitsplätze sichert. Sie wird durch ein reichhaltiges kulturelles und sportliches Angebot in den Kurorten selbst oder durch Fahrten zu Sehenswürdigkeiten in der Umgebung ergänzt.

site www.vogtlandkreis.de provides current information about placements for grammar school pupils and students under the heading "Ärztekonzept"; it summarises the vacancies and which hospitals and rehabilitation centres are available, with which the Vogtland district has signed agreements and where people can apply for initial or further training. The district took measures to counter the threat of a lack of specialists at an early stage and provides information about doctors' practices that are becoming vacant where a successor is needed. The concept aims to tie young doctors to the region. Cooperation between the health centres and the future specialists begins even while they are still at school. The "Obergöltzsch" Hospital, for example, regularly has open days for grammar school pupils who want to pursue a medical career in future. Every profession, except medical studies, can be learned in the Vogtland region. So the hospitals maintain very close relations with the training centres. After medical studies, specialist training can be completed in local hospitals. Some students have already signed supervision agreements with their future place of work. The financial allowances for people on placements and medical students on placements and pupils doing holiday work must be unique. All these measures are designed to give pupils, students and young doctors a future perspective in the region.

Rehabilitation is also an element for closing any gaps in the system. The Statutory Accident Insurance Clinic for Work-Related Sicknesses, which is primarily used by the statutory accident insurance schemes for their patients, was created out of the former East German government sanatorium. Doctors not only diagnose and treat, but also issue medical assessments. The latest spa clinics can be found at the Bad Elster/Bad Brambach spa centres in the Upper Vogtland area. The spa clinics with their various owners provide a wide range of services. There are few generally recognised types of treatment which are not offered to patients here. But patients and doctors no longer just rely on traditional medicine, but also increasingly use integrative medicine using the latest knowledge. The spas have their own "white industry", which has developed into a major economic factor and guarantees many jobs. It is complemented by a wide range of cultural and sporting events in the spa towns themselves and by trips to sights in the surrounding area.

Rundum gut versorgt
In Very Good Hands

Das Leistungsspektrum des Klinikums Obergöltzsch Rodewisch ist breit gefächert. Es werden in allen Kliniken hochwertige medizinische Leistungen den Patienten der Region und darüber hinaus angeboten. Im Jahr 2006 wurden im Klinikum 17.500 ambulante Patienten und 12.700 stationäre Patienten behandelt.

Dem Patienten wird eine **durchgehende Behandlungskette** geboten, beginnend mit der Überweisung durch den niedergelassenen Arzt, der rund um die Uhr besetzten Notfallambulanz bzw. den Chefarztambulanzen bis hin zum stationären Bereich. Unser Leistungsspektrum umfasst des weiteren das ambulante Operieren, die Möglichkeit der vor- und nachstationären Behandlung sowie die ambulante physiotherapeutische Betreuung.

Mit hochqualifizierten Teams aus Ärzten und Pflegepersonal in **interdisziplinärer Zusammenarbeit** sowie mit modernster technischer Ausstattung erfüllt das Klinikum alle Vorraussetzungen für eine optimale und umfassende Versorgung der Patienten in einem hotelähnlichen Ambiente und freundlicher Atmosphäre.

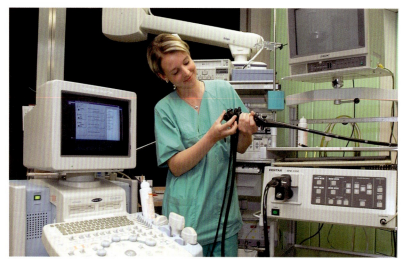

Um die Versorgungsqualität der ambulanten Behandlungen noch weiter zu verbessern, wurde im September 2006 das **Ambulante OP-Zentrum** am Klinikum Obergöltzsch eröffnet, in dem sich die Patienten den ambulanten Eingriffen fachkompetent unterziehen können.

Im Zuge der zunehmenden Vernetzung des ambulanten und des stationären medizinischen Sektors und weiterer Qualitätsverbesserungen für die Patienten wurde im Oktober 2007 ein **Medizinisches Versorgungszentrum (MVZ)** am Klinikum Obergöltzsch mit einer Augenarzt- und HNO-Arzt-Praxis eröffnet. Der Zusammenschluss von Ärzten aus verschiedenen Fachrichtungen trägt dazu bei, die Betreuung der Patienten zu optimieren und deren Wege zu verkürzen.

Ebenfalls im Oktober 2007 wurde das **Beckenbodenzentrum** im Klinikum Obergöltzsch in Betrieb genommen. Die Behandlung von proktologischen Erkrankungen sowie Harn- und Stuhlinkontinenz durch das qualifizierte Fachpersonal stehen dabei im Mittelpunkt.

Es ist bereits am Klinikum zur Tradition geworden, regelmäßig **„Samstagsakademien"** zur Information der interessierten Bevölkerung durchzuführen. Bei diesen Veranstaltungen werden den Besuchern interessante und aktuelle medizinische Themen durch unser kompetentes Fachärzte-Team im Rahmen eines Vortrages nahegebracht. Informationen zu den jeweiligen Veranstaltungen werden vom Klinikum in einem jährlich erscheinenden Flyer sowie regelmäßig in der Tagespresse veröffentlicht.

Das Klinikum Obergöltzsch Rodewisch ist zertifiziert nach KTQ (Kooperation für Transparenz und Qualität). Ebenfalls ist das bestehende Brustzentrum Vogtland nach den hohen Qualitätsanforderungen der Deutschen Krebsgesellschaft e. V. und der Deutschen Gesellschaft für Senologie zertifiziert.

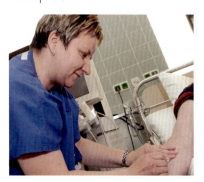

The range of services provided by the Obergöltzsch Clinic in Rodewisch is very broad. High-quality medical services are provided for patients from the surrounding region and beyond at all the clinics. 17,500 outpatients and 12,700 in-patients were treated at the centre in 2006.

Patients are provided with an ongoing chain of treatments, starting with a referral from a local doctor, an accident and emergency department that is manned around the clock or the head doctor's clinic and the hospital wards. Our range of services also includes out-patient operations, the option of receiving treatment before or after your hospital stay and out-patient physiotherapy care.

The clinic is fully equipped to provide patients with ideal and comprehensive care in a hotel-like and friendly atmosphere – with its highly qualified teams of doctors and nursing staff working in an interdisciplinary way and the latest technical equipment.

The out-patient operating theatre was opened at the Obergöltzsch Clinic in September 2006 to improve the quality of care for out-patient treatment even further. Patients are operated on here in a professional and competent manner.

As a result of the increasing integration of the out-patient and in-patient medical sector and further improvements in quality for patients, a Medical Care Centre was opened at the Obergöltzsch Clinic in October 2007 with an eye specialist and ENT practice. This amalgamation of doctors from various specialist areas plays a role in improving care for patients and having everything on the spot.

(Fotos/Photos by Franco)

(Übersetzung/Translated by David Strauss)

Klinikum Obergöltzsch in Rodewisch

Kompetenz
Vertrauen
Geborgenheit

Das Klinikum Obergöltzsch Rodewisch (310 Betten) umfasst folgende Kliniken und Abteilungen:

The Pelvic Floor Centre at the Obergöltzsch Clinic was also opened in October 2007. It focuses on treating proctological illnesses or aconuresis and encopresis.

The clinic has also established a tradition of regularly providing "Saturday academies" to inform interested people about issues. Interesting and current medical subjects are introduced to visitors at these events by our competent team of specialists who give a lecture. Information on these events is published by the clinic in a leaflet that appears every year and they are regularly mentioned in the local press.

The Obergöltzsch Clinic in Rodewisch is certified according to KTQ (Cooperation for Transparency and Quality in Healthcare). The Vogtland Breast Centre has also been certified by the German Cancer Society and the German Society for Senology that it meets their high quality standards.

- Medizinische Klinik mit den Sektionen
  - Allgemeine Innere Medizin
  - Kardiologie
  - Gastroenterologie
- Chirurgische Klinik
- Klinik für Unfall- und Gelenkchirurgie
- Frauenklinik
- Klinik für Anästhesie, Intensiv- und Schmerztherapie
- Klinik für Kinder- und Jugendmedizin
- HNO-Belegabteilung
- Radiologisches Institut/Computertomographie/Mammotome®

- Physiotherapie
- Funktionsdiagnostik
- Psychoonkologin
- Sozialdienst
- Seelsorge
- Zentrallabor
- Zentralapotheke
- Notfallambulanz (Tag und Nacht dienstbereit)
- Wund- und Fußambulanz
- Ambulantes OP-Zentrum
- Zertifiziertes Brustzentrum
- Mutter-Kind-Zentrum
- Beckenbodenzentrum
- Medizinisches Versorgungszentrum mit Augenarzt- und HNO-Arzt-Praxis

Weitere Einrichtungen:
- Frauenarztpraxis
- Logopädiepraxis
- Sanitätsfachgeschäft
- Hörgeräteakustiker

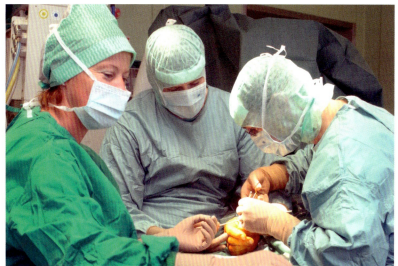

Klinikum Obergöltzsch Rodewisch
Stiftstraße 10, 08228 Rodewisch
Telefon +49 (0) 3744 361-0
Telefax +49 (0) 3744 32907

www.klinikum-obergoeltzsch.de
postmaster@klinikum-obergoeltzsch.de

Im Mittelpunkt steht der Mensch

People are the Focus of Attention

Das Sächsische Krankenhaus für Psychiatrie und Neurologie Rodewisch (SKH) ist eine Einrichtung mit langer Tradition und gutem Ruf national als auch international auf dem Gebiet der psychiatrischen und neurologischen Diagnostik und Therapie.

Im SKH Rodewisch werden Kinder, Jugendliche und Erwachsene mit jeglichen psychiatrischen, psychosomatischen und neurologischen Erkrankungen und Störungen behandelt. Über 500 Mitarbeiter, Ärzte, Pflegepersonal, Beschäftigte in den diagnostisch-therapeutischen als auch in den Verwaltungs- und technischen Diensten setzen sich für die Genesung ihrer Patienten ein. Träger der Einrichtung ist der Freistaat Sachsen, vertreten durch das Sächsische Staatsministerium für Soziales. „Wir betrachten unsere Patienten ganzheitlich, mit all ihren persönlichen und kulturellen Besonderheiten", so heißt es im Leitbild, das zur Orientierung und Hilfestellung in der täglichen Arbeit dient. Es beinhaltet die Wertvorstellungen und Zielsetzungen, nach denen die Mitarbeiterinnen und Mitarbeiter handeln. Diagnostisch-therapeutisches Handeln unter Berücksichtigung der körperlichen, seelischen und sozialen Seiten der Erkrankung zählen ebenso dazu wie therapeutisch-pflegerische Wertschätzung und einfühlendes Verstehen unter Achtung der Würde und Selbstbestimmung der Patienten.

Zum Krankenhaus gehört die Klinik für Psychiatrie und Psychotherapie mit den Fachbereichen Allgemeine Psychiatrie, Gerontopsychiatrie und der Station für geistig Behinderte. Sie verfügt über 144 vollstationäre Betten, 20 tagesklinische Plätze und eine Institutsambulanz. Angegliedert ist eine Rehabilitationseinrichtung für Alkohol- und Medikamentenabhängige mit 30 Therapieplätzen. Die Klinik steht in Tradition der „Rodewischer Thesen", die für eine grundlegende Erneuerung der Psychiatrie auf einem internationalen Symposium für psychiatrische Rehabilitation 1963 verabschiedet worden sind. Darüber hinaus orientiert man sich an den Zielsetzungen der modernen psychiatrischer Versorgungskonzepte. Durch Aufklärung, Verhandeln und Transparenz soll der Patient zum eigenverantwortlichen Mitwirken an der Behandlung und Rehabilitation motiviert werden. Die auf den individuellen Hilfebedarf ausgerichtete Therapie und Pflege erfolgt in multiprofessionellen Teams. In diesen arbeiten Ärzte, Pflegepersonal, Diplompsychologen, Sozialarbeiter, Ergotherapeuten, Physiotherapeuten, Sport- und Bewegungstherapeuten, Kunsttherapeuten sowie weitere soziotherapeutische Mitarbeiter zusammen.

The roots of the Saxon Hospital for Psychiatry and Neurology in Rodewisch (SKH) go back a long way and it has a good reputation in Germany and internationally in the field of psychiatric and neurological diagnosis and treatment. Children, young people and adults suffering from all kinds of psychiatric, psychosomatic and neurological sicknesses and dysfunctions are treated at the SKH Rodewisch. More than 500 members of staff, doctors, nursing personnel and employees in the diagnostic/therapeutic and administrative and technical departments are there to help patients recover. The Free State of Saxony, represented by the Saxon State Ministry for Social Affairs, is the body responsible for the centre.
"We view our patients as a whole, with all their personal and cultural peculiarities," is the message in the hospital's mission statement, which helps to provide a sense of direction and assistance for the staff's daily work. This document contains the moral concepts and goals, which dictate staff practices. Diagnostic/therapeutic action taking into account the physical, emotional and social aspects of the sickness are just as much a part of procedures here as the therapeutic/nursing assessment and empathetic understanding shown – while not neglecting patients' sense of dignity and right to determine their own lives.

The Clinic for Psychiatry and Psychotherapy with its general psychiatry and geriatric psychiatry departments and the ward for the mentally retarded are all part of the hospital. The clinic has 144 inpatient beds, 20 day clinic places and an out-patients' clinic. A rehabilitation centre for people suffering from alcohol or drug addiction with 30 places is housed in an annex. The clinic upholds the tradition of the "Rodewisch Theses", which were passed at an international symposium for psychiatric rehabilitation in 1963 and called for a fundamental new approach to psychiatry. The hospital is also guided by the goals set by modern psychiatric care concepts. Patients are motivated to take responsibility for themselves and play their role in the treatment and rehabilitation process based on clarification, discussion and transparency. The treatment and care, which is designed to give patients individual help, is provided by teams involving people in various professions. Doctors, nursing staff, trained psychologists, social workers, occupational therapists, physiotherapists, sports and movement therapists, art therapists and other social therapeutic staff all work together.
The Clinic for Children's and Young People's Psychiatry and Psychotherapy

(Fotos/Photos by Igor Pastierovic, Hartmut Briese, Übersetzung/Translated by David Strauss)

Sächsisches Krankenhaus für Psychiatrie und Neurologie Rodewisch

Die Klinik für Kinder- und Jugendpsychiatrie und Psychotherapie mit den Tageskliniken in Plauen und Annaberg, der Institutsambulanz, der Jugendforensik und der Klinikschule sind ein wichtiger Bestandteil des Sächsischen Krankenhauses in Rodewisch. Das Aufgabengebiet umfasst die Prävention, Diagnostik, Behandlung und Rehabilitation von Entwicklungsstörungen sowie von psychischen und psychosomatischen Störungen und Erkrankungen bei Kindern, Jugendlichen und Heranwachsenden. Die Klinik verfügt über die anerkannten Möglichkeiten der komplexen und multiprofessionellen Diagnostik und Therapie (medizinisch, psychologisch, pädagogisch-erzieherisch) unter Einbeziehung der Bezugspersonen. Es stehen 50 Plätze zur stationären kinder- und jugendpsychiatrischen Behandlung sowie 20 tagesklinische Plätze in Plauen und Annaberg-Buchholz zur Verfügung. Die jugendpsychiatrische Forensik ist auf 18 Plätze begrenzt.

Die Neurologische Klinik befindet sich in einem neu erbauten Gebäude. Neben dem Bettenbereich sind Intensivabteilung und Stroke-Unit, einer Schlaganfall-Spezialeinheit, Physiotherapie, Neuropsychologie, Neuroradiologie einschließlich MRT, Neurophysiologie, Ergotherapie, Logopädie und Sozialdienst untergebracht. Mit einer Kapazität von 32 Betten, darunter 4 Schlaganfalls- und 4 Intensivbetten und im Durchschnitt 6,5 Ärzte werden hier alle Krankheiten des peripheren und zentralen Nervensystems sowie Muskelerkrankungen diagnostiziert und behandelt.

Die Klinik für Forensische Psychiatrie für männliche Erwachsene arbeitet in zwei Bereichen: 1. strafrechtliche Begutachtung und 2. Maßregelvollzugsbehandlung. Im weiteren Sinne deckt das Fach Forensische Psychiatrie jenen breiten Überlappungsbereich zwischen Recht und Psychiatrie ab, der sich aus den rechtlichen Problemen im Umgang mit psychisch Kranken und Gestörten ergibt. Im Maßregelvollzug befinden sich Personen, die erhebliche Straftaten begangen haben. Im Rahmen des Strafverfahrens ist dafür eine forensische Begutachtung erforderlich. Maßgebend für die Einweisung ist aber gleichzeitig die Annahme einer weiteren erheblichen Gefahr für die Allgemeinheit infolge der vorliegenden psychischen Störung.

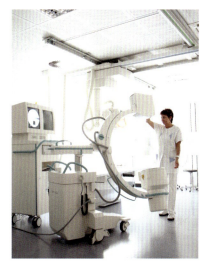

Zu den diagnostisch und therapeutischen Diensten des SKH Rodewisch gehören die physiotherapeutischen Behandlungen (zum Beispiel Hippotherapie, Manuelle Therapie, Reflexzonenmassage, manuelle Extension der WHS, medizinische Wannenbäder, Unterwasserdruckmassage uvm.) und die ergotherapeutischen Angebote für die Fachbereiche Psychiatrie und Neurologie. Im Fachbereich Psychiatrie werden handwerklich kreative Tätigkeiten in verschiedenen Therapieformen und Therapiemethoden genutzt, um z.B. eingeschränkte Basisfähigkeiten, wie Kontaktverhalten, Konzentration und Ausdauer zu trainieren. Angeboten werden diese Therapiemaßnahmen auf den Stationen und in der Tagesklinik. Im Fachbereich Neurologie bestehen die Ziele der Behandlung in einer Verbesserung der grobmotorischen und feinmotorischen Fähigkeiten: Beübung der Bewegungskoordination, der Wahrnehmungsstörungen, der Körperwahrnehmung und der Sensibilität sowie von Konzentrations-und Gedächtnisstörungen.

in the day clinics in Plauen and Annaberg, the outpatients' clinic, the young people's forensic centre and the clinic school are an important part of the Saxon Hospital in Rodewisch. This department deals with the prevention, diagnosis, treatment and rehabilitation of people with development problems and mental and psychosomatic problems and dysfunctions in children, young people and adolescents. The clinic has at its disposal the recognised facilities to provide complex and multi-professional diagnosis and treatment (medical, psychological and educational) and involve the individual's friends and family. There are 50 places to provide inpatient psychiatric treatment for children and young people and 20 day clinic places in Plauen and Annaberg-Buchholz. But there are only 18 places in the youth psychiatry forensic centre.

The Neurological Clinic is located in a new building. This not only houses wards with beds, but also an intensive care and stroke unit, a special area for people who have suffered a stroke, physiotherapy, neuropsychology, neuroradiology including MRT, neurophysiology, occupational therapy, speech therapy facilities and social workers. It has space for 32 beds, 4 of which are for stroke patients and 4 for intensive care. On average there are 6.5 doctors diagnosing and treating all kinds of sicknesses of the peripheral and central nervous system and muscular disorders.

The Clinic for Forensic Psychiatry for male adults works in two main areas: 1. carrying out appraisals related to criminal cases and 2. providing treatment for criminals with psychological problems. In a broader sense, forensic psychiatry covers a wide area of overlap between law and psychiatry; this is caused by the legal problems of dealing with the mentally sick and disturbed. People who have committed serious crimes are kept in the secure hospital unit. A forensic assessment is often needed as part of the criminal process. Patients are only referred if it is assumed that they pose a threat to society on account of the mental dysfunction from which they are suffering.

Physiotherapy treatment (for example, hippotherapy, manual therapy, reflex zone massage, manual extension of the cervical spinal column, medical baths, underwater pressure massage etc) and occupation therapy for the psychiatry and neurology departments are all part of the diagnostic and therapeutic treatments provided by the SKH Rodewisch. In the psychiatric field, various creative activities are used as treatment in order to train limited basic abilities like social contact, concentration and stamina. This treatment is provided on the wards and in the day clinic. In the neurological field, specialists aim to improve the basic and precise capabilities of the body's movements: this involves help with the coordination of movements, perception disorders, body perception and sensibility as well as concentration and memory problems.

Sächsisches Krankenhaus für
Psychiatrie und Neurologie Rodewisch
Bahnhofstraße · D-08228 Rodewisch
Telefon   +49 (0) 3744 366-0
Telefax   +49 (0) 3744 366-1199
www.skh-rodewisch.de
poststelle@skhro.sms.sachsen.de

Berufsgenossenschaftliche Klinik für Berufskrankheiten Falkenstein

Nachhaltige Gesundung in der grünen Lunge des Vogtlandes

Long-term Recovery in the Natural Vogtland Air

Schon der erste Eindruck vermittelt Ruhe und Geborgenheit. Die moderne Berufsgenossenschaftliche Klinik für Berufskrankheiten Falkenstein liegt eingebettet in einer herrlichen Parkanlage mit altem Baumbestand, kleinen Seen und Wegen, die zum Ausschwärmen einladen. Körperliches und geistiges Wohlbefinden finden hier gleichwertige Beachtung. Medizinische Funktionsabteilungen und Therapien auf dem neuesten wissenschaftlichen Stand unterstützt durch umfangreiche Physio-, Sport- und Ergotherapie gepaart mit koordinierten Bewegungsprogrammen in der Natur, in der Sporthalle oder im Bewegungsbad gehören in der Klinik ebenso zum Genesungsprogramm wie der Saunabesuch und die zahlreichen abgebotenen Freizeitvergnügen. Schwimmbad, Billard, automatische Kegelbahn, Tischtennis, Außenschach, Minigolf, Fahrradtouren mit den kostenlos zur Ausleihe stehenden Trekkingrädern, Spaziergänge in der Parkanlage, kulturelle Abendveranstaltungen, Ausflüge mit dem klinikeigenen Bus, – „Luft zum Atmen" gibt es auf vielfältige Art und Weise, hier gibt es für jeden Geschmack Abwechslung oder Ruhe und Entspannung.

Rund 90 Mitarbeiterinnen und Mitarbeiter kümmern sich um die Belange und das Wohl der Patienten. Der Chefärztin Dr. med. Nicola Kotschy-Lang steht ein Team aus sieben Ärztinnen und Ärzten zur Seite. Gemeinsam mit 15 Schwestern und Pflegern werden bei einer Aufnahmekapazität von 127 Betten im Jahr ca. 1350 Patienten betreut. Freundlich eingerichte Einzel- und Doppelzimmer mit Dusche, WC, Telefon, TV und Balkon stehen den Klinikpatienten und eventuellen Begleitpersonen zur Verfügung. Gemeinsame Aufenthaltsräume laden zu Gesellschaftsspielen und zu geselligen Film- und Fernsehabenden ein. Die im Eingangsbereich befindliche Cafeteria und der Kiosk für Souvenirs, Postkarten und Gebrauchsartikel lassen Raum für spontane Genüsse und Bedürfnisse.

Weil Essen und Trinken Leib und Seele zusammenhalten gehört ein schmackhaftes, abwechslungsreiches und vor allem gesundes Essen zu den Eckpfeilern der erfolgreichen Behandlung. Morgens und am Abend ein reich gedecktes Buffet mit Diätecke und mittags zwei Gerichte á drei Gänge sorgen für das leibliche Wohl. Neben Vollkost bietet die mit dem RAL-Siegel ausgezeichnete Küche des Hauses ballststoff- und kalziumreiche, purin- und cholesterinarme Mahlzeiten und Diabetikerkost an.

Initial impressions convey a sense of ease and comfort. The modern Statutory Accident Insurance Clinic for Work-Related Sicknesses in Falkenstein is embedded in a beautiful park with plenty of trees, small lakes and footpaths, which encourage people to move about. Equal attention is paid to people's physical and mental well-being. Medical departments and the latest treatments backed by physiotherapy, sports therapy and occupational therapy and coupled with coordinated exercise programmes in the fresh air, the sports hall and the exercise pool are just as much part of the recovery programme as visits to the sauna and the many leisure pursuits on offer. A swimming pool, billiards, an automatic skittle alley, table tennis, outdoor chess, miniature golf, cycling tours on mountain bikes that can be hired free of charge, walks in the park, cultural evenings, excursions in the clinic's bus – there are plenty of ways of "breathing in the fresh air" – there is something here to cater for every taste: having a change, a rest or some relaxation.

About 90 employees cater for the needs and well-being of the patients. The head physician Dr. med. Nicola Kotschy-Lang is supported by a team of seven doctors. 15 nurses help care for about 1350 patients every year; the clinic has 127 beds. Well-equipped single and double rooms with a shower, WC, telephone, TV and balcony are available for the clinic's patients or accompanying relatives. Common lounges encourage people to join in games and enjoy film and TV evenings together. The cafeteria in the entrance area and the kiosk for souvenirs, post cards and daily items for personal use allow people to indulge themselves or satisfy their needs.

Food and drink keep body and soul together, so tasty, varied and healthy meals form a major part of any successful treatment. A splendid buffet with dishes for those on a special diet is provided in the mornings and evenings and there is a choice of two three-course meals at midday. The centre's cuisine, which has been awarded a prize for its quality, provides meals that are full of fibre and calcium and low in purine and cholesterol, as well as food suitable for diabetics.

(Fotos/Photos by Igor Pastierovic, Übersetzung/Translated by David Strauss)

Berufsgenossenschaftliche Klinik für Berufskrankheiten Falkenstein

In der Klinik werden berufsbedingte Lungen- und Atemwegserkrankungen diagnostiziert, behandelt und gutachterlich beurteilt. Schwerpunktmäßig behandelt man Patienten, die an einer Silikose, Asbestose, an einer durch allergiesierende-, chemisch-irritative oder toxische Stoffe verursachten obstruktiven Atemwegserkrankungen leiden sowie Patienten im Rahmen der Nachsorge beruflich verursachter Bronchialkarzinome. Desweiteren werden beruflich bedingte Hauterkrankungen therapiert.

Zur Abklärung der Krankheitsbilder stehen hochmoderne, patientengerechte diagnostische Methoden zur Verfügung. Beispielsweise führt man im Lungenlabor zur abgrenzenden Diagnose von Erkrankungen des Herz-Kreislaufsystems verschiedene Formen des EKGs, Langzeitblutdruckmessung und eine Farbdopplerchografie durch. Eine besonders wichtige Behandlungsform bei chronischen Lungen- und Atemwegserkrankungen ist die physikalische Therapie., deren Basis die verschiedenen Inhalationen darstellen. Ergänzend dazu werden Atemtherapien und Atemschulungen sowie Lungensport durchgeführt.

Die Patienten sind infolge des Krankheitsbildes sowohl körperlich als auch sozial erheblich eingeschränkt. Ganzheitlich ausgerichte Rehabilitationskonzepte im Kontext mit der beruflichen Biografie therapieren den gesamten Menschen. Einheit von Körper und Geist ist in der Berufsgenossenschaftlichen Klinik für Berufskrankheiten in Falkenstein gelebte Realität.

Über die Atemwege vollzieht sich der wichtigste energetische Austausch des Menschen mit seiner Umwelt. Diese Bedeutung bezieht sich sowohl auf die biochemischen und physiologischen Prozesse als auch auf die Gewinnung neuer Lebensenergie durch bewußte Atemtechniken, gesunder Lebensweise, innerer Besinnung und Freude an ausreichender Bewegung. Das Erlangen neuer Sichtweisen auf den eigenen Körper, innere Ruhe und Kraft, neue Mobilität und die damit verbundene bessere Lebensqualität befördern einen nachhaltigen Gesundungsprozess über den in der Regel vierwöchigen stationären Klinikaufenthaltes hinaus.

Experts at the clinic diagnose, treat and assess work-related lung and respiratory problems. The main focus is on treating patients suffering from silicosis, asbestosis, obstructive respiratory problems caused by allergies, chemical irritants or toxic substances, and patients requiring aftercare for lung cancer, which has been caused by working conditions. Skin diseases caused by working conditions are also treated.

Extremely modern, patient-oriented diagnostic methods are used to monitor conditions. Various forms of ECG, long-term blood pressure monitoring and a colour Doppler ecography machine are used in the lung laboratory to diagnose the extent of cardiac and circulatory diseases. Physical treatments are an important form of treatment for chronic lung and respiratory illnesses. Various inhalations form the basis of this. Breathing treatment and training and lung exercises are also provided.

Patients are subject to major restrictions physically and socially due to their physical condition. Holistic rehabilitation concepts related to the patients' professional career cater for the whole person. The unity of body and soul is a reality that is lived out at the Statutory Accident Insurance Clinic in Falkenstein.

The most important energy swap in human beings takes place in the lungs. This not only relates to the biochemical and physiological processes, but also gaining new energy through conscious breathing techniques, a healthy lifestyle, inner reflection and a sense of pleasure at being able to move about. Patients' ability to view their own body differently, gain peace of mind and strength, new mobility and the increase in the quality of life associated with this encourage a long-term process of recovery, which continues beyond the normal four week stay at the clinic.

BGKF
Berufsgenossenschaftliche
Klinik für Berufskrankheiten
Falkenstein/Vogtland

Lauterbacher Straße 16
D - 08223 Falkenstein
Telefon +49 (0) 3745 746-0
Telefax +49 (0) 3745 746-5204
info@klinik-falkenstein.de
www.klinik-falkenstein.de

Kur & Rehabilitation / Spa Facilities and Rehabilitation

Klinik Bad Brambach: Mit Radon gegen Rheuma
Bad Brambach Clinic – Fighting Rheumatism with Radon

Etwas außerhalb des Ortskerns im Kurviertel von Bad Brambach liegt die 1994 neu errichtete Klinik Bad Brambach. In der landschaftlich reizvoll gelegenen Einrichtung werden entzündlich-rheumatische sowie orthopädische und Herz-Kreislauf-Erkrankungen behandelt. Den Klinikpatienten stehen über 200 Einzel- und 10 Doppelzimmer in moderner Ausstattung mit Balkon zur Verfügung. Neben verschiedenen konservativen Behandlungsmaßnahmen wie der Krankengymnastik, Wärme-, Kälte- und Elektrotherapie, Lymphdrainage, Massagen oder Sport- und Bewegungstherapie, setzt die Klinik besonders bei der Therapie von rheumatoider Arthritis und Morbus Bechterew auf das ortsgebundene Heilmittel Radon. Radon ist ein natürliches, geruchloses, farbloses, radioaktives Edelgas und wird traditionell zur Behandlung entzündlich-rheumatischer Erkrankungen eingesetzt. Die in Bad Brambach entdeckten Quellen weisen einen sehr hohen Radongehalt auf, der zusammen mit großen Mengen an gelöstem Kohlendioxid und Mineralsalzen eine weltweit einzigartige Kombination darstellt. Radon wirkt nachweislich schmerz- und entzündungshemmend. Weiterhin wirkt sich die Radonbehandlung positiv auf die Gelenkbewegungsfunktion und die körpereigenen Abwehrkräfte aus. In der Klinik wird die Radontherapie mittels Wannenbädern und Trinkkuren durchgeführt. Neben Behandlung und Therapie bietet die Klinik verschiedene Möglichkeiten während des Aufenthaltes die Freizeit aktiv zu gestalten. Zum einen laden die gemütliche Cafeteria und die Aufenthaltsräume zum Verweilen ein, zum anderen können die Patienten sich bei geführten Wanderungen, beim Tischtennis, bei der Tanztherapie, im Bewegungsbad, beim Billard oder beim Freilandschach sportlich betätigen. Das kulturelle Leben kommt während eines Klinikaufenthaltes auch nicht zu kurz- so finden regelmäßig Konzerte, Filmvorführungen und interessante Vorträge statt.

Bad Brambach Clinic, which was newly built in 1994, is located just outside the centre of town in the spa district. The clinic, which is situated in charming countryside, treats patients suffering from rheumatic inflammation, orthopaedic problems or heart and circulation diseases. More than 200 single and 10 double rooms with modern equipment and a balcony are available for clinic patients. The clinic uses traditional treatments like physiotherapy, heat therapy, cryotherapy and electrical stimulation therapy, lymph drainage, massage, sports or exercise, but also treats rheumatoid arthritis and ankylosing spondylitis with radon, which occurs naturally in the area. Radon is a natural, odourless, colourless, radioactive inert gas and is traditionally used to treat rheumatic inflammation. The springs discovered in Bad Brambach have a very high radon content and when used with large amounts of dissolved carbon dioxide and mineral salts, provides a unique combination. It has been proven that radon inhibits pain and inflammation. The radon treatment also has a positive effect on joint movements and the body's own defence mechanisms. Radon treatment is provided in the form of baths and drinking the waters. The clinic not only provides treatment for patients, but also gives them a variety of opportunities to actively enjoy their leisure time. The cosy cafeteria and day rooms encourage people to spend time there, but patients can also go on guided walks, play table tennis, go dancing, swimming or play billiards or open-air chess. There is no shortage of culture during a stay at the clinic either – there are regular concerts, film shows and interesting lectures.

Dr. Ebel Fachkliniken GmbH & Co.
Rehabilitationsklinik Bad Brambach KG
Christian-Schüller-Straße 14
D-08648 Bad Brambach
Telefon +49 (0) 37438 96-510
Telefax +49 (0) 37438 96-105
patientenservice@klinik-bad-brambach.de
www.ebel-klinik.de
www.klinik-bad-brambach.de

(Fotos/Photos by Klinik Bad Brambach, Übersetzung/Translated by David Strauss)

Kur & Rehabilitation / Spa Facilities and Rehabilitation

Gesundheit gewinnen - Vitalität erleben - Erholung genießen

Gaining Health - Experiencing Vitality - Enjoying Relaxation

In bester Lage, am sonnendurchfluteten Südhang des Brunnenberges, in der traditionsreichen Kultur– und Festspielstadt Bad Elster liegt die Fachklinik für Kardiologie und Orthopädie.
Die Klinik ist in beiden Fachgebieten spezialisiert und überregional bekannt durch ihr differenziertes und erfolgreiches Leistungsprofil bei den Indikationen:

Kardiologie
Herz-Kreislauf-Erkrankungen, Anschlussrehabilitation nach Herz-, Herzklappenoperation, Bypassoperation Z.n. Myocardinfarkt, Z.n. PTCA u. Stentimplantation, Funktionelle Herzsyndrome, Schlaganfall

Orthopädie
Erkrankungen der Wirbelsäule und des Muskel- und Bandapparates, Arthrose der großen und kleinen Gelenke, Z.n. endoprothetischer Versorgung von Knie-, Hüft- und Schultergelenken, Wurzelkompressionssyndrome, Z.n. Wirbelsäulen OP, Behandlung nach Gliedmaßenamputationen, Osteoporose etc.

Wir sind Partner der Rentenversicherungsträger und Krankenkassen.
Ganzjährig bietet die Klinik individuelle, indikationsspezifische Privataufenthalte, Pauschalkuren und Präventionsprogramme an. Für Wiederkehrer gibt es ein attraktives Rabattsystem. Die Aufnahme von Begleitpersonen und deren Teilnahme an den Aktivangeboten zur Prävention ist im Klinikkonzept fest verankert. Die aktuellen Privatangebote sind jederzeit bei uns buchbar.
Das Behandlungszentrum umfasst die Anschlussheilbehandlung/Anschlussrehabilitation (AHB/AR), medizinische Leistungen zur stationären Rehabilitation (Heilverfahren), ambulante/teilstationäre Rehabilitation, berufsgenossenschaftliche stationäre Weiterbehandlung (BGSW) sowie die ambulante physio- und ergotherapeutische Behandlungen für die Indikationen Orthopädie und Kardiologie.
Unseren Patienten und Gästen stehen 236 zum größten Teil behindertengerecht ausgestattete Einzelzimmer mit separater Nasszelle, Telefon und TV zur Verfügung. Neben einer modern und großzügig ausgestatteten medizinisch-diagnostischen sowie therapeutischen Abteilung bestehen vielfältige Möglichkeiten der Freizeitgestaltung. Die medizinische Leitung des Hauses obliegt Herrn Chefarzt Dr. Breitbeck (Orthopädie) und Herrn Chefarzt Dr. Siegel (Kardiologie).
Unsere neue Seniorenresidenz Brunnenbergblick bietet sowohl vollstationäre – als auch Kurzzeitpflege, Betreuung mit Herz und Verstand für Senioren, die ein neues zuhause suchen. Für Pflegebedürftige und Angehörige bieten wir das Programm "PflegePlus" (Preise auf Anfrage).

Wir freuen uns auf Sie.

The Specialist Clinic for Cardiology and Orthopaedics is situation in an ideal location on the sun-drenched south slope of the Brunnenberg in the traditional cultural and festival town of Bad Elster.
The clinic specialises in both areas and is known nationally for its sophisticated and successful skills in tackling the following symptoms:

Cardiology
Sicknesses of the heart and circulation system, rehabilitation after heart, heart valve, bypass operations, conditions after heart attacks, conditions after PTCA and stent implantations, functional heart syndromes, Strokes

Orthopaedics
Diseases of the spinal column and muscles and ligaments, arthritis in major and minor joints, conditions after the endoprothetic replacement of knee, hip and shoulder joints, root compression syndromes, conditions after operations on the spinal column, treatment after limbs have been amputated, osteoporosis etc.

We are partners of pension and health insurance schemes.
The clinic provides private treatment for patients with specific individual symptoms, normal spa treatments and prevention programmes. There is an attractive discount system for patients who return to the centre. The clinic welcomes relatives or friends who are accompanying the patient and they can take part in the activities for preventing medical problems. Private treatment can be booked at any time.
The treatment centre comprises follow-up treatment and rehabilitation, medical services for inpatient rehabilitation (therapy), outpatient/part-inpatient rehabilitation, further inpatient treatment as part of the statutory accident insurance system and physiotherapy and occupational therapy treatment for outpatients suffering from orthopaedic and cardiological symptoms.
There are 236 single rooms, most of them equipped for disabled persons, with a separate shower, telephone and TV for patients and guests. The clinic has a modern, well-equipped medical diagnostic and therapeutic department and there are many opportunities for people to enjoy their free time. Dr. Breitbeck (orthopaedics) and Dr. Siegel (cardiology) are the head doctors responsible for the medical work performed at the clinic.

Our new old people's residential home called Brunnerbergblick provides full inpatient and short-term care with an appreciation and understanding for the needs of old people who are looking for a new home. We provide the "PflegePlus" (care plus) programme for those needing care and their relatives (prices available on request).

We look forward to seeing you

Zertifiziert nach
DIN EN ISO 9001:2000

MediClin Klinik am Brunnenberg
Fachklinik für Kardiologie und Orthopädie
Endersstrasse 5
08645 Bad Elster
Telefon +49 (0) 37437 8-3223
Telefax +49 (0) 37437 8-3201
info@brunnenberg.mediclin.de
www.mediclin.de

(Fotos/Photos by Klinik am Brunnenberg, Übersetzung/Translated by David Strauss)

Wir setzen alles in Bewegung / We Get Everything Moving

Immer nah für Sie da

Always Available Locally

Die Bundesregierung sieht gerade im öffentlichen Personennahverkehr (ÖPNV) einen wichtigen Baustein zur Sicherung einer nachhaltigen Mobilität. Busse und Bahnen entlasten nicht nur Ballungsräume vom Individualverkehr und gewährleisten gleiche Lebensverhältnisse in den Regionen. Sie leisten auch wichtige Beiträge zur Entlastung der Umwelt und zur Reduzierung klimarelevanter Emissionen.

Nur ein kundenfreundlicher und effizienter ÖPNV kann im Wettbewerb mit seinem Hauptkonkurrenten dem PKW bestehen. Frühzeitig erkannten die Vogtländer, dass nur ein einfaches und flexibles Nahverkehrssystem den ÖPNV attraktiv und zukunftsfähig macht. Im Vogtland zeichnet sich für diese Koordinierung und Gestaltung der Verkehrsverbund Vogtland verantwortlich.

Zu den Zielen und Aufgaben des Verbundes zählen die Zusammenführung des Bus- und Bahnnetzes zu einem integrierten ÖPNV-System, die Abstimmung des Linienkonzeptes von Bahn und Bus, Schaffung einer der Nachfrage gerechten Versorgung mit Nahverkehrsleistungen, Schaffung nutzerfreundlicher Umsteigebedingungen an den Schnittstellen des ÖPNV und zügiger Übergänge zwischen den Verkehrsmitteln, die Einbindung des motorisierten Individualverkehrs in Form von Park-and-Ride Plätzen, Erhöhung der Reisegeschwindigkeit durch den Einsatz moderner Leichtbauniederflurbetriebswagen, Einführung des 1-Stunden-Taktes des schienengebundenen ÖPNV auf stark frequentierten Strecken, Umsetzung eines einheitlichen Tarifkonzeptes in Form des Verbundtarifes (Ein Fahrschein für alles: Im gesamten Personennahverkehr Vogtland, also im Vogtlandkreis und der kreisfreien Stadt Plauen, gilt der Verbundtarif Vogtland [VTV]. Es gibt streckenbezogene Fahrscheine und Netzfahrscheine, die in allen öffentlichen Verkehrsmitteln anerkannt werden. Es besteht eine linienübergreifende Umsteigeberechtigung.), Erhöhung der Sicherheit des Fahrgastes, Einführung eines Systems zum Fahrscheinkauf per Handy (TeleFahrschein), Schaffung eines modernen Fahrgastabfertigungs- und Informationssystems, Einführung einer Vogtland-Card-Mobil und des E-Ticketing mit Chipkarte, Einsatz von Funkgeräten in allen Fahrzeugen zur Koordinierung der Verkehrsdurchführung, ebenso für den Fall von Notsituationen, Pannen, Witterungseinflüssen, Schaffung weiterer Zugangsstellen zur Optimierung des Verkehrssystems im Vierländereck der Euregio Egrensis. Einige Ziele sind schon erreicht, manches wird verbessert und ausgebaut.

Das EgroNet – In den 90er-Jahren als Projekt für die Weltausstellung „Expo 2000" in Hannover ins Leben gerufen, zeigt sich das grenzüberschreitende Nahverkehrssystem im Herzen Mitteleuropas bis heute zukunftsweisend. Es bietet die Möglichkeit, mit Straßenbahnen, Bussen und Zügen die Vierländerregion zu erkunden. Das EgroNet umfasst eine Fläche von ca. 13.000 Quadratkilometern zwischen Karlovy Vary (Karlsbad), Marianske Lazne (Marienbad), Cheb (Eger), Weiden, Bayreuth, Hof, Lobenstein, Schleiz, Zeulenroda, Gera, Plauen, Reichenbach, Zwickau, Aue und Johanngeorgenstadt. Hier leben ca. drei Millionen Einwohner. Im Geltungsbereich kooperieren 54 Verkehrsunternehmen sowie 13 kreisfreie Städte, Landkreise und Verbünde. Weitere Informationen erhalten Sie unter www.vogtlandauskunft.de oder der Service-Nummer 03744 19449.

The German federal government believes that local public transport networks are an important component for guaranteeing sustainable mobility. Buses and trains not only relieve major cities from individual traffic – they also guarantee stable living conditions in the regions. And they play a major role in relieving the environment and reducing emissions that affect the climate.

But only a customer-friendly and efficient local public transport network can compete effectively with its main rival, the motor car. People in the Vogtland region recognised at an early stage that its local public transport network would only be attractive and capable of surviving if it was kept simple and flexible. The Vogtland Transport Network is responsible for coordinating and arranging its activities in the Vogtland region.

The goals and tasks of the network include bringing together the bus and train network to create a coordinated local public transport system, harmonising the route concept for trains and buses, creating the local public transport services to meet demand, creating user-friendly conditions for changing from one mode of transport to another, providing quick transfer times between the different types of transport, integrating motorised individual traffic in the form and park & ride areas, increasing the speed of journeys by using lightweight, low-floor vehicles, introducing a regular hourly timetable for well-used local public transport routes on the railways, using a unified pricing concept in the form of a network tariff (one ticket for everything: the Vogtland Network Tariff [VTV] applies in the all the Vogtland local public services – i.e. in the Vogtland district and the urban district of Plauen.) There are tickets for particular routes and network tickets, which are accepted on all public modes of transport. Passengers can change from one route to another. Passenger safety is being increased, a system is being introduced to purchase tickets using a mobile phone (teleticket), a modern passenger departure and information system is being created, a mobile Vogtland card and e-ticketing with a chip card are being introduced, radios are being used in all vehicles to coordinate the movement of traffic and cover emergency situations like breakdowns, the effects of the weather and create other access points to optimise the transport system in the Euregio Egrensis, where four states meet. Some of these goals have already been met – others are being improved and extended.

The EgroNet, which was formed in the 1990s as an "Expo 2000" World Fair project in Hanover, is still setting the trend for the future of cross-border local public transport networks at the heart of Central Europe. It provides passengers with the opportunity of discovering the four states region on trams, buses and trains. The EgroNet covers an area measuring approx. 13,000 square kilometres between Karlovy Vary, Marianske Lazne, Cheb, Weiden, Bayreuth, Hof, Lobenstein, Schleiz, Zeulenroda, Gera, Plauen, Reichenbach, Zwickau, Aue and Johanngeorgenstadt. Approx. 3 million people live here. 54 transport companies and 13 urban and rural districts and associations cooperate within the ticket's geographical limits.

You can obtain further information at www.vogtlandauskunft.de or
phone the service number:
03744 19449.

(Fotos/Photos by VVV, Übersetzung/Translated by David Strauss)

Zukunft braucht Bewegung
Mobility is Essential for the Future

Mit unseren Angeboten im Schienenpersonenverkehr bieten wir für die Region ein maßgeschneidertes Mobilitätsangebot. So verbindet der Franken-Sachsen-Express die Region im Einstundentakt mit Chemnitz und Dresden sowie Nürnberg. Mit dem Bäder-Express sichern wir eine schnelle Verbindung nach Leipzig mit Anschlüssen an den Fernverkehr nach Berlin und Frankfurt/M.

Unsere modernen Triebwagen der Baureihen 612 verfügen u.a. über Klimaanlage und geräuschgedämmte Fahrgasträume. Durch den Einsatz der mit Neigetechnik ausgestatteten Fahrzeuge konnten u.a. auf der kurvenreichen Sachsen-Franken-Magistrale attraktive Reisezeiten erzielt werden. Im Interesse der Umwelt können wir so auf einen extensiven Streckenausbau verzichten.

Attraktive Tarifangebote des Verkehrsverbundes Vogtland wie etwa die Familientageskarten gelten selbstverständlich auch in den unseren Nahverkehrszügen. Das Egronet-Ticket bietet darüber hinaus die Möglichkeit, mit Bussen, Zügen und Straßenbahnen das Vierländereck Böhmen, Bayern, Thüringen und Sachsen zu erkunden.

Bahn-Angebote wie das Sachsen-Ticket lassen nicht nur Sachsen per Bahn zum Erlebnis werden, sondern können auch für die Weiterfahrt in der Straßenbahn und den Bussen im Verkehrsverbund genutzt werden. Für einen Ausflug in die nördlichen Regionen Tschechiens bieten wir z.B. mit den Sachsen-Böhmen-Tickets maßgeschneiderte Angebote.

We provide the region with tailor-made mobility with our passenger rail services. The Franconia-Saxony Express connects the region with Chemnitz, Dresden and Nuremberg every hour. The Spa Express provides quick journey times to Leipzig with connections to long-distance services to Berlin and Frankfurt/Main.

Our modern 612 series trains provide air-

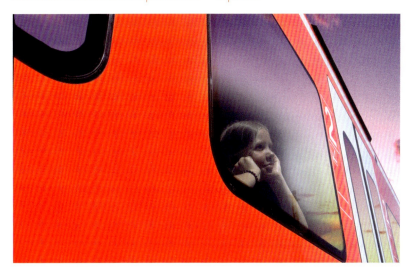

conditioning and noise-insulated compartments. By using trains equipped with tilt technology, journey times have been reduced on the winding Saxony-Franconia main line. So we have been able to avoid laying extensive new track, which has helped protect the environment.

Attractive offers from the Vogtland Transport Network such as family daytickets are valid on all our regional services too. The EgroNet ticket also enables people to discover the Czech Republic, Bavaria, Thuringia and Saxony on buses, trains and trams.

Rail offers, like the Saxony ticket, not only allow passengers to discover Saxony by train, but it can also be used for ongoing journeys by tram and bus. The Saxony-Bohemia tickets and other tailor-made offers enable people to enjoy outings to the northern regions of the Czech Republic.

DB

DB Regio AG
Region Südost
Verkehrsbetrieb Südostsachsen
Hansastraße 4
D-01097 Dresden
Telefon +49 (0) 351 8600
Telefax +49 (0) 351 8606
www.bahn.de

Beste Verbindungen durch Engagement und Leidenschaft für die Schiene
THE BEST CONNECTIONS FOR RAIL TRAVEL ACHIEVED THROUGH COMMITMENT AND ENTHUSIASM

„Alex" heißt das neueste Angebot, mit dem die Vogtlandbahn GmbH in das zwölfte Jahr ihres erfolgreichen Bestehens startet. Mit dem Fahrplanwechsel am 9.12.2007 hat das vogtländische Nahverkehrsunternehmen den „Alex"-Zugbetrieb auf den Linien Hof/Prag - Schwandorf - München und München - Lindau/Oberstdorf aufgenommen und damit sein Streckennetz um 700 auf fast 1600 Kilometer erweitern können.

Mitte 1996 schlug die Geburtsstunde der Vogtlandbahn GmbH, die zum Konzern der Regentalbahn AG gehört. Mit einem schlüssigen und durchdachten Konzept hatte die Regentalbahn AG damals die europaweite Ausschreibung des Freistaates Sachsen für zwei Bahnstrecken im Vogtland für sich entscheiden können. Im Herbst 1996 wurde der Verkehr zwischen Bad Brambach und Zwickau aufgenommen und in der Folge die „Vogtlandbahn GmbH" als Tochter mit Sitz zunächst in Reichenbach gegründet. Von Anfang an war es das Bestreben aller Mitarbeiter durch hohes Engagement, gutes Fachwissen, Mut zum gesunden Risiko und Entscheidungsfreude den Fahrgästen eine neue und vor allem bessere Qualität auf der Schiene zu bieten. Diesem Anspruch ist das Unternehmen treu geblieben. Was vor mehr als einem Jahrzehnt klein begann, ist heute im Verbund der Regentalbahn-Unternehmen einer der stärksten Leistungsträger. Seit ihrer Gründung hat die Vogtlandbahn ihre Angebote für die Fahrgäste und ihr Bediengebiet stetig erweitert. Heute erbringt das Unternehmen Nahverkehrsleistungen nicht nur über Länder - sondern über Staatsgrenzen hinweg. Bereits seit 2000 rollen die modernen Vogtlandbahn-Triebwagen der Typen RegioSprinter und DESIRO nicht mehr nur im Vogtland und in Westsachsen, sondern auch in Ostthüringen, in Oberfranken, der Oberpfalz und in Kooperation mit zwei tschechischen Bahngesellschaften auch in Nordwestböhmen. Damit ist das Unternehmen am euro-regionalen Nahverkehrsprojekt „EgroNet" der Euregio Egrensis maßgeblich beteiligt. Täglich verkehren zum Beispiel bis zu 34 Vogtlandbahnzüge grenzüberschreitend zwischen Deutschland und Tschechien.

Im Sommer 2005 gelang der Vogtlandbahn die Wiederinbetriebnahme der von der Deutschen Bahn 2001 eingestellten Direktverbindung von Plauen nach Berlin. Damit erstreckte sich nun ihr Bediengebiet auf die Region zwischen Zwickau, Gera, Hof, Regensburg, Marianske Lazne (Marienbad), Karlovy Vary (Karlsbad) bis hin zur Bundeshauptstadt.

Unter dem Markennamen „Die Länderbahn" hatte die Regentalbahn AG in Kooperation mit der schweizerischen SBB seit 2002 Erfahrungen mit Nahverkehrsleistungen auf dem Streckenabschnitt zwischen München - Oberstdorf sammeln können. Im Herbst 2005 und im Frühjahr 2006 konnte „Die Länderbahn" die europaweite Ausschreibung zwischen München und Hof sowie die Weiterführung des heutigen Alex-Verkehrs der Vogtlandbahn ab Dezember 2007 für sich entscheiden. Mit dem neuen „Alex" bietet die Vogtlandbahn jetzt Fernverkehrsniveau zum Nahverkehrspreis. Dafür wurden zu den 44 bisherigen Triebwagen extra 15 neue Lokomotiven und 60 modernisierte Reisezugwagen angeschafft. Jährlich befördert die Vogtlandbahn rund 5 Millionen Fahrgäste. Mit „Alex" werden es künftig über 15 Millionen sein. Auch die Mitarbeiteranzahl hat sich dadurch verdoppelt und so steht die Vogtlandbahn GmbH in der sächsisch-bayrischen Region mit insgesamt 280 Mitarbeitern auch in sozialer Verantwortung. Hinzu kommen etwa 130 Mitarbeiter des Schwesterunternehmens Regentalwerke an den Standorten Neumark, Schwandorf und Viechtach, die für die Wartung der Züge sorgen. Zusätzlich kümmern sich seit November 2007 vier Mitarbeiter des Kundencenters um alle Anliegen der Fahrgäste.

Und mit dem ARRIVA-Konzern, einem der größten Personenverkehrsunternehmen in Europa, wurde über die Regentalbahn ein leistungsfähiger, strategischer Investor gewonnen, der auch für die Vogtlandbahn garantiert, dass für das kommende Jahrzehnt die Weichen auf „Freie Fahrt!" stehen.

„Alex" is the name of the latest service provided by the Vogtland Railway Limited (Vogtlandbahn GmbH) in the twelfth year of its successful existence. The timetable change on 9 December 2007 allowed the local Vogtland railway service to take over the "Alex" services on the Hof/Prague – Schwandorf- Munich and Munich – Lindau/Oberstdorf lines, so expanding its network from 700 to almost 1600 kilometres.

The Vogtlandbahn, a subsidiary of Regentalbahn AG, was founded in the middle of 1996. Using a coherent and well conceived concept, Regental AG was able to win the contract from the Free State of Saxony to take over two railway lines in the Vogtland region. Operations began on the line between Bad Brambach and Zwickau in the autumn of 1996 and the "Vogtlandbahn GmbH" was founded as a subsidiary company based initially in Reichenbach. From the very beginning, all the employees made a great deal of effort to provide new and better levels of quality on the railways through a high level of commitment and endeavour, sound knowledge, the courage to step out in new ways and decisiveness. The company has remained true to its principles. What began as a small concern more than ten years ago is now one of the strongest performers in the Regental Railway group of companies. Since the founding of the company, the Vogtlandbahn has steadily increased its services for passengers and its network. The local railway company

(Fotos/Photos by Igor Pastierovic [5], Vogtlandbahn-GmbH, Text/Text by Ekkehard Glaß, Übersetzung/Translated by David Strauss)

Wir setzen alles in Bewegung / We Get Everything Moving

now not only crosses state borders, but also national ones. Since 2000 the modern trains (Regiosprinter and DESIRO) not only travel within the Vogtland region and West Saxony, but also in East Thuringia, Upper Franconia, the Upper Palatinate and in the north of the Czech Republic in cooperation with two Czech railway companies. This makes the company an important participant in the regional project called the "EgroNet" in the Euregio Egrensis region. As many as 34 Vogtlandbahn trains cross the border between Germany and the Czech Republic every day.

The Vogtlandbahn successfully restarted the direct line between Plauen and Berlin in the summer of 2005, a route abandoned by Deutsche Bahn in 2001. This enabled the Vogtlandbahn to extend its service between Zwickau, Gera, Hof, Regensburg, Marianske Lazne and Karlovy Vary as far as the German capital. Using the name "The States Railway", Regentalbahn AG had been able to gain experience in running regional railway services on the line between Munich and Oberstdorf in co-operation with the Swiss SBB railways since 2002. The States Railways, after tendering on a Europe-wide basis, won the contract for the Munich – Hof route as from December 2007 and to continue the "Alex" services as they are now known. The new "Alex" enables the Vogtlandbahn to provide long-distance travel at local travel prices. In order to do this, 15 new engines have been added to the 44 multiple units in service, together with 60 modernised long-distance carriages.

The Vogtlandbahn transports around five million passengers every year. This figure will rise to 15 million per annum with the advent of the "Alex" services. The number of employees has doubled to 280 as a result and ensures that the Vogtlandbahn takes seriously its social responsibilities in the Saxony/Bavaria region. In addition, around 130 people are employed by the sister company, Regentalwerke, in Neumark, Schwandorf and Viechtach; they maintain the trains. Four employees have been dealing with customer enquiries since 2007. The ARRIVA Company, one of the largest passenger transport companies in Europe, has proved to be a competent, strategic investor, guaranteeing that the Vogtlandbahn will continue to be able to provide its services in the coming decade.

vogtlandbahn

Vogtlandbahn-GmbH
Ohmstraße 2 · D-08496 Neumark
Hotline   0180 123-123-2*
info@vogtlandbahn.de
www.vogtlandbahn.de

*) Kosten pro Minute aus dem Festnetz der T-Home:
3,9 Cent, aus anderen Netzen gelten andere Tarife.

Einkaufen im Plauener Zentrum
Shopping in the City of Plauen

Nicht nur in der Altstadt und an anderen historischen Stätten treffen sich die Plauener mit ihren Gästen. Vom Bahnhof aus, wo sich auch die zentrale Bushaltestelle befindet, zieht sich die Bahnhofstraße als beliebte Flaniermeile hinunter zum Zentrum. Und jenseits des Postplatzes führt die Neundorfer Straße in die entgegengesetzte Richtung bis ins Westend hinaus. Viele Geschäfte verlocken zum Einkaufen, Restaurants, Cafés, kleine und große Kneipen sowie im Sommer zahlreiche Biergärten laden zum Verweilen ein. An manchen Ecken wird noch gebaut, wie zum Beispiel am alten Postgebäude, in das ebenfalls Geschäfte einziehen sollen. Fertig gestellt ist die Stadtgalerie, der Treffpunkt schlechthin. Seit 2001 besuchen dieses Einkaufs- und Kulturzentrum täglich unzählige Menschen. Sie kommen nicht nur aus der Stadt, sondern aus dem gesamten Umland, ja sogar aus der Partnerstadt Hof in Bayern. Einkaufen in der Innenstadt machen genügend Stellplätze in den Parkhäusern einfach. Die Stadtgalerie bietet einen Branchen-Mix aus ca. 80 Fachgeschäften. Schwerpunkte sind der Mode- und Textilbereich sowie Dienstleistung und Gastronomie. Das Bummeln und Einkaufen wird besonders dann zum Erlebnis, wenn sich das ganze Haus vor Ostern in einen Frühlingsgarten oder in der Adventszeit in Weihnachtsmannwerkstatt und Märchenzimmer verwandelt. Übers Jahr wird noch mehrmals thematisch umdekoriert. Außerdem finden Modenschauen, musikalische Highlights und zahlreiche Aktionen statt.

Viele Plauener Einzelhändler waren nicht begeistert über den Bau dieses Einkaufstempels der Stadt. Manch einer mußte die Segel streichen, andere überlebten, bildeten Werbegemeinschaften und bieten ein interessantes Angebotsspektrum, nicht nur im Zentrum, an der Bahnhofstraße oder Neundorfer Straße. Es lohnt sich, Abstecher auch in die Seitenstraßen zu unternehmen. Die Stadt ließ damals die Bürger entscheiden, ob die Stadtgalerie gebaut werden soll. Die Mehrheit war dafür, und heute will keiner mehr das Zentrum im Zentrum missen.

Einige Zeit vor der Stadtgalerie eröffneten bereits die Kolonnaden. Die moderne, gläserne Eckfassade schiebt sich an der unteren Bahnhofstraße dem Zentrum entgegen und ist von der Zentralhaltestelle der Straßenbahn am Postplatz aus nicht zu übersehen. Auch die Kolonnaden, der Name geht auf früher an dieser Stelle gestandene kleine Häuschen mit Geschäften zurück, bieten eine bunte Palette an Einkaufsmöglichkeiten und gastronomischen Angeboten.

Local people not only meet others in the old city and the other historical sites. Starting at the railway station, where the central bus station is also situated, Bahnhof Street makes its way down to the city centre as the main promenade. And on the other side of the Post Square, Neundorfer Street takes you as far as the Westend district in the other direction. There are plenty of shops for buying things, restaurants, cafés, small and large pubs and in summer many beer gardens where people can wile away the hours. Building work is still continuing on many corners, e.g. the old post office building, where shops are due to move in. The City Gallery has been finished and it is the meeting point par excellence. Countless numbers of people have visited this shopping and cultural centre since 2001. They do not just come from the city, but from the surrounding area and even from the city's twin town, Hof in Bavaria. It is easy to go shopping as there is adequate space in the car parks. The City Gallery provides a mix of facilities with approx. 80 specialist shops. Many of these specialise in fashion and textiles or services and catering. Strolling around and buying goods is a real experience, especially when the whole building is turned into a spring garden before Easter or a Father Christmas workshop and fairy tale rooms during Advent. The centre is decorated to reflect various themes throughout the year. There are also fashion shows, musical highlights and many events.

Many Plauen retailers were not thrilled about the construction of this shopping temple in the city. Many of them were forced to close down, others survived and formed trade associations and provide an interesting range of services, not just in the centre, on Bahnhof Street or Neundorfer Street. It is worth your while making a quick detour down the side roads. The city gave its residents an opportunity to decide whether the City Gallery should be built or not. The majority supported the plan and today nobody would like to forego the centre in the centre.

The Colonnades opened some time before the City Gallery. The modern, glass corner façade edges into the lower part of Bahnhof Street and you cannot miss it if you get off the central tram stop at Post Square. The name Colonnades can be traced back to a small house with shops, which used to occupy this area. The centre provides a wide range of shops and catering facilities.

Plauen – eine Reise wert / Plauen - Worth a Visit

Einkaufsmagnet für das Vogtland
Shopping Magnet for the Vogtland Region

Die Stadt-Galerie in Plauen ist mit ihrer modernen, großstädtischen Architektur und ihren attraktiven Einzelhandelsangeboten der Einkaufs- und Erlebnistreffpunkt im Herzen der Vogtland-Metropole.

■ Standort/Lage:
Die kreisfreie Stadt Plauen mit ihren ca. 70.000 Einwohnern ist das wirtschaftliche und kulturelle Zentrum des Vogtlandes im Vierländereck Sachsen, Thüringen, Bayern und Böhmen. Die Stadt-Galerie befindet sich in zentraler Citylage zwischen der Fußgängerzone „Bahnhofstraße" und der Altstadt.

■ Branchen- und Mietermix:
ca. 14.000 Quadratmeter Verkaufsfläche auf drei Ebenen mit rund 80 Fachgeschäften, darunter ein Fachmarkt für Unterhaltungselektronik, ein Bekleidungshaus, ein Warenhaus, ein Schlemmerbereich sowie Dienstleistungs- und Gastronomiebetriebe.

■ Verkehrsanbindung:
Mit dem Auto: sehr gut zu erreichen über die Autobahnen A 9 (München-Leipzig-Berlin) und A 72 (Hof-Dresden) sowie die Bundesstraßen B 92, B 173 und B 282.
Mit öffentlichen Verkehrsmitteln: Alle Straßenbahnlinien halten direkt an der Stadt-Galerie.

■ Kundenservice:
rund 750 Stellplätze im Center, Kundeninformation, Parkhausbüro, Telefon- und Postservice, behindertengerechte Aufzüge, Wickelraum, Kid Cars.

The City Gallery in Plauen with its modern city architecture and attractive retail shopping facilities is the meeting place for shoppers and those seeking something special in the heart of the Vogtland capital.

■ Site/situation:
The independent city of Plauen with its 70,000 or so inhabitants is the business and cultural centre of the Vogtland region in the area where the German states of Saxony, Thuringia and Bavaria and the Czech Republic meet. The City Gallery lies at the heart of the city between the "Railway Street" pedestrian precinct and the old city.

■ Mix of sectors and tenants:
the centre contains approx. 14,000 square metres of shopping space on three floors with about 80 specialist dealers, including a specialist market for entertainment electronics, a clothes shop, a department store, a food area and service and catering companies.

■ Transport links:
By car: easy to reach if you are travelling on the A 9 (Munich-Leipzig-Berlin) and A 72 (Hof-Dresden) motorways and the B 92, B 173 and B 282 main roads
By public transport: all the tram lines stop right by the City Gallery.

■ Customer services:
about 750 parking spaces at the Centre, customer information, car park office, telephone and postal services, lifts for the disabled, a changing room, kid cars.

STADT-GALERIE
PLAUEN
Schöner einkaufen im Vogtland.

ECE-Center-Management
Postplatz 1
D-08523 Plauen
Telefon +49 (0) 3741 1486-0
Telefax +49 (0) 3741 1486-99
info@stadtgalerie-plauen.de
www.stadtgalerie-plauen.de

Projektentwicklung, Generalplanung und Vermietung:
ECE Projektmanagement
Heegbarg 30 · 22391 Hamburg
Telefon +49 (0) 40 60606-0
Telefax +49 (0) 40 60606-230
info@ece.de
www.ece.de

Plauen - die Stadt in der „Klingenden Ferienregion Vogtland"

Plauen – the City in the "Vogtland Musical Holiday Region"

Plauen, die größte und kreisfreie Stadt in der Ferienregion Vogtland – Deutschlands Wanderregion Nr. 1 des Jahres 2005 – lädt ein:

Zu einem Bummel durch die aufblühende Innenstadt und die romantische Altstadt mit ihren kleinen, schmalen Gassen;
zum Besuch des einzigen Spitzenmuseums Deutschlands oder der Schaustickerei Plauener Spitze, des Vogtlandmuseums oder der ständigen Ausstellung zu Leben und Werk des bekannten Zeichners „e.o. plauen" in der gleichnamigen Galerie;
zu erholsamen Wanderungen oder Radtouren in die idyllische vogtländische Umgebung;

zu erlebnisreichen Stunden im mehr als einhundertjährigen Vogtland Theater, das für seine spektakulären Aufführungen wie Titanic, Jesus Christ Superstar, Rocky Horror Show oder Freiluftopernspektakel wie Aida, Nabucco, Carmen oder Der fliegende Holländer weit über die Grenzen des Vogtlandes hinaus bekannt ist;
zu einem gemütlichen Bier in einem urigen Altstadtlokal oder gar in Plauens ältester Gastwirtschaft, der „Matsch",
zu einer zünftigen Stadtrundfahrt in einer der historischen Straßenbahnen oder am besten bei einem „kühlen Blonden" in der Bierelektrischen;

zu einem Aufenthalt mit viel Kurzweil. Oder planen Sie bald Ihre Hochzeit? Wie wäre es mit einem romantischen Brautkleid aus Plauener Spitze und der Trauung extravagant in einer der historischen Plauener Straßenbahnen? All das hat Plauen zu bieten und noch mehr!

Plauen, the largest city in the Vogtland holiday region and an urban district in its own right – Germany's no. 1 walking region in 2005 – invites you to:

stroll through the flourishing inner city and romantic old city with its small, narrow streets;
visit the only lace museum in Germany or the Plauen Lace Exhibition Embroidery Works, the Vogtland Museum or the permanent exhibition on the life and work of the well-known artist "e.o. plauen" in the gallery named after him;
go on walks or cycle tours of the idyllic Vogtland surroundings;

spend an exciting time in the Vogtland Theatre, which is more than 100 years old and is well known beyond the boundaries of the Vogtland region for its spectacular performances like Titanic, Jesus Christ Superstar, the Rocky Horror Show or open-air opera spectacles like Aida, Nabucco, Carmen or the Flying Dutchman;
enjoy a homely beer in a traditional old city pub or even in Plauen's oldest restaurant, the "Matsch";
go on an excellent city tour in one of the historical trams or preferably enjoy a light beer in the "Beer Tram";
spend time here and have plenty of fun.

Or are you planning to marry soon? How about a romantic wedding dress made of Plauen lace and marrying in style in one of the Plauen's historic trams? Plauen has all this to offer and much more!

(Fotos/Photos by Stadtverwaltung Plauen, Text/Text by Stadtverwaltung Plauen, Übersetzung/Translated by David Strauss)

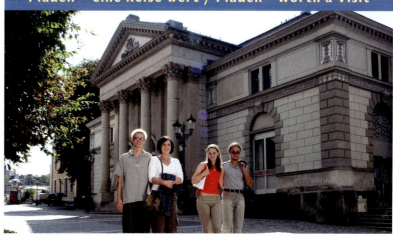

Plauen – eine Reise wert / Plauen – Worth a Visit

Plauen, eingebettet in die wunderschöne vogtländische Kuppenlandschaft, ist mit fast 70 000 Einwohnern die größte und bedeutendste Stadt der Region.
Zahlreiche Höhen und Tiefen hatte die Stadt in ihrer wechselseitigen Geschichte bereits zu überwinden.
Mit der Entwicklung der Plauener Spitze und der damit verbundenen Industrialisierung hatte einst der wirtschaftliche Aufschwung in der Vogtlandstadt eingesetzt. Innerhalb nur weniger Jahre, von 1880 bis 1912, vervierfachte sich die Einwohnerzahl. 1912 zählte Plauen 128.000 Einwohner.
Leidgeprüft die Stadt im zweiten Weltkrieg – Plauen wurde zu 75 Prozent zerstört.

Der Wiederaufbau stand im Zeichen der damaligen SED-Regierung. An der Grenze zu Bayern wurden die Stadt und ihr Umland ignoriert bzw. bewusst vernachlässigt.
In der Zeit des politischen Umbruchs 1989 waren es neben den Leipzigern vor allem die Bürger Plauens, die mit wöchentlichen Samstagsdemonstrationen, beginnend bereits am 7. Oktober 1989, ihre Stadt zu einer Wiege der friedlichen Revolution erhoben.
Seit der Grenzöffnung am 9. November 1989 ist Plauen aus seinem Schattendasein an der ehemaligen deutsch-deutschen Grenze, vom Mauerblümchendasein der DDR-Diktatur, wieder in die Mitte Deutschlands und mit der EU-Osterweiterung in die Mitte Europas gerückt.

Wer Plauen aus den Jahren vor der Wiedervereinigung kennt, staunt über das neue Antlitz der Stadt und die städtebaulichen Veränderungen.
Der alte Stadtkern um den Altmarkt, sorgfältig und liebevoll restauriert, ist Anziehungspunkt für viele Touristen. Herrschaftliche Häuser zeugen noch heute vom ehemaligen Reichtum der Stadt. Dort findet der Gast das Vogtlandmuseum mit Wissenswertem über regionales Brauchtum und das Plauener Malzhaus, Kultur- und Kommunikationszentrum, Heimstätte für Rock, Jazz, Blues und Folk, wo alljährlich beim Plauener Folkherbst um den „Eisernen Eversteiner" gerungen wird, der einzige Europäische Folkpreis, der in Deutschland vergeben wird. Mit der Sanierung des Malzhauses, dessen Entstehungsgeschichte bis ins 11. Jahrhundert zurückreicht, wurde ein architektonisches Schmuckstück geschaffen.
Das Plauener Spitzenmuseum, einzigartig in Deutschland, dokumentiert in den Gewölben des Alten Rathauses die Entwicklung der Spitzen- und Stickereiindustrie des Vogtlandes bis zur Gegenwart.
Plauen lockt gleichermaßen mit Einkaufs- und Kulturvielfalt.
Da wären zum Beispiel das Vogtland Theater, Musentempel mit über hundertjähriger Tradition, oder die Galerie e.o. plauen, die in einer ständigen Ausstellung die Werke des bekannten Zeichners und Sohnes der Stadt, Erich Ohser – e.o. plauen, zeigt. Wer kennt sie nicht, die lustigen Geschichten vom schnauzbärtigen Vater und seinem spitzbübigen Sohn?
Alljährlich findet im Juni das größte aller Plauener Feste – das Spitzenfest - statt. Seit 1996 küren die Plauener die Spitzenprinzessin.
Das „Festival Mitte Europa" ist ein weiterer Höhepunkt im Kulturleben Plauens. Klassische Konzerte höchsten Niveaus, Ausstellungen und Lesungen zeitgenössischer Künstler und Autoren werden in der Euroregion Sachsen – Bayern – Thüringen - Böhmen in den Sommermonaten geboten.

Plauen, embedded in the beautiful Vogtland hills, is the largest and most important city in the region with its population of almost 70,000 people.
The city has had to overcome many highs and lows in its varied history. The Vogtland city first experienced a period of boom when Plauen lace was developed and the industrialisation process that accompanied this. During a matter of just a few years, from 1880 to 1912, the population quadrupled. Plauen had 128,000 residents in 1912.
The city was seriously damaged in the Second World War – 75 percent of Plauen was destroyed.

The reconstruction of the city was affected by the East German communist party. The city and its surrounding region was ignored or deliberately neglected because it bordered on Bavaria.
During the time of political upheaval in 1989, the citizens of Plauen along with their counterparts in Leipzig made their city into a cradle of the peaceful revolution with their weekly Saturday demonstrations starting on 7 October.
Since the border was opened on 9 November 1989, Plauen has risen from its shadowy existence along the former East German/West German border and its Cinderella status under the East German regime, and has moved back into the heart of Germany and the heart of Europe following EU enlargement.

Those who knew Plauen before German reunification will be amazed by the new face of the city and the changes to the buildings.
The old heart of the city round the old market square has been carefully and lovingly restored and is now a major attraction for many tourists. Stately buildings still bear testimony to the city's former wealth. Visitors will find the Vogtland Museum with much to discover about regional customs and the Plauen Malt House, the cultural and communication centre, the home of rock, jazz, blues and folk, where the "Iron Everstein" competition is held every autumn – the only European folk prize, which is awarded in Germany. The redevelopment of the Malt House has created an architectural jewel – the origins of the house go back to the 11th century.
The Plauen Lace Museum is unique in Germany; it is located in the vaults of the old city hall and documents the development of the lace and embroidery industry in the Vogtland region right up to the present day.
But Plauen is just as attractive for those wishing to go shopping or enjoy some culture: the Vogtland Theatre, for example, a temple of the muses with traditions going back more than one hundred years, or the "e.o.plauen" gallery, which has a permanent exhibition of the works of the well-known artist and son of the city, Erich Ohser – e.o. plauen. Who is not familiar with these amusing stories of the father with his walrus moustache and his mischievous son? The largest of the all the Plauen festivals – the lace festival – takes place every June. The people of Plauen have crowned a lace princess since 1996.
The "Central Europe Festival" is another highpoint in Plauen's cultural life. Classical concerts of a very high standard, exhibitions and readings by contemporary artists and authors are provided in the Saxony – Bavaria – Czech Republic Euroregion during the summer months.

Plauen – eine Reise wert / Plauen - Worth a Visit

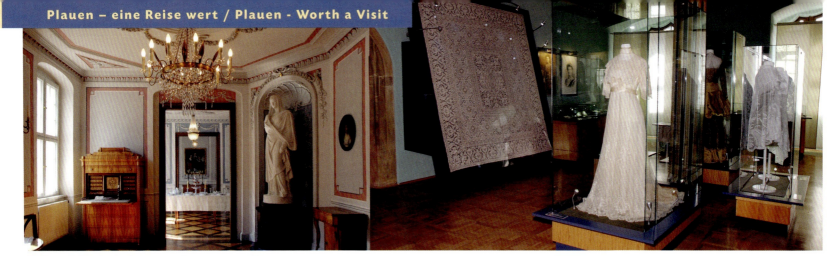

Und während eines Einkaufsbummels oder auch nach einem Konzert oder Ausstellungsbesuch laden zahlreiche Restaurants und Gaststätten unterschiedlichster Couleur in der Altstadt wie auch in den traditionellen Einkaufslagen zum Verweilen ein, im Sommer natürlich schattige Biergärten.

Aus den sprichwörtlichen „Nähten zu platzen" scheint die Plauener Innenstadt während der jährlich stattfindenden Stadtfeste „Plauener Frühling", „Plauener Herbst" und „Plauener Spitzenfest" (immer am dritten Juniwochenende), die tausende Plauener und Gäste anlocken.

Mit viel Engagement erschließen in ehrenamtlicher Tätigkeit seit einigen Jahren die Mitglieder des „Vogtländischen Bergknappenvereins zu Plauen" e.V. die „Unter-Tage-Welt" im Plauener Stadtzentrum. Es ist die Faszination, sich mitten im Herzen der Stadt „unter Tage" in unterschiedliche Zeitepochen zu begeben und „über Tage" zugleich das innerstädtische Flair aus Bummeln, Einkaufen, Verweilen und Kultur des Plauener Stadtzentrums genießen zu können. Und bei einer spannenden Schatzsuche ist schon so manches Kind im Manne erwacht.

Mehr zu, um und über Plauen unter www.plauen.de.

And while you are out shopping or after a concert or visit to a gallery, there are many restaurants and inns of various kinds waiting to serve you in the old city and the traditional shopping areas; and there are beer gardens with some shade in the summer.

The inner city in Plauen seems to be bursting at the seams during the annual "Plauen Spring", "Plauen Autumn" and "Plauen Lace" festivals (the latter is always on the third weekend in June); they attract thousands of Plauen residents and guests.

The members of the "Vogtland Miners Association in Plauen" have shown a great deal of commitment in unearthing the "underground world" in the Plauen city centre on a voluntary basis over the past few years. It is fascinating to go underground to various periods of history right at the heart of the city and then enjoy the inner city flair above ground strolling, shopping, spending time and enjoying the culture of the Plauen city centre. And during a treasure hunt, the little boy in many a man has been resurrected.

You will find more about Plauen at www.plauen.de

Geschichte

- 1122
Erste Erwähnung als „vicus plawe"
- 1224
Plauen erhält Stadtrecht
- 15. Jh.
Die Tuchmacherei entwickelt sich
- 16. Jh.
Verbreitung der Baumwollweberei
- 1602
Plauen wird Hauptstadt des „Voigtländischen Kreißes"
- 1881
Bau der ersten Stickmaschine - Begründung des Maschinenbaus in Plauen
- 1889
Bau der ersten Rotationsdruckmaschine
- 1900
Auf der 1. Weltausstellung in Paris wird die „Plauener Spitze" mit dem Grand Prix ausgezeichnet
- 1907
Plauen wird kreisfreie Stadt
- 1912
wird die höchste Einwohnerzahl mit 128 014 erreicht
- 1945
Plauen wird zu 75 % zerstört
- 1989
von Plauen gehen maßgebliche Impulse zur Einleitung der politischen Wende in der ehemaligen DDR aus
- 2001
Eröffnung der Stadt-Galerie einschließlich neuer Zentralhaltestelle der Straßenbahn
- 2004
Der Nachlass von Erich Ohser/e.o. plauen wird an die Stadt Plauen übergeben
- 2005
Gründung der Erich Ohser/e.o. plauen-Stiftung

History

- 1122 First mentioned as „vicus plawe"
- 1224 Plauen received its town charter
- 15th century: cloth making developed
- 16th century: cotton weaving works spread
- 1602 Plauen became capital of the "Voigtland District"
- 1881 The first embroidery machine was made – start of engineering manufacturing in Plauen
- 1889 The first rotation printing machine was built
- 1900 "Plauen lace" was awarded a grand prix at the 1st World Fair in Paris
- 1907 Plauen because an urban district
- 1912 The highest population figure was reached: 128, 014
- 1945 75% of Plauen was destroyed
- 1989 Plauen played a major role in triggering the political upheaval in former East Germany
- 2001 Opening of the City Gallery shopping centre and a new central tram stop
- 2004 The estate of Erich Ohser/e.o. plauen was handed over to the city of Plauen
- 2005 Founding of the Erich Ohser/ e.o. plauen Trust

Besuchen Sie das Plauener Spitzenmuseum

Plauener Spitzenmuseum
Altmarkt · 08523 Plauen

www.plauenerspitze.info

Telefon: 03741 222355
Öffnungszeiten: Mo. bis Fr. 10–17 Uhr
Sa. 9–14 Uhr
Gruppenbesuche am
So. nach Vereinbarung

Betreiber: Förderverein Plauener Spitzenmuseum e.V. © Branchenverband Plauener Spitze® und Stickereien e.V

Ihre kommunalen Partner für Mobilität in und um Plauen
Your Local Mobility Partners in and around Plauen

Sie haben sich für eine kulturvolle, lebendige Stadt entschieden, die Spitzenstadt Plauen, eine Stadt mit Tradition. Lebendig bedeutet aber auch: Verkehrsprobleme gehören zum Alltag. Setzen Sie deshalb auf das gut ausgebaute Netz der Plauener Straßenbahn GmbH. Wir bieten Ihnen auf 5 Straßenbahn- und 4 Stadtbuslinien allen Komfort, um schnell und sicher von einem Teil der Stadt Plauen in den anderen Teil zu gelangen.

Wollen Sie mehr erfahren? Bitte!

Wir setzen täglich auf durchschnittlich 26 Kursen moderne Straßenbahntriebwagen und Busse ein, die unseren Fahrgästen einen hohen Komfort bieten.
Außerdem gibt es die Möglichkeit, unsere Stadt mit einer unserer Sonderbahnen zu erkunden und dabei zum Beispiel in der „Bier-Elektrischen" gemütlich das bekannte Plauener Bier zu genießen.

Nun haben Sie es sich überlegt? Werden Sie unser Kunde? Wie? Ganz einfach!

Wir können Ihnen ein breites, für jeden Bedarf zugeschnittenes, Fahrscheinsortiment anbieten.

Fahren Sie täglich und viel?
Dann haben wir für Sie die verschiedensten Zeitkarten im Angebot: Jahreskarten, Monatskarten, Wochenkarten.

Oder wollen Sie es erst einmal probieren? So bieten wir Ihnen Einzel- und Sammelfahrscheine.

Nun, wir hoffen Ihnen einen kleinen Einblick in unsere Leistungsfähigkeit und unser Serviceangebot gegeben zu haben und Sie bald als unseren Fahrgast begrüßen zu dürfen.

Für weitere Informationen steht Ihnen gern unser geschultes Serviceteam in unserem PSB-Service-Gebäude am Tunnel zur Verfügung.

Sie erreichen uns außerdem unter der Servicetelefonnummer 03741 19449 oder im Internet unter:
www.strassenbahn-plauen.de.

Wir wünschen Ihnen einen guten Start in der Spitzenstadt Plauen, denn Plauen ist echt Spitze.

You have decided to come to a lively city with plenty of culture – Plauen, the top address, and not just for lace. It is a city with traditions going back a long way. But a lively city means that traffic problems are a daily occurrence. So put your trust in the Plauen Tram Company's well developed network. We provide you with all the comfort you need to get from one part of the city of Plauen to another quickly and safely on 5 tram lines and 4 bus routes.

Would you like to know more? Yes please!

We use modern trams and buses every day usually on 26 routes and these provide our passengers with a high degree of comfort.
You also have a chance to discover our city on one of our special trams and, for example, enjoy the well-known Plauen beer in the comfort of the "Beer Tram".

Have you really thought it through now? You want to become one of our customers? But how? It's very easy!

We can provide you with a broad range of tickets suitable for any requirements. Do you travel every day or a great deal? Then we have various season tickets available: annual seasons, monthly seasons or weekly season tickets.

Or do you first want to try out our services? We can provide you with an individual ticket or tickets valid for several journeys.

We hope that we have given you a glimpse of our efficient range of services and we look forward to welcoming you as one of our passengers in the near future.

Our trained service team at our PSB service building by the "Tunnel" in Plauen will be happy to give you further information.

You can also get in touch with us on our service number: 03741 19449
or go to the Internet at:
www.strassenbahn-plauen.de.

We wish you a good start in the lace city of Plauen, for Plauen is really the top address.

(Fotos/Photos by PSB GmbH, Übersetzung/Translated by David Strauss)

Altes Bewahren – Neues wagen
Cherishing the Old – Daring the New

Slawisches Dorf, Berg- und Ackerbürgerstadt, blühende Industriestadt – all das war Oelsnitz/Vogtl. in seiner Geschichte. Das eng gedrängte mittelalterliche Ensemble der Giebel und Türme hinter einer wehrhaften Stadtmauer wich nach dem großen Stadtbrand von 1859 der offenen spätklassizistischen Stadtanlage.

Stagnation und Bevölkerungsrückgang in der DDR, die politische Wende und der Zusammenbruch vieler Firmen, die Erneuerung der Infra-Struktur, Ansiedlung neuer Industrie, die Rekonstruktion der Bausubstanz und die Lösung des drängenden Verkehrsproblems bestimmten die Jahre seit dem Herbst 1989.

Mit dem 72 Hektar großen Industriegebiet am Johannisberg verfügt die große Kreisstadt Oelsnitz/Vogtl. über ein bedeutendes Wirtschaftsareal. Am 16. September 1991 setzten Wirtschaftsminister Dr. Kajo Schommer, Landrat Bernd Abele und Bürgermeister Kurt Reichel den symbolischen ersten Spatenstich. Damit nahmen Oelsnitz und der damalige Landkreis eine Vorreiterrolle in Sachsen ein.

Zu der erforderlichen Investition von 43 Millionen Mark trug das Land 37 Millionen Mark bei, das entspricht einer Förderung von 90 Prozent. Voraussetzung dafür war die Ansiedlung von überwiegend produzierendem Gewerbe. Begünstigt wurde das Genehmigungsverfahren durch die Ansiedlung der Beaulieu-Gruppe, eines europaweit agierenden Großunternehmens, das nun in Oelsnitz/Vogtl. als Ideal Automotive firmiert und Zulieferer der Autoindustrie ist. 2002 – nach zehn Jahren – war das Industriegebiet am Johannisberg voll belegt. Rund 2000 Arbeitsplätze sind hier entstanden.

Mit den Stadtwerken hat sich auch ein zu 100 Prozent kommunaler Betrieb angesiedelt, der wichtige Aufgaben für Oelsnitz/Vogtl. wie die Gas- und Stromversorgung, den Winterdienst und die Betreibung des Stadtbads übernimmt. Mehrere Firmen haben inzwischen ihre ursprüngliche Investition aufgestockt und ihre Ansiedlung im Industriegebiet erweitert wie Meiser Gitterroste oder Tul-Tec. Insgesamt rund 40 Firmen in einem Branchenmix aus Maschinen- und Anlagenbau, Textilindustrie, Glasverarbeitung, Recycling, Baustoffen und Dienstleistungsgewerbe sind am Johannisberg zu finden genauso wie ein Bäckereiunternehmen und die Behindertenwerkstatt des Obervogtländischen Vereins für Innere Mission.

Slav village, mining and agricultural town, prosperous industrial centre – the large county town of Oelsnitz in the Vogtland region has been all of those things in the course of its history. After fire swept through the town in 1859, the medieval gables and towers tightly packed behind a defensive wall were replaced by an open, late classical ensemble.

Stagnation and population decline during the East German era, the fall of the Berlin Wall and the consequent collapse of many companies, the renewal of its infrastructure, the arrival of new industries, the restoration of the town's building fabric and the search for a solution to its acute traffic problems have dominated the period since the autumn of 1989.

The 72-hectare Johannisberg industrial park is an important economic asset for Oelsnitz. Saxony's economics minister Dr. Kajo Schommer, the chief administrative officer Bernd Abele and Mayor Kurt Reichel took part in the symbolic ground-breaking ceremony on 16 September 1991, which gave Oelsnitz and its then rural district a pioneering role in Saxony.

The state of Saxony contributed DM 37 million of the necessary DM 43 million, equating to 90 percent of the cost. One important condition was attached to the funding: the majority of the companies setting up there had to be from the manufacturing sector. The approval procedures were given a boost by the arrival of the Beaulieu Group, a concern with operations throughout Europe, which now supplies the motor industry from its base in Oelsnitz operating under the name Ideal Automotive. By 2002 – after just ten years – the Johannisberg industrial park was full. Some 2,000 jobs have been created there.

The 100 percent publicly-owned company, which provides important local services such as the supply of gas and electricity, winter gritting and snow clearance and the operation of the town swimming pool, also set up shop there. A number of companies, such as Meiser Gitterroste and Tul-Tec, have meanwhile topped up their original investment and expanded their presence on the industrial park. A total of about 40 companies from a wide range of sectors, including mechanical engineering and plant construction, textiles, glass processing, waste-recycling, building supplies and the service sector, can be found at Johannisberg, as well as a large-scale bak-

(Fotos/Photos by Oelsnitzer Stadtmarketing und Tourismus GmbH, Renate Wöllner, Harald Sulski, Text/Text by Renate Wöllner, Übersetzung/Translated by David Strauss)

Oelsnitz/Vogtland

Fast zeitgleich mit dem Industriegebiet entstand in Oelsnitz/Vogtl. ein Gewerbegebiet an der Untermarxgrüner Straße – das im Volksmund die „Automeile" genannt wird. Hier allerdings flossen keine öffentlichen Mittel. Neben den Autohäusern haben sich großflächige Handelseinrichtungen aus der Lebensmittelbranche und dem Gartenbedarf angesiedelt. Jüngste Investition ist der Bau Saxnet GmbH.

Ein neues Industriegebiet hat die Stadt im Ortsteil Taltitz/Neue Welt ausgewiesen. 22 Hektar Fläche unmittelbar neben der Autobahn erwarten den Investor, die Voltavis AG. Reserveflächen hält das ebenfalls bereits ausgewiesens Industriegebiet „Moritzbach" an der B 92 oberhalb von Untermarxgrün bereit.

Die Industriebrache des Halbmond-Werks, das sich auf einen Teil der ehemaligen Betriebsfläche zurück gezogen hat, gibt der Stadt die Möglichkeit, in der Nähe des Bahngeländes und der Umgehungsstraße weitere interessante Flächen für den Wirtschaftsstandort Oelsnitz/Vogtl. zu schaffen. Mit den Halbmond-Teppichwerken hat ein Unternehmen der Altindustrie erfolgreich die Talsohle nach der Wende durchschritten und ist wieder auf Wachstumskurs.

Mit der Einweihung der Umgehungsstraße am 18. November 2006 überwand Oelsnitz/Vogtl. eines seiner schwerwiegendsten, urbanen Probleme – den Schwerlastverkehr mitten durch das Stadtzentrum. Das staatliche Großvorhaben von rund 25 Millionen Euro Umfang – vertreten durch das Straßenbauamt Plauen - nahm rund vier Jahre in Anspruch und wurde trotz starker Einschnitte ins innerstädtische Verkehrsgeschehen fristgerecht realisiert. An der Verkehrsführung in Oelsnitz/Vogtl.

wird weiter gearbeitet. Eine verkehrsberuhigte Zone ist vor dem Rathaus ausgewiesen und der angrenzende Marktplatz wird ab 2008 neu gestaltet. Der gesamte Bereich soll barrierefrei gestaltet, neu bepflanzt und mit attraktiven Elementen geschmückt werden. Vorgesehen sind unter anderem die Pflasterung im Stil eines Teppichmusters und die Rekonstruktion des historischen Brunnens.

Mit dem Landkreisarchiv gewann die Stadt eine neue Perspektive für Schloss Voigtsberg. Die neu gestalteten Schlosshöfe auf unterschiedlicher Höhe – verbunden durch die frei gelegte mittelalterliche Bogenbrücke – dienen als reizvolles Veranstaltungsgelände für das jährliche Historische Schlossfest. Durch weitere Bauarbeiten der Stadt am ehemaligen Polyka-Gebäude und dem Torhaus rückt die Wiedereröffnung des Teppichmuseums und der mittelalterlichen Kernburg in greifbare Nähe. Schon jetzt kann im Fürstensaal mit seiner gotischen Burgkapelle geheiratet werden.

ery and the workshop for handicapped people run by the Upper Vogtland Association for Home Mission Work.

A business park in Untermarxgrüner Street in Oelsnitz – referred to colloquially as the "car mile" – was set up at almost the same time as the industrial park, although this did not involve any public funding. In addition to car dealerships, large-scale retail operations from the food and gardening supplies sectors have also set up shop here. Saxnet GmbH is the latest company to invest in premises there.

The town has now also earmarked the Taltitz/Neue Welt district for a new industrial park, providing the investor there, Voltavis AG, with a 22-hectare site right next to the motorway. Overflow capacity is also available at yet another site, the Moritzbach industrial park on the B 92 main road near Untermarxgrün.

The former Halbmond factory location has also given the town an opportunity to create more sites of importance for Oelsnitz as a business location near the railway sidings and the ring road. The Halbmond carpet factory has now withdrawn to one part of its former works and is one of the old industrial companies that has successfully weathered the post-reunification recession and is now growing once again.

The opening of the ring road on 18 November 2006 solved one of Oelsnitz's most serious urban problems – the passage of heavy goods traffic through the town centre. This major public project, which was directed by the Highways Department in Plauen and cost approximately € 25 million, took four years to complete and, in spite of considerable disruption to traffic in the town itself, was completed on schedule. Work on the town's traffic system is continuing: a restricted zone is planned in front of the town hall and the adjacent marketplace is due for a redesign starting in 2008. All the barriers will be removed and the whole area will be replanted with trees and vegetation and decorated with attractive elements. Planned features include paving with a carpet pattern and the reconstruction of the historical fountain.

By attracting the district archives to Voigtsberg Castle, the town has opened up new prospects for the building. The remodelled courtyards, which are at different heights and are linked by a medieval arched bridge that has been uncovered, are a charming setting for the annual historical castle festival. Further building work on the former Polyka building and the gatehouse means that the carpet museum and the keep should both reopen in the foreseeable future. It is already possible to get married in the Prince's Chamber with its Gothic chapel.

Oelsnitz/Vogtland

Mit der Sanierung des Zoephelschen Hauses, dem ältesten erhaltenen Wohnhaus der Stadt mit Fachwerkgiebel, gewann Oelsnitz/Vogtl. Mitte der neunziger Jahre ein blickträchtiges innerstädtisches Kulturzentrum, in dem die Bibliothek und das Fremdenverkehrsamt einzogen. Ausstellungen, Vorträge und Konzerte bereichern hier das kulturelle Leben.

Mit dem Umbau der Katharinenkirche an der Egerstraße wurde ein Veranstaltungszentrum für rund 170 Besucher gewonnen. Es wird gemeinsam von Stadt und Kirchgemeinde genutzt.

Im Dezember 1357 wurde Oelsnitz/Vogtl. erstmals urkundlich als Stadt erwähnt. Mit einer Festwoche vom 25. Mai bis 3. Juni 2007 und dem 11. Tag der Vogtländer feierten die Oelsnitzer ihr 650-jähriges Jubiläum. Sechs Festtage mit einem Wochenende, das von Höhepunkten nur so strotzte, fanden trotz des regnerischen Sommers Riesen-Resonanz. Höhepunkt war der Historische Festumzug, den das Heimatwerk Oelsnitz e. V. in über einjähriger Vorbereitung engagiert und einfallsreich gestaltet hatte. Zusammen mit dem großen Landkreis-Umzug zum Tag der Vogtländer, der sich nahtlos anschloss, waren 1600 Leute in 90 Bildern auf den Beinen – ein neuer Rekord in der Geschichte des Vogtländertags.

Ihre Bewährungsprobe bestand dabei die neu ins Leben gerufene Stadtmarketing- und Tourismus GmbH unter Leitung von Eckardt Scharf. Sie hatte seit Jahresbeginn das Ereignis vorbereitet und hielt die organisatorischen Fäden zusammen mit Gabriele Klug vom Landratsamt und dem Oelsnitzer Gewerbeverband in der Hand. Das Stadtfest zum Tag der Vogtländer und zur 650-Jahrfeier von Oelsnitz/Vogtl. übertraf von seiner Dimension alles, was bisher an kulturellen Höhepunkten in Oelsnitz stattgefunden hatte.

The restoration of the Zoephelsches Haus, the town's oldest surviving dwelling with its half-timbered gables, in the mid-1990s gave Oelsnitz an attractive cultural centre at the heart of the town housing the library and tourist office. Exhibitions, lectures and concerts enrich cultural life here.

The conversion of the St. Catherine's Church in Eger Street has created a performance location with seating for about 170 guests. It is used by both the town and the parish.

The first official mention of Oelsnitz as a town was in December 1357. The people of Oelsnitz celebrated their 650th anniversary with a festival week from 25 May to 3 June 2007 and the 11th Vogtland Festival. The six days and one weekend of festivities with their innumerable highlights brought in huge crowds in spite of the rainy weather. The climax was an imaginative historical parade which took the Oelsnitz Folk Crafts Association more than a year to organise. Together with the big rural district parade at the Vogtland Festival, which linked in without a hitch, it involved 1600 participants in 90 scenes – a new record for the Vogtland Festival.

The event was also a litmus test for the newly established town marketing and tourism agency directed by Eckardt Scharf. It had worked on the preparations for the event since the start of the year and, together with Gabriele Klug from the rural district office and the town's Business Association, was responsible for the overall coordination of events. The town celebrations at the Vogtland Festival and the town's 650th anniversary outshone all of Oelsnitz's earlier cultural highlights.

OEWOG
Oelsnitzer Wohnungsbaugesellschaft mbH

Oelsnitzer Stadtmarketing und Tourismus GmbH

Dr.-Friedrichs-Straße 42
D-08606 Oelsnitz/Vogtl.
Telefon +49 (0) 37421 70973

emm@oelsnitz-vogtland.com
www.oelsnitz.de

(Fotos/Photos by Renate Wöllner, Harald Sulski, Text/Text by Renate Wöllner, Übersetzung/Translated by David Strauss)

Kompetenz in Sachen Energie
Competence in Energy

Ger Bauer – der Geschäftsführer (Manager) der SWOE

Aus dem Wunsch, die kommunalen Wirtschaftsbetriebe zusammenzufassen, wurden am 30. Juni 1993 die Stadtwerke Oelsnitz (SWOE) gegründet.

Seitdem liegt die Versorgung mit Strom und Gas in den Händen der zu 100 Prozent städtischen Gesellschaft. Der Bauhof mit seinem Dienstleistungsangebot kam wenig später noch hinzu. Anfang 2002 übernahmen die Stadtwerke auch das Freibad an der Elster, den heutigen „Elstergarten", und 2003 die Betreuung der Sportstätten und den Hausmeisterservice. Unter einer von der Verwaltung unabhängigen Geschäftsführung sind damit alle wirtschaftlichen Betätigungen der Stadt vereint. Die Bereiche im Rathaus wurden entlastet. Als leitender Kopf von Anfang an wirkt Ger Bauer, ein Vogtländer mit niederländischem Pass. In einer Doppelspitze arbeitete in den ersten Jahren der verdienstvolle Geschäftsführer Hans Kunte mit. Rund 60 Mitarbeiter kümmern sich um die vielfältigen Aufgaben.

Die erfolgreiche wirtschaftliche Betätigung widerspiegelt sich in jährlichen Gewinnausschüttungen, mit denen die Stadtwerke Vorhaben der Kommune unterstützt. Um Synergie-Effekte und steuerliche Vorteile zu nutzen gründete die Stadt Ende 2005 die Kommunale Holding, eine Klammer für ihre Eigenbetriebe. Diesem Verbund gehören auch die Stadtwerke an.

Bei Preisvergleichen günstiger Energieanbieter ist auch der Name des

Oelsnitzer Versorgers zu lesen. Das Unternehmen nutzt seine Möglichkeiten, um Preise zu optimieren und die Vorteile an die Kunden weiterzureichen. Alle Bemühungen reichen aber nicht, den Preisauftrieb für Öl, Gas und Strom zu stoppen, der auch auf die Preisgestaltung bei den Stadtwerken durchschlägt. Hier ist der Gesetzgeber zur Problemlösung gefragt, um zum Beispiel die Benutzung der Transportnetze neu zu regeln.

In Zukunft will der städtische Versorger sein Leitungsnetz ausbauen und weitere Aufgaben von der Stadt als Beitrag zum Umweltschutz übernehmen. Ger Bauer schwebt ein Kompetenz-Zentrum rund um die Energie mit ausgezeichneter Kundenberatung vor.

The Oelsnitz Public Utilities Company (SWOE) was set up on 30 June 1993 to bring all the public utilities under one roof.

Since then, electricity and gas supplies have been managed by the agency, in which the town owns a 100 percent stake. Building services were added a short time later. At the beginning of 2002, the SWOE also took over the open air swimming pool by the river Elster, now known as the "Elster Garden", and in 2003 the management of the town's sports facilities and property management services. That brought all the town's economic activities together to be managed by an agency that is independent of the town council, thereby relieving it of responsibility for these areas. Ger Bauer, a Vogtland resident with a Dutch passport, has headed the agency since its inception. During the first few years, he shared the top job with managing director Hans Kunte. Some 60 employees are responsible for a wide range of tasks.

The success of this economic activity is reflected in the annual profits, which go towards supporting the town's other projects. In order to capitalize on the synergy effects and tax advantages, the town set up a public holding company for its own operations at the end of 2005. This now also belongs to the SWOE.

The Oelsnitz energy utility's prices bear comparison with those of the cheaper energy providers. The company does everything possible to optimize its costs and pass on the advantages to its customers. However, in spite of all its efforts, the rising costs of oil, gas and power are having an effect on its pricing. The government needs to find a solution to the problem: changing the way transport networks are used, for example, would be one option.

The company intends to expand its supply network in future and take over more of the town's functions as its contribution towards environmental protection. Ger Bauer is currently looking at the possibility of setting up a specialised centre dealing with all aspects of energy and offering a first-class customer advisory service.

Stadtwerke Oelsnitz (Vogtl.) GmbH

Boxbachweg 2
D-08606 Oelsnitz/Vogtl.
Telefon +49 (0) 37421 408-0
Telefax +49 (0)37421 29491
info@vogtland-energie.de
www.swoe.de

(Fotos/Photos by Stadtwerke Oelsnitz/Vogtland GmbH, Text/Text by Renate Wöllner, Übersetzung/Translated by David Strauss)

Elstergarten in Oelsnitz/Vogtland

Freizeit, Sport und Erholung

Leisure, Sport and Relaxation

Eine grüne Oase nahe am Stadtzentrum ist das Oelsnitzer Freibad in der Elsteraue. Ab dem Herbst 2004 wurde es von den Stadtwerken zu einer modernen Freizeitanlage umgebaut. Undichte Wasserbecken und veraltete Badtechnik zeigten damals dringenden Handlungsbedarf an. Rund fünf Millionen Euro investierte der Oelsnitzer Eigenbetrieb.

Mit Begeisterung nahmen die Badelustigen im Mai 2006 ihren neuen „Elstergarten" wieder in Besitz, einen Ort der Ruhe und Erholung, der sportlichen, schulischen und kulturellen Aktivitäten. Dafür sorgt das innovative Konzept, welches die Stadtwerke zusammen mit dem Architekten Klaus Fleischmann umgesetzt hatten.

Eine kreisrunde Plattform verbindet drei Wasserflächen - eine 50-Meter-Bahn für Schwimmer, den Nichtschwimmerbereich und ein 3,80 Meter tiefes Becken mit dem Fünf-Meter-Sprungturm, dessen Gestalt aus den Initialen von Oelsnitz im Vogtland entstand. Mit dem ersten Sprung vom Fünfmeterbrett weihten Oberbürgermeisterin Eva-Maria Möbius und Stadtwerke-Geschäftsführer Ger Bauer den Elstergarten ein.

Durch ein Blockheizkraftwerk kann das Wasser in kühlen Zeiten bis 24 Grad Celsius aufgeheizt werden. Aufwärmen können sich Badegäste außerdem im Glashaus mit offenem Kamin. Moderne Filtertechnik sorgt in der Unterwelt für das zügige Umwälzen des Badewassers und eine hygienische Mikrobiologie. Auch auf Anregungen aus dem Stadtrat hin blieb das wettkampftaugliche Schwimmerbecken erhalten.

Ins Auge springt die futuristische Dachkonstruktion mit einer 2500 Quadratmeter großen Photovoltaik-Anlage, die Strom ins Netz einspeist. Etwa 2017 sollen sich die Anlage amortisiert haben – und dann zur Kostenersparnis beitragen. Das wuchtige Dach ist gleichzeitig ein Schlechtwetterschutz für den Beach-Volleyball-Platz.

Das Oelsnitzer Freibad hat sich zwar umfassend verändert, doch es ist trotzdem wiedererkennbar geblieben. Die Liegewiese mit den alten Platanen, die Lage am Fluss inmitten der Auenlandschaft, die historischen Pfahlbauten mit den Umkleidekabinen, die ganzjährig gemietet werden können, sorgen weiterhin für Flair. Eine besondere Note setzt die künstlerische Gestaltung. Unmittelbar vor Ort schufen die Holzbildhauerstudenten Nora Leschinski und Benjamin Hahn große, hölzerne Stelen aus der Welt des Urtümlichen, die nun die Badeplattform säumen.

Auch das Umfeld des Elstergartens haben die Oelsnitzer Stadtwerke neu gestaltet. Der Eingangs- und Kassenbereich wurde zum Fluss hin verlegt, den eine neue Stahlbrücke überspannt. Sie ist von dem eigens geschaffenen Parkplatz erreichbar, der zugleich die Verbindung zur neuen Ortsumgehungsstraße schafft. So wurde die bereits historisch geplante Wegeführung aufgenommen. Denn die Geschichte des Oelsnitzer Freibades reicht ein Jahrhundert zurück.

The open-air swimming pool in the water meadows alongside the river Elster is a green oasis close to the centre of the town. By the autumn of 2004, action was urgently needed to deal with leaking tanks and obsolete swimming pool technology, so the SWOE launched a project to turn it into a modern leisure facility. The company invested approximately € 5 million in the conversion work.

In May 2006, eager swimmers were delighted to reclaim their new "Elster Garden", a place of calm and relaxation and sporting, school and cultural activities. They were able to do so thanks to an innovative concept realised by the SWOE in collaboration with the architect Klaus Fleischmann.

A circular platform connects three pools – 50-meter lanes for swimmers, an area for non-swimmers and a 3.8 metre deep pool with a five metre high diving platform in the shape of the initials of "Oelsnitz im Vogtland". Mayor Eva-Maria Möbius and the Stadtwerke's managing director Ger Bauer inaugurated the "Elster Garden" by being the first to jump from the five metre diving board. When it is cold, the water can be heated to 24 degrees Celsius by a combined heat and power station and swimmers can also warm themselves up in a glasshouse with its open fire. Modern filter technology means the water can be quickly circulated and its microbiological content regulated in the interests of hygiene. The town council was also keen to retain a swimming pool where competitions could be held.

People are immediately struck by the futuristic roof with its 2,500 square metres of solar panels feeding into the electricity grid. The unit should have paid for itself by about the year 2017, after which it will help cut costs greatly. The huge roof also protects the beach-volleyball court from bad weather.

The open-air swimming pool in Oelsnitz may have changed a lot, but not out of all recognition. The sunbathing lawn with its ancient plane trees, its location on the water meadows by the river and the historical pile dwellings with their changing rooms that are available for rent all year round still provide a touch of flair. Its artistic design also gives sets a particular tone. Right on the spot, two students of wood sculpture, Nora Leschinski and Benjamin Hahn, have created huge wooden steles that hark back to a more primitive world and these now line the bathing platform.

The Oelsnitz utilities company has also remodelled the "Elster Garden's" surroundings. The entrance and ticket office were moved towards the river, which is spanned by a new steel bridge. It is accessible from the specially built car park, which is also linked to the new ring road. This integrates it into the historical road layout, which is apt, because the history of the open-air pool in Oelsnitz goes back a century.

Elstergarten

Oelsnitz (Vogtl.)

An der Elsteraue 15
D-08606 Oelsnitz/Vogtl.
Telefon +49 (0) 37421 22619
Telefax +49 (0)37421 72998
info@elstergarten.de
www.elstergarten.de

(Fotos/Photos by Renate Wöllner, Harald Sulski, Text/Text by Renate Wöllner, Übersetzung/Translated by David Strauss)

Eine Gabe für nachfolgende Generationen
A Gift to Future Generations

Glück gehabt hat die Oelsnitzer Katharinenkirche. Die ehemalige Hospital- und Friedhofskirche, erbaut 1617 vor dem Egerer Tor, überlebte unbeschadet den großen Stadtbrand von 1859. Sie ist damit eins der wenigen Bauwerke von Alt-Oelsnitz – und ein (Neben)schauplatz der Geschichte. In den Befreiungskriegen gegen Napoleon Buonaparte 1813 bis 1815 wurde die kleine Kirche als Heulager und Lazarett zweckentfremdet. Für ihre Wiederherstellung spendete der russische Zar Alexander 1000 Taler.

Aus Richtung Adorf ist das Gotteshaus stadtbildprägend. Der barocke Dachreiter bildet zusammen mit den neugotischen Türmen der Jakobikirche eine charakteristische Silhouette. Manch ein „Sperk" weiß sich hier getauft oder erlebte in der Kirche seine Konfirmation. Doch in der DDR genügte die große Stadtkirche Sankt Jakobi dem religiösen Leben der evangelisch-lutherischen Gemeinde. Die Innenausstattung der Katharinenkirche wurde aufgelöst, das Gebäude verfiel. Erst nach der Wende konnte der Dachstuhl saniert werden. Ein Projekt zur Erneuerung blieb aber für fast ein Jahrzehnt Zukunftsmusik, weil Gemeinde und Landeskirche durch die Sanierung von Sankt Jakobi und seiner Jehmlich-Orgel finanziell stark belastet waren.

Erst mit der gemeinsamen Nutzung und dem Umbau zum "Gemeinde-, Stadt- und Kommunikationszentrum" sowie dem Verzicht auf die Widmung als Gotteshaus fanden Kirche und Stadt 2004 die Lösung. Wegen der städtebaulichen Bedeutung des Gebäudes bewilligte der Stadtrat großzügig Mittel aus dem Förderprogramm Städtebaulicher Denkmalschutz in Höhe von rund 580 000 Euro und übernahm damit den größten Teil der Bausumme von

nahezu 900 000 Euro. Der Innenraum der Kirche blieb in seiner sakralen historischen Form erhalten und erhielt wieder eine Empore. Der Chor mit seinem Kreuzgewölbe wurde denkmalgerecht rekonstruiert, der Zuschauerraum mit modernen Elementen und Materialien gestaltet. Augenfällig im Außenbereich ist ein Funktionsanbau, welcher mit dem Hauptgebäude durch ein gläsernes Treppenhaus verbunden ist.

Nach rund einjähriger Bauzeit wurde die Katharinenkirche am 7. Juli 2007 mit einem Benefizkonzert der Chursächsischen Philharmonie unter Leitung von Florian Merz feierlich wieder eröffnet. Die ersten Takte im neu gestalteten Haus stammten von einem Oelsnitzer Kind, dem Barockkomponisten Johann Rosenmüller. Oberbürgermeisterin Eva-Maria Möbius sieht die Sanierung als „unsere Gabe an nachfolgende Generationen". „Altes bewahren – Neues wagen", habe man sich bei der Sanierung zum Ziel gesetzt, erklärte Diplomingenieur Harald Schneider vom Oelsnitzer Architekturbüro, welches mir der Planung des Projektes beauftragt war.

St. Catherine's Church in Oelsnitz has been fortunate. The former hospital and cemetery church, which was built in 1617 in front of the Eger Gate, survived the great fire of 1859 unscathed. That means it is one of the few buildings that are left from the old town – and one which played a role, albeit perhaps minor, in historical events. During the War of Liberation against Napoleon Bonaparte from 1813 to 1815, the small church was used as a hay barn and a field hospital. Afterwards, the Russian Czar Alexander I donated 1,000 thalers towards its restoration.

If you are coming from Adorf, the church is a major feature of the townscape; its Baroque ridge turrets combine with the neo-Gothic towers of the Saint Jakobi Church inside the town to form a characteristic silhouette. Many local "sparrows" were once baptised or confirmed here. However, during the East German period, the larger Saint Jakobi was deemed sufficient for the religious life of the Lutheran Protestant parish. The interior of St. Catherine's Church was stripped and the building became derelict. The restoration of the roof truss had to wait until after the fall of the Berlin Wall and even then complete refurbishment was little more than a pipe dream for almost another decade as the parish and regional church authorities were under considerable financial strain because of the restoration of Saint Jakobi and its organ, originally built by the renowned Jehmlich family.

The church and town authorities finally hit on a solution in 2004: St. Catherine's Church would not be reconsecrated as a church but instead turned into a non-profit "Parish, Town and Communications Centre." Because of the building's architectural importance, the town council authorized a generous contribution of some € 580,000 from the listed building preservation fund, which accounted for the biggest share of the total refurbishment cost of € 900,000. The interior of the church retained its old ecclesiastical form and was given a new gallery. The choir with its cross vault was restored to its original state and an auditorium created using modern elements and materials. To increase the amount of usable space, a striking outside building was added and linked to the main building by a glass stairwell.

The restoration work took about a year. St. Catherine's Church was formally reopened with a benefit concert given by the Chursächsisch Philharmonic orchestra conducted by Florian Merz. The first notes to sound through the newly converted building came from a native of Oelsnitz, the Baroque composer Johann Rosenmüller. The Mayor, Eva-Maria Möbius, sees the restoration as "our gift to future generations". The aim of the restoration was to "Cherish the Old and Dare the New," says Harald Schneider, an engineer from the architectural practice in Oelsnitz responsible for planning the project.

(Fotos/Photos by Eva-Maria Müller, Text/Text by Renate Wöllner, Übersetzung/Translated by David Strauss)

9,5 Kilometer Akten ziehen um in das Schloss Voigtsberg

9.5 Kilometres of Files Move into Voigtsberg Castle

Von einem Sorgenkind zu einem Paradepferd hat sich Schloss Voigtsberg in Oelsnitz gemausert. Als im Sommer 2005 ein Lkw der Firma Seidel-Umzüge an die rückwärtige Rampe rollte, zog neues Leben in das ehemalige Frauengefängnis. Aus Falkenstein kamen die ersten Aktenkartons dort wieder an, von wo sie vor rund drei Jahren ausgezogen waren, als der Bau des neuen Landkreisarchivs begann. Die logistisch schwierige Aufgabe des Umzugs bewältigten Archivleiterin Sigrid Unger und ihren acht Mitarbeitern in Wochen harter Arbeit. Rund 9,5 Kilometer historischer Aktenbestände aus dem Vogtlandkreis zogen in die Gebäudeteile aus dem 18. und 19. Jahrhundert.

Mehrfach entspannen sich nach der Wende Diskussionen, wie der Gebäudetrakt, der nach dem Auszug der Berufsschule in großen Teilen leer stand, sinnvoll genutzt werden kann. Die desolate Bausubstanz tauchte die Zukunft des Gemäuers für fast zehn Jahre ins Dunkel. Auch der Abriss wurde erwogen. Das Heimatwerk Oelsnitz e. V. äußerte erstmals öffentlich die Idee, das Schloss als Vogtländisches Kreisarchiv einzurichten.

Anfang des neuen Jahrtausends votierte der Kreistag in diesem Sinn, nachdem die Stadt ein schlüssiges Konzept vorgelegt hatte. Die Abgeordneten beschlossen die langjährige Mietbindung des Landkreises. Damit und mit Hilfe von Fördergeldern aus dem Programm für städtischen Denkmalschutz konnte die Stadt Oelsnitz den sogenannten Neuteil von Schloss Voigtsberg umfassend sanieren. Während die Fassade denkmalgerecht wiederhergestellt wurde,

musste das Innere – in dem noch einige Gefängniszellen und große Arbeitssäle vorhanden waren - entkernt und nach den Anforderungen modernen Archivwesens gestaltet werden.

Aufbewahrt werden die wertvollen Dokumente und Sachzeugen in den Rollregalen des Magazins. Die 2,75 Meter hohen Regale lasten mit einem Druck von 10 Kilonewton (Kn) pro Quadratmeter auf der Rohdecke. Jeweils die drei obersten Etagen des Faktorenhauses und des Neuen Zellenhauses sowie zwei Etagen im Alten Zellenhaus enthalten Magazinräume, während die Erdgeschosse als Öffentlichkeitsbereich dienen und die Untergeschosse der Verwaltung vorbehalten sind.

Im ersten Halbjahr nach der Eröffnung am 25. August 2005 strömten über 600 Bürger zum „Schnuppern" in die Einrichtung. Schüler und Studenten suchen Material für Belegarbeiten, Heimat-, Familien- und Namensforscher geben sich die Klinke in die Hand. Dokumente zu Rechts- und Grundstücksangelegenheiten und zur Vereinsgeschichte sind gefragt. Ein Wissenschafter aus den USA studierte Unterlagen zur Weimarer Republik für seine Dissertation und wurde unter anderem zu Max Hölz fündig. Für alle Archiv-Nutzer und die Mitarbeiter haben sich die Arbeitsbedingungen und Auffindemöglichkeiten wesentlich verbessert.

Als die Akten von Schloss Voigtsberg auszogen, herrschte in den alten Räumen Feuchtigkeit, und der Salpeter drang durch die Mauern. Im winzigen Arbeitsraum gab es gerade mal einen Nutzerplatz. Heute stehen 12 Nutzerplätze in modernen Kabinen zur Verfügung, von denen einige verglast sind - falls jemand auf seinem Notebook klappern möchte.

Während des Umbaus durch die Stadt Oelsnitz kamen im Außenbereich Teile der ursprünglichen Anlage wie die Bogenbrücke wieder zum Vorschein, über welche die Archiv-Besucher jetzt laufen. Ein Stück Mittelalter kehrte nach den Worten der Oelsnitzer Stadtbaumeisterin Karin Schuberth wieder ins Bild zurück. Mit Rhododendron-Rabatten und einem plätschernden Brunnen präsentiert sich der Schlosshof in neuer Attraktivität.

Durch die Anordnung der Gebäude ergeben sich drei in sich geschlossene Hofebenen. Sie bieten Raum für verschiedenste kulturelle Events bieten. Besonders reizvoll sind die Veranstaltungen im historischen Ambiente, die jeweils in den Sonderankündigungen im Internet und in den Tagespressen nachzulesen sind. Trauungen können mit dem örtlichen Standesamt vereinbart werden. Das Areal kann für Feste gemietet werden.

Ein Besuch von Schloss Voigtsberg lohnt zu jeder Jahreszeit. Die umfangreichen Sanierungsarbeiten bilden die Basis für den Erhalt der einmaligen Burganlage des oberen Vogtlandes. Jeder Bauabschnitt wirkt getrennt für sich selbst. Die Besucher können vor Ort die Entwicklung von Schloss Voigtsberg miterleben und beim Spaziergang durch die Burganlage das beeindruckende Gebäudeensemble bestaunen.

(Fotos/Photos by Renate Wöllner, Harald Sulski, Oelsnitzer Stadtmarketing und Tourismus GmbH , Text/Text by Renate Wöllner, Übersetzung/Translated by David Strauss)

Schloss Voigtsberg Oelsnitz/Vogtland

Voigtsberg Castle in Oelsnitz has turned from a problem child into a flagship. When a truck from the Seidel removals company rolled up the ramp at the back of the building in summer 2005, the former women's prison took on a whole new lease of life. The first crates of files were brought back from Falkenstein, where they had been stored when the construction work on the new rural district archives started three years earlier. It took head archivist Sigrid Unger and her eight staff weeks of hard work to manage the logistically complex move. Some 9.5 kilometres of historical documents from the Vogtland district were moved into the parts of the building that date back to the 18th and 19th centuries.

The debate about the how to make the best use of the building, large parts of which had been left empty after the vocational school moved out, had flared up from time to time since the fall of the Berlin Wall. For almost ten years, the castle's terrible structural condition left its future shrouded in gloom and there was even some talk of demolishing it completely. The Oelsnitz Folk Crafts Association was the first to go public with the idea of turning the castle into the Vogtland District Archives.

Once Oelsnitz had come up with a convincing concept at the start of the new millennium, the district council voted in favour of the idea and committed the rural district to a long-term fixed rental agreement. This, together with funding from the listed building preservation fund, allowed the town to embark on a comprehensive restoration of the so-called "new section" of Voigtsberg Castle. While the outer facade was being returned to its original state, the interior – which still contained several prison cells and large workrooms – was gutted and rebuilt in accordance with the requirements of modern archival practice.

The valuable documents and papers are housed on rolling shelves in the repositories. The 2.75 metre high shelves exert a pressure of 10 kilonewtons (Kn) per square metre on the concrete slab floors. Repositories have been established on each of the top three stories of the Upper Lusatian-style half-timbered house and new prison buildings and on two floors of the old prison building, while the ground floors serve as a public area and the cellars are reserved for the archive's administration.

In the first six months after the archive opened on 25 August 2005, more than 600 locals came to look around. School pupils and students go there to look for materials for their studies, and local historians and people researching their family trees also make extensive use of the facilities. Documents relating to legal and property matters and the history of local societies are particularly sought after. A graduate student from the USA examined the documents there for his dissertation on the Weimar Republic and, amongst others, came across Max Hölz. The working conditions and accessibility of materials have improved greatly for both users and staff at the archives.

After the files were removed from Voigtsberg Castle, the old rooms became damp and saltpetre made its way through the walls. The tiny workroom only used to have space for one user. Today there are 12 workspaces in modern cubicles, some of which are glassed in to cut down the sound of people typing on their laptops.

During the restoration work, some of the castle's original external features such as the arched bridge, over which visitors now walk, also remerged. As Karin Schuberth, the town's head of construction services, put it, a bit of the Middle Ages has returned to the townscape. Rhododendron bushes and a splashing fountain have also imbued the castle courtyard with a new attractiveness.

The arrangement of the buildings has led to enclosed courtyards on three levels. They provide room for various cultural events and those that capitalize on the castle's medieval atmosphere are particularly appealing: details about these can be found in special announcements on the Internet or in the daily press. It is also possible to arrange weddings there with the local registry office and the site can be rented for parties.

A visit to Voigtsberg Castle is worthwhile at any time of the year. The comprehensive restoration project means the Upper Vogtland district has been able to keep its unique castle complex. Each phase of the construction work stands alone, which means visitors can experience the way the castle is developing and marvel at the impressive architecture as they stroll through it.

Weitere Informationen erhalten Sie im Fremdenverkehrsamt der Stadt Oelsnitz im „Zoephelschen Haus"/Further information in the tourist information office in Oelsnitz
Grabenstraße 31
D-08606 Oelsnitz
Telefon +49 (0) 37421 20785
Telefax +49 (0) 37421 20794
kul-tour@oelsnitz-vogtland.com
www.oelsnitz.de

KLINGENTHAL – Musik- und Wintersportstadt
Music and Winter Sports Town

Weltruf erlangte Klingenthal durch seine mehr als 300 jährige Tradition des Musikinstrumentenbaus. Böhmische Exulanten brachten in der Mitte des 17. Jahrhunderts dieses Wissen in die damals kleine Hammersiedlung und machten mittels Geigen-, Holz- und Metallblasinstrumentenbau daraus ein klingendes Tal. 1852 begann die Fertigung der Handharmonikas, woraus sich das Akkordeon entwickelte und dessen Fabrikation Klingenthal schließlich zu einem weltweiten Zentrum der Handzuginstrumentenherstellung machte.

Die schon länger als 100 Jahre andauernde Tradition des Skisports brachte mehr als 20 Weltmeister und Olympiasieger in den nordischen Disziplinen hervor. Das erste Paar Ski wurde in Klingenthal bereits 1886 nach norwegischem Vorbild gebaut, der erste Wintersportverein 1908 gegründet. Deshalb gibt es in der Stadt einige Skisprungschanzen zu besichtigen, die größte und neueste steht in der Vogtland Arena. Außerdem ist das Gebiet rund um die Stadt von ausgedehnten Wander- und Radfahrwegen, sowie Skiloipen durchzogen.
Klingenthal ist staatlich anerkannter Erholungsort und liegt an den westlichen Ausläufern des Erzgebirges im Südosten des Vogtlandkreises unmittelbar an der Grenze zur Tschechischen Republik. Das 10,5 Kilometer lang gestreckte Stadtgebiet reicht von 533 Metern ü.NN im Zwotatal bis hinauf zum 936 Meter

Klingenthal has gained global fame as a result of its long history of making musical instruments, which stretches back more than 300 years. Exiles from across the border in Bohemia brought this knowledge to the small hammer mill settlement in the middle of the 17th century and turned the place into a musical valley by making violins, woodwind and brass instruments. The production of melodeons started in 1852 and this led to the development of the accordion. The production of this instrument finally made Klingenthal into a global centre for making instruments with bellows.

The tradition of winter sports, which goes back more than 100 years, has produced more than 20 world champions and Olympic winners in the Nordic skiing disciplines. The first pair of skis was constructed in Klingenthal in 1886 based on a Norwegian design and the first winter sports club was founded in 1908. So there are a few ski-jumps to see in the town, the largest and newest of them is at the Vogtland Arena.
The area around the town is covered with extensive footpaths and cycle paths – and of course cross-country ski tracks.
Klingenthal is a recognised resort and is located by the western foothills of the Ore Mountains in the south-east of the Vogtland district right on the border with the Czech Republic. The town area, which stretches for 10.5 kilometres, ranges from 533 metres above sea level in the Zwota Valley up to the

(Fotos/Photos by Touristinformation Klingenthal, Schaumanufaktur BGK GmbH [1], Übersetzung/Translated by David Strauss)

Klingenthal

hohen Aschberg und den Ortsteil Mühlleithen. Klingenthal ist von ausgedehnten Fichtenwäldern umgeben. Durch Klingenthal fließen die Brunndöbra und die Zwota die sich vereinigen und in die Eger münden.

Stadtrecht erhielt Klingenthal am 1. Oktober 1919. Die Stadt besitzt eine Verkehrsanbindung zur Wirtschaftsregion Westsachsen und direkt nach Tschechien. Die Infrastruktur bietet alles, was von einer intakten Kommune erwartet wird: Kindergärten, Schulen, Jugendzentrum, zahlreiche touristische Einrichtungen und ein medizinisches Betreuungsnetz mit Allgemeinmedizinern, Fachärzten und Pflegediensten.

Aschberg, which is 936 metres high and the district of Mühlleithen. Klingenthal is surrounded by extensive pine forests. The Brunndöbra and Zwota rivers flow through Klingenthal and merge and flow into the river Oh e.

Klingenthal received its town charter on 1 October 1919. The town has major roads linking it to the West Saxon business region and a direct link to the Czech Republic. The infrastructure provides everything expected of a functioning community: nurseries, schools, a youth centre, many tourist facilities and a medical care network with general practitioners, specialists and nursing services.

Museen:
Musik- und Wintersportmuseum Klingenthal
Schaumanufaktur für Akkordeonbau Klingenthal
Harmonikamuseum Zwota

Sehenswürdigkeiten:
Großschanze in der Vogtland Arena (K125)
Rundkirche „Zum Friedefürsten"
Sommerrodelbahn
Tierpark Klingenthal
Wanderaussichtsturm „Otto-Hermann Böhm" auf dem Aschberg
Naturlehrpfad Radiumquelle

Kontakt:
Touristinformation Klingenthal
Schloßstraße 3
D-08248 Klingenthal

+49 (0) 37467 / 64832
www.klingenthal.de

Treuen – internationaler Wirtschaftsstandort in der Mitte des Vogtlandes
Treuen – International Business Centre in the Centre of the Vogtland Region

Logistisches Drehkreuz im Dreiländereck Sachsen. Bayern. Tschechien / Logistic Hub Where Saxony, Bavaria and the Czech Republic Meet

Die Kleinstadt Treuen entwickelte sich in ihrer über 600-jährigen Geschichte aus einem Ackerbürgerstädtchen und nach Jahrhunderten als „Weberstadt" mit einseitigem Wirtschaftsgefüge zum heutigen modernen Wohn- und Gewerbestandort mit vielseitigem Branchenmix, in der rund 9000 Einwohner ihr Zuhause und zum Teil auch ihren Arbeitsplatz haben.

Ein wesentlicher Einflussfaktor für das Wachstum der Stadt war und ist seine günstige Verkehrslage und -anbindung.

Der politische und wirtschaftliche Umbruch durch die Wiedervereinigung Deutschlands 1990 schuf eine völlig neue Situation. Mit dem vierspurigen Ausbau der A 72 Hof-Chemnitz war Treuen seit Oktober 1992 zu einem exponierten Standort im Vogtland und zum Tor in den Freistaat Sachsen geworden. Über das Autobahnnetz besteht der Anschluss an die sächsischen und bayerischen Verdichtungsräume, wie Chemnitz, Dresden, Nürnberg oder Regensburg und darüber hinaus zu anderen Regionen Deutschlands und seine Nachbarländer, wie Tschechien oder Polen.

An keiner anderen Stelle im Vogtland treffen Anschlussstelle von Autobahn, Bundesstraße und Eisenbahn in unmittelbarer Stadtnähe zusammen. Die relativ ebene Hochfläche links und rechts an der Straße zwischen der Stadt und der Autobahn sowie am Gleisbogen der Eisenbahn westlich der Autobahn bot beste Bedingungen für die Ansiedlung neuer Gewerbe.

Im Industrie- und Gewerbegebiet „Goldene Höhe, Teilgebiete I und II" siedelten sich auf rund 33,5 Hektar verschiedene mittelständische Betriebe, Handwerker, Logistikunternehmen und Dienstleister aus der Stadt und der Region, aber auch aus den alten Bundesländern an, wie zum Beispiel die Firma GOLDBECK Bau GmbH, die als erstes Unternehmen die Standortvorteile nutzte und 1991 den Grundstein für ihr neues Werk in Treuen legte.

Mittlerweile sind auf diesem Areal 43 Firmen ansässig, die rund 970 Arbeitnehmern Lohn und Brot geben. Entwickelt hat sich ein gesunder Branchenmix, der modernen und innovativen Betrieben unter anderem die Möglichkeit zu interessanter Zusammenarbeit bietet.

Bereits während der Bauphase der beiden Teilgebiete wurde auf einer Fläche von 26,8 Hektar mit der Vorbereitung für das Industrie- und Gewerbegebiet „Goldene Höhe, Teilgebiet III" begonnen. Es befindet sich gegenüber dem Teilgebieten I und II, zwischen der Herlasgrüner Straße und der neuen Umgehungsstraße S 298. Das Gebiet, kürzlich noch landwirtschaftliche Nutzfläche, verändert täglich sein Gesicht. Neben einem einheimischen Investor, der erst 2008 eine Produktionsstätte errichten will, ist bei zwei anderen Unternehmen rege Bautätigkeit sichtbar.

Für die Produktionsstätte der Physiotherm Holding GmbH aus Oesterreich werden momentan die Erdmassen für die Fundamente bewegt und die Grundsteinlegung wird in absehbarer Zeit durchgeführt. In Treuen soll die Herstellung von Holzelementen für Infrarotkammern erfolgen. Der Produktionsstart ist für März 2008 vorgesehen.

Währenddessen wurde bei der japanischen Firma MIM Steel Processing GmbH bereits Richtfest für die neue Werkhalle gefeiert. „In vier Monaten Bauzeit ist ein schönes Bauwerk entstanden", lobte Dieter Pfortner, Geschäftsführer von Magnetto Automotive Treuen. Mit Interesse verfolgt er von der anderen Seite der Autobahn den Fortgang der Bauarbeiten, ist doch das neue Werk, die MIM Steel Processing GmbH, ein Joint

The small town of Treuen has developed a great deal during its 600-year history; it started life as a small farming community and after several centuries became a "weaving centre" focussing on just one kind of business; today it is a modern residential and business centre and is home to a wide variety of business sectors. 9,000 people live in Treuen and some of them work there too.

One of the most important factors behind the town's growth is and was its favourable location and transport links.

The political and economic upheaval caused by German reunification in 1990 created a completely new situation. Once the A72 motorway from Hof to Chemnitz had been upgraded into a four-lane road in 1992, Treuen became an outstanding location in the Vogtland region and the gateway to the Free State of Saxony. The motorway network provides links to the densely populated areas in Saxony and Bavaria like Chemnitz, Dresden, Nuremberg or Regensburg – and beyond to other regions in Germany and neighbouring countries like the Czech Republic and Poland.

There is no other place in the Vogtland region where the motorway, main road and railway meet so close to the centre of town. The relatively flat plateau to the left and right of the road between the town and the motorway and next to the bend in the railway track west of the motorway provided ideal conditions to attract new businesses.

Various medium-sized companies, trades, logistics and service companies from the town and region have set up in business on the "Goldene Höhe, Sections I and II" industrial and business park on an area measuring approx. 33.5 hectares; some of the companies come from Western Germany like GOLDBECK Bau GmbH, which was the first firm to make use of the advantages of the area ; it laid the foundation stone for its new factory in Treuen in 1991.

This area is now home to 43 different companies, which provide work for 970 people. A healthy mix of companies has developed and this provides modern and innovative companies with the opportunity of working with other companies on interesting projects. Even while the building work was going on to set up these two sections, work also started on preparing for the "Goldene Höhe, Section III" industrial and business park on an area measuring 26.8 hectares. It is located opposite sections I and II between Herlasgrüner Street and the new S 298 bypass. This area, which was still agricultural land until recently, changes its appearance every day. One local investor plans to build a production facility in 2008 and there is plenty of building work going on for two other companies

The earthworks are being moved to prepare the foundations for a production factory for Physiotherm Holding GmbH from Austria. The laying of the foundation stone is planned for the near future. Wood elements for infra-red chambers will then be made in Treuen. Production is due to begin in March 2008.

Meanwhile, the topping-out ceremony has already been held for the new factory for the Japanese company, MIM Steel Processing GmbH. "A beautiful building has been created in just four months," says Dieter Pfortner, managing director of Magnetto Automotive Treuen, full of praise for the construction. He is following the progress in the building work from the other side of the motorway; the new factory, MIM Steel Processing GmbH, is after all a joint ven-

(Fotos/Photos by Stadtverwaltung Treuen, Text/Text by Stadtverwaltung Treuen, Übersetzung/Translated by David Strauss)

Venture Unternehmen mit der italienischen Magnetto Gruppe.

Um der wachsenden Nachfrage nach Flachbild - Fernsehern in Europa gerecht zu werden, haben zahlreiche japanische Hersteller Werke in Europa errichtet. Für die Rückwände und einige Innenteile der TV-Geräte werden verstärkt hochwertige Stähle benötigt, die in Zukunft auch aus Treuen kommen sollen.

Mittlerweile haben schon weitere Ansiedlungswillige diese überaus exponierte Lage in Treuen erkannt und Interesse bekundet.

Mit der Umgehungsstraße S 298, die in naher Zukunft auch zu den Zentren ins Göltzschtal führt, wird Treuen zum logistischen Sprungbrett zu den Wirtschaftsstandorten im östlichen Vogtland, im Westerzgebirge und in Tschechien.

Schon zeitig erkannten wir in Treuen, dass neben der Flächenverfügbarkeit auch eine günstige Verkehrsanbindung neue wichtige Standortfaktoren für die Logistik sind. Gerade bei der Just-intime-Produktion der Fertigungsindustrie in Ballungsräumen - wie zum Beispiel im Fahrzeugbau - werden großflächige Lager- und Fertigungshallen an verkehrsgünstigen Lagen errichtet, um jederzeit störungsfreie Zu- und Auslieferungen zu gewährleisten. All das können wir in Treuen bieten.

Eingerahmt von der A 72, der Bahnstrecke und der B 173 wurde im Jahr 2002 das neue Industrie- und Gewerbegebiet „Goldene Höhe, Teilgebiet IV" förmlich aus dem Boden gestampft, um dem italienischen Automobilzulieferer Magnetto Automotive Deutschland GmbH die Möglichkeit zur Ansiedlung zu geben. Durch einen rasanten Bauablauf konnte bereits im März 2003 Richtfest gefeiert und im April 2004 die Serienproduktion von Karosserieteilen gestartet werden.

Noch in der Bauphase von Magnetto wurde im November 2002 ein weiterer Ansiedlungsvertrag mit dem META WERK Zwickau abgeschlossen, hier befindet sich die Scherdel Schweiß- und Umformtechnik GmbH Treuen.

Mit dem aus der Schweiz stammenden Unternehmen Weidmann Plastics Technology AG reihte sich 2004 eine weitere Firma in den Automobilzuliefererstandort „Goldene Höhe" in Treuen ein. In diesem 1. Bauabschnitt (von Teilgebiet IV) sind gegenwärtig rund 500 Personen beschäftigt.

Unsere Industrie- und Gewerbegebiete verändern endgültig die Industriestruktur der ehemaligen Textilstadt. Der vielseitige Branchenmix aus produzierendem Gewerbe (Metallverarbeitung, grafisches Gewerbe, Bau von technischen Ausrüstungen, Textilindustrie mit Stickerei und Konfektionsbetrieben) sowie Dienstleistungsunternehmen sind ein gesunder Ausgangspunkt für die Stadtentwicklung von Treuen im 21. Jahrhundert.

ture with the Italian Magnetto Group.
Many Japanese manufacturers have set up factories in Europe to meet the growing demand for flat-screen TV monitors in Europe. High-quality steel is required for the rear panels and some of the inner parts in the TVs and they will come from Treuen in future.

Other companies have already recognised the value of this outstanding location and have signalled interest in setting up in business there.

The S 298 bypass will soon be extended to link up with the towns in the Göltzsch valley and this will make Treuen the logistical springboard to the business centres in the east of the Vogtland region, the western part of the Ore Mountains and the Czech Republic.

We in Treuen recognised at an early stage that we did not just have to provide space for companies, but also favourable transport links; they are the new important factors for logistics. In the case of just-in-time production in manufacturing industry in the major conurbations – for example, in the automotive industry – huge storage and manufacturing facilities are built at locations with favourable transport links so that supplies can be transported to and from the factories without any difficulty at any time. We in Treuen can provide all that.

Surrounded by the A 72 motorway, the railway line and the B 173 main road, the new "Goldene Höhe, Section IV" industrial and business park was conjured up out of nothing in 2002 in order to provide space for the Italian automobile supplier Magnetto Automotive Deutschland GmbH to build a factory. The topping-out ceremony was already being celebrated in March 2003 as a result of the fast building work and series production of bodywork parts began in April 2004.

While the building work was going on for Magnetto, another contract was being signed with META WERK Zwickau in November 2002 and the Scherdel Schweiss- und Umformtechnik GmbH Treuen company is now located there.

Another company moved into the "Goldene Höhe" automobile supplier site in 2004 in the shape of Weidmann Plastics Technology AG based in Switzerland. About 500 people are now employed on this initial construction site of (Section IV),

Our industrial and business parks are conclusively changing the industrial structure of the former textile town. The mix of business sectors from manufacturing industry (metal processing, the graphics business, the construction of technical equipment, the textile sector with embroidery and the clothing industry) and service companies are a healthy basis for the development of the town of Treuen in the 21st century.

Stadtverwaltung Treuen
Markt 7 · D-08233 Treuen
Telefon   +49 (0) 37468 638-0
Telefax   +49 (0) 37468 63860
stadtverwaltung@treuen.de
www.stadt-treuen.de

Auerbach

Mehr als drei Türme
More than Three Towers

Auerbach – die Große Kreisstadt im Herzen des Vogtlandes - grüßt ihre Gäste schon aus der Ferne. Der Schlossturm, die St. Laurentiuskirche und die Katholische Kirche sind die Wahrzeichen der Drei-Türme-Stadt. Im Jahr 2007 feierte Auerbach bereits das 725. Jubiläum. Dabei zog die Bürgerschaft eine stolze Bilanz:

Spannende Geschichte zwischen den drei Türmen

Auerbach blickt auf eine lange und interessante Geschichte zurück, aus der - bedingt durch zehn große Stadtbrände zwischen 1430 und 1861 - nur noch wenige historische Quellen erhalten geblieben sind. Am Fuße des Burgberges und dem östlichen Ufer der Göltzsch entstand in der ersten Hälfte des 14. Jahrhunderts die Stadt Auerbach. Das erste urkundliche Zeugnis stammt aus dem Jahre 1402. Mit Gründung der Stadt sind die Pfarrkirche St. Laurentius und der Marktplatz (Altmarkt) entstanden.
Ein Großbrand im Jahr 1757 zerstörte die Stadtkirche vollkommen. Danach bauten die Auerbacher eine der „schönsten Kirchen" des Landes Sachsen, die aber bei einem weiteren Stadtbrand im Jahre 1834 wieder vernichtet wurde. Der heutige Bau wurde 1839 geweiht. Die Kirche wurde nach dem Jahr 2000 umfangreich saniert und modernisiert. Am 18. Mai 2003 erfolgte die Neueinweihung der St. Laurentiuskirche sowie die gleichzeitige Eröffnung des Kirchenmusikalischen Zentrums Vogtland
Die industrielle Entwicklung war die Ursache für eine wesentliche räumliche Ausdehnung der Stadt und für das sprunghafte Anwachsen ihrer Einwohnerzahl am Ende des 19. Jahrhunderts. Auerbach erweiterte sich nach Osten in Richtung Hinterhain, nach Süden in Richtung Falkenstein und nach Westen in Richtung Rebesgrün / Reumtengrün. In diesem Zuge entstand die Kaiserstraße mit anspruchsvollen Bürgerhäusern im Jugendstil und verschieden historischen Stilelementen, die den wirtschaftlichen Aufstieg der Stadt und ihrer Bürger repräsentierten.
Der historische Stadtkern von der Nicolaikirche über den Altmarkt bis zum Neumarkt, vom Schlossbereich bis zum Ufer der Göltzsch mit Museum, Stadtkirche und Schloss sind Anziehungspunkte für den historisch interessierten Besucher.

Lebendige Wirtschaft

Neben Ackerbau und Viehzucht bildeten in der Vergangenheit die riesigen Wälder in der Umgebung Auerbachs mit Pech-, Ruß- und Harzgewinnung einen wichtigen Erwerbszweig für die Bürger. Stark vertreten war das bürgerliche Handwerk, besonders Weber, Gerber, Kürschner und Nadler.
Zu Beginn des 20. Jahrhundert entwickelten sich die Baumwollweberei und Stickerei zur Großindustrie. Auerbach wurde mit Gardinen, Wäsche, Kinder- und Berufskleidung sowie Stickereierzeugnissen weit über die Grenzen Deutschlands bekannt.
Heute ist Auerbach durch den sprichwörtlichen Gewerbefleiß seiner Bürger ein wichtiges Wirtschafts-, Handels- und Dienstleistungszentrum im östlichen Vogtland. Neben mittelständischen Betrieben in der Innenstadt befindet sich am westlichen Stadtrand das rund vierzig Hektar große voll erschlossene Industriegebiet. Es besitzt sämtliche infrastrukturellen Anforderungen.

Auerbach heute

Am 1. April 1997 erhielt die Stadt den Status einer „Großen Kreisstadt" als Ausgleich dafür, dass Auerbach durch die Bildung des Vogtlandkreises seinen Kreissitz verlor. Die Ortschaft Beerheide wurde am 1. Januar 1994, die Ortschaft Schnarrtanne/Vogelsgrün am 1. Januar 1999 und die Ortschaften Rebesgrün und Reumtengrün am 1. Januar 2003 eingemeindet. Auerbach ist mit seinen rund 21.000 Einwohnern das Zentrum des Mittelzentralen Städteverbundes im Oberen Göltzschtal. Seit dem Jahr 1990 veränderte sich die Stadt atemberaubend. Industrie- und Gewerbegebiete wurden erschlossen, neue Wohngebiete entstanden, die Stadtsanierung sowie die Rekonstruktion und die Modernisierung von Bildungs- und Sozialeinrichtungen kamen mit hohem Tempo voran. Allein in den Ausbau der Infrastruktur, in die Sanierung und Modernisierung von Schulen, Kindergärten, Straßen und Plätzen wurden seit dem Jahr 1990 stolze 126 Millionen Euro von der Stadt investiert.

Shoppen und genießen

Die sanierte Innenstadt mit ihren attraktiven Einzelhandelsgeschäften und gastronomischen Einrichtungen laden zum Bummeln, Einkaufen und Einkehren ein. Besucherfreundlich sind die zahlreichen Parkmöglichkeiten im Stadtzentrum mit günstigen Parkzeiten und -preisen. Wer ohne Auto mobil sein will, kann das umfangreiche Citybuslinennetz benutzen.

Auerbach – the major district town at the heart of the Vogtland region – welcomes its guests from afar. The Castle Tower, the St. Laurentius Church and the Catholic Church are the landmarks of the three-tower town. Auerbach celebrated its 725th anniversary in 2007. It was an occasion for the town to take a proud look back on its history: :

Exciting History between the Three Towers

Auerbach can look back on a long and interesting history – but few historical sources have remained on account of the ten major fires in the town between 1430 and 1861.
The town of Auerbach was founded at the foot of the Burgberg and on the eastern bank of the river Göltzsch in the first half of the 14th century. The first mention of the town in official records was in the year 1402. The St. Laurentius Church and the market square (old market) were built when the town was founded.
A major fire in 1757 completely destroyed the town church. After this the people of Auerbach built one of the "most beautiful churches" in the state of Saxony, which was destroyed again in another town fire in 1834. The current building was dedicated in 1839. The church was rebuilt extensively and modernised in 2000. The rededication of St. Laurentius church took place on 18 May 2003 and the Vogtland Church Music Centre was opened at the same time.
Industrial developments were the reason for a major expansion of the town and for the sudden jump in the population

(Fotos/Photos by Hagen Hartwig, Text/Text by Stadtverwaltung Auerbach, Übersetzung/Translated by David Strauss)

Ein Herz für den Tourismus

Für Besucher der Auerbacher Innenstadt ist das am Burgberg liegende Schlossviertel mit einem Ensemble kultureller Einrichtungen ein attraktiver Anziehungspunkt. Nur wenige Meter daneben erwarten das Fremdenverkehrsamt und die neue Bibliothek ihre Gäste.

Verkehrstechnisch ist Auerbach aus allen Richtungen gut zu erreichen. Durch die Stadt führt in Nord-Südrichtung die B169 von Aue nach Plauen über Falkenstein. Die Autobahn 72 ist über die Anschlussstellen Plauen-Ost, Treuen, Reichenbach oder Zwickau-West schnell erreichbar. Bahnverbindungen bestehen über Falkenstein nach Klingenthal bis nach Böhmen, über Lengenfeld nach Zwickau und über Treuen/Herlasgrün nach Reichenbach oder Plauen.

at the end of the 19th century. Auerbach expanded to the east towards Hinterhain, towards Falkenstein in the south and towards Rebesgrün/Reumtengrün in the west. As a result, Kaiser Street was built with its sophisticated houses in Art Nouveau style and various historical styles, which reflected the economic upturn in the town and its people.

The historical heart of the town from the Nicolai Church via the old market square to the new market square, from the castle to the banks of the river Göltzsch with the museum, town church and castle are attractions that visitors who are interested in history should not miss.

Buoyant Economy

The huge forests surrounding Auerbach provided an important source of income for people who extracted pitch, soot and resin as well as working as arable and livestock farmers. There were also many tradesmen, including weavers, tanners, furriers and needle-makers.

Cotton weaving and embroidery work developed into major industries at the start of the 20th century. Auerbach was well-known far beyond the borders of Germany for its curtains, underwear, children's clothing and works clothing.

Auerbach is now an important business, trade and service centre in the east of the Vogtland region as a result of the proverbial industrious of its people. The forty hectare business park with all utilities available and meeting every kind of infrastructural need is located on the western edge of the town, while the centre of town is home to medium-sized businesses.

Auerbach Today

The town has had the status of a "major district town" since 1 April 1997 as compensation for the fact that Auerbach lost its own county when the Vogtland district was formed. The village of Beerheide became a part of Auerbach on 1 January 1999, Schnarrtanne/Vogelsgrün followed suit on 1 January 1999 and Rebesgrün und Reumtengrün did the same on 1 January 2003. Auerbach forms the centre of the central network of towns in the Upper Göltzsch valley with its 21,000 or so inhabitants.

The town has changed in a breath-taking fashion since the year 1990. Industrial and business parks have developed, new residential areas have been created, the town has been cleaned up and the reconstruction and modernisation of educational and social centres has been pursued at high speed. The town has invested no less than € 126 million in expanding infrastructure, redeveloping and modernising schools, nursery schools, roads and squares since 1990.

Shopping and Enjoyment

The redeveloped town centre with its attractive retail shops and places to eat is ideal for a stroll, shopping or stopping for a bit to eat. The many car parks in the town centre with low charges are helpful to visitors. And those who do not own a car can use the comprehensive local bus network.

A Heart for Tourism

The castle district located at the foot of the Burgberg with its collection of cultural centres is an attractive destination for visitors to the town centre. The tourist information office and the new library await their guests just a few metres away.

Auerbach is easy to reach from any direction. The B169 main road from Aue to Plauen via Falkenstein runs north-south through the town. The A72 motorway can be reached quickly at the Plauen East, Treuen, Reichenbach or Zwickau West exits. There are railway connections to Klingenthal and into the Czech Republic via Falkenstein or to Zwickau via Lengenfeld or to Reichenbach or Plauen via Treuen/Herlasgrün,

Stadtverwaltung Auerbach
Nicolaistraße 51
D-08209 Auerbach
Telefon +49 (0) 3744 825-0
Telefax +49 (0) 3744 212585
www.stadt-auerbach.de
post@stadt-auerbach.de

Sternwarte mit Planetarium und das Renaissance-Schlößchen sind die Wahrzeichen der Stadt
Observatory with planetarium and the Renaissance Castle are the town's landmarks

Lebendig, dynamisch, fortschrittlich und traditionell zugleich
Living, Dynamic, Progressive and Yet Still Traditional

Rodewisch als junge Stadt mit ihrem Stadtrecht seit 1924 kann im Jahr 2011 auf 600 Jahre erste urkundliche Erwähnung des Ortes „Rodewisch" verweisen. Verkehrsgünstig gelegen an der B 94, der B 169 und nur 10 Kilometer von der A 72 entfernt, entwickelten sich in Rodewisch mittelständige Wirtschaft, vielfältiges Handwerk und gut funktionierendes Dienstleistungsgewerbe. Die Firma ERTEX Jacquard zum Beispiel ist Produzent von feinsten Jacquardgeweben und sorgt mit einer Exportquote von rund 70 Prozent dafür, dass Rodewisch Weltruf hat.

Die beiden Gesundheitseinrichtungen, das Klinikum Obergöltzsch und das Sächsische Krankenhaus für Psychiatrie und Neurologie wurden in den vergangenen Jahren mit erheblichen finanziellen Mitteln auf den modernsten Stand gebracht und gewährleisten somit eine ausgezeichnete medizinische Versorgung für die gesamte Region.

Mit Grundschule und Gymnasium mit derzeit 720 Schülern, einem Beruflichen Schulzentrum für Wirtschaft (2007: 50-jähriges Schuljubiläum) mit rund 1000 Schülern und der Musikschule, an der momentan 650 Kinder musizieren, kann sich Rodewisch zurecht als Stadt der Bildung bezeichnen. Eine weit verbreitete Anerkennung für das hohe Bildungsniveau ist nur ein Grund dafür, dass die Absolventen des Beruflichen Schulzentrums für Wirtschaft besonders gute Chancen auf dem internationalen Arbeitsmarkt haben.

Ausreichende Kindergartenplätze, kinder- und familienfreundliche Wohngebiete mit kurzen Wegen sowie die guten Erziehungs- und Bildungsangebote bilden die Grundlage für ein günstiges Lebensumfeld. Vertrautheit, Geborgenheit, Gemeinschaft, Miteinander der Generationen und gegenseitige Fürsorge bilden den Rahmen der kinder- und familienfreundlichen Stadt.

Mit den erneuerten Grundmauern des „Festen Hus" (mittelalterliche Wasserburg) hat Rodewisch ein Kleinod aus der frühesten Besiedlung der Nachwelt erhalten können. / Rodewisch has preserved a treasure from the earliest settlement period for posterity having restored the foundations of the "Feste Hus" (medieval Water Castle).

Wie unschwer im Stadtwappen der Stadt zu erkennen, hat Kegeln in Rodewisch Tradition. Doch damit nicht genug: In über 50 Vereinen fühlen sich die Rodewischer wohl und gehen ihren Freizeitbeschäftigungen nach. Von Blasmusik über Volkskunst bis hin zu sportlicher Betätigung reicht die Palette. Mit drei Sportvereinen ist Rodewisch in der Bundesliga vertreten. So spielt man schon seit der Gründung der Fachschule für Ökonomie 1957 erfolgreich Schach. Inzwischen bestreiten die „Rodewischer Schachmiezen" ihre zwölfte Saison in der 1. Bundesliga. Den Judoverein IPPON Rodewisch gibt es seit 1990. Der Verein ist sächsischer Landesleistungs- und Talentestützpunkt und zählt 250 Mitglieder, davon sind 70 Prozent Kinder und Jugendliche. Die 1. Männermannschaft kämpft seit 1998 in der 1. Judo-Bundesliga. Zu erwähnen sind auch die Gewichtheber von der TSG Rodewisch, die in der 2. Bundesliga aktiv sind und als sächsisches Leistungszentrum fungieren. Erfolge sind u. a. Titel- und Podestplätze bei Deutschen Jugendmeisterschaften. Die Rodewischer springen aber auch von Schanzen und davon haben sie gleich vier, die für den Kinder- und Nachwuchsbereich zur Verfügung stehen. Der Kultur- und Heimatverein Rodewisch e. V. hat sich die Pflege des Brauchtums, der Mundart und der Traditionen zur Aufgabe gestellt. Zu den größten und bekanntesten Veranstaltungsorten des Göltzschtals gehört der Ratskellersaal, der sich durch niveauvolle Konzerte, Theateraufführungen und Vereinsfeste einen Namen gemacht hat. Für Festveranstaltungen, Hochzeiten und kleinere Konzerte eignet sich besonders das Renaissance-Schlößchen auf der Schloßinsel. Die Göltzschtalhalle wartet jährlich mit mehreren Großsportveranstaltungen im Judo und Gewichtheben auf.

Rodewisch is a young town, which only obtained its town charter in 1924; but it will mark the 600th anniversary of the first mention of Rodewisch in official documents in 2011. Favourably located on the B 94, B 169 main roads and only 10 kilometres from the A 72 motorway, medium-sized businesses, many types of trades and efficient service companies have developed in Rodewisch. The ERTEX Jacquard company, for example, produces the finest jacquard fabrics and, with an export quota of about 70 percent, ensures that Rodewisch has an international reputation.

The two health centres, the Obergöltzsch Hospital and the Saxon Hospital for Psychiatry and Neurology, have been thoroughly modernised over the past few years as a result of considerable financial investments and they guarantee that medical care in the whole region is outstanding.

Rodewisch can justifiably call itself an educational centre: 720 pupils currently attend the primary and grammar schools, there is a Vocational Business College with about 1,000 students (it celebrated its 50th anniversary in 2007) and 650 pupils attend courses at the local music school. Graduates of the Vocational Business College have particularly good opportunities of finding work on the international market because of the widespread recognition of the high level of training provided.

Sufficient places at nursery schools, residential areas that are kind to children and families, having everything on the spot and good education and training facilities form the basis of a positive living environment. Familiarity, security, a sense of community, a mixture of generations and mutual care form the framework of this

(Fotos/Photos by Silke Keller-Thoß [2], Stadtverwaltung Rodewisch, Übersetzung/Translated by David Strauss)

Das aus dem 15. Jahrhundert stammende Renaissance-Schlößchen auf der Schloßinsel ist zum Wahrzeichen der Stadt geworden. Gleich nebenan befindet sich das Museum Göltzsch. Den Grundstock für das 1951 eröffnete Museum bildeten die Ausgrabungsstücke der alten Wasserburg, die von 1937 bis 1939 auf dem Inselgelände freigelegt wurden. Diese europaweit einmalige Sammlung gibt Einblick in die Lebensweise der früheren Bewohner des Rittergutes „Göltzsch". Pünktlich zum 1. Advent öffnet die traditionelle Weihnachtsausstellung ihre Pforten. Pyramiden, Schwibbögen, Nussknacker, Weihnachtsmänner, Moosmänner, Eisenbahnen, Spielzeug für die „Kleinen" und der „Erzgebirgische Bergaufzug" faszinieren immer wieder die Gäste.

Die Sternwarte und das Planetarium „Sigmund Jähn" Rodewisch bieten ein vielfältiges Programm, um den Sternhimmel zu erleben und die Astronomie zu begreifen. Eine Sternenreise durch Raum und Zeit in der 8-m-Kuppel des Planetariums sind ein unvergessliches Erlebnis. Flimmernde Sterne, wandernde Planeten, die Lichtgestalten des Mondes, die strahlende Sonne, Kometen, Sternschnuppen und Sternbilder sind zu beobachten und man bekommt so einen Einblick in die Vielfältigkeit und Schönheit des Weltalls. In regelmäßigen Abständen wird das Programm aktualisiert und unter eine spezielle Thematik gestellt. Darüber hinaus gibt es für Besuchergruppen aller Altersstufen spezielle Angebote. Neben der traditionellen Satellitenbeobachtung werden in Kursen, Arbeitsgemeinschaften und Unterrichtsveranstaltungen die Handhabung von traditionellen Fernrohren, modernste Beobachtungstechniken, die Erdfernerkundung durch die Raumfahrt sowie die Nutzung der eigenen Wettersatellitenempfangsstation präsentiert.

town that welcomes children and families. It is not hard to see that bowling is a tradition in Rodewisch in the town's crest. But that is not the whole story: Rodewisch people feel at home in more than 50 clubs and are able to pursue their leisure activities. They range from brass music and folk art to all kinds of sports. Three sports clubs in Rodewisch are in the top German leagues. Chess has been played with success since the founding of the Economics College in 1957. The "Rodewisch Chess Cats" are now playing their fifteenth season in the country's top league. The IPPON judo club has existed since 1990. The club is a centre of excellence and training for the next generation of stars in Saxony and has 250 members, 70 percent of whom are children and young people. The 1st men's team has been competing in the top German league since 1998. Mention should also be made of the TSG Rodewisch weightlifters, who compete in the 2nd national division and are a centre of excellence in Saxony. They have also won titles or other medals at the German Youth Championships. But residents of Rodewisch also leap from ski-jumps – of which they have four – for use by children and the next generation of stars. The Rodewisch Cultural and Local History Club concentrates on ensuring that old customs, the dialect and traditions are maintained. The town hall cellar room is one of the largest and best known events sites in the Göltzsch valley and it has made a name for itself with high-quality concerts, theatre performances and club festivals. The Renaissance castle on the castle island is particularly suitable for festive occasions, weddings and smaller concerts. The Göltzsch Valley Hall provides the setting for several major sports events in judo and weightlifting every year.

The 15th century Renaissance Castle on the castle island has become the town's landmark. The Göltzsch Museum is located right next door to this. The archaeological excavations of the old Water Castle, which were uncovered in the period 1937 - 1939, account for a large proportion of the exhibits in the museum, which was opened in 1951. This collection, which is unique in Europe, provides some insight into the life of the early residents of the "Göltzsch" Manor. The traditional Christmas fair opens its doors punctually on the first Sunday in Advent. Pyramids, illuminated arches, nutcrackers, Father Christmases, Moss Men, railways, toys for the children and the "Ore Mountains miners' procession" always fascinate visitors.

The observatory and the Rodewisch "Sigmund Jähn" planetarium provide a varied programme for people to experience the sky at night and understand astronomy. A journey through time and space in the 8 metre dome of the planetarium is an unforgettable experience. Twinkling stars, moving planets, the various phases of the moon, the shining sun, comets, shooting stars and constellations can be observed and this gives people a glimpse of the variety and beauty of space. The programme is brought up to date and a special theme is highlighted at regular intervals. There are also special offers for groups of visitors of all ages. The centre enables people to watch satellites, but also arranges courses, working groups and teaching events to inform people how to use traditional telescopes, the latest observation techniques, discovering the depths of space and using the centre's own weather satellite terminal.

In der Göltzschtalhalle finden hochkarätige Sportveranstaltungen statt und hier haben die zahlreichen Vereine und Schüler auch besonders gute Trainingsmöglichkeiten./Top sports events take place in the Göltzsch Valley Hall and it also provides very good training facilities for many clubs and schoolchildren.

Das Pestalozzigymnasium ist bekannt für gute Bildungsarbeit. Unterrichtliche und vielfältige außerunterrichtliche Angebote fördern die Interessen, Begabungen und Selbstständigkeit der Schüler./The Pestalozzi Grammar School is well-known for its high educational standards. Both the teaching and many kinds of extra-curricular activities foster pupils' interests, abilities and sense of independence.

Stadtverwaltung Rodewisch
Wernesgrüner Straße 32
D-08228 Rodewisch
Telefon +49 (0) 3744 3681-0
Telefax +49 (0) 3744 34245
www.rodewisch.de
stadt@rodewisch.de

Falkenstein

Die Kleinstadt mit dem großstädtischen Flair
The Small Town with the Flair of a City

Als im Mittelalter die Schätze aus dem Schoss der Erde versiegten, galt es in der Freien Bergstadt Falkenstein, neue Ideen zu haben und Möglichkeiten zum Broterwerb zu finden. Dies geschah zunächst, indem man geschlagenes Holz aus den dichten Wäldern einholte und per Floß weiterbeförderte. Aus der kleinen Ansiedlung an der Göltzsch wurde eine wohlhabende Stadt, von der auch die zahlreichen Dörfer im Umfeld profitierten. Später entwickelte sich in Falkenstein angesehene Weberei und große Textilfirmen entstanden. 1721 gründete sich die Falkensteiner Weberinnung, die als stärkste Innung im gesamten Vogtland galt. Prachtvolle restaurierte Fabrikantenhäuser künden noch heute von dieser Zeit.

Von der Dynamik einer Industriestadt mit landschaftlichem Flair und besonderer Lebensqualität hat Falkenstein nichts verloren. Das Gewerbegebiet mit zwölf Firmen ist bereits voll ausgelastet. Ein weiteres entsteht auf dem Gelände der ehemaligen Falkensteiner Gardine (Falgard), einer als Modellprojekt in Sachsen vorbildlich rekultivierten Industriebrache. Im Industriegebiet stehen für Investoren Flächen bis zu 25 ha zur Verfügung. Durch die Stadt Falkenstein wird eine aktive Wirtschaftsförderung betrieben, die es den Unternehmen ermöglicht, „Service aus einer Hand" zu bekommen. Ein echtes „Falkensteiner Kind" ist das Unternehmen ERFAL Erler e. K. (ERFAL ist die Abkürzung für Erler und Falkenstein). Das Familienunternehmen begann seine Laufbahn mit der Gründung der Drechslerei Jörg Erler. Heute beliefert das Unternehmen als Hersteller von Sonnenschutz, Dekoration und Insektenschutz rund 2000 Stammkunden in der Raumausstatterbranche. Mit vier repräsentativen Niederlassungen in Ost- und Mitteldeutschland haben die regionalen Hersteller den Sprung zum überregionalen Anbieter geschafft. Und überall, wo die Marke „ERFAL" in Erscheinung tritt, schwingt auch ein Stück Falkenstein mit.

Den Vorteil der Kleinstadt nutzen – alles ist überschaubar, kurze Wege und Geborgenheit – weiß man in Falkenstein durchaus mit den Vorzügen einer Großstadt zu verbinden. Dabei sind Familienfreundlichkeit und hohe Lebensqualität Schwerpunkte, auf die die Stadtväter setzen. Die Innenstadt lockt mit charmanter Fußgängerzone und zahlreichen attraktiven Fachgeschäften. Die Verkehrsanbindung, auch mit öffentlichen Verkehrsmitteln, ist sehr gut und die soziale Infrastruktur allseitig ausgebaut. Moderne Kindertagesstätten, Schulen, ärztliche Versorgung, Freizeitangebote von Museum, Kino, Fitnessstudio, Talsperre über Tierpark bis hin zu den vielfältigen Vereinsangeboten der 51 Vereine sorgen für ein harmonisches Miteinander von Jung und Alt. Mit vier städtischen und einer privaten Kindereinrichtung, einer aktiven Mittelschule, Horten an allen Grundschulen – allesamt neu gestaltet, dem Vereinsfördersystem, dem Freizeitzentrum und Jugendbüro und einer breiten Palette an Gemeinschaftsaktionen wie Weihnachtsspendenaktion oder Zuckertütenbaum, kann sich Falkenstein mit seinen Ortsteilen zurecht als „Familienfreundliche Stadt" bezeichnen. Die jährlich auf dem Veranstaltungsplan stehenden Stadt-Feste wie Straßenfest, Weinfest und Bornkinnlmarkt sind fester Bestandteil des Falkensteiner Lebens und sorgen für angenehme Unterbrechungen des Alltags.

When the treasures from the depths of the earth dried up in the Middle Ages, the free mining town of Falkenstein had to come up with some new ideas and people needed to find a way of earning a living. The first idea was to bring wood that had been cut down out of the forests and send it downstream on rafts. The tiny settlement on the river Göltzsch turned into a prosperous town, which also benefited the many villages in the vicinity. Later Falkenstein developed a respectable weaving industry and major textile companies were created. The Falkenstein weavers' guild was formed in 1721 and it was considered to be the strongest guild in the whole Vogtland region. Magnificent, restored houses, which belonged to factory owners, still bear witness to this time.

Falkenstein did not lose anything of its dynamism as an industrial town with country flair and a particular quality of life. The business park with twelve companies is already full. Another one is being created on the site of the former Falkensteiner Gardine (Falgard) works, one of the former industrial sites, which is being redeveloped to provide an example of how this is done in Saxony. Sites measuring up to 25 hectares are available on the industrial park. Falkenstein provides active business support and this allows companies to obtain "service from a single source". ERFAL Erler e. K. (ERFAL is an abbreviation of Erler and Falkenstein) is a real "Falkenstein baby". The family business began when the Jörg Erler wood turning works were set up. The company now manufactures sun and insect protection equipment and decorations and supplies about 2,000 regular customers in the interior decorations sector. The company now has four impressive branches in Eastern and Central Germany and has made the leap to become a national supplier. Everywhere where the name "ERFAL" appears, it takes the name of Falkenstein with it.

Using the advantages of a small town – everything is straightforward, there are no long distances and there is a feeling of security – is one side of the coin, but Falkenstein also has the advantages of a city. A family-friendly atmosphere and a high standard of living are major focuses, which the town's fathers underlined. The centre of town has a charming pedestrian zone and many attractive specialist shops. Transport links, including public transport, are very good and the social infrastructure has been expanded in all sorts of directions. Modern nursery schools, schools, medical care, leisure activities ranging from a museum, cinema, fitness studio, reservoir to the zoo and many kinds of activities in 51 clubs provide a harmonious atmosphere for people of all ages to live together. Falkenstein can well be called a "family-friendly town" with its four town nurseries and one private child centres, an active middle school, daycare centres for children at all the primary schools – all of them modernised, the club support system, the leisure centre and youth office and a wide range of joint activities like the Christmas gift programme or the cone-shaped sweet package tree. The town festivals like the street festival, wine festival and the Bornkinnl market, which take place every year, are a permanent feature in Falkenstein's calendar and provide a pleasant break from everyday life.

Stadtverwaltung Falkenstein
Willy-Rudert-Platz
D-08223 Falkenstein
Telefon +49 (0) 3745 741-0
www.stadt-falkenstein.de

(Fotos/Photos by Hartmut Briese, Übersetzung/Translated by David Strauss)

An die Spitze durch Innovationen und besten Service
At the Top because of Innovations and the Best Service

Auf Expansionskurs – ERFAL

Das vor mehr als 20 Jahren mit der Gründung der Drechslerei Jörg Erler im vogtländischen Falkenstein zugleich die Grundlagen für die spätere Firma ERFAL geschaffen wurden, konnte zum damaligen Zeitpunkt keiner ahnen. Anfänglich konzentrierte sich das Familienunternehmen insbesondere auf die Herstellung von erzgebirgischer und vogtländischer Volkskunst wie Räuchermännchen, Nussknacker, Kunstgewerbe und Spielzeug, fertigte aber auch bereits Gardinenstangen – in der DDR-Ära Mangelware. Die politischen Veränderungen des Jahres 1989 erforderte eine Neuorientierung der Firma ERFAL. Aufbauend auf die guten Erfahrungen als Hersteller von Gardinenstangen wurde das Warensortiment systematisch mit Vorhangschienen aus Aluminium, Lamellenvorhängen, Jalousien, Rollos, Plissees, Raffvorhangtechniken und Flächenvorhangsystemen erweitert.

Mittlerweile hat sich das mittelständische, inhabergeführte Unternehmen zu einem der führenden Hersteller von Sonnenschutzprodukten und Dekorationsartikeln entwickelt und das Sortiment seit einigen Jahren mit der Herstellung hochwertiger Insektenschutzsysteme ergänzt. Der auftragsbezogene Vertrieb der zumeist maßgefertigten Produkte erfolgt nahezu ausschließlich über den Raumausstatterfachhandel. ERFAL ist stolz darauf, dass sich die Zahl der Kunden jährlich vergrößert und sieht insbesondere im gezielten Aufbau einer Kundenbetreuung und Belieferung des gesamten deutschsprachigen Raumes eine wesentliche Aufgabe der nächsten Jahre. Mit dem Neubau der mittlerweile dritten Produktionsstätte am Standort Falkenstein schafft ERFAL die hierfür notwendigen Voraussetzungen.

Um den ständig wechselnden Wohn- und Einrichtungstrends sowie individuellen Vorstellungen der Endkunden bestmöglich zu entsprechen, werden die für jede Produktgruppe vorhandenen Stoff- bzw. Farbkollektionen ständig aktualisiert und durch neue innovative Lösungen ergänzt. Darüber hinaus stellen hohe Qualitätsanforderungen während der Produktion ein wesentliches Erfolgselement des Unternehmens dar. Grundlage hierfür sind neben teilautomatisierten Fertigungsmaschinen und modernen Produktionstechnologien insbesondere die motivierten Mitarbeiter in den einzelnen Abteilungen. Gegenwärtig sind im Unternehmen rund 235 Mitarbeiter beschäftigt – darunter 31 Auszubildende.

On a growth path – ERFAL

Nobody realised at the time when Jörg Erler set up his wood turning works in the Vogtland town of Falkenstein more than 20 years ago that it would lay the foundations for the ERFAL company to emerge later. The family business initially concentrated on manufacturing Ore Mountains and Vogtland folk art like smoking men, nutcrackers, arts and crafts and games, but was already making curtain rods too – which were in short supply in East German times. The political changes in 1989 meant that the ERFAL company had to move in a new direction. Building on its good experience as a manufacturer of curtain rods, the range of products was systematically expanded to include curtain rails made of aluminium, vertical blinds, blinds, roller blinds, pleated fabrics, gathered blinds and panel curtains.

The medium-sized company managed by its owner has now developed into one of the leading manufacturers of sunshade products and decorative articles and the range has been expanded by including insect protection systems for several years now. Most of the products are usually tailor-made and are almost exclusively sold to interior decoration specialists. ERFAL is proud to have increased the number of its customers every year and believes that it should deliberately set up customer care facilities and supply the whole of the German-speaking part of Europe over the next few years. ERFAL is creating the framework for this by building a third new production site at Falkenstein.

In order to best meet the constantly changing trends in living accommodation and equipment and individual ideas from final customers, the material and colour collections for each product group are constantly being updated and supplemented with new innovative solutions. In addition, one of the major success factors at the company has been the high quality standards it sets for production processes. Partly automated manufacturing equipment and modern production technology are part of the reason for this success – but motivated members of staff in the individual departments are also an essential element. About 235 people are currently employed by the company – including 31 trainees.

ihr partner für
sonnenschutz, dekoration, insektenschutz

ERFAL Erler e. K.
Gewerbering 8 · D-08223 Falkenstein
Telefon   +49 (0) 3745 750-0
Telefax   +49 (0) 3745 750-299
info@erfal.de · www.erfal.de

(Fotos/Photos by ERFAL Erler e. K., Übersetzung/Translated by David Strauss)

Im Mittelpunkt der Mensch
People are the Main Focus

Die beste Methode ein Unternehmen einzuschätzen, ist die Menschen in ihm zu betrachten. „In einem vertrauensvollen Miteinander werden wir in Einheit die Wirtschaftlichkeit für die Zukunft sichern. Jeder Mitarbeiter übernimmt auf seinem Platz Verantwortung für den Erfolg des Unternehmens. In partnerschaftlicher Zusammenarbeit steigern wir unser Leistungsvermögen. Die ethischen Grundwerte wollen wir achten und mit Menschen, Familie und Umwelt vertrauensvoll umgehen." Mit diesen Worten beschreibt das 400 Mitarbeiter zählenden Bauunternehmen seine Firmenphilosophie und den Grund, warum das Unternehmen auf ein solides Wachstum verweisen kann.

Mit den Niederlassungen in Falkenstein, Zwickau und dem thüringischen Gotha ist die VOBA in Mittel- und Süddeutschland präsent. Doch es werden auch Leistungen im gesamten Bundesgebiet ausgeführt. Durch die 100ige Tochterfirma, die Bauträger und Schlüsselfertigbau GmbH, bietet die VOBA für die Errichtung von Wohneigentum sowie für Betreuungs- und Pflegeeinrichtungen die gesamte Palette von der Planung über die Finanzierung bis zur schlüsselfertigen Erstellung der Projekte an.

Stellt man sich die Firmenstruktur als einen Kuchen vor und schneidet diesen in Teile, dann wäre das größte Stück der Hochbau mit 140 Mitarbeitern, der Tiefbau mit 90 Mitarbeitern, die Baunebengewerke mit 40 und der Spezialtiefbau mit 10 Mitarbeitern. Das sind die Produktionsanteile der Firma. 45 Auszubildende, 15 Mitarbeiter der Werkstatt, des Mietparks und des Bauhofes sowie 60 Angestellte, die als Ingenieure und Techniker sowie in der Verwaltung arbeiten, komplettieren das Gesamtunternehmen.

Nach der Wende und der Neufirmierung zur VOBA Bau GmbH im Jahr 1990 hat as Unternehmen zahlreiche kleinere und größere Bauvorhaben fertiggestellt. Der Kreis der Auftraggeber erweitert sich ständig. Viele Bauherren sind schon über Jahre Stammkunden, weil diese die Arbeit der VOBA kennen und schätzen. Termintreue, wirtschaftliche Unternehmensführung, fairer Umgang mit Kunden und Geschäftspartnern, ständige Kontrolle und Korrektur des Arbeitsprozesses, Dynamik, marktgerechtes Produktionspotential und hohes technisches Niveau gehören zu den Qualitätsmerkmalen des Unternehmens.

Durch Ausbildung von Azubis, Durchführung von Fachseminaren und Delegierung von fähigen Mitarbeitern zum Studium investiert die VOBA in die Zukunft. Mit der Weiterentwicklung des Oualitäts-Management-Systems nach DIN EN ISO 9001 Ausgabe 2000 macht sich das Unternehmen fit, um im Wettbewerb immer vorn dabei zu sein. Hinter dem Unternehmen steht als Gesellschafter die Raiffeisen-Handelsgenossenschaft Schöneck e. G.

The best way of assessing a company is to look at the people working there. "We shall guarantee profitability for the future as we pull together and work with each other in a trusting manner. Each member of staff takes responsibility for the success of the company at their place. We shall increase our capabilities as we work together in partnership. We want to respect ethical principles and deal with people, families and the environment in a trustworthy manner." These words describe the company philosophy of the building company, which employs 400 members of staff, and it is the reason why the company can point to solid growth.

VOBA works in Central and Southern Germany and has branches in Falkenstein, Zwickau and Gotha in Thuringia. But work is carried out all over Germany. Using its 100 percent subsidiary, Bauträger und Schlüsselfertigbau GmbH, VOBA provides the whole spectrum of services for constructing residential property and support and care centres, ranging from planning to funding and even the construction of complete projects so that they are ready for people to move in.

If we imagine that the company structure is a cake and is divided up into parts, the largest section would be the building construction department with 140 employees, civil engineering with 90 employees, related trades with 40 members of staff and special civil engineering work with 10 members of staff. They are the various production departments in the company. The company structure is rounded off by 45 trainees, 15 people in the workshops, the rental department and the building yard and 60 employees, who work as engineers and technicians and in the administration department.

After the fall of the Berlin Wall and the renaming of the company to VOBA Bau GmbH in 1990, the company completed many fairly small and larger building projects. The circle of customers is expanding constantly. Many clients have become regular customers because they know and appreciate the work done by VOBA. Adherence to deadlines, efficient company management, fair dealings with customers and business partners, constant checks and corrections made to working procedures, dynamism, production potential in line with market requirements and a high technical level are just some of the company's quality features.

By training apprentices, putting on specialist seminars and sending capable members of staff to study, VOBA is investing in the future. By further developing the quality management system according to DIN EN ISO 9001 (2000 edition), the company is equipping itself to always be ahead of the competition.
The Raiffaisen-Handelsgenossenschaft Schöneck e. G is a partner in the company.

Einige Beispiele der verschiedenen Bauprojekt, die die VOBA im Vogtland durchgeführt hat. Fotos von oben nach unten: Sanierungsmaßnahmen an der denkmalgeschützten Moltke Brücke in Auerbach; Neubau der Sparkasse Vogtland; neukonzipiertes Bürogebäude bei Neoplan mit angeschlossener Werkstatt

VOBA Bau GmbH Hammerbrücke
Neue Straße 20
D-08269 Hammerbrücke
Telefon   +49 (0) 37465 70-0
Telefax   +49 (0) 37465 7250
VOBA.BAU@t-online.de
www.voba-bau.de

(Fotos/Photos by VOBA, Übersetzung/ Translated by David Strauss)

Schweiker GmbH in Grünbach

Arbeiten wo andere Urlaub machen
Working Where Others Go on Holiday

Im Höhenluftkurort Grünbach ist die Luft noch sauber. Der in Wald eingebette Ort bietet viel Natur, die Menschen haben Musik im Blut und der Moosmann nennt es sein zu Hause. Hier hat die Firma Schweiker GmbH ihren Sitz und schuftet ordentlich für die Umwelt. Die nachhaltige Entlastung unserer Umwelt bedeutet, die vorhandene Energie effizient zu nutzen und energiesparende Maßnahmen beginnen zuerst mal bei Fenster und Türen.

Die Firma ist der größte Arbeitgeber in Grünbach und aus ehemals fünf sind heute mehr als 150 Mitarbeiter geworden. Allesamt kommen aus dem Vogtland. Produziert werden maßgeschneiderte Türen und Fenster, sowie hochwertige Rollladen und Rolltore aus Kunststoff und Aluminium.

Fenster kauft man nicht von der Stange – so bieten die bei Schweiker arbeitenden, handwerklich hervorragend ausgebildeten Mitarbeiter höchste Qualität und Flexibilität für den Kunden.

Ende 2007 wurde die Produktionsfläche um 1200 Quadratmeter erweitert. In einer nunmehr neuen Produktionshalle laufen die Prozesse effektiver ab, die Kunden werden noch schneller und individueller bedient. „Mit der Erweiterung werden die positiven Erwartungen der Firma an den Standort Grünbach unterstrichen", so Geschäftsführer Gerd Tunger.

In Zeiten ständig steigender Energiepreise entwickeln sich die Fenster von Schweiker fast schon zu einem Muss, denn sie halten die Wärme da, wo sie hingehört und geben so ihrem zu Hause Geborgenheit und Ruhe. Die modernste Dämmtechnik hilft, kostbare Heizenergie zu sparen und – ganz nebenbei – die Umwelt zu schonen.

The air in the high altitude holiday resort of Grünbach is still clean. The town nestles between forests, has retained its natural surroundings, the people have music in their blood and the Moss Man calls it his home. The Schweiker company has its headquarters here and it is working away for the environment. The long-term relief of our environment means that existing energy sources are used efficiently and energy-saving measures start with windows and doors.

The company is the largest employer in Grünbach. There used to be just five members of staff – now there are more than 150. All of them come from the Vogtland region. Tailor-made doors and windows and high-quality shutters and roller shutters made of plastic and aluminium are all manufactured.

People do not buy windows off the shelf – so the members of staff who work at Schweiker with their outstanding qualifications provide top quality and flexibility for customers.

The production area was expanded by 1,200 square metres at the end of 2007. The processes now work more efficiently in the new production hall and customers can be served more quickly and their needs met down more directly. Managing director Gerd Tunger says: "The company's positive expectations with regard to Grünbach are underlined by our expansion."

Schweiker's windows are almost a must in times of constantly rising energy prices – they retain the heat where it belongs and provide your home with security and peace and quiet. The latest insulation techniques help save valuable heating

Die neue Produktionshalle wurde Ende 2007 fertig gestellt.

SCHWEIKER

Schweiker GmbH
Falkensteiner Straße 39
D-08223 Grünbach
Telefon +49 (0) 3745 7802-0
Telefax +49 (0) 3745 5469
info@schweiker.de
www.schweiker.de

(Fotos/Photos by Hartmut Briese, Übersetzung/Translated by David Strauss)

Natürlich, fröhlich und traditionell
Natural, pleasant and traditional

Wem Freundlichkeit und Gastlichkeit gefallen, wer fröhliche Feste und traditionelle Veranstaltungen liebt, der findet dies alles in der mitten im schönen Vogtlandwald gelegenen Gemeinde Grünbach/Muldenberg. Gastfreundlichkeit bedeutet den Menschen hier mehr, als bloß ein Dach überm Kopf und Kost zu bieten. Alle Gastgeber wünschen, dass sich die Touristen auch in der Ferne geborgen fühlen können, ihr Urlaubsdomizil eben echt als Heimat erleben. Zu allen Jahreszeiten laden Hotels, Pensionen, Gasstätten und private Ferienunterkünfte freundlichst ein unter anderem auch das 100 Jahre alte Hotel „Der Bayerische Hof", welches Tradition und modernen Komfort auf einmalige Art und Weise verbindet.

Zu den weiteren Attraktionen in Grünbach gehören die Kirmes, Dorfgemeinschaftsabende, das Pfingstsingen, Countryfeste, sportliche Veranstaltungen, ein bestens markiertes Wanderwegenetz, gespurte Loipen geräumte Winterwanderwege sowie Skihang mit Tellerlift im Göltzschtal, außerdem der Wendelstein, der Rehhübel, das Göltzschgesprenge mit Bastei und die Rißfälle.

In Muldenberg findet man in der Ortsmitte einen glasklaren Badesee und eine Minigolfanlage. Zu den traditionell bekannten Festen weit über das Vogtland hinaus, gehört das jährlich mehrfach stattfindende Schauflößen. Neben einer Trinkwassertalsperre hat Muldenberg ein Wasserwerk, das Technische Denkmal des Floßgrabensystems und ein Flößerdorf zu bieten. Ein Ferienparadies für die ganze Familie, in dem es sich auch gut leben lässt.

If you value friendliness and hospitality, celebrating in style and enjoying traditional events, the community of Grünbach/Muldenberg situated in the middle of a huge forest area is just the place for you. Hospitality means much more to the people here than just having a roof over your head and eating meals. Any host wants to provide comforts to tourists so that they really feel at home at their holiday destination. Various hotels, guest houses, restaurants and private accommodation will be delighted to see you at any time of the year, including the 100-year-old "Der Bayerische Hof" hotel, which combines tradition and modern comforts in a unique way.

Grünbach has plenty of attractions on offer: the annual fair, village evenings, singing at Whitsun, country music festivals, sporting events, a well marked network of footpaths, cross-country skiing runs, footpaths, which even are cleared in winter, and a downhill slope with a button lift in the Göltzsch valley. And do not forget Wendelstein hill, the Rehhübel rock face, the Göltzschgesprenge river source with its bastion and the small Rissfälle waterfalls.

Muldenberg has a lake with extremely clear water and a mini-golf course at its centre. The annual log rafting festival celebrated on several occasions each year is well-known far beyond the Vogtland region. Muldenberg not only has a drinking water reservoir, but also a water works, the engineering memorial for the log rafting ditch system and a rafting village. It is a holiday paradise for the whole family – where people can enjoy very high standards.

(Fotos/Photos by Gemeinde Grünbach, Igor Pastierovic [2], Joachim Thoß [1], Hartmut Briese)

Wintersport in den schönsten Loipengebieten

Der Ort Grünbach mit seiner Höhenlage von bis 788 Metern, garantiert bis in den Monat März hinein ideale Wintersportbedingungen. Das heißt 28 Kilometer hervorragend markierte und gespurte Loipen aller Schwierigkeitsgrade, für den Skilanglauf in Richtung Muldenberg, Schöneck, Rißfälle, Rißbrücke-Hammerbrücke. Für alpine Wintersportler steht im Göltzschtal ein Skihang mit Tellerlift in schneesicherer Nordlage zur Verfügung. Das Abfahrtsterrain wird mit modernen Pistenraupen präpariert und gewalzt.

Spaziergänger finden gut geräumte Wanderwege vor. Fahrten mit dem Pferdeschlitten werden durch verschneite Winterwälder und herrlicher Natur zu einem unvergesslichen Erlebnis.

Im Nachbarort Muldenberg mit einer Höhenlage bis zu 830 Metern ist traditionsgemäß einer der günstigsten Ausgangspunkte für Skitouren in das schneesichere Kammgebiet Schneckenstein-Mühlleithen-Aschberg-Carlsfeld-Johanngeorgenstadt. Durch dieses Gebiet führt die 36 Kilometer lange Kammloipe, die hervorragend gespurt ist und im oberen Teil zu den schneesichersten Loipen Deutschlands, mit blauen Loipenschildern gekennzeichnet, gehört. Vom Wanderparkplatz im Ortszentrum führt eine Anschlussloipe mit orangener Markierung zur 2,5 Kilometer entfernten Kammloipe. Vom Wanderparkplatz „Schneidersberg" ist der direkte Einstieg in die Kammloipe möglich. Als Rundloipe ist der Muldenberger Rundkurs bestens für Familiensport geeignet. Über das gesamte Loipennetz sind die Orte Grünbach, Hammerbrücke, Schöneck und Mühlleithen erreichbar.

Winter Sports in the Most Beautiful Cross-Country Ski Routes

Grünbach, which is situated 788 metres above sea level, guarantees ideal winter sport conditions well into March. This means 28 kilometres of well-marked ski routes with all kinds of grades of difficulty along the tracks leading to Muldenberg, Schöneck, the Rissfälle and Rissbrücke-Hammerbrücke. And for downhill skiers there is a ski slope with a button lift in a north-facing area in the Göltzsch valley; this guarantees that there will be snow. The downhill area is prepared and rolled using modern snow cats.

Hikers will find well cleared footpaths here. Trips on the horse-drawn snow plough are an unforgettable experience through snowy winter forests and beautiful scenery.

Parts of Muldenberg nearby are 830 metres above sea level and this is one of the best starting points for skiing tours along the Schneckenstein-Mühlleithen-Aschberg-Carlsfeld-Johanngeorgenstadt snow-covered ridge. A ridge ski route runs through this area for 36 kilometres; the tracks are well marked and, with their blue signs, this is one of the areas in Germany where you can be pretty sure of finding snow at its highest points in winter. A connecting track with orange markings takes people the 2.5 kilometres to the ridge route from the hiking car park at the centre of the village. It is possible to get straight on to the ridge route from the „Schneidersberg" hiking car park. The Muldenberg circuit is ideally suited for families. Grünbach, Hammerbrücke, Schöneck and Mühlleithen can all be reached using the network of ski routes.

Ganz neu in Grünbach ist der gemeinnützige Verein Kinderspiel Vogtland e.V., liebevoll auf den Namen „Kispi" getauft. Klettern, Rutschen, Toben, Schmökern, Geburtstag feiern, Playmobil spielen, Aktionsbühne, Kinderwerkstatt und spielen, spielen, spielen, all das kann man nach Herzenslust auf einem 650 Quadratmeter großen Indoor-Spielplatz.

The non-profit-making association called the Vogtland Children's Play Centre, affectionately known as "Kispi", is quite new in Grünbach. Children can climb, slide, go wild, browse through books, celebrate birthday parties, play with Playmobil, go on stage or to the children's activity centre and just play, play, play. They can do all this and more at the 650 square metre indoor play area.

Steckbrief zu Grünbach mit dem Ortsteil Muldenberg

- Grünbach ist Höhenluftkurort
- Prädikat „familienfreundliches Dorf"
- Ruhe und Geborgenheit in einer waldreichen Umgebung mit immergrünen Fichtenbeständen
- Brauchtum wie Mundart, Liedgut und Flößerei werden besonders gepflegt
- Trinkwassertalsperre Muldenberg besitzt die längste Drucksteinmauer Europas (Länge 92 Meter)
- Sport- und Kulturveranstaltungen haben Tradition

Fact file on Grünbach including Muldenberg

- Grünbach is a resort certified for its clean air
- Awarded the title "family-friendly village"
- Peace and quiet in a forested environment with evergreen firs
- Local customs such as the dialect, songs and log rafting are maintained
- Muldenberg drinking water reservoir has the longest quarry stone wall in Europe (92 metres long)
- Sports and cultural events have a long tradition here

Gemeindeverwaltung Grünbach/Muldenberg
Rathausstraße 4
D-08223 Grünbach
Telefon +49 (0) 3745 5303
Telefax +49 (0) 3745 5925
www.gruenbach.de
info@gruenbach.de

Familienfreundlich, grün, erholsam und beständig
Family-friendly, Green, Relaxing and Stable

Erlbach - Staatlich anerkannter Erholungsort im Naturpark Erzgebirge/Vogtland

Der Erholungsort Erlbach liegt im Landschaftsschutzgebiet „Oberes Vogtland" und im Gebiet des Naturparks „Erzgebirge/Vogtland". Die Ausläufer des Elstergebirges mit markanten Bergen bis 800 Meter prägen von drei Seiten die Silhouette für den malerisch gelegenen ruhigen Ort.

Im Jahre 1303 findet Erlbach erstmalig urkundliche Erwähnung. Die ehemals freien Siedler gelangten bald in Abhängigkeit von Adel und Kirche. Im Durchzugsgebiet von Böhmen nach Sachsen gelegen, wurde Erlbach von vielen kriegerischen Auseinandersetzungen heimgesucht. Durch besondere Verdienste gegenüber den meißnisch-sächsischen Landesherren wurden die Grundherren von Erlbach privilegiert, Salz verkaufen, brauen, Jahrmarkt abhalten und Handwerker ansiedeln zu dürfen. Dies kam vielen Exulanten zugute, die während des 30jährigen Krieges und danach das nahe Böhmen verlassen mussten und ihr Musikinstrumentengewerbe ins obere Vogtland mitbrachten. Hier verbreitete es sich schnell, denn viele Kleinbauern und Häusler waren gezwungen, sich in einem Nebengewerbe zu verdingen. Es entstanden „Ackerbürger", die im Sommer Land- und Viehwirtschaft betrieben und im Winter Musikinstrumente und deren Bestandteile herstellten. Um die Jahrhundertwende bildeten sich viele Handwerksbetriebe in Heimarbeit heraus. So gab es 1925 in Erlbach 76 Geigenbauer und 93 Geigenbogenmacher. Noch heute sind über 30 Handwerksmeister in Erlbach ansässig, die in kleinen Familienbetrieben Streich-, Zupf- und Blechblasinstrumente in sehr guter Qualität herstellen.

Durch seine landschaftlich reizvolle Lage ist Erlbach Anziehungspunkt für zahlreiche Tagestouristen, Sommer- und Winterurlauber. Der Ort verfügt über ca. 450 Gästebetten und verbucht jährlich ca. 35 000 Übernachtungen. 34 Vereine bestimmen das kulturell-sportliche Angebot des Ortes. Das obere Vogtland ist ein beliebtes Wandergebiet. Es gibt ein gut ausgebautes Wanderwegenetz mit Routenvorschlägen, auch grenzüberschreitend sowie viele organisierte Wanderaktivitäten. Neben Klingenthal und Schöneck verfügt Erlbach über ein ansprechendes Wintersportareal mit modernen Liftanlagen und gespurten Loipen.

Aufgrund der demographischen Entwicklung bemüht sich Erlbach um ständige Angebote für junge Familien. 2006 wurde Erlbach als erster familienfreundlicher Ort Sachsens zertifiziert. Interessante Natur- und Abenteuerspielplätze, ein Familienzentrum, Kindertagesstätte, Angebote im Freilichtmuseum Eubabrunn, Reittouristik uvm. werden für Einheimische und Gäste angeboten.

Im Vogtländischen Freilichtmuseum Eubabrunn sind auf einer vier Hektar großen Fläche drei original eingerichtete Höfe mit entsprechenden Nebengebäuden, Hausgärten, Tiere und bewirtschaftete Felder zu besichtigen. Es gibt besondere Höhepunkte und Events,

Erlbach is a state recognised resort in the Ore Mountains/Vogtland National Park.

The resort of Erlbach is located in the "Upper Vogtland" nature reserve and in the Ore Mountains/Vogtland National Park. The foothills of the Elster Mountains with their striking hills rising to a height of 800 metres dominate the silhouette of the picturesque, quiet town on three sides.

Erlbach was first mentioned in official records in 1303. The free settlers at that time soon came to depend on the nobility and church. Located in the area where many people passed from Bohemia to Saxony, Erlbach was affected by many military conflicts. As a result of special services rendered to the Meissen/Saxon rulers, the lords of the manor in Erlbach were privileged to be able to sell salt, brew beer, hold annual fairs and draw in trades people. This benefited many exiles, who were forced to leave Bohemia over the border during the 30 Years War and afterwards, and they brought their musical instrument business to the Upper Vogtland region. This spread very quickly, for many farmers and rural labourers were forced to seek employment in a second line of business. This gave rise to what were known as "farming residents", who looked after the land and cattle in summer and made musical instruments and components for them in winter. Many trades companies working at home were formed at the turn of the last century. There were 76 violin makers and 93 violin bow makers in Erlbach in 1925. There are still more than 30 master craftsmen in Erlbach today and

(Fotos/Photos by Gemeinde Erlbach, Hartmut Briese, Harald Sulski, Übersetzung/Translated by David Strauss)

ERLBACH

besondere Höhepunkte und Events, die sich dem Jahreslauf im früheren Dorfleben anpassen. Der Riedelhof in Eubabrunn hat eine ca. 400jährige Geschichte und wurde unter denkmalpflegerischen Gesichtspunkten rekonstruiert. Zahlreiche besondere architektonische Details sowie die idyllische Hanglage mit Blick auf das sich weitende Tal ließen das alte Gehöft als unbedingt erhaltenswert erscheinen. Der Hof fungiert jetzt als Begegnungsstätte für Kunst und Kultur, als Ort für ökologische Projekte und bäuerliche Direktvermarktung.

Erlbach hat seit 1563 Brautradition. Die ehemaligen Gebäude der ländlichen Brauerei werden jetzt als Handwerkliche Schaubrauerei mit Gaststätte betrieben. Das Erlbacher Brauhaus mit seinem Biergarten bietet 200 Gästen Erlebnisgastronomie in rustikaler Art verbunden mit allerlei hauseigenen Bierspezialitäten.

master craftsmen in Erlbach today and they make stringed, plucking and brass instruments of a very high quality in small family businesses.

Erlbach is also a favourite destination for many day visitors and summer and winter holiday makers because of its beautiful scenery. There are approx. 450 beds for visitors in the town and some 35,000 overnight stays are registered here every year. 34 clubs provide the cultural and sporting facilities in the town. The Upper Vogtland region is a popular walking area. There is a well developed network of footpaths with route suggestions – some of them cross the border into the Czech Republic – and many organised hiking activities. Like Klingenthal and Schöneck, Erlbach also has an attractive winter sports centre with modern lifts and cross-country skiing tracks.

Because of the latest demographic developments, Erlbach is constantly seeing to provide facilities for young families. Erlbach was the first town in Saxony to be certified as a family-friendly location in 2006. Local people and visitors can use fascinating open-air and adventure playgrounds, a family centre, a day-care centre, facilities in the Eubabrunn open air museum or go horse-riding and enjoy much more.

Three farms in their original state with the relevant outbuildings, gardens, animals and cultivated fields can be seen at the Vogtland Open-Air Museum in Eubabrunn on an area measuring four hectares. Particular highlights and events are held, which relate to the different times of the year in village life in earlier times. The history of the Riedel Farm in Eubabrunn goes back about 400 years and it has been reconstructed taking into account the requirements for listed buildings. Many special architectural details and the idyllic location on a slope with a view of the valley opening out meant that the old farm was particularly worth preserving. The farm now functions as a meeting place for art and culture, a location for ecological projects and the direct marketing of farm products.

Erlbach has been brewing beer since 1563. The former country brewery buildings are now used as an exhibition brewery with a restaurant. The Erlbach Brewery with its beer garden provides excellent cuisine for 200 guests in a country style atmosphere and combines this with all kinds of special local beers.

Gemeindeverwaltung Erlbach

D-08265 Erlbach
Klingenthaler Straße 1
Telefon +49 (0) 37422 6225
Telefax +49 (0)37422 6225
erlbach@t-online.de
www.erlbach.de

Das Beste aus Erlbach

The Best of Erlbach

Die Besonderheiten dieses Kleinodes im oberen Vogtland verdienen es hier konkret und in Einzelheiten beschrieben zu werden.
Seit November 2006 darf sich der idyllische staatlich anerkannte Erholungsort mit dem Prädikat „Familienfreundlicher Ort" schmücken. Erlbach hat in Sachen Familie durchaus die Nase vorn in Sachsen. Nach Prüfung durch die Tourismusmarketinggesellschaft Sachsen wurde die Gemeinde als erster „Familienfreundlicher Ort" in Sachsen zertifiziert. Doch warum ist das so?
Vor allem die Einigkeit im Gemeinderat hat dazu begetragen, dass im Ort Investitionen in kinderfreundliche Maßnahmen getätigt werden konnten. Im Jahre 2003, dem 700-jährigen Bestehens Erlbachs, zahlte die Gemeinde 700 Euro Begrüßungsgeld an jeden Neubürger. Die Früchte der konsequenten Familienpolitik im Ort kann man bereits ernten. So ist die Geburtenrate höher als die Sterberate. Und die findige Gemeinde wird sich nun mit der Schaffung weiterer Kinderbetreuungsplätze beschäftigen.
Kindern stehen in Erlbach qualitativ hochwertige Bildungs- und Erziehungsmöglichkeiten zur Verfügung. Die 6- bis 10-jährigen aus dem gesamten Umland und Markneukirchen besuchen die Grundschule in Erlbach. Im Kindergarten an der Forststraße haben die Knirpse die Möglichkeit, sich frei und unbeschwert im Einklang mit der Natur zu entwickeln. Großer Spielplatz und kindgerechte Bewegungsförderung geben dem Nachwuchs Raum für eine allseitige und gesunde Entwicklung. Ein Barfußpfad und der Sinnesgarten führen die Kinder zu einem ganzheitlichen Lebens- und Gemeinschaftsgefühl.
Und in Erlbach kann man natürlich was erleben! Die Spielplätze sind kleine Freizeitparks. Da gibt es den Kinderspielplatz im Erlbacher Park und den Abenteuerspielplatz in Eubabrunn. Mit zahlreichen Aktionen und Veranstaltungen sorgen die Verantwortlichen für Abwechslung. Der Naturlehrpfad „Natur live erleben" erweist sich als wahre Fundgrube für kleine Naturliebhaber. Das Familienzentrum „Altes Schloss" ist eine Begegnungsstätte für die gesamte Familie. Kinderbetreuung,

The special features of this treasure in the Upper Vogtland region are worth describing here in detail.
The idyllic, state recognised resort has been allowed to bear the title "Family-friendly Location" since November 2006. Erlbach is leading the way when it comes to the family in the state of Saxony. The community was certified as the first "family-friendly location" in Saxony after an inspection by the Saxon Tourism Marketing Association. But why is this?
The unity on the local council has enabled the town to make investments in child-friendly activities. The community paid a welcome sum of € 700 to each new person moving there in 2003, the 700th anniversary of Erlbach's existence. The fruits of this consistent family policy in the town are already being harvested. The birth rate is higher than the death rate. And the resourceful community is now seeking to create more child care places.
There are high-quality education and training facilities for children in Erlbach. The 6-10 year-olds from the surrounding area and Markneukirchen attend the primary school in Erlbach. Youngsters have the opportunity to develop freely and without any cares natural surroundings at the nursery school in Forst Street. A large playground and activity equipment suitable for children give them the space to develop in an all-round and healthy manner. A barefoot path and the "garden of senses" provide children with an all-round feeling for life and community.
And there is also plenty to enjoy in Erlbach! The playgrounds are small leisure parks. There is a play area in Erlbach Park and an adventure playground in Eubabrunn. Those responsible ensure that there is plenty of variety by arranging special activities and events. The "Experiencing Nature Live" nature trail is a real treasure trove for young nature lovers. The "Old Castle" family centre is a meeting place for the whole family. Child care, all kinds of lectures, English for kids and the "toddlers' group" for moth-

Erlbach

Vorträge aller Art, Englisch für Kids und die „Krabbelgruppe" für Mütter mit Kleinstkinder sind nur einige Beispiele für die vielseitigen Angebote. Im Kunstkeller der Kegelbergvilla trifft sich Jung und Alt zum Töpfern, Basteln oder Malen.

Eine breite Skala von Ereignissen bereichern das soziale und kulturelle Leben in Erlbach. Mundarttage, Schäfertag, deutsch-tschechische Kernobstschau und Erdäpfelzeit sind nur einige der interessanten Veranstaltungen, die im Vogtländisches Freilichtmuseum Eubabrunn oder im Riedelhof stattfinden. Den Veranstaltungskalender des musikalischen Traditionsortes füllen zahlreiche musikalische Darbietungen von Folkmusik oder Blasmusik bis hin zu Konzerten mit Gitarre oder Mandoline. Ein besonderes Event ist das Internationale Zupfinstrumentenfestival. Gitarrenliebhaber haben die Möglichkeiten zum Kennenlernen neuer Techniken des Gitarrespiels und anderer innovativer Techniken unter Anleitung von Künstlerpersönlichkeiten von internationalem Ruf. Das Holzbildhauersymposium zieht ebenfalls Künstler und Interessierte aus nah und fern in den beschaulichen Ort.

Seit 2004 gibt es die grenzüberschreitende Partnerschaft mit der Stadt Luby, Fester Bestandteil der Beziehung sind das jährliche Grenzfest im August mit rund 1000 Besucher, der Stollenanschnitt (Stollen misst 5 Meter) in Luby und der grenzüberschreitende Lehrpfad „Natur live".

Legendär ist auch die Erlbacher Kirmes (Kirchweihe), die „Kirwe". Zum Kirmes-Wochenende Mitte Oktober kommen 120 Händler und Schausteller auf den Erlbacher Marktplatz. Das Programm ist bunt und abwechslungsreich. Vereine präsentieren Ihr Können, ein zünftiges Schlachtfest, Tanz am Samstagabend im Schloß und am Sonntag die Luftgitarrenweltmeisterschaft sind beliebte Höhepunkte des Ereignisses.

Für Leben, Verbundenheit und Traditionspflege sorgen im Ort 34 Vereine. Sie kümmern sich um vielfältige Aktionen und Veranstaltungen in den Bereichen Sport, Kultur und traditionelles Handwerk wie den Musikinstrumentenbau.

Die Plakette „Familienfreundlicher Ort" bezieht sich natürlich auch auf die touristischen Aspekte – den familienfreundlichen Urlaub. Familien mit Kindern sind in Erlbach gut aufgehoben. Tagsüber hat die abwechslungsreiche Landschaft viel für große und kleine Entdecker zu bieten. Thematische Veranstaltungen wie Kinderfeste, Pferdefest, Rodelabende, Fackelwanderungen und vieles mehr sind wahre Besuchermagnete. Den fleißigen und geschickten Musikinstrumentenbaumeistern darf über die Schulter geschaut werden. Auch beim Schmied, beim Landwirt oder beim Imker kann man viel erfahren. Es gibt Tiere zum Streicheln und Füttern, eben richtiges Landleben. Abends machen familienfreundliche Gastgeber den Aufenthalt stressfrei und unkompliziert. So gibt es zum Beispiel im Landhotel „Lindenhöhe" eine extragroße Spielecke. Doch Kinder sind am liebsten im Freien, da kann man toben, matschen, rennen und die Welt erforschen. Beim Wandern kann man richtig viele Abenteuer erleben: Insekten beobachten, über Steine im Fluss balancieren, ein Versteck im Wald bauen – wenn Entdecken, Aktionen und Spaß an erster Stelle stehen, wird die Wanderung ein nachhaltiges Erlebnis, weil es die Sinne schärft

ers with tiny children are just some of the examples of the variety of facilities available. People of all ages meet in the art cellar in the Kegelberg villa to do pottery, make things or paint.

A broad range of events enrich Erlbach's social and cultural life. Dialect days, shepherds' days, German-Czech core fruit shows and potato fairs are just of the interesting events that take place in the Vogtland Open-Air Museum in Eubabrunn or Riedel Farm. Many musical events fill the calendar in this traditional music centre, ranging from folk music to brass music and even concerts featuring the guitar or mandolin. The International Plucking Instrument Festival is a very special event. Guitar lovers have an opportunity to get to know new ways of playing the instrument and other innovative techniques under the direction of artists of international repute. The wood carving symposium also draws artists and interested parties from near and far to the tranquil town.

A cross-border partnership has existed with the town of Luby since 2004. The annual border festival in August, which attracts about 1000 visitors, the stollen cutting ceremony (the stollen cake measures 5 metres) in Luby and the cross-border "Nature Live" nature trail are already permanent features of the partnership.

The Erlbach parish fair, the "Kirwe" is also legendary. 120 traders and showmen come to the Erlbach market square for the parish fair in the middle of October. The programme is colourful and varied. Clubs show off their skills and popular highlights at the event are the hearty festival with freshly prepared meat, dancing in the castle on the Saturday evening and the imaginary guitar competition on the Sunday.

34 clubs in the town provide animation, close ties and help maintain traditions. They provide a variety of programmes and events in the fields of sports, culture, traditional skills and musical instrument making.

The "Family-friendly Location" label also relates to the tourism facilities – family-friendly holidays. Families with children are well provided for in Erlbach. The varied countryside has plenty to offer large and small during the daytime. Topical events like children's festivals, horse-riding galas, sledging evenings, torchlight walks and a great deal more are real tourist magnets. People can look over the shoulders of industrious master musical instrument makers or they can learn a lot watching a blacksmith, a farmer or a bee-keeper at work. There are animals to stroke and feed – it is a taste of real country life. Hosts with a heart for families will make your stay relaxing and uncomplicated in the evenings. There is an extra large play area at the "Lindenhöhe" country hotel, for example. But children love being out in the open air – romping around, splashing around, running and finding out about the world. And there is plenty to discover when out on walks: observing insects, crossing rivers on stones, building a hiding place in the woods – if discoveries, action and fun are your first priority, walks will be a real experience, for they quicken people's senses and reveal the beauty of nature. A family holiday in Erlbach

Erlbach

und die Schönheiten der Natur erkennen läßt. Der Familienurlaub in Erlbach bringt die Freizeitgestaltung von Kindern und Erwachsenen perfekt unter einen Hut. Ob kindgerechte Wanderwege, Museen oder Führungen, abenteuerliche Ausflüge, spektakuläre Naturschauspiele oder Freizeitparks – für jedes Kind und jeden jung gebliebenen Erwachsenen ist etwas dabei. Die Wander- und Radwanderwege in Erlbach verfügen über kindgerechte Abschnitte und sind in kürzeren Etappen auch für kurze Beine zu bewältigen. Für den „Familienfreundlichen Ort" stehen Wohlfühlen und Spaß für alle Altersgruppen an oberster Stelle. Das Eichhörnchenmaskottchen „Hörnchen" führt Familien zu allen interessanten Orten wie dem Abenteuerspielplatz oder dem Sinnesgarten. Eine Tafel verrät, wo es kindgerechte Einrichtungen gibt oder Wanderwege, die man getrost mit Kinderwagen genießen kann.

Doch auch Aktivurlauber ohne Kinder sind in Erlbach herzlich willkommen. Der Infoparkplatz am Ortseingang mit Tourist-Terminal gibt anhand des aktuellen Ortplanes Auskunft zur Verfügbarkeit, Lage und Beschaffenheit von Unterkünften und Sehenswertem im Ort. Wandern, Radeln, Reiten, Baden – hier kommt jeder auf seine Kosten. Wer die Schönheit der Berglandschaft zu genießen weiß, der kann sich verzaubern lassen, von stillen Wäldern, weiten Ausblicken, von fröhlichem Vogelgesang. Der Erholungsort Erlbach bietet mit ausgedehnten Wander- und Radwegen die Möglichkeit, Natur aktiv zu erleben. Reizvolle Aussichtspunkte und rustikale Rastplätze laden zum Verweilen ein. Ganz gleich ob man den Bergweg entlang der deutsch-tschechischen Grenze, das Eubabrunner Tal, die romantische Landesgemeinde oder Wernitzgrün erwandern möchte, es führen über 100 km gut ausgebaute und übersichtliche Wanderwege mit vielen Erlebnisbereichen an das gewünschte Ziel. Die Erlbacher Bergwanderung im Mai oder die Erlbacher Wanderwoche im September erfreuen sich größter Beliebtheit. Die Bergwanderung gibt es bereits seit 28 Jahren und zählte zuletzt 1092 Teilnehmer.

Bei appetitlichem Duft von Hopfen und Malz im Erlbacher Brauhaus können sich die Besucher über die traditionelle Kunst des Bierbrauens informieren, ein echtes „Erlbacher Zwickelbier" probieren und dazu vogtländische Hausmannskost genießen. Ein besonderes Kleinod ist das Obervogtländische Dorfmuseum am Lindenplatz, ein Doppelstubenblockhaus mit Holzschindeldach aus dem Jahre 1726. In der Ausstellung wird die Geschichte des Ortes dokumentiert und das Musikinstrumentengewerbe dargestellt.

Im Winter erwartet das Skigebiet am Kegelberg seine Besucher. Für alpines Skivergnügen sorgen ein Doppelschlepplift (700 Meter lang, 160 Meter Höhendifferenz, Beschneiungsanlage), günstige Skipasspreise und ein 80 Meter langer kleiner Skilift für Kinder, Anfänger und Skischule. Imbissversorgung und Rodelverleih runden das Angebot ab. Wer mit dem Skiern lieber die Natur erkunden möchte, dem stehen die Hoher-Brand-Loipe 9 km, eine Familienringloipe 5 km, die Rundloipe Zauberwald 3 km und die Skiwanderwege Erlbach-Wernitzgrün-Landwüst (Grenzloipe) 9 km und Eubabrunn-Landesgemeinde zur Verfügung.
(Schneetelefon: 037422 6225)

perfectly combines leisure activities for children and adults. There is something for every child or adult with a young heart – walks suitable for children, museums or guided tours, excursions full of adventure, spectacular natural spectacles or leisure parks. The footpaths and cycle paths in Erlbach have sections that are suitable for children and they can be tackled in shorter stages so that little legs do not get too tired. Well-being and fun for all age groups is the top priority at this "family-friendly location". The squirrel mascot guides families to interesting places like the adventure playground or the "garden of senses". One sign reveals where there are facilities suitable for children or footpaths that can be enjoyed with children without any difficulty.

But those seeking an active holiday without children are also welcome in Erlbach. The information car park at the entrance to the town with its tourist terminal provides information on the location and type of accommodation available and sights in the town by means of an up-to-date map. Walking, cycling, riding, swimming – everybody will find something interesting to do. Those who enjoy the beauty of the hills will be captivated by tranquil forests, wide views and the cheerful song of birds. The resort of Erlbach provides people with an opportunity to experience nature actively on a wide network of footpaths and cycle paths. Beautiful viewpoints and natural picnic areas encourage people to stay. More than 100 km of well developed footpaths with many adventures will take you to your destination – the hill route along the German-Czech border, the Eubabrunn valley, the romantic country community or Wernitzgrün. The Erlbach hill climbing event in May or the Erlbach walking weekend in September are very popular. The hill climbing event has been held for 28 years and 1,092 people took part last time.

Visitors can find out about the traditional art of brewing beer with the appetizing smell of hops and malt at the Erlbach brewery, try out a genuine "Erlbach Zwickel beer" and enjoy a good Vogtland homely meal to go with it. The Upper Vogtland village museum on Linden Square is a special treat – it has a blockhouse design with two downstairs rooms with a wood shingle roof dating from 1726. The history of the town is documented in the exhibition and there is plenty on musical instrument making for people to enjoy.

The skiing area on the Kegelberg is there for winter sports enthusiasts. A double t-bar tow (700 metres long, 160 metres difference in altitude, snowmaking unit), cheap skiing passes and an 80 metre small ski lift for children, beginners and the ski school provide downhill skiing pleasure. A snack bar and sledge hire round off the facilities available. Those who prefer to discover the natural surroundings on skis can use the Hoher Brand track (9 km), the family ring track (5 km), the Enchanted Forest circular track (3 km), the Erlbach-Wernitzgrün-Landwüst border track (9 km) or the Eubabrunn country parish track. (Snow hotline: 037422 6225).

Lebendige Traditionen

Living Traditions

Das Vogtländische Freilichtmuseum Eubabrunn wird seit 1992 in dem zur Gemeinde Erlbach gehörigen Ortsteil gleichen Namens aufgebaut. Seit seiner offiziellen Eröffnung im Jahr 1995, wurde es von zahlreichen Besuchern aus nah und fern besichtigt.

Eubabrunn liegt unmittelbar an der Grenze zum historischen Egerland, zu dem von alters her rege Handelsbeziehungen bestanden. Die Fähigkeit zum Bau von Musikinstrumenten brachten Glaubensflüchtlinge im 17. Jahrhundert mit, ein Fakt, der die Region auch heute noch prägt.

Die Besiedlung durch nordbayrische Kolonisatoren und dem Egerland hinterließen ihre Spuren auch in der Mundart. Das Südvogtländische grenzt sich von den anderen vogtländischen Dialekten ab.

Diese museale Einrichtung präsentiert Zeugnisse der Volksarchitektur des südlichen Vogtlandes aus der Zeit um 1720 bis Anfang des 20. Jahrhunderts. Von den derzeit 18 Gebäuden sind die meisten zu besichtigen.

In derzeit drei Höfen finden die Besucher Sonder- u. Dauerausstellungen zu verschiedenen Themen.

Das Areal des Museums erstreckt sich in einer am Bachlauf gelegenen Tallage auf eine Fläche von ca. 4 Hektar.

Die Gebäude sind alle von verschiedenen Orten der Region nach hier umgesetzt worden. Die weit auseinandergezogene Anordnung der Höfe entspricht der, solcher ursprünglich nach deutschem Recht, angelegten Dörfer.

Verschiedene, teils vom Aussterben bedrohte Haustierrassen sind je nach Jahreszeit in den Ställen oder auf den Wiesen zu finden. Auf den Feldern wird historisches Saatgut angebaut.

Sehr anschaulich wird das Leben vergangener Generationen bei einem geführten Rundgang oder bei verschiedenen museumspädagogischen Programmen vermittelt.

Im Laufe des Jahres finden verschiedene Veranstaltungen statt. Sie sind auf den jahreszeitlichen Ablauf bezogen, haben aber auch bestimmte Themen zum Inhalt.

Im Museumsgelände befindet sich die Gaststätte „Grünes Tal".

Das Museum befindet sich seit 2002 in Regie des 1. Fördervereines Vogtländisches Freilichtmuseum Eubabrunn e.V. Es wird als regionalbedeutsame Einrichtung durch den Kulturraum Vogtland gefördert.

Work has been going on to set up the Vogtland Open-Air Museum in Eubabrunn in the parish that bears its name and belongs to Erlbach since 1992. Many visitors from near and far have crossed the threshold since it was opened in 1995.

Eubabrunn is situated directly on the border with the historic Bohemian region called Egerland, where brisk trading ties go back a long way. Religious refugees from there brought with them the ability to make musical instruments in the 17th century and this is still a major factor in the region today.

Settlement by North Bavarian colonisers and people from Bohemia has left its mark on the dialect too. The Southern Vogtland speech is quite different from the other Vogtland dialects.

This museum shows items recalling the folk architecture of the Southern Vogtland district from the period around 1720 to the beginning of the 20th century. Most of the 18 buildings can be visited. Visitors will find special and permanent exhibitions on various themes at the three farms.

The museum covers an area of approx. 4 hectares along a stream in a valley.

The buildings have all been moved here from various places in the region. The arrangement of the farms, located at a distance from each other, corresponds to the arrangement of villages, originally dictated by German law.

Various domestic pets, some of them threatened with extinction, can be found in the stables or in the fields, depending on the time of year. Historical seed is cultivated in the fields.

The life of previous generations can be well appreciated if you join one of the guided tours or one of the many teaching programmes at the museum.

Various events take place during the course of the year. They relate to procedures at that particular time of the year, but also deal with special themes.

The "Green Valley" restaurant is located on the museum compound.

The museum has been managed by the 1st Vogtland Open-Air Museum Eubabrunn Development Association since 2002. It is sponsored as a significant regional institution by the Vogtland Cultural Region.

VOGTLÄNDISCHES FREILICHTMUSEUM EUBABRUNN

www.freilichtmuseum-eubabrunn.de
E-mail: freilichtmuseum@web.de
Telefon +49 (0) 37422 6536
Telefax +49 (0) 37422 47301 o. 6537

Öffnungszeiten
Die bis So von 10.00 bis 17.00 Uhr
(Ab 1. November. bis 31. Januar
von 10.00 bis 16.00 Uhr)

Elsterberg – im grünen Tal der Weißen Elster

Elsterberg – in the Green Valley of the "Weisse Elster"

Das Städtlein Elsterberg breitet sich an den Hängen und im Tal der Weißen Elster aus. Die Lage ist hervorragend für Wanderer, Naturfreunde und Denkmalinteressierte.

Das markanteste Bauwerk des malerisch gelegenen Ortes ist die altehrwürdige Burgruine, die auf einem Bergsporn liegt und von der Weißen Elster in weitem Bogen umflossen wird. Um 1200 kamen die Herren von Lobdeburg in die Elsterberger Gegend. Sie erbauten sich vor 1225 den neuen Herrschersitz, die jetzige Burgruine. Zu ihren Füßen entwickelte sich im Laufe der Zeit die Stadt Elsterberg. Als 1394 die Lobdeburger ausstarben, übernahmen die Bünaus das Schloss und von 1636 bis 1736 war es Eigentum des Reichen Carol Bose bzw. seiner Nachkommen. Danach wechselten die Besitzer ständig. Bedingt durch Geldmangel und adlige Vernachlässigung verfiel das Schloss sehr schnell. Um 1750 war es schon nicht mehr bewohnbar.
Erst im Jahre 1909 besann man sich seiner Verantwortung und die Stadtgemeinde

Altehrwürdige Mauerreste der größten Burganlage Sachsens/ Ancient remains of walls in Saxony's largest castle

Elsterberg erwarb die Ruine vom Rittergutsbesitzer Adler auf Coschütz. Es begannen notwendige Restaurierungsarbeiten. Der damalige Gebirgsverein veranstaltete Ruinenfeste, um den Erlös für die Erhaltung des historisch wertvollen Geländes einzusetzen. Der Sinn und Zweck der Ruinen- und Heimatfeste hat sich bis in die heutige Zeit erhalten. Stadtverwaltung, Heimatverein und ein großer Teil der Elsterberger Bürger organisieren und gestalten im 4-jährigen Rhythmus dieses schöne traditionelle Fest. Das 1,5 Hektar große, frei zugängliche Ruinengelände mit seinen eigenartigen Mauerresten, den Wehrtürmen und Kellern ist dann Schauplatz und großartige Kulisse.
Das gesamte Ruinengelände steht unter Denkmalschutz.
In einem der gut erhaltenen Wehrtürme befindet sich die Elsterberger Heimatstube, in einem weiteren ein kleines Museum. Beide geben Einblicke in die Vergangenheit der Stadt. Anschaulich wird die Entwicklung von den Anfängen bis zur Gegenwart dargestellt.

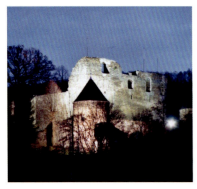
Die Burgruine im Abendlicht/ The castle ruins in evening light

(Fotos/Photos by Arno Hiller, Igor Pastierovic [5], Übersetzung/Translated by David Strauss)

Blick auf Elsterberg/ View of Elsterberg

The little town of Elsterberg is located in the Weisse Elster valley surrounded by hillsides. This makes it an ideal spot for hikers, nature lovers and people interested in listed buildings.
The most distinctive building in the picturesque town is the ancient castle ruin situated on a hilltop surrounded by the waters of the Weisse Elster. The lords of Lobdeburg came to the region near Elsterberg in about 1200. They established a new base in today's castle ruin in 1225. The town of Elsterberg slowly developed at the foot of the hill over the years. When the Lobdeburg family died out, the castle was taken over by the Bünau family. From 1636 to 1736 it belonged to a rich man called Carol Bose and his descendants. From 1736 onwards the castle changed hands continually. Due to a lack of money and neglect by the aristocrats, the castle deteriorated very quickly. By 1750 it was uninhabitable.
Elsterberg did not take on any responsibility for the castle until 1909 and bought it from the manor owner Adler auf Coschütz. The necessary restoration work soon started. The Mountain Society arranged festivals on the ruin at that time to invest the proceeds in the preservation of this historically valuable building. The nature of the local festivals on the castle ruins has been retained right up to the present day. The town, local clubs and many local residents organise these attractive traditional festivals every four years. The freely accessible castle grounds, which cover an area measuring 1.5 hectares, and its unique ruins, fortified towers and cellars have become the ideal setting for the festival.

Festumzug zum Ruinen- und Heimatfest /Festival procession during one of the castle ruin and local festivals

The entire castle ruins are a listed building.
One of the well-preserved fortified towers is home to a local exhibition about Elsterberg, while another tower hosts a little museum. Both provide insight into the town's past and show how Elsterberg has developed from its origins to the present day.
Elsterberg was a simple country town until 1700 and all local production was for home consumption. Hand weaving soon started and was to become a main source of income for the majority of the population. From 1800 onwards muslin, cotton and gabardine weaving played an important role. In 1882 the first mechanical weaving mill opened and in 1919 a publicly owned company for spinning fibres was set up. The "Elsterberger Kunstseide" brand (artificial silk from Elsterberg) became famous nationally and internationally. The production of leather and stoves was no less important for Elsterberg, which by then had become a modern industrial town. The links with the railway network from 1875 onwards had very beneficial effects. It helped at-

Elsterberg

Denkmalgeschütztes Marktplatzensemble/ View of the listed market square

Evangelisch-lutherische Laurentiuskirche/ St Laurentius Church (Lutheran)

Schule Elsterberg/ The school in Elsterberg

Bis etwa 1700 war Elsterberg ein reines Landstädtchen; demzufolge diente alle Erzeugung dem Eigenbedarf. Es begann auch die Zeugmacherei, die später den Hauptteil der Bevölkerung ernährte; die Musselin-, Baumwoll- und Kammgarnweberei kamen nach 1800 auf, 1882 erfolgte die Eröffnung der ersten mechanischen Weberei und 1919 wurde die „Spinnfaser-Aktiengesellschaft" gegründet. Der Name „Elsterberger Kunstseide" wurde im In- und Ausland bekannt. Aber auch die Leder- und Herdfabrikation war von nicht zu unterschätzender Bedeutung. Elsterberg entwickelte sich zur modernen Industriestadt. Der Anschluss an das Eisenbahnnetz im Jahr 1875 wirkte sich dabei sehr günstig aus. Er war mit Sicherheit ausschlaggebend für die Ansiedlung neuer Betriebe und die weitere Entwicklung der Neustadt.

1952 erfolgte im Zuge der Gebietsreform die Einordnung der Stadt Elsterberg in den Bezirk Gera und damit nach Thüringen. Am 1. April 1992 konnte auf Drängen der Bevölkerung die Rückgliederung nach Sachsen vollzogen werden.

Durch die veränderten Bedingungen nach der politischen Wende 1989/90 wurde die Textilindustrie fast völlig zum Erliegen gebracht. Viele hoch qualifizierte Fachleute wurden arbeitslos. Infolgedessen gründeten sich mittelständische Betriebe, die die Grundlage für eine gut funktionierende Wirtschaft sind.

In den Jahren 1991 bis heute wurde in Elsterberg viel Positives geschaffen. So konnte das Waldbad vollkommen rekonstruiert werden. Der Neubau der Umgehungsstraße führte zur Entlastung des historischen Stadtkerns. Modernisierte Wohngebäude, Schulen, Kindereinrichtungen und das sanierte Seniorenzentrum tragen zur Verbesserung der Lebensqualität der Elsterberger bei.

Zu jeder Jahreszeit lockt Elsterberg mit seiner wundervollen Landschaft Wanderer, Natur- und Heimatfreunde. Zu den bevorzugten Ausflugszielen gehören das wildromantische Landschaftsschutzgebiet „Steinicht" und der 407 Meter hohe „Kriebelstein". Wer den Aufstieg geschafft hat, wird überrascht sein vom herrlichen Panoramablick auf Elsterberg und seine Umgebung.

Heute leben in Elsterberg und den sieben Ortsteilen etwa 5000 Einwohner. Bereits 1972 wurde Noßwitz eingemeindet, 1993 folgten Görschnitz, 1994 Coschütz, Kleingera, Losa und Scholas und 1995 Cunsdorf.

tract new companies to the town so that new areas of Elsterberg could be further developed.

In the course of a local government reform in 1952, Elsterberg was assigned to the district of Gera in Thuringia. But at the instigation of the local people, a referendum was held on 1 April 1992 and the town reverted to Saxony.

The changes introduced by the fall of the Berlin Wall in 1989/90 signalled the almost total collapse of the textile industry in the area. Many skilled and highly qualified workers lost their jobs. But small and medium sized businesses were set up and have become the foundation of a thriving economy.

A great deal has been achieved in Elsterberg since 1991. The swimming pool in the woods has been restored. A bypass has relieved the heart of the town of a great deal of traffic. The quality of life in Elsterberg has been improved by modernising buildings, schools, children's facilities and an old people's centre.

Elsterberg attracts hikers, nature lovers and people interested in local history at any time of the year because of the wonderful scenery here. The romantic "Steinicht" natural conservation area and the "Kriebelstein", which is 407 metres high, are popular destinations for outings. Anyone who climbs to the top will be surprised by the magnificent panoramic view over Elsterberg and its surroundings. Elsterberg and its 7 districts now have a population of approximately 5,000 inhabitants. Nosswitz was incorporated into the town in 1972. Görschnitz followed in 1992, Coschütz, Kleingera, Losa and Scholas in 1994 and Cunsdorf in 1995.

Das idyllisch gelegene Waldbad im Tremnitzgrund/ The idyllic location for the swimming pool in the woods

Landschaftsschutzgebiet „Steinicht / "Steinicht" nature conservation area

Kleingera - Küchenteich des Rittergutes / Kleingera – the manor pond

Stadtverwaltung Elsterberg

D-07985 Elsterberg · Marktplatz 1
Telefon +49 (0) 36621) 881-0
Telefax +49 (0) 36621) 881-11
stadtverwaltung@elsterberg.de
www.elsterberg.de

Mylau

Geschichte bewahren, Zukunft gestalten

Enshrine History, Design Future

Das Tal der Göltzsch bildet den landschaftlichen Rahmen für die Kleinstadt Mylau mit ihren 3000 Einwohnern. Hoch über der Mündung zwischen Göltzsch und Raumbach wurde um 1180 auf einem Felssporn ein romanischer Wehrbau als Reichsdienstmannensitz Kaiser Barbarossas errichtet. Aus dieser Zeit stammen der 27 Meter hohe Bergfried, die zwei Viereckstürme, der Rote Turm und der Glockenturm der Burg. Das Stadtrecht erhielt Mylau im Jahr 1367 durch Kaiser Karl IV., der seitdem das Stadtwappen ziert. Der Einzug von Kaiser Karl wird alljährlich zum Burgfest nachgestaltet. Auf den Spuren der Kaiser kann man in Mylau auf dem Kaiserpfad wandeln. Er beginnt am Markttor der Burg und führt über die Vorburg bis in den Kaiserhof. An 13 Stationen lernen die Burgbesucher das mittelalterliche Bauwerk mit seinen Türmen, Toren, Mauern und Bastionen, dem Graben und auch den Relikten aus der Zeit der böhmischen Könige Karl IV., Wenzel IV. und Sigismund kennen. Über einen zweiten Burgpfad, den "Ritterpfad", gelangt man vom Markttor über den Markt zum Ortsteil Obermylau. Das dort befindliche Rittergut war einst Wohnsitz und Wirtschaftshof der Mylauer Herrschaften. Die Mitglieder des 1998 gegründeten Fördervereins Burg Mylau organisieren neben ihrer denkmalpflegerischen Mitwirkung bei der Erhaltung der Burg Veranstaltungen wie das Puppenspielfest im Februar oder das Burgfest im September. Die Burg Mylau ist die größte und am besten erhaltene Burganlage im sächsischen Vogtland. Das Museum besitzt die größte Naturkundesammlung des Vogtlandes, zu der 15.000 Insekten, 1000 Vogelpräparate, 700 Säugestiere und etwa 2000 Gesteine gehören. Ein Teil davon wird im historischen Naturalienkabinett gezeigt. Eine Kostbarkeit der Sammlung ist ein Wisent mit der stattlichen Höhe von 1,75 Metern und einer Länge von 2,70 Metern, der aus Westrussland stammt. Andere Räume informieren über die Geschichte der Burg und der Stadt, den Bau der Göltzschtalbrücke, über Geologie und Bergbau im Vogtland oder würdigen bedeutende Mylauer. Im Elfriede-Mäckel-Zimmer wird in einer ständigen Ausstellung Kunst aus dem Vogtland präsentiert. Die im Barocksaal ausgestellten 40 Veduten europäischer Barockresidenzen um 1750 stellen eine Rarität dar. Der Musikverein Mylau/Reichenbach probt und residiert im historischen Ambiente der Mylauer Burg. Unter dem Motto „It's time for Blasmusik" treten die Mitglieder mit einem vielseitigen und abwechslungsreichen Repertoire auf.

Die Kirche ist eine der Mylauer Sehenswürdigkeiten. Der große neogotische Backsteinbau mit einem 72 Meter hohen Turm entstand 1890 und ersetzte die um 1250 gebaute romanische Kirche, die dem Heiligen Wenzel geweiht war. Die Originalausstattung mit Altar, Kanzel, Lesepult, Orgelprospekt und Kirchengestühl ist weitgehend erhalten. Aus dem Vorgängerbau wurde das Orgelwerk von 1731 übernommen. Es stammt von Gottfried Silbermann, dem bedeutendsten Orgelbauer des Spätbarocks. Zu den Schätzen des Kirchenarchivs gehört ein Tabulaturbuch, das vermutlich aus der Zeit des Orgelbaus stammt. Der damalige Kantor Johann Christoph Traeger könnte die Noten von 176 Stücken unbekannter, aber auch so bedeutender vorbachscher Komponisten wie Johann Pachelbel oder Johann Krieger für seine Arbeit in der Kirche zusammengefasst haben.

The little town of Mylau with its 3,000 inhabitants is situated in the scenic Göltzsch valley. Romanesque fortifications were built for the castle trustees serving Emperor Barbarossa in about 1180, high above the point where the Göltzsch and Raumbach rivers meet. The 27 metre high keep, the two corner towers and the castle's Red Tower and Bell Tower all date from this period. Mylau was recognised as a town in 1367 by Emperor Karl IV and he adorns the town's coat of arms. Emperor Karl's entry into the town is re-enacted every year at the town's castle festival. Visitors can follow the Emperor's footsteps along the imperial path. It starts at the castle's Market Gate and takes people to the Emperor's court via the bailey. At 13 different points, visitors to the castle can find out all about this medieval building with its towers, gates, walls and bastions, its moat and also the relics from the time of the Bohemian Emperors Karl IV, Wenceslas IV and Sigismund. And there is a second castle pathway, the "Knights' Path", which takes visitors from the market gate to the part of town known as Upper Mylau. The manor there was once the residence and business centre for the Mylau gentry. As well as looking after the castle's listed building status when maintaining the building, the members of the Mylau Castle Support Group, founded in 1998, also organise events like the Puppet Festival in February or the Castle Festival in September. Mylau Castle is the largest and best preserved castle in the Saxon Vogtland region. The museum houses the largest natural history collection in the Vogtland region. It includes 15,000 insects, 1,000 stuffed birds, 700 mammals and about 2,000 different rock formations. Some of these are on display in the natural history cabinet. One of the treasures of the collection is a bison, which comes from western Russia and is 1.75 metres tall and 2.70 metres long. The other rooms provide information for visitors on the history of the castle and the town, the construction of the Göltzsch Valley Bridge, geology and mining in the Vogtland region or famous sons and daughters of Mylau. There is a continuous art exhibition of works from the Vogtland region in the Elfriede-Mäckel Room. The 40 veduta of European baroque residences in about 1750, which are on display in the Baroque Room, are almost unique. The Mylau/Reichenbach Music Association is based at and practises in the historical atmosphere of Mylau Castle. Under the heading "It's time for brass music", the members have a versatile and varied repertoire.

The church in Mylau is really worth visiting. The large neo-Gothic brick building with its 72 metre high tower was first built in 1890 to replace the Romanesque church built in about 1250, which had been dedicated to Wenceslas IV. The original furnishings with the altar, pulpit, lectern, organ front and church seating have been largely retained. The organ built in 1731 for the previous building was also taken over. It was built by Gottfried Silbermann, the most important late baroque organ builder. The church archives also house treasures, including a collection of organ compositions, which probably stems from the time when the organ was built. The choirmaster at the time, Johann Christopher Traeger, may have been able to collect the notes of 176 pieces from unknown and more familiar pre-Bach composers like Johann Pachelbel or Johann Krieger for his work in the church.

Erfolg für Mylauer Mädchen bei den Deutschen Meisterschaften 2008: Im Bild Karoline Zillmann (links für den ESC Erfurt startend) und Denise Roth (rechts vom TSV Vorwärts Mylau 1891 e.V.) Karoline konnte bei den Einzelstrecken-DM in Erfurt eine Bronzemedaille und eine Goldmedaille in der U23 (unter 23jährige)-Wertung über die 1500 Meter erringen. Denise schaffte als erst 19jährige die Überraschung sich in der Damenkonkurrenz den 100-Meter-Titel, nach der Qualifikation über die 500 Meter Angangszeiten und einem Semifinallauf, zu sichern. Über 1000 Meter konnte sie zudem noch eine Bronzemedaille in der U23 ergattern.

Deutsche Meisterschaften 2008: Im Bild Karoline Zillmann (links) und Denise Roth (rechts) beide TSV Vorwärts Mylau 1891 e.V.. Karoline konnte bei den Einzelstrecken-DM in Erfurt eine Bronzemedaille und eine Goldmedaille in der U23 (unter 23jährige)-Wertung über die 1500 Meter erringen. Denise schaffte als erst 19jährige die Überraschung sich in der Damenkonkurrenz den 100-Meter-Titel, nach der Qualifikation über die 500 Meter Angangszeiten und einem Semifinallauf, zu sichern. Über 1000 Meter

Stolz kann Mylau aber auch auf seine Sportvereine sein. Die Liste zahlreicher besonders erfolgreicher Sportler aus der Abteilung Eisschnelllauf des TSV Vorwärts Mylau 1891 e. V. kann sich sehen lassen. Keine ruhige Kugel schiebt, allen voran die Deutsche Vizemeisterin Petra Werner, aus dem Kegelsportclub Reichenbach/Mylau.

Im Ortsteil Obermylau gibt es mehr Arbeitsplätze als Einwohner, denn dort befindet sich der größte Mylauer Gewerbestandort. Auf dem Gelände der früheren Renak-Werke hat sich die Firma Fissek im Bereich Maschinenbau und Instandsetzung zum weltweit gefragten Wirtschaftspartner entwickelt. In Mylau produzierte Teile der Firma VCST (Vehicle Components, Systems and Transmissions) Reichenbach, einer 100%igen Tochter von Industrial Products Belgien stecken in der Hälfte aller in Europa gefertigten Autos. Beim Textilgroßhandel Meisner & Forbrig OHG werden täglich 25 Tonnen Kleidung und fünf Tonnen Schuhe sortiert und in die Länder West- und Ostafrikas sowie nach Asien und Osteuropa weitergegeben. In der Mylauer Niederlassung der Schüchen International GmbH & Co KG werden auf 12.000 Quadratmetern Gesamtfläche vor allem Zulieferteile der Automobilindustrie umgeschlagen.

Im Gewerbehof am Schillerweg haben sich vor allem Handwerksbetriebe niedergelassen. Dort befindet sich auch die Reichenbacher Außenstelle der Volkshochschule des Vogtlandkreises. Kurse von Englisch für Kindergärtnerinnen über Yoga und Entspannungstraining oder Computer und Internet bis zum Orientalischen Tanz können an dieser Weiterbildungseinrichtung belegt werden. In Sachen Bildung hat die Kleinstadt Mylau noch mehr zu bieten. Am Fuße der Burg hat seit 01.01.2007 das Evangelische Gymnasium Mylau „FUTURUM Vogtland" sein Domizil. Träger dieses Gymnasiums ist der Evangelische Schulverein Vogtland e. V. Seit dem Eröffnungstag am 1. September 2007 besuchen 44 Mädchen und Jungen dieses Gymnasium, welches sich am Lehrplan des Landes Sachsen orientiert. Die Schüler legen in der 10. bzw. 12. Klasse die allgemeingültigen Prüfungen ab. Das Bildungswerk der Sächsischen Wirtschaft bildet in Mylau Jugendliche in unterschiedlichen Berufen aus. In der ehemaligen Thyssen-Niederlassung hat der Bildungsträger die über Regionalgrenzen hinaus bekannte und vom Deutschen Verband für Schweißen und verwandte Verfahren e. V. (DVS) anerkannte Ausbildungsstätte für Schweißer.

Größter Arbeitgeber der Stadt ist die Behr Industry Mylau GmbH mit etwa 300 Beschäftigten. In der Reichenbacher Tochtergesellschaft Behr Motorradtechnik arbeiten weitere 80 Fachkräfte. Im Auftrag der internationalen Behr-Gruppe entstehen Wärmeüberträger, Heiz- und Klimageräte oder Kraftstoffbehälter für die Automobil-, Motorrad- und Bahnfahrzeugindustrie. Die Firma GeDaCom bietet ein breites Spektrum im Bereich Hard- und Software sowie Web-Design. Seit 1984 hat sich die Kelterei „Göltzschtal" e.G. von der Lohnmosterei zum modernen Industriebetrieb entwickelt. Der zu 100% aus frisch gepressten Äpfeln bestehende Apfelsaft ist weit über die Grenzen des Vogtlandes hinaus begehrt. Handwerksbetriebe verschiedener Gewerke, Werkstätten und Einkaufszentren kümmern sich um die Versorgung mit Waren und Dienstleistungen.

Mylau also has good reason to be proud of its sports clubs. The list of many speed skating athletes from TSV Vorwärts Mylau 1891 e.V. speaks for itself. The German national runner-up in ten pin bowling, Petra Werner, does not hold back either. She's a member of the Reichenbach/Mylau club.

Upper Mylau has more jobs than residents. This is where the largest business park in Mylau is situated. Fissek has its production facilities on the former Renak site and has developed into a mechanical engineering and maintenance company that is in demand around the world. Parts manufactured in Mylau by VCST (Vehicle Components, Systems and Transmissions) Reichenbach, a 100% subsidiary of Industrial Products Belgium, are found in half of all the cars manufactured in Europe. The textile wholesalers Meisner & Forbrig OHG sort 25 tonnes of clothes and 5 tonnes of shoes every day and send them on to West and East Africa as well as Asia and Eastern Europe. Vehicle components are also the main items shipped on 12,000 square metres of land by the Mylau branch of Schüchen International GmbH & Co KG.

Tradesmen companies have mainly set up business at the Schillerweg business park. The area is also home to the Reichenbach branch of the Vogtland district's adult education centre. Students can attend courses at this further education centre ranging from English for nursery school teachers or yoga and relaxation training, computers and the Internet or even oriental dancing. And the small town of Mylau has even more on offer on the education front. The evangelic grammar school Mylau "FUTURUM Vogtland" has had its domicile at the foot of the castle since January 1, 2007. The responsible body of the grammar school is the evangelic school society Vogtland e. V.. Since the opening day on September 1, 2007, 44 girls and boys have attended this school, which is geared to the curriculum of the country Saxony. The pupils take their general exams in the 10th and respectively in the 12th grade. The Saxon Business Training Centre also trains young people in various trades in Mylau. The training centre for welders, which is well known far beyond the local sphere and is recognised by the German Association for Welding and Linked Procedures (DVS), is housed in the former Thyssen works.

Behr Industry Mylau GmbH is the town's largest employer with about 300 members of staff. Another 80 workers are employed at the Reichenbach subsidiary, Behr Motorradtechnik. The companies make heat exchangers, heating and air-conditioning units or fuel tanks for the automobile, motorcycle and railway industries on behalf of the international Behr Group. GeDaCom provides a wide range of hardware and software, as well as web design services. The "Göltzschtal e.G." fruit juice company has been turned from a part-work fruit juice works into a modern industrial company. The apple juice, which is completely made from 100% freshly pressed fruit, is a sought after product well beyond the borders of the Vogtland region. Companies providing various trades, workshops and shopping centres ensure that there are sufficient goods and services available for local people.

Stadtverwaltung Mylau
Reichenbacher Straße 13
D-08499 Mylau
Telefon   +49 (0) 3765 3850
Telefax   +49 (0) 3765 392808
www.mylau.de
info@mylau.de

(Fotos/Photos by Michael Knabe, Wolfgang Zahn, TSV Vorwärts Mylau)

Gutes für Leib und Seele / Good for Body and Soul

Was gut schmeckt im Vogtland

Wie schmeckt es denn nun im Vogtland? Wirft man einen Blick in die lange Liste der hier beheimateten Nahrungs- und Genussmittelhersteller, so gibt es auf die Frage eigentlich nur eine Antwort: Es schmeckt mindestens so verschieden, wie die Geschmäcker der Menschen in der Region sind.

Im Grunde kann das Vogtland die Vogtländer und ihre Gäste ernähren, abgesehen von exotischen Früchten und Gewürzen oder Wein und Kaffee, die in unseren Breiten nicht wachsen. Die Bauern sorgen für Fleisch, Getreide und Kartoffeln, die als Grundlage für viele vogtländische Gerichte dienen. Die „tolle Knolle" wird nachweislich seit dem Ende des 30-jährigen Krieges angebaut und fand zuerst im Gebiet um den Kapellenberg ihre Verbreitung. Von dort aus begann der Siegeszug ins Vogtland, nach Thüringen und ins Erzgebirge. Die ersten Knollen kamen nach 1647 aus dem fränkischen Pilgramsreuth, heute Ortsteil von Rehau. Es ist also anzunehmen, dass die Vogtländer sich schon von ihrem „Nationalgericht" Bambes oder der Kartoffelsuppe ernährten, lange bevor Friedrich der Große 1756 seinen Propagandafeldzug für die Kartoffel startete. Nicht umsonst sind gerade diese beiden Gerichte in jedem vogtländischen Kochbuch zu finden.

Der Grundsatz „Vom Acker bis zum Teller" wird in der Region mit Leben erfüllt, wobei der Anteil der Betriebe mit Direktvermarktung und Hofladen ständig zunimmt. Einige von ihnen findet man freitags in der Marktscheune Rothenkirchen. Andere haben nur ein Schild mit dem Hinweis auf den Verkauf von Kartoffeln, Eiern oder anderen landwirtschaftlichen Erzeugnissen vor ihrem Bauernhof stehen.

Einen wahren Goldregen gibt es alljährlich bei der Vogtländischen Wurstprüfung, zu der einheimische Fleischermeister Spitzenprodukte vorstellen. 2007 hagelte es elf Mal „Vogtlandgold" und fünf Mal „Vogtlandsilber" für die 16 Variationen von Leberwurst und Salami über Roster bis zum Schinken. Von überregionalen Wurstprüfungen kehren die vogtländischen Fleischermeister regelmäßig mit Trophäen zurück. Gerade die Fleischverarbeitungsbetriebe setzen auf das Vertrauen der Kunden und entwickeln dafür immer neue Angebote. Hoffeste, Tage der offenen Tür oder Besichtigungsmöglichkeiten in Produktionsstätten sind gute Beispiele. Ähnlich wie den Fleischermeistern geht es den Bäckerhandwerksbetrieben, die ihre Produkte jedes Jahr in der Vorweihnachtszeit für die Vogtländische Stollenprüfung anmelden. Begehrter Titel ist der „Stollen-Oscar". Was Weihnachtsspezialitäten aus den Bäckereien angeht, so lassen sich die Meister immer wieder Neues einfallen. Jürgen Schneider aus Neumark bäckt den mit 1,80 Meter längsten Stollen, der dann auf dem Weihnachtsmarkt im Ort für einen guten Zweck verkauft wird. In der Bäckerei Donner in Mylau wurde ein Stollen-Eis kreiert, das sich großer Beliebtheit erfreut.

Für Abwechslung auf dem Speiseplan sorgen Agrarbetriebe wie die „Marienhöher Direktvermarktung", die mit „Vogtlandliebe" eine eigenes Label entwickelt hat, unter dem nicht nur Fleisch und Wurstwaren, sondern auch Käse, Joghurt, Quark und andere Milcherzeugnisse vermarktet werden.

Sowohl für gesunde Säfte als auch für Biere und hochprozentige Tropfen gibt es mehrere Anbieter mit Tradition. Ganze Generationen von Vogtländern wuchsen mit Kinella-Säften auf und greifen auch heute noch nach dieser Marke, wenn es um gesunde Ernährung im Baby- und Kleinkindalter geht. Die 1934 gegründete Ein-Mann-Süßmosterei in Ellefeld entwickelte sich nach der Enteignung und Verstaatlichung in der DDR seit 1991 unter dem Namen Ackermanns Haus Flüssiges Obst GmbH & Co. KG zu einem anerkannten Produzenten von Frucht- und Gemüsesäften sowie Säuglingszusatznahrung.

1984 wurde die Vogtland Kelterei Göltzschtal als reiner Lohnmostbetrieb gegründet. Noch heute herrscht vor allem im Frühherbst Hochzeit auf dem Firmengelände in Mylau oder in den anderen Aufkaufstellen, wenn Hobbygärtner ihre reiche Apfelernte bringen. Der Favorit ist 100-prozentiger, frisch gepresster Apfelsaft. Darüber hinaus produziert die Genossenschaft ein umfassendes Sortiment an Fruchtsäften und Wellness-Getränken.

Vollendete Braukunst verspricht die Wernesgrüner Brauerei, deren Geschichte sich bis ins Jahr 1436 zurückverfolgen lässt. Damit gehört dieser Bierproduzent zu den Firmen mit der längsten Erfahrung bei der Herstellung des Gerstensaftes. Der Werbeslogan „Alles im grünen Bereich" bezieht sich nicht nur auf die Braukunst in ihrer Einheit von Tradition und Moderne, sondern auch auf die vielfältigen Angebote im Brauerei-Gutshof. Die „Wernesgrüner Musikantenschenke", „Rock im Saustall" oder Live-Konzerte mit Stars wie Peter Maffey spielen eine gewichtige Rolle beim erfolgreichen Vormarsch der Pils-Legende.

Genau 150 Jahre am Markt ist die Sternquell-Brauerei Plauen. 1857 wurde der „Aktienbrauverein" im Syratal gegründet. 1995 erfolgte die Auslagerung der kompletten Logistik in das Gewerbegebiet Neuensalz, direkt an der A 72. Gebraut wird bis heute in der Dobenaustraße, wo die erfolgreiche Brauereigeschichte einst begann. „Sternquell" macht auch durch gemeinsame Aktionen mit anderen Partnern auf sich aufmerksam, wie zum Beispiel durch die alljährliche Spielplatzaktion „Gemeinsam geht's besser" mit Brambacher und „Freie Presse".

Wer wie die Vogtländer gern deftig isst, braucht ab und zu auch einen Verdauungsschnaps. Feinster Magenbitter wird seit 1891 nach einem Rezept von Robert Adler hergestellt und als „Adler-Tropfen" verkauft. Im Rittergut Planschwitz kann man den Produzenten über die Schulter schauen und das auch als Medizin bezeichnete Getränk im historischen Laden verkosten. Wenn es beim Vogtländer „E Drecketer" heißt, dann ist damit garantiert kein Schmutzfink gemeint. So nennt der Volksmund einen bekömmlichen Kräuterbitter, der nach Geheimrezeptur ohne Zuckerzusatz aus erlesenen Kräutern, Wurzeln und Gewürzen gemixt wird. Auf dem Etikett steht natürlich „Grün-Bitter", und so sieht er auch aus. Diese Hausmarke hat den Ruf der Firma Zill & Engler in Reichenbach begründet, die seit 1887 auf dem Markt ist.

Gutes für Leib und Seele / Good for Body and Soul

Die beste Instantsuppen-Fabrik in Europa: Das Werk in Auerbach steht für eine fast 65-jährige Tradition der Lebensmittelherstellung. Seit 2001 gehört das Werk Auerbach zu Unilever, welche eine der weltgrößten FMCG Firmen ist. Wegen ihrer hohen Qualität und ihres ausgezeichneten Geschmacks sowie dem hohen Anteil an Gemüse, Pasta, Croutons und Reis, haben es die Auerbacher Produkte geschafft, sich am Markt zu etablieren und Millionen anspruchsvolle und zufriedene Kunden in mehr als 22 Ländern Ost- und Westeuropas für sich zu gewinnen.

Alkohol verdünnt man am besten mit Wasser, und auch hier haben die Vogtländer ihre Stammmarke. Bereits um 1800 wurden in Bad Brambach wild ablaufende Quellen als Erfrischungsgetränk genutzt. Mittlerweile werden unter dem Namen Bad Brambacher außer natürlichen Mineralwassern auch Limonaden, Fruchtsaftschorlen und Säfte angeboten.

Der gesunden Ernährung hat sich die Lebensgarten GmbH verschrieben. Sie gilt deutschlandweit als einziger Hersteller für Reiswaffeln oder -taler mit Schokoladenüberzug in Bioqualität. Auch Dinkelwaffeln oder Müsli-Komponenten verlassen täglich das Werk. Außerdem ist die Firma Zulieferer für andere Marken im Natur- und Reformbereich. Jährlich werden 70 Tonnen Schokolade sowie rund 120 Tonnen Reis verarbeitet und etwa 40 Tonnen Waffeln und Waffelröllchen produziert. Die 2002 auf einem brachliegenden Güterbahnhofsgelände in Adorf errichteten Firmenräume mussten bereits 2005 um zwei Hallen für die Produktion und die Kommissionierung erweitert werden.

Auf gesunde Kost setzt auch die Firma Schlichting in Plauen, die 1882 vom Kaufmann Edmund Schlichting als „Erste Vogtländische Sauerkohlfabrik, Gurkeneinlegerei, Kolonialwaren und Landesprodukte" gegründet wurde. Seitdem gehört das frische vogtländische Sauerkraut aus dem Fass vor allem in der kalten Jahreszeit zu den begehrten Produkten der einheimischen Küche. Ähnlich wie Witwe Bolte bei Wilhelm Buschs „Max und Moritz" schwärmen auch die Vogtländer besonders für die aufgewärmte Variante. Die Tochterfirma GEVEMO GmbH mitten im traditionellen Weißkohlanbaugebiet des Altenburger Landes sorgt dafür, dass frisch geerntetes Weißkraut aus kontrolliertem Anbau verarbeitet werden kann. Schon 1960 begannen die Mitarbeiter, das Sauerkraut in praktische Plastebeutel abzufüllen. Damals waren sie die ersten in der DDR. Heute sind die Abpackungen für Gurken in flexiblen Standbeuteln mit Wiederverschluss ein Markenzeichen der Firma.

In der vogtländischen Welt der Konserven ist ein Unternehmen in Stützengrün aktiv, direkt am Tor zum Erzgebirge. Unter dem Dach und mit dem unverwechselbaren Sammelbegriff „DIE KONSERVEN" werden Marken wie „BWF" (Fertiggerichte), „Metzger Meyer" (Fertiggerichte) und „NP Naturprodukte" (Fertiggerichte) produziert. Rund 150 verschiedene Artikel gehören zum Sortiment. Das 1880 von Gustav Fuchs für die Veredlung von Waldprodukten gegründete Unternehmen wird heute in vierter und fünfter Generation geführt. Die sechste steht bereits in den Startlöchern.

Eher ein Nischenprodukt bietet die Firma Heinrich Karow Nachf. KG aus Plauen an. 1948 begann in dem von Willy Bäume gegründeten Großhandel für Bäckereien und Lebensmittelgeschäfte die Herstellung von Aromen, Pasten und Lebensmittelfarben. Die Firma war stets in privater Hand. Nachfrage und Produktion stiegen kontinuierlich. Schon in den 50er Jahren wurden die heute noch begehrten Orangen- und Zitronenschalenpasten entwickelt. Das Unternehmen setzt auf natürliche und naturidentische Backaromen, Dessertsoßen, Pasten für die Speiseeisherstellung und weitere Produkte für den Bäckereibedarf.

Das Vogtland war einst für seine vielen Mühlen bekannt. Nur wenige produzieren noch Mehl. Die Vogtland-Mühlen sind ein gutes Beispiel. Seit 1276 wird am gleichen Standort in Straßberg Getreide zu Mehl gemahlen. Heute ist vor allem das markenrechtlich geschützte Malfa-Kraftma-Spezial-Brotmehl der Renner unter den Mehlen und Backmischungen.

Vogtländischen Honig kann man auf Märkten, aber auch beim Vogtländischer Imkertag im Freilichtmuseum Landwüst kaufen. Die Fischereigenossenschaft Plauen und viele Teichbesitzer und -pächter sorgen für frischen Fisch.

Viele Vogtländer setzen auf Selbstvermarktung und bauen nach wie vor Obst und Gemüse in ihren Gärten an, wobei der Trend zu alten, in der Region erfolgreichen Sorten wie zum Beispiel dem Safranapfel ungebrochen ist. Allein zum Regionalverband Göltzschtal der Kleingärtner gehören mehr als 160 Kleingartensparten. Regelmäßig stattfindende Ausstellungen der Kleintierzüchter demonstrieren Zuchterfolge bei Kaninchen und Geflügel, wobei die nicht ganz so erfolgreichen Tiere sich hervorragend als Weihnachtsbraten eignen. Hausschlachtene Wurst von Tieren aus der Region und hergestellt von vogtländischen Fleischern kommt frisch und geräuchert vor allem im Herbst und Winter auf den Tisch, während Konserven das ganze Jahr über angeboten werden. Auch die Hausbäckerei von Stollen hat eine lange Tradition. In den Adventswochen bringen viele Familien ihren zuhause gekneteten Stollenteig zum Bäcker und lassen dort ihre Stollen ausbacken.

(Fotos/Photos by Igor Pastierovic, Wernesgrüner Brauerei, Text/Text by Petra Steps)

Gutes für Leib und Seele / Good for Body and Soul

Der Tradition im Vogtland verbunden
Robert Adlers Tropfen – der König unter den Kräuterbittern in der Region

Keeping up Traditions in the Vogtland Region
Robert Adler's Drops – the king among the herbal liqueurs in the region.

Als Medizin galten sie einst, die Magenbitter aus Klosterkellern und Apotheken. Von Genießern werden sie bis heute geschätzt. Auch das Vogtland hat seine Traditionsmarke. Adler-Tropfen haben eine weit über 100-jährige Geschichte. Die Rezeptur des beliebten Kräuterbitters stammt von Robert Adler, der sein Geschäft 1891 in Adorf begründete. Seine „Tropfen" kamen so gut an, dass er damit 1906 in Zwickau die königlich-sächsische Goldmedaille „Friedrich August König von Sachsen" errang. Erneut ausgezeichnet wurden die Adlertropfen 2006 von Prinz Albert von Sachsen auf der 100. WestSachsenschau in Zwickau.

1952 wurde die Produktion aufgrund der damaligen wirtschaftlichen und politischen Verhältnisse eingestellt. Doch etwas Erstaunliches geschah, die Marke blieb über vier Jahrzehnte in Erinnerung. 1997 kehrten die Adler-Tropfen ins Vogtland zurück. Heute wird der Magenbitter von Frank Felberg hergestellt, als einziger noch in handwerklicher Tradition. 2006 zog die Produktionsstätte der Adler-Tropfen in das sanierte Rittergutsgebäude von Planschwitz.

Die Rezeptur des Kräuterbitters ist geheim. Nur soviel verrät der Hersteller, dass die Spirituose nicht destilliert wird, sondern aus Kräutern und Wurzeln extrahiert. Bei immer mehr Kennern und Genießern finden Adler-Tropfen Anklang. Dazu tragen auch die hochwertigen Etiketten bei.

Als vogtländisches Markenprodukt ist der Magenbitter als typisches Souvenir bei den Urlaubern beliebt und wird von den Lokalpolitikern bei offiziellen Anlässen Gästen gern als Geschenk überreicht. Zu kaufen gibt es den Magenbitter in der Hauptverkaufsstelle im Getränkemarkt am Oelsnitzer Stadion. Im Verkaufsraum des Ritterguts mit dem Flair eines Kolonialwarenladens und im weitläufigen, aufwändig restaurierten Gewölbe des Rittergutes können Adler-Tropfen und dazu noch edle Weine verkostet werden. Das Gewölbe mit seinen 300 Quadratmetern Fläche kann für Feiern und Geschäftspräsentationen gemietet werden.

The bitter cordials from monasteries and chemist's shops were once viewed as medicine. They are still appreciated by connoisseurs today. And the Vogtland region has its own special brand too. The history of Adler Drops goes back far more than a century. The recipe for the popular herbal liqueur comes from Robert Adler, who opened his shop in Adorf in 1891. His "drops" were such a hit that he won the "Friedrich August King of Saxony" gold medal in Zwickau in 1906 for his product. The Adler Drops won an award again in 2006 presented by Prince Albert of Saxony at the 100th West Saxon Show in Zwickau.

Production was halted in 1952 on account of the economic and political circumstances at the time. But something amazing occurred – people did not forget the brand name during the four intervening decades. The Adler Drops returned to the Vogtland region again in 1997. The bitter cordial is made by Frank Felberg today – he is the only one upholding this craftsman's tradition. The production site for Adler Drops was moved into the redeveloped manor building in Planschwitz in 2006.

The recipe for the herbal liqueur is a secret. The manufacturer will only reveal that the spirit is not distilled, but is extracted from herbs and roots. Adler Drops are becoming more and more popular with connoisseurs and gourmets. The high-quality labels play their part in this.

The bitter cordial is popular as a Vogtland region souvenir with holiday-makers and local politicians are happy to pass it on as a gift at official occasions. The bitter cordial can be bought at the main sales point in the drinks market by the stadium in Oelsnitz. Adler Drops and other high-class wines can be tasted in the sales room in the manor house, which has the flair of an old grocer's shop, and in the manor's spacious and elaborately restored vaults. The vaults, which cover an area measuring 300 square metres, can be hired for celebrations or business presentations.

Fa. Adler-Tropfen · Inhaber Frank Felberg
Altes Rittergut · Kirchpöhlweg 1–3
08606 Oelsnitz OT Planschwitz
Telefon/Fax 037421 26833
www.adler-tropfen.de

(Fotos/Photos by Igor Pastierovic, Text/Text by Renate Wöllner, Übersetzung/Translated by David Strauss)

Über 570 Jahre Brautradition
More than 570 Years of Brewing Tradition

Die erfolgreiche Pils Legende mit Jahrhunderte langer Brautradition

Im Jahre 1436 wurde in Wernesgrün den Brüdern Schorer das Braurecht verliehen und damit der Grundstein für eine der ältesten Brauereien der Welt gelegt. Deren Erfolgsgeschichte hat Wernesgrün weit über die Grenzen Deutschlands bekannt gemacht. Über die Jahrhunderte hinweg eroberte das Pils die Sympathien zahlreicher Bierfreunde in Deutschland und sogar in Übersee. Mittlerweile ist die Wernesgrüner Brauerei eine der bekanntesten und erfolgreichsten Brauereien in den Neuen Bundesländern. Auch international ist die Pils Legende beliebt und bereits auf vier Kontinenten erhältlich.

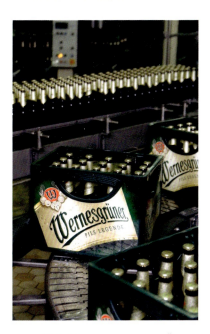

Doch was hat Wernesgrüner eigentlich zur Pils Legende gemacht? Die besondere Premiumqualität verbunden mit dem einzigartigen Geschmack wissen Pilsgenießer zu schätzen. Sie beruht auf der Verwendung erlesenster Zutaten und dem besonderen Wasser aus den Höhen des Naturparks Erzgebirge-Vogtland. Die jahrhundertlange Brauerfahrung trägt natürlich auch ihren Teil zur beständigen Qualität des legendären Biers bei. Doch Wernesgrüner bietet mehr als nur klassischen Pilsgenuss. Nach erfolgreicher Einführung von Wernesgrüner Lemon erfreut sich die Pils Legende auch als fruchtig-frischer Biermix wachsender Beliebtheit. In Ostdeutschland zählt Wernesgrüner Lemon mittlerweile zu den Top-Marken im Segment der Lemon- und Radlerprodukte.

Auch wenn Wernesgrüner inzwischen im deutschen Pilsmarkt fest verankert ist, vergisst die Brauerei nicht, wo ihre Wurzeln liegen. Als Sponsor für den Reitsport, für den sächsischen Landessportbund und Fußballverband sowie einer Vielzahl sächsischer Vereine ist sie insbesondere in der direkten Nachbarschaft aktiv und auch Partner der Vogtland-Arena. Zudem holte die Pils Legende schon viele bekannte Musiker nach Sachsen. Nationale und internationale Stars der Pop-, Rock-, Country- und Volksmusik geben im historischen Wernesgrüner Brauerei-Gutshof regelmäßig umjubelte Auftritte. Die Pils Legende konnte für die Konzerte bereits Stars wie Sasha, Christina Stürmer und Peter Maffay gewinnen.

Informationen zu Veranstaltungen/
Information on events:
Telefon   +49 (0) 37462 61-7399

The successful pils legend with centuries of brewing tradition

The Schorer brothers were given to right to brew beer in Wernesgrün in 1436 and this laid the foundation for one of the oldest breweries in the world. This success story has made the name Wernesgrün famous far beyond the borders of Germany. Down through the years this pils has captured the hearts of many beer fans in Germany and overseas. The Wernesgrüner brewery is now one of the best known and most successful in Eastern Germany. The pils legend is also popular internationally and is available on four continents.

But what has made Wernesgrüner beer into a pils legend? Pils lovers enjoy its special premium quality coupled with its unique flavour. This is because the most select ingredients and special water from the mountains in the Ore Mountains/Vogtland National Park are used. Centuries of brewing experience also contribute to the consistent quality of this legendary beer. But Wernesgrüner beer provides more than normal pils enjoyment. After the successful introduction of Wernesgrüner Lemon, the legendary pils is also becoming increasingly popular as a fruity, refreshing mixed drink. Wernesgrüner Lemon is now one of the top brands in the lemon and shandy product sector in Eastern Germany.

Even if Wernesgrüner is now a permanent part of the German pils market, the brewery has not forgotten where its roots lie. It is actively involved in local events, whether as a sponsor for riding sports, the Saxon State Sports Association and Football Association or a number of Saxon clubs - and it is also a partner of the Vogtland Arena. The pils legend has also attracted many musicians to Saxony. Domestic and international stars in the pop, rock, country and folk music scenes regularly give performances that are cheered in the Wernesgrüner Brewery Estate. The pils legend has been able to attract stars like Sasha, Christina Stürmer and Peter Maffay for concerts.

Wernesgrüner Brauerei
Bergstraße 4 · D-08237 Wernesgrün
Telefon   +49 (0) 37462 61-0
Telefax   +49 (0) 37462 61-7383
info@wernesgruener.de
www.wernesgruener.de

(Fotos/Photos by Wernesgrüner Brauerei, Übersetzung/Translated by David Strauss)

Unilever Deutschland GmbH & Co. OHG Werk Auerbach

Die beste Instantsuppen-Fabrik in Europa

The Best Instant Soup Factory in Europe

Das Werk Auerbach steht für eine fast 65-jährige Tradition der Lebensmittelherstellung. Nach vielen turbulenten Jahren und Veränderungen ist das Werk Auerbach 2004 schließlich zu einer hoch spezialisierten und effektiven Suppenproduktionsstätte geworden. Seit 2001 gehört das Werk Auerbach zu Unilever, welche eine der weltgrößten FMCG Firmen ist.

Wegen ihrer hohen Qualität und ihres ausgezeichneten Geschmacks sowie dem hohen Anteil an Gemüse, Pasta, Croutons und Reis, haben es die Auerbacher Produkte geschafft sich am Markt zu etablieren und Millionen anspruchsvolle und zufriedene Kunden in mehr als 22 Ländern Ost- und Westeuropas für sich zu gewinnen.

Das sehr gute Image des Werkes Auerbach resultiert aus der Kombination ausgezeichneter Produkte mit hoch automatisierten Produktionsmaschinen und einem überdurchschnittlich motivierten und sehr gut ausgebildeten Team. Besonders engagiert sich das Werksmanagement für die Entwicklung aller Mitarbeiter, und so wurde ein mitarbeiterfreundliches Arbeitsklima mit ausgezeichneten Arbeitsbedingungen geschaffen. Die Werksmitarbeiter sind der Schlüssel zum Erfolg der Fabrik. Gegenwärtig beschäftigt das Werk Auerbach 220 Mitarbeiter, davon 12 Auszubildende, welche in fünf verschiedenen Berufsbildern geschult werden. Dieses großartige Team hat kontinuierlich dazu beigetragen, seine Fabrik in ein Werk mit höheren Standards und ausgezeichneten hygienischen Bedingungen bei vertretbaren Kosten umzuwandeln.

Aufgrund der Produktion einer Vielzahl verschiedener Produkte für viele Länder um die Bedürfnisse der verschiedenen Kunden zu erfüllen, ist die Produktion im Werk Auerbach sehr komplex.

Daraus resultiert die Einlagerung von 750 Komponenten, welche für die Produktion von 700 Artikeln für die weltbekannten Marken Knorr und Unox und die Sub-Marken Spaghetteria und Croutinos benötigt werden.

Alle Mitarbeiter nehmen an einem sehr umfassenden Entwicklungsprogramm namens TPM (Total Production Management) teil, welches Verbesserungen forciert und jedem einzelnen Mitarbeiter ein Stück Verantwortung für die Weiterentwicklung des Werkes überträgt. Während der letzten fünf Jahre wurden diese Fortschritte, Errungenschaften und großartigen Resultate zweimal von JIPM (Japanese Institute of Planned Maintenance) ausgezeichnet. 2003 war das Werk Auerbach das erste Knorr-Werk weltweit, welches den TPM Excellence Award in Japan entgegennehmen konnte. 2005 erhielt das Werk Auerbach den zweiten TPM Consistent Award. Im Oktober 2007 fand nun das Abschlussaudit von JIPM für den dritten Special Award statt. Alle diese Preise beweisen, dass Auerbach sich erfolgreich am Markt etabliert hat und seine starke Position in der ersten Liga der Lebensmittel produzierenden Unternehmen behaupten kann. Das Motto des Werkes spricht für sich: „Wir wollen das beste Instantsuppenwerk in Europa für unsere Kunden sein."

The factory Auerbach stands for an almost 65-year-long tradition of producing food. After a very turbulent history of many changes and modifications, the factory has finally been transformed into a highly specialized and efficient soup producing plant in 2004. Since 2001 the Auerbach factory has belonged to Unilever which is one of the biggest global FMCG companies.

Due to its high quality and excellent taste, the high content of vegetables and a lot of other components such as pastas, croutons and rice, the Auerbach products have finally managed to establish themselves on the market and gained millions of demanding and satisfied customers in more than 22 countries in Western as well as Eastern Europe.

The combination of very good products with highly automated production equipment and an excellently motivated and well-skilled factory team results in a very good image of the factory. The factory management takes very good care of the development of all the employees and has created an employee-friendly environment with excellent working conditions. The factory staff is the key to the success of the plant. The Auerbach factory is currently employing 220 people, 12 of them being apprentices who are trained in 5 different areas. This great team has continuously been contributing to transforming its factory into one of higher standards and an excellent hygienic environment at appropriate costs.

Producing so many different products for so many different countries and trying to meet the needs of so many different customers lead to a high complexity of the Auerbach plant. This results in more than 750 components, which have to be stored and are used to produce almost 700 finished products of the very well known brands Knorr and Unox and the sub-brands Spaghetteria & Croutinos.

All the employees are involved in a comprehensive program called TPM (Total Production Management) which enforces improvements and hands over some responsibility for the factory's development to every employee. During the last five years those efforts, achievements and great results have been awarded by JIPM (Japanese Institute of Planned Maintenance) twice. In 2003 Auerbach was the first Knorr plant world-wide to receive the TPM Excellence Award in Japan. In 2005, the plant received the second TPM Consistent Award. The final audit provided by JIPM for the third Special Award was carried trough in October 2007.

All those awards prove that Auerbach has established and asserted its strong position in the very first league of food-producing factories.

The factory motto speaks for itself: "We want to be the best instant soup factory in Europe for our customers!"

Unilever Deutschland Produktions GmbH & Co. OHG
Werk Auerbach
Dr.-Wilhelm-Külz-Straße 21
D - 08209 Auerbach/V.
Telefon +49 (0) 3744 257-0
Telefax +49 (0) 3744 257-220
info@unilever.com
www.unilever.de

Sensibel, modern, verantwortungsbewusst – Landwirtschaft im Vogtland
Sensitive, Modern, Responsible – Agriculture in the Vogtland Region

Die Landwirte im Vogtland fühlen sich ihrer Heimat mit ihren reizvollen Landstrichen besonders verpflichtet. Neben der landwirtschaftlichen Produktion geht es ihnen vor allem darum, das ihnen anvertraute Acker- und Grünland bodenschonend und umweltverträglich zu bewirtschaften. Besonders die Landwirte aus Markneukirchen, die sich in der „Agrarprodukte Direktvermarktung Oberes Vogtland" GmbH zusammengeschlossen haben, versuchen dabei stets die neuesten wissenschaftlichen Erkenntnisse und Verfahren anzuwenden. So produzieren sie Braugerste, Keks- und Brauweizen, aber auch Raps und Leguminosen nach umweltgerechten Anbauverfahren. Der Raps deckt dabei den Bedarf an eigenem Biodiesel, der im vogtländischen Großfriesen hergestellt wird. Die direkten Kontakte zu Mühlen und Mälzern aus dem benachbarten Franken und Thüringen garantieren dabei eine ständige Qualitätskontrolle der heimischen Produkte. Seit 2007 stellen die Landwirtschaftsbetriebe der Kooperation, deren größter Betrieb die Agro-Dienst-Marktfrucht GmbH ist, ihre gesamte Tierproduktion auf die Bioproduktion um. Noch 2007 erfolgt für das Grünland die ökologische Zertifizierung und Anerkennung. Dies ist wieder ein Schritt mehr, den Kundenwünschen gerecht zu werden. Alle produzierten Tiere der Kooperation werden in Jacob's Bauernmarkt verarbeitet und vermarktet. Damit wird den Kunden eine stets gleich bleibend hohe Qualität an stets frischen und ökologisch hergestellten Produkten garantiert. Auch in vielen Hotels und Gaststätten hat sich mittlerweile herumgesprochen, dass man mit den Qualitätsprodukten der vogtländischen Landwirte bei den Gästen und Touristen unserer Heimat gut ankommt. Somit sind die von den vogtländischen Bauern initiierten regionalen Kreisläufe mit Leben gefüllt. Sie garantieren eine umweltgerechte und biologische Landbewirtschaftung und Tierhaltung und tragen so zum Vertrauen der Bevölkerung in die heimische Landwirtschaft und deren anschließende Verarbeitung bei. Ein Grund mehr für unsere Bauern, auf ihren Beruf stolz zu sein.

Farmers in the Vogtland region feel particularly committed to their beautiful countryside. They not only want to achieve high agricultural yields, but also use the farmland and grasslands in an environmentally-friendly manner without damaging the soil. The farmers in Markneukirchen, who have joined forces in what is known as the "Upper Vogtland Agricultural Products Direct Marketing Company" are trying to use the latest scientific knowledge and procedures. They grow malt barley, wheat for bread and beverages, rape seed and legumes using environmentally-friendly methods. The rape seed is used to provide biodiesel for the farmers' own use and it is produced in Grossfriesen in the Vogtland district. Direct contacts with mills and maltsters in Franconia and Thuringia guarantee that local products are subject to constant quality controls. The farms in the cooperative, whose largest farm is Agro-Dienst-Markt GmbH, switched their complete livestock faming to organic methods in 2007. Organic certification and recognition was also granted in 2007. This is another step towards meeting customer demands. All the animals on the cooperative are processed and marketed at Jacob's farmers' market. This guarantees customers consistently high quality for fresh, organic products. Word is spreading at many hotels and restaurants – they realise that customers enjoy high-quality natural products from Vogtland farmers. So the regional supply chains started by Vogtland farmers are working well. They guarantee organic farming and livestock keeping and are increasing people's sense of confidence in local agriculture and its products. This is just another reason for farmers to be proud of their job.

Damwildhaltung

Getreideernte

Umweltverträglicher Pflanzenschutz

Produktion von Qualitätslammfleisch

Artgerechte Schweinemast

Vogtländisches Rotvieh – Erhaltung genetischer Ressourcen

Moderne Aussaat

Grünlandpflege

Einsatz modernster GPS-Technik

Agro-Dienst-Marktfrucht GmbH
Inhaber Reimund und Siegbert Jacob
An der Papiermühle 1
D - 08258 Markneukirchen
Telefon +49 (0) 37422 558-0
Telefax +49 (0) 37422 558-10
adm@agrodienst.de · www.agrodienst.de

(Fotos/Photos by Ralf Jakob, Harald Sulski [1], Text/Text by Ralf Jakob, Übersetzung/Translated by David Strauss)

Jacob's Bauernmarkt

Vom Bauern direkt - das schmeckt

Direct from the Farm – with a Great Taste

Die Landfleischerei in Ihrer Nähe!

Neben der reizvollen Landschaft und einer bewegten Geschichte hat das Vogtland auch kulinarisch einiges zu bieten, so zum Beispiel in Markneukirchen bei der Landfleischerei Jacob's Bauernmarkt. Nach traditionellen Rezepten werden hier noch von Meisterhand beste Fleisch- und Wurstwaren hergestellt und in der Region vermarktet. Bei der Produktion arbeiten alle Hand in Hand, vom 76jährigen Meister, bis zu den Lehrlingen, die hier das Fleischerhandwerk erlernen und die Erfahrungen aus vielen Jahrzehnten Berufstätigkeit vermittelt bekommen.

Die Schlachttiere stammen ausschließlich aus eigener Produktion oder von Vertragsbauern aus dem Vogtland und werden vor Ort geschlachtet und verarbeitet. Dadurch wird Transparenz für den Kunden geschaffen und die tägliche Frische der Ware garantiert, die in den insgesamt vier Filialen und auf den Wochenmärkten des oberen Vogtlandes verkauft wird. Zusätzlich wird ein täglich wechselndes Mittagsmenü angeboten. Der Partyservice richtet kleine und große Feiern aus und bietet vom belegten Brötchen bis zum Buffet für 1000 Personen die optimale Lösung für jede Veranstaltung. Auch werden zahlreiche Gaststätten des Vogtlandes von Jacob's Bauernmarkt beliefert, so etwa das Landhotel Lindenhöhe in Erlbach (www.landhotel-lindenhoehe.de).

Neben Schweinen und Rindern wird auch Damwild und frisches Weidelamm aus eigener Aufzucht geschlachtet, das vor allem um Ostern und Weihnachten sehr gefragt ist. Um der gestiegenen Nachfrage gerecht zu werden, wird ab 2008 noch Rind- und Lammfleisch aus rein biologischer Aufzucht angeboten.

Adorfer Straße 65
08258 Markneukirchen
Telefon 037422 6111
Telefax 037422 558-10

Markt 6
08626 Adorf
Telefon 037423 788113

Johann-Christoph-Hilf-Str. 1
08645 Bad Elster
Telefon 037437 48001

Hauptstraße 621
08261 Schöneck
Telefon 037464 33758

Wochenmärkte
Erlbach: Do
14.00-17.00 Uhr
Oelsnitz: Fr
08.00-14.00 Uhr

Wochenmärkte
Klingenthal: Mi
08.00-12.00 Uhr
Grünbach: Do
09.00-13.00 Uhr

Freundliches Verkaufspersonal sorgt für optimale Kundennähe

Traditionelles Handwerk in modernster Umgebung

Besonders beliebt: Catering zu großen und kleinen Events -

The Vogtland region not only provides people with beautiful countryside and a rich history, it also has special dishes – found, for example, at Jacob's country butcher's in Markneukirchen. Meat dishes and sausages are still made here by master butchers and are then marketed in the region. Everybody pulls their weight, from the 76-year-old master butcher down to the trainees, who are learning their trade and gaining experience from those with more years under their belt.

The meat only comes from Jacob's own farm or other local farmers in the region. The animals are slaughtered on the spot and then processed. This provides customers with transparency and guarantees that goods sold in the four branches and at markets in the Upper Vogtland area are fresh every day. The shop also offers a special lunch menu, which changes every day. The party service arranges small and large celebrations and provides the ideal solution for any kind of event ranging from filled rolls to a buffet for 1,000 people. Jacob's farming market supplies many restaurants in the Vogtland area, including the Lindenhöhe Hotel in Erlbach (www.landhotel-lindenhoehe.de).

The business slaughters pigs and beef cattle, deer and fresh lamb from its own farms. The latter are particularly in demand at Easter and Christmas. Organic beef and lamb will be available from 2008 onwards to satisfy the increase in demand.

(Fotos/Photos by Christian Passon ,Text/Text by Christian Passon)

Ein Ort der Bildung, Begegnung & Entspannung

A place of Education, Encounters & Recreation

Der Gläserne Bauernhof Vogtland e. V.

In Mitten des reizvollen Tales des Ebersbachs im Poetenwald an den Fischteichen in Markneukirchen OT Siebenbrunn befindet sich der Gläserne Bauernhof. Hier findet der Besucher seine verdiente Ruhe, kann sich entspannen und ganz nebenbei auch noch viel Wissenswertes über die Natur erfahren. Die Vereinsmitglieder wollen mit Ihrer Arbeit allen Naturfreunden die Möglichkeit bieten, die Kreisläufe in der Natur und die Produktionsweise einer integrierten Landwirtschaft verstehen zu lernen und sich zu einer Vielzahl anderer naturnaher Themen zu informieren. Darüber hinaus bietet der Verein über das Jahr verschiedene kulturelle Veranstaltungen zu den verschiedensten Anlässen an. Musik und Spaß für Groß und Klein sollen so auf dem Hof nicht zu kurz kommen.

Freizeitangebote

Rundwanderwege laden zum Erkunden der näheren Umgebung ein, Gondeln, mit Tieren auf Du und Du stehen, Angeln, Lagerfeuerromantik genießen – all das und vieles mehr kann man auf dem Hof erleben. Und da sich an der frischen Luft bekanntlich der Appetit auf eine zünftige Mahlzeit von ganz allein einstellt, werden im neu errichteten Bildungs- und Begegnungszentrum frischer Fisch und viele andere vogtländische Spezialitäten angeboten. Wollen Sie zünftig feiern und dabei die Natur genießen, dann ist der Verein Ihr Partner – Kinderfeste, Filmvorführungen, Betriebsfeiern oder Ihre ganz private Party – es wird alles getan werden, um Sie rund herum zufrieden zu stellen. Auch für Senioren ist das Begegnungszentrum geeignet, um einen gemütlichen Nachmittag mit gutem Essen und Musik zu erleben.

Mit Spaß von & in der Natur lernen

Besonders Kinder liegen dem Verein am Herzen: Er hilft bei einer sinnvollen Freizeitgestaltung, organisiert den nächsten Projekttag und fördert das Verständnis für die Natur bei unseren Jüngsten. Ferienspiele in der Natur – so machen Ferien Spaß: Musik und Natur erleben, der Natur die Klänge ablauschen, den Wald erkunden, einen Schultag in der Natur verbringen, mit den Kleinsten den Hühnern beim Eierlegen zusehen, Wissenswertes über Fische erfahren, mit Naturmaterialien Musikinstrumente basteln, etwas über die gesunde Ernährung erfahren und vieles mehr. Gemeinsam mit den Erziehern wird ein passendes Programm zusammengestellt – und das zu kinderfreundlichen Preisen.

The Vogtland Transparent Farm Association

The transparent farm is situated in the middle of the beautiful valley of Ebersbach in the Poets' Forest by the fish ponds in the Markneukirchen district of Siebenbrunn. Visitors will find plenty of peace and quiet, relaxation and a wealth of information about the natural surroundings. The members of the association aim to help nature lovers understand natural cycles, production methods at integrated farms and provide information on a number of other subjects related to nature. The association also puts on various cultural events during the year. So people of all ages can enjoy plenty of fun and music at the farm.

Leisure time activities

There is plenty to enjoy on the farm – circular trails allow people to explore the surroundings, there are gondolas, visitors can get close to the animals, fish or enjoy the romantic atmosphere round a campfire. And as people's appetites for a hearty meal are automatically stimulated by the fresh air, fresh fish and other Vogtland specialities are available in the newly built education and meeting centre. If you want to celebrate in style and enjoy natural surroundings at the same time, this association is just the place for children's parties, cinema shows, works parties or your very private occasion. Everything will be done to make you feel at home. The meeting centre is also suitable for the elderly to enjoy a pleasant afternoon with good food and music.

Learning about nature in natural surroundings – and having fun

Children have a special place in the association's heart. It helps provide meaningful leisure pursuits, organises project days and helps young people learn more about nature. Wide games in natural surroundings make holidays a great deal of fun: experiencing music and nature, listening to natural sounds, exploring a forest, spending a school day out in the open, watching hens lay their eggs, finding out all about fish, making musical instruments from natural materials or learning something about healthy food and much more. The centre organises the programme in conjunction with the teachers – and it all comes at affordable prices.

Gläserner Bauernhof Vogtland e. V.
Breitenfelder Straße
D - 08258 Markneukirchen
Telefon +49 (0) 37422 74759
Handy +49 (0) 171 4498294
adm@agrodienst.de
www.landschule.de

(Fotos/Photos by Ralf Jakob ,Text/Text by Ralf Jakob)

Landwirtschaft/Farming

Landwirtschaft ist unser Leben.
FARMING IS OUR LIFE

Selbst wenn die Region des Vogtlandes vom Ertragswert des Bodens, von den klimatischen Bedingungen und zum Teil auch von der Höhenlage eher als für die Landwirtschaft benachteiligte Region einzustufen ist, so ist es den Landwirten über Generationen hinweg gelungen, durch kluges Handeln eine effiziente Landwirtschaft zu betreiben, das natürliche Umfeld als Lebens- und Ernährungsgrundlage der Bevölkerung zu bewahren und dies auch für die zukünftige Generation zu sichern. Die Landwirte haben es verstanden, sich mit den Nachteilen der Region zu arrangieren und insbesondere die Vorzüge dieses reizvollen Landstrichs in den Dienst der Sache zu stellen.

Heute stellen die etwa 1100 Landwirtschaftsbetriebe in verschiedenen Rechts- und Bewirtschaftungsformen einen bedeutenden Wirtschaftsfaktor der Region dar. Die Landwirtinnen und Landwirte haben sich den gesellschaftlichen und wirtschaftlichen Wandlungen sowie den Erfordernissen der Zeit und der Region in ihrer internen Betriebsstrukturierung angepasst. Aus heutiger Sicht bedeutet dies, dass die Betriebe neben pflanzlicher und tierischer Produktion bereits neue, zusätzliche Betätigungsfelder gefunden haben und sich die Beschäftigten dieser Branche insgesamt im ländlichen Raum zukünftig noch sehr viel mehr und verschiedenartiger engagieren werden. Nicht zuletzt wegen dieser neuen, alternativen Leistungen – wie man es zum Beispiel durch Urlaubs- und Kinderangebote oder Dienstleistungen im Umweltbereich zur Kenntnis nehmen kann – werden sie von der gesamten Bevölkerung, den Besuchern und Gästen des Vogtlandes nicht mehr nur als Erzeuger pflanzlicher und tierischer Produkte wahrgenommen sondern als Betriebe und Betriebsleiter mit besonderer, beispielloser und interessanter Ausrichtung.

Dennoch: Ackerbau, Futterbau und Viehhaltung sind die typischen traditionellen und auch zukünftig wichtigsten Produktionsrichtungen der vogtländischen Bauern. Unter diesen natürlichen Gegebenheiten der sanften Hügellandschaft mit einem Höhenunterschied von 250 bis über 900 Meter und einer Jahresdurchschnittstemperatur von 6,4° C erreichen die Landwirte Spitzenleistungen in den Ställen und auf den etwa 56.000 Hektar landwirtschaftlicher Nutzfläche.

Even though the Vogtland region has to live with relatively low yields, the effect of the climate and in part the problems of farming on high ground – all of which makes it a tough area to farm – generations of farmers have been successful as a result of their business prowess; they have retained the natural environment as a source of livelihood and food production for people and have ensured that the next generation will be able to continue the process. Farmers have understood not only how to come to terms with the disadvantages of the region, but also make full use of this delightful area.

The 1100 farms or so operating in varying types of farming and legal structures are now an important economic factor. The farmers have adapted to the changes in business and farming structures as well as the demands of the current time and the region. From today's perspective, it means that the farms have discovered new types of business, in addition to crop production and husbandry, and the employees will have to dedicate far more time and attention to these in future. As a result of these new, alternative services – for example, providing holidays or children's attractions, or actively engaging in environmental issues – farms are not only viewed by the local population, visitors and guests as producers of plant and animal products, but also as companies and company managers with a special, unique and interesting focus.

But arable farming, producing animal feedstuffs and cattle farming are the typical traditional practices and they will also be the most important types of farming in the Vogtland region in future. Given the natural conditions of rolling hills with an altitude varying from 250 to 900 metres and an average annual temperature of 6.4 degrees centigrade, farmers produce amazing results not only in the farm buildings, but also on the 56,000 hectares of useable land.

(Fotos/Photos by Staatliches Amt für Landwirtschaft, Text/Text by Staatliches Amt für Landwirtschaft, Übersetzung/Translated by David Strauss)

Landwirtschaft/Farming

Gerste, vorwiegend als Braugerste mit Spitzenqualität, weitere Getreidearten, Ölfrüchte wie Raps aber auch Mais und Grünland als wichtige Futterpflanze für die Rinderhaltung und Kartoffeln für den Eigenbedarf sind nachhaltig etabliert.

Leistungsstarke Viehherden, insbesondere hochleistungsfähiges Milchvieh, sind zu Recht der Stolz vieler Landwirte. Die Herdenführung sowie das gesamte betriebliche Management erfolgen nach dem Höchststand von Wissenschaft und Technik.

Der weithin mögliche Blick auf moderne Stallungen, neu- oder umgebaute bzw. umgenutzte Gebäude ergänzt die Erkenntnis vom Erfolg des Bemühens zur Bewahrung des landwirtschaftlich-kulturellen Erbes über die Generationen hinweg und für die Zukunft.

Gepflegte Felder, Wiesen, Weiden und Wälder verleihen dem Besucher wie dem Einheimischen oder auch dem Durchreisenden zu allen vier Jahreszeiten den Wunsch des Seins und Bleibens in dieser Region.

Für ihre verantwortungsvolle und umweltgerechte Landbewirtschaftung, für ihr Engagement zum Erhalt von Umwelt und Landschaft erhalten die Landwirte einen finanziellen Ausgleich von Land, Bund und der europäischer Union.

Viel Neues entdeckt man heute in den Gemeinden. Aber man stößt auch durchaus auf notwendig zu Ergänzendes. So ist es in den kommenden Jahren ein dringendes Gebot, dass sich der ländliche Raum als Gesamtensemble weiter entwickelt. Viele Mitwirkende und zahlreiche wirtschaftliche Ansätze hat dieses Gebot bereits. Ihm wird sich auch die Landwirtschaft nicht entziehen. So erfreut sich bereits heute die direkte Vermarktung landwirtschaftlicher Erzeugnisse bzw. auch die erste Verarbeitung dieser sowie die Schaffung von Verkaufsmärkten und Verkaufsstellen – oft auch in historischem Ambiente – immer stärkerer Beliebtheit bei Gästen und bei der einheimischen Bevölkerung.

Die landwirtschaftlichen Betriebe sind ebenfalls bereit für neue Produktionszweige in ihren Betrieben. So ist die Ressourcen schonende Erzeugung von Energie aus Biostoffen längst etabliert.

Die Vielfalt zukünftiger Einkommensalternativen bestimmen aber letztendlich die Landwirte selbst. Für den Beobachter und Besucher bleibt damit ein bisschen Spannung auf die Zukunft bestehen.

Der hohe Bildungsstand der Landwirte, ihre Bodenständigkeit und ihr sicheres, von den Altvorderen übernommenes Gefühl für den Einklang zwischen Wirtschaftlichkeit und den Erfordernissen, die die Erhaltung der natürlichen Gegebenheiten ihnen abverlangen, sind Garant für die Bewahrung der Landwirtschaft und die weitere Mitgestaltung dieser Region und den Erhalt der besonderen Reize des Vogtlandes.

The well established crops include barley, mainly used for high-quality beer, other cereals, oil crops such as rape seed, and also corn and grassland, which are important for feeding cattle, and potatoes for human consumption.

Many farmers are justifiably proud of their high-quality cattle and especially their cows, which produce high yields of milk. Herd and farm management is carried out using the latest knowledge from the worlds of science and technology.

Modern stables, both new or those that have been modernised or adapted from unused farm buildings, demonstrate the success and care that has gone into preserving the heritage of the farming culture over generations and for the future.

Fields, meadows and woods, which are well cared for, give both visitors to the region and those who live there and even those who are just passing through the desire to stay longer, whatever the time of year.

Farmers receive financial compensation from the state, central German government and the European Union for their responsible attitude and environmentally-friendly farming methods and their commitment to maintain the environment and countryside.

There are plenty of new things to discover in communities, but there are also things that still require a lot of attention. It is essential that rural areas are developed as a whole over the next few years. Many of those involved have made suggestions and economic approaches have been proposed. Agriculture will not be able to escape this process. The direct marketing of agricultural products and the initial processing of these or the creation of sales markets and sales points – often in an historical setting – are becoming more and more popular with visitors and the local population. Agricultural businesses are ready for new production methods. It has long been possible to harness energy from organic sources. But the farmers themselves are the ones who will determine which of the many future sources of income should be exploited. So observers and visitors will have to hold their breath with regard to what is going to happen in future.

The high standard of training of farmers, their down-to-earth approach and their positive sense adopted from their forefathers to harmonise economic requirements and the need to preserve the natural surroundings guarantee that agriculture will survive and continue to shape the area and maintain the treasures of the Vogtland region.

Staatliches Amt für Landwirtschaft mit Fachschule für Landwirtschaft Plauen
Europaratstr. 7 · 08523 Plauen
Telefon +49 (0) 3741 103100
Telefax +49 (0) 3741 103140
poststelle.afl01@smul.sachsen.de
www.landwirtschaft.sachsen.de/afl/plauen

Guter Geschmack aus Tradition

A Great Traditional Taste

Wenn am Sonnabend die frischen Brötchen auf dem Tisch durften, der Kaffee in der Tasse dampft und der Familienvorstand zur Zeitung greift, dann denkt keiner daran, wie viel Arbeit notwendig war, damit all das zum Frühstück bereitsteht. Nehmen wir zum Beispiel die Brötchen. Erst muss das Feld bestellt, das Korn gesät, das Getreide geerntet und gedroschen werden. Kaum hat der Bauer die Ernte eingeholt, steht der Müller auf dem Hof und prüft, ob die Qualität seinen Ansprüchen gerecht wird. Einer, der noch auf Tradition setzt, ist Müllermeister Dietrich Klopfer aus Lengenfeld. Gemeinsam mit Sohn Michael betreibt er seit 1990 die letzte Wassermühle im Vogtland – 45 soll es einst an der Göltzsch gegeben haben. Damit müsste schon die fünfte Klopfer-Generation dem Beruf nach eigentlich Müller heißen, denn am 16. Juni 1863 übernahm Christian Gotthilf Klopfer, der Urgroßvater von Dietrich Klopfer, die Mahleinrichtung. Dessen Sohn mit gleichem Namen führte sie von 1899 bis 1952 und übergab alles an seinen Sohn Franz Gotthilf Klopfer.

Die denkmalgeschützte Mühle ist wesentlich älter. Erstmals urkundlich erwähnt wurde sie als „Hoyersmühle" im Jahre 1438. In den Jahren 1531, 1576 und 1722 waren die Mühlenbesitzer die größten Steuerzahler in Lengenfeld. Von so etwas wagt Dietrich Klopfer nicht einmal zu träumen. Im Familienbetrieb werden jährlich etwa 900 Tonnen Roggen und Weizen verarbeitet. Abnehmer des Mehls und der Backmischungen sind Bäckereien im Umkreis von 30 Kilometern. An der traditionellen Verarbeitung hat sich wenig verändert. Das angelieferte Getreide wird gereinigt, kommt dann in die Vermahlung und von da in die Verpackung. Wenn die Göltzsch genügend Wasser führt, treibt das Flüsschen das Mahlwerk direkt an, über eine 1968 eingebaute Turbine. Ansonsten sorgt ein Elektromotor für die notwendige Energie. Auf dem Mühlengelände betreibt die Familie einen Naturkostladen und einen Futtermittelhandel. Wenn alljährlich zum Pfingstmontag der Mühlentag begangen wird, strömen Hunderte auf das hübsch hergerichtete Grundstück an der Zwickauer Straße. Den Mühlenbetrieb kann man auch sonst besichtigen. Hier ist eine Voranmeldung notwendig. Der Mühlenladen und das kleine Mühlenmuseum haben von montags bis sonnabends geöffnet.
www.klopfermuehle.de

(Fotos/Photos by Petra Steps, Text/Text by Petra Steps, Übersetzung/Translated by David Strauss)

Klopfermühle

When fresh bread rolls are placed on the breakfast table, the coffee is steaming in a cup and the head of the family is reading the newspaper on a Saturday morning, nobody actually realises how much work was needed to provide everything for this meal. Let us start with the rolls, for example. First of all the field has to be ploughed, the corn has to be sown, the grain needs to be harvested and finally threshed. As soon as the farmer has gathered in the harvest, a miller is standing there to check whether the grain fulfils his quality standards. One of them is master miller Dietrich Klopfer from Lengenfeld, who seeks to uphold old traditions. He and his son Michael have operated the last water mill in the Vogtland region since 1995 – there were supposed to have been 45 of them along the river Göltzsch at one time. Miller would probably be a more appropriate surname for them, since Dietrich and Michael Klopfer are the fifth generation of the family running the mill. Christian Gotthilf Klopfer, the great-grandfather of Dietrich Klopfer, took over the mill on 16 June 1863. His son with the same name managed it from 1899 to 1952 and then handed it over to his son Franz Gotthilf Klopfer. The mill, which is a listed building, is much older. It was first mentioned in a document as the "Hoyersmühle" in 1438. And in the years 1531, 1576 and 1722 the mill owners were the largest taxpayers in Lengenfeld – but Dietrich Klopfer is not even dreaming of emulating this feat. The family-run business currently processes approximately 900 tons of wheat and rye every year. Bakeries in a 30 km radius are the main customers for the flour and baking mixtures. The traditional processes have hardly changed down through the years. The grain is delivered, cleaned, ground and packed. If the river Göltzsch has enough water, it can drive the mill directly through a turbine that was fitted in 1968. Otherwise an electric motor provides that power that is required. The family also runs a food shop with natural ingredients and an animal feedstuff centre at the mill site. During the annual Mill Day on Whit Monday, hundreds of visitors come to the tidy property on Zwickau Street. The mill can also be visited if people make an appointment in advance. The mill shop and the little mill museum are open from Monday to Saturday.

Auf dem Weg zur energieautarken Region
On the Way to Becoming a Self-Sufficient Region in Energy

Wer sich in Sachsen über den Einsatz erneuerbarer Energien informieren will, kommt am Vogtland nicht vorbei. Sicherlich stehen in unserer Region nicht Anlagen in Rekordgröße, doch können wir auf eine sehr lange Tradition bei der Nutzung verweisen. Aber, und das ist besonders hervorzuheben, die Vogtländer bereichern diesen Sektor mit vielen innovativen Ideen und Lösungen.

Historisch gesehen bestanden Anfang des 20. Jahrhunderts im Vogtland über 120 Wasserkraftanlagen, in denen zuerst vorrangig Wasserkraft in mechanische Energie umgewandelt und später auch in einigen Fällen Strom erzeugt wurde. Diese technischen Lösungen können heute noch in einigen Mühlen und, leider ungenutzt, in verschiedenen Industriebrachen besichtigt oder vorgefunden werden.

Bereits in den 80er Jahren entstand in Zobes eine Anlage in der organische Abfälle vergoren und somit zur Energiegewinnung genutzt werden sollten. Nach der politischen Wende wurde diese Anlage im Osten Deutschlands zum Modellprojekt einer Biogasanlage umgebaut, in welcher alle Arten dieser Abfälle umgesetzt werden können. Diese Anlage arbeitet auch 17 Jahre danach zuverlässig und ist wesentlicher Bestandteil einer ökologisch sinnvollen und schadstoffarmen Abfallentsorgung im Vogtland.

Mitte der 90er Jahre entstand in Großfriesen die erste sächsische Anlage zur Herstellung von Biodiesel aus regional angebautem Raps. Dies war ein erster Meilenstein bei der Entwicklung regionaler Stoffkreisläufe unter Nutzung erneuerbarer Energien.

Diese Beispiele verbunden mit einer breiten Öffentlichkeitsarbeit des Landkreises haben nach der Jahrtausendwende dazu geführt, dass das Vogtland in Sachsen bei der Vielfalt der Anlagen zur Nutzung erneuerbarer Energien eine Spitzenstellung einnimmt. So bestehen inzwischen 14 Biogasanlagen in der Landwirtschaft und über 340 Anlagen zur Nutzung von Erdwärme. Weiterhin zu nennen sind ca. 13.000 Anlagen, in denen Biomasse zum Beispiel in Form von Holz verbrannt wird.

Those who wish to find out about the use of renewable energy sources in Saxony, will not be able to avoid coming to the Vogtland region. There may not be any record size plant operating in our region, but we can point to a very long tradition in using renewables. And this needs to be said: Vogtland people are enriching this sector with many innovative ideas and solutions.

Historically there were more than 120 water power stations in the Vogtland region at the start of the 20th century. Usually water power was turned into mechanical energy and electricity was generated in a few cases later. These technical solutions can still be seen or found in old mills and on various old industrial sites – but unfortunately they are not being used now.

A unit was made in Zobes in the 1980s, where organic waste was fermented and used to generate energy. After the fall of the Berlin Wall, this unit became a model project for biogas plant in Eastern Germany and was adapted to one where any waste of this kind could be converted. This plant is still working reliably 17 years later and is a major part of the ecologically efficient waste disposal system in the Vogtland region; this system does not produce many pollutants.

The first Saxon plant for manufacturing biodiesel from regionally harvested rape seed was built in the mid-1990s. This marked a first milestone in the development of regional material cycles using renewable energy.

These examples coupled with the broad PR work carried out by the rural district created a situation after the turn of this millennium where the Vogtland region now occupies a leading position with regard to the variety of plant using renewable energy sources in Saxony. There are now 14 biogas units used in agriculture and more than 340 units using geothermal energy. The 13,000 or so units where organic waste – for example in the form of wood – is burned should also be mentioned.

ORC-Modul Danpower Schöneck

Fa. J. Chemnitz Pausa – Einbau eines Motor Blockheizkraftwerkes

Die Firma Brunner aus Morgenröthe-Rautenkranz projektiert und baut hochwertige Energiesparhäuser.

(Fotos/Photos by Landratsamt Vogtlandkreis Umweltamtfachbereich RP Chemnitz Uwe Hergert, Text/Text by Landratsamt Vogtlandkreis Umweltamt, Übersetzung/Translated by David Strauss)

Erneuerbare Energien / Renewable Energies

Photovoltaikanlage auf dem Dach der Firma RaLux in Oelsnitz/Vogtl.

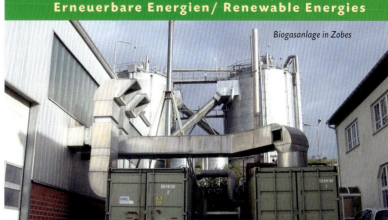
Biogasanlage in Zobes

Die Verantwortung, die in den genannten Beispielen die Vogtländer übernommen haben, um über Nutzung erneuerbarer Energien das Klima zu schützen, wird inzwischen auch für immer mehr Großanlagenbetreiber deutlich. Sicherlich ist das Vogtland nur eine kleine Fläche auf unserer Erde. Trotzdem haben wir auf Grund unserer technischen und meteorologischen Voraussetzungen eine Verantwortung im Großen. Einerseits durch Nutzung erneuerbarer Energien tragen wir zum direkten Klimaschutz bei. Andererseits hat vogtländischer Erfindergeist zu Projekten geführt, welche pilothaft Erstlösungen bzw. -nutzungen bestimmter Verfahren darstellen. Dabei ist es unwesentlich, wer letztendlich der Ideengeber ist, Verwaltungen, Verbände, Firmen oder Bürger. Wenn man die Projekte sieht, muss man feststellen, dass die vogtländischen Lösungen durchaus funktionieren und verallgemeinerungswürdig sind. Besonders interessant sind dabei noch die Lösungen, wo es gelungen ist, mehrere Arten von erneuerbaren Energien einzubinden. Besonders hinzuweisen ist in diesem Zusammenhang auf das Stadtbad Plauen, in welchem Erdwärme, Photovoltaik, Solarthermie und Kraft-Wärme-Kopplung zum Einsatz kommen. Ähnlich komplexe Lösungen existieren inzwischen auch in einzelnen Wohngebäuden, so zum Beispiel in einem Wohnhaus in Markneukirchen. Aber auch sächsische bzw. deutschlandweite Erstlösungen wie beispielsweise die ORC-Anlage in Schöneck, die CO_2-neutrale Beheizung eines Feuerwehrhauses in Neustadt, der Einsatz eines Pflanzenöl-BHKW in einem Mehrfamilienhaus in Plauen, die Nutzung der Erdwärme zur Beheizung einer Produktionshalle in Hammerbrücke oder auch erste Ergebnisse mit Luftwärmetauschern zeigen, dass vogtländische Lösungen durchaus für Nachnutzer interessant sind. Die rege Beteiligung bei den vogtländischen Energiekonferenzen zeigt das Interesse an der Nachnutzung derartiger Ergebnisse.

Im Vogtland haben sich einzelne Regionen das Erreichen einer echten Energieautarkie auf ihre Fahnen geschrieben. Einige davon sind auf dem besten Wege dazu, dies auch zu erreichen. Ein Miteinander von Verwaltung, Gewerbetreibenden und Bürgern ist ein Garant dafür, dass dadurch Klimaschutzziele erreicht werden und andererseits für die Energienutzer eine spürbare Entlastung des Portmonee sichtbar werden kann. Und was noch wichtiger ist, dabei werden regionale Stoffkreisläufe aufgebaut. Die Gelder, die sonst zum Kauf der Rohstoffe in die Taschen großer Strom- oder Erdölkonzerne fließen würden, bleiben in der Region und helfen dabei, weitere Arbeitsplätze zu schaffen. Das Vogtland ist auf einem guten Weg, wir dürfen nur nicht anhalten, um die hochgesteckten Ziele wirklich zu erreichen.

The responsibility that the Vogtland people have assumed in the above mentioned examples to protect the climate by using renewable sources of energy is now becoming clear for more and more large plant users. It is true that the Vogtland region only occupies a small area on our planet. But because of our technical and meteorological capabilities, we have a responsibility for a large part of it. We play a role in protecting the climate directly by using renewable sources of energy. But the Vogtland spirit of invention has already created projects, which represent pilot solutions or uses for particular procedures. It is unimportant who gave birth to the idea – the authorities, associations, companies or individuals. When you see the projects, you have to agree that the Vogtland solutions work well and general conclusions can be drawn from them. Those solutions, where several types of renewable energy sources have been combined, are particularly interesting. Particular mention should be made here of the Plauen City Baths, where geothermal heat, solar energy, solar heat and combined heat and power are used. Similarly complex solutions now exist in individual places of residence – for example, in a house in Markneukirchen. But firsts in Saxony or Germany – e.g. the ORC plant in Schöneck, the heating system in the fire station in Neumark, which is CO_2 neutral, the use of a vegetable oil combined block heat and power plant in an apartment building in Plauen, the use of geothermal heat to heat a production facility in Hammerbrücke or the first results with air heat exchangers – all show that Vogtland solutions are very interesting for other users. The lively participation at Vogtland energy conferences shows that many are interested in imitating these results.

Individual regions in the Vogtland district are publicly aiming to reach genuine self-sufficiency in energy. Some of them are well on the way to achieving this. When the authorities, manufacturers and individuals get together, this guarantees that climate protection goals are reached and energy users' bills are significantly reduced. What is even more important is that regional material cycles are being established. The money, which otherwise would flow into the pockets of major power or oil conglomerates, remains in the region and helps create more jobs. The Vogtland region is well on the way, but we must not stop now in order to really reach the very high goals that have been set.

Stadtbad Plauen

Sicher – das Haus der Zukunft

A Good Investment – the House of the Future

Der Traum vom eigenen Haus, wer träumt ihn nicht. Doch unkalkulierbar weiter steigende Energiekosten könnten den Traum auch zum Alptraum werden lassen. Seit 1993 entwickelt, plant und baut ein Netzwerk von vogtländischen Technikern, Architekten, Ingenieuren und Fachhandwerksmeistern unter der Leitung von Dipl.-Ing. Arndt Brunner aus Morgenröthe-Rautenkranz hochwertige Energiesparhäuser. Das Spezialistenteam besitzt inzwischen die Facherfahrung und das Know-how von über 140 realisierten Vorhaben. Die ständig steigenden Energiepreise bestätigten die Richtigkeit der konsequenten vorausschauenden, und kontinuierlichen Entwicklung zu immer weniger benötigter Heizenergie. Im Jahr 2005 wurde dann unter dem Dach der BRUNNER GmbH das „Holzsolarhaus" entwickelt und bereits mehr als 10 mal erfolgreich realisiert. Das Hauskonzept steht auf drei Säulen: einem optimalen Wärmeschutz im KfW 40 Energiesparhaus, einer intelligenten Haustechnik und einer Ganzdach-Solarstromanlage. Das Haus wird in moderner hoch gedämmter Holzständerbauweise errichtet und funktioniert wärmebrückenfrei wie eine große „Thermoskanne". Die Fenster haben eine Dreischeibenwärmeschutzverglasung, die mit Edelgas gefüllt ist. Die Wärmedämmung entspricht höchsten Standards, so dass kaum Heizenergie verloren geht. Neben den intensiven Wärmeschutzmaßnahmen besitzt das Holzsolarhaus eine genau auf den minimalen Energieverbrauch fein abgestimmte einfache Haustechnik. Ein kleines Wärmepumpenkompaktgerät mit nur noch 600 W Anschlussleistung übernimmt die Funktionen Heizung, Warmwasserbereitung und Komfort-Wohnraumlüftung und sorgt damit für gute saubere Raumluft und spürbar angenehme Behaglichkeit. Kernelement des Holzsolarhauses ist eine Photovoltaikanlage, die ohne Umweltbelastung sauberen Strom erzeugt. Mit der 20 Jahre gesetzlich garantierten Einspeisevergütung dieser Anlage werden alle anfallenden Energiekosten im Haus gedeckt, einschließlich des Stromes für Heizung, Warmwasser und Haushaltstrom, sowie in Zukunft auch der Strom für den Betrieb eines Elektroautos. Montiert man eine Ganzdachanlage mit etwa 10 kWp Leistung, wird mehr Strom durch die Sonne produziert, als im Haus selbst verbraucht wird. In dieser Kombination ist das Holzsolarhaus nicht nur ein sehr gutes Energiesparhaus, sondern bereits ein Energieüberschusshaus. Der Hausherr ist damit langfristig unabhängig! Er benötigt KEIN Oel, KEIN Gas und wohnt kostenlos und sehr behaglich bei mietähnlicher Monatsbelastung! Das Bankkonto freut sich dabei und unsere Umwelt wird deutlich entlastet.

Termine zu Hausbesichtigungen und genauere Informationen zu den Vorteilen beim Hausbau der Zukunft im Beratungszentrum in Morgenröthe-Rautenkranz, Bahnhofstraße 3A (gleich neben der neuer Raumfahrtausstellung) und unter **Telefon +49 (0) 37465 41752** und **www.brunner-holzhaus.de**

Netzwerkpartner/ Network partner:
www.brunner-holzhaus.de
www.schmiedigen.com
www.mh-roth.de
www.elektro-seidel.de
www.waehner-gmbh.de
www.auerbacher-fensterbau.de
www.dachdecker-guetter.de

Who has not dreamt of owning their own house? But energy costs, which might continue to rise to an incalculable degree, could turn a dream into a nightmare. A network of Vogtland technicians, architects, engineers and master craftsmen led by engineer Arndt Brunner from Morgenröthe-Rautenkranz has been developing, planning and building high-quality energy-saving houses since 1993. The expert team now has the special experience and expertise that it has gained from completing more than 140 projects. Constantly rising energy prices have confirmed how correct it is to consistently and continually look ahead and introduce further developments so that people require less energy. The "wood solar house" was developed under the direction of BRUNNER GmbH in 2005 and it has been built more than 10 times so far. The concept of the house is based on three foundations: ideal insulation to prevent loss of heat in the "KfW 40 energy-saving house", the intelligent use of domestic equipment and a solar panel that covers the whole roof. The house is constructed using a modern, highly insulated timber frame style and works without any thermal bridges, rather like a large "thermos flask". The windows have triple glazing, which is filled with inert gas, to provide heat insulation. The heat insulation levels meet the highest standards, so that hardly any heat is lost. As well as intensive heat insulation measures, the wood solar house also has equipment, which is finely tuned to ensure minimum energy consumption. A compact heat pump using only 600 W looks after the heating, hot water preparation and ventilation in the living areas, so ensuring clean air in rooms and a comfortable atmosphere that people really notice. The core element of the wood solar house is a solar power unit, which produces clean electricity without causing any ecological damage. Given the fact that the government has guaranteed payment for feeding in electricity from this kind of equipment for 20 years, all energy costs in the house are covered and include electricity for heating, hot water and household use, in addition to power for operating an electric car some time in the future. If the roof is covered by a 10 kWp unit, the sun generates more electricity than the house uses. This means that the wood solar house not only saves energy, but also generates surplus energy. So the owner of the house will be independent in the long term! He does NOT need any oil or gas and he can live free of charge and very comfortably for no more than a normal monthly rent! The bank account breathes a sigh of relief and less damage is done to the environment. You can arrange appointments to visit one of these houses and obtain more detailed information on the advantages of building a house of the future from the advisory centre in Morgenröthe-Rautenkranz, Bahnhofstrasse 3A (next to the new space travel exhibition) or **by phoning +49 (0) 37465 41752** or **www.brunner-holzhaus.de**

(Fotos/Photos by Brunner, Übersetzung/Translated by David Strauss)

Regionaler Marktführer für Solartechnik und alternative Energien

Regional Market Leader for Solar Technology and Alternative Energy Sources

Die Klimaveränderung mit den wirtschaftlichen Konsequenzen, wie dem Einsatz erneuerbarer Energien und dem sparsamen Umgang mit den natürlichen Ressourcen, sorgt auch in den vogtländischen Unternehmen für Umdenken und führt zu innovativen Angeboten für die Kundschaft. Zu diesen kreativen Firmen gehört der Handwerksbetrieb J. Chemnitz in Pausa.

Die am 1. Juli 1990 von Joachim Chemnitz als Zwei-Mann-Betrieb in der nordwestvogtländischen Stadt gegründete Firma für Heizung, Solar und Bad bietet derzeit als Knüller eine Wärmepumpe mit Bohrung und Direktverdampfung an. Der Firmenchef hatte dieses Produkt eines französischen Herstellers im vergangenen Jahr auf einer Messe in Prag gesehen und war beeindruckt. Durch diese Technik wird die Erdwärme für die Heizung eines Hauses optimal eingesetzt. Günstiger Preis und eine schnelle Installation sprechen weiterhin für diese umweltfreundliche Art des Heizens. Dafür müssen die Mitarbeiter des Unternehmens aus Pausa in Richtung Kältetechnik weitergebildet werden.

Generell legt der Firmenchef großen Wert auf Weiterbildung seiner 13 Mitarbeiter, dazu gehört immer ein Lehrling, der nach Abschluss der Ausbildung auch übernommen wird.

Gerade bei den Offerten zur Nutzung erneuerbarer Energie kann der Betrieb auf viel Erfahrung verweisen, die dank der guten Ausbildung zustandekam. Bereits vor 15 Jahren baute Chemnitz die erste Solarthermieanlage. Im Lauf der Jahre entstanden so 10.000 Quadratmeter, auf denen dank dieser von den Vogtländern installierten Anlagen Sonnenenergie genutzt wird. Die größten von J.Chemnitz gebauten Anlagen stehen im Schwarzwald und auf einem Haus in Pausa, mit jeweils rund 110 Quadratmeter Fläche.

Nächstes Firmenhighlight ist ein Pflanzenöl-Blockheizkraftwerk mit einer dezentralen Wärmeversorgung für Mehrfamilienhäuser, aber auch größere Objekte wie Industrie- und Gewerbebetriebe. Der Firmenchef sieht dieses Angebot als einen zukunftsträchtigen Zweig des Unternehmens aus Pausa an, das Mitglied im BUSO Bund Solardach ist, Europas größter Einkaufsgenossenschaft im Bereich Solar.

So nutzt das Unternehmen im Nordwestzipfel des Vogtlandes optimal die Möglichkeiten, die sich aus der Klimaveränderung ergeben.

Climate change and its economic consequences, such as the increasing use of renewable energies and the conservation of natural resources, have led to a change of thinking at a lot of Vogtland-based companies. This has triggered innovative ideas for helping customers. One of these creative companies is the J. Chemnitz company in Pausa in the north western part of the Vogtland district.

The two-man company specialising in heating, solar technology and bathroom installations was founded on 1 July 1990. One of its top selling products at the moment is a geothermal heat pump; the package includes the drilling work and direct evaporation. Last year the company director saw this French product at a trade fair in Prague and was immediately fascinated by it. This technology involves using warmth from the earth to heat a house in the best possible way. A reasonable price and fast installation work are further advantages of this environmentally-friendly heating system. This new product also means that the staff at the company in Pausa have had to be trained in refrigeration techniques.

As a matter of principle, the company director attaches great importance to providing additional training for his 13 employees. They include an apprentice who, after completing his training, is taken on by the company.

The company has had plenty of experience when it comes to using renewable energy sources. This is largely due to having highly qualified staff. They built their first solar thermal installation 15 years ago. Over the years the Vogtland company has installed solar systems on an area measuring approximately 10,000 m². The largest systems built by J. Chemnitz, each measuring about 110m², are located in the Black Forrest and on a house in Pausa.

The next highlight at the firm will be a combined heat and power station run on vegetable oil with a local heat supply for apartment buildings or larger buildings such as industrial or business parks. In the eyes of the business director, this product range is a promising sector for the Pausa based company, which is a member of the BUSO Solar Roof Association, Europe's largest purchasing cooperative for the solar sector.

This means that the company based in the north-western corner of the Vogtland district is making the best of the economic opportunities provided by climate change.

Firma J. Chemnitz Heizung-Solar-Bad
Braugasse 4a · D-07952 Pausa
Telefon +49 (0) 37432 5080-0
Telefax +49 (0) 37432 5080-18
www.chemnitz-pausa.de

(Fotos/Photos by Igor Pastierovic, Text/Text by Bert Walther, Übersetzung/Translated by David Strauss)

Natur und Umwelt / Nature and the Environment

Wir machen Ihren Abfall zu unserer Sache.
We Make Your Waste Our Business.

Zukunftssicher

Die vogtlandeigene mechanisch-biologische Abfallbehandlungsanlage MBS Vogtland hat wesentliche Bedeutung für die Gewährleistung der Entsorgungssicherheit in der Region. Das im Industriegebiet Oelsnitz gelegene Werk ermöglicht unabhängigeres Entsorgen und flexibles Reagieren aufs Marktgeschehen.

Jährlich werden hier etwa 30.000 t Ersatzbrennstoff (EBS) hergestellt. Ein Beitrag gegen die Verbrennung fossiler Brennstoffe, hat EBS doch einen ähnlich hohen Heizwert wie Braunkohle (zum Vergleich: EBS 16.000 kJ/kg, Braunkohle 19.000 kJ/kg.).

Auch in der Deponiewirtschaft unternimmt der EVV seit Jahren Anstrengungen zum Klimaschutz. An den Deponien Adorf und Schneidenbach verbrennen Fackelanlagen das ozonschädliche Deponiegas Methan. In Zobes produzieren Gasmotoren daraus sogar jährlich ca. 2,4 Mio kWh Elektroenergie.

Kompetent

Im Dienstleistungscenter Abfallwirtschaft verwaltet der EVV alle abfallwirtschaftlichen Daten für den Vogtlandkreis, realisiert Abfallberatung, Gebührenbescheid- und Kassenwesen.

Die MBS Vogtland in Zahlen

Erster Spatenstich: 4. April 2006
Richtfest: 13. Oktober 2006
Inbetriebnahme: 29. Mai 2007
Anlagenerrichter: Nehlsen AG
Bauherr und Besitzer: Deponie Schneidenbach GmbH im Auftrag des EVV
Betreiber: Gesellschaft für Abfallbehandlung MBS Vogtland mbH
Verfahren: Mechanisch-biologische Abfallstabilisierung
Investitionskosten: 24 Mio Euro
Input: Hausmüll, Gewerbemüll
Durchsatz: 50.000 t/a + 15.000 t/a
Anzahl der Rottecontainer: 100

Assured of a Good Future

The Vogtland region's own mechanical/biological waste treatment plant (MBS Vogtland) is very important for guaranteeing the waste disposal services in the region. The centre, which is based on the Oelsnitz Industrial park, allows disposal procedures to continue more independently and makes it easy to respond to events in the market place flexibly.

Approx. 30,000 t of refuse derived fuels (EBS) are produced here every year. This is one way of preventing the use of fossil fuels. EBS has about the same calorific value as lignite (for comparison purposes: EBS 16,000 kJ/kg, lignite: 19,000 kJ/kg).

The Vogtland Waste Disposal Association (EVV) has been making efforts to protect our climate for years when handling waste. Flares at the Adorf and Schneidenbach sites burn off the methane found on rubbish tips as this gas damages the ozone layer. Gas engines produce approx. 2.4 million kWh of electrical energy from this at Zobes.

Competent

The EVV manages all the data related to waste for the Vogtland district at its waste service centre and provides advisory services for waste and handles demands for fees and cash accounting.

The MBS Vogtland in Figures

Ground-breaking ceremony: 4 April 2006
Topping-out ceremony: 13 October 2006
Commissioned: 29 May 2007
Plant constructor: Nehlsen AG
Principal and owner: Deponie Schneidenbach GmbH on behalf of the EVV
Operator: Gesellschaft für Abfallbehandlung MBS Vogtland mbH
Processes: Mechanical/biological waste stabilisation
Investment costs: € 24 million
Input: domestic waste, commercial waste
Operational capacity: 50,000 t/a + 15,000 t/a
Number of rotting containers: 100

Gesellschaft für Abfallbehandlung mbH MBS Vogtland
Alte Reichenbacher Str. 76
08606 Oelsnitz
Telefon +49 (0) 37421 25210
Entsorgungsverband Vogtland
Dienstleistungscenter Abfallwirtschaft
Theumaer Str. 3 · 08606 Oelsnitz
Telefon +49 (0) 37421 40270
dlc@entsorgungsverband-vogtland.de
www.entsorgungsverband-vogtland.de

(Fotos/Photos by EVV, Übersetzung/Translated by David Strauss)

Natur und Umwelt / Nature and the Environment

Damit die Natur zurückerhält, was wir ihr genommen haben.
So That Nature Recoups What We Have Removed.

Naturnah

Früher hatte nahezu jede Gemeinde ihre eigene Deponie. Heute verleiht der Entsorgungsverband Vogtland diesen ehemaligen Müllkippen durch naturnahe Sicherung und Sanierung ein umweltgerechtes Gesicht. Kosten und Aufwand sind unterschiedlich hoch. Vielfach finden die Arbeiten Unterstützung durch Fördermittel des Freistaates Sachsen oder der Europäischen Union. Insgesamt betreut der EVV für den Vogtlandkreis und die Stadt Plauen weit über 200 alte Deponien.

Am Ende soll sich die Natur das Gelände wieder zurückholen können. Diese landschaftsangepasste Renaturierung kann auf unterschiedliche Weise geschehen:

- Das sanierte Areal erhält als Starthilfe eine ortstypisch-heimische Ansaat bzw. Bepflanzung und wird seinem weiteren natürlichen Bewuchs überlassen.

- Wasserableitsysteme werden statt in Rohren möglichst unter freiem Himmel im Schotterbett oder zur Hochwasserprophylaxe in geländeangepassten Kaskaden verlegt. Flora und Fauna können sich auf natürliche Art ansiedeln und frei entfalten. Biotope können entstehen.

- Wo naturschutzfachlich gewünscht, werden Bereiche auch völlig ihrer natürlichen Entwicklung überlassen, so dass sich das Gelände je nach Anflug naturgemäß entfalten kann.

Umweltbewusst

Was Hänschen nicht lernt, lernt Hans nimmermehr! Unter diesem Motto engagiert sich der Verband vogtlandweit auf dem Gebiet der Umwelterziehung für Vor- und Grundschulkinder. Die EVV-Umweltfrauen sensibilisieren die kleinsten Vogtländer für wachsames Abfallverhalten und schulen deren Sinne bei naturnah-kindgerechtem Er-Fühlen, Be-Greifen und Wahr-Nehmen.

In den letzten zehn Jahren haben weit über 3000 Kinder Bekanntschaft mit dem EVV-Maskottchen Don Camüllo machen können. Der beliebte Frosch ist gemeinsam mit seinem Freund, dem Kompostwurm Kompostone, bei den wöchentlichen Einsätzen der Umweltfrauen zugegen und hilft überaus erfolgreich, die Kinder mit Anekdoten, Spielen und Basteleien für den Umweltschutzgedanken zu begeistern.

Close to Nature

In the old days almost every community had its own waste tip. Nowadays the EVV puts an environmentally-friendly face on former rubbish dumps by providing clean-up facilities that protect the natural surroundings. This work is often supported by subsidies from the Free State of Saxony or the European Union. Overall the EVV looks after far more than 200 rubbish tips on behalf of the Vogtland district and the city of Plauen.

In the end nature should be in a position to take over any site again. This process of renaturation, which is adapted to the landscape in question, can take place in different ways.

- The area that has been cleaned up is given a boost at the start in the form of typical local seeds being planted; the area is then left to develop naturally.

- Water drains are not laid in pipes, but are left open on a gravel base or small waterfalls are adapted to the site and provide protection against flooding. Flora and fauna can then settle and develop in a natural way. Biotopes may be created.

- If it is desirable from a nature conservation point of view, areas are completely left to develop in a natural manner, so that the site can evolve naturally and depend on normal pollination.

Ecology-Minded

You cannot teach an old dog new tricks! This is the motto that the association uses to teach pre-school and primary school children about the environment throughout the Vogtland region. The EVV environment ladies create an awareness in the youngest members of the Vogtland community of how to deal with waste in a vigilant manner and train their senses to feel, grasp and perceive things in a child-like way. Well over 3,000 children have been able to get to know the EVV mascot, Don Camüllo. The popular frog and his friend, the compost worm Kompostone, are always present when the environment ladies go about their task and they play a role in enthusing children about the concept of protecting the environment with anecdotes, games and modelling sessions.

Entsorgungsverband Vogtland
Geschäftsstelle
Boxbachweg 2 · 08606 Oelsnitz
Telefon + 49 (0) 37421 4020
postmaster@entsorgungsverband-vogtland.de
www.entsorgungsverband-vogtland.de

Natur und Umwelt / Nature and the Environment

Wasser und Abwasser – alles aus einer Hand
Water and Sewage – Everything from One Source

Wasser ist unser höchstes Gut und der Ursprung allen Lebens. Der Mensch kommt vielleicht zwei bis drei Wochen lang ohne feste Nahrung aus, aber nur drei Tage ohne Wasser. Doch der Wasserbedarf ist insgesamt um ein Vielfaches höher als der direkte Trinkwasserbedarf. Wasser ist lebensnotwendig in der Landwirtschaft, um unsere Grundnahrungsmittel zu erzeugen. In vielen anderen Produktionszweigen ist Wasser nicht wegzudenken. Es ist für uns selbstverständlich und kein besonderer Luxus, unseren hygienischen Ansprüchen nachzukommen: regelmäßig zu duschen, zu baden, Wäsche zu waschen und vieles mehr.

Dafür, dass diese lebenswichtige Ressource im Vogtland immer verfügbar ist und Trinkwasser zudem in bester Qualität und damit das in Zukunft auch so bleibt, arbeitet der Zweckverband Wasser und Abwasser Vogtland, kurz ZWAV genannt. Die politischen Grenzen des Vogtlandkreises stellen dabei auch die Grenzen des Tätigkeitsgebietes dar. Der Zweckverband Wasser und Abwasser Vogtland leistet für alle 47 vogtländischen Städte und Gemeinden eine sichere Trinkwasserversorgung. Für einen großen Teil des Vogtlandes betreibt der verband auch die Abwasserentsorgung. Der ZWAV ist eine Körperschaft des öffentlichen Rechtes und arbeitet ohne Gewinnerzielungsabsichten.

Trinkwasser für das Vogtland

Der ZWAV liefert zuverlässig Trinkwasser für 99,6 Prozent der Vogtländer. Dazu sind 45 Wasserwerke, 222 Trinkwasserbehälter und ein 2350 Kilometer langes Leitungsnetz in Betrieb. Wasser bezieht der ZWAV zu 60 Prozent über eine Fernwasserversorgung aus Talsperren und zu 40 Prozent aus eigenen lokalen Quellgebieten. Eine intakte Natur ist für die Schutzräume der Talsperren und Quellgebiete von oberster Bedeutung. Deshalb hat der ZWAV seit 1990 rund 500 Millionen Euro in Neubau und Sanierung von Wasserwerken, Kläranlagen und Netzen investiert.

Water is our most precious commodity and the origin of all life. People can survive without solid food for two or three weeks, but only three days without water. But the need for water is much greater than just drinking water. Water is essential in agriculture in order to produce our basic foodstuffs. And it is impossible to imagine other production sectors without water. Water has become a fact of life and is not a luxury so that we can keep ourselves clean and take a regular shower or bath, wash our clothes and do a great deal more.

The Vogtland Special Purpose Association for Water and Sewage, known as ZWAV, works to ensure that this essential resource is and will always be available in the Vogtland region and that people have access to top-quality drinking water. The political boundaries of the Vogtland district are also the limits of the association's fields of activities. The Vogtland Special Purpose Association for Water and Sewage guarantees that all 47 Vogtland towns and communities have access to quality drinking water. The company also treats sewage for a large part of the Vogtland region. The ZWAV is a public body and operates without seeking to make a profit.

Drinking Water for the Vogtland Region

The ZWAV provides reliable supplies of drinking water for 99.6 percent of people living in the Vogtland region. For this purpose it uses 45 water works, 222 drinking water holding tanks and a network of pipes that runs for 2,350 kilometres. The ZWAV obtains 60 percent of its water via long-distance pipes from reservoirs and 40 percent from its own local sources.

It is vital that the natural surroundings near the reservoirs and water springs are kept intact. This is why the ZWAV has invested about € 500 million in new building work and redeveloping water works, sewage plant and networks.

(Fotos/Photos by ZWAV, Übersetzung/Translated by David Strauss)

Natur und Umwelt / Nature and the Environment

Abwasser

Auch die Abwasserentsorgung und -reinigung gewährleistet der ZWAV an 365 Tagen im Jahr. Dafür betreibt der Verband 72 Kläranlagen, Abwasserpumpstationen, Regenrückhaltebecken und ein ausgedehntes Kanalnetz. Vogtlandweit werden insgesamt 500 große und kleine Anlagen zur Wasserver- und Abwasserentsorgung betrieben, so ist „Wasser rund um die Uhr" eine Selbstverständlichkeit für die Menschen des Vogtlandes.

Einen wichtigen Beitrag zum Naturschutz leistet der ZWAV beim Schutz des Naturraumes der Flussperlmuschel im Dreiländereck Bayern-Böhmen-Sachsen. Hier werden ca. acht Millionen Euro in infrastrukturelle Maßnahmen investiert, um über ein neues Abwassernetz das häusliche Abwasser aus einem sensiblen Naturraum herauszuleiten. Dieser Einsatz hilft das Überleben der Flussperlmuschel in unserer Region zu sichern. Da alle großen Kläranlagen modernstem Reinigungsstand entsprechen, konnte in den letzten 10 Jahren die Qualität der Flüsse enorm verbessert werden. Die Gewässer entwickeln sich seither zu echten Lebensräumen für Pflanzen und Tiere.

Sewage

The ZWAV guarantees that sewage is disposed of and purified 365 days a year. The association operates 72 sewage works, sewage pumping stations, rainwater storage reservoirs and an extensive network of sewers. 500 large and small units are operated around the Vogtland region to provide water and treat sewage – this means that the residents of the Vogtland region have access to "water round the clock" without having to bat an eyelid.

The ZWAV is making an important contribution to natural conservation in protecting the natural habitat of the freshwater pearl mussels in the area where Bavaria, Saxony and the Czech Republic meet. About € 8 million have been invested in infrastructure to drain off domestic sewage from a sensitive natural area using a new network of sewers. As all the major sewage works meet the latest standards of purity, the quality of rivers has improved dramatically over the past 10 years. The rivers and streams are developing into real habitats for plants and animals.

Zukunftsausblick

Der Zweckverband Wasser und Abwasser Vogtland gehört mit 260 000 zu versorgenden Einwohnern zu den größeren Wasserversorgern Deutschlands. Eine gesunde Kostenstruktur gewährleistet auch zukünftig bezahlbare Preise und eine sichere den hohen Qualitätsanforderungen gerecht werdende Wasserver- und Abwasserentsorgung.

Das kommunales Unternehmen arbeitet nach den Anforderungen eines Umwelt- und Qualitätsmanagements. Damit leistet man einen hohen Beitrag für ein lebenswertes Vogtland mit naturnahen Lebensräumen. Der ZWAV ist für die zukünftigen Herausforderungen gut vorbereitet und gerüstet: „Wasser und Abwasser ist unser Auftrag für die Region, heute, morgen und auch übermorgen."

Prospects for the Future

The Vogtland Special Purpose Association for Water and Sewage is one of the largest suppliers of water in Germany as it serves 260,000 residents. A healthy cost structure ensures that prices will be affordable in future and that water supplies and sewage facilities will meet the high quality standards without any difficulties.

The local company satisfies the requirements of an environmental and quality management system. This means that the ZWAV plays an important role in providing natural surroundings where people can enjoy life. The association is well prepared to meet future challenges too: "Water and sewage is our assignment for the region, today, tomorrow and the day after tomorrow."

Zweckverband Wasser und Abwasser Vogtland
Hammerstraße 28
D-08523 Plauen
Telefon +49 (0) 3741 402-0
Telefon +49 (0) 3741 402-160
post@zwav.de
www.zwav.de

Talsperren im Vogtland
Reservoirs in the Vogtland District

Die sechs Talsperren des Vogtlandes sind, eingebettet in die Hügellandschaft, nicht nur aus Sicht der Wirtschaft und Umwelt von großer Bedeutung. Auch die landschaftlichen Reize setzen Akzente. Menschen, Pflanzen und Tiere haben auch die relativ neuen Wasserspeicher angenommen. Sogar neue Tierarten siedelten sich an. Während die Talsperren Muldenberg, Werda und Dröda vor allem der Trinkwasserversorgung dienen und daher vor schädlichen Stoffen geschützt werden müssen, werden die Brauchwassertalsperren Pöhl, Pirk und Falkenstein vielseitig für das Erholungswesen und den Tourismus genutzt. Pöhl, Pirk und Dröda sind außerdem fischereiwirtschaftlich von Bedeutung.

Für den Menschen ist Wasser die wichtigste natürliche Ressource. Wasser wird uns von der Natur zu verschiedenen Zeiten in unterschiedlichen Mengen bereitgestellt. Trockenwetter und Hochwasser beschert sie uns. Beidem sollen die Talsperren gerecht werden und die Menschen vor extremen Ereignissen schützen. So wurde bereits um 1900 mit dem Bau der Talsperre Werda der Grundstein für eine langfristig gesicherte Wasserversorgung gelegt. Die Talsperre Muldenberg folgte 1925, die in Dröda 1972. Die Trinkwasserversorgung im Vogtland stabilisierte sich. Etwa 70 Prozent der öffentlichen Wasserversorgung wird mit den Talsperren erreicht. Mit dem Bau der Talsperren Pirk 1939, Pöhl 1964 und Falkenstein 1975 wurde der Hochwasserschutz erweitert, die Niedrigwassererhöhung verbessert beziehungsweise der Industrie direkt Brauchwasser zur Verfügung gestellt (Talsperre Falkenstein). In begrenztem Rahmen ist durch alle Talsperren die Energiegewinnung möglich.

The six reservoirs in the Vogtland district are embedded in the hilly countryside and are not only very important from an economic and environmental point of view. Their beauty has left its mark on the area. People, plants and animals have all accepted the relatively new reservoirs. And some new species of animals have also been attracted to the area. The Muldenberg, Werda and Dröda reservoirs are mainly used as sources of drinking water and therefore have to be protected from any contamination, while the Pöhl, Pirk und Falkenstein industrial water reservoirs are used in many ways as centres of recreation and tourism. Pöhl, Pirk und Dröda are also important for the fishing industry.

Water is the most important natural resource available to human beings. Nature provides us with water in varying amounts at different times. It gives us dry weather and floods. The reservoirs should be able to cope with both and protect people from major disasters. So when building work started on the Werda reservoir back in 1900, the foundation stone was laid for long-term local water supplies. Muldenberg reservoir followed in 1925 and Dröda in 1972. This has stabilised drinking water supplies in the Vogtland district. The reservoirs provide about 70 percent of public water needs. Flood protection was expanded when Pirk reservoir was built in 1939, Pöhl in 1964 and Falkenstein in 1975, the amount of water available during dry periods was improved and industrial-grade water was made available to industry directly (Falkenstein reservoir). Power generation is possible at all the reservoirs to a limited degree.

(Fotos/Photos by Igor Pastierovic,, Text/Text by Brigitte Kempe-Winkelmann, Übersetzung/Tranlated by David Strauss)

Kleinste in Europa

Im Vogtland hat man alles – Berge und Täler, Wälder und Wasser. In dieser Region entspringen die Weiße Elster, die Zwickauer Mulde und die Göltzsch. Ein idealer Lebensbereich und für Urlauber ungeheuer reizvoll. Nicht zuletzt tragen dazu die sechs Talsperren bei, die unter anderem von den genannten Flüssen gespeist werden. Halt! Eigentlich sind es ja sieben Talsperren, wenn man das Minibauwerk in Oberpirk bei Mehltheuer mit dazu zählt.

Obwohl ohne überregionale Bedeutung, soll das Stauwerk in Oberpirk nicht unbeachtet bleiben. Immerhin gilt diese Talsperre als die wahrscheinlich kleinste in Europa. Zweieinhalb Meter hoch ist das Bauwerk nur, und die Mauer hat eine Länge von sechs Metern, darf aber nicht betreten werden. 1954 ist die Talsperre mit Zu- und Abfluss errichtet und 1998 saniert worden. In keiner Karte ist sie verzeichnet. Dennoch wird sie vor allem von Wanderern gern aufgesucht. Ab und an finden sogar Talsperrenfeste statt. Das angestaute Wasser dient der Feuerwehr als wichtiges Reservoir.

Talsperre Pöhl

Machen wir einen Sprung von der kleinsten zur größten Talsperre im Vogtland. In Sachsen ist die Talsperre Pöhl nach der Talsperre Eibenstock die zweitgrößte. Das Feriengebiet „Vogtländische Schweiz", dessen Mittelpunkt das Vogtlandmeer, wie die Talsperre auch liebevoll genannt wird, ist, gehört zu den größten Sommererholungsgebieten im Freistaat. Bis zu einer Million Urlauber und Besucher werden in ganz tollen Sommern registriert. Dazu zählen auch rund 10 000 Camper aus 17 Nationen.

Hauptgrund für den Bau der Talsperre: Hochwasserschutz. Schäden von rund 75 Millionen DDR-Mark hatte das Hochwasser 1954 in den damaligen Vogtlandkreisen angerichtet. Neben dem Hochwasserschutz gab es einen weiteren Grund: Die Industrie brauchte kontinuierlich Wasser, vor allem die Wismut. Im Januar 1958 erfolgte der symbolische erste Spatenstich. Zuvor war das Dorf Pöhl geräumt worden. Die Bewohner zogen nach Jocketa, Plauen und in andere Ortschaften. Schule, Kirche, Friedhof und Betriebe wurden umgesiedelt beziehungsweise an anderer Stelle neu errichtet. Was sich hier so einfach liest, war eine dramatische Zeit für alle, die sie miterlebten. Anfang Oktober 1964 wurde die 312 Meter lange Staumauer für den Verkehr freigegeben. Pöhl war versunken, lebt jedoch im Namen der Talsperre und dem des Gemeindeverbandes weiter. Vor einigen Jahren, als das Wasser sehr weit abgelassen werden musste, wurden die Grundmauern von Gebäuden wieder sichtbar.

Den Hauptstau bildet die Trieb, ein Nebenfluss der Weißen Elster. Aber auch kleinere Bäche werden angestaut. Der Stauinhalt, einschließlich der Vorsperren Neuensalz und Thoßfell beträgt 63,4 Millionen Kubikmeter. Die überstaute Fläche beträgt 425 Hektar. Die Talsperre hat eine Ausdehnung von sieben Kilometern und ist an der breitesten Stelle zwei Kilometer breit. Die Hochwasserentlastung wird mit einem Kronenüberlauf, mit einem breiten Feld

The Smallest in Europe

The Vogtland region has everything – hills and valleys, forests and water. The Weisse Elster, Zwickauer Mulde and Göltzsch rivers all have their source in this region. It is an ideal place to live and is extremely attractive for holidaymakers. The six reservoirs play their part in this and some of them are fed by the rivers just mentioned. But wait a moment. Actually there are seven reservoirs, if the mini-reservoir in Oberpirk near Mehltheuer is counted as well.

Although it does not have any national importance, the dam at Oberpirk deserves a mention. The reservoir is probably the smallest in Europe. The dam is just two-and-a-half metres high and the wall is six metres long, but cannot be walked across. The reservoir was provided with its inlet and outlet in 1954 and was repaired in 1998. It is not marked on any map. But hikers often visit it and reservoir parties are even held here from time to time. The reservoir is an important reserve source of water for the fire brigade.

Pöhl Reservoir

Let us move from the smallest to the largest reservoir in the Vogtland district. Pöhl reservoir is the second largest in Saxony after Eibenstock. The "Vogtland Switzerland" recreational area centred on the Vogtland Sea, as the reservoir is affectionately called, is one of the largest summer holiday areas in the Free State. As many as a million holiday-makers and visitors come here during good summers. This figure includes about 10,000 campers from 17 different countries.

The main reason why the reservoir was built was to protect the area from flooding. The floods in 1954 caused the Vogtland administrative districts of the time damage amounting to approx. 75 million East German marks. But there was another reason besides flood protection: industry needed water continually, particularly the Wismut mining works. The ceremonial groundbreaking ceremony took place here in January 1958. The village of Pöhl had been evacuated prior to this. Residents were moved to Jocketa, Plauen and other places. The school, church, cemetery and industries were relocated or rebuilt at a different site. It may be easy to read, but it was a dramatic time for all those who lived through it. The 312 metre long dam was opened to traffic at the beginning of October 1964. Pöhl was submerged, but its name lives on in the reservoir and the local council. A few years ago, when the water was drained off to a large degree, it was possible for people to see the foundations of buildings again.

The river Trieb, a tributary of the White Elster, is the main water source. But smaller streams are dammed here too. The reservoir, including the auxiliary dams at Neuensalz and Thossfell, can hold 63.4 million cubic metres. The reservoir covers an area measuring 425 hectares. The reservoir extends for seven kilometres and is two kilometres wide at its broadest point. A crest overflow, a wide field and a waterfall into the absorption basin relieve the reservoir at times when water levels are high. Major repair work was carried out

Natürliche Ressourcen / Natural Resources

und mit Wassersprungschanze ins Tosbecken gewährleistet. 2003 begannen erstmals seit Inbetriebnahme umfangreiche Sanierungen an der Staumauer. Dazu gehörten zunächst die Hochwasserentlastung und Teile der Überlaufeinrichtung, die das Wasser bei Vollstau kontrolliert überlaufen lassen in der ersten Bauphase. Im zweiten Bauabschnitt wurde die Staumauer auf der Wasserseite saniert (2004). Die Arbeiten an der Luftseite des Stauwerkes dauerten vom Juli 2005 bis Juli 2007. Insgesamt kostete die Sanierung der Staumauer in Pöhl zirka 5,6 Millionen Euro, die vollständig aus dem Haushalt der Landestalsperrenverwaltung bezahlt wurden.

Die malerischen Täler der Trieb und der Weißen Elster sind ein Paradies für Wanderfreunde. 100 Kilometer umfasst das ausgebaute Wandernetz. Ein 4,5 Kilometer langer Lehrpfad führt durch das Naturschutzgebiet Triebtal-Eisenberg, vorbei an der Elstertalbrücke bei Jocketa (281 m lang, 69 m hoch), der kleinen Schwester der Göltzschtalbrücke bei Mylau/Netzschkau.

Der zirka 22 Kilometer lange Rundweg um die Talsperre Pöhl bietet herrliche Ausblicke auf das „Vogtländische Meer". Beliebtes Wandergebiet ist auch das Naturschutzgebiet Steinicht mit seinen Kletterfelsen.

Erholungssuchende, aber auch jene, die in ihrer Freizeit Action lieben, kommen rund um die Talsperre auch anderweitig auf ihre Kosten. Die Fahrgastschiffe „Pöhl" und „Plauen" laden zu Rundfahrten ein. Die Route führt auch unter der Autobahnbrücke der A 72 entlang, der einzigen Brücke mit „nassen Füßen", denn ihre Pfeiler sind seit dem Bestehen der Talsperre umflutet. Gleich neben der Anlegestelle nahe der Hauptsperre können Ruder- und Tretboote ausgeliehen werden. Baden ist am 27 Kilometer langen Ufer rund um die Talsperre fast überall möglich. Einen FKK-Strand gibt es bei Helmsgrün. In den vergangenen Jahren wurden auch Hundestrände ausgewiesen. In unmittelbarer Nähe des mehrfach ausgezeichneten Campingplatzes Gunzenberg befindet sich das Naturfreibad mit einer großen Liegewiese, Beachvolleyballplatz, Abenteuerspielplatz und der Gaststätte „Pöhl-Oase".

(Fotos/Photos by Igor Pastierovic)

on the dam itself in 2003 for the first time since it had been commissioned. The first phase of the building work included the high water relief facilities and parts of the overflow system, which allow the water to flow out in a controlled manner. The water side of the dam was repaired in the second building phase (2004). The work on the air-side of the dam continued from July 2005 until July 2007. The repair work on Pöhl dam cost approx. € 5.6 million and this sum was provided by the State Reservoir Authority in full.

The picturesque Trieb and Weisse Elster valleys are a paradise for hiking enthusiasts. The network of footpaths in the area extends 100 kilometres. A nature trail, which is 4.5 kilometres long, takes people through the Trieb Valley-Eisenberg nature reserve past the Elster Valley Bridge near Jocketa (281 metres long, 69 metres high), the little sister of the Göltzsch Valley Bridge near Mylau/Netzschkau. The circular path round Pöhl reservoir, which is approx. 22 kilometres long, gives people magnificent views of the "Vogtland Sea". The Steinigt nature reserve with its climbing rocks is also a popular walking area.

People seeking recreation, but also those who love some action in their leisure time, will find plenty to do in other ways around the reservoir. The "Pöhl" and "Plauen" pleasure boats take people round the lake. Their route passes under the A 72 motorway bridge, the only one with "wet feet", as its piers have been flooded since the reservoir has existed. Rowing and pedal boats can be hired out next to the mooring point for the large boats. It is possible to go swimming along almost the whole length of the 27 kilometre beach round the reservoir. There is a nudist beach near Helmsgrün. Special dog swimming areas have also been set up over the past few years. The open-air swimming pool with a large green area, a beach volleyball area, an adventure playground and the "Pöhl-Oase" café are all right next to the Gunzenberg campsite, which has won numerous awards.

Those who are fond of sports can attend surfing and sailing schools, diving courses or enjoy themselves

Wer es sportlich mag, kann Surf- und Segelschulen besuchen, Tauchkurse absolvieren, sich im Sportpark beim Minigolf, Volleyball, Tischtennis oder Großschach vergnügen, an Fahrten mit dem Drachenboot teilnehmen, Rad fahren oder auf der Golfanlage bei Möschwitz vorbeischauen. Zwischen Schiffsanlegestelle und Naturfreibad befindet sich der Kletterwald Pöhl, der 2004 eröffnet wurde und seither schon zig Tausende anlockte. Wer wollte sich nicht schon immer mal wie Tarzan von Baum zu Baum schwingen, in luftiger Höhe auf wackligen Balken balancieren oder mit dem Skateboard übers Seil fahren? Aber auch Freunde des Pferdesports oder des Nordic Walkings finden an der Talsperre Angebote und ideale Bedingungen.

Sportlich und kulturell gibt es übers Jahr etliche Höhepunkte. Das Langstrecken-Pöhlschwimmen, der traditionelle Triathlon, Segelregatten, Beachvolleyball-Turniere, Drachenbootrennen begeistern Teilnehmer wie Zuschauer. Alljährlich findet im Juli das Strand- und Laternenfest statt. Am letzten Juni-Wochenende darf man sich das Ruinenfest Liebau nicht entgehen lassen, das vom Vogtländischen Volksmusikverein „De Gockeschen" veranstaltet wird. Open-Air-Konzerte an der Freilichtbühne am „Talsperrenblick", Sommerfest in den Bungalowdörfern und die Sommeraktionen von Kirche Unterwegs sind ebenfalls Anziehungspunkte.

Auf sechs Jahrescampingplätzen finden zirka 7000 Jahrescamper, Segelsportler und Mitglieder anderer Sportvereine Erholung. Auf dem Campingplatz Gunzenberg werden sowohl Jahrescamper als auch Touristen bedient. Zehn Prozent der Gäste kommen aus dem Ausland, insbesondere aus den Niederlanden, der Schweiz und aus Dänemark. Deutsche Gäste reisen überwiegend aus Sachsen, Thüringen, Hessen und Nordrhein-Westfalen an. In den drei Bungalowsiedlungen Voigtsgrün, Rodlera und Neudörfel können über 500 Bungalows genutzt werden. In den Orten rings um die Talsperre bieten 32 Hotels, Gasthöfe, Pensionen und Privatvermieter Unterkünfte an.

Seit 1991 kümmert sich der Zweckverband Talsperre Pöhl um die Freizeit- und Erholungsregion. Mitglieder sind die Gemeinden Neuensalz und Pöhl sowie der Vogtlandkreis.

in the sports park playing mini-golf, volleyball, table tennis or large-size chess, go on trips in the dragon boat, cycle or call in at the golf course near Möschwitz. The Pöhl climbing forest, which was opened in 2004 and has attracted people in their thousands, is located between the boats' mooring point and the open-air swimming pool. Who would not like to swing through the forest from tree to tree like Tarzan, balance on shaky beams at dizzy heights or ride over a rope on a skateboard? But fans of horse-riding and Nordic walking will also find facilities and ideal conditions by the reservoir.

There are several sporting and cultural highlights during the year. The long-distance Pöhl swimming race, the traditional triathlon, sailing regattas, beach volleyball tournaments and dragon boat races all delight participants and spectators. The beach and lantern festival takes place every year in July. The Liebau Ruin Festival, which is put on by the Vogtland Musical Association called "De Gockeschen", should not be missed during the last weekend in June. Open-air concerts on the open-air stage by the "Talsperrenblick" restaurant, a summer festival in the bungalow villages or the summer campaigns by "Church on the Road" are other highlights.

About 7,000 long-term campers, sailing sports fans and members of other sports clubs enjoy their activities at six all-year campsites. Long-term campers and tourists feel at home at the Gunzenberg campsite. Ten percent of the visitors come from abroad, particularly from Holland, Switzerland and Denmark. Most German visitors come from the states of Saxony, Thuringia, Hessen and North Rhine-Westphalia. More than 500 bungalows can be used at the three bungalow villages at Voigtsgrün, Rodlera und Neudörfel. 32 hotels, guest houses and private rooms provide accommodation in the villages round the reservoir.

The Pöhl Reservoir Special Purpose Association has been promoting the leisure and holiday region since 1991. The communities at Neuensalz, Pöhl and the Vogtland rural district are all members of this body.

Natürliche Ressourcen / Natural Resources

Talsperre Pirk

Ebenfalls ein sehr beliebtes Ausflugsziel und Erholungsgebiet ist die Talsperre Pirk im Verwaltungsbereich der Stadt Oelsnitz nahe der Autobahn 72. Errichtet wurde das Stauwerk bereits 1939. Ihre Funktionen sind der Hochwasserschutz, die Niedrigwasserauffüllung in Trockenperioden, die Energieerzeugung und der Tourismus.

10,3 Millionen Kubikmeter Wasser können gestaut werden. Zufluss ist die Weiße Elster. Als Hochwasserentlastung dient ein seitlicher Kronenüberlauf mit sechs Feldern, von denen zwei mit hydraulischen Fischbauchklappen ausgeführt sind. Diese können 2,30 Meter abgesenkt werden. Die leicht gekrümmte Staumauer ist 250 Meter lang und ist begehbar. An der engsten Stelle in der Breite befindet sich die Staumauer der Vorsperre.

In den vergangenen Jahren wurden die zwei Grundablassschieber generalüberholt, die Mauerkrone wurde saniert und Brückenelemente über der Hochwasserentlastung sowie Stahlklappenwehre erneuert. Auch die Hangtreppe und die Treppe zur Mauerkrone wurden saniert.

In Planung befand sich im Jahr 2007 die Absenkung des Wasserspiegels, um im Vorsperrenbereich Sedimente abtragen zu können. Die sollen zu zwei Inseln zwischen Dobeneck (dort befindet sich auch eine Jugendherberge) und dem Einlauf Oelsnitz angehäuft und befestigt werden. Mit dieser Maßnahme, so hofft Staumeister Rainer Degenkolb, könnte auch die Algenausbildung gemindert werden, die in manchen Sommern das Badevergnügen einschränkte.

Baden, Segeln, Surfen, Tauchen, Angeln – dafür bietet die Talsperre Pirk beste Voraussetzungen. Angesiedelt hat sich zum Beispiel der TSV Oelsnitz, Abteilung Segeln, der Regatten austrägt. Der Motorsportclub Plauen organisiert Modellsportveranstaltungen. Und neuerdings starten in Taltitz Motorgleitschirmflieger. Urlauber und Touristen können sich Ruderboote ausleihen. Die Wasserrettungswache sorgt für die Sicherheit der Besucher. Imbissgaststätten und eine mobile Angebote für die Camper sichern die Versorgung der Urlauber und Touristen.

Bis zu 10 000 Erholungssuchende kommen im Jahr an die Talsperre. Rund 500 Stabilzelte sind von Dauercampern bewohnt. Für den Wechseltourismus stehen 60 Parzellen zur Verfügung, so mit Zelten oder Wohnwagen Station gemacht werden kann. Für die touristischen Aufgaben ist seit 2003 die Naherholung Talsperre Pirk GmbH verantwortlich.

Pirk Reservoir

Pirk Reservoir, which is managed by the town authorities in Oelsnitz, is also a very popular destination for outings; this recreation area is located near the A 72 motorway. The dam was built in 1939. It provides protection against flooding, is a source of water during dry periods, it is used to generate energy and is a tourist attraction.

10.3 million cubic metres of water can be stored. The White Elster river flows into the reservoir. A crest overflow with six fields helps to provide relief when water levels are high and two of the fields are equipped with hydraulic fish bellied flaps. They can be lowered 2.30 metres. The slightly curved dam is 250 metres long and it can be walked across. The dam for the auxiliary reservoir is located at the narrowest point. General repairs have been made to the two discharge sluices over the past few years, the crest of the wall has been repaired and bridge elements over the high water level relief system and the steel flap weirs have been renewed. The sloped steps and the steps to the crest of the wall have also been repaired.

Plans were drawn up in 2007 to lower the water level to remove sediment in the auxiliary reservoir area. This sediment is due to be piled up and made secure on two islands between Dobeneck (where the youth hostel is situated) and the Oelsnitz inlet. The dam manager, Rainer Degenkolb, hopes that this could reduce the formation of algae, which has often caused problems for those wanting to swim during the summer.

Pirk Reservoir is an ideal spot for swimming, sailing, surfing, diving and fishing. The sailing branch of the Oelsnitz sports club, for example, is based here and organises regattas. The Plauen motor sports club organises model sports events. And recently motorised paragliders have begun taking off in Taltitz. Holiday-makers and tourists can hire rowing boats. The emergency services ensure that visitors do not have any accidents. Snack bars and mobile facilities for campers round off the facilities available for holiday-makers and tourists.

As many as 10,000 holiday-makers come to the reservoir every year. Some 500 permanent tents are used by long-term campers. There are 60 plots for campers coming and going, who can stay here for a short period in their tent or caravan. The Pirk Reservoir Recreation Company has been responsible for organising tourist facilities since 2003.

(Fotos/Photos by Harald Sulski, Hartmut Briese)

Natürliche Ressourcen / Natural Resources

Talsperre Falkenstein

Die jüngste und kleinste Talsperre mit Freizeitmöglichkeiten im und am Wasser ist die Talsperre Falkenstein. Die Talsperre ist einen Kilometer lang und bis zu 250 Meter breit. Die tiefste Stelle beträgt 20 Meter. Bei Betriebsstau fasst die Talsperre 0,843 Millionen Kubikmeter Wasser. Gestaut wird die Weiße Göltzsch, die sich kurz darauf mit der Roten Göltzsch zur Göltzsch vereinigt und später in die Weiße Elster mündet. Der Staudamm der Talsperre ist ein Steinschüttdamm mit Innendichtung aus Beton. Die 234 Meter lange Dammkrone ist begehbar.

Die Talsperre wurde in erster Linie für die Brauchwasserversorgung der Industrie, vor allem der Falgard, gebaut. 1977 ging sie offiziell in Betrieb. Da es nun hier keine Betriebe mehr gibt, die Brauchwasser benötigen, dient der Stausee nur noch der Freizeiterholung und dem Hochwasserschutz. Seit dem Jahrhunderthochwasser hat die Talsperre als Hochwasserstauraum an Bedeutung gewonnen. Modernisierungsmaßnahmen am Betriebssteg und moderne Messtechnik im Inneren der Staumauer machen es möglich, dass jede kleinste Bewegung im Bauwerk aufgezeichnet werden kann und anschließend per Computer aus der Staumeisterei abrufbar ist. Diese Investitionen wurden von der Landestalsperrenverwaltung Sachsen finanziert.

Für die Entwicklung des Tourismus an der Talsperre hat die Stadt Falkenstein den Hut auf. Der Stausee ist ebenfalls ein geprüftes EU-Badegewässer. Es gibt einen mit Sand bedeckten befestigten Uferbereich mit Liegewiesen. Ein privater Betreiber am Bootssteg verleiht Ruderboote und lädt mit seinem Imbissstand zum Verweilen ein. Angeln ist praktisch nicht möglich. Im Stausee gibt es keine Fische, weil das Wasser zu sauer ist. Die Umgebung lädt zu ausgedehnten Spaziergängen und Wanderungen ein. Um die Talsperre gibt es einen Rundweg. Die Stadt plant, weitere Wanderwege auszuweisen.

Falkenstein Reservoir

Falkenstein Reservoir is the newest and smallest reservoir with recreational facilities in and next to the water. The reservoir is one kilometre long and up to 250 metres wide. The deepest point is 20 metres. When full, it can store 0.843 million cubic metres of water. The White Göltzsch river, which joins the Red Göltzsch shortly afterwards to become the Göltzsch and later flows into the White Elster, feeds the reservoir. The dam on the reservoir is a rock-fill dam with an internal seal made of concrete. The crest of the dam, which is 234 metres long, can be walked across.

The reservoir was primarily constructed to provide industrial-grade water for local industry, particularly the Falgard textile works. It was officially opened in 1977. But as the companies, which needed the industrial-grade water, have now disappeared, the reservoir is only used for recreational purposes and flood protection now. Since the major floods in 2002, the reservoir has become more important as a flood water storage point. Modernisation work on the works catwalk and modern measuring technology within the dam mean that even the smallest movement in the construction can be recorded and made available to the dam manager by computer. The Saxon State Reservoir Authority financed these investments. The municipal authorities in Falkenstein are responsible for developing tourism at the reservoir. The reservoir is also a swimming area, which has been tested by the EU. There is a beach area with sand and a sunbathing area where people can relax. A private operator by the boat mooring point hires out rowing boats and encourages people to spend time at the snack bar. Fishing is not an option here as there are no fish in the reservoir. The water is too acid. The surrounding area is ideal for long walks or hikes. There is a circular path round the reservoir. The town is planning to signpost other footpaths.

Natürliche Ressourcen / Natural Resources

Talsperre Muldenberg

Die Trinkwassertalsperre Muldenberg bietet einen möglichen Stauraum von 6,2 Millionen Kubikmetern Wasser. Oberhalb des gleichnamigen Ortes, zwischen Schöneck und Hammerbrücke im oberen Vogtland gelegen, dient sie neben der Trinkwassergewinnung auch dem Hochwasserschutz und der Niedrigwassererhöhung in Trockenperioden. Erbaut wurde die Talsperre von 1920 bis 1925. Die Rote und die Weiße Mulde, die sich nach der Staumauer zur Zwickauer Mulde vereinigen, sowie der Saubach bringen das Wasser. Die Hochwasserentlastung bildet ein mittiger Kronenüberlauf mit 18 Feldern. Die Staumauer ist eine gekrümmte Gewichtsstaumauer aus Bruchsteinmauerwerk. Mit ihren 525 Metern Länge gehört sie zu den längsten in Deutschland. Sichtbar sind allerdings nur 470 Meter, der Rest verläuft unterirdisch. Bislang war das Stauwerk aus Sicherheitsgründen nicht begehbar. Doch das soll sich ändern. Mit dem Ende der umfassenden Sanierungsarbeiten soll die Mauer ab dem Frühjahr 2008 für Fußgänger und Radfahrer passierbar sein.

Aller 80 bis 100 Jahre, so der Staumeister Jürgen Görner, wird eine grundhafte Sanierung notwendig. Im Herbst 2001 hat man an der Talsperre Muldenberg damit begonnen. Die Mauerkrone wurde zunächst abgebrochen und neu aufbetoniert sowie auf der Luftseite wieder mit Bruchsteinen versehen. Dann begann die Sanierung der Staumauer auf der Luftseite. Zudem sind Dauerfelsanker in den Untergrund eingebracht worden, um die Standsicherheit zu verbessern und selbst für Erdbeben zu rüsten. Für die Sanierung der Wasserseite im zweiten Bauabschnitt musste die Talsperre im Januar 2005 komplett abgelassen werden. Eine neue Dichtwand aus wasserundurchlässigem Stahlbeton entstand. Weiterhin wurden die Einlaufbauwerke saniert, die Wassertechnik erneuert und der Schutzdamm zur Bahn über zirka 400 Meter neu aufgebaut und abgedichtet. Bis Ende 2007 soll der Bau der zwei Vorsperren abgeschlossen werden. Letzte Arbeiten sind dann die Errichtung der Fußgängerbrücke über die Bahn und die Erneuerung der Elektrotechnik. Bereits im Sommer 2007 begann die erste Probestauphase. Es wird wohl bis zum Spätsommer 2008 dauern, bis die Talsperre wieder vollgelaufen ist.

Baden, Angeln und Freizeitsport sind an diesem Stausee nicht möglich. Eingebettet in Wälder ist die Umgebung der Talsperre aber ein wunderschönes Wandergebiet. Unterhalb und oberhalb der Talsperre befinden sich mehrere kleinere Becken, die früher zum Flößen von Holz angelegt worden sind.

Talsperre Dröda

Das jüngste Trinkwasserreservoire im Vogtland ist die Talsperre Dröda in der Gemeinde Burgstein, nach dem gestauten Fluss aus Feilebach-Talsperre genannt. Erbaut wurde sie in den Jahren 1965 bis 1971. Das Wassereinzugsgebiet hat einen Umfang von 53,5 Quadratkilometern. Die Talsperre hat eine Kleinwasserkraftanlage, zwei Vorsperren (Bobenneukirchen, Ramoldsreuth) und neun Vorbecken. Gestaut wird neben dem Feilebach auch der

Muldenberg Reservoir

Muldenberg drinking water reservoir can hold 6.2 million cubic metres of water. Located above the village with the same name between Schöneck and Hammerbrücke in the Upper Vogtland area, it is used to provide drinking water and provide flood protection and top up water supplies during dry periods. The reservoir was built between 1920 and 1925. The Red and White Mulde rivers, which join after the dam to form the Zwickauer Mulde, and the Saubach feed the reservoir. A central crest overflow with 18 fields forms the flood plain. The dam itself is a curved gravity dam made of rubble masonry. It is one of the largest in Germany and is 525 metres long. But only 470 metres are visible. The remainder runs underground. In the past the dam could not be walked across for safety reasons. But that is all about to change. Once the comprehensive repair work has been completed, the wall will be open to pedestrians and cyclists from the spring of 2008 onwards.

Dam manager Jürgen Görner says that major repair work is needed every 80 - 100 years. This started at Muldenberg reservoir in the autumn of 2001. The wall crest was first demolished and made secure with concrete and new rubble masonry was added to the air side. Then work started on repairing the dam on the air side. Permanent rock anchors were fitted in the underground section to improve the dam's stability and make it strong enough to even withstand earthquakes. The water had to be drained from the dam completely in January 2005 to repair the water side during the second building phase. An impermeable new sealing wall made of reinforced concrete has been installed. The inlet units were also repaired, the water technology was renewed and the protective wall next to the railway line was renewed and sealed along about 400 metres. Work on constructing the two auxiliary dams should have been completed by the end of 2007. The final work involves constructing the pedestrian bridge over the railway line and renewing the electrical equipment. The first water storage test phase began in the summer of 2007. But it will be the late summer of 2008 before the reservoir is full again.

Swimming, fishing or leisure sports are not available at this reservoir. But the area surrounding the reservoir is a beautiful for walks as the reservoir is embedded in forests. There are several smaller pools, which were once used for log rafting, below and above the reservoir.

Dröda Reservoir

The newest drinking water reservoir in the Vogtland district is the one at Dröda in the community of Burgstein and it is named after the dammed river flowing from the Feilebach reservoir. It was built during the years 1965-1971. The water drainage area covers 53.5 square kilometres. The reservoir has a small hydro-electric power station, two auxiliary reservoirs (Bobenneukirchen and Ramoldsreuth) and nine pools further upstream. The water not only comes from the Feilebach stream, but also the Schafbach, both of which are tributaries of the White Elster. The dam

(Fotos/Photos by Hartmut Briese)

Natürliche Ressourcen / Natural Resources

Schafbach, beides Nebenflüsse der Weißen Elster. Das Bauwerk hat auch die Funktion des Hochwasserschutzes. 18 Millionen Kubikmeter Wasser können gestaut werden. In Sachsen steht die Talsperre von der Größe her an achter Stelle. Plauen, Oelsnitz, Adorf und weitere Ortschaften werden von hier aus mit Trink- und Brauchwasser versorgt.

Die Sperrmauer ist eine geradlinige Schwergewichtsmauer und besteht aus 25 Feldern. Sie enthält ein Kontrollgangsystem mit umfangreichen Messeinrichtungen. Die drei mittleren Mauerfelder sind als Hochwasserüberlauf ausgebildet, der direkt ins Tosbecken führt. Das 375 Meter lange Stauwerk ist für die Öffentlichkeit nicht zu begehen. Freizeitsport im und am Stausee ist wegen der Wasserreinhaltung untersagt. Angler allerdings kommen auf ihre Kosten.

Wer sich die Talsperre südwestlich von Oelsnitz anschauen möchte, kann dies per pedes oder mit dem Rad tun. Dröda und Umgebung im Feilebachtal haben landschaftlich Schönes zu bieten. Im Nordosten erhebt sich der Hohe Kulm mit 515 Metern. Sehenswert ist die Kirche von Dröda. Viele Wege führen zu idyllischen Orten im Burgsteingebiet.

also serves to provide protection from flood waters. 18 million cubic metres of water can be stored. The reservoir is the eighth largest in the state of Saxony. Plauen, Oelsnitz, Adorf and other places are provided with drinking and industrial-grade water from here.

The dam is a straight gravity wall and consists of 25 sections. It contains a monitoring access system with plenty of measuring equipment. The three middle wall sections act as the high water overflow facility, which feeds directly into the absorption basin. The dam, which is 375 metres long, cannot be walked along by the general public. No leisure sports on or by the reservoir are allowed so as to keep the water pure. But anglers have plenty of opportunities to practise their sport.

Those wishing to look at the reservoir located to the south-west of Oelsnitz can do so on foot or on their bikes. Dröda and the surrounding area in the Feilebach valley are extremely attractive. The Hohe Kulm hill rises 515 metres to the north east. The church at Dröda is also worth a visit and there are plenty of footpaths taking people to attractive destinations in the Burgstein area.

Talsperre Werda

Die älteste Talsperre im Vogtland und zweitälteste in Sachsen ist die Talsperre Werda. Sie ist auch unter dem Namen Geigenbachtalsperre bekannt, benannt nach dem gestauten Bach. Erbaut wurde sie 1904 bis 1909 mit der ersten Filteranlage Deutschlands. Die Trinkwasserversorgung und der Hochwasserschutz sind ihre Hauptaufgaben. Die Hochwasserentlastung erfolgt über einen seitlichen Abflussgraben mit Kaskadenabstürzen. Ein Speichervolumen von 5 Millionen Kubikmetern steht zur Verfügung. Saniert wurde die Talsperre in den Jahren 1985 bis 1992. Die Bruchsteinmauer aus Fruchtschiefer ist 311 Meter lang und seit der Sanierung wieder begehbar.

In der Werdaer Umgebung laden einige, gut ausgeschilderte Wege zum Wandern ein, zum Beispiel auch der Exkursions- und Wanderpfad um die Talsperre. Auch die Route nach Grünbach führt über die Talsperre. Eine Aussichtsplattform lädt zum Verweilen ein. Werda bietet etliche Sehenswürdigkeiten. Zum Beispiel die Ringwallanlage „Wasserburg Werda", das Wasserwerk, das Rittergut und die Jahnsmühle – alles Kulturdenkmale wie auch die Talsperre Werda selbst.

Werda Reservoir

Werda reservoir is the oldest in the Vogtland district and the second oldest in Saxony. It is also known as the Geigenbach reservoir, named after the stream that flows into it. It was built between 1904 and 1909 and had the first filter unit in Germany. It mainly serves to supply drinking water and offer protection against flooding. A side drainage ditch with waterfalls ensures that water can be released if levels are too high. The reservoir can hold 5 million cubic metres of water. It was repaired during the period 1985-1992. The quarry stone wall made of grey slate is 311 metres long and can be walked over again now that it has been repaired. There are some well-signposted footpaths in the Werda area for hikers – for example, the nature trail round the reservoir itself. The route to Grünbach also takes people past the reservoir. A viewing platform encourages people to come to the area. Werda has several sights, including the "Wasserburg Werda" ringed embankment, the water works, the manor and the Jahns mill – all of them cultural highlights like the Werda reservoir itself.

Der Naturpark Erzgebirge/Vogtland

The Ore Mountains/Vogtland National

An der sächsisch-böhmischen Grenze erstreckt sich zwischen dem vogtländischen Bad Elster und dem osterzgebirgischen Holzhau der Naturpark „Erzgebirge/Vogtland".

Das Gebiet von etwa 1495 Quadratkilometer Gesamtgröße liegt überwiegend in Höhen oberhalb 500 mNN. 60 Prozent des Naturparkgebietes sind Waldfläche, 31 Prozent landwirtschaftliche Nutzfläche und 9 Prozent Siedlungsfläche. Getragen wird der Naturpark von einem Zweckverband, den die Landkreise, auf deren Territorium das Gebiet liegt, gegründet haben. Mit ca. 325.000 Einwohnern gehört der Naturpark zu den am dichtesten besiedelten Mittelgebirgsregionen Europas.

Das Naturparkgebiet zählt aufgrund der naturräumlichen Voraussetzungen, des naturschutzrelevanten Inventars und der Jahrhunderte währenden Landnutzung zu den landschaftlich wertvollsten Teilen des südsächsischens Raumes.

In den höheren Lagen des Erzgebirges sind zahlreiche Pflanzen- und Tierarten nachgewiesen, die europaweit stark gefährdet sind. Derzeit befinden sich 228 Flächennaturdenkmale, 16 Landschaftsschutzgebiete (LSG), 41 Naturschutzgebiete (NSG) und 3 international anerkannte Vogelschutzgebiete im Areal des Naturparks. Etwa 20 Erweiterungen bzw. Neuausweisungen von NSG und LSG sind vorgesehen. Damit nimmt in Zukunft der geschützte Bereich mehr als 71 Prozent der Gesamtfläche ein.

Viele Orte und Regionen des Erzgebirges und oberen Vogtlandes sind traditionelle Urlaubs- und Naherholungsgebiete. Herbe landschaftliche Schönheit, mittelgebirgstypisches Klima, mannigfaltige Natur, reiche Kultur, umfangreiche Beherbergungskapazitäten, gut markierte Wanderwege, vielfältige Sportmöglichkeiten u.a.m. bilden die Grundlagen einer ganzjährigen Erholungsnutzung für Tagestouristen und Feriengäste.

The Ore Mountains/Vogtland National Park stretches along the Saxon/Czech border from Bad Elster in the Vogtland region to Holzhau in the eastern Ore Mountains.

Most of the territory, which covers about 1495 square kilometres, is higher than 500 metres above sea level. 60 percent of the national park area is covered by forests, 31 percent is for agricultural use and 9 percent is covered by settlements. The national park is backed by a special purpose organisation, which the rural districts within the park have set up. The national park is one of the most densely populated central upland regions in Europe with approx. 325, 000 inhabitants.

The national park area is one of the valuable parts of southern Saxony on account of its natural conditions, the natural features that need to be preserved and the land use, which has continued for centuries.

There are many species of plants and animals in the higher areas of the Ore Mountains, which are under serious threat around Europe. There are currently 228 protected areas, 16 landscape conservation areas, 41 protected areas and 3 internationally recognised bird protection areas within the park. Plans have been drawn up to extend about 20 of the protected areas and landscape conservation areas. This means that protected areas will make up more than 71 percent of the whole park in future.

Many areas and regions in the Ore Mountains and Upper Vogtland district are traditional holiday and recreation centres. Harsh landscape beauty, a typical central uplands climate, a variety of nature, a rich culture, comprehensive overnight accommodation facilities, well marked footpaths, many sports facilities etc form the basis for all-year-round recreation for day visitors and holiday guests.

(Fotos/Photos by Zweckverband „Naturpark Erzgebirge/Vogtland", Text/Text by Landratsamt Vogtlandkreis in Zusammenarbeit mit Zweckverband „Naturpark Erzgebirge/Vogtland", Übersetzung/Translated by David Strauss)

Natürliche Ressourcen / Natural Resources

Erzgebirge und Vogtland repräsentieren ein reichhaltiges kulturhistorisches Erbe. Besonders die Geschichte des über Jahrhunderte landschaftsprägenden Bergbaus ist durch zahlreiche Sachzeugen nachvollziehbar. Grubenbaue mit Tagesöffnungen, Schürfe, Schächte und Bingen finden sich im gesamten Gebiet des Naturparks. Oft sind sie Lebensraum speziell angepasster Arten wie Moose, Flechten und der immer seltener werdenden Fledermäuse.

In den Kammlagen des Naturparks, mit ausgedehnten Wäldern, befinden sich die größten und ergiebigsten Wassereinzugsbereiche, deren Quellaustritte und Bäche oft eine sehr gute Wasserqualität aufweisen. Von den 9 Talsperren im Naturparkgebiet dienen gegenwärtig 8 der Trinkwasserversorgung.

Die landwirtschaftliche Produktionsstruktur ist maßgeblich vom Mittelgebirgscharakter der Landschaft geprägt, was sich in dem hohen Grünlandanteil ausdrückt. Die historische Entwicklung der bäuerlichen Strukturen hat zur Entstehung des heute typischen Landschaftsbildes von Erzgebirge und Vogtland geführt. Zur Erhaltung der Kulturlandschaft ist es unerlässlich, die landwirtschaftliche Nutzung im Naturparkgebiet extensiv und ökologisch weiterzuführen.

The Ore Mountains and Vogtland region represent a rich cultural and historical heritage. Evidence of the history of mining, which went on for centuries, can be seen all over the place. Mine openings, exploration work, shafts and depressions are found at many places in the national park. They often house specially adapted mosses, lichens or bats, which are becoming increasingly rare.

The largest and most prolific water sources, where the springs and streams are often of a very high water quality, are found along the ridge of the national park in the extensive forests. 8 of the 9 reservoirs in the national park area are currently used for drinking water.

The agriculture in the region is largely determined by the central uplands character of the landscape, which is seen in the high proportion of grassland. The historical developments of peasant structures led to the creation of what is now a typical landscape in the Ore Mountains and Vogtland region. If the cultural landscape is going to be retained, it is essential to continue using the agricultural areas in the national park both extensively and ecologically.

Bildbeschreibungen

Linke Seite unten: von links Ebereschen bei Klingenthal, Schönberger Teiche im LSG „Oberes Vogtland", Flächennaturdenkmal „Schneckenstein" – ein interessantes Wanderziel

Rechte Seite: oben von links Fachwerkhaus in Raun – Egerländer Giebel, Vogtländisches Freilichtmuseum Landwüst – Einblick in historische bäuerliche Lebens- und Wirtschaftsweisen, holzverschalte Häuser am Aschberg; Bild darunter zeigt den traditionellen Kammlauf in Mühlleithen, der für viele seit Jahren ein sportlicher Höhepunkt ist. / Bottom left: Mountain ash trees near Klingenthal, Schönberg ponds in the "Upper Vogtland" landscape conservation area "Schneckenstein" protected area – an interesting destination for a walk

On the right: top from the left: half-timbered house in Raun – Czech gables, Vogtland Open-Air Museum in Landwüst – View of historic farming lifestyle and business, weather boarded houses on the Aschberg; Photo below shows the traditional ridge track in Mühlleithen, which has been a sporting highlight for many for years.

Natürliche Ressourcen / Natural Resources

Der westliche Teil des Parks verfügt über ein sehr wertvolles Potential gefährdeter Waldtypen, wie verschiedenartige naturnahe Fichtenwälder in der Kammregion, Flechten-Höhenkiefernwälder im Elstergebirge, Spirken-Moorwälder und Reste von (Tannen-) Rotbuchenwäldern. Hoch-, Zwischen- und Flachmoore prägen ebenso das Landschaftsbild wie Quellfluren, mäandrierende Bäche, Teiche mit Röhricht und Großseggenriedern, sowie artenreiche Bergwiesen und bodensaure Borstgraswiesen. Sie sind nicht nur besonders reizvolle Landschaftsbestandteile, die jeden Wanderer begeistern, sondern auch Lebensräume vieler seltener, europaweit stark gefährdeter Tier- und Pflanzenarten. Bei großer Aufmerksamkeit und mit ein wenig Glück sieht man unterwegs vielleicht Sperlingskauz, Birkhuhn, Uhu, Eisvogel, Tannenhäher und Fichtenkreuzschnabel. Im Dreiländereck mit gleichnamigen Naturschutzgebiet finden wir die letzten sächsichen Vorkommen der Flußperlmuschel und der Bachmuschel. Bachrenaturierungen und strengste Schutzmaßnahmen sollen die Restbestände stabilisieren und erhalten. In den Teichen und Tümpeln finden wir den Kamm-, Berg-, Teich- und Fadenmolch oder beobachten eventuell die selten gewordene Kreuzotter und die Ringelnattern. Auf den Bergwiesen werden Sumpfdotterblumen und Buschwindröschen von Veilchen, Teufelskralle, Kuckuckslichtnelke, Glockenblume und Magariten abgelöst. Etwa 500 Arten farbenprächtiger Schmetterlinge umgaukeln das Blütenmeer. Auf trockenen Standorten finden wir Augentrost und Berufskraut und auf Moorstandorten Sonnentau, Fettkraut, Wollgras, Moos-, Rausch- und Krähenbeere. Zu den besonderen Schmuckstücken der Flora gehören Feuerlilie, Arnika und mehrere Orchideen- und Enzianarten.

Der interessierte Gast kann sich durch ein vielfältiges Publikationsangebot über den Naturpark „Erzgebirge/Vogtland" informieren. Ein Faltblatt, das auch in tschechischer und englischer Übersetzung vorliegt, zeichnet ein Kurzporträt der Region. Detaillierte Darstellungen vermittelt die Wanderausstellung „Naturerleben weckt Naturverständnis" ebenso wie der repräsentative Naturpark-Bildband und ein Videofilm, die zu begehrten Souvenirs geworden sind.

The western part of the park is a very high proportion of endangered wood types – for example, various kinds of spruce forests along the ridge, lichen/upper Scots pine forests in the Elster Mountains, mountain pine-marsh forests and the remains of (pine and) common beech forests. High, medium and flat moor lands also dominate the scenery along with many springs, meandering streams, ponds with common reeds and tufted sedge, many types of hill meadows and acid soil mat grass fields. They are not only beautiful elements in the scenery, which delight walkers, but they also form the habitat for many rare, threatened species of animals and plants in Europe. If you look carefully and have some luck, you might see a Eurasian pygmy owl, a black grouse, an eagle owl, a kingfisher, a nutcracker or a common crossbill. At the point where three states meet are the last Saxon freshwater pearl mussels and thick shelled river mussels. Stream renaturation and most stringent protective measures are aimed at stabilising and retaining the remaining stock. You can find the crested, Alpine, common and palmate newts in ponds and pools and possibly see an adder or grass snake. Marsh marigolds and anemones are replaced by violets, devil's claw, ragged robin, Canterbury bells and marguerites on the hill meadows. About 500 species of colourful butterflies flutter around the sea of flowers. You can find eyebright and annual fleabane at dry places and sundew, common butterwort, cotton grass and cranberries, bog blueberries and crowberries on marshy ground. The tiger lily, arnica and several species of orchids and gentians are just some of the magnificent flora that can be seen.

Any interested guests can gain information about the Ore Mountains/Vogtland National Park from a wide variety of publications. A leaflet, which is also available in English and Czech, describes the region in brief. The "Natural life arouses an understanding of nature" exhibition and the prestigious colour illustrated book on the national park and a video film, which have become treasured souvenirs, provide more detailed information.

**Zweckverband
Naturpark „Erzgebirge/Vogtland"**

Geschäftsstelle Schlettau
Schlossplatz 8
09487 Schlettau
Telefon   +49 (0) 3733 622106
Telefax   +49 (0) 3733 612107
naturpark@tira.de
Außenstelle Tannenbergsthal
Zum Schneckenstein 42
08262 Tannenbergsthal
OT Schneckenstein
Telefon   +49 (0) 037465 / 22 24
Telefax   +49 (0) 037465 / 41871
schneckenstein.naturpark@tira.de

www.naturpark-erzgebirge-vogtland.de

(Fotos/Photos by Zweckverband „Naturpark Erzgebirge/Vogtland" [3], Archiv Tourismusverband Vogtland e.V. [1])

Schützenswert
Worth Protecting

Ausschnitt aus dem Naturschutzgebiet „Feilebach". Noch gut ist der Aufbau der ehemaligen Grenzanlagen zu erkennen (von rechts nach links): Kolonnenweg mit Spurensicherungsstreifen, Kfz-Sperrgraben, Minenfeld, vorgelagertes Hoheitsgebiet/ Section of the "Feilebach" nature conservation area. The composition of the former border fortifications can still be recognised (from right to left): former vehicle track with detection strip, vehicle traps, minefield, "border of the sovereign territory".

Grünes band

Früher „Todesstreifen", heute „Grünes Band" – die ehemals innerdeutsche Grenze begrenzt den Vogtlandkreis gen Bayern im Westen auf einer Länge von 42 Kilometern. Acht Naturschutzgebiete, zwei Flächennaturdenkmale und drei Geschützte Landschaftsbestandteile beherbergen den zwischen 70 und mehrere hundert Meter breiten ehemaligen Grenzstreifen. Dank seiner Unterschutzstellung und der Umsetzung des von den Naturschutzbehörden erarbeiteten Pflege- und Entwicklungskonzeptes existieren hier eine besonders artenreiche Flora und Fauna. Ob Braunkehlchen und Neuntöter (zwei charakteristische Vogelarten), Dukatenfalter, Ringelnatter, Sumpfblutauge oder Waldläusekraut – eine Vielzahl heute seltener oder gefährdeter Tier- und Pflanzenarten tummelt sich im längsten Schutzgebietssystem Südwestsachsens, unmittelbar an der Landesgrenze zu Bayern. Am ehemaligen Kolonnenweg können Naturliebhaber dieses einmalige Biotopverbundsystem zwischen Pabstleithen im Süden über Posseck, Gassenreuth, Sachsgrün, Blosenberg und Grobau im Norden per pedes erleben. Auch der Laie erkennt, dass die hier vorhandenen Biotope keine Durchschnittslandschaft darstellen und ausgesprochen artenreich sind.

Mit dem Naturschutz abgestimmte Maßnahmen helfen, die Artenmannigfaltigkeit des reich strukturierten Biotopkomplexes zu erhalten: blütenbunte Wiesen im so genannten „Vorgelagerten Hoheitsgebiet" werden extensiv zur Heugewinnung genutzt, zwischen den ehemaligen Sperranlagen Kolonnenweg, Kfz-Sperrgraben und Minenfeld pflegt eine 500-köpfige Schafherde die verschiedenartigsten Offenlandbiotope. Feucht- und Nasswiesen – Lebensstätten besonders vieler gefährdeter Spezies – werden zu deren Erhaltung einmalig im Spätsommer oder Herbst gemäht. Deutschlandweit nimmt der vogtländische Abschnitt des „Grünen Bandes" Modellcharakter ein. Auch viele Jahre nach der Grenzöffnung sind der ehemalige Grenzaufbau noch weitgehend zu erkennen und das schützenswerte Arteninventar fast vollständig vorhanden.

Für die Schutzgebiete des „Grünen Bandes" gilt ein Wegegebot. Zum Radfahren ist der Kolonnenweg wegen seiner großen Löcher eher ungeeignet. Und zu guter Letzt: Hunde gehören im „Grünen Band" an die Leine.

Green Strip

It used to be known as "death strip" – but now it is the "green strip" – what used to be the frontier between East and West Germany runs along the border between the Vogtland district and Bavaria to the west for 42 kilometres. Eight nature conservation areas, two natural monuments and three protected areas cover the former border strip, which is between 70 and 100 metres wide. Many species of flora and fauna exist here thanks to the preservation and development concept drawn up by the nature conservation authorities and by placing the area under protection. A wide variety of rare or threatened species of animals and plants live freely in the longest protected area in South West Saxony, right on the state border with Bavaria – including whinchats, red-backed shrikes (two typical species of birds), scarce coppers, grass snakes, purple marshlocks or lousewort. Nature-lovers can walk along the former track used by East German guards and experience this unique habitat between Pabstleithen in the south via Posseck, Gassenreuth, Sachsgrün, Blosenberg and Grobau in the north. Even lay people will recognise that the biotope here is not a typical landscape and contains a huge variety of species.

Measures attuned to match the principles of nature conservation are helping to maintain the variety of species in this richly structured biotope: blossoming meadows in what was known as the "border of the sovereign territory" (of East Germany) are extensively used to make hay and a flock of sheep numbering 500 look after the open biotope landscape between the former border fortifications, the vehicle track, vehicle barriers and minefields. Marsh areas – habitats for particularly threatened species – are mown once a year in late summer or autumn to conserve them. The Vogtland section of the "green strip" is proving to be a model for the whole country. The former border can still be seen many years after the border was opened and the number of species here worth protecting have almost all been preserved.

No footpaths are allowed to cross the "green strip". The vehicle track area is not suitable for cycling because of its huge holes. And last but not least: dogs have to be on a lead in the "green strip".

Ausschnitt aus dem Naturschutzgebiet „Fuchspöhl". Extensive Mähwiesen, Feldgehölze und Brachestrukturen bilden ein kleinräumiges Biotopmosaik/Section of the "Fuchspöhl" nature conservation area. Extensive meadows, hedges and fallow ground form a small biotope mosaic.

(Fotos/Photos by T. Findeis,/Text by Landratsamt Vogtlandkreis in Zusammenarbeit mit dem Regierungspräsidium Chemnitz, Abteilung Umwelt, Außenstelle Plauen) (Übersetzung/Translated by David Strauss)

Natürliche Ressourcen / Natural Resources

Flussperlmuscheln im kleinsten vogtländischen Perlbach (Foto: T. Findeis)
Freshwater pearl mussels in the smallest Vogtland stream. (Photo by: T. Findeis)

Flussperlmuschel

Die letzten sächsischen Vorkommen der europaweit vom Aussterben bedrohten Flussperlmuschel (Margaritifera margaritifera) leben in vogtländischen Bächen. Waren einst die Weiße Elster und ein Großteil ihrer Zuflüsse im Oberen Vogtland mehr oder weniger durchgängig und in mehreren hunderttausend Exemplaren von dieser faszinierenden Großmuschel besiedelt (Perlfischerei!), haben im Zuge der Industrialisierung und Intensivierung der Landnutzung einhergehende Gewässerbelastungen die Art an den Rand des Aussterbens gebracht.

Die Flussperlmuschel, die existenziell auf saubere, sauerstoffreiche Fließgewässer angewiesen ist, weist eine hochinteressante Biologie auf: weibliche Tiere geben jährlich bis zu 4 Millionen befruchtete und ausgebrütete Eier (Glochidien) in das Freiwasser ab. Die mit einem „Schnappreflex" ausgestatteten Muschellarven müssen dann von einem Wirtsfisch (im Vogtland ausschließlich die Bachforelle) eingeatmet werden, wo sie sich an deren Kiemen festbeißen und im Kiemengewebe zur Jungmuschel entwickelt. Nach mehreren Monaten werden die dann nur ca. 0,5 mm großen Muscheln vom Wirtsfisch abgestoßen. Ab diesem Moment ist sie sich völlig selbst überlassen. Auf Grund ihrer geringen Masse ist die Jungmuschel gezwungen, sich im Bachsubstrat einzugraben, wo sie die ersten Lebensjahre verbringt.

Da die meisten ehemaligen Perlbäche mit Sedimenten und anderen Schadstoffen belastet sind, bleibt seit mehreren Jahrzehnten die Verjüngung dieser anspruchsvollen Muschelart aus. Schutzbemühungen der vergangenen 20 Jahre lassen jedoch hoffen, die Art auch für unsere Kinder und Enkel zu erhalten. Neben erforderlichen Maßnahmen zur Abwasserentsorgung, der landwirtschaftlichen Extensivierung bachnaher Flächen und Gewässerrenaturierungen gehört dazu auch die Nachzucht von Jungmuscheln unter Laborbedingungen.

Als Indikator sauberer Fließgewässer zeigt uns die Flussperlmuschel heute, wo die Wasserqualität noch weitgehend intakt ist. Die Bäche beherbergen deshalb eine Vielzahl weiterer, z.T. gefährdeter Arten wie z.B. Elritze, Edelkrebs, Zweigestreifte Quelljungfer und Blauflügel-Prachtlibelle.

Im Adorfer Heimatmuseum zeugt eine 800 Exponate umfassende Ausstellung vom vogtländischen Gewerbe der Perlmuttverarbeitung des vergangenen Jahrhunderts.

Freshwater Pearl Mussels

The last examples of freshwater pearl mussels (Margaritifera margaritifera) in Saxony – a species threatened with extinction in Europe – live in Vogtland streams. The White Elster river and many of its tributaries in the Upper Vogtland region were once more or less universally populated by several thousands of examples of this fascinating large mussel (pearl fishing!); but water pollution as a result of industrialisation and the intensification of use of the land has driven this species to the brink of extinction.

Freshwater pearl mussels, which depend on clean flowing water with plenty of oxygen for their very existence, are very interesting in biological terms: females lay up to 4 million fertilised and hatched eggs (larvae) in the fresh water every year. The mussel larvae, which are equipped with a "snap reflex" then need to be breathed in by a host fish (only brown trout in the Vogtland region), where they hold tight to its gills and develop into young mussels in the gill tissue. Several months later the host fish discards the mussels, which are only approx. 0.5 mm long. They are completely left to their own devices from this time onwards. The mussels are forced to dig into the substrate of the stream because of their small size and they spend their early years there.

As most of the former pearl streams are polluted with sediment and other contaminants, the regeneration of this sophisticated type of mussel died out for several decades. But protective measures introduced over the past 20 years are suggesting that this species may be preserved for our children and grandchildren. Necessary steps are being taken like disposing of waste water, decreasing the agricultural use of land near streams and water renaturation – and young mussels are also being bred in laboratory conditions.

The freshwater pearl mussels now demonstrate how clean our rivers are and where the water quality is still high. The streams also carry a variety of species, many of which are also under threat – e.g. minnows, European crayfish, golden-ringed dragonflies and beautiful demoiselle damselflies.

The local history museum in Adorf has 800 exhibits on the Vogtland business of processing pearl mussels in the last century.

Verschieden alte Flussperlmuscheln
Various old freshwater pearl mussels
(Foto/Photo by: M. Lange, INTERREG III A – Projekt „Flußperlmuschel Dreiländereck")

Natürliche Ressourcen / Natural Resources

Borstgrasrasen mit Arnika im Naturschutzgebiet „Zeidelweide und Pfaffenlohe"
False oat grass with arnica in the "Zeidelweide and Pfaffenlohe" nature conservation area
(Foto/Photo by: T. Findeis)

» *Wer die Natur betrachtet, wird vom Geheimnis des Lebens gefangen genommen.* « Albert Schweitzer

» *Those who observe nature will be captivated by the secret of life.* « Albert Schweitzer

Bergwiesen

Auf Höhenlagen über 500 m NN und somit vor allem auf das südliche und östliche Vogtland ist das Vorkommen von Bergwiesen beschränkt. Im Gegensatz zum EU-Einheitsgrün stechen die auch aus kulturhistorischer Sicht wertvollen Bergwiesen durch ihren Arten- und Blütenreichtum positiv hervor. Wegen der Belebung des Landschaftsbildes und ihrer Funktion als Lebensraum für eine Vielzahl gefährdeter Tiere und Pflanzen sind sie für den Natur- und Artenschutz so wertvoll. Die Arnika – auch Bergwohlverleih genannt – ist eine typische Bergwiesenart. Früher massenhaft vorkommend, wurden ihre Blüten zur Gewinnung von Essenzen als Heilmittel gesammelt. Heute steht die Art, wie viele andere auch, unter dem besonderen Schutz des Naturschutzgesetzes, womit die Entnahme aus der Natur nicht gestattet ist. Weitere typische Pflanzen der vogtländischen Bergwiesen sind z.B. Bärwurz, Wald-Storchschnabel, Schwarze Teufelskralle, Rundblättrige Glockenblume und Perücken-Flockenblume. Aber auch für die Fauna stellen Bergwiesen ein wichtiges Refugium dar. Schmetterlinge wie der Lilagold-Feuerfalter, die Kleine Goldschrecke und hunderte weiterer Insektenarten profitieren vom Blüten- und Strukturreichtum der Bergwiesen. Aber auch Wirbeltiere wie Braunkehlchen und Wiesenpieper, Kreuzotter, Blindschleiche und Waldeidechse gehören zu den typischen Bergwiesenbewohnern.

Auch wenn es mit Storchschnabel-Goldhafer-Bergwiesen, Berg-Glatthafer-Frischwiesen und Borstgrasrasen verschiedenste Ausprägungen von Bergwiesen gibt – eines ist ihnen allen ge-meinsam: entstanden sind sie durch jahrzehnte- oder gar jahrhundertelange Mahdnutzung, weitgehend ohne Düngung. Vielfältige Gefährdungsursachen haben den einst auch im Vogtland weiter verbreiteten Biotoptyp stark dezimiert: Nutzungsintensivierung, -änderung (Aufforstung, Umbruch) oder aber auch Brachfallen durch Nutzungsaufgabe. Deshalb gehören die Bergwiesen zu den in Sachsen per Gesetz besonders geschützten Biotoptypen (§ 26 SächsNatSchG).

Schwerpunkte vogtländischer Bergwiesenvorkommen existieren am Aschberg bei Klingenthal, Mühlleithen, um Schöneck, in Gottesberg bei Tannenbergsthal und bei Hennebach, nahe Bad Brambach.

Mühlleithen – eingebettet in verschiedenste Typen von Bergwiesen/ Mühlleithen – embedded in various types of hill meadows (Foto/Photo by: W. Böhnert)

Hill Meadows

There are only hill meadows above 500 metres and so most of them are restricted to the southern and eastern parts of the Vogtland region. In contrast with standard EU greenery, these hill meadows, which are valuable from a cultural history point of view, stand out because of the richness of species and flowers that they contain. They are so valuable for protecting nature and species because they brighten up the landscape and provide a habitat for so many threatened animals and plants. The arnica – also known as Arnica montana – are a typical type of hill meadow. There used to be plenty of them and their flowers were picked to obtain essences for medicinal purposes. Nowadays this type of meadow – along with many others – is protected by the Nature Conservation Act; this means that they must be conserved. Other typical plants on the Vogtland hill meadows are the spignel, woodland geranium, black rampion, bluebell and centaurea pseudophrygia. But hill meadows also provide an important refuge for fauna. Butterflies like the purple-edged copper, the brown mountain grasshopper and hundreds of other species of insects benefit from the wealth of flowers and structures on the hill meadows. Vertebrates like the whinchats, adders, grass snakes and common lizards are just some of the creatures living on hill meadows.

Even if there are different types of hill meadows with woodland geranium/ golden oats meadows, hill/false oat grass meadows and ornamental onion meadows – they all have one thing in common: they were created by decades and centuries of mowing, largely without any fertilisation. Many threats have almost decimated what was once a familiar biotope in the Vogtland region: agricultural use, changes (forestation, radical change) or fallow land after farmers abandoned it. This is why the hill meadows are one of the biotopes that are protected by law in Saxony (Section 26, Saxon Nature Conservation Act).

The main hill meadows in the Vogtland region can be found on the Aschberg near Klingenthal, Mühlleithen, around Schöneck, in Gottesberg near Tannenbergsthal and at Hennebach, near Bad Brambach.

Natürliche Ressourcen / Natural Resources

Von der Natur lernen
Learning from Nature

Natur- und Umweltzentrum Vogtland

Waren Sie schon einmal in Oberlauterbach? Noch nicht – dann wird es aber Zeit! Der Ort, bestehend aus den Dörfern Oberlauterbach und Unterlauterbach, belegte bereits dreimal erste Plätze im Kreisausscheid des Wettbewerbes „Unser Dorf soll schöner werden, unser Dorf hat Zukunft". 1999 wurde sogar im sächsischen Landeswettbewerb der dritte Platz belegt.

Die erste urkundliche Erwähnung geht auf das Jahr 1421 zurück. Ausgangspunkt der bäuerlichen Entwicklung in Unterlauterbach war das Rittergut. Das Herrenhaus des Rittergutes und weitere Gebäude wurden nach der Wende neu aufgebaut bzw. saniert. Seit dem Jahr 2000 ist das bereits 1992 gegründete Natur- und Umweltzentrum Vogtland Mieter des Herrenhauses und prägt seitdem mit seinem Programm und seinen Aktivitäten das dörfliche Leben und darüber hinaus den weiteren Umkreis entscheidend mit. Gemeinsam mit den ortsansässigen Vereinen leben traditionelle Dorffeste wieder auf.

Im Jahr 2005 wurde der Verbindungsbau zweier Gebäude im Osten des Rittergutsgeländes, die so genannte Ostlücke, fertig gestellt und kann nun ebenfalls durch das Natur- und Umweltzentrum Vogtland und den Landschaftspflegehof des Vogtlandkreises genutzt werden. Wiederum mit Fördermitteln der Europäischen Union wurde in den Jahren 2006 und 2007 ein Gebäudeteil zur Naturherberge mit insgesamt 36 Betten ausgebaut und zur Nutzung übergeben.

Unter dem Motto „Umwelt erleben mit allen Sinnen" ist das Programm des Natur- und Umweltzentrums Vogtland auf eine ganzheitliche Betrachtungsweise unserer Umwelt ausgerichtet. Es werden zu allen Teilen des Umweltschutzes, wie Naturschutz, Abfallberatungen, Wasser, Klimaschutz und alternative Energien bis hin zur Ernährungsberatung, Kenntnisse vermittelt und teils spielerisch umgesetzt.

Besonders interessant sind Fledermaus- und Vogelstimmen-, Kräuter-, Pilz- und botanische Wanderungen oder – alles verbindend – eine Waldrallye. Interessenten, welche allein die Umgebung von Oberlauterbach erkunden wollen, können dies auf dem Lehrpfad „Klassenzimmer Natur" und dem Bienenlehrpfad tun. Ein auf die einzelnen Altersklassen abgestimmtes Programm kann besonders bei Projekttagen für Schulen und andere Kindereinrichtungen umgesetzt werden. Bei den kleineren Kindern steht dabei die spielerische Vermittlung von Kenntnissen und bei den Jugendlichen die Vermittlung im Zusammenhang mit der Selbsterarbeitung von Wissen im Vordergrund.

Großes Augenmerk der Arbeit des Natur- und Umweltzentrums Vogtland liegt in der Berücksichtigung von Familien, Senioren und benachteiligten Menschen. Entsprechend diesen Anforderungen sind Feste, Exkursionen und Projekttage gezielt ausgerichtet, vor allem auch, um gemeinsame Erlebnisse zu schaffen.

Vogtland Nature and Environment Centre

Have you been to Oberlauterbach? Not yet – then it is time to do so! It consists of the villages of Oberlauterbach and Unterlauterbach and has already captured first place in the district competition entitled "Our village should be more beautiful – our village has a future". It was even third in the Saxon-wide state competition in 1999.

The location was first mentioned in official records in 1421. The starting point for agricultural developments in Unterlauterbach was the manor house. The stately manor home and other buildings were reconstructed or restored after the fall of the Berlin Wall. The Vogtland Nature and Environment Centre, which was set up in 1992, has been a tenant in the building since 2000 and has had a marked effect on village life and beyond with its programme and activities. Traditional village festivals have flourished again in conjunction with local associations.

The building that connects two others on the eastern part of the manor house estate, what is known as the eastern gap, was completed in 2005 and can now be used by the Vogtland Nature and Environment Centre and the Vogtland district's landscape conservation centre. One part of the building was extended to form a country hostel with a total of 36 beds in 2006 and 2007 and was handed over for use.

Under the motto "Experiencing the Environment with Every Sense", the programme of the Vogtland Nature and Environment Centre is directed at viewing things from an all-round perspective. Information is provided about all kinds of ways of protecting the environment – nature conservation, advice on waste, water, protecting our climate, alternative energy sources and even advice on nutrition – and some of these are communicated in the form of games.

The bat, birdsong, herbs, mushrooms and botanical walks are particularly interesting – or something that combines every element – a wood tour. Those who are just interested in discovering the surroundings in Oberlauterbach can do so using the "Nature Classroom" nature trail and the bee nature trail. A programme adjusted to the needs of individual school classes can be used particularly for project days at schools and other children's centres. Younger children can learn much by playing games and young people learn a great deal by working through knowledge themselves.

The Vogtland Nature and Environment Centre attaches great importance to families, old people and those at a disadvantage. Festivals, excursions and project days are deliberately aimed at these groups to provide them with opportunities to enjoy events together.

(Fotos/Photos by Landratsamt Vogtlandkreis Umweltamt, Text/Text by Landratsamt Vogtlandkreis Umweltamt, Übersetzung/Translated by David Strauss)

Natürliche Ressourcen / Natural Resources

Eine besondere Berücksichtigung finden die Aspekte „Umweltbildung" und auch das Basteln mit Naturprodukten bzw. das Basteln mit verwertbaren Abfällen bei den größeren Festen im Hofbereich, wie z. B. anlässlich des Frühlingserwachens der Wanderer, zu Himmelfahrt, im Rahmen der Vogtlandradtour und des Teichfestes. Bei diesen Festen wird auch ein weiteres Handlungsfeld deutlich, die Förderung der regionalen und ökologischen Landwirtschaft. Zu diesen Anlässen können einheimische Erzeuger landwirtschaftlicher Produkte diese zum Verkauf anbieten. Eine Möglichkeit, die rege genutzt wird. Auch im Rahmen der Vorträge findet dieses Thema große Beachtung.

Das Natur- und Umweltzentrum Vogtland ist eines der fünf Regionalzentren im Netzwerk Umweltbildung Sachsen. In dieser Funktion werden gemeinsame Aktivitäten koordiniert und Programme abgestimmt. Netzwerkpartner werden in die eigenen Programme einbezogen und können sich auch auf anderen Veranstaltungen mit vorstellen. Durch diese Vernetzung konnte die Umweltbildung im Vogtland effektiviert werden und es gelang, durch gezieltes gemeinsames Marketing den Erfolg der Veranstaltungen, besonders im Hinblick auf die Beteiligung und die Qualität der nachhaltigen Wissensvermittlung, zu erhöhen. Die Netzwerkpartner unterstützen auch die bis zu zweimal monatlich jeweils Mittwochs durchgeführten Vortragsveranstaltungen und Ausstellungen in den Räumen des Natur- und Umweltzentrums Vogtland. Dabei werden in erster Linie Themen angeboten, die regional von Interesse sind und andererseits populärwissenschaftliche Themen aus vielfältigen Interessensgebieten.

Ein wesentliches Thema ist auch die Meditation von Problemen im Umweltbereich, die von verschiedenen Interessengruppen kontrovers diskutiert werden, so u. a. die Themen „Mobilfunk", „Umsetzung der Wasserrahmenrichtlinie" und „Akzeptanz für den Naturschutz".

"Environmental training" is particularly taken into consideration and this includes making things with natural products or recycled waste at the major festivals at the centre – e.g. the spring awakening for walkers, on Ascension Day, as part of the Vogtland cycling tour or the pond festival. These occasions also underline another sphere of activity – promoting regional and ecological agriculture. Local producers of agricultural goods can offer them for sale on these occasions. They make full use of this opportunity. This subject is also important in the lectures that are given.

The Vogtland Nature and Environment Centre is one of five regional centres in the Saxon Environmental Education Network. As a result, joint activities are coordinated and programmes are adjusted accordingly. Partners in the network are drawn into the programme and can introduce their facilities at other events. This network has enabled environmental education to be communicated more effectively in the Vogtland region and the success of events has been increased as a result of deliberate joint marketing – particularly in terms of the quality of the information that has been communicated and those communicating it. The network partners also support the lectures, which are held on a Wednesday sometimes twice a month, and the exhibitions in the rooms of the Vogtland Nature and Environment Centre. These primarily deal with subjects of regional interest and also popular scientific themes from many fields of knowledge.

One major theme involves thinking about problems in the environmental field, which are controversial to people in different pressure groups: e.g. mobile phones, implementing the Water Framework Directive and acceptance of the idea of nature conservation.

Natürliche Ressourcen / Natural Resources

Sicherlich ist es schwer, den Erfolg eines solchen Zentrums zeitnah zu messen. Wir sind aber bestrebt, die Gedanken des Umweltschutzes so zu vermitteln, dass sich die Besucher auch damit identifizieren können und somit ihr langfristiges Handeln entsprechend ausrichten. Als positives Beispiel hierzu steht die Anwendung von erneuerbaren Energien. Hier sind wir der Meinung, dass das Natur- und Umweltzentrum Vogtland durch die vielfältigen Veranstaltungen einen wesentlichen Beitrag dazu geleistet hat, dass die Zahl der Anwender im Landkreis im Gegensatz zum Rest des Freistaates überproportional gestiegen ist.

Sie waren noch nicht in Oberlauterbach und haben nach dem Lesen dieser Zeilen und Betrachten dieser Bilder Interesse gefunden und wollen uns einmal besuchen? Nutzen Sie unsere Hoffeste bzw. Vorträge, um uns kennen zu lernen, oder vereinbaren Sie einfach einen Termin unter der Telefonnummer 03745/75105.
Und falls Sie länger bleiben wollen, können Sie auch in unserer Naturherberge übernachten und am nächsten Morgen ein regionales Frühstück genießen.

It is certainly difficult to measure the success of a centre like this at this time. But we are seeking to transmit the ideas of protecting the environment in such a way that visitors can identify with them and therefore change their long-term habits as a result. The use of renewable energies is one positive example of this. We believe that the Vogtland Nature and Environment Centre has played a major role in this with its various events – the number of users of these types of energy in the rural district has risen above average in comparison with the rest of the Free State.

So you have not been to Oberlauterbach yet, but you are now interested in coming after having read these few lines and seen the photos and would like to visit us? Use our festivals or lectures to get to know us or make an appointment by phoning us on 03745/75105.

And in case you would like to stay longer, you can spend the night in our country hostel and enjoy a regional breakfast after a good sleep.

Natur- und Umweltzentrum Vogtland
Treuener Straße 2
08239 Oberlauterbach
OT Unterlauterbach
Telefon +49 (0) 3745 75105-0
Telefax +49 (0) 3745 75105-35
nuz@nuz-vogtland.de
www.nuz-vogtland.de

Natürliche Ressourcen / Natural Resources

Gelebte Traditionen / Traditions Perpetuated

Orgelpfeifen für Putin
Organ Pipes for President Putin

In der vom Musikinstrumentenbau geprägten vogtländischen Landschaft gibt es nur eine Orgelbaufirma, und die ist abseits vom traditionellen Musikwinkel zuhause. Orgelbaumeister Thomas Wolf aus Netzschkau lernte seinen Beruf in der Greizer Firma Schüßler, die er 1997 übernahm. Als die Werkstatt aus allen Nähten platzte, verlegte er sein Unternehmen 2002 in ein ehemaliges Webereigebäude in Limbach, das zuvor mit hohem Aufwand renoviert und umgebaut wurde. Seitdem firmiert der Orgelbaumeister unter Vogtländischer Orgelbau Thomas Wolf. Zu seinem Team gehören neun Mitarbeiter, darunter drei Lehrlinge. In Ausbildung befindet sich auch Tochter Patricia, die sich zurzeit auf die Gesellenprüfung vorbereitet.

Die Liste der Orgelstandorte, an denen Thomas Wolf mit seinen Mitarbeitern Spuren hinterlassen hat, ist lang. Zu den herausragenden Arbeiten dürfte schon das Meisterstück gehören, Orgelpositiv mit vier Registern, welches das ganze Jahr auf Wanderschaft an bekannten Konzertorten ist und auch schon bei den Händel-Festspielen in Halle erklang. Seine erste große Orgel baute Thomas Wolf 2006 am Gymnasium Albertinum Coburg. Für die Restaurierung und Rekonstruktion der Röver-Orgel in der Salvatorkirche Gera erhielt die Firma den Handwerkerpreis der Stadt für die denkmalpflegerischen Leistungen. Die Restaurierung der Eule-Orgel in Tannenbergsthal brachte dem Orgelbaumeister ein Empfehlungsschreiben von Frauenkirchenkantor Matthias Grünert. Zu den interessanten Projekten gehören die Restaurierung der Trampeli-Orgel in Sirbis, die Restaurierung und Rekonstruktion der 1764 gebauten Gerhard-Orgel in Jena-Ziegenhain, die Instandsetzung der Jehmlich-Orgel in der Methodistischen Kirche Netzschkau oder die Restaurierung einer Röver-Orgel in Neinstedt/Harz, an der die Firma gegenwärtig arbeitet.

2007 fertigten die Limbacher Orgelbauer Pfeifen für den Neubau einer Orgel im russischen Kaliningrad/Königsberg, die kein geringerer als Präsident Putin in Auftrag gab. Die längste dafür in Limbach gebaute Holzpfeife war über fünf Meter lang und wog 66 Kilogramm.

Ein Blick in die Orgelwerkstatt von Thomas Wolf verrät, was so ein Instrumentenbauer alles beherrschen muss. Das Repertoire reicht von Holz- und Metallbearbeitung bis zu musikalischen Kenntnissen für das Intonieren oder Wissen in Baustilkunde und Kunstgeschichte. Der Orgelbauer bietet auch besondere Leistungen an. Zum Beispiel werden in Limbach die Platten für die Zinnpfeifen noch selbst gegossen.

There is only one organ building company in the Vogtland region, which is so dominated by musical instrument making. Surprisingly it is not situated in the traditional Musicon Valley area. Organ builder Thomas Wolf from Netzschkau learned his profession at the Schüßler company based in Greiz, which he took over in 1997. When his workshop was about to burst at the seams in 2002, he relocated his company to a former weaving mill in Limbach, which had previously been renovated and converted with a great deal of effort. Since that time the company has been operating under the name of Vogtländischer Orgelbau Thomas Wolf (Thomas Wolf Vogtland Organ Building). He has nine employees, including three trainees. His daughter Patricia is also an apprentice and is currently preparing for her final professional exams.

The list of locations where Thomas Wolf and his staff have left their mark on organs is long. One of his most praised works may be his master piece, a transportable organ with four stops, which is currently touring famous concert locations and has already been played at the Handel Festival in Halle. Thomas Wolf built his first large organ in 2006 at the Albertinum grammar school in Coburg. The company was awarded the craftsmen's award by the city of Gera for its work in the historic preservation of a masterpiece – restoring and reconstructing the Röver organ in the Salvator Church. The restoration work on the Eule organ in Tannenbergsthal brought a letter of reference for the organ builder from Matthias Grünert, the church musician at the Church of Our Lady in Dresden. Other interesting projects for the company have included the reconstruction of the Trampeli organ in Sirbis, the restoration of the Gerhard organ in Jena-Ziegenhain, which was built in 1764, the renovation of the Jehmlich organ in the Methodist church in Netzschkau and the restoration of a Röver organ in Neinstedt in the Harz Mountains; the company is still working on this project.

The organ builders from Limbach built the organ pipes for the new organ being constructed in the Russian city of Kaliningrad in 2007. The order came from no less a figure than the Russian President Vladimir Putin. The longest wooden pipe built for this project in Limbach was more than five metres long and weighed 66 kilograms.

A glance at Thomas Wolf's workshops proves that an instrument builder of this kind has to be a master of many trades. His repertoire includes wood and metal processing as well as musical knowledge for the intonation of instruments and a knowledge of architectural styles and art history. The organ builder also provides special services. For example, the company still casts the sheets for the pipes made of tin itself.

(Fotos/Photos by Petra Steps/Text by Petra Steps, Übersetzung/Translated by David Strauss)

Gelebte Traditionen / Traditions Perpetuated

Kunst kommt von Können
Ability Gives Birth to Art

„Licht und Farbe das ganze Jahr" verspricht Kunstverglaserin Dagmar Müller aus Reichenbach. In ihrer kleinen Werkstatt in der Lutherstraße kann man erahnen, was sie damit meint. Glas in verschiedenen Farben und Designs sowie Bleisprossen warten auf die Verarbeitung. Zum Firmenangebot gehören die Restaurierung und die Neuanfertigung von Bleiverglasungen. Ein neues Betätigungsfeld ist die Fensterbildherstellung. Während sie bei großen Arbeiten auf die künstlerischen Motive vergangener Generationen festgelegt ist, kann sie hier ihrer Fantasie freien Lauf lassen. Im Laufe der Zeit entstanden bunte Schmetterlinge, Blüten und eine ganze Weihnachtskollektion. Oder Dagmar Müller gestaltet Glasmalereien zu Fensterbildern. In der Werkstatt hängen davon mehrere Beispiele.
Zurzeit steigt das Kundeninteresse am Umarbeiten historischer Bleiglasfenster in moderne Isolierverglasungen. Die Bleiglasfelder müssen dabei in mühevoller Kleinarbeit von der Kunstverglaserin in Einzelteile zerlegt und neu verbleit werden. Anschließend wird es im Glaswerk ähnlich einem Sandwich zwischen zwei Scheiben zu einer Isolierglasscheibe gepresst.
Mit ihrem uralten Kunsthandwerk hat sich die Reichenbacherin in eine Männerdomäne eingeschlichen. Zum Berufsalltag gehören Tätigkeiten wie Fenster ein- und ausbauen, Bleiglasornamente neu fertigen oder alte reparieren. Sie muss Entwürfe, Zeichnungen und Schablonen erstellen, Glas zuschneiden, das Blei um die Teile legen und an den Enden verlöten. Ohne Baustilkunde geht nichts, denn niemand will ein mit Jugendstilornamenten verunstaltetes Klassizismusfenster. Was bei der Demonstration auf Handwerkermärkten ganz leicht aussieht, kann in schwere Knochenarbeit ausarten, denn so ein Fenster oder eine Türverglasung wiegen etliche Kilogramm.
Das Handwerk erlernte Dagmar Müller erst im dritten Anlauf, nach Abitur, mehreren anderen Berufen und Tätigkeiten sowie einem jahrelangen Aufenthalt in den alten Bundesländern. Seit 1996 lebt sie wieder in ihrer vogtländischen Heimat. Manchmal wird Dagmar Müller als Frau erst skeptisch beäugt. Doch daran hat sie sich längst gewöhnt, denn ihre gute Arbeit ist anerkannt. Die Aufträge kommen nicht mehr nur aus der Region, sondern auch aus Bayern oder Baden-Württemberg. An und in vielen Gebäuden hat Dagmar Müller schon ihre Spuren hinterlassen.

"Light and colour all year round" is the promise made by glazing artist Dagmar Müller from Reichenbach. And you can imagine what she means if you go to her little workshop in Luther Street. Glass in many different colours and designs and lead came is waiting to be processed. The company carries out restoration work as well as new lead glazing work. The production of window pictures is a new line of business. While larger projects often limit her creativity to traditional artistic motives from past generations, window pictures allow her to follow her own imagination. In the course of time she has created a variety of colourful butterflies, floral arrangements and a whole Christmas collection. Or Dagmar Müller designs glass painting for window pictures. Some examples can be seen in her workshop.
Nowadays some customers are increasingly interested in preserving historical lead glass windows in modern double glazing. To do this, the lead glass windows have to be dismantled step by step into single fragments by the glazing artist and re-leaded afterwards. Then the window is put between two plates of glass and is compressed into one double glazing pane rather like a sandwich.
The lady from Reichenbach has also slipped into what was a male domain with her traditional artwork. Her day-to-day work routine includes tasks like mounting and removing windows and producing new leaded glass ornaments or repairing old ones. She has to produce blueprints, drafts and templates, cut out the glass, set the lead around each piece and solder it at the ends. She has to have a profound knowledge of architectural styles: after all, nobody wants to see a Classicist window ruined by an Art Nouveau ornament. What may look easy at a demonstration at a craft fair can be very tough physical work at times; after all, windows or door glazing like this can be very heavy.
Dagmar Müller learnt her trade at the third attempt: after completing her final school exams, she tried several other jobs and professions and spent several years in western Germany. But she has lived in her home Vogtland region again since 1996. Sometimes people look at her rather strangely because she is a woman. But she has got used to that because people appreciate her good work. Nowadays she not only receives job orders from the local region, but also from Bavaria or Baden-Württemberg. So Dagmar Müller has left her mark on many a building.

Kunstverglasung Reichenbach
Inhaberin Dagmar Müller
Lutherstraße 35
D-08468 Reichenbach
Telefon/Fax: + 49 (0) 3765 711414
Dagmar-Mueller-Glas@t-online.de
www.kunstverglasung-reichenbach.de

(Fotos/Photos by Hartmut Briese/Text by Petra Steps, Übersetzung/Translated by David Strauss)

Echte Handarbeit spricht sich rum
Word Gets Around about Real Craftsmanship

Egal, ob man auf den Hund gekommen ist oder sich dem Reitsport verschrieben hat – in der Sattlerei von Stefan Reißmann in Oberreichenbach stößt man auf offene Ohren, wenn Hunde- oder Reitsportartikel aus Leder gebraucht werden. Die Arbeitsräume befinden sich in einem Bauerngut fernab der Hauptverkehrsstraßen. „Die Werkstatt braucht kein Schild – die Leute finden mich auch so", ist sich der Sattler sicher. So viele, die sich noch der echten Handarbeit verschrieben haben, gibt es in der Region nicht.
Gleich nach der Schule erlernte der Reichenbacher seinen Traumberuf ist. Wenn er von seiner Tätigkeit erzählt, dann kommt er regelrecht ins Schwärmen. Leder ist sein Element, damit arbeitet er schon seit 15 Jahren. 2005 ergriff er die Gelegenheit beim Schopfe und wagte den Schritt in die Selbstständigkeit.
Stefan Reißmann geht gern auf die Wünsche seiner Kunden ein und versucht dabei, seine kreativen Ideen umzusetzen. Bei Neuanfertigungen spielen auch Modeerscheinungen eine Rolle, zum Beispiel Farben fernab des normalen Schwarz-Weiß-Braun-Angebotes. Oder Verzierungen, wie die gegenwärtig gefragten Swarovski-Kristalle auf Hundehalsbändern. Auf Messen holt sich der Fachmann dafür die Anregungen.
Manchmal kommen Oldtimer-Freunde mit Spezialaufträgen in die Werkstatt. Neben Neuanfertigungen hat sich der Sattler auch der Reparatur verschrieben, und da geht es von der geliebten winzigen Handtasche bis zum respektablen Forstgeschirr. Gern erinnert er sich an einen Spezialauftrag, bei dem er für eine Pferdefreundin das Geschirr für die Verbindung zwischen Pferd und Sulky gefertigt hat. Seine Maßarbeit war jetzt schon zwei Mal bei Deutschen Meisterschaften und bei anderen Wettbewerben im Distanzfahren dabei.
Sein Handwerkszeug hält Stefan Reißmann in Ehren. Einige Teile wie der Halbmond zum Lederschneiden sind schon über 100 Jahre alt. Auch das Nähross, auf dem der Sattler beim Nähen sitzt, hat schon viele Jahre auf dem Buckel. Manche Hausfrau würde bestimmt neidisch, wenn sie sähe, wie schnell und akkurat der Fachmann Stich für Stich mit der Hand setzt.

It is irrelevant whether people have gone to the dogs or have dedicated their life to riding – they will find an open ear at Stefan Reissmann's saddlery in Oberreichenbach if they need leather sporting items for dogs or horses. The workshops are located in a farm building right off the beaten track. "The workshop doesn't need a signboard – people find me anyway," the saddler is confident. There are not that many people in the region who have committed themselves to producing genuine hand-made products.
The native of Reichenbach learned the job of his dreams straight after leaving school. When he starts talking about his work, he becomes really enthusiastic. Leather is his thing – he has been working with this material for 15 years. He jumped at the opportunity in 2005 and summoned up the courage to go self-employed.
Stefan Reissmann is very happy to respond to his customers' wishes and he tries to produce his creative ideas at the same time. When making new products, fashion also plays a role – for example, in the choice of colours that move away from the normal black or white or brown. Or in the case of decorations – some people want Swarovski crystal on the collar for their dog. The specialist goes to trade fairs to pick up new ideas.
Fans of vintage cars sometimes come to the workshops with special requests. The saddler not only produces new items, but also carries out repair work. This ranges from a precious tiny handbag to massive harnesses for forestry purposes. He can well remember a special order where he made the harness for the link between the horse and sulky for a horse-lover. His made-to-measure work has now been used twice at German championships and other long distance horse race competitions.
Stefan Reissmann has respect for his tools. Some of them, like the half moon used to cut leather, are more than 100 years old. Even the sewing stool, where the saddler sits for sewing, has been around for a few years. Many housewives would be envious if they could see how quickly and accurately this expert sews his stitches by hand.

(Fotos/Photos by Petra Steps/Text by Petra Steps, Übersetzung/Translated by David Strauss)

Gelebte Traditionen / Traditions Perpetuated

Kompetenz lässt Leistung reifen
Expertise Allows Performances to Mature

Saßen wir nicht schon alle einmal ehrfürchtig auf dem Rücken eines Pferdes und schauten hinab zur entfernten Erde. Auf dem Fohlenhof Schöniger haben sich die Kinder daran längst gewöhnt, sie genießen es vielmehr, denn sie kommen zum Training in den Talentstützpunkt Ponyreiten. Und sie sind hier an der absolut richtigen Stelle, weil die Voraussetzungen passen. Ob in der eigenen Reithalle, auf dem Reitplatz oder der Geländestrecke- alle Trainingsmethoden und –möglichkeiten können ausgeschöpft werden. Gunter Schöniger ist Trainer und Besitzer des Fohlenhofes und er gibt es preis- sein reichhaltiges Fachwissen. Bei Championaten, deutschen Meisterschaften und der Beschickung der Europameisterschaften ist er als Mitglied der nationalen Reiterlichen Vereinigung (FN) verantwortlich für die Ponyvielseitigkeit. Außerdem sitzt er im sächsischen Vielseitigkeitsausschuss. Kinder ab 5 Jahre werden hier ausgebildet vom Anfänger bis zum erfolgreichen Turnierreiter. Nehmen die Schützlinge vom Fohlenhof Schöniger an Championaten und Meisterschaften in Deutschland teil, kehren sie meist erfolgreich ins Vogtland zurück. Beim Vierkampf, der sich über zwei Tage verteilt, muss der Reiter zunächst 50 Meter Schwimmen und 3000 Meter Laufen. Am folgenden Tag wird die Dressur und das Springen absolviert. Bei der „Vielseitigkeit" handelt es sich um Dressur, Springen und Geländereiten.

Sachsenmeisterschaft Grimma 2007 (Springen Klasse A): im Bild Reiterin Antje Schöniger mit Urano (Foto: db-fotos.de)

Auerbach 2007 (Stilspringen Klasse A): im Bild Reiterin Sandra Möckel mit Mars (Foto: db-fotos.de)

Erfolge der Reiter Fohlenhof Schöniger
Antje Schöniger, 19:
   5malige Sächsische Meisterin,
   10. Platz Deutsche Meisterschaft 2003
Sandra Möckel, 16:
   Sieger Landesbestenermittlung
   mehrfache sächsischer Vizemeister,
   Vielseitigkeit und Dressur
Julius Gerisch, 14:
   Sächsischer Meister Vielseitigkeit Pony,
   Sächsischer Vizemeister Vielseitigkeit
   Junioren und Pony Dressur
Michellé Mothes, 12:
   Sächsischer Meister Springen,
   3. Platz Sächsische Meisterschaft Dressur
   2007 Sächsische Meisterin Vierkampf
Desiree Müller, 13:
   Sieger Landesbestenermittlung Vielseitigkeit
Nastasja Marquard, 12:
   6. Platz Bundeschampionat Vielseitigkeit
Lukas Wappler, 13:
   Teilnehmer Bundeschampionat Vielseitigkeit

Have we not all set on a horse's back with a sense of awe and looked down to the earth far below us? The children have long since grown accustomed to this at Schöniger Riding Stables – they tend to enjoy the experience, for they come to train at the pony riding talent centre. And they are in exactly the right place, because the conditions here are ideal. All the training methods and opportunities can be fully exploited – at the indoor or outdoor riding areas or on the cross-country course. Gunter Schöniger is the trainer and owner of the riding stables and he is prepared to pass on his expert knowledge to others. At competitions, German championship and when sending delegates to European Championships, he is the member of the national Equestrian Association (FN) who is responsible for pony eventing. He is also a member of the Saxon Eventing Committee. Children from the age of 5 are trained here – from beginners to successful tournament riders. If protégés from the Schöniger Riding Stables take part in competitions and championships, they usually return to the Vogtland region with plenty of trophies. During the four discipline event, which is spread over two days, the rider first has to swim 50 metres and run 3,000 metres. The dressage and horse jumping have to be completed on the second day. "Eventing" includes dressage, horse jumping and cross country riding.

Fohlenhof Schöniger kurz & knapp:
60 Hektar Grünland in Bewirtschaftung
60 Pferde und Reitponys mit Zucht
(3 gekörte Hengste und jährlich 4-6 Fohlen mit Aufzucht u. Ausbildung)

Fohlenhof Schöniger: im Bild Reiter Julius Gerisch mit Kaiserstolz (Foto: Marion Partenfelder)

Fohlenhof Schöniger: im Bild Reiterin Nastasja Marquard mit King (Foto: Fohlenhof)

FOHLENHOF Schöniger
- Reitbetrieb
- Zucht
- Pension
- Reitsportartikel

Polenzstraße 25 · 08485 Lengenfeld
Tel. 037606 2795 · Fax 037606 32721
info@fohlenhof-schoeniger.de
www.fohlenhof-schoeniger.de

(Übersetzung/Translated by David Strauss)

Gelebte Traditionen / Traditions Perpetuated

Tradition heißt weitergeben

Tradition Means Passing Things

Das Vogtland gehört zu den Regionen in Deutschland, die auf mannigfaltige Traditionen verweisen können und wo diese auch noch gelebt werden. „Traditio" steht im Lateinischen für „Überlieferung". Und Tradition beschreibt das Überliefern und Bewahren von Sitten und Bräuchen, von Gepflogenheiten und Handlungsmustern, die einem bestimmten Menschenschlag eigen sind. Dass sich gerade im Vogtland noch viele solcher gewachsenen Bräuche und Verhaltensweisen bewahrt haben, liegt an seiner geografischen Lage, an seiner Landschaft und der damit verbundenen Ausprägung des Menschenschlags.

Der geografische Vogtlandbegriff hat seine Wurzeln im frühen Mittelalter, als das Gebiet im 12. Jahrhundert in den Besitz der Reichsministerialen, der Herren von Weida, kam. Aus deren Geschlecht gingen die späteren, Namen gebenden Voigte hervor, zu deren Besitzungen neben den heute sächsischen Gebie-ten auch angrenzende Landstriche in Franken (Hof), Böhmen (Asch) und Thüringen (Greiz) gehörten. Zwar nie eine wirkliche politische Verwaltungseinheit, konnte sich jedoch über heutige Landes- und Staatsgrenzen hinweg damals ein eigen-ständiger Kultur- und Siedlungsraum bilden.
Was wir heute „Euregio Egrensis" nennen, begründet seine Tradition somit bereits im Mittelalter. „Die historischen Verflechtungen im Gebiet der Euregio Egrensis, ob siedlungsgeschichtlich, kirchenpolitisch oder ethnographisch sind ausgesprochen eng", stellte Ronny Hager vom Verein für vogtländische Geschichte 2006 nach einem Treffen von Heimatforschern und Ortschronisten fest. So sind zum Beispiel Elemente der vogtländischen Tracht, wie „de Dachmütz", die Schirmmütze der Männer, oder die „Buckelhaube" der Frauen im sächsischen, thüringischen, bayrischen und böhmischen Vogtland gleichermaßen zu finden, wenn auch letztere im Raum um Asch und Hof in etwas abgewandelter Form. Dank des Engagements von Heimatvereinen und Folkloregruppen, wie zum Beispiel den Trachtengruppen aus Elsterberg, Weischlitz oder Oelsnitz, den „Gockechen" aus Jocketa oder den Grünbacher Folkloristen, wurde die Tracht, die sich als landschaftstypische Kleidung im 19. Jahrhundert entwickelt hat, bewahrt. Heute erlebt sie eine Renaissance, allerdings ohne bereits im großen Stil wieder den Eingang in die Alltagsmode gefunden zu haben, wie das bei unseren bayerischen Nachbarn der Fall ist.
Seit dem 8. Jahrhundert durch Slawen und ab dem 11. Jahrhundert durch Franken besiedelt, war das Vogtland schon immer ein Durchgangsland. Die großen mittelalterlichen Handelshauptstraßen – etwa von Regensburg nach Leipzig oder von Bamberg nach Dresden – trafen in Plauen zusammen. Dieser Umstand hat regionaltypische Tradition geprägt, insbesondere die Sprache. Der Vogtländer ist geliebt, aber auch verschrieen ob seines sprachlichen Singsangs, mit dem er sich deutlich und auch immer wieder nachdrücklich betont von sächsischer Zunge abhebt. Wie er ja auch nicht müde wird, zu konstatieren, dass er sich zwar gern dem Freistaat Sachsen angehörig fühlt,

The Vogtland region is one of those in Germany, which can point to a variety of traditions and it is also one where they are still being lived out. The Latin word "traditio" means "handing things down". And tradition describes passing on and maintaining customs and practices, habits and ways of acting, which are the mark of a particular group of people. The Vogtland region's geographical location, its scenery and the type of people here affected by them are the reason why many of these customs and behaviour patterns that have grown up are still part and parcel of life here.

The geographical term "Vogtland" has its roots in the early medieval period, when the region came under the rule of the imperial ministerials, the lords of Weida, in the twelfth century. They later gave birth to the reeves or Vögte, who gave the region its name; their territory included what is now Saxon Vogtland, as well as adjacent land in Franconia (Hof), Bohemia (Aš) and Thuringia (Greiz). It was never a political administrative unit, but was able to develop its own culture and became a self-contained residential region beyond today's state and national borders.
So the traditions in the area that we now call the "Euregio Egrensis" go back to the medieval period. "The historical links in the Euregio Egrensis region are very close, regardless of whether they relate to settlement patterns, church life or ethnographical issues," said Ronny Hager from the Association for Vogtland History in 2006 following a meeting of local history experts and chroniclers. Elements of Vogtland traditional dress, for example, "de Dachmütz", a peaked cap for men, or the "Buckelhaube" (bonnet) for women are the same in the Saxon, Thuringian, Bavarian and Bohemian parts of the Vogtland region, even if they have been slightly modified in the area near Aš and Hof. Thanks to the efforts made by local history associations and folklore groups – e.g. traditional costume groups in Elsterberg, Weischlitz or Oelsnitz, the "Gockechen" in Jocketa or the folklore group in Grünbach, the traditional costume, which developed as typical dress in the area in the 19th century, has been retained. It is experiencing a renaissance now, but has not once again become part of everyday fashion, as is the case with our Bavarian neighbours.
The Vogtland region was settled by the Slavs from the 8th century and by the Franks from the 11th century onwards and was always a transit area. The major medieval trade routes – e.g. from Regensburg to Leipzig or from Bamberg to Dresden – met in Plauen. This fact shaped regional traditions – especially the local language. People from the Vogtland region are well-liked, but are notorious for their sing-song speech, which clearly distinguishes them for other Saxon dialects, as people regularly point out. Local people do not tire of pointing out that they definitely feel part of the Free State of Saxony, but are not Saxons. Vogtland speech has a special place among German dialects. It forms a bridge between Upper and Central German speech and has absorbed elements from both. Dialect experts have subdivided the Vogtland region into several clearly defined speech

(Fotos/Photos by Harald Sulski, Igor Pastierovic [5], Foto-Dick [1] Text/Text by Ekkehard Glaß, Übersetzung/Translated by David Strauss)

aber keinesfalls ein Sachse sei. Das Vogtländische nimmt eine Sonderstellung unter den deutschen Mundarten ein. Es schlägt die Brücke zwischen den oberdeutschen und mitteldeutschen Spracheigenheiten, hat Elemente von beiden absorbiert. Gegliedert in mehrere, von den Mundartforschern klar abgegrenzte Sprachräume, zeigt sich das Vogtländische jedoch sehr differenziert. „So wandelt sich zum Beispiel der ‚Käse' in seiner sprachlichen Form von ‚Käs' im südlichen, über ‚Kees' im mittleren zu ‚Kaas' im nördlichen Vogtland", dozierte Dr. Friedrich Barthel, der Nestor der vogtländischen Mundartforschung.

Auch wenn in der Hochsprache – vor allem unter der Jugend – immer mehr Anglizismen und Internationalismen Eingang gefunden haben: Der Vogtländer hat sich seine Mundart erhalten. Und sie wird gepflegt, nicht nur in Heimatgruppen und Ensembles. In die Phalanx der gestandenen Mundartschreibenden sind junge Nachwuchsautoren vorgestoßen. Mit der zweiten Auflage der Vogtländischen Mundarttage, bei der 2007 immerhin 20 Autoren aus dem Vogtland, dem Erzgebirge und Bayern agierten, ist ein wirksames, öffentliches Podium für Mundart entstanden, dass vor allem auch den Weg in die Schulen gefunden hat und so auch schon bei den Jüngsten das Interesse für die landschaftlich gefärbte „Muttersprache" weckt. Und der nun schon seit mehreren Jahren veranstaltete „Guschenziehauf" – das Mundarttheatertreffen im „Bayerischen Hof" zu Grünbach – hat seine Fangemeinde quer durch alle Altersklassen.

Die Mundart gehört eben zu diesem Landstrich wie seine weitläufigen Höhenlagen, seine vor allem von Fichten beherrschten Wälder, die meist hügeligen Felder und Wiesen, die vielen Fluss- und Bachläufe. Und eben diese Landschaft ist es, die so prägend war für typisch vogtländische Traditionen und die auch in unseren Tagen noch in besonderem Maße auf die vogtländische Volksseele wirkt. Julius Mosen (1803 bis 1867), des Vogtlands berühmtester Dichter, hat dieses „Liebesverhältnis" einst mit folgenden Worten auf den Punkt gebracht: „Mit meinen Landsleuten habe ich immer die Anhänglichkeit an die heimatliche Erde des Vogtlandes gemeinsam gehabt. Wie es Menschen gibt, von welchen man, hat man sie einmal liebgewonnen, nie wieder lassen kann, so geht es uns auch mit Ortschaften und Gegenden."

Das einstige Land der Voigte war und ist nicht gerade mit fetten Böden gesegnet. Nur schwer konnte der Landmann der Scholle reiche Erträge abringen. Bis, ja bis – dem Entdeckergeist eines Christoph Kolumbus und vogtländischer Experimentierfreude sei's gedankt – die Kartoffel im 17. Jahrhundert von hier aus ihren Siegeszug als Grundnahrungsmittel nach ganz Sachsen und Thüringen antrat. Schon 1680 soll der feldmäßige Anbau der nährenden Knolle für unser Gebiet erwähnt sein, bereits ein halbes Jahrhundert bevor der Alte Fritz der Kartoffel in Preußen zu Ehren verhalf. Unsere Vorfahren müssen wahre Experten im Anbau der Erdäpfel gewesen sein, wird doch das Vogtland in älterer Literatur auch als das „Kartoffelland" bezeichnet. Verständlich, dass sich die Knolle ein

areas and the language spoken here is very varied. "For example, the word "Käse" (cheese) is pronounced "Käs" in the south, "Kees" in the central area and "Kaas" in the northern Vogtland area," says Dr. Friedrich Barthel, the doyen of Vogtland dialect research.

Even if more and more Anglicisms and international expressions are creeping into standard language – especially among young people – the Vogtland people have retained their dialect. And it is being cultivated – and not just in local history or theatre groups. Young authors are forging ahead and are now members of the phalanx of established dialect writers. An effective, public platform for dialect was created in the shape of the second meeting of the Vogtland Dialect Conference in 2007 and it attracted no less than 20 authors from the Vogtland region, the Erzgebirge Mountains and Bavaria. It has found its way into the schools and has even generated some interest in the native language coloured by the local scenery among the very young. The "Guschenziehauf" – the dialect theatre meeting that has been held at "Der Bayerische Hof" hotel in Grünbach for a number of years – has its fans in every age group.

The dialect is just as much a part of this swathe of land as its rambling hills, its forests consisting mainly of coniferous trees, the fields and meadows, most of which are not flat, and the many rivers and streams. It is this scenery which has played such a crucial role in Vogtland traditions and still has a particular effect on the Vogtland psyche. Julius Mosen (1803 – 1867), the Vogtland region's most famous poet, once summarised this "love relationship" very poignantly: "I have always had this sense of devotion to my Vogtland home in common with my fellow countrymen. There are people, whom you can never drop once you have got to know them, and it is just the same for us with our villages and countryside."

The territory formerly ruled by the reeves (Voigte) was and is not exactly blessed with fertile soil. Farmers have struggled to get rich yields from the clods. Until – thanks to the spirit of adventure of Christopher Columbus and a Vogtland willingness to experiment – potatoes began their triumphal march as a staple food from here to the whole of Saxony and Thuringia in the 17th century. Records suggest that these nourishing tubers were planted in fields as early as 1680, half a century before Frederick the Second of Prussia helped potatoes become accepted there. Our forefathers must have been real experts in cultivating potatoes, as the Vogtland region is called "potato land" in some old literary works. So it comes as no surprise that potatoes rank high on the list of what is otherwise a rather modest culinary collection in the Vogtland region. Whether as "Spalken" (stew), Späkle (fried potatoes) or Bambes (potato pancakes), the traditional dishes of old still hold their own among many consumers in the face of competition from today's döner kebabs, pizzas, suvlakis and nasi gorengs. And in its luxury form as the "Griegeniffter" (potato dumplings), they still play a significant role at Sunday lunchtime. And if they are accompanied by what is known as "Schwammebrieh" – mushroom sauce, Vogtland people feel as if they are in a

Gelebte Traditionen / Traditions Perpetuated

für allemal einen Spitzenplatz im ansonsten eher bescheiden anmutenden kulinarischen Pantheon der Vogtländer erobert hat. Ob als Spalken (Eintopf), Späkle (Bratkartoffeln) oder Bambes (Kartoffelpuffer) – die traditionellen Gerichte von einst können auch heute noch ganz gelassen zwischen all den Döners, Pizzas, Suvlakis und Nasi Gorengs auf reichlichen und genussvollen Verzehr hoffen. Und gar in ihrer Luxusausführung, als „Griegeniffter" – als Grüner Kloß – ist die Kartoffel von keinem sonntäglichen Mittagstisch wegzudenken. So es denn dazu dann auch noch „Schwammebrieh" – Pilzsoße – gibt, schwelgt der Vogtländer lukullisch im siebten Himmel. Die Pilze dazu werden natürlich selbst gesammelt. „Nei de Schwamme giehe" – das hat Tradition. Was früher zur Aufbesserung des meist kärglichen täglichen Brotes notwendig war, ist in unseren Tagen schon zu einer Art Breitensportbewegung avanciert. In der Saison stehen an den Waldrändern die Autos der Pilzsucher zuhauf und viele Vogtländer sind Experten, was die Bestimmung der Vielzahl an Schwamme-Sorten angeht. Sie wissen sich dabei in guter Tradition mit „Pilzvater" Edmund August Michael, dem Begründer der modernen Mykologie. Der war zwar kein Vogtländer, wirkte und lebte aber viele Jahre bis zu seinem Tode 1920 im vogtländischen Auerbach.

Mit ihrem Wald sind die Vogtländer in besonderem Maße verbunden und das nicht nur, weil in ihm der Moosmann hausen soll. Unter den Sagengestalten nimmt er samt seinem Weibe eine Sonderstellung ein. Feen, Waldgeister und Kobolde treiben aller Orten ihr (Un)wesen. Einen Moosmann hat nur das Vogtland zu bieten. Er ist ureigenes Kulturgut, unantastbar, unnachahmlich – basta! Und wenn es eines Beweises bedarf, dass alt überlieferte Traditionen fest verwurzelt sind, weitergegeben und neu belebt werden, dann ist der Geselle im moosgrünen Rock dafür beredtes Beispiel. Er ziert nicht nur in guter Schnitztradition als kleines Holzmännlein die Weihnachtsstuben oder in lebensgroßer Variante Plätze und Eingangsbereiche. Nein, mit Werner Köhler aus Gürth oder mit Dieter Seidel vom Waldpark Grünheide hat er in unseren Tagen seine Fleischwerdung als touristischer Werbeträger bzw. Animateur erfahren. Plauen richtet gar ein jährliches Moosleute-Treffen aus. Nicht von ungefähr ist der Moosmann zum Maskottchen der neuen Vogtland Arena, der hochmodernen Sprungschanze am Schwarzen Berg zu Klingenthal avanciert, führt dort quasi die alteingesessene Skisport-Traditon zu neuen Ufern. Doch zurück zum Wald, an dem das Vogtland so reich ist: Dessen gewerbliche Nutzung steht in alter Tradition. Ob Harzgewinnung, Rußbrennerei, Holzeinschlag oder häusliches und gewerbliches Schnitzhandwerk – der Wald bot und bietet den Menschen im Vogtland einen wichtigen Broterwerb und hat dementsprechend seine Spuren im Brauchtum hinterlassen. Der rührige Flößerverein zu Muldenberg zum Beispiel hat nicht nur das alte Handwerk des Flößens mit neuem Leben erweckt, sondern es auch geschafft, dass sich Muldenberg seit 2007 stolz und hochoffiziell „1. Flößerdorf Deutschlands" nennen darf – Traditionspflege par excellence!

seventh heaven. Of course, they pick the mushrooms themselves. Going off to pick mushrooms is a real tradition here. Formerly they were needed to brighten up what was usually people's rather plain daily bread, but gathering them has now become a kind of sport for the masses. During the season you will see mushroom pickers' cars parked on the edge of forests and many Vogtland people have become real experts in recognising the wealth of mushroom varieties. They are maintaining a good tradition with the father of mushrooms, Edmund August Michael, the founder of modern mycology. He did not originate from the Vogtland region, but lived and worked in Auerbach/Vogtland for many years until his death in 1920.

Vogtland people also feel particularly attached to their forests – and not just because the Moss Man is supposed to live there. He and his wife assume a particular position among the legendary figures. Pixies, forest spirits and gremlins are up to mischief all over the place. But only the Vogtland region has a Moss Man. He is an original part of the local culture – sacrosanct and inimitable! And if there is any need for evidence that old traditions are still firmly rooted, passed on and reinvigorated, then the man in the moss-green attire is proof of this. He not only decorates rooms at Christmas time as a carved wooden figure or squares and entrances in life-size form. No, with Werner Köhler from Gürth or Dieter Seidel from Grünheide Forest Park, he has been brought to life as an advertising medium for tourists or an entertainer in the recent past. Plauen even holds an annual Moss Man meeting. It is no accident that the Moss Man has become the mascot of the new Vogtland Arena, the extremely modern ski-jumping facility on the Black Hill in Klingenthal. It is as if he is extending the tradition of skiing to new limits.

But back to the forests, of which the Vogtland region has so many. Their commercial use has a long tradition – whether it is for extracting resin, pine soot works, felling or domestic or commercial carving – forests provided and still provide Vogtland people with an important source of income and this has left its mark on customs. The active log rafting association in Muldenberg, for example, has not only breathed new life into the old craft of log rafting, but also managed to ensure in 2007 that Muldenberg may now proudly and officially call itself "Germany's 1st log rafting village" – cultivating tradition par excellence!

Gelebte Traditionen / Traditions Perpetuated

Wie die 350-jährige Geschichte der Instrumentenbauer im vogtländischen Musikwinkel. Nicht gefangen in verstaubten Konventionen, sondern aufbauend auf altem Meisterkönnen und mit neuen Ideen gestaltend, sind sie angetreten, an die weltweite Bedeutung, die die vogtländische Musikindustrie Mitte des 19. Jahrhunderts genoss, anzuknüpfen. Sie sind in guter Gesellschaft mit den Stickern.. „Plauener Spitze" adelte schon vor über 125 Jahren die vogtländische Stickereiindustrie und tut es heute wieder. Weberei und Spinnerei, Gardinenfertigung, Teppichherstellung oder Weißwarenindustrie – textiles Gewerbe und Industrie waren und sind vogtländische Tradition.

Und wo gearbeitet wird, da soll auch gefeiert werden. Der Vogtländer genießt dies ausgiebig. Wenn auch das benachbarte Erzgebirge als das deutsche „Weihnachtsland" schlechthin gilt: Das Vogtland partizipiert davon und hat Eigenständiges beigesteuert. Traditionsgemäß ist die Region zwischen Greiz und Bad Brambach, zwischen Steinberg und Mühltroff jedoch das „Kirmesland". Fast jedes Dorf und jede Stadt feiert das Kirchweihfest althergebracht nach wie vor als großes Ereignis. Doch neben den überlieferten haben sich vor allem in den vergangenen Jahrzehnten und besonders nach der Wende auch neue Feste etabliert, die selbst schon Traditionen begründen: allen voran der Tag der Vogtländer und das Spitzenfest in Plauen, die Alt und Jung gleichermaßen ansprechen und einbinden.

Wo also Traditionen fest verwurzelt sind und gelebt werden, schweißen sie Generationen zusammen, geben Halt und können Werte vermitteln. Sicher, aus Traditionsbewusstsein kann rasch auch schnöde Heimattümelei entstehen, und manchmal sind die Grenzen fließend. Doch wo Überliefern und Bewahren nicht stures Festhalten heißt, sondern kreatives Fortführen und Erneuern, da werden Traditionen auch weiterhin lebendig bleiben. Denn wie ließ Goethe schon seinen Faust erkennen: „Was du ererbt von deinen Vätern hast, erwirb es, um es zu besitzen."

Quellen:
Internetplattform Wikipedia
„Unser Vogtland" Band 20, Heft V, 1897
„Das große buch vom Vogtland" Blechschmidt/Walther 1999
„Ein vogtländischer Mundartabend", Reinhard Glaß 1977
„Kreis-Journal", Ekkehard Glaß 14. Otnat-Gespräch 2006

(Foto/Photo by Michael Rischer/Christian Suhr)

Or just take the 350-year history of musical instrument making in the Vogtland Musicon Valley. The skilled workers have not remained trapped in dusty old traditions, but have sought to build on their ancient skills and add new ideas and are seeking to forge links with the global importance that the Vogtland music industry enjoyed in the middle of the 19th century. They are in good company with the embroiderers. "Plauen lace" raised the Vogtland embroidery industry to dizzy heights more than 125 years ago and is doing so again today. Weaving and spinning, curtain making, carpet making or the white goods industry – the textile business and the textile industry were and are a tradition in the Vogtland region.

And those who work hard can celebrate too. Vogtland people are able to do this in style. If the neighbouring Erzgebirge Mountain area is knows as the German "Christmas land", the Vogtland region participates in this and has added its own unique contribution. Traditionally the region between Greiz and Bad Brambach, between Steinberg and Mühltroff is known as "funfair land". The traditional church dedication festival is still a major event for almost every village or town. But alongside traditional celebrations, new festivals have made their mark in the past few decades, particularly since the fall of the Berlin Wall, and they are laying the foundation for new traditions: especially the Vogtland Day and the Lace Festival in Plauen, which appeal to old and young and involve them too.

If traditions are a firmly rooted and are lived out, they bind generations to each other, provide moral support and can impart values. It is true that local tradition can quickly be over-exaggerated in a negative manner and sometimes the boundaries are fluid. But where tradition and preservation do not represent stubborn adherence, but promote creative perpetuation and renewal, traditions remain a living thing. Goethe once put the following words in the mouth of his character Faust: "Acquire what you have inherited from your fathers in order to possess it."

Im Vogtland zu Hause: Von einst über 10.000 gebauten VOMAG-Lastwagen sind heute weltweit keine zwei Dutzend Komplettfahrzeuge mehr bekannt. Einige der Raritäten werden in ihrer Heimat liebevoll gepflegt./At home in the Vogtland region: of the 10,000 VOMAG lorries built, there are probably no more than two dozen complete vehicles left today. Some of these rare vehicles are lovingly cared for at their home base.

Gelebte Traditionen / Traditions Perpetuated

Mekka des Sports
The Mecca for Sports Lies in the Vogtland Region

Das Vogtland ist ein Mekka des Sports. Das ist bereits seit Jahrzehnten so und wird es auch in Zukunft bleiben. Vor allem im Wintersport hat das Vogtland eine große Anzahl national und international erfolgreicher Athleten vorzuweisen. Immerhin ist der eigentliche Pionier der deutschen Skispringer ein Klingenthaler – Harry Glaß. Er holte 1956 bei den Olympischen Spielen in Cortina D'Ampezzo als erster Mitteleuropäer mit Bronze im Spezialspringen eine olympische Medaille. Drei Jahre später weihte er die Große Aschbergschanze ein, die 1990 abgerissen wurde und 2005 als modernste Großschanze in Europa ihre Wiedergeburt feierte. Neben Glaß haben bisher weitere 22 Sportlerinnen und Sportler, deren Werdegang mit Klingenthal eng verbunden ist, bei Ski-Weltmeisterschaften und Olympischen Winterspielen Medaillen geholt. Genannt seien solche Namen wie Gert-Dietmar Klause, Matthias Buse, Henry Glaß, Manfred Deckert, Christel Meinel, Klaus Ostwald, Marlies Rostock, Uwe Dotzauer und Björn Kircheisen. Letzterer ist gegenwärtig das hoffnungsvolle Aushängeschild für das Landesleistungszentrum und den Vogtländischen Skiclub (VSC) Klingenthal – dem größten Wintersportverein in Sachsen. Beim VSC werden in den Sektionen Nordische Kombination, Spezialsprunglauf, Alpin und Snowboard Hunderte aktive Sportler und Nachwuchstalente von erfahrenen Trainern betreut. Der Verein betreibt auch die Großschanze in der Vogtland Arena, ist seit Jahren Veranstalter hochkarätiger Wettkämpfe und hat dank zahlreicher Helfer mit hervorragenden Wettkampfbedingungen für Aufsehen in der ganzen Welt gesorgt.

Wer von einer vogtländischen Kaderschmiede im Wintersport spricht, denkt zugleich an die weiteren Schanzen und Loipen, auf denen sich die jungen Athleten messen. Einst gab es in vielen Orten eigene Sprungschanzen – insgesamt etwa 100 an der Zahl. Das erklärt auch die Begeisterung für das Skispringen, das sich heute bei den Wettkämpfen auf der Klingenthaler Großschanze anhand Tausender Zuschauer zeigt. Die neue Schanze ist ein markantes Zeichen für die Skisport besessenen Vogtländer. Als die Aschbergschanze abgerissen werden musste, war klar, dass sie wie Phönix aus der Asche schöner und top modern wieder erstehen musste. Dass sie Landrat Dr. Tassilo Lenk zur Chefsache machte und gegen so manche Unkenrufe Wirklichkeit werden ließ, bringt sportlich und touristisch einen riesigen Aufschwung in die Region. Sie ist Magnet für die besten Springer und Nordisch Kombinierer aus aller Welt. Und natürlich auch für den eigenen Nachwuchs. Hervorragende Bedingungen finden junge Athleten in dem Sportgymnasium in Klingenthal, das seit 1998 Eliteschule des Sports ist.

The Vogtland region is a Mecca for sports. This has been the case for decades and will remain so in future. The Vogtland region has a particularly large number of athletes who have been successful nationally and internationally in winter sports disciplines. The real pioneer of German ski-jumping came from Klingenthal – Harry Glass. He was the first Central European to win an Olympic medal in special jumping at the Olympic Games in Cortina D'Ampezzo in 1956. Three years later he inaugurated the Large Aschberg Jump, which was demolished in 1990 and celebrated its renaissance as the most modern ski-jumping facility in Europe in 2005. So far apart from Glass, another 22 sportsmen and sportswomen, whose careers are closely linked to Klingenthal, have carried off medals at skiing world championships or the Winter Olympics. These include names like Gert-Dietmar Klause, Matthias Buse, Henry Glass, Manfred Deckert, Christel Meinel, Klaus Ostwald, Marlies Rostock, Uwe Dotzauer and Björn Kircheisen. The latter is currently the most promising star at the State Sports Centre and the Vogtland Ski Club (VSC) in Klingenthal – the largest winter sports club in Saxony. Hundreds of active athletes and young stars are coached by experienced trainers at the VSC in the Nordic combination, special ski-jumping, downhill skiing and snowboarding disciplines. The club also runs the large ski-jump facility in the Vogtland Arena and has organised top-quality competitions for years; it has also gained a respect around the world for the outstanding conditions that it provides for competitions thanks to its many helpers.

Those who talk about the anvil for shaping the next generation of talent in winter sports automatically think of the other ski-jump facilities and cross-country skiing tracks, where young athletes compete. In earlier times many places had their own ski-jump – there used to be about 100 of them. This also explains the enthusiasm for ski-jumping, which is evident from the thousands of spectators who turn up for competitions at the Klingenthal ski-jump facility nowadays. The new jump is a striking sign of the Vogtland people's passion for winter sports. When the Aschberg ski-jump facility was demolished, it was clear that it would have to rise from the ashes again like Phoenix, only in a modern and more beautiful form. Chief administrative officer, Dr. Tassilo Lenk, made it a top priority himself and ensured that the structure was built in the face of many prophets of doom; this has brought an enormous boost to the region, both in terms of tourism and sporting activities. It is a magnet for the best jumpers and Nordic combination athletes from all over the world. And quite naturally, for young people too. Young athletes find outstanding conditions at the sports grammar school in Klingenthal, which has been an elite sports school since 1998.

(Fotos/Photos by Harald Sulski/Text/Text by Marjon Thümmel, Übersetzung/Translated by David Strauss)

Gelebte Traditionen / Traditions Perpetuated

Beste Bedingungen für den Schul- und Leistungssport im sanierten und umgebauten Schulgebäude „Am Amtsberg": Hier können die Schüler/-innen der Mittelschule und des Sportelitegymnasiums – eine Außenstelle des kreislichen Julius-Mosen-Gymnasiums Klingenthal – optimal trainieren. Entsprechend der sportorientierten Ausrichtung des Schulkomplexes können die Schüler nach abgestimmten Schul- und Trainingsplänen lernen und trainieren.

Was Skisport in Klingenthal ist, ist der Eislaufsport in Mylau, Judo in Rodewisch, Ringen in Markneukirchen, Gewichtheben in Plauen und so weiter. Das Spektrum ist sehr weit gefächert. In jedem Jahr werden bei einer Sport-Gala die besten vogtländischen Sportlerinnen, Sportler und Mannschaften sowie erfolgreiche Nachwuchssportler geehrt. Es sind Frauen und Männer, die bei Deutschen-, Europa- oder Weltmeisterschaften sowie olympischen Spielen den Ruf des Vogtlandes als sportliche Region immer wieder mit Bravour verteidigen. Und weil die Förderung des Sports nicht nur eine Floskel sein soll, gibt es eine Sporthilfe Vogtland. „Wir haben uns vor neun Jahren mal das Ziel von drei Millionen Euro gesteckt, jetzt liegen wir bei 2,6 Millionen Euro. Wir haben 260 000 Einwohner im Vogtland und sind deutschlandweit die einzigste Region, die eine solche Sportstiftung auf die Beine gestellt hat und so mehr als das Übliche für den Nachwuchs tut. Im Vogtland gibt es 300 Sportvereine mit mehr als 30 000 Mitgliedern, darunter 10 000 Kinder und Jugendliche. Hinter diesen Zahlen steckt ein tolles Engagement ehrenamtlicher Helfer. Während landesweit die Zahl junger Leute in den Vereinen abnimmt, steigt sie bei uns. Das ist toll", sagte Landrat Dr. Lenk zur Sport-Gala 2007. Der Breitensport ist die Basis für Leistungssport. Und bei einer solchen Anzahl Aktiver braucht es nicht allein den Blick in die Gegenwart und Vergangenheit, um von einer vogtländischen Sport-Elite zu sprechen.

What Klingenthal is for winter sports, Mylau is for ice skating, Rodewisch for judo, Markneukirchen for wrestling, Plauen for weight-lifting and so on. The range of sports is very broad. Each year the best Vogtland sportsmen and sportswomen and teams and successful young athletes are honoured. They are men and women, who have repeatedly defended the reputation of the Vogtland region as a sports centre at German, European and World Championships or Olympic Games with their brilliance. And because promoting sports should not be an empty phrase, there is such a thing as the Vogtland Sports Fund. "We set ourselves the target of € 3 million nine years ago; we now have about € 2.6 million. We have 260,000 residents in the Vogtland region and we are the only region in Germany, which has managed to set up a sports endowment fund and is therefore doing more than what is normal for the next generation. There are 300 sports clubs in the Vogtland region with more than 30,000 members, including 10,000 children and young people. The commitment of voluntary helpers is what keeps these figures so high. While the number of young people in clubs is decreasing across the state, it is rising here. That is fantastic," said chief administrative officer, Dr. Lenk at the 2007 Sports Gala. Sport for the masses is the foundation for competitive sports. And with this number of people involved, the present or past do not tell the final story about a sports elite in the Vogtland region – there will be a future too.

Sportgala 2007 – Ehrung der Sportlerinnen des Jahres

Sportgala – Wahl der Vogtlandsportler des Jahres: In gemeinsamer Arbeit der Sportämter des Vogtlandkreises und der Stadt Plauen, der Sportbünde und der Medien des Vogtlandes werden die Ehrungen der besten vogtländischen Sportlerinnen und Sportler, Mannschaften, Nachwuchssportler und verdienter Sportfunktionäre, die im Rahmen der Sportgala vorgenommen.

Gelebte Traditionen / Traditions Perpetuated

Da liegt Musik im Blut
When Music Runs in the Blood

Liebe auf den ersten Blick mit sechs Jahren? Sebastian Zippel aus Reichenbach hat damit Erfahrung. Als er mit seinen Eltern das erste Mal bei einem richtigen Konzert war, funkte es gewaltig. Ausgerechnet die Tuba, die damals noch ein paar Zentimeter höher als der Knirps war, hatte es ihm angetan. Unterricht auf dem Riesenblechblasinstrument für einen Sechsjährigen, das ging nun wirklich nicht. Deshalb begann er an der Musikschule Vogtland mit dem etwas kleineren Bariton, um schon zwei Jahre später zur B-Tuba zu wechseln. Inzwischen ist Sebastian 18 Jahre alt und kann auf über elf Jahre musische Ausbildung zurückblicken. Zum Lieblingsinstrument gesellten sich Klavier, Orgel, Fagott, die musiktheoretische Ausbildung und die Lehre im Komponieren. Er spielt in verschiedenen Ensembles und kann auf eine ganze Reihe von Konzerterfahrungen verweisen. 2005 führte ihn eine Konzertreise mit dem Sächsischen Landesjugendblasorchesters nach China, wo mit 2000 Gästen gefüllte Säle die Norm waren. Im gleichen Jahr gastierte er mit seinem Quintett und anderen Gruppen der Reichenbacher Musikschule in Tolna/Ungarn. Er nahm an Tourneen der Jungen Deutsch-Polnischen Philharmonie Niederschlesien in Polen und Deutschland, Auftritten des Landesjugendblasorchesters oder Konzertreisen mit der Jungen Dresdner Philharmonie nach Linz und in andere Orte teil. Die Mappe mit Urkunden füllt sich rasch. Darunter sind Förderpreise der Musikschule, Preise beim Wettbewerb „Jugend musiziert" oder beim bundesweiten Carl-Schröder-Wettbewerb, Förderpreise und Diplome verschiedener Orchester. Lang ist auch die Liste der Ensembles, mit denen Sebastian auftritt. Neben den Landes-Jugendorchestern des Freistaates Sachsen sind das zu Beispiel das Brass Ensemble Hannes Mück München, die Hirschsteiner Musikanten Reichenbach und Canaletto Brass Dresden. In mehreren Bläsergruppen schrieb er Geschichte der Musikschule Vogtland mit. Seit 2006 lernt Sebastian am Landesgymnasium für Musik in Dresden. Schon mit 13 Jahren wurde er für die Begabtenförderung des Landes Sachsen ausgewählt.

Ähnlich erfolgreich ist seine Schwester Julia, die ebenfalls an mehreren Wettbewerben „Jugend musiziert" und dem bundesweiten Carl-Schröder-Wettbewerb teilnahm und seit 2005 als begabtes Nachwuchstalent gefördert wird. Sie war bereits mit zwölf Jahren mit der Jungen Deutsch-Polnischen Philharmonie Niederschlesien auf Tournee. Auf ihre Orchesterdiplome ist sie besonders stolz. Sie bescheinigen ihr neben herausragenden musikalischen Leistungen das Bewältigen der Fremdsprache Englisch und der italienischen Orchesterfachtermini. Die jetzt 14-Jährige begann nach der musikalischen Früherziehung mit dem Flötenspiel. Seit 2003 lernt sie Trompete und nimmt Schlagzeug-Unterricht an der Musikschule Vogtland. Sie spielt in mehreren Ensembles, in denen nicht nur ihr Bruder, sondern auch Vater Peter Zippel als Trompeter und Organisator aktiv ist, während sich Mutter Simone Zippel mehr dem sakralen Chorgesang widmet. Von den Eltern dürfte ein guter Teil des musikalischen Talents der beiden Nachwuchsmusiker stammen.

Love at first sight at six years of age? Sebastian Zippel from Reichenbach knows what that is all about. When he went to see his first proper concert with his parents, he fell in love immediately. Of all the instruments, it was the tuba that attracted his attention – and at that time it was a couple of centimetres taller than him. Lessons for a six-year-old on this giant instrument were out of the question. So he started to learn the slightly smaller baritone at the Vogtland Music School. He switched to his beloved B flat tuba two years later. Sebastian is now 18 years old and can look back on eleven years of musical training. In addition to his favourite instrument, he has also learned to play the piano, the organ, and the bassoon and has been given training in musical theory and composing. He plays in several ensembles and has gained a great deal of concert experience. In 2005 he went on a concert tour with the Saxon Regional Youth Wind Orchestra, which took him to China, where he regularly played in front of an audience of 2,000 people. He also played in Tolna in Hungary with his quintet and other groups from the music school from Reichenbach in the same year. He has participated in tours throughout Poland and Germany with the Lower Silesia Young German - Polish Philharmonic Orchestra, has performed with the Regional Youth Wind Orchestra or has gone on concert trips with the Young Dresden Philharmonic Orchestra to Linz and other destinations. His certificates file is filling up quickly. These include prizes from music schools, prizes from the "Young People Make Music" contest or the nationwide Carl Schröder Contest, as well as prizes and diplomas from various orchestras. The list of ensembles where Sebastian performs is just as long. It includes the Brass Ensemble Hannes Mück in Munich, the Hirschstein Musicians in Reichenbach and Canaletto Brass in Dresden, as well as the Regional Youth Orchestras of the Free State of Saxony. He also wrote history for the Vogtland Music School by playing in various brass bands. Sebastian has been attending the state grammar school for music in Dresden since 2006. He was selected for a scholarship to help gifted children by the state of Saxony at the age of 13.

His sister Julia is equally successful. She has also participated in several "Young People Make Music" contests and the nationwide Carl Schröder Contest. She has been sponsored as a young music talent since 2005. She went on tour with the Lower Silesia Young German - Polish Philharmonic Orchestra at the age of 12. Her orchestra diplomas are her pride and joy. They prove that she has also acquired a knowledge of the English language and specialist orchestra terms in Italian in addition to her musical skills. The 14-year-old started her musical training by playing the flute. She has been learning to play the trumpet since 2003 and has drums lessons at the Vogtland Music School. She plays in various ensembles, not only with her brother, but also her father. Peter Zippel is actively involved as a trumpeter and organiser, while their mother Simone Zippel specialises in singing sacred chorales. It seems that these two children have inherited a lot of musical talent from their parents.

(Fotos/Photos by Petra Steps/Text by Petra Steps, Übersetzung/Translated by David Strauss)

Musikschule hat eine lange Tradition im Vogtland
Music Schools have a Long Tradition in the Vogtland

Die Geschichte der vogtländischen Musikschulen reicht bis in die erste Hälfte des 19. Jahrhunderts zurück. Es waren vor allem gewerbliche Interessen des sich entwickelnden Musikinstrumentenbaus, die zur Gründung der Musikschulen 1834 in Markneukirchen, 1843 in Klingenthal, 1909 in Erlbach und 1911 in Schöneck führten. „Jeder Lehrling, welcher zum Gesellen gesprochen werden will, hat nachzuweisen, dass er mindestens zwei Jahre die hiesige Gewerbe- und Musikschule besucht habe." Dieses duale Prinzip, festgehalten im Statut der Geigenmacherinnung, wurde viele Jahre beibehalten. Erst 1951 kam es mit der Bildung der Volksmusikschule Markneukirchen zur Trennung von der gewerblichen Berufsschule. In den Folgejahren wechselten die vogtländischen Musikschulen mehrmals ihre Bezeichnungen und Träger. Am 14.12.1998 gründete sich in Plauen der Verein „Musikschule Vogtland e.V.", der mit Wirkung vom 01.01.1999 die Trägerschaft über die bis dahin kreislichen Musikschulen Reichenbach, Auerbach und Markneukirchen mit der Außenstelle Klingenthal übernahm. Zu den die Musikschule Vogtland finanzierenden Vereinsmitgliedern gehören neben dem Vogtlandkreis unter anderem die als Standortkommunen geltenden Städte Reichenbach, Auerbach, Markneukirchen und Klingenthal. Weitere Unterstützung und Förderung erfährt die Musikschule Vogtland durch den Freistaat Sachsen und als regional bedeutsames Projekt durch den Kulturraum Vogtland.

Gegenwärtig nutzen ca. 1.400 Schülerinnen und Schüler die zahlreichen Ausbildungsangebote der Musikschule Vogtland. Sie werden fachlich angeleitet und betreut von engagierten Lehrkräften. In rund 200 öffentlichen Veranstaltungen jährlich präsentiert sich die Musikschule als eine vielseitige und leistungsfähige musikalische Bildungseinrichtung. Die Musikschule Vogtland ist offen für alle musikalisch interessierten Menschen. Im Kurs „Musikgarten" werden die kleinsten Musikschulbesucher liebevoll an die Musik herangeführt. Über die „Musikalische Früherziehung" und die „Musikalische Grundausbildung" gelangen die meisten Kinder zu „ihrem Wunschinstrument". Der Musikunterricht wird entsprechend den Empfehlungen des Verbandes deutscher Musikschulen, dem die Musikschule Vogtland seit ihrer Gründung als Mitglied angehört, in verschiedenen Ausbildungsstufen erteilt. Von der Grundstufe bis zur studenvorbereitenden Ausbildung, von frühbarocker Musik bis Jazz, von Gruppenunterricht bis individueller Begabtenförderung reicht das Spektrum der musikalischen Möglichkeiten. Es gibt eine Vielzahl von Ensembles, wie Blas- und Streichorchester, Chor, Big Band sowie unterschiedlichste gemeinschaftliche Musizierformen, in denen sich die Schülerinnen und Schüler musikalisch betätigen können.

Die Musikschule Vogtland pflegt die Zusammenarbeit mit Schulen und anderen Kinder- und Jugendeinrichtungen sowie verschiedenen kulturellen Einrichtungen und Vereinen. Es finden regelmäßig Schülerkonzerte für die Kinder der ersten bis vierten Klassen statt. In Markneukirchen begleitet die Musikschule Vogtland das Projekt „Klassenmusizieren mit Blasinstrumenten" am dortigen Gymnasium. Nicht nur gemeinsame Musicalproduktionen verbinden die Musikschule Vogtland und das Goethe-Gymnasium Reichenbach. Früherziehungsangebote und Blockflötenkurse gibt es an zahlreichen Kindereinrichtungen und Grundschulen. Mit der Vogtland Philharmonie Greiz/Reichenbach, dem Stadtorchester Markneukirchen und anderen Musikvereinen gestaltet die Musikschule Vogtland regelmäßig gemeinsame Konzerte.

The history of the Vogtland music schools goes back to the first half of the 19th century. Commercial interests on the part of the developing musical instrument making industry led to the formation of music schools in Markneukirchen in 1834, Klingenthal in 1843, Erlbach in 1909 and Schöneck in 1911. "Each apprentice, who wants to qualify as an assistant, must prove that they have attended a commercial and music school for at least two years." This dual principle, which is enshrined in the statutes of the violin makers' guild, was upheld for many years. The foundation of the public music school in Markneukirchen in 1951 marked the first separation from a commercial training school. The Vogtland music schools changed their labels and backers on several occasions during the next few years. Then the "Vogtland Music School" Association was set up in Plauen on 14 December 1998 and it took over responsibility for the music schools in the districts of Reichenbach, Auerbach and Markneukirchen and the branch in Klingenthal with effect from 1 January 1999. The Vogtland district and the towns of Reichenbach, Auerbach, Markneukirchen and Klingenthal are all members of the association and fund the Vogtland music schools. The Vogtland schools also receive subsidies and support from the Free State of Saxony and the important local "Vogtland Cultural Region" project.

Some 1,400 pupils currently make use of the many education facilities at the Vogtland music schools. Committed teachers provide children with guidance and care. The music schools demonstrate their variety and high degree of productivity at about 200 public events every year. The music schools are open to anyone interested in music. The youngest pupils are lovingly introduced to the world of music in the "nursery music" course. Most children find the instrument they want to ply using the "early musical training" and "basic music training" courses. Musical tuition is provided for different age groups in line with the principles of the Association of German Music Schools, of which the Vogtland Music School Association has been a member since it was set up. The spectrum of music on offer ranges from basic tuition to training for pupils wanting to study music, from early Baroque to jazz and from group tuition to individual support for highly talented children. There are a variety of ensembles like the brass and stringed orchestras, the choir and big band and there a huge variety of different opportunities for children to get involved in musical activities.

The Vogtland music schools work closely with schools, other children's and young people's centres and various cultural centres and associations. Pupils' concerts for children in the first four grades take place regularly. The Vogtland Music School Association backs the "Class Music with Brass Instruments" project at the grammar school in Markneukirchen. And it is not only musical productions that link the Vogtland Music School Association and the Goethe grammar school in Reichenbach. There are early talent courses and recorder lessons at many children's centres and primary schools. The music school regularly holds joint concerts with the Greiz/Reichenbach Vogtland Philharmonic, the town orchestra in Markneukirchen and other music associations.

(Fotos/Photos by Landratsamt Vogtlandkreis; Text by Andreas Häfner, Übersetzung/Translated by David Strauss)

Ein Dorf im SR2-Fieber
A Village in SR2 Fever

Traditionstreffen für Freunde des Kultmopeds in Kürbitz

Jedes Jahr im August gibt der Kürbitzer Löwe Gas. Was heißen soll, dass zum Löwenspektakel, dem Dorffest im Weischlitzer Ortsteil Kürbitz, auch das SR2-Treffen stattfindet. 2008 wird das Spektakel der SR-Freunde bereits zum 13. Mal über die Bühne gehen. Was einst mit 14 Startern begann, nimmt derweil ungeahnte Ausmaße an. Seit Jahren toppen die Veranstalter – Montagsclub, Freiwillige Feuerwehr, Dorfclub und Sportverein – die Teilnehmerzahl und schaffen den Eintrag ins Guinessbuch der Rekorde. 2007 bewältigten 403 Fahrer die 26 Kilometer lange, bergige Rundfahrt. Sie kommen aus dem Vogtland, von der Ostsee, aus Dresden, Bad Salzungen, Riesa, Berlin, Magdeburg und sogar aus Ungarn. Allein in Kürbitz stehen über 100 der legendären Zweiräder aus der Suhler DDR-Produktion in Höfen, Garagen und Scheunen. Liebevoll werden sie von ihren Besitzern restauriert. Zur Rundfahrt sieht man aber nicht nur chromblitzende Mopeds. Manch Gefährt erregt Aufsehen wegen seiner Naturbelassenheit und dicken Rostschicht. Oder auch wegen humorvoller Aufrüstungen. Da werden lustige Figuren mitgeführt. Da geht es mit Schwimmflossen an den Start oder es lassen Sonderaufbauten staunen – von Vogelkäfigen über Kohlenkasten bis hin zu Würstchenkocher und Getränkelager. Nicht minder spaßig sind die Verkleidungen der Fahrer. Den Vogel schießt meist Arnd Maul ab, der die Rundfahrt schon als Mohr, Lotto-Fee, Bauer oder als verwirrter Altenheimbewohner eröffnete.

Wenn sich Boxengasse, Dorfplatz und Elsterbrücke in Benzinduft hüllen, ist am Straßenrand kaum noch ein Durchkommen. Auch der Besucheransturm ist alljährlich rekordverdächtig. Trotz der heutigen Vielfalt der Auto- und Motorradmarken lösen die Chassis und Motorleistungen von einst Bewunderung und Begeisterung aus. Und das gilt auch für Motor getriebene Zweiräder, wie SR1 und SR2, der Stolz eines jeden Mopedfreaks in den 1960er und den Anfängen der 1970er Jahre in der DDR. Der erste Kürbitzer, der sein gutes Stück nach der Wende auf dem Heuboden vorm Verschrotten rettete, war Frank Stumpf. Weitere Besitzer entdeckten ihre „Moped-Liebe" wieder, trafen sich und drehten Runden. Seither freuen sie sich Jahr für Jahr auf das SR2-Treffen, um mit Gleichgesinnten fachsimpeln zu können, Ersatzteile austauschen und Spaß an der Rundfahrt zu haben.

Traditional Meeting for Friends of the Cult Moped in Kürbitz

Every year the Kürbitz lion puts his foot down – or put in another way, the SR2 meeting takes place as part of the Lion Spectacle, the village festival in the Weischlitz suburb of Kürbitz. The spectacle will be held for the 13th time in 2008. It all started with just 14 participants, but has now expanded to an unbelievable degree. The organisers – the "Monday Club", the voluntary fire brigade, the village club and sports association – have been increasing the number of participants for years and have managed an entry in the Guinness Book of Records. In 2007, 403 drivers covered the 26 kilometre long, hilly course. They came from the Vogtland region, from the Baltic coast, from Dresden, Bad Salzungen, Riesa, Berlin, Magdeburg and even from Hungary. In Kürbitz alone, there are more than 100 of the legendary bikes, which were made in the East German town of Suhl, in gardens, garages or barns. They are carefully restored by their owners. But mopeds with gleaming chrome are not the only bikes that spectators see on the course. Some of them have been left in their natural state with a thick layer of rust – and attract people's attention as a result. Or there are others with amusing extras. Comical figures enjoy the ride too. Others arrive at the starting point wearing flippers or build special superstructures to enthral the visitors – ranging from bird cages to coal boxes or even sausage cookers and a drinks store. The clothes worn by the drivers are just as amusing. Arnd Maul often carries off the prize for the most outlandish gear; he has opened the course dressed as a carrot, a lottery girl, a farmer or as a confused resident in an old people's home.

When the pit lane, the village square and the Elster bridge are enshrouded in petrol fumes, there a huge crowds at the side of the road. The hordes of visitors set new records every year. Despite the variety of brands of cars and motorbikes on the market today, the chassis and engine performance of yesteryear trigger a sense of admiration and enthusiasm. The same is true of motorised bikes, like the SR1 and SR2, which were the pride of any moped fan in the 1960s and early 1970s in East Germany. The first person in Kürbitz, who saved his bike in a hay loft from being turned into scrap metal after the fall of the Berlin wall, was Frank Stumpf. Other owners also discovered their "love of mopeds", met and did some laps. Since then they look forward to the SR2 meeting every year so to be able to talk shop with like-minded people, exchange spare parts and have their fun during the race.

(Fotos/Photos by B. Kempe-Winkelmann, Text/Text by B. Kempe-Winkelmann, Übersetzung/Translated by David Strauss)

Gelebte Traditionen / Traditions Perpetuated

Die Erinnerung an August Horch in Reichenbach wird gewahrt.
The Memory of August Horch Is Being Kept Alive in Reichenbach.

August Horch – der Autopionier (geboren 1868 Winningen/Mosel, gestorben 1951 Münchberg/Oberfranken)

„Wir erhalten die Horch-Fabrik in Reichenbach". Mit diesem Slogan warb die Arbeiterwohlfahrt Vogtland, Bereich Reichenbach (AWO) beim Tag der Sachsen im September 2007, allerdings noch mit einem kleinen Fragezeichen. Seit Anfang November ist klar: In der Kramer'schen Fabrik, die August Horch von 1902 bis zu seinem Weggang 1904 nach Zwickau als Produktionsstätte nutzte, entsteht das neue AWO-Domizil mit Büroräumen sowie 12 Wohneinheiten für das Betreute Wohnen. 2,6 Millionen Euro kostet das Projekt, das zur Landesgartenschau 2009 fertig sein soll. Ausgehend vom jetzigen Zustand gilt der Umbau als echte Herausforderung. Und Geschäftsführer Steffan Günther setzt noch eins drauf: In Gemeinschaftsräumen sowie einem angebauten Pavillon wird es eine Gedenkausstellung zu Ehren des Autopioniers geben. Dazu hat er bereits viele Kontakt geknüpft, zum Beispiel zu Hans-Jürgen Löffler. Er gehört zu den Horch-Freunden des Reichenbacher Oldtimerclubs und ist Besitzer eines 835 Horch Sport-Cabrios Baujahr 1938. Seit Jahren setzt er sich für die Bewahrung der Tradition ein, kämpfte um den Horch-Weg in Reichenbach und pflegt Verbindungen zum Horch-Club Deutschland. Gemeinsam mit dem Oldtimerclub sorgte er für die Aufstellung eines Erinnerungsschildes an der Fabrik und lockte die Teilnehmer der Horch-Ausfahrten sowie Horchfreunde aus ganz Europa mehrfach ins Vogtland. Die Horch-Freunde unterhalten enge Beziehungen zu August Horchs Enkelin, Heike Müller oder zu Edgar Friedrich, dem letzten Lehrling des Automobilbauers.

August Horch (1868 bis 1951) zog aus Köln-Ehrenfeld nach Reichenbach und begann hier mit der Umsetzung seiner Kölner Entwicklungen. In die Reichenbacher Zeit fällt die Probefahrt des ersten Zweizylinderautos mit Kardanantrieb auf dem legendären Liebauberg. 1903 wurde der erste Vierzylinderwagen gebaut. Dieser vermutlich älteste noch erhaltene Horch, ein roter 10/12 Tonneau aus Reichenbacher Produktion, gehört dem Deutschen Museum und steht als Leihgabe im Museum Mobile Ingolstadt.

„We are acquiring the Horch factory in Reichenbach." This was the slogan used by the Reichenbach branch of the Vogtland Industrial Welfare Organisation (AWO) at the Saxon Festival in September 2007 – but at the time a question mark still hung over the project. But that issue was cleared up in November 2007. The new AWO centre with offices and 12 flats for sheltered accommodation will be built in the Kramer'schen factory, which August Horch used as a production site from 1902 until he moved away to Zwickau in 1904. The project is costing € 2.6 million and it is due to have been completed by the 2009 National Horticultural Show.
Looking at the current state of the building, the conversion work will be a real challenge. Managing director Steffan Günther has gone one step further: there will be an exhibition in honour of the automobile pioneer in common rooms and a pavilion, which will be built on. He has already made many contacts for this purpose, for example, with Hans-Jürgen Löffler. He is a member of the supporters of Horch at the Reichenbach Vintage Car Club and owns a Horch sports convertible dating from 1938. He has been pleading for this tradition to be maintained, he fought for the Horch Way in Reichenbach and he is in close contact with the German Horch Club. He and the vintage car club ensured that a memorial sign was erected by the factory and he has encouraged many participants on Horch excursions and Horch fans from all over Europe to come to the Vogtland region. The Horch fans maintain close relations to August Horch's granddaughter, Heike Müller or even Edgar Friedrich, the last apprentice at the car maker.

August Horch (1868-1951) moved from Cologne-Ehrenfeld to Reichenbach and began building what he had developed in Cologne. The test run of the first two-cylinder car with a fully suspended drive system took place during the Reichenbach period on the legendary Liebauberg. The first four-cylinder car was built in 1903. What is probably the oldest remaining Horch, a red 10/12 tonneau from the Reichenbach factory, belongs to the German Museum and is on loan to the Ingolstadt Museum Mobile.

Fotos von links:
Der letzte Lehrling von August Horch, Edgar Friedrich aus Hof, mit Horch-Besitzer Gerold Zeidler vor dessen Horch Baujahr 1933 beim Bergpreis in Mühlwand (Fahrerlager); Modell der Horch-Fabrik; Hans-Jürgen Löffler und seine Familie im Horch 835 H, Baujahr 1938 beim Tag der Sachsen

(Fotos/Photos by Petra Steps/Text/Text by Petra Steps, Übersetzung/Translated by David Strauss)

„De Gockeschen" und ihre Ziebele — Vogtländischer Volksmusikverein pflegt Traditionen
"De Gockeschen" and Their Ziebele — Vogtland Traditional Music Club Fosters Traditions

Volksmusik, Tanz, Gesang, Brauchtum und Mundart – das Unverwechselbare und Urwüchsige aus Vergangenheit und Gegenwart unserer vogtländischen Heimat prägen den Charakter des Ruinenfestes Liebau. Veranstalter ist der Vogtländische Volksmusikverein „De Gockeschen". Alljährlich am letzten Juni-Wochenende treffen sich Gruppen aus Franken, Thüringen und Böhmen, um gemeinsam mit den Vogtländern zu musizieren, zu tanzen und zu singen. Zum 18. Mal wird im Jahr 2008 dieses Fest im kleinen Dörfchen Liebau bei Jocketa stattfinden. „De Gockeschen" allerdings bestehen schon seit 1965. Damals nannten sie sich noch Singgruppe. Der vogtländischen Folklore verschrieben sich die Mitglieder ab Mitte der 70er Jahre. Lieder und Texte in Mundart wurden ins Programm aufgenommen und auch vogtländische Tänze einstudiert. Die Singgruppe, die hauptsächlich vor Urlaubern aufgetreten ist, entwickelte sich zu einem Ensemble, das weit übers Vogtland hinaus bekannt wurde. Fortan trugen sie den Namen „De Gockeschen", verweisen damit auf den Ort Jocketa, den die Einheimischen in ihrem Dialekt „Gocke" nennen.

Ob beim Tag der Sachsen, beim Kuchensingen im Erzgebirge, bei Folkloretreffen in Polen oder Ungarn, bei Fernsehaufzeichnungen und Auftritten in vielen Städten und Dörfern bekennen sich die Volksmusikanten mit ihrer bodenständigen, traditionellen Musizierweise konsequent zu ihrer vogtländischen Heimat. Zwei Mal weilten sie sogar in den USA, im Staat Indiana. Die vogtländische Tracht, anhand von Originalen authentisch nachgearbeitet, ist ihre Auftrittskleidung.

15 Musikanten, Sänger, Tänzer und Mundartsprecher gehören zum Ensemble. Die musikalische Leitung liegt in den Händen von Ursula Albert. Sie ist übrigens die einzige noch Aktive aus der Gründerzeit. Nur kurze Zeit später kam ihr Mann Ulrich Albert hinzu. Aus der Familie Albert heraus entstand 1979 die Nachwuchsgruppe „De Gockeschen Ziebele". Bis 2006 wurde sie von Irina Pörner geleitet.

Das Repertoire des Volksmusikvereins widerspiegelt das vogtländische Dorfleben im Jahreslauf. Bekannt sind die Kirmesprogramme, zum Beispiel in Landwüst oder Eubabrunn. Landauf, landab sind die Auftritte der „Gockeschen" in der Advents- und Weihnachtszeit besonders beliebt. Wenn es am Jahresende heißt „Muestmaa kumm, dei Zeit is do" (Moosmann komm, deine Zeit ist da), ist es zum Beispiel seit Jahren Brauch, die Gäste im Gemeindesaal der Jocketaer Kirche zu unterhalten. Denn vor allem dort wird es verstanden, wenn der Weihnachtsmann noch Rupperich genannt wird und der Raachermaa (Räuchermann) seine Kringel pafft.

Traditional music, dancing, singing, customs and the dialect – the unmistakeable and typical features from the past and present in our Vogtland homeland dominate the character of the Liebau Ruins Festival. The organiser is the "De Gockeschen" Vogtland Music Club. Groups from Franconia, Thuringia and the Czech Republic meet on the last weekend in June every year to make music, dance and sing with the Vogtland people. This festival will be celebrated in the little village of Liebau near Jocketa for the 18th time in 2008.
The "De Gockeschen" group, however, has existed since 1965. They still called themselves a singing group in those days. The members committed themselves to upholding Vogtland folklore from the mid-1970s onwards. They included songs and texts written in dialect in their programme and rehearsed Vogtland dances. The singing group, which mainly performed to holiday-makers, developed into an ensemble, which became known far beyond the borders of the Vogtland region. They then adopted the name "De Gockeschen", referring to the town of Jocketa, which the locals call "Gocke" in their dialect.
Regardless of whether they are appear at the Saxon Festival, cake singing occasions in the Erzgebirge Mountains, folklore meetings in Poland or Hungary, television recordings or performances in many towns or villages, the traditional musicians consistently refer to their Vogtland home with their down-to-earth, traditional way of making music. They have even been to the USA on two occasions, to the state of Indiana. They appear for performances in Vogtland traditional dress, authentically reworked using originals.
The ensemble consists of 15 musicians, singers, dancers and dialect speakers. Ursula Albert is the musical director. By the way, she is the only active member still in the group from the time that it was founded. Her husband Ulrich Albert joined a short while afterwards. The young people's group "De Gockeschen Ziebele" was created by the Albert family in 1979. It was led by Irina Pörner until 2006.
The repertoire of the traditional music club reflects Vogtland village life in the course of a year. The performances at parish fairs, for example in Landwüst or Eubabrunn, are well known. Appearances by "De Gockeschen" are particularly popular in the Advent and Christmas period all over the place. When it is time to say "Moss man come, the time is here" at the end of the year, the group has been entertaining guests in the parish room at the church at Jocketa for years. For people there will really understand when Father Christmas is called "Rupperich" or when the "smoking man" puffs his rings of smoke.

(Fotos/Photos by B. Kempe-Winkelmann, Text/Text by B. Kempe-Winkelmann, Übersetzung/Translated by David Strauss)

Gelebte Traditionen / Traditions Perpetuated

Schönes bewahren und Leidenschaften pflegen
Preserving Beauty and Cultivating Passion

Wenn einmal im Jahr Tausende Vogtländer „Mal wieder Land sehen" wollen, wie es als Motto des sachsenweiten Tages des offenen Hofes 2007 angekündigt war, dann haben auch die vogtländischen Landfrauen Hochkonjunktur. Bei Festen in der Region sind sie garantiert mit dabei, beim Hoffest genau so wie beim Tag der Sachsen 2007 in Reichenbach, als sie einen Stand auf der Schlemmermeile betreuten und am Festumzug teilnahmen. 24 aktive Frauen mit den verschiedensten Berufen und aus mehreren Generationen zählt der Irfersgrüner Landfrauenverein. Sie kommen regelmäßig zusammen, um ihre Freizeit gemeinsam zu verbringen oder sich mit Themen zu beschäftigen, die Frauen auf dem Lande interessieren. Sie treiben gemeinsam Sport oder gehen wandern.

Seit 2002 werden jährlich auf dem Hoffest der Marienhöher Milchproduktion in Waldkirchen die schönsten Exemplare von Erntekränzen und Erntekronen im Rahmen des Vogtländischen Erntekronenwettbewerbes ausgestellt und prämiert. Der Irfersgrüner Landfrauen e. V. und der Regionalverein Vogtland des Landfrauenverbandes, ebenfalls mit Sitz in Irfersgrün, haben die ländliche Tradition des Erntekronenbindens wieder aufleben lassen. Ein Großteil der Hofbesucher strömt alljährlich in die Ausstellung und wählt seinen ganz speziellen Favoriten.

Schon Monate vorher beginnen die Landfrauen mit der Planung für ihre Ausstellungsstücke, denn das Getreide oder andere Pflanzen müssen gesät oder angebaut, gehegt, gepflegt und zum rechten Zeitpunkt geerntet werden. Zum Getreide kommen bunte Farbtupfer aus Stroh- und Lampionblumen oder Schafgarbe und anderen Blütenpflanzen. Experimentierfreudige Frauen verarbeiten auch Obst und Gemüse oder Brot und Semmeln.

Um ein wirklich schönes Exemplar zu binden, muss man eine bestimmte Technik beherrschen und Zeit und Geduld aufbringen. Während im Winter die Treffen im Zwei-Wochen-Rhythmus ausreichen, wird im Sommer zwei Mal pro Woche zusammen gebastelt. Gespannt warten jedes Mal alle Teilnehmerinnen auf die Auswertung und Preisübergabe, die im voll besetzten Festzelt beim Hoffest stattfindet. Die Erntekronen sind natürlich nicht nur für das eine Wochenende gemacht. In Kirchen und landwirtschaftlich orientierten Ausstellungen im gesamten Vogtland kann man in Spätsommer oder Frühherbst Erntekränze und -kronen der Landfrauen bewundern.

Once a year thousands of Vogtland people want to "See the Countryside again", as the motto of the 2007 Saxon Open Farm Day announced. Then the Vogtland Country Women have plenty to do. They often take part in festivals around the region – for example, the Farm Festival or the 2007 Saxony Fair in Reichenbach, where they had a stand offering snacks in the food area; they also took part in the festival procession. 24 active ladies from many walks of life and several generations are members of the Country Women's Association in Irfersgrün. They meet on a regular basis and spend their free time together or devote their attention to matters of interest to women in the countryside. They practise sports together or go for walks.

The best harvest wreaths or harvest crowns have been exhibited and prizes have been awarded as part of the Vogtland Harvest Crown Competition at the annual Farm Festival at the Marienhof Milk Farm in Waldkirchen since 2002. The Country Women's Association in Irfersgrün and the Regional Association of Country Women in the Vogtland region, which also has its headquarters in Irfersgrün, have revived the rural tradition of making harvest crowns. Many of the visitors to the Farm Festival come to see the exhibition and vote for their special favourites. The Country Women start planning their exhibits months in advance since the grain or other plants have to be sown or planted, nourished, cared for and finally harvested at the right moment. Colourful materials such as strawflowers, Chinese lantern plants, blood-wort or other flowers are added to the corn. Ladies who are happy to try out new things may also use fruit, vegetables, bread or rolls for their creation.

In order to bind a particularly pretty wreath, the ladies need the right technique and have a lot of patience and time. While the Country Women's meetings are held every other week during the winter, they meet twice a week during the summer to do their handcrafts together. Every year the participants eagerly wait for the results of the competition and the presentation of the prizes at the award ceremony, which takes place in the party tent at the Farm Festival. But harvest crowns are not just made for this one weekend. The Country Women's harvest wreaths and crowns can be enjoyed in many churches or agricultural exhibitions all over the Vogtland region in the late summer or early autumn.

Herzlich und interessiert ging es zu bei der Begegnung mit den Landfrauen aus Irfersgrün. Ein noch recht junger Verein von Frauen aus den verschiedensten Berufen, die sich mit Tagesgeschehen, veränderter Infrastruktur, mit Arbeitsbeschaffungsproblematik und allgemeinen Themen befassen, und dabei Geselligkeit, Tradition und Zusammenhalt pflegen. Kontakt: Gudrun Schwarz Sächsischer Landfrauenverband e.V. Regionalverein Vogtland

There is plenty of interest and enthusiasm when the Country Women from Irfersgrün meet. This is still a young association of women from a wide range of walks of life, who talk about daily events, changes to infrastructure, the problems of creating jobs and general subjects and enjoy each other's company and maintain traditions and a sense of community. Contact: Gudrun Schwarz Saxon Country Women's Association Vogtland Regional Association

(Fotos/Photos by Petra Steps, Text/Text by Petra Steps/Translated by David Strauss)

Gelebte Traditionen / Traditions Perpetuated

Das Plauener Spitzenmuseum –
Branchenmuseum der vogtländischen Spitzen- und Stickereiindustrie mit Tradition und Zukunft
The Plauen Lace Museum – Specialist Museum of the Vogtland Lace and Embroidery Industry with Traditions and a Future

Im Juni 1984 öffnete im Plauener Alten Rathaus das Plauener Spitzenmuseum als „museale Abteilung" des damaligen VEB Plauener Spitze. Gemeinsame Interessen der Stadt und der Industrie ermöglichten erstmals in der mehr als 100-jährigen Geschichte der *Plauener Spitze*® ein Branchenmuseum zu präsentieren, das in architektonisch wertvollen Räumen die Branchengeschichte unter der damaligen Sicht der Dinge darstellte und kostbare Spitzen und Stickereien aus der historischen Sammlung und aktuellen Kollektionen zeigte.

Im Verlauf der Jahre hat sich das Museum weit über die Grenzen Plauens hinaus einen guten Ruf erworben und zum festen Bestandteil der vogtländischen Museumslandschaft entwickelt. Anlässlich des 20-jährigen Jubiläums im Jahr 2004 entschloss sich der Verein zur umfassenden Rekonstruktion und Renovierung sowie inhaltlichen Neugestaltung der in die Jahre gekommenen Ausstellung. Entstanden ist eine selbstführend konzipierte Dauerausstellung, die denkmalgeschützte Architektur berücksichtigt und die vogtländische Spitzen- und Stickereiindustrie in das Zentrum der musealen Präsentation stellt.

Das Museum versteht sich als Einrichtung, insbesondere für touristische Besucher der Stadt Plauen, die in einer überschaubaren Zeit alles Wissenswerte zur *Plauener Spitze*® erfahren wollen.

Der erste Ausstellungsraum gibt einen Überblick zur „Technologie der Stickerei auf Großstickmaschinen". Am Beispiel der Fertigung einer Wickeldecke wird der hohe Grad der Veredlung geringster Rohstoffmengen zu einem Markenprodukt gezeigt. Im Mittelpunkt steht dabei eine über 80-jährige Pantografenstickmaschine – Typ Kappel, auf der Vorführungen stattfinden. Herausragende Stickereien verschiedener Epochen komplettieren diesen Teil des Museums. Die Geschichte der Branche wird mit ausgewählten Daten, Bildern und Dokumenten vom frühen 19. Jahrhundert bis ins neue Jahrtausend hinein dargestellt.

Der zweite Ausstellungsabschnitt zeigt „Plauener Spitze und Mode" im Wandel der Zeiten. Ausgewählte kostbare Damenkleider und Accessoires sowie Wäsche und Heimtextilien dokumentieren das erfolgreiche Wirken der heimischen Industrie.

Der meisterlich nach Originalbefund restaurierte Mittelgang mit gotischem Netzrippengewölbe, 1382 erstmals urkundlich erwähnt, bietet als architektonische Sehenswürdigkeit den Rahmen für den dritten Ausstellungsabschnitt zum Thema „Höchstleistungen der Maschinenstickerei". Gezeigt werden Stickereien und Spitzen mit besonders kreativer Musterung in technologisch meisterlicher Ausführung, die beim Betrachter Bewunderung hervorrufen.

Im vierten Ausstellungsabschnitt wird die Kleinmaschinen-Stickerei als typischer früherer Erwerbszweig im Vogtland gezeigt.

Der Mittelgang und der Zugang zum Informations- und Designzentrum wird für wechselnde Sonderausstellungen genutzt.

Im Anschluss an die Ausstellungsräume befindet sich die historische Mustersammlung im Informations- und Designzentrum. Interessenten an wissenschaftlicher Arbeit und für Studienzwecke steht der von der Stadt Plauen erworbene Fundus textiler Kostbarkeiten nach Voranmeldung zur Verfügung.

Im Museums-Shop wird *Plauener Spitze*® aus aktuellen Kollektionen der heimischen Produzenten sowie Fachliteratur zum Kauf angeboten.

The Plauen Lace Museum, which was opened as a "museum department" of the then Plauen lace combine, was opened at Plauen's old city hall in June 1984. Interested parties from the city and industry were able to present a specialist museum covering more than 100 years of Plauen lace (*Plauener Spitze*®). It portrays the history of this sector from the standpoint of the time in a splendid architectural setting. It exhibited precious lace and embroidery items from historical and modern collections.

The museum obtained a good reputation well beyond the boundaries of Plauen down through the years and developed into a fixed element in the Vogtland museum landscape. In 2004 on the 20th anniversary of the museum, the association decided to carry out comprehensive reconstruction and repair work to the exhibition, which had become somewhat dated. The permanent exhibition is now designed to enable people to find their way round, the listed architecture has been carefully preserved and the Vogtland lace and embroidery industry has become the focus of the museum's presentation.

The museum is a centre for tourists who come to the city of Plauen and wish to learn about everything worth knowing about Plauen lace (*Plauener Spitze*®) in a manageable time.

The first exhibition room provides an overview of "embroidery technology on large embroidery machines". The high level of finish using very small amounts of raw materials and making them into a brand product is demonstrated by the example of manufacturing a table cloth. A pantograph embroidery machine, which is more than 80 years old, is the central focus – a Kappel model, which is used to demonstrate the process. Outstanding embroidery work from various periods completes this part of the museum. The history of the sector is shown using selected data, photos and documents from the early 19th century to the current century.

The second part of the exhibition shows "Plauen lace and fashion" down through the ages. Selected precious ladies' dresses and accessories and underwear and home furnishings document how successfully the local industry worked.

The middle corridor, which has been restored in a masterful fashion with a Gothic vaulted ceiling, was first mentioned in documents in 1382 and it provides an architecturally interesting framework for the third section of the exhibition on the theme of "Top embroidery work carried out on machines". Embroidery work and lace with particularly creative patterns, made with outstanding technological skill, are on display and amaze visitors.

The fourth part of the exhibition shows embroidery work carried out on small machines – a typical business in the Vogtland region.

The middle corridor and the entrance to the information and design centre are used for temporary special exhibitions.

The historical collection of patterns is found in the information and design centre next to the exhibition rooms. The pool of textile treasures acquired by the city of Plauen is available to those interested in scientific studies and study purposes if they apply to come in advance.

Plauen lace (*Plauener Spitze*®) from the latest collections of local manufacturers and specialist literature are on sale in the museum shop.

PLAUENER SPITZENMUSEUM
Altes Rathaus, Altmarkt
D-08523 Plauen · Unterer Graben 1
Telefon   +49 (0) 3741 222355
Telefon   +49 (0) 3741 223713
Telefax   +49 (0) 3741 281192
www.plauenerspitze.info
bv.plauenerspitze@t-online.de
Öffnungszeiten: Mo – Fr 10 – 17 Uhr
                  Sa   9 – 14 Uhr
Sonntag für Gruppenbesucher nach Vereinbarung

(Fotos/Photos by Branchenverband Plauener Spitze und Stickereien e.V., Text/Text by Jürgen Fritzlar Branchenverband Plauener Spitze und Stickereien e.V., Übersetzung/Translated by David Strauss)

Adel verpflichtet - Schönheit ist nicht genug
High Class Brings Responsibilities — Beauty Is Not Enough

„Gruß aus Sachsen, wo die schönen Mädchen wachsen", stand um 1900 auf Postkarten, die um den Erdball gingen. Daran hat sich wohl nichts geändert. Dass ein ganzer Teil der schönen Mädchen im sächsischen Vogtland beheimatet ist, verrät ein Blick in die Liste der amtierenden Königinnen, Prinzessinnen und anderen Hoheiten. Nehmen wir zum Beispiel die Sächsische Sektprinzession 2006/07. Sie heißt Sandra Pavlik und stammt nicht etwa aus einem Weinanbaugebiet, sondern aus Bad Brambach. Die Kosmetikerin arbeitet im Staatsbad, trinkt am liebsten Traminer und möchte das sächsische Spitzengetränk auch im Vogtland bekannt machen. Ähnlich ist es um die Herkunft der Sächsischen Milchkönigin bestellt. Julia Floß aus Pausa wurde auf der „agra 2007" gekrönt. Bei einem Casting musste die Landwirtschaftsstudentin ihr Wissen zu den Themen Milch, Kuh und Melken unter Beweis stellen. Beim Tag der Sachsen 2007 in Reichenbach erhielt die Sächsische Ernteprinzessin von Landtagspräsident Erich Illtgen ihren Kopfschmuck. Sie hat ihre Wurzeln im Treuener Ortsteil Wetzelsgrün, wo ihre Mutter Marion einen modernen Bauernhof betreibt.

Zu den gesamtsächsischen Hoheiten kommen noch viele regionale und lokale Würdenträgerinnen. Vor allem im Oberen Vogtland scheinen Krönungen äußerst beliebt zu sein. Das ist nicht weiter verwunderlich, denn die sächsischen Staatsbäder hatten zu Zeiten von König Albert schon einmal eine Blütezeit. In Bad Elster residiert die Brunnenkönigin Catharina Liebold, die sogar schon beim „Kutschentheater"

als Darstellerin zu erleben war. Über das Wasser in Bad Brambach herrscht die Quellenprinzessin Franziska Ernst.
Die Oelsnitzer Sperkenprinzessin heißt Romina Siegel. Die Oberhermsgrünerin wurde bereits 2005 für drei Jahre gewählt. Zur 650-Jahr-Feier der Sperkenstadt Oelsnitz präsentierte sie sich in ihrem neuen Kleid in den Oelsnitzer Stadtfarben gelb-schwarz. Gleich um die Ecke in Planschwitz schwingt Yvonne Engelbrecht das Zepter als Apfelprinzessin. Zu den dienstältesten, jedoch weniger bekannten Majestäten gehört die Musikwinkelkönigin Sandra Müller aus Zwota.
Das nördliche Vogtland hat nur zwei richtige Prinzessinnen. Seit 1996 wird in Plauen die Spitzenprinzessin gekürt. Neben Schönheit und dem publikumswirksamen Auftritt muss sie auch ein umfangreiches Wissen über die Plauener Spitze in Geschichte und Gegenwart präsentieren. 2007 konnte sich die Reichenbacherin Sophie Gürtler gegen ihre Mitbewerberinnen durchsetzen. Die letzte im Bunde ist die Vogtländische Reiterprinzessin, die beim Reit- und Springturnier in Lengenfeld gekrönt wurde Theresa Weck vom RFV Lengenfeld ist die achte Pferdefreundin, die diesen Titel führen darf.

Zu den Adelsdamen – Herren vermisst man hier gänzlich – kommen noch viele Schärpenträgerinnen, die sich bei Misswahlen durchsetzen konnten, oder Darstellerinnen historischer Persönlichkeiten. Hier sei vor allem Sandra Gerlach als „Neuberin" erwähnt.

"Greetings from Saxony where you can find the most beautiful girls", was the text on postcards from the region in 1900, which were sent around the globe. It seems that nothing has changed. A glance at a list of the reigning beauty queens, princesses and other titles reveals that quite a number of these beauties come from the Saxon Vogtland area. Sandra Pavlik, the 2006-07 Saxon Sparkling Wine Princess is just one example, but she does not come from a wine-growing region, but Bad Brambach. The beautician works at the health spa in the town, likes to drink Traminer wine and is interested in promoting this top quality wine from Saxony in her Vogtland home region. The origins of the Saxon Milk Queen are very similar. Julia Floß from Pausa was crowned at the 2007 "agra2007" Agricultural Fair. During a casting, the agriculture student had to prove her knowledge on subjects like milk, cows and milking. During the 2007 Saxony Fair in Reichenbach, the Saxon Harvest Princess was crowned by Erich Illtgen, the president of the Saxon state parliament. Her roots are in the Treuen district of Wetzelsgrün, where her mother Marion runs a modern farm.
There are also a number of local and regional dignitaries in addition to all these Saxon royal highnesses. Coronations seem to be very popular, especially in the Upper Vogtland region. However, this is far from surprising since the Saxon Spa towns had their first Golden Age during the time of King Albert. Catharina Liebold, the reigning Fountain Queen, lives in the spa town of Bad Elster and has already participated in one of the famous "carriage theatre"

performances, which re-enact historical events. The waters at Bad Brambach, on the other hand, are guarded by the Well Princess, Franziska Ernst.
The Sparrow Princess in Oelsnitz is called Romina Siegel. She was born in Oberhermsgrün and was elected for three years in 2005. She appeared in a new dress sporting the town colours of Oelsnitz, black and yellow, at the celebrations for the 650th anniversary of Oelsnitz, which is also known as "sparrow town". Yvonne Engelbrecht, the reigning Apple Princess, holds sway just around the corner in Planschwitz. One of the longest-serving but less famous royal personages is the Queen of Musicon Valley, Sandra Müller from Zwota. The northern part of the Vogtland only has two real princesses. A Lace Princess has been crowned in Plauen since 1996. Besides her beauty and her audience appeal, she also has to possess extensive knowledge of Plauen lace in the past and present. In 2007 Sophie Gürtler from Reichenbach won the crown, beating off the other contestants. Last but not least, there is the Vogtland Riding Princess, who is crowned during the horse jumping show at Lengenfeld. Theresa Weck from the RFV Lengenfeld equestrian club is the eighth horse lover to hold this office.

Besides these royal ladies – after all, there are no gentlemen in this business at all – there are a number of sash bearers who have won beauty pageants or represent historical personalities in the Vogtland region. Sandra Gerlach, representing the theatre reformer Friedericke Caroline Neuber, is just one example.

(Fotos/Photos by Petra Steps, Text/Text by Petra Steps/Translated by David Strauss)

Menschen mit Format / People of Calibre

Ein edles Beispiel macht die schweren Taten leicht (Johann Wolfgang von Goethe)

A GOOD EXAMPLE MAKES DIFFICULT TASKS EASY.

Was macht den Charme einer Region aus? Ist es wie im Vogtland die herrliche Natur, oder sind es die Menschen, die durch ihr Tun keinen Stillstand zulassen und andere zum Mitmachen bewegen können? Beides werden viele sagen und doch auf jene Akteure verweisen, die das Werk der Vorfahren mit neuen Ideen und Visionen fortsetzen und den Namen Vogtland weit über dessen Grenzen hinaustragen. Beispiele gibt es viele und nicht alle lassen sich nennen.

Wie breit gefächert das Engagement auf verschiedene Bereiche ist, zeigt die Verleihung des Ehrenpreises, der höchsten Auszeichnung im Vogtlandkreis. Ihn erhielt 2003 der erste deutsche Kosmonauten Dr. Sigmund Jähn für sein Lebenswerk und die Förderung der Raumfahrtregion Vogtland. Ein Jahr später wurden zwei Künstler geehrt: Zum einen Leonore Klotz, die „Vogtländische Mundartkönigin" und Talentemutter für ihre unermüdliche Förderung von Brauchtum, Tradition und der Bewahrung der vogtländischen Sprache und des hiesigen Liedgutes. Zum anderen Eberhard Hertel, der gemeinsam mit seiner Tochter Stefanie musikalische Botschafter des Vogtlandes sind. Für sein unternehmerisches Geschick als Geschäftsführer der Goldbeck Bau Treuen, sein Wirken in wirtschaftlichen Gremien Sachsens und sein Engagement beim Bau der Großschanze in Klingenthal wurde 2005 Dr. Rüdiger Kroll die hohe Auszeichnung zuteil. Dass die Michaeliskirche in Wiedersberg, im einstigen Grenzgebiet gerettet und wiederaufgebaut werden konnte, verdankt sie dem Verein der Kirche und seinem Vorsitzenden Kurt Geipel. Dafür erhielt er 2006 den vogtländischen Ehrenpreis. In diesem Jahr wurden die Verdienste von Christoph Mann und damit sein Engagement für Natur- und Umweltschutz sowie Landschaftspflege, Ökomärkte und grenzüberschreitende Zusammenarbeit gewürdigt.

In der Stadt Plauen werden hervorragende Leistungen mit der höchsten Auszeichnung – der Ernennung zum Ehrenbürger geehrt. Diese Würdigung erfuhren seit 1990 der damaligen Superintendenten Thomas Küttler, der bei den Demonstrationen im Herbst 1989 Garant für eine friedliche Wende war, der Zeichner Lothar Rentsch, der erste freigewählte Oberbürgermeister Dr. Rolf Magerkord und der Ärztliche Direktor und Leiter der Psychiatrie am Vogtland-Klinikum, Professor Dr. Klaus-Dieter Waldmann. Hinzu wurde in den vergangene Jahren mehr als 30 Mal die Stadtplakette verliehen.

Doch bei all den genannten Menschen mit Format sollen auch all jene nicht vergessen werden, die sich in ihrer Freizeit selbstlos um Kinder, Jugendliche und Senioren kümmen, ob auf kulturellem oder sportlichen Gebiet, in den Feuerwehren oder Vereinen und Verbänden. Die genannten und die zahllosen ungenannten Vogtländer sind in ihrem Wirken wie kleine Mosaiksteinchen, die dem reizvollen Bild vom Vogtland erst die unverwechselbare Farbe geben.

What makes a region charming? Is it the beautiful countryside or is it people who through their conduct leave nothing undone and motivate other people to get involved, as is the case in the Vogtland region? A lot of people would say both and yet point to those protagonists, who are continuing their forefathers' work with new ideas and visions and are carrying the reputation of the Vogtland region well beyond its borders. There are a lot of examples, not all of which can be mentioned.

The awarding of the Vogtland Prize, the highest accolade in the region, demonstrates how widespread these endeavours can be. The first German astronaut, Dr Sigmund Jähn, was awarded the prize in 2003 for his life's work and for promoting the Vogtland areas as a space travel region. A year later, two artists were honoured: one was Leonora Klotz, the Vogtland "Dialect Queen" and huge talent for her tireless support for customs and traditions and the preservation of the Vogtland dialect and local songs. The other was Eberhard Hertel, who, together with his daughter Stefanie, is the Vogtland region's musical ambassador. Dr Rüdiger Kroll was awarded this great honour for his skill as managing director of the Goldbeck Bau Treuen company, his work on business committees in Saxony and his endeavours in the construction of the ski-jump facility in Klingenthal. The fact that St Michael's Church in Wiedersberg in the former East German/West German border area was saved and could be rebuilt was due to the organisation set up to restore the church under the chairmanship of Kurt Geipel. He was awarded the Vogtland Prize in 2006, together with Christoph Mann for his endeavours in preserving nature and the environment as well as the countryside, organic markets and cross-border initiatives.

In Plauen, outstanding achievements are awarded the highest accolade, the freedom of the city. This honour was first presented to the then Lutheran Church Superintendent Thomas Küttler in 1990, who during the demonstrations in the autumn of 1989, was one of those who ensured that the Berlin Wall came down peacefully; it was also presented to the artist Lothar Rentsch, the first democratically elected mayor, Dr Rolf Magerkord, and the medical director and manager of the psychiatric department at the Vogtland Clinic, Professor Dr Klaus-Dieter Waldmann. Since then, more than 30 awards have been presented.

Besides all the people mentioned above, who have done something important, we should not forget the many people who spend their free time helping children, young people and the elderly in cultural areas or sports, the voluntary fire brigade or in clubs and organisations. Those named and the many unnamed people in the Vogtland region are like small pieces of a mosaic, which give the area its unique colour.

(Fotos/Photos by, Text/Text by Marjon Thümmel /Translated by David Strauss)

Gesicht zeigen

Show Your True Colours

Der berühmteste Reichenbacher in der Sparte Bildende Kunst ist zweifellos Wolfgang Mattheuer. Am 7. April 1927 wurde er in Reichenbach geboren. Sein Vater arbeitete als Buchbinder im polygrafischen Großbetrieb Carl Werner. In dieser Firma lernte Mattheuer nach dem Schulabschluss den Beruf eines Lithografen. Die ersten Grundlagen für sein späteres druckgrafisches Werk hat er also 1941 bis 1944 in der Neuberinstadt erworben.

Aus einem sozialdemokratischen Elternhaus stammend, lehnte er den Beitritt zur Hitlerjugend ab. Schon als 15-Jähriger hatte er seine Liebe zur Heimat, aber auch das Fernweh entdeckt. Er unternahm Wanderungen durch das Vogtland sowie Radtouren nach Bayern und Österreich, zu einem Zeitpunkt, als andere im Gleichschritt marschierten ... Die unstillbare Sehnsucht nach einem Blick hinter den Horizont, die Suche nach Erkenntnis und Wahrheit – all das trieb Wolfgang Mattheuer schon damals an und wurde später zur Quelle seines Schöpfertums.

Wie den meisten jungen Männern seiner Generation blieb ihm der Krieg nicht erspart. 1944 wurde er zu den Gebirgsjägern nach Salzburg einberufen und bei einem Einsatz in der Slowakei verwundet. Der geglückten Flucht aus russischer Kriegsgefangenschaft verdankt Mattheuer, dass er nicht nach Sibirien kam. Zurückgekehrt nach Reichenbach, wartete ein einschneidendes Erlebnis auf ihn: Seine Firma Carl Werner wurde demontiert, die Maschinen in die Sowjetunion abtransportiert. Und er musste dabei auch noch helfen.

Während in der Nachkriegszeit noch vieles in Schutt und Asche lag, widmete sich Wolfgang Mattheuer bereits wieder der Kunst. 1946/47 besuchte er die Kunstgewerbeschule Leipzig und begegnete dort seiner späteren Frau Ursula Mattheuer-Neustädt. Die aus Plauen stammende Künstlerin begleitete ihn von nun an. Gemeinsam studierten sie an der Hochschule für Grafik und Buchkunst. Beide schlossen mit dem Grafikdiplom ab.

Bereits 1954 nahm der Wahl-Leipziger an der Kunstausstellung des Bezirkes Leipzig teil. Es folgten ungezählte Ausstellungen und Ausstellungsbeteiligungen in beiden Teilen Deutschlands, in Schweden und Tokio. Wolfgang Mattheuer entdeckte zunehmend die Malerei für sich. Es gab keine Kunstausstellung in der DDR, bei der die interessierte Besucherschar nicht Ausschau nach neuen Werken des vogtländischen „Bildermachers" hielt. Nach der Wende standen auch ihm die Türen zur Welt offen. Davon zeugen verschiedene Ausstellungen. Zeit seines Lebens behielt er seinen kritisch-realistischen Blick. Fast legendär sind die Worte anlässlich der Eröffnung der Mattheuer-Retrospektive zu seinem 75. Geburtstag in den Chemnitzer Kunstsammlungen. Auf die Frage, warum er immer noch DDR-Symbole verwende, antwortete er: „Ja glauben Sie denn, alles ist besser geworden?" Damals, 2002, dachte noch keiner daran, dass die Zeit für und mit Wolfgang Mattheuer endlich ist. Völlig unerwartet verstarb er an seinen 77. Geburtstag am 7. April 2004 in einem Leipziger Krankenhaus.

The most famous artist in Reichenbach is undoubtedly Wolfgang Mattheuer, who was born in Reichenbach on 7 April 1927. His father worked as a bookbinder in a large polygraphic company called Carl Werner. After leaving school, Mattheuer trained as a lithographer at the company. So he acquired the initial foundations for his later printing work between 1941 and 1944 in Reichenbach. Coming from a Social Democratic family, he did not join the Hitler Youth movement. As a fifteen year old, he had already fallen in love with his home region, but had discovered other places too. He went on walks through the Vogtland region and went on cycling tours through Bavaria and Austria at a time when other people were marching in step. This insatiable thirst for a glimpse of what lay beyond the horizon, the search for recognition and truth all affected him early on and would be the source of his creativity later on.

Like most young men of his generation, the war did not pass him by. He was called up in 1944 and joined the mountain infantry in Salzburg and was wounded in action in Slovakia. He owes his successful escape from a prisoner of war camp in Russia to the fact that he was not sent to Siberia. On his return to Reichenbach, he was confronted by a far-reaching event. His firm, Carl Werner, was stripped down and the machines were transported to the Soviet Union. And he had to lend a helping hand.

During the period after the war, when a great deal lay in ruins, he turned his attention back to art. In 1946-7 he went to art college in Leipzig, where he met the lady who was to become his wife, Ursula Mattheuer-Neustädt. From then on, the artist from Plauen accompanied him wherever he went. They studied together at the Academy of Visual Arts. Both left with a qualification in graphics.

Mattheuer took part in the art exhibition in the Leipzig district in 1954, the city of his choice. Many exhibitions followed in both parts of Germany, Sweden and Tokyo. He also discovered painting. Every exhibition in East Germany included the new works from the "picture maker" from the Vogtland region for interested visitors. After the fall of the Berlin Wall, the doors to the rest of the world and its exhibitions lay open. Many exhibitions bear testimony to this. He maintained his self-critical outlook throughout his lifetime. At the opening of his exhibition at the Chemnitz Art Collection to mark his seventy-fifth birthday, his opening words were almost legendary. In response to a question about why he still used East German symbols, he replied: "Do you think everything has improved?" At that time, in 2002, nobody thought that the time for and with Wolfgang Mattheuer would come to an end. His death came totally unexpectedly on his seventy seventh birthday, on 7 April 2004, in a Leipzig hospital.

(Fotos/Photos by Petra Steps, Text/Text by Petra Steps/Translated by David Strauss)

Reichenbach und das Vogtland hatten für Wolfgang Mattheuer immer eine besondere Bedeutung. Gern hielt er sich in seinem Elternhaus nahe der „Schönen Aussicht" auf und ließ sich von der Landschaft inspirieren. Erst wenige Jahre vor seinem Tod hatte die Stadt wieder engere Kontakte zu ihrem Ehrenbürger geknüpft. Es ist ein Glücksfall, dass der Künstler seiner Geburtsstadt die wohl neben dem „Jahrhundertschritt" bedeutendste Plastik „Gesicht zeigen", auch „Großer Maskenmann" genannt, schenkte. Sie steht vor dem Zugang zum Reichenbacher Rathaus und mahnt die Vorüberziehenden, nicht alles hinzunehmen. Fünf Exemplare wurden aus Bronze gegossen. Sie stehen im Museum der Bildenden Künste Leipzig, gehören dem Museum Heilbronn und der Berliner Nationalgalerie. Eine weist an Wolfgang Mattheuers Grabstätte auf dem Südfriedhof in Leipzig auf den bedeutenden Künstler hin.

Reichenbach and the Vogtland region were always special to Wolfgang Mattheuer. He enjoyed spending time in his parents' house near the "beautiful view" and allowed the landscape to inspire him. Reichenbach did not regain any interest in its well-known citizen until a few years before his death. It was a stroke of fortune that the artist gave the town of his birth what was probably his most significant sculpture – apart from his "Step of the Century" in Leipzig – entitled "Show Your True Colours", also known as the "Large Masked Man". The latter is in the entrance to the town hall in Reichenbach and warns people going past not to accept everything. Five examples were cast in bronze. They are in the Museum of Visual Arts in Leipzig, but belong to the Heilbronn Museum and the Berlin National Gallery. One of them highlights the important artist at Wolfgang Mattheuer's gravestone in the Southern Cemetery in Leipzig.

Es ist ein Glücksfall, dass der Künstler seiner Geburtsstadt die wohl neben dem „Jahrhundertschritt" bedeutendste Plastik „Gesicht zeigen", auch „Großer Maskenmann" genannt, schenkte. Sie steht vor dem Zugang zum Reichenbacher Rathaus und mahnt die Vorüberziehenden, nicht alles hinzunehmen.
Der Maler und Grafiker Wolfgnag Mattheuer gehörte zu den profiliertesten Vertretern des kritischen Realismus in Deutschland. Er starb am 7. April 2004, seinem 77. Geburtstag, an Herzversagen. Er bestand darauf, ein „Bildermacher" zu sein, wollte nicht „im Topf der Maler verrührt werden". Er mischte sich ein mit seinen Bildern und Plastiken. Sisyphos und Ikarus, Kain und Abel zeigte er nicht als Figuren aus ferner Vergangenheit, sondern als unsere Zeitgenossen
It was a stroke of fortune that the artist gave the town of his birth what was probably his most significant sculpture – apart from his "Step of the Century" in Leipzig – entitled "Show Your True Colours", also known as the "Large Masked Man". The latter is in the entrance to the town hall in Reichenbach and warns people going past not to accept everything.
The painter and graphic artist Wolfgang Mattheuer was one of the best known representatives of critical realism in Germany. He died of heart failure on 7 April 2004, his seventy-seventh birthday. He insisted on being called a "picture maker" and didn't want to be mixed up with common painters. He meddled with history in his pictures and sculptures. He did not portray Sisyphus and Icarus, Cain and Abel as figures from the distant past, but as our contemporaries.

Thomas Kropff - Weltenbummler mit vogtländischen Wurzeln
Globe Trotter with Vogtland Roots

Eichendorffs vertontes Gedicht „Wem Gott will rechte Gunst erweisen, den schickt er in die weite Welt," muss sich der gebürtige Reichenbacher Thomas Kropff zu Herzen genommen haben. Nach Schulabschluss und Lehre zog es ihn gen Westen. Der Mauerfall ersparte ihm die Ausreise. Dem Abi auf dem zweiten Bildungsweg folgte ein Studium. Doch weil die Sehnsucht nach der Ferne zunahm, begann er sich auf den Weg zu machen. Ein einschneidendes Ereignis ereilte ihn dabei 1997 bei einer Südamerikatour. Kolumbien hätte nach der Entführung durch Guerilleros im Urwaldgebiet El Darien das Ende seines Lebens bedeuten können.

Thomas Kropff hat inzwischen mehr als 40 Länder auf fünf Kontinenten bereist und arbeitet heute nebenberuflich als Reiseleiter in Vietnam und als Vortragsreferent. Er organisiert die Vortragsreihe „Kulturen der Erde" in mehreren Orten Mitteldeutschlands. Durch seine Initiative kam der bedeutende Survivalexperte Rüdiger Nehberg ins Reichenbacher Neuberinhaus, die Gäste konnten den Bergsteiger Hans Kammerlander erleben oder den Vorträgen von Thomas Kropff lauschen.

Zu den besonderen Abenteuern des mittlerweile in Dresden lebenden Vogtländers gehört eine sechsmonatige Radtour durch Vietnam, Laos, Kambodscha und Thailand. Zusammen mit einem Freund fuhr er mit einem alten russischen Jeep an den Baikalsee, den die Abenteuerlustigen bei bis zu Minus 40 Grad zu Fuß überquerten. Spektakulär war ein Tandemgleitschirmflug vom Elbrus, dem mit 5621m höchsten Berg des Kaukasus. Mit dem Vortrag „GO EAST" über diese Russlandreise begeisterten die beiden in vielen Städten Deutschlands, aber auch in Österreich und der Schweiz. Szenen aus dem mit Schirm- und Handkamera gedrehten Video vom Gleitschirmflug wurden im MDR gesendet.

Seine Verbundenheit mit dem Vogtland zeigt der 37-Jährige nicht nur bei Vorträgen in der Heimat. In Dresden mischt er bei der seit 13 Jahren halbjährlich stattfindenden „Vogtlandfete" mit, zu der inzwischen über 700 Leute kommen.

Mit zwei Partnern betreibt Thomas Kropff den Club „Sputnik" in der Dresdner Neustadt, der sich schon kurz nach der Eröffnung zu einer der angesagtesten Locations der Dresdner Partyszene entwickelt hat. Ein Café wird folgen.

Heute stellt Thomas Kropff nicht ohne Selbstironie fest: „Irgendwann hab ich mich gefragt, was ich eigentlich wirklich richtig gut kann. Mir fielen nur zwei Dinge ein: Party und Reisen. Und das habe ich perfektioniert und zu meinem Beruf gemacht."

The native of Reichenbach, Thomas Kropff, must have taken to heart Eichendorff's poem set to music: "Those whom God really favours, He sends off to the big, wide world." After finishing school and his training, he moved to western Germany. The fall of the Berlin wall saved him having to apply to leave East Germany. Having completed his final school examinations at evening school, he went to university. But a longing to travel overwhelmed him and he began to head off. A dramatic event overtook him during a tour of South America in 1997. Columbia could have cost him his life after guerrilla fighters kidnapped him in the El Darien tropical forest.

Thomas Kropff has now travelled to more than 40 countries on five continents and works part-time as a tour guide in Vietnam and as a lecture speaker. He organises the "Cultures of the Earth" series of lectures in several towns in Central Germany. As a result of his initiatives, the eminent survival expert, Rüdiger Nehberg, came to the Neuberinhaus Theatre in Reichenbach, guests were able to experience the mountaineer Hans Kammerlander live or listen to Thomas Kropff's lectures.

The native of the Vogtland region, who now lives in Dresden, has had many adventures including a six-month cycling tour through Vietnam, Laos, Cambodia and Thailand. He drove an old Russian jeep to Lake Baikal with a friend and the two adventurers crossed the lake on foot in temperatures of minus 40 degrees Celsius. The tandem paragliding flight from the Elbrus, the highest mountain in the Caucasus at 5,621 metres, was also highly spectacular. The two men brought great pleasure to people in many towns in Germany, Austria and Switzerland with their "GO EAST" lecture on this journey to Russia. Scenes from the video of their flight filmed with a camera fixed to the paraglider and a video camera were shown on regional German television.

The 37-year-old not only demonstrates his links with the Vogtland region by giving lectures on his home turf. In Dresden he is involved in the six-monthly "Vogtland Fete", which has been held for the past 13 years and to which more than 700 people come.

Thomas Kropff runs the "Sputnik" club with two partners in the Neustadt district of Dresden; the club has turned into one of the most popular locations in the Dresden party scene. A café is due to be added.

Thomas Kropff admits with a touch of irony: "At some stage I asked myself what I could do really well. I could only think of two things: partying and travelling. I've perfected the art of both and have made them my profession".

Baikalsee im Winter

Mit dem Fahrrad durch Laos

(Fotos/Photos by Petra Steps, Text/Text by Petra Steps/Translated by David Strauss)

Menschen mit Format / People of Calibre

Der „weltgrößte Zuckertütenshop"

The "Largest Cone-Shaped Sweet Package Shop in the World"

● ● ● ist in Reichenbach

Die Idee ist so ausgefallen wie schön: Barbara Kurpiers aus Reichenbach setzt in ihrem 1990 eröffneten Schicki-Micki-Geschäft seit 2002 auf Zuckertüten, und das nicht nur in der heißen Phase vor dem Schulanfang, sondern über das ganze Jahr. Natürlich ist im Sommer Hochsaison für die großen, bunten und manchmal schweren Tüten, die die Schulanfänger bei ihrem Start in den neuen Lebensabschnitt erhalten. Gründe, jemandem den Alltag oder ein besonderes Ereignis zu versüßen, gibt es aber viele. Da muss die kreative Geschäftsfrau gleich mal 70 kleine Tüten für ein Klassentreffen packen. Oder Eltern brauchen ein Hochzeitsgeschenk, in dem sie nette Kleinigkeiten wie Liebesperlen und ein paar Scheine für den gemeinsamen Lebensweg unterbringen. Diese Zuckertüten sind besonders hübsch, meist mit einem Bärchenpaar und einem Klapperstorch verziert.

Bei den Schulanfängertüten fehlt kaum ein Motiv im Regal. Seit Jahren lieben die Mädchen Barbie, Pferde und Katzen, während die Jungs eher auf Spongebob, Lego oder Autos stehen. Die traditionellen Märchentüten fristen hingegen ein Schattendasein. Kundenwünsche haben für die Reichenbacherin oberste Priorität: Wenn jemand eine patriotische Tüte in den Sachsen-Farben will, dann bekommt er auch die.

Was anfangs für die Region gedacht war, erfreut sich großer Beliebtheit quer über den Erdball. Die liebevoll gepackten Tüten in spezieller Schicki-Micki-Technik gingen nach Kanada und Australien. Eine philippinische Familie war so begeistert, dass sie gleich vier große Exemplare mit auf die Insel nahm. Bestellungen aus Holland, Dänemark, Frankreich und vor allem Österreich sind schon Normalität. Ein Hotelier aus der Schweiz erfreute seine Geschäftskunden mit den lustigen Tüten. Auch in Guadeloupe lacht in manchem Kinderzimmer eine in Reichenbach verpackte Diddl-Maus. Zu den Stammkunden gehört eine Einrichtung in Brandenburg, die ihre Kinder in der Frühförderung mit Zuckertüten aus dem Vogtland verabschiedet. Selbst in den alten Bundesländern, aus denen anfangs nur Eltern mit ostdeutschem Hintergrund die Schultüten orderten, ist die typische Schulanfangstradition auf dem Vormarsch. Als eine Kundin ausrief „Hier ist ja der weltgrößte Zuckertütenshop", ließ sich Barbara Kurpiers ein Schild mit genau dieser Aufschrift anfertigen.

● ● ● is in Reichenbach

The idea is as outlandish as it is attractive: Barbara Kurpiers from Reichenbach opened her "Schicki-Micki" shop in 1990 and has been specialising in cone-shaped sweet packages since 2002 – and not just when it is really busy before the start of the school year, but all year round. Of course, the summer is the high season for these large, colourful and sometimes heavy cone-shaped packages, which those starting school receive as they begin this new phase in their lives. There are many reasons to sweeten up everyday life or turn something into a special event. The creative business lady has to pack up 70 small cones for a meeting of former schoolchildren. Or parents need a wedding present, into which they can put a few little titbits like small sweets and a few banknotes for the couple. These cone-shaped sweet packages are particularly attractive and are usually decorated with a couple of little bears and a stork.

There is no shortage of motifs on the cones for those starting school. Girls have loved Barbie, horses and cats for years and boys love SpongeBob, Lego or cars. But traditional fairy tale cones have been eclipsed. The Reichenbach shopkeeper regards customer wishes as her top priority: if somebody wants a patriotic cone in Saxon colours, he or she will get it.

A concept that was initially designed for the region is becoming popular right round the globe. The cones lovingly packed with a special "Schicki-Micki" technique have gone to Canada and Australia. One Philippine family was so excited that they took four large cones with them to their island. It is quite normal for the shop to receive orders from Holland, Denmark, France and especially Austria. One hotelier from Switzerland delighted his business guests with the amusing cones. A Diddl mouse packed in Reichenbach is even laughing in several children's rooms on the island of Guadeloupe. Her regular customers include a centre in Brandenburg, which says goodbye to its children in the nursery school with cone-shaped sweet packages from the Vogtland region. In West Germany, orders initially only came from parents with an Eastern German background, but the typical tradition when children start school is catching on. When one customer shouted: "Here's the largest cone-shaped sweet package shop in the world", Barbara Kurpiers had a sign made with exactly the same text.

SCHICKI-MICKI · Inh. Barbara Kurpiers
Zenkergasse 18 · 08468 Reichenbach · Telefon/Fax: +49 (0) 3765 12122
info@schicki-micki.de · Onlineshop: www.schicki-micki.de

(Fotos/Photos by Petra Steps, Text/Text by Petra Steps/Translated by David Strauss)

Menschen mit Format / People of Calibre

Alles Große in unserer Welt geschieht nur, weil jemand mehr tut, als er muss.
(Hermann Gmeiner, 1919-1986, Gründer der SOS-Kinderdörfer)

"Anything great in our world only happens because somebody does more than is required."
(Hermann Gmeiner, 1919-1986, Founder of the SOS Children's Village Organisation)

Es gibt Leute, die können gar nicht anders – sie müssen einfach helfen. Zu dieser ganz besonderen Spezies gehört Annemarie Schramm aus Reichenbach. Die Erwerbsunfähigkeitsrentnerin erfuhr vom damaligen Pfarrer ihrer Kirchgemeinde von Menschen, die in Not geraten waren. Als folgerichtig 1998 der Leuchtturm e. V. gegründet wurde, schrieb sie sich als eine der ersten in die Mitgliederliste ein. Es dauerte nicht lange, und sie musste die Verantwortung als Vereinsvorsitzende übernehmen.

Der Leuchtturm-Verein kümmert sich um sozial Schwache, Obdachlose, Straffällige und Strafgefangene, seelisch und geistig Behinderte, Suchtkranke und Menschen, die zeitweilig oder dauerhaft Hilfe und Unterstützung brauchen. Er hat sein Domizil in einem ehemaligen Schulhort, Am Graben 57 in Reichenbach. Waren es anfangs rund 30 Hilfesuchende, so kommen heute regelmäßig fast 100 zu den regelmäßigen Öffnungszeiten.

Der Schwerpunkt der Vereinstätigkeit hat sich in Richtung Jugendarbeit und Betreuung junger Familien verändert. Daran hat Annemarie Schramm einen großen Anteil, denn Kinder und Jugendliche liegen ihr besonders am Herzen. Voller Hingabe widmet sie sich der Reintegration, Resozialisierung oder Prävention. Mit den Jugendlichen bleibt sie jung und fit und sieht am ehesten Erfolge, auch wenn es immer mal wieder Rückschläge gibt. Gern würde sie noch mehr Zeit mit ihnen verbringen, aber die gezielte Erarbeitung immer neuer Projekte, die Suche nach Sponsoren und Helfern, Termine in Ämtern und Behörden sowie der überdurchschnittlich gewachsene bürokratische Teil fordern nicht nur einen enormen Zeitaufwand, sondern auch eine gute Kondition. Oftmals gelangt die Vereinsvorsitzende dabei bis an ihre Grenzen und nimmt sich unerledigte Dinge mit nach Hause. Einen leeren Schreibtisch kennt sie nicht. Manchmal geht sie fast in der Papierflut unter und sucht selbst nach dem rettenden Leuchtturm, der dann in Gestalt von Mitarbeitern und ehrenamtlichen Helfern auftaucht. Einen unerschöpflichen Kraftquell sieht sie in ihrem Glauben an Gott. In kritischen Situationen hilft auch ein Dankeschön der Leuchtturmbesucher, denn Geld steht für die Vereinsvorsitzende nicht an erster Stelle. Das braucht sie vor allem, um den Bedürftigen ihren Zufluchtsort zu erhalten.

Some people cannot do anything but help others. Annemarie Schramm from Reichenbach is one of these exceptional people. The lady, who was pensioned off because of a disability, first heard of people in need from the former pastor of her parish. So when the "Lighthouse" Association was set up in 1998, Annemarie Schramm was one of the first to join up. It was not long before she was forced to take over responsibilities as manager of the association. The "Lighthouse" takes care of the socially disadvantaged or homeless, delinquents and prisoners, the mentally and emotionally disabled, addicts or people with other disadvantages, who need temporary or permanent support. The association is based in a former after-school care centre at Am Graben, 57 in Reichenbach. At the outset, only 30 people sought help from the association, but now almost 100 people regularly come during opening hours.

The focus of the association's activities has shifted towards youth work and providing support for young families. Annemarie Schramm has played a major role in this change of emphasis, since she has a real heart for children and young people. She devotes her energy fully to the processes of reintegration, social rehabilitation and prevention. Working with young people keeps her young and fit and allows her to see some success, even though there are the occasional setbacks. She would very much like to spend even more time with the youngsters, but unfortunately she has to draw up new projects, look for sponsors and helpers, make appointments with administrative and public authorities and cope with a growing amount of administrative tasks; this not only takes up an enormous amount of time, but also means that she has to be fit. Sometimes she is at the end of her tether and has to take work home to finish it. She does not know what an empty desk is. Sometimes she seems to be drowning in paperwork and urgently needs some help herself. This often comes in the shape of colleagues and voluntary helpers. Her faith in God is another inexhaustible source of strength. In critical situations, she is motivated by a simple "thank you" from one of the people seeking help at the "Lighthouse". Money is not her first priority. But she needs it to provide a place of refuge for people in need.

(Fotos/Photos by Petra Steps, Text/Text by Petra Steps/Translated by David Strauss)

Erfahrungen und Leidenschaft weitergeben
Passing on Experience and Enthusiasm

Nicht jeder hat das Glück, Hobby und Beruf so kreativ vereinbaren zu können wie Beate Schad. Die Schaustickerei im Plauener Obstgartenweg, deren Leiterin sie ist, vermittelt Besuchern die Geschichte von den Anfängen der Maschinenstickerei bis zur Automatenstickerei. Sonderausstellungen zu Themen der Textilgeschichte werden organisiert und Projektarbeit mit Schülern und Studenten geleistet. „Unser Credo lautet, ein lebendiges Museum zu bieten und den Bogen von der Historie zur Zukunft zu spannen", so Frau Schad.

Der Weg bis zur Eröffnung der Schaustickerei 1997 war jedoch alles andere als leicht.

Die Pädagogin (Frau Schad lehrte Geschichte und Russisch) arbeitete nach ihrem Umzug nach Plauen acht Jahre im Vogtlandmuseum, wo bereits mit dem Sammeln von Maschinen und Anlagen der Textilindustrie begonnen wurde. Aus diesem Projekt heraus entstand schließlich der Verein „Vogtländisches Textilmuseum". Die Idee, ein Vogtländisches Textil- und Industriemuseum aufzubauen, konnte nicht verwirklicht werden. Man entschloss sich, klein anzufangen und mit der Schaustickerei gelebte Geschichte anzubieten. Standort wurde das Objekt im Obstgartenweg, das früher einmal eine Stickerei war. Projektträger ist heute der Verein „Vogtländische Textilgeschichte Plauen". Der Maschinenbestand wurde ergänzt. Zu den Pantographenstickmaschinen kamen Adler- und Kurbelstickmaschinen sowie Singer-Nähmaschinen zum Einsatz. Schauvorführungen vermitteln einen lebendigen Eindruck von der Vielfalt der Fabrikation von Spitzen und Stickereien. Die Schaustickerei wurde zur touristischen Attraktion in Plauen.

Beate Schad wird nicht müde, ihre historischen Kenntnisse an junge Leute weiterzugeben. Sie organisiert Workshops mit Studenten der Westsächsischen Hochschule oder aus Tschechien, in denen beispielsweise auf alten Maschinen experimentiert wird. Zum museumspädagogischen Programm der Schaustickerei gehören Projekte mit Schülern, in denen Grundlagen im Erlernen einer speziellen Technik aus dem textilen Handwerk erworben und experimentell angewendet werden. Sie ist froh, dabei ihre pädagogischen Fähigkeiten anwenden zu können. „Es macht einfach sehr viel Spaß und gibt mir sowie vielen Teilnehmern Impulse für neue Wege der Textilindustrie."

So lassen sich zum Beispiel Designer und Studenten auch im Informations- und Designzentrum für Spitzen und Stickereien inspirieren. Dieses Zentrum im Plauener Rathaus hat Beate Schad aufgebaut und befindet sich in Trägerschaft des Spitzenmuseums.

Unermüdlich ist die 57-Jährige auch zehn Jahre nach Eröffnung der Schaustickerei auf der Suche nach Förderprogrammen, die die Projekt bezogenen Zuschüsse der Stadt und des Kulturraumes Vogtland ergänzen.

Not everybody is as fortunate as Beate Schad: she can combine her hobby and her job. The exhibition embroidery works in Obstgartenweg in Plauen where she is director informs visitors about the history of this art from the beginnings of embroidery on machines to automated embroidery work. Special exhibitions on subjects related to the history of textiles are organised and project work is carried out with pupils and students. "Our credo is to provide a living museum and form a bridge between history and the future," says Ms Schad.

But the preparation work before the exhibition embroidery works were opened in 1997 was anything but easy.

After moving to Plauen, the teacher (Ms Schad taught history and Russian) worked for eight years in the Vogtland Museum; this is where they made a start on collecting machines and equipment related to the textile industry. This project gave birth to the association called "Vogtland Textile Museum". The idea of setting up a Vogtland textile and industry museum did not materialise. So they decided to start up in a small way and provide living history at the exhibition embroidery works. The building in Obstgartenweg used to be an embroidery works. The "Vogtland Textile History of Plauen" association is the backer of the project. The inventory of machines has been built up. Pantograph embroidery machines were used in addition to Adler and crank handle embroidery machines and Singer sewing machines.

Guided tours provide a living impression of the variety of lace making and embroidery work. The exhibition embroidery work has become one of Plauen's tourist attractions.

Beate Schad never tires of passing on her knowledge of history to young people. She organises workshops with students from Zwickau University of Applied Sciences or from the Czech Republic, where they carry out experiments on old machines, for example. The teaching programme at the exhibition embroidery works includes projects with pupils, where the principles of learning a special technique in textile craftsmanship are acquired and then used to carry out experiments. She is happy to be able to use her teaching ability. "I gain a lot of enjoyment and this provides me and many participants with ideas for new approaches in the textile industry."

Designers and students allow the Design Centre for Lace and Embroidery to inspire them, for example. Beate Schad set up this centre in the Plauen city hall and it is supported by the Lace Museum.

The 57-year-old works tirelessly, even ten years after the exhibition embroidery works were opened; she is constantly on the lookout for subsidy programmes, which will complement the funds made available by the city and the Vogtland Cultural Region for specific projects.

(Foto/Photo by Igor Pastierovic, Text/Text by B. Kempe-Winkelmann, Übersetzung/Translated by David Strauss)

Kulturraum – Raum für Kultur
Room for Art

Wo gibt es das schon noch in Deutschland, zwei sinfonische Orchester – mit den Plauener Theater-Philharmonikern sogar drei – auf engstem Raum? Setzt man die Berufsmusiker mit den Einwohnern des Vogtlandes ins Verhältnis, so darf sich die vogtländische Orchesterlandschaft wohl zu Recht als die dichteste weltweit bezeichnen. Dazu kommen auf die gut 188.000 Einwohner des Vogtlandes und der Stadt Plauen noch zwei Theater. Die Vogtländer leisten sich so viel Kultur eben. Auch wenn das einen finanziellen Kraftakt bedeutet und eine aktuelle Studie aus der Landeshauptstadt diesbezüglich eine „Überkapazität in der Region" konstatiert.

Der Kulturraum Vogtland, sowohl in seiner territorialen und historisch gewachsenen Ausrichtung als auch in seiner politischen Manifestation als Pflichtzweckverband bietet ein überaus reichhaltiges kulturelles Angebot aller Genres, von der Breitenkultur in ihrer gesamten Vielfalt bis zur so genannten Hochkultur. Ob internationales Festival, Sinfoniekonzert, Schauspiel, Opernabend, Ballett, Kabarett, große Unterhaltungsshow, Kunstausstellung oder Kleinkunst - die Vogtländer haben all das vor ihrer Haustüre. So viel Kultur will finanziert sein.

Seit dem 18.11.1994 gibt es per sächsischem Gesetz als politisches Gremium den „Kulturraum Vogtland", der sich der Förderung regional bedeutsamer kultureller Einrichtungen und Projekte verpflichtet fühlt. Mitglieder sind der Vogtlandkreis und die Stadt Plauen. Rund 8 Millionen Euro fließen über den „Kulturraum" jährlich in den vogtländischen Kulturbereich. Und da der Landkreis und Plauen nun schon seit Jahren das Maximum an eigener Kulturumlage bereit stellen, konnten bisher auch immer maximale Fördersummen aus Dresden abgerufen werden.

Zu den 24 vom Kulturraum geförderten bedeutsamen Einrichtungen gehören zwei Sinfonieorchester und die Theater in Plauen und Bad Elster. Seit seinem Bestehen unterstützt der „Kulturraum Vogtland" die Vogtland Philharmonie Greiz/Reichenbach, die per Staatsvertrag zwischen Sachsen und Thüringen seit 1992 als länderübergreifendes Sinfonieorchester agiert – auch das dürfte einmalig in Deutschland sein. Auftritte in der gesamten Bundesrepublik und Gastspiele im Ausland begründen den Ruf des Ensembles als „musikalischer Botschafter" des Vogtlandes. Mit der beliebten Veranstaltungsreihe „Philharmonic Rock" hat sich das Orchester unter der Leitung von Musikdirektor Stefan Fraas zudem einen besonderen Besuchermagnet geschaffen, der sich stetig steigender Resonanz erfreut, wie der Tag der Sachsen im September 2007 in Reichenbach einmal mehr eindrucksvoll unter Beweis stellte.

Seit 1998 kooperiert die Vogtland Philharmonie Greiz/Reichenbach mit der Chursächsischen Philharmonie Bad Elster. Dieses Ensemble steht seit 1992 unter der Leitung von Musikdirektor Florian Merz und ist wie die Vogtland Philharmonie ein Kulturbotschafter der Region. Der Chursächsischen Philharmonie und dem Wirken der Chursächsischen Veranstaltungs GmbH in der Sächsischen Staatsbäderregion ist es vor allem zu danken, dass Bad Elster

Where else in Germany can you find two symphony orchestras so close together – in fact three, if the Plauen Theatre Philharmonic is included? If we compare the ratio of professional musicians to the inhabitants of the Vogtland region, the Vogtland orchestral landscape could probably be called the densest in the world. Then there are also two theatres for the 188,000 inhabitants of the Vogtland district and the city of Plauen. The people in this area can afford to treat themselves to so much culture. Even if this is a huge financial challenge and a recent study from the Saxon capital states that there is an "overcapacity in the region."

The Vogtland cultural region, both in its territorial and historically based orientation and its political shape as a special purpose association, provides an extremely rich cultural feast for all kinds of genres, ranging from popular culture to what is known as high culture. Whether it is an international festival, a symphony concert, a play, an opera evening, ballet, cabaret, a major entertainment show, an art exhibition or variety shows – Vogtland people have everything on their doorstep. But all this culture has to be funded.

Since 18 November 1994, Saxon law dictates that there must be a political body known as the "Vogtland Cultural Region", which is obliged to promote regionally important cultural centres and projects. The Vogtland rural district and the city of Plauen are members of this body. Some € 8 million flow via the "Cultural Region" into

(Text/Text by Ekkehard Glaß, Übersetzung/Translated by David Strauss)   Foto/Photo by Igor Pastierovic

Raum für Kunst / Room for Art

Vogtland cultural activities every year. And as the rural district and Plauen have now provided the maximum cultural funds for years, the maximum amount of support has always been demanded from Dresden.

Two symphony orchestras and the theatres in Plauen and Bad Elster are among the 24 centres supported by the "Cultural Region". Since its existence it has supported the Greiz/Reichenbach Vogtland Philharmonic, which has operated as a cross-state symphony orchestra between Saxony and Thuringia since 1992 by state decree – and that too must be unique in Germany. Performances all over Germany and guest appearances abroad justify the ensemble's reputation as the "musical ambassador" of the Vogtland region. The orchestra under musical director Stefan Fraas has also created a particularly successful magnet for visitors with its popular "Philharmonic Rock" concerts and this attracts an increasing number of supporters, as the Saxon Festival in Reichenbach in September 2007 once again proved in an impressive manner.

The Greiz/Reichenbach Vogtland Philharmonic has been cooperating with the Chursächsisch Philharmonic in Bad Elster since 1998. This ensemble has been directed by Florian Merz since 1992 and, like the Vogtland Philharmonic, is a cultural ambassador for the region. It is largely due to the efforts made by the Chursächsisch Event Organisation Company and the Chursächsisch Philharmonic in the Saxon spa region that Bad Elster has once again been able to link up with its former glory days and may justifiably be called a culture and festival town again. A really "royal" programme is arranged for local people and spa guests, whether it is for the "Chursächsisch Festival", the "Saxon/Bohemian Festival of Culture", the "Mozart Weeks" or "Winter Dreams". And Bad Elster has many theatre and event centres at the KunstWandel Hall, the Royal Spa Centre, the King Albert Theatre, which was reopened in 2004, and the open-air theatre, which was brought to life again like a sleeping beauty in 2007.

If the King Albert Theatre can trace its roots back to the year 1919, the Vogtland Theatre Plauen's traditions go back even further. The theatre in Plauen was opened on 1 October 1898 with a performance of Schiller's "The Maid of Orleans". One year later the first opera performed was Weber's "Freischütz". The theatre was closed in 1944 because of the Second World War, but was reopened again in October 1945. It was renamed the "Vogtland Theatre Plauen" in 1991 and then became a company run by the city. Due to economic pressures, the Vogtland Theatre merged with its counterpart in Zwickau in 2000 to become a theatre that transcends different cultural regions. The new Plauen-Zwickau Theatre under general manager Dr. Ingolf Huhn with its extended ensembles for performances involving music, drama and ballet, its orchestra and the puppet theatre provides stage performances for every age. Spectacular open-air performances have become the trade mark of the merged theatre over the past few years with productions of Verdi's operas "Aida", "Nabucco" and "The Troubadour", Wagner's "The Flying Dutchman", "The Gypsy Baron" by Johann Strauss or the play entitled "Knight Runkel's Great Hour", based on the famous mosaic of comic stories written by Martin Verges and set to music by Karsten Wolf; this had its premiere on 1 September 2007 at Plauen's Park Theatre.

The two partners, the Vogtland district and the city of Plauen, have provided huge sums of money to preserve the two theatres and other cultural facilities. The Vogtland district is the only cultural region in Saxony, which has been able to provide investments to repair and modernise cultural infrastructure every year since 1999. These projects have included renewing the stage mechanics in the theatres in Plauen and Bad Elster, rebuilding the German Space Exhibition at Morgenröthe-Rautenkranz or funding the conversion of the festival hall in Plauen. Comprehensive modernisation work has also been carried out at the facilities belonging to the Vogtland Cultural Company. This company, which belongs to the Vogtland district and was set up in 1997, looks after the maintenance and expansion of cultural events in the region. Five centres – the Neuberin Theatre in Reichenbach, the Nicolai Church in Auerbach, the Chapel in Neuensalz, the Landwüst open-air museum and the Tannenberg Exhibition Mine put on their specific events under the umbrella of the company and provide for particular cultural sectors. In addition, there are a variety of attractive entertainment centres like the Wernesgrün Beer House, the Markneukirchen Music Hall, the Malt House in Plauen, the Royal Spa Centre and KunstWandel Hall already mentioned in Bad Elster, the Landwüst Cultural Barn or the Riedel Farm in Eubabrunn, which put on a wide range of varied cultural events throughout the year. Open-air stages are used in the summer and the new Vogtland Arena in Klingenthal has provided a unique open-air setting since 2006; it can accommodate up to 30,000 people.

(Fotos/Photos by Igor Pastierovic,)

heute auch wieder kulturell an alte Glanzzeit anknüpfen kann und sich zu Recht Kultur- und Festspielstadt nennen darf. Ob „Chursächsische Festspiele", „Sächsisch/Böhmisches Kulturfestival", „Mozartwochen" oder „Winterträume", Einheimischen und Kurgästen wird ein wahrhaft „königliches" Programm geboten. Und mit der KunstWandelhalle, dem Königlichen Kurhaus, dem 2004 wieder eingeweihten König Albert Theater als Prunkstück sowie dem 2007 aus dem Dornröschen-Schlaf erweckten Naturtheater stehen in Bad Elster Spiel- und Event-Stätten par excellence zur Verfügung.

Führt das König Albert Theater seinen Ursprung auf das Jahr 1919 zurück, so hat das Vogtland Theater Plauen die längere Tradition. Mit Schillers „Jungfrau von Orleans" wurde das Plauener Theater bereits am 1. Oktober 1898 eröffnet. Ein Jahr später gab es mit Webers „Freischütz" die erste Opernaufführung. 1944 infolge des 2. Weltkrieges geschlossen, eröffnete es schon im Oktober 1945 wieder. 1991 wurde es in „Vogtland Theater Plauen" umbenannt und in der Folge ein Eigenbetrieb der Stadt Plauen. Ökonomischen Zwängen gehorchend fusionierte das Vogtland Theater im Jahr 2000 mit dem Zwickauer zu einem kulturraumübergreifenden Theater. Das neue Theater Plauen-Zwickau bietet unter Leitung von Generalintendant Dr. Ingolf Huhn mit seinen erweiterten Ensembles im Musiktheater, Schauspiel und Ballett, mit seinem Orchester und mit dem Puppentheater Bühnenerlebnisse für jedermann. Zum Markenzeichen des Fusionstheaters sind in den vergangenen Jahren vor allem spektakuläre Open-Air-Produktionen geworden, wie die großen Verdi-Opern „Aida", „Nabucco" und „Der Troubadour", Wagners „Der fliegende Holländer", „Der Zigeunerbaron" von Johann Strauß oder das nach den berühmten Mosaik-Comic-Geschichten von Martin Verges geschriebene und von Karsten Wolf vertonte Bühnenstück „Ritter Runkels große Stunde", das am 1. September 2007 Premiere im Plauener Parktheater hatte.

Für den Erhalt der beiden Theater wie auch anderer kultureller Einrichtungen haben die beiden Partner Vogtlandkreis und Stadt Plauen nicht unerhebliche Mittel zur Verfügung gestellt. Als einziger Kulturraum Sachsens schafft es der vogtländische nun schon seit 1999, jährlich Investitionen für die Sanierung und Modernisierung der kulturellen Infrastruktur bereit zu stellen. So war es unter anderem möglich, die Bühnentechnik in den Theatern Plauen und Bad Elster zu erneuern, den Neubau der Deutschen Raumfahrtausstellung in Morgenröthe-Rautenkranz zu realisieren oder den Umbau der Festhalle in Plauen zu finanzieren. Umfangreiche Modernisierungsmaßnahmen konnten so auch in den Einrichtungen der Vogtland Kultur GmbH umgesetzt werden. Die kreiseigene GmbH, die 1997 gegründet wurde, sorgt sich um Erhalt und Ausbau des kulturellen Angebots in der Region. Fünf Einrichtungen - das Neuberinhaus Reichenbach, die Nicolaikirche Auerbach, die Kapelle Neuensalz, das Freilichtmuseum Landwüst und das Besucherbergwerk Grube Tannenberg bieten unter dem Dach der Kultur GmbH ihre spezifischen Angebote und decken ganz bestimmte kulturelle Bereich ab. Zudem bieten eine Vielzahl attraktiver Veranstaltungshäuser wie die Wernesgrüner Biertenne, die Musikhalle Markneukirchen, das Malzhaus Plauen, das eingangs erwähnte Königliche Kurhaus und die KunstWandelhalle in Bad Elster, die Kulturtenne Landwüst oder der Riedelhof Eubabrunn ganzjährig ein breites Spektrum abwechslungsreicher Kulturveranstaltungen. Im Sommer kommen Freilicht- und Naturbühnen hinzu und seit 2006 steht mit der neuen Vogtland-Arena in Klingenthal ein einzigartiges Open-Air-Areal zur Verfügung, das bis zu 30.000 Gäste fassen kann.

Fotos/Photos by Igor Pastierovic

Eine solche Vielfalt von Veranstaltungsstätten bietet natürlich nicht nur heimischen, sondern auch internationalen Künstlern eine ansprechendes Auftrittspodium. So hat sich zum Beispiel das „Festival Mitte Europa" als großes, Kunst- und Staatsgrenzen überschreitendes Musikfestival seit 1992 fest etabliert. Die Veranstaltungsorte befinden sich dabei im Vogtland, in Bayern und in Tschechien. Neben namhaften Künstlern der Festivalregion gastieren Künstler „aus aller Herren Länder". Mit hochkarätigen Wettbewerben macht der „Musikwinkel" seinem Namen alle Ehre. Seit 1966 richtet Markneukirchen den Internationalen Instrumentalwettbewerb aus, einen Vergleich von Rang, wie nicht zuletzt die seit 2005 bestehende Schirmherrschaft des weltbekannten Dirigenten Professor Kurt Masur beweist. Künstlerisch anspruchsvoll und auf Weltniveau präsentiert sich auch die Musikstadt Klingenthal mit ihrem Internationalen Akkordeonwettbewerb, der seine Tradition bis ins Jahr 1963 zurückführen kann. Künstler von Weltruf treffen seit 1993 bei den Internationalen Meisterkursen für Gitarre und Mandoline in Erlbach auf Musiker und Nachwuchskünstler aus aller Welt.

International ist das Flair auch beim Plauener Folkherbst. Seit 15 Jahren wird dort im Malzhaus mit dem „Eisernen Eversteiner" der einzige europäische Folkpreis verliehen und Folkmusikern aus ganz Europa gilt die Stadt an der Weißen Elster als wahres Eldorado.

Auch in der Bildenden Kunst gibt sich das Vogtland weltoffen. Bei den jährlichen Holzbildhauer-Symposien in Erlbach/Eubabrunn geben renommierte Künstler aus Europa und Asien dem Rohstoff Holz künstlerische Form. Und die Internationalen Sommerakademien im Weisbachschen Haus zu Plauen sind ein interdisziplinäres und grenzüberschreitendes Arbeitsforum für junge Gestalter, geleitet von international anerkannten Künstlern.

Such a variety of event sites not only provides local, but also international artistes with a forum for their appearances. For example, the Central Europe Festival has made a name for itself since 1992 as a major music festival, which crosses artistic and national boundaries. The events take place in the Vogtland region, Bavaria and the Czech Republic and feature not just well-known artists from the festival region, but performers from all over the world. "Musicon Valley" does justice to its name with top-class competitions. Markneukirchen has organised the International Instrumental Competition since 1966, a high-quality contest, not least demonstrated by the fact that the world-famous conductor Kurt Masur has been a patron since 2005. The music town of Klingenthal also show offs its world-class credentials in a sophisticated manner with its International Accordion Competition, which can trace its roots back to the year 1963. World renowned artists have been meeting musicians and young artists from all over the world at the International Master Courses for guitar and mandolin in Erlbach since 1993. The flair found at the Plauen Folk Autumn Festival is also international. The only European folk prize, the "Iron Eversteiner", has been awarded at the Malt House there for the past 15 years and the town by the White Elster river is known to folk musicians all over Europe as a real El Dorado.

The Vogtland region is also cosmopolitan in the fine arts. Renowned artists from all over Europe and Asia craft the raw material wood into artistic shapes at the annual Wood Carvers Symposia in Erlbach/Eubabrunn. And the International Summer Academies in the Weisbach House in Plauen are an interdisciplinary and cross-border working forum for young designers, led by internationally recognised artists.

It is no wonder that the "culturally fertile" soil of the Vogtland region has a distinct art and artistic scene and gifted craftspeople. And this has a long tradition. The names of well-known artistic personalities from the past are closed linked to the Vogtland region: Friederike Caroline Neuber, for example. The German theatre reformer was born in Reichenbach in 1697. Johann Rosenmüller und Johann Caspar Kerll, both celebrated composers in the 17th century, were born in Oelsnitz and Adorf respectively. Julius Mosen (1803-1876), the poet who wrote the Tyrolean national anthem – the "Andreas Hofer song" – grew up in the Vogtland region. This links him to Hermann Vogel (1854-1921), who was one of Germany's most respected painters in his time. Erich Ohser (1903-1944) is still a well-loved figure after his death; he created the popular father-son stories as a cartoonist using the pseudonym "e.o.plauen". More recent well-known figures include Wolfgang Mattheuer (1927-2004), an important German painter and sculptor, who was born in Reichenbach, Jürgen Hart (1942-2002), the cabaret artist and leader of the Leipzig "akademixer" group for many years, who came from Treuen, Jürgen B. Wolff, who came from Plauen and was one of the founders of the German folk scene in what was East Germany, or the hit singer, Stefanie Hertel, who is acclaimed all over Germany and comes from Oelsnitz/Vogtland.

Fotos/Photos by Igor Pastierovic, Stadtverwaltung Plauen [1], Harald Sulski [1])

Auf solch' „kulturträchtigem" Nährboden ist es nicht verwunderlich, dass das Vogtland über eine ausgeprägte Kunst- und Künstlerszene sowie begabte Kunsthandwerker verfügt. Und das hat Tradition, sind doch auch historische Namen bekannter Künstlerpersönlichkeiten eng mit dem Vogtland verbunden: Friederike Caroline Neuber zum Beispiel. Die Reformerin des deutschen Theaters wurde 1697 in Reichenbach geboren. Die Wiegen von Johann Rosenmüller und Johann Caspar Kerll, zu ihren Lebzeiten im 17. Jahrhundert gefeierte Komponisten, standen in Oelsnitz und Adorf. Julius Mosen (1803 - 1876), der Dichter der Tiroler National-Hymne - des „Andreas-Hofer-Liedes" - war ein Kind des Vogtlandes. Das verbindet ihn mit Hermann Vogel (1854 bis 1921), der zu seiner Zeit zu Deutschlands geachtetsten Malern gehörte. Einen hohen Bekanntheitsgrad über seine Lebenszeit hinaus erwarb sich auch Erich Ohser (1903 bis 1944), der als Zeichner unter dem Pseudonym e.o.plauen die beliebten Vater-Sohn-Geschichten schuf. Aus unseren Tagen seien genannt der in Reichenbach geborene Wolfgang Mattheuer (1927 bis 2004), bedeutender deutscher Maler und Bildhauer, der aus Treuen stammende Kabarettist und langjährige Leiter der Leipziger „akademixer" Jürgen Hart (1942 – 2002), der Plauener Jürgen B. Wolff, der mit seinen „Folkländern" die Deutsch-Folk-Szene in der damaligen DDR mitbegründete oder unser im gesamten deutschen Sprachraum gefeierter Schlagerstar Stefanie Hertel aus Oelsnitz/Vogtland.

Raum für Kunst / Room for Art

Was das Vogtland in kultureller Hinsicht jedoch ganz besonders macht, ist neben der Hochkultur, den großen Festivals oder den national und international beachteten Künstlern vor allem der hohe Stellenwert der Breitenkultur. In ihrer einzigartigen Vielfalt ist sie stabile Grundlage für Brauchtum und Tradition sowie Wiege für den künstlerischen Nachwuchs aller Genres. So kann das Vogtland auf über 330 Kulturvereine und -gruppen verweisen, deren Palette von Musikgruppen aller Art über Folklore- und Heimatgruppen, Kunst-, Literatur- und Geschichtsvereine bis hin zu Karneval- und Countryclubs reicht. Besonders gepflegt wird dabei durch zahlreiche Mundartgruppen und Trachtenvereine das vogtländische Brauchtum. Der „Tag der Vogtländer" – das größte Kulturfest der Region – liefert jährlich ein eindrucksvolles Beispiel dieser breit gefächerten Vereinstätigkeit.

Äußerst vielfältig präsentiert sich auch die Museenlandschaft des Vogtlandes. 27 Museen, 12 Heimatstuben, sechs Ständige Ausstellungen, sechs Galerien und fünf Schauwerkstätten und -anlagen laden zum Besuch und zum Erkunden ein, darunter so bedeutende Einrichtungen wir das Spitzenmuseum in Plauen, das einzige seiner Art in Deutschland, und das Musikinstrumentenmuseum in Markneukirchen.

Und natürlich gehören auch die Bibliotheken zur Kulturlandschaft Vogtland. In den vergangenen Jahren konnte die computergestütze Vernetzung der öffentlichen Bibliotheken im Kulturraum vorangebracht werden. Und mit dem Bücherbus, der „Rollenden Bibliothek" zeigt der Vogtlandkreis Flagge für die „literarische Grundversorgung" der Landbevölkerung.

Solch' eine kulturelle Vielfalt wie sie das Vogtland bietet birgt aber auch Probleme in sich. Da überschneiden sich oftmals am Wochenende die hochkarätigen Angebote und der Konsument hat die Qual der Wahl. Und manchmal treten Künstler nur vor all zu leeren Stuhlreihen auf. Trotzdem: Wenn es wohl auch in Zukunft immer schwieriger werden wird, Kultur staatlicherseits zu finanzieren, die jährlich rund 8 Millionen Euro aus der Kulturkasse des „Kulturraums Vogtland" sind gut angelegtes Geld. Auf das kann die Kulturlandschaft Vogtland nicht verzichten, soll sie auch künftig in ihrer so vielfältigen Ausprägung Bestand haben.

Quellen
Veröffentlichungen Landratsamt SG Kultur
Internet-Recherchen
VogtlandATLAS Teil 1
Ein vogtländischer Mundartabend, Reinhard Glaß 1977

But what makes the Vogtland region very special from a cultural point of view is not just its high culture, the major festivals or artists, who are respected nationally and internationally, but the importance given to popular culture. Its unique variety also provides a home for customs and traditions and it is the cradle for the next generation of artists in every genre. The Vogtland region has more than 330 cultural associations and groups. Their focus ranges from music groups of all kinds to folklore and heritage groups, art, literary and historical associations and even includes carnival and country clubs. Vogtland customs are particularly fostered by the many dialect and traditional dress associations. The "Vogtland Festival" – the largest cultural festival in the region – provides an impressive example of the wide range of activities pursued by these associations every year.

The museums in the Vogtland region are also very varied. People can visit 27 museums, 12 heritage centres, six permanent exhibitions, six galleries and five exhibition workshops – and discover a great deal. These include important centres like the Lace Museum in Plauen, the only one of its kind in Germany, and the Musical Instrument Museum in Markneukirchen.

It goes without saying that the libraries are also a vibrant part of the Vogtland cultural landscape. Over the past few years it has been possible to provide a computer-based network of libraries in the cultural region. And the Vogtland district demonstrates how important it is to provide local people with "basic literary nourishment" with its book bus, the "library on wheels".

But the amount of culture, as found in the Vogtland region, has its drawbacks too. The high-quality performances often clash at weekends and consumers are spoilt for choice. This means that artists often appear at half-empty auditoriums. Nevertheless: if it becomes harder and harder to back cultural events with state funds in future, the 8 million or so euros provided by the "Vogtland Cultural Region" every year is money well invested. The Vogtland cultural landscape depends on this, if it is going to maintain this level of variety in future.

Fotos/Photos by Igor Pastierovic)

Landwirtschaft küsst Muse
FARMING INSPIRED BY LIGHT ENTERTAINMENT

Wenn im Vogtland die Erdäpfelzeit beginnt, dann wird bei Familie Gündel in Rotschau jede helfende Hand gebraucht. Ulrich und Birgit Gündel hatten vor ein paar Jahren die Idee, aus ihrem alten Kuhstall einen Kulturstall zu machen. Seitdem bieten sie „Musikalische Wein- und Kartoffelproben der besonderen Art" an. Aus der als Freizeitspaß gedachten Aktion wurde aufgrund der großen Nachfrage ein Betätigungsfeld für Sohn Swen, der mit gerade 20 Jahren und erfolgreich abgeschlossener Lehre als Landwirt den Schritt in die Selbstständigkeit wagte.

Die Landwirtschaft und die Musik tragen zum Erfolg des Konzeptes bei. Für die Veranstaltungen bauen Gündels traditionelle oder seltene Kartoffelsorten an. Hinter Namen wie „Blauer Schwede", „Red Cardinal" oder „Mr. Breese" stecken blaue, rote oder gelbe Erdäpfel. Zum Kartoffelgemisch kommt die musikalische Vielfalt der „Vinotheker", zu denen die ehemaligen Studienkollegen Gerald Tomat aus Podelwitz bei Altenburg und Holger Streit aus Beelitz bei Potsdam gehören. In der gemeinsamen Studienzeit mit Ulrich Gündel an der Martin-Luther-Universität Halle spielten sie Bauern- und Gesellenlieder auf traditionellen Instrumenten mit modernen Arrangements und waren als Gruppe „Ackerfolk" zumindest in der DDR-Folkszene bekannt. Die Freundschaft blieb, das Hobby auch. Ulrich Gündel fungiert als Ideengeber, dem beim Joggen die besten Einfälle kommen. Eigene Titel wie der „Kartoffel-Rock'n'Roll" oder das „Diätwein-Lied" entstanden. Swen spielt Schlagzeug, bei den „Vinothekern", und in der Band „7 Days". Gerald Tomat beherrscht Tenorhorn, Flöte und Mundharmonika. Holger Streit lässt Bassgitarre, Mandoline und alles, was Saiten hat, erklingen. Ulrich Gündel tritt als Schauspieler, Kabarettist, Sänger und Texter in Erscheinung. Die Versuche mit der Gitarre hat er längst aufgegeben. Dafür ist seine Frau Birgit zuständig, die als Musiklehrerin natürlich auch singen kann.

Mit dem „Kulturstall" kann Swen Gündel den erlernten Beruf und sein Hobby prima verbinden und seine Eltern entlasten. Neben den Wein- und Kartoffelverkostungen gibt es immer wieder besondere Veranstaltungen. „Weinhexen zur Walpurgisnacht" heißt ein literarisch-musikalischer Weinabend mit anschließendem Hexenfeuer. Der Kulturstall kann auch gemietet werden.

When the potato harvest begins, the Gündel family in Rotschau needs all the help it can get. A couple of years ago Ulrich and Birgit Gündel hit on the idea of turning the old cowshed into a "culture shed". Since then, they have offered a very special kind of "Musical Wine and Potato Tasting" sessions. This leisure activity has proved so popular, that their son Swen, aged 20, has taken the bold step of going self-employed since finishing his training as a farmer. This combination of farming and music has proved very successful. The Gündels cultivate traditional and rare potatoes for these events. "Blue Congo", "Red Cardinal" and "Mr Breese" are just some of the blue, red or yellow potatoes available. In addition to the potatoes, a variety of music is provided by the group called "Vinotheker", which features former students Gerald Tomat from Podelwitz near Altenburg and Holger Streit from Beelitz near Potsdam. During their student days at the Martin Luther University in Halle with Ulrich Gündel, they played modern arrangements of peasant and journeymen's songs on traditional instruments and were at least well-known in the East German folk scene. Their friendship lasted - as did their hobby. Ulrich Gündel is the ideas man, most of which come when he is out jogging. He has written his own songs such as "Potato-Rock 'n' Roll" and "the Diet Wine Song". Swen plays the drums with the "Vinotheker" and also the "Seven Days" band. Gerald Tomat plays the baritone horn, flute and mouth organ. Holger Streit plays the bass guitar, mandolin – and anything with strings. Ulrich Gündel is the actor, cabaret artist, singer and songwriter. He gave up trying to play the guitar a long time ago. His wife Birgit does that and, as a music teacher, she can also sing, of course.

The "culture shed" means that Swen Gündel can combine his profession and hobby and take some of the pressure off his parents. There are always special events in addition to the wine and potato tasting sessions. One example is "Wine witches for Walpurgis Night" – the name of a musical and literary evening with wine, which concludes with a witches' fire. The "culture shed" can also be hired.

(Fotos/Photos by Petra Steps, Text/Text by Petra Steps, Übersetzung/Translated by David Strauss)

Ideen werden phantastische Wirklichkeit
When Ideas become Fantastic Reality

Christoph Krumbiegel, waschechter Treuener und Vogtländer, hat nach dem Abitur 1991 seine Liebe zum Schreiben entdeckt. Damals reichte er seine erste Geschichte beim „Magazin" ein – sie kam prompt zurück. Die harten Hinweise des Lektors waren Motivation und Hilfe zugleich: Schon den zweite Versuch krönte der Erfolg – die Magazin-Leser bekamen die skurrile Erzählung als Unterhaltungskost serviert. Zu diesem Zeitpunkt lagen die Prioritäten des Treueners bereits beim Studium, das seine ganze Energie forderte, denn er wollte Apotheker in seinem Heimatort werden.

Das Skurrile und bisweilen auch Kriminelle fesselte Christoph Krumbiegel schon in jungen Jahren. Im Bücherschrank der Eltern griff er deshalb nicht nach Goethe, Schiller oder Thomas Mann. Ihn faszinierte der makabre Humor eines Roald Dahl, oder er las die Sherlock-Holmes-Bücher von vorn nach hinten und wieder zurück.

Zum Schreiben braucht der Hobbyautor Motivation oder ein Ziel. Der vogtländische Literaturwettbewerb, gekrönt durch die „Lange Nacht des Buches" in der Kapelle Neuensalz, war so eine Triebfeder, die zum längeren Verweilen am Schreibtisch verführte. Gleich mit der ersten Teilnahme 2003 erschrieb sich Christoph Krumbiegel die Trophäe. Seitdem landete er regelmäßig auf vorderen Plätzen.

Ideen kommen dem Hobbyautoren bei Beschäftigungen, die mit einem freien Kopf verbunden sind – bei der Körperpflege, beim Wandern, beim erfolglosen Warten auf den Fisch am Angelhaken. In der ersten Sekunde entscheidet sich, ob die erfundenen Figuren eine Zukunft haben. Einfälle zum falschen Zeitpunkt versinken leider manchmal im Vergessenen.

Der erste Ausflug ins Mörderische trägt den Titel „Kleines totes Meer" und spielt an der Talsperre Pöhl. Er erscheint 2008 in der Anthologie Mords-Sachsen II. „Irreale Sachen kann man nur erfinden, wenn man mit beiden Beinen fest im Leben steht", meint Christoph Krumbiegel. Seine Familie und die vogtländische Heimat bilden für ihn dieses Fundament.

Verbundenheit zur Heimat demonstriert der 1972 Geborene gemeinsam mit seinem Freund Alexander Spitzner im Vogtland-Online-Shop, für den beide Produktideen entwickelten und umsetzten, vom vogtländischen Schwammemesser bis zu bedruckten T-Shirts.

Christoph Krumbiegel, who is from Treuen and is a true Vogtland character, discovered his love for writing in 1991 after passing his final school exams. At that time he presented his first piece of work to a journal called "Magazin" - only to have it sent back immediately. The harsh comments by the editor of the magazine helped and motivated him at the same time: his second try was an immediate success and the readers of "Magazin" were served up his strange story as entertainment. At this point the young man from Treuen was concentrating his efforts on his university course; he wanted to become a chemist in his home town.

Christoph Krumbiegel was fascinated by absurd or crime matters at a young age. So he did not pick up works by Goethe, Schiller or Thomas Mann from his parents' book shelves. No, he was fascinated by the macabre humour of Roald Dahl or he read Sherlock Holmes books from cover to cover.

The part-time writer needs motivation or a purpose in order to write. The Vogtland literature competition, the highlight of which is the "Long Night of Books" in Neuensalz Chapel, was one of these incentives that tempted him to spend a little more time at his desk. Christoph Krumbiegel walked away with the trophy the very first time that he participated in 2003. Ever since then he has regularly been one of the top writers.

The part-time writer gains his inspiration when he is involved in activities that do not require his full concentration – personal hygiene, a walk or when he is waiting for fish to take the bait from his hook. He decides whether the character has a future or not as soon as he has the idea. Ideas that come at the wrong moment may never be pursued. His first foray into the world of murders is called "Kleines totes Meer" (Little Dead Sea) and is set at Pöhl reservoir. It is being published in 2008 as part of the "Murderous Saxons II" anthology. Christoph Krumbiegel is convinced of one thing: "You can only come up with those surreal ideas if you have a good grip on life in the first place." His family and his Vogtland home provide him with this foundation. The native of the Vogtland region, who was born in 1972, and his friend Alexander Spitzner demonstrate their close links with their home region at the Vogtland Online Shop where they market their own product ideas, ranging from the Vogtland knife for picking mushrooms to printed T-shirts.

(Fotos/Photos by Petra Steps, Text/Text by Petra Steps, Übersetzung/Translated by David Strauss)

Täterin im Geiste
Perpetrator in Thought

Manche Menschen leben ihre Phantasien im Verborgenen aus. Ganz anders Maren Schwarz aus Rodewisch. Sie hat 2003 erstmals öffentlich preisgegeben, dass ihr das Kriminelle besonders liegt. Allerdings ist sie nur eine „Täterin im Geiste": Sie schreibt auf, was andere denken, tun oder vielleicht gern machen würden. Bisher sind fünf Krimis sowie mehrere Kurzgeschichten in verschiedenen Anthologien erschienen. Einige der Mordfälle hat sie auf der Insel Rügen und im Erzgebirge angesiedelt. Als wahres Mekka der Mordslust gilt jedoch ihre vogtländische Heimat, die immer neue Inspirationen für entsetzliche Taten zu bieten scheint. Mit „Grabeskälte" begibt sie sich an die Göltzschtalbrücke. „Dämonenspiel" stellt die dunklen Seiten des Burgsteingebietes vor. „Zwiespalt" spielt auf dem kleinen, verborgenen Lochbauernhof hinter Rodewisch. Auch den Flößern in Muldenberg hat Maren Schwarz ein kriminelles Denkmal gesetzt – in einem Kurzkrimi.

In der Region ist die Krimiautorin häufig bei Lesungen zu erleben, zum Beispiel bei den Ostdeutschen Krimitagen. Manchmal holt sie auch gleich ein Dutzend und mehr ihrer Kollegen ins Vogtland – wenn der sächsische Krimistammtisch turnusmäßig hier tagt oder sich die „Mörderischen Schwestern" treffen – ein Netzwerk von Krimiautorinnen.

Wer die sympathische Frau erlebt, kann sich kaum vorstellen, dass hinter der liebenswürdigen Fassade ein solch grauenhaftes Gedankengut schlummert.

Geschrieben hat Maren Schwarz schon immer gern, aber die kriminellen Geschichten formten sich erst in den vielen schlaflosen Nächten, als die zuletzt in der Versicherungsbranche tätige Finanzwirtschafterin ihren Job verlor. Das war nach der Geburt der zweiten Tochter. Inzwischen hat sich die Familie weiter vergrößert. 2004 wurde ein Sohn geboren, der für durchwachte Nächte und die Entstehung vieler neuer Ideen sorgte. An Einfällen mangelt es nicht, höchstens an der Zeit und Muße zum Aufschreiben.

Der Laptop, auf dem sie ihre ersten Gehversuche als Krimiautorin wagte, hat inzwischen ausgedient. Ein neuer musste her, und mit dem kann sie über das Internet Verbindung mit anderen Autoren oder ihren Lesern halten. Das erleichtert auch die Recherchetätigkeit, denn die Mitglieder im „Syndikat", der Vereinigung deutschsprachiger Krimiautoren, helfen sich gegenseitig.

Many people live out their fantasies in secret. But not Maren Schwarz from Rodewisch. She first admitted in 2003 publicly that she is very interested in criminal acts. However, she is only a "perpetrator in thought". She writes what other people think, do or perhaps would like to do. She has published five detective stories and several short stories so far in various anthologies. Some of her murder cases are based on the Island of Rügen or in the Erzgebirge Mountains. But the real Mecca for her lust to kill is her Vogtland home area, which always seems to provide her with fresh inspiration for terrible deeds. The Göltzsch Valley Bridge is the setting for "Grabeskälte". The story "Dämonenspiel" introduces the dark side of the Burgstein area. "Zwiespalt" is played out at a small, hidden farm with an enclosed courtyard near Rodewisch. Maren Schwarz has also set up a monument for the log rafters in Muldenberg – in a short detective story.

The detective story writer can often be heard at readings – e.g. the Eastern German Detective Story Festival. Sometimes she brings a dozen or more colleagues with her to the Vogtland region – if the Saxon detective story writer group meets here on a rotational basis or when the "Murderous Sisters" – a network of female detective story writers – congregate.

Those who know this likeable lady can hardly imagine that such terrible thoughts could lodge in her brain behind such a genial façade!

Maren Schwarz has always enjoyed writing, but she only began thinking up detective stories during sleepless nights after she lost her job as a financial expert in the insurance sector. That was after the birth of her second daughter.

The family has now grown even more. A son was born in 2004 – and he gave her a few more broken nights to think up new plots. She does not lack ideas – but often the spare time to write them down.

The laptop that she used to take her first tentative steps as a detective story writer is now worn out. She had to buy a new one and uses it to keep in touch with other authors or her readers via the Internet. This also makes it easier for her to carry out research, for the members in the "syndicate", the association of German-speaking detective story writers, are more than happy to help each other out.

(Fotos/Photos by Petra Steps, Text/Text by Petra Steps, Übersetzung/Translated by David Strauss)

Malerin Susanne Söllner-Burr
Painter Susanne Söllner-Burr

Aus der Natur schöpft sie ihre Kraft. Und aus ihren Bildern, die in Aquarell, Acryl und Öl die Schönheiten des Vogtlandes zeigen. Auch dem Experiment gibt sie viel Raum. Susanne Söllner-Burr ist Mitglied im Plauener Kunstverein und Leiterin dessen Malzirkels. Ihr Heim hat sie in Pirk-Türbel in der Burgsteingemeinde.

1997 kehrte die damals 60-Jährige nach über 30-jähriger Tätigkeit als Kunstlehrerin in Solingen und Düsseldorf in ihr Elternhaus zurück. Ein Künstlerhaus, versteckt hinter hohen Bäumen, in einem idyllischen, naturbelassenen Garten. Früher fanden dort Dichterlesungen statt und es wurden anregende Gespräche mit Freunden sowie Eltern und Brüdern geführt. Kurt Arnold Findeisen, ein Schriftsteller aus Dresden, war des öfteren zu Gast und hat im Obergeschoss mit weitem Blick ins Vogtland geschrieben. Auch über den kleinen Bahnhof in Pirk, von dem aus die Malerin als Kind zur Schule fuhr. Findeisen habe prophezeit, dass die Pirker Autobahnbrücke einmal fertig gestellt werden würde, so die Künstlerin. Sie durfte das erleben. Auch den kleinen Bahnhof entdeckte sie neu. Und hatte eine Idee: Die ehemalige Schalterhalle in einen Ausstellungsraum umzufunktionieren und Menschen zusammenzuführen, die Kunst und Handwerk zu ihrem Hobby machten beziehungsweise zu ihrem Beruf. Es ist ihr mit Unterstützung des Ortschaftsrates und der Bürgermeisterin gelungen. Diese Sonntagsausstellungen in den Sommermonaten sind zu einer Attraktion geworden. 24 Veranstaltungen haben zwischen 2002 und 2007 schon Hunderte von Besuchern erfreut. Auch die Malerin selbst stellte ihre Arbeiten im Bahnhof aus. Susanne Söllner-Burr, examinierte Werbe- und Fotografikerin, hatte auch Freie Kunst an der Kunsthochschule Westberlin studiert. Wissen und Erfahrungen, die sie in ihrem Leben begleiteten. Einzel- und Gemeinschaftsausstellungen in vielen Orten Deutschlands, in Holland, Frankreich, Kolumbien, Paraguay und Argentinien zeugten von ihrer Kreativität und ihrer Experimentierfreude. Auch Radierungen, Illustrationen für Bücher, Linolschnitte, Rohrfeder- und Bleistiftzeichnungen gehören zu ihren Arbeitsergebnissen. In der Vogtlandregion stellte die Künstlerin zum Beispiel schon der Kapelle Neuensalz, im Rittergut Pirk, in Bad Elster, im Malzhaus und im Plauener Theater aus. Zu Hause, einem Ort der Stille, wird Susanne Söllner-Burr inspiriert. Dort malt sie in einer kleinen Scheune – ihrem Atelier ohne elektrischen Strom oder im Garten. Bescheiden und zurückhaltend weiß sie dennoch ganz klar, was sie will: „Ich möchte noch lange malen und mich an meinem Häuschen und Garten erfreuen können, zusammen mit meiner Familie und den Freunden."

She draws her strength from nature – and from her paintings, which show off the beauty of the Vogtland region in water colours, acrylic or oil paints. She leaves plenty of room for experimentation. Susanne Söllner-Burr is a member of the Plauen Art Association and leads its painting group. She has her home in Pirk-Türbel in the Burgstein parish.

She returned to her parental home as a 60 year-old in 1997 after working as an art teacher in Solingen and Düsseldorf for more than 30 years. It is an artist's home, hidden behind tall trees and located in an idyllic garden full of local plants. Years ago poetry readings took place here and lively discussions were held with friends and parents and brothers. Kurt Arnold Findeisen, a writer from Dresden, was often a guest here and wrote on the upper floor with a wide view of the Vogtland region – and the little railway station at Pirk, from which the painter went to school as a child. Findeisen prophesied that the Pirk motorway bridge would be completed one day, the painter says. She has been privileged to experience this. She also rediscovered the little station – and had an idea: she decided to transform the old ticket office into an exhibition room and bring together people who have made art and crafts their hobby or their profession. With the support of the local council and the mayor, she has been successful. The Sunday exhibitions in the summer months have become a real attraction. 24 events between 2002 and 2007 have given pleasure to hundreds of visitors. The painter also exhibited her works at the station.

Susanne Söllner-Burr, qualified advertising and photo graphics specialist, also studied free art at the West Berlin School of Art. This knowledge and experience has accompanied her down through her life. Individual and joint exhibitions at many places in Germany, in Holland, France, Colombia, Paraguay and Argentina have shown her creativity and her love of experimentation. Her work also includes etchings, illustrations for books, linocuts, reed pen and pencil drawings. The artist has exhibited her works in Neuensalz Chapel, Pirk Manor, in Bad Elster, the Malt House and at the Plauen theatre in the Vogtland region. Susanne Söllner-Burr gains her inspiration at home in the quietness. She paints in a small barn – her studio without any electricity – or in the garden. Despite her modesty and shyness, she knows what she wants: "I would like to continue painting for a long time and enjoy my little house and garden with my family and friends."

(Fotos/Photos by B. Kempe-Winkelmann, Text/Text by B. Kempe-Winkelmann, Übersetzung/Translated by David Strauss)

Mario Urlaß – Kunst, die begeistert
Mario Urlaß – Art that Delights Others

Mit gerade einmal 37 Jahren wurde Mario Urlaß aus Schönbach Professor. Das war 2003. Seitdem unterrichtet er Kunst und Didaktik an der Pädagogischen Hochschule Heidelberg. Davor lagen Lehrtätigkeiten an der damaligen Pädagogischen Hochschule Zwickau, an der Universität Chemnitz sowie am Lehrstuhl für Kunsterziehung der Universität Erlangen-Nürnberg.

Eng verbunden mit der beruflichen Tätigkeit ist auch der künstlerische Werdegang von Mario Urlaß. Schon mit zehn Jahren wurde er in das Förderstudio für Malerei und Grafik Zwickau aufgenommen. Später gehörte er der Künstlergruppe 5+1 an und ist seit 2002 Mitglied im Verein „Freunde aktueller Kunst". 1993 erhielt er ein Stipendium des Sächsischen Ministeriums für Wissenschaft und Kunst, das ihm einen Aufenthalt in Civitella d'Agliano, einem italienischen Künstlerdorf, ermöglichte. Malereien, Grafiken und Objekte von Mario Urlaß wurden vor allem in sächsischen sowie bayrischen Galerien und Museen ausgestellt. Seine größte Arbeit trägt den Titel „Werden, Wachsen und Vergehen" und hängt im Heinrich-Braun-Krankenhaus Zwickau. Im Rahmen des Wettbewerbes „Kunst am Bau" hatte er die Ausschreibung für das 2 mal 7 Meter große Triptychon, eine Malerei auf Leinwand, gewonnen. Wenn es um Verbesserungen im Kunstunterricht geht, mischt sich Mario Urlaß gern ein. Er arbeitete in verschiedenen Lehr- und Bildungsplankommissionen mit und organisiert selbst Kunstausstellungen und -Konferenzen. Ein Glanzstück gelang ihm zum Ende des Sommersemesters 2007: Gemeinsam mit zwei weiteren Professoren konnte er den InSEA-Forschungs- und Entwicklungs-Kongress erstmals seit 20 Jahren wieder nach Deutschland holen. 350 Gäste aus 45 Ländern nahmen an der Tagung des von der UNESCO anerkannten Weltverbandes aller im kulturellen/künstlerischen Bildungssektor Lehrenden und Forschenden teil. In seinem Vortrag hatte der Kunstpädagoge über ein Projekt referiert, das er gemeinsam mit Schülern der Reichenbacher Weinholdgrundschule durchgeführt hat. Sein Auftreten brachte ihm eine Einladung zum nächsten Kongress nach Osaka/Japan ein. Dort wird er als „Keynote-Speaker" einen Impulsvortrag halten, in dem auch die Arbeit mit den Grundschülern wieder eine Rolle spielt. Viel zu wenig Zeit bleibt ihm für die eigene künstlerische Arbeit in seinem Atelier am Schönbacher Erlengrund.

Mario Urlaß from Schönbach became a professor in 2003 at the age of just 37. Since then he has been teaching arts and didactics at the University of Education in Heidelberg. Prior to this, he had also been teaching at the former educational college in Zwickau, at Chemnitz University and the Chair of Art Education at the University of Erlangen-Nuremberg.

Mario Urlaß's artistic development is closely connected to his professional career. At the age of 10, he was accepted as a member of the Studio Promoting Painting and Graphics in Zwickau. Later he was a member of the artist group "5+1" and has been member of the "Friends of Contemporary Art" Association since 2002. He was awarded a scholarship by the Saxon Department for Arts and Sciences in 1993; this gave him the opportunity of spending some time in the Italian artists' village of Civitella d'Agliano. Paintings, graphics and items by Mario Urlaß have been displayed in a number of Saxon and Bavarian galleries and museums. His greatest work is called "Werden, Wachsen und Vergehen" (Becoming, Growing and Dying Away) and is displayed in the Heinrich Braun hospital in Zwickau. In the course of the "Art in Buildings" competition, he was awarded the job of producing the 2 by 7 metre large triptych, a painting on canvas.

Mario Urlaß likes to get involved when it comes to improving art education. He has worked on a number of syllabus and curriculum commissions and he organises art exhibitions and conferences. At the end of the summer term in 2007 he brought off a coup: for the first time in 20 years he and two fellow-professors were able to bring back to Germany the InSEA Research and Development Congress (the International Society for Education through Art). 350 guests from 45 countries participated in this conference organised by an association of tutors and research scientists working in the cultural or artistic education sectors; this association is recognised by UNESCO. In his speech, the arts lecturer presented a project that he had produced with pupils from the Weinhold Primary School in Reichenbach. His presentation resulted in an invitation to the next congress in Osaka, Japan. He will be the main speaker there and give a keynote lecture that will also cover his work with primary school pupils. He has far too little spare time for his own artistic work in his studio in the Erlengrund district of Schönbach.

(Fotos/Photos by Petra Steps, Text/Text by Petra Steps, Übersetzung/Translated by David Strauss)

Ideen werden phantastische Wirklichkeit
Von einem, der seine Ideen zu bewegten Bildern macht

Das Hobby zum Beruf gemacht hat Jörg Halsema aus Mylau. Der 45-Jährige verdient seinen Lebensunterhalt als Trickfilmzeichner und Illustrator. Richtig begonnen hat er damit erst im Jahr 2000, nach einer selbstständigen Tätigkeit mit einer Handwerksfirma. Schuld war ein Auftrag in einem Zwickauer Altenheim. Dort las er in einer Mittagspause einen Zeitungsartikel über ein Dresdner Trickfilmstudio. Nach einem Anruf dort durfte er sich mit seiner Zeichenmappe vorstellen und war im Geschäft. Nebenberuflich malte er oft bis spät in die Nacht, um eines Tages festzustellen, dass es so nicht mehr geht und ein Berufswechsel ansteht.

Seitdem hat Jörg Halsema bereits Jahre am Zeichentisch zugebracht, denn pro Sekunde Film braucht es 24 Bilder. Bei großen Filmen wie „Der kleine Eisbär" war er einer von etwa 120 Zeichnern. An der Serie „Das Wiesenspektakel", die beim Sandmann gesendet wurde, entwarf der Mylauer die Figuren und gestaltete die Hintergründe. Ein ganzes Jahr Arbeit war für die 13 Teile zu jeweils fünf Minuten notwendig. Zeichentrickfilme für Kinder sind das Hauptbetätigungsfeld, aber nicht ausschließlich. Zurzeit arbeitet er an einem Projekt für Erwachsene, das Bilder und Musik der 20er Jahre verbindet.

Sein Talent zum Zeichnen bemerkte Jörg Halsema schon zeitig. Der Kunstunterricht sorgte für die einzige 1 auf dem Zeugnis. Später besuchte er in Reichenbach einen Mal- und Zeichenzirkel und versuchte sich in allen möglichen Genres. Dabei stellte er fest, dass es die kleinen Männchen und Kritzeleien auf dem Bildrand waren, die besonders gut ankamen. Und so war der Karikaturist geboren. Die häufig gesellschaftskritischen Bilder waren und sind in vielen Ausstellungen zu sehen, zum Beispiel im Greizer Sommerpalais zu mehreren Triennalen, in der Burg Mylau, im Schloss Netzschkau, im Reichenbacher Neuberinhaus, aber auch in Göttingen und Hannover oder im Sächsischen Finanzministerium. Die Ideen für die Karikaturen kommen spontan – die Wirklichkeit findet er oft noch schlimmer als seine Darstellungen. In mehreren Kinderbüchern hat Jörg Halsema seine Handschrift hinterlassen. Ein von ihm illustriertes Buch heißt „Märchen und Geschichten aus dem Vogtland".

Jörg Halsema from Mylau has turned his hobby into his profession. The 45-year-old earns his living as a cartoon drawer and illustrator. It all really started in 2000 after he was working for a tradesman's company on a self-employed basis. He was working at an old people's home in Zwickau – and picked up a newspaper article about a cartoon studio in Dresden during his lunch break. After a phone call, he was able to present his file of drawings and was accepted! He often painted until well into the night for pleasure, but then discovered on the next day that he could not live like this, so he changed jobs.

Since that time Jörg Halsema has spent years at his drawing table, for there are 25 images for each second in a film. He was one of about 120 illustrators for big films like "The Small Polar Bear". The native of Mylau designed the figures and the background for the "The Meadow Spectacle" series, which was broadcast on the Sandmann children's programme. He spent a whole year on the 13 episodes, each of which lasted five minutes. His main area of work is cartoon films for children, but that is not all he does. He is currently working on a project for adults, which combines images and music from the 1920s.

Jörg Halsema noticed his talent for drawing at an early age. Art was the only subject where he got the best possible mark. He later attended a painting and drawing group in Reichenbach and tried out every possible genre. He discovered that the little men and the scribble at the edge were the most successful elements. This gave birth to the caricaturist in him. His drawings, which often point the finger at society, can be seen at many exhibitions – at the Greiz Summer Palace every three years, Mylau Castle, Netzschkau Castle, the Neuberin Theatre in Reichenbach, but also in Göttingen and Hanover and the Saxon Finance Ministry. The ideas for his caricatures come to him spontaneously – he often finds that reality is worse than his drawings. Jörg Halsema has also left his mark on several children's books. One of the books illustrated by him is called "Fairy Tales and Stories from the Vogtland Region".

(Fotos/Photos by Igor Pastierovic, Text/Text by Petra Steps, Übersetzung/Translated by David Strauss)

Ein ganzes Leben mit der Musik
A WHOLE LIFE WITH MUSIC

Der wohl größte Raum im Hause von Dr. Rolf und Dr. Isolde Seidel ist das Musikzimmer. Es ist der Treffpunkt zum gemeinsamen Musizieren sowohl mit Familienmitgliedern als auch mit Freunden. Der Hausmusikkreis Dr. Seidel ist ein Begriff bei Kennern klassischer Musik in Jocketa und weit darüber hinaus.

Schon in den Elternhäusern von Rolf und Isolde Seidel wurde musiziert. Er drängte bereits mit neun Jahren darauf, Klavierunterricht zu bekommen. Mit 14 erlernte er das Orgelspielen. „In Zwickau habe ich bei dem Domorganisten Günther Metz sehr gründlichen Unterricht bekommen. Und als Medizinstudent habe ich extern die Kirchenmusikschule in Dresden besucht." Posaune, Trompete und Geige kamen später als Instrumente dazu. Sie genoss Cello- und Gambe-Unterricht. „Das Klavierspielen ist dann etwas untergegangen."

Als Medizinstudenten haben sich die heute in Jocketa Lebenden kennen gelernt. In der Familie von Frau Isolde in Plauen existierte schon frühzeitig eine Musiziergemeinschaft, in die beide 1959 einstiegen. Seit 1960 wurde zu verschiedenen Gelegenheiten öffentlich musiziert – auch in der Markuskirche. Nachdem Seidels zur Hochzeit des Ehepaares Pflug aus Ruppertsgrün aufgespielt hatten, entwickelte sich eine Freundschaft, die zum Hausmusikkreis führte, dem sich weitere Interessierte anschlossen, insbesondere das Ehepaar Ebert aus Jocketa.

Seit 1997 leitet Dr. Seidel außerdem das Kammerorchester der Plauener Musizierfreunde. Auch seine Frau und die große Tochter Christiane (Geige, Blockflöte) gehören dazu.

Beide Töchter, so berichten die inzwischen 73-Jährigen stolz, haben vom musikalischen Haus profitiert. Bettine (Gesang) lebt in Leipzig, Christiane mit Familie im Elternhaus in Jocketa. Sechs Enkel zwischen sieben und 18 Jahren machen Seidels ebenfalls viel Freude. Alle musizieren – Harfe, Trompete, Cello, Gambe, Posaune und Horn sind die Instrumente, die beherrscht werden. Zu Familienfeiern und Festtagen, wie Weihnachten, kommt dann das Familien"orchester" zusammen und füllt das Musikzimmer mit schönsten Klängen.

Aus Jocketa nicht wegzudenken ist die Veranstaltungsreihe der Orgelvespern. Seit 1980 wird von Ende Juni bis September jeden Samstag in die Jocketaer Kirche eingeladen. Konzerte, die Rolf Seidel organisiert und dazu aus anderen Musizierkreisen Ausführende einlädt. Solisten, Chöre und Kantoren sind zu Gast und bieten dem breiten Publikum ein Spektrum ihres Könnens. Die beliebten Orgelvespern finanzieren sich durch die Kollekte, mit Fördergeldern und über ein Konto, auf das Kantor Dr. Seidel sein Geld überweist, das er sich bei den Gottesdiensten an der Orgel erspielt. Übrigens: In 27 Bänden hat Rolf Seidel alles gesammelt, was an Dokumenten zu den Orgelvespern vorhanden ist, einschließlich der 2465 Programme. Eine chronistische Arbeit, für die ihm Nachfolgende sicher einmal dankbar sein werden.

Das musikalische Schaffen von Isolde und Rolf Seidel wäre unvollständig, würde die Vogtländische Bassgemeinschaft, in der sie beide musizieren, und das Fränkisch-Vogtländische Gambenconsortium, dem sie angehört, nicht erwähnt.

Und wenn man dann noch erfährt, dass Seidels Sinfonie-, Kammer- und Kirchenkonzerte besuchen, gerne wandern und Rad fahren und seit sieben Jahren an der Volkshochschule Englisch lernen, bekommt man vielleicht einen kleinen Eindruck von einem ausgefüllten Leben auch im Ruhestand.

Probably the biggest room in Drs Rolf and Isolde Seidel's house is the music room. This is where the family and friends meet to make music together. The Dr Seidel music group is not only well known to classical music lovers in Jocketa, but also outside the town. Music was played in their parents' houses. Rolf started to have piano lessons when he was nine years old. He began to have organ lessons at the age of fourteen. "I received a good grounding in my music lessons from the organist Günther Metz in Zwickau, and as a medical student I visited the church music school in Dresden. He later added the trombone, trumpet and violin to the list of instruments he learned to play. Isolde had cello and viola da gamba lessons. "But then piano playing took a back seat."

The couple, who now live in Jocketa, got to know each other as medical students. There was a musicians' group in Mrs Isolde's family in Plauen from an early stage and both of them joined it in 1959. From 1960 this group performed in public places, including the Markus Church. After the Seidels played at the Pflug's wedding in Ruppertsgrün, a friendship developed, which led to the home music group, which other people joined, in particular the Eberts from Jocketa.

Dr Seidel has also led the chamber orchestra of Plauen amateur musicians since 1997. Both his wife and elder daughter Christiane (she plays the violin and recorder) are members.

Both daughters, the 73 year old parents explain, have benefited from their musical home. Bettine, who sings, lives in Leipzig, while Christiane lives in her parents' house with her family. Six grandchildren aged seven to eighteen give their grandparents a lot of pleasure. All of them are learning an instrument – including the harp, trumpet, cello, viola da gamba, trombone and horn. The family "orchestra" gets together at family celebrations and festivals such as Christmas and fills the music room with wonderful sounds.

It is hard to imagine life in Jocketa without the series of organ meditation concerts. People can attend these in the church at Jocketa every Saturday evening from the end of June until the beginning of September – and this has been going on since 1980. Rolf Seidel organises concerts and invites other musical groups to take part. Soloists, choirs and church musicians are invited to perform and offer a wide variety of musical treats to their listeners. These popular events are financed through collections and sponsorship money and an account to which Dr Seidel transfers the money he receives for playing the organ for church services. Dr Seidel has collected all the information about these events in 27 volumes, including the 2465 programmes. The work is chronological, for which his successors will be grateful.

The musical accomplishments of Isolde and Rolf Seidel would be incomplete without mentioning the Vogtland Bass Society, where both play, and the Franconian-Vogtland Viola da Gamba Consortium, of which they are also members.

The Seidels also attend symphony, chamber and church concerts. They enjoy walking and cycling and have been learning English at evening classes for the last seven years. This gives you some insight into how full life can be, even in retirement.

(Fotos/Photos by Hartmut Briese, Text/Text by B. Kempe-Winkelmann, Übersetzung/Translated by David Strauss)

Gute Musik ist der kürzeste Weg in die Herzen
Good Music is the Quickest Way to People's Hearts

Als am 19. September 1992 der Fusionsvertrag zwischen dem Staatlichen Vogtlandorchester Reichenbach in Sachsen und dem Staatlichen Sinfonieorchestern im thüringischen Greiz zur Vogtland Philharmonie Greiz/Reichenbach unterzeichnet wurde, war der Grundstein zu einer Erfolgsgeschichte gelegt. Denn 15 Jahre danach, im Jahr 2007, hat sich das in Deutschland einzigartige Länder übergreifende Projekt nicht nur bestens bewährt, sondern besitzt mittlerweile viel beachteten Modellcharakter.

When the merger contract was signed between the Reichenbach State Vogtland Orchestra in Saxony and the State Symphony Orchestra in Greiz in Thuringia to become the Greiz/Reichenbach Vogtland Philharmonic on 19 September 1992, the foundation for a success story had been laid. 15 years later, in 2007, the unique German project, which transcends state borders, has not only proved its worth, but is now admired by many as a model for the future.

(Fotos/Photos by Vogtland Philharmonie, Text/Text by Ekkehard Glaß, Übersetzung/Translated by David Strauss)

Raum für Kunst / Room for Art

Der Klangkörper, der durch beide Länder, den Kulturraum Vogtland, den Vogtlandkreis, den Landkreis Greiz und die Städte Reichenbach und Greiz gefördert und budgetiert wird, zeichnet sich durch Kontinuität und Vielseitigkeit sowie durch wirtschaftlichen Erfolg aus. Zu rund 23 Prozent finanziert sich der Kulturbetrieb selbst – ein Novum in der Orchester- und Theaterlandschaft. Mitgetragen wird die künstlerische Arbeit der 65 Musiker des Orchesters von einem starken Förderverein. Der zählt mittlerweile über 600 Mitglieder und gehört damit zu den größten seiner Art in Deutschland.

In ihrem 15-jährigen Wirken ist die Vogtland Philharmonie Greiz/Reichenbach durch zahlreiche Konzertangebote, kammermusikalische Abende oder Unterhaltungsprogramme nicht nur zu einem festen Veranstaltungspartner in der Region geworden. Als „Kulturbotschafter des Vogtlandes" wirkt das Orchester weit über die Grenzen Sachsens und Thüringens hinaus. Konzertreisen führten und führen das Ensemble regelmäßig in verschiedene deutsche Städte. Auslandsgastspiele gab es unter anderem in China, Österreich, den USA, Dänemark, Frankreich oder in der Tschechischen Republik. Für 2010 ist ein Gastspiel in Spanien im Gespräch.

Für Generalmusikdirektor Stefan Fraas, den Geschäftsführer und Intendant, ist eine solche kulturell-künstlerische Außenwirkung natürlich wichtig für das nationale und internationale Renommee des Klangkörpers. Doch das Hauptfeld ist und bleibt für die Philharmonie die weiter gefasste heimische Region. Denn gerade hier haben sich in den vergangenen Jahren neue, interessante infrastrukturelle Möglichkeiten ergeben. So stehen zum Beispiel mit neu gebauten Hallen in Schleiz, Ronneburg oder Weida potenzielle Spielstätten für das Orchester zur Verfügung, und neue, ständige Auftrittsorte haben sich die Musiker in West-Thüringen, im Erzgebirge und in Franken erschlossen.

Seit 13 Jahren fest im Veranstaltungskalender verankert ist das von der Vogtland Philharmonie Greiz/Reichenbach mit ins Leben gerufene Projekt „Philharmonic-Rock", das auf einzigartige Weise Klassik und Rockmusik und damit Fans beider Musikrichtungen vereint. 140 Titel sind mittlerweile dafür in Spezialarrangements von Jens Pfretzschner produziert worden. Die Aufführungen erweisen sich jedes Mal als wahrer Publikumsmagnet. Wie auch die „Sounds of Hollywood", ein weiteres populäres Projekt der Philharmoniker, das seit nunmehr sechs Jahren auf Großleinwand Ausschnitte aus Filmklassikern mit live gespielter Filmmusik verbindet. Allein 14 solcher Konzerte gab es in der letzten aktuellen Spielzeit. Laut Intendant Fraas ist ein weiteres Projekt in Vorbereitung. Ab der Spielzeit 2008/09 sollen die Hits der britischen Rockgruppe „Queen" in rock-sinfonischem Arrangement zur Aufführung gebracht werden.
In Vorbereitung ist auch eine weitere CD, von denen das Ensemble bisher über 20 Stück eingespielt hat. Diesmal werden es Fagottkonzerte sein.

The orchestra, which is funded by both states, the Vogtland Cultural Area, the Vogtland District, the Rural DIstrict of Greiz and the towns of Reichenbach and Greiz, is characterised by continuity and variety – and it is an economic success. The cultural organisation covers about 23 percent of its own costs – something quite new in the world of orchestras and theatres. The artistic work performed by the 65 musicians in the orchestra is backed by a strong supporting association. It now has more than 600 members and is therefore one of the largest of its kind in Germany.

In its 15 years of existence, the Greiz/Reichenbach Vogtland Philharmonic has not only become a permanent event partner in the region with its many concerts, chamber music evenings or entertainment programmes. The orchestra also functions as a "cultural ambassador of the Vogtland region" beyond the borders of Saxony and Thuringia. Concert trips have taken the ensemble to many German cities. There have been guest appearances abroad in China, Austria, the USA, Denmark, France and in the Czech Republic. A tour of Spain is being considered for 2010.

A cultural and artistic public image is naturally important for general music director Stefan Fraas, the managing director and orchestra's conductor; this underpins the domestic and international renown of the orchestra. But the main area of operations for the Philharmonic is still its home region, viewed in very broad terms. For new infrastructure opportunities have opened up here over the past few years. Newly built concert halls in Schleiz, Ronneburg or Weida mean potential sites where the orchestra could play; and the musicians have tapped into new permanent performance sites in West Thuringia, the Ore Mountains and in Franconia.

"Philharmonic Rock" has become a permanent feature in the event calendar of the Greiz/Reichenbach Vogtland Philharmonic over the past 13 years; it combines classical and rock music in a unique manner and appeals to fans of both genres. Jens Pfretzschner has now produced special arrangements for 140 titles. The performances are a real attraction for the public every time. Then there is the "Sounds of Hollywood", which is another popular project performed by the orchestra. It has now combined excerpts from classical films on a huge screen with live music being played – and has been held for the past six years. There were 14 such concerts along during the last music season. Director Stefan Fraas says that another project is being prepared. The hits of the British rock group "Queen" are due to be played in a rock-symphony arrangement from the 2008-09 season onwards.
Another CD is also being prepared. The ensemble has already recorded 20 tracks. This time it will primarily feature bassoon concerts.

Raum für Kunst / Room for Art

Seit 1992 leitet **Stefan Fraas** die Geschicke der Vogtland Philharmonie Greiz/Reichenbach als Dirigent und Geschäftsführer. 1995 wurde er zum Intendant. In Würdigung seines Engagements um das Ensemble ernannte ihn Reichenbachs Oberbürgermeister Dieter Kießling im Oktober 2007 zum Generalmusikdirktor.

Nach einem Studium der Schulmusik in Zwickau hatte Stefan Fraas an den Musikhochschulen „Franz Liszt" in Weimar und „Carl Maria von Weber" in Dresden studiert. Seine Studienfächer waren Klavier, Gesang sowie Chor- und Orchesterdirigieren. Seine Arbeit beim damaligen Vogtlandorchester Reichenbach begann der Vogtländer 1988 als Kapellmeister. Von 2000 bis 2006 leitete Fraas als Chefdirigent auch noch das Folkwang Kammerorchester Essen. Aus Zeitgründen hat er diese Tätigkeit aufgegeben. Nach wie vor führen ihn aber Konzertreisen in bedeutende Musikzentren und viele Länder der Welt. So dirigierte er zum Beispiel im September ein Konzert im fernen sibirischen Irkutsk.

Stefan Fraas has directed the fate of the Greiz/Reichenbach Vogtland Philharmonic as conductor and managing director since 1992. He became the director in 1995. Reichenbach's mayor Dieter Kießling appointed him to the position of general musical director in October 2007 in recognition of his commitment to the orchestra. After studying at the Zwickau School of Music, Stefan Fraas studied at the "Franz Liszt" School of Music in Weimar and the "Carl Maria von Weber" School of Music in Dresden. He studied the piano, singing and conducting choirs and orchestras. The native of the Vogtland region began his work at what was then the Reichenbach Vogtland Orchestra as band master. Fraas was also head conductor of the Folkwang Chamber Orchestra in Essen from 2000 until 2006. He then gave up this position for time reasons. But concert trips still take him to major music centres and many countries in the world. He conducted a concert in the Siberian city of Irkutsk in September.

» *Philharmonic-Rock – ob an der Göltzschtalbrücke oder der Vogtland Arena – hier werden eindrucksvolle Kulissen mit außergewöhnlichem Klangerlebnis verbunden zu einem unvergesslichem Ereignis.* «

» *Philharmonic-Rock – regardless of whether it is held at the Göltzsch Valley Bridge or the Vogtland Arena – impressive settings with extraordinary sound experiences combine to provide an unforgettable event.* «

(Foto/Photo by Igor Pastierovic)

Raum für Kunst / Room for Art

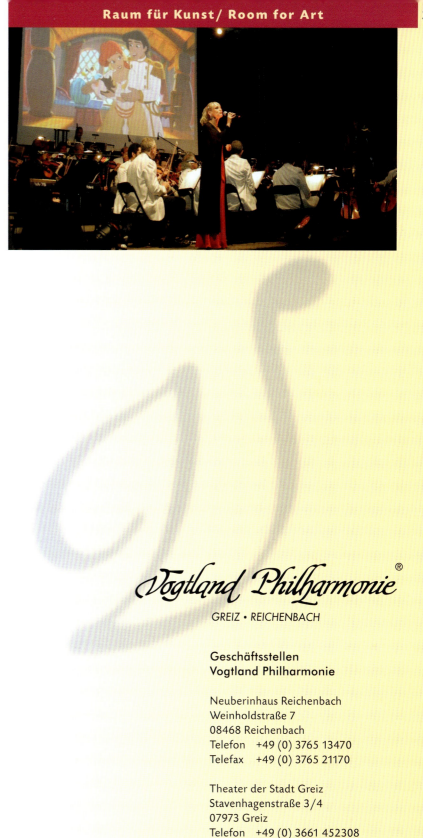

Mit **Jiří Malát** hat die Vogtland Philharmonie Greiz/Reichenbach seit September 2004 einen erfahrenen Chefdirigenten. Der gebürtige Prager studierte am Prager Konservatorium und an der Prager Akademie der musischen Künste. Seine Fächer waren Viola, Dirigieren und Komposition. 1981 wurde er Chefdirigent an der Oper Pilsen und 1985 Dirigent des Rundfunk-Sinfonieorchesters Pilsen, dessen Chefdirigent er von 1990 bis 1992 war. Stationen führten ihn zur Philharmonie in Ostrava, ans Prager Nationaltheater und als Chefdirigent zum Kurpfälzischen Kammerorchester in Mannheim. Seit 1998 wirkt er als ständiger Gastdirigent an der Staatsoper Prag.

Als Ehrendirigent bereichert der Weimarer **Lothar Seyfarth** seit der Spielzeit 2004/05 die künstlerische Ausstrahlung der Vogtland Philharmonie. Seyfarth war unter anderem Chefdirigent des DEFA-Sinfonieorchesters und Dirigent der Dresdner Philharmonie. Er arbeitete ebenfalls als Musikalischer Oberleiter am Deutschen Nationaltheater Weimar und als Dirigent an der Komischen Oper Berlin. Bis 1991 war er Chefdirigent des Staatlichen Sinfonieorchesters Thüringen und ist seitdem als freischaffender Dirigent tätig. Lothar Seyfarth setzt sich intensiv für die Wiedererschließung und Aufführung „vergessener" Kompositionen ein.

The Greiz/Reichenbach Vogtland Philharmonic has had an experienced chief conductor in the shape of **Jiří Malát** since September 2004. The native of Prague studied at the Prague Conservatory and the Prague Academy of Musical Arts. He studied the viola, conducting and composition. He became chief conductor at the Pilsen Opera House in 1981 and conductor of the Pilsen Radio Symphony Orchestra; he was chief conductor here from 1990 until 1992. Various stages of his career took him to the Philharmonic in Ostrava, the Prague National Theatre and as chief conductor to the Kurpfälzisch Chamber Orchestra in Mannheim. He has been a regular guest conductor at the Prague State Opera since 1998.

Lothar Seyfarth from Weimar has been enriching the artistic appeal of the Vogtland Philharmonic since the 2004-05 season as an honorary conductor. Seyfarth has held positions as head conductor at the DEFA Symphony Orchestra and conductor of the Dresden Philharmonic. He has also worked as Senior Musical Director at the Weimar German National Theatre and as a conductor at the Comic Opera in Berlin. He was head conductor at the State Symphony Orchestra in Thuringia until 1991 and has worked as a self-employed conductor since then. Seyfarth is particularly interested in rediscovering and performing "forgotten" compositions.

Vogtland Philharmonie®
GREIZ • REICHENBACH

Geschäftsstellen Vogtland Philharmonie

Neuberinhaus Reichenbach
Weinholdstraße 7
08468 Reichenbach
Telefon +49 (0) 3765 13470
Telefax +49 (0) 3765 21170

Theater der Stadt Greiz
Stavenhagenstraße 3/4
07973 Greiz
Telefon +49 (0) 3661 452308
Telefax +49 (0) 3661 455544

www.vogtland-philharmonie.de
info@vogtland-philharmonie.de

Kultur erleben im Vogtland
Culture to experience in the Vogtland

„Kultur erleben" – Einwohner und Gäste des Vogtlandes in den Einrichtungen der Vogtland Kultur GmbH. Fünf unterschiedliche Einrichtungen des Vogtlandkreises werden seit 1997 durch die Vogtland Kultur GmbH betrieben, deren alleiniger Gesellschafter der Vogtlandkreis ist. Die Vogtland Kultur GmbH ist in ihrer Struktur neuartig in Deutschland. Zentrale Aufgabe ist der Erhalt und Ausbau des kulturellen Angebots in der Region.

Die Vogtland Kultur GmbH wird durch den Vogtlandkreis und den Kulturraum Vogtland gefördert.

Alle Einrichtungen der Vogtland Kultur GmbH sind mit ihren spezifischen Angeboten für die Region einmalig und jede Einrichtung birgt für sich das Potential zur Profilierung in einem bestimmten kulturellen Bereich.

In einer Zeit, in der der Faktor Freizeit eine immer größere Rolle einnimmt, werden attraktive Angebote zur sinnvollen Nutzung dieser Freizeit angeboten und Möglichkeiten zur Regeneration der Arbeitskräfte zur Verfügung gestellt. Alters- und interessengerechte Erlebnisse werden immer mehr als Anlass für Reisen oder Tagesausflüge genutzt, in deren Planung und Durchführung immer auch andere Dienstleistungsträger in Anspruch genommen werden.

Die kulturellen Einrichtungen der Vogtland Kultur GmbH leisten damit einen wichtigen Beitrag zur Umwegrentabilität des Dienstleistungs- und tourismustangierenden Gewerbes. Aber nicht nur für Touristen sind attraktive Angebote erforderlich. Die Bürger des Vogtlandkreises nutzen die vielfältigen Angebote der Einrichtungen der Vogtland Kultur GmbH, die ihre Lebensqualität wesentlich beeinflussen. Die positive Ausstrahlung der Vogtland Kultur GmbH schafft Identität und fördert Heimatliebe. Die kulturelle Infrastruktur ist ein entscheidender Faktor bei der Standortfrage für die Ansiedlung oder Ausweitung von Unternehmen.

Die Vogtland Kultur GmbH stellt Arbeitsplätze zur Verfügung und sichert durch die Vergabe von Leistungen an die heimische Wirtschaft auch Arbeitsplätze. Unsere Mitarbeiter und Mitarbeiterinnen sind fachlich gut ausgebildet und motiviert, Veränderungen für die Besucher mitzutragen, neue Konzepte zu entwickeln und auf aktuelle Trends zu reagieren. Alle Angebote der Vogtland Kultur GmbH sind ganzjährig nutzbar, d.h. dass alle unsere Einzelleistungen unter dem Anspruch „KULTUR ERLEBEN" dem Gesamtprodukt Kultur und Tourismus im Vogtland zur Verfügung stehen. Niveauvolle, vielfältige Veranstaltungen und museale Kostbarkeiten tragen zur Attraktivität des Standortes Vogtland bei, in wirtschaftlicher wie auch touristischer Sicht.

Entdecken Sie in den Einrichtungen der Vogtland Kultur GmbH wahre kulturelle Schätze, besuchen Sie niveauvolle Veranstaltungen, lassen Sie sich mit kulinarischen Köstlichkeiten verwöhnen oder geben sich das „Ja – Wort" in besonders schönem Ambiente. Die Vogtland Kultur GmbH plant und organisiert auch Ihre Präsentationen, Tagungen, Betriebs- und Familienfeiern.

"Culture to experience" – for the inhabitants and guests of the Vogtland in the public buildings of the "Vogtland Kultur Ltd.". Five of the most different facilities of the district Vogtland are prosecuted by the Vogtland Kultur Ltd. since 1997, the administration of the district Vogtland is the only acting partner of it. The Vogtland Kultur Ltd. is a complete new structure in Germany. The main commission is the preservation and development of the cultural proposals in the region of the Vogtland. The Vogtland Kultur Ltd. is grant-aided through the administration of the district Vogtland and the "Kulturraum Vogtland".

All public buildings of the "Vogtland Kultur Ltd." are unique with their very specific proposals for the region and each constitution contains the own potential for there image in a special cultural area.

At this times, where the leisure time factor develops an ever increasing role, we offer attractive proposals for a suggestive application and capabilities for the regeneration of the human resources. The occasions to travel are more and more in conformity with age and interests, and many people use service provider for arrangements and transaction.

The public buildings of the "Vogtland Kultur Ltd." afford an important contribution for the profitabilities of the service and touristic industry. But these attractive sources are not only necessary for tourists. The citizens of the district Vogtland use the varied offers of the „Vogtland Kultur Ltd.", to influence the quality of life, the positive vibes of the "Vogtland Kultur Ltd." creates identity. The cultural infrastructure is a decisive factor for the question of locations of the establishing companies.

The "Vogtland Kultur Ltd." adds jobs and secures other jobs because of the placing of commissions. Our employees are well qualified and motivated. They're taking responsibility for the visitors and guests, develope new proposals and respond by setting a new trend. All public buildings of the "Vogtland Kultur Ltd." are all season to harness., that means all our products are always in connection with the slogan "Culture to experience in the Vogtland", for top-culture and top-tourism in our area. Sophisticated, multiplex events and valuables of the museums support the attraction of the region of Vogtland, in economically and touristic vision.

Discover in the public buildings of the "Vogtland Kultur Ltd." true cultural treasures, visit sophisticated concerts and events, and let us spoil you with culinary deliciousness or get married in a very beautiful atmosphere. The "Vogtland Kultur Ltd." will plan and organize your special presentation, meetings and congresses, ceremonies and celebrations.

Vogtland Kultur GmbH
Weinholdstr. 7 · D-08468 Reichenbach
Telefon +49 (0) 3765 12743
Telefax +49 (0) 3765 612013
www.vogtland-kultur.de
info@vogtland-kultur.de
Ihr Ansprechpartner/*Your contact person*
Herr Bernd Weck,
1. Geschäftsführer/*1st Managing Director*

(Fotos/*Photos by* Vogtland Kultur GmbH, Text/*Text by* Vogtland Kultur GmbH, Übersetzung/*Translated by* Vogtland Kultur GmbH)

Kunst und Kultur

Telefon +49 (0) 3765 12188
Telefax +49 (0) 3765 12425
info@neuberinhaus.de

Ihr Ansprechpartner
Your contact person
Herr Jens Pfretzschner, Manager
Neuberinhaus Reichenbach

Als attraktives und modernes Veranstaltungshaus mit vielfältigsten Angeboten präsentiert sich das **Neuberinhaus Reichenbach (1)**. Die Palette der angebotenen Veranstaltungen reicht von Konzerten, Shows, Tanzabenden, Theateraufführungen und Kinderprogrammen bis hin zu Kabarett, Vorträgen und Ausstellungen. Das Neuberinhaus bietet auch beste Bedingungen für Konferenzen, Messen, Firmenpräsentationen oder Familienfeierlichkeiten. Dafür stehen verschiedenste Räumlichkeiten zur Verfügung. Bei der Planung und Durchführung Ihrer Veranstaltungen steht Ihnen ein motiviertes Team mit Rat und Tat zur Seite. Modernste Technik garantiert hervorragende Bedingungen.

The **Neuberinhaus Reichenbach (1)** is an attractive and modern event location. The scale of events in this house is: classical and rock concerts, shows, dancing parties, theatre and children shows. The Neuberinhaus offers best conditions for conferences, different fairs, presentations and ceremonies of companies. Therefore we have several rooms and halls at one's disposal. We offer you a competent and motivated team for the preparation and performance of your event. Our modern equipment guarantees outstanding results.

Telefon +49 (0) 3741 413290
Telefax +49 (0) 3741 411108
kapelle.neuensalz@t-online.de

Ihr Ansprechpartner
Your contact person
Frau Angela Görner, Manager
Konzert- und Ausstellungszentrum
Kapelle Neuensalz

Mit niveauvollen Veranstaltungen und interessanten Kunstausstellungen präsentiert sich Ihnen das **Konzert- und Ausstellungszentrum Kapelle Neuensalz (2)**. Das historische und architektonische Kleinod hat seinen Ursprung bereits im 13. Jahrhundert. Unter Denkmalschutz gestellt, erfolgte eine sechsjährige Rekonstruktion und Restaurierung. Heute ist die Kapelle ein ideales Domizil für Kunst und Musik. Ob Vortragsreihen, Kammermusik, Autorenlesungen, moderne Konzerte oder Kabarett, hier finden Sie immer etwas für einen genüsslichen oder vergnüglichen Abend. Für private Familienfeiern, Trauungen und Firmenfeierlichkeiten ist die Kapelle durch ihr wunderschönes Ambiente inzwischen zum Geheimtipp geworden.

With sophisticated events and interesting exhibitions we highly advise the **Konzert- und Ausstellungszentrum Kapelle Neuensalz (2)**. The historical and architectural jewel was first mentioned in the 13th century. To be under preservation order, the little chapel was reconstructed and restored during six years. Today it is an ideal domicile for art and music, recitations, lectures, modern concerts and comedy is finding place here. You can always choose the right performance for a pleasurable evening. In addition to that you can book the location for your private ceremony or marriage. Meanwhile the chapel is enjoying a very good reputation because of the wonderful ambience.

Kunst und Kultur

www.vogtland-kultur.de

Telefon +49 (0) 37422 2136
Telefax +49 (0) 37422 6836
vogtl.freilichtmuseum@t-online.de

Ihr Ansprechpartner
Your contact person
Frau Gabriele Maiwald, Manager
Vogtländisches Freilichtmuseum Landwüst

Zu einem interessanten und lehrreichen Rundgang lädt das **Vogtländische Freilichtmuseum Landwüst (3)** ein. In den vielen historischen Gebäuden erfährt der Besucher wie unsere Vorfahren gelebt haben, Tierhaltung betrieben, Felder und Wiesen bewirtschafteten und im Nebenerwerb Teile für den Musikinstrumentenbau fertigten. Empfehlenswert ist ein Spaziergang zu jeder Jahreszeit. Im historischen Backhaus können die Besucher selbst Brot backen oder zuschauen. An Sonntagen sorgt die beliebte Veranstaltungsreihe „Musik aus der Scheune" für beste Unterhaltung. Live-Musik mit Anspruch wird samstags im rustikalen Ambiente der Kulturtenne geboten. Lebendige Thementage vermitteln bei Vorführungen Wissens- und Sehenswertes zur Imkerei, zu Handwerk und Landtechnik, zu Kräutern und zur Ernte. Für Gruppen werden Führungen angeboten und Pauschalprogramme bereitgehalten.

We invite you for a very interesting and instructive tour in the **Vogtländisches Freilichtmuseum Landwüst (3).** In the various historical buildings the visitor is finds out, how many ancestors used to live there, used to keep animals, farmed fields and meadows and additional constructed parts of musical instruments . Recommendable is a walk to any season. In our historical baking-house the visitors can bake bread on your own or watch other people by doing this. On Sundays you can enjoy yourself with the production series "Musik aus der Scheune". Sophisticated Live Music is taken place on saturday in the "Kulturtenne". Even there you can experience the country style of the museum. „Days of a subject" convey very lively worth knowing and seeing contents like: beekeeping, handcraft, herbs and harvest home. We offer special conditions and guidance for groups.

Telefon +49 (0) 37465 41993
Telefax +49 (0) 37465 41825
grube-tannenberg@t-online.de

Ihr Ansprechpartner
Your contact person
Herr Steffen Gerisch, Manager
Besucherbergwerk „Grube Tannenberg"

Interessante Einblicke in die Bergbau - und Industriegeschichte des oberen Vogtlandes gespickt mit Legenden und Geschichten der Bergleute vermitteln Ihnen unsere Bergwerks-Führer im **Besucherbergwerk „Grube Tannenberg" (4)** auf einer unterirdischen Tour. Sehen Sie technische Zeitzeugen, die den Abbau der Schätze aus unseren Bergen in den verschiedensten Zeiten ermöglichte. Die eindrucksvolle Kulisse eines unterirdischen Sees ist der Höhepunkt einer jeden Führung. Auf 40.000 qm präsentieren wir Ihnen im **Vogtländisch – Böhmischen Mineralienzentrum** Steine und Edelsteine, ergänzt durch eine Edelsteinschleiferei, eine Naturkundeausstellung mit lebenden Reptilien, eine Lesegesteinshalde und vieles Interessantes mehr. Eine Wanderung zum nahe gelegenen Schneckenstein – der einzige Topasfelsen Europas - ist sehr empfehlenswert. Mit leckeren vogtländischen Gerichten bewirten wir Sie in unserer Erlebnisgaststätte „Zum alten Zechenhaus", welche auch für private Feiern genutzt werden kann.

Very interesting insights of mining - and the history of industry of the upper Vogtland added with legends and stories of the colliers you can get from our mining-guides in the **Besucherbergwerk „Grube Tannenberg" (4)** on a mining tour. See the technical contemporary witness, which allows you to understand the exploitations of the treasures of the soil in our region in different epochs. These most impressive scenery with a subterranean sea is the highlight of each guidance. On 40.000 square meters (9.88422 acres) we'd like to introduce you the **Vogtländisch – Böhmisches Mineralienzentrum** – there we inform you about gemstones and minerals, completed by gemstone cutter, natural history, living reptiles and many more highlights. You can take a walk to the highest mountain in our area the "Schneckenstein" – this is the one and only topaz-rock in europe – highly recommended!
With most delicious meals of the region we invite you in our country-style restaurant „Zum alten Zechenhaus", which you can hire for your own private celebrations too.

(5) (5) (6)

Telefon +49 (0) 3744 211815
Telefax +49 (0) 3744 213903
goeltzschtalgalerie@t-online.de

Ihr Ansprechpartner
Your contact person
Frau Romy Koglin, Manager
Göltzschtalgalerie Nicolaikirche Auerbach

Weit über die Grenzen der Stadt Auerbach hinaus bekannt ist die **Göltzschtalgalerie Nicolaikirche (5)**. Hier finden Veranstaltungen aller Genres statt. In wechselnden Ausstellungen wird meist zeitgenössische Kunst gezeigt, daneben werden auch Themen aus Umwelt- und Naturschutz, Politik und Geschichte präsentiert. Die gebotenen Veranstaltungen sollen möglichst vielen Interessierten gerecht werden. So finden Kammermusikabende, Kabarett- und Theatergruppen, Rock, Pop und Hip Hop, Jazz, Vorträge und Lesungen gleichberechtigt ein Podium. Für die Kleinsten werden viele Kreativangebote bereitgehalten. Das Haus kann ganz oder teilweise gemietet werden, als Ort mit stilvollem Ambiente für die Trauung, ob Saal oder Technik für eine Firmenpräsentation gebraucht werden oder nur die Kellerbar für den Geburtstag im kleinen Kreis.

Well known in the city of Auerbach and around the whole area is the **Göltzschtalgalerie Nicolaikirche (5)** Auerbach. Here you can experience lots of different events. In rotative exhibitions they show mostly contemporary pictorial art, as well as themes of environment and nature, politics and history. The offered events are arranged for all types of target groups and all different generations. So you can find chamber music, cabaret and theatre, rock, pop and hip hop, jazz, recitations and readings on equal terms on stage. For the little children we offer a lot of creative courses . You can hire a part or the whole house, for having a classy marriage ceremony and celebration afterwards, whether you need the hall or only the technical equipment for your company-presentation, we help you in any ways. Even the beautiful cellar is the right place to have an extraordinary birthday party.

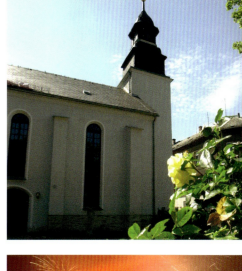
(5)

Telefon +49 (0) 3741 413290
Telefax +49 (0) 3741 411108

Ihr Ansprechpartner
Your contact person
Frau Angela Görner, Manager
Gelände an der Göltzschtalbrücke

Am Fuße der **Göltzschtalbrücke (6)** befindet sich ein Areal für verschiedenste Veranstaltungen. Die Kulisse dahinter ist gigantisch: Auf vier Etagen überspannen 81 Bögen die Göltzsch. Die größte Ziegelsteinbrücke der Welt gilt als technische und ästhetische Meisterleistung. Das Gelände vor der Brücke eignet sich für Open Air Konzerte, Zirkus, Performances, Firmenpräsentationen und Feste aller Art. Ein erhöhter Fotopunkt garantiert beste Ausblicke auf die Brücke. Die kleinen Gäste können sich auf dem Spielplatz, gestaltet aus vielen Ziegelsteinen, so richtig austoben. Ergänzt wird das Gelände mit Ziegelstein-Skulpturen deutscher und tschechischer Künstler.

Right in front of the **"Göltzschtal bridge" (6)** is an open air area prepared for different events. The scenery is sensational: Eightyone bows build on four floors are overstretching the valley of the "Göltzsch". The biggest red brick bridge of the world ranks as the most incredible masterpiece technical and aesthetically ways. The area in front of this bridge is very practical to arrange big events like concerts, company presentations and other different performances and festivals. An exalted point for taken photographs guarantees you the best view. Children can enjoy themselves on a playground made of bricks, just like the worlds biggest bridge. Further on, a couple of well known german and czech artists made brick - sculptures next to the footpath.

(6)

(6)

Das Vogtland – die klingende Ferienregion
The Vogtland Region – the Musical Holiday Area

Das Vogtland ist eine Region im südlichsten Teil des Freistaates Sachsen, im Viereldändereck zwischen Sachsen, Bayern, Thüringen und Böhmen. Zu früheren Zeiten war es das mittelalterliche Herrschaftsgebiet der Vögte, daher der Name. Geografisch liegt das Vogtland zwischen Fichtelgebirge, Erzgebirge und Thüringer Schiefergebirge. Über 70 vogtländische Orte tragen das Wörtchen „grün" im Namen. Verschiedene Landschaftsformationen mit sanften Hügeln, romantischen Bach- und Flusstälern, ausgedehnten Wäldern und buntblühenden Wiesen machen das Vogtland zu einem beliebten und abwechslungsreichen Ausflugsziel. Eine reiche Kulturlandschaft mit einmaligen Sehenswürdigkeiten prägt die Landschaft ebenso wie viele neu geschaffene touristische Attraktionen. Die Vogtland Arena in Klingenthal mit der modernsten Sprungschanze Europas (mehr dazu auf Seite 212), die neue Deutsche Raumfahrtausstellung in Morgenröthe Rautenkranz oder die Skiwelt Schöneck sollen nur drei Beispiele sein. Ein Geheimtipp ist auch der 220 Kilometer lange Vogtland Panorama Weg®, der in 12 Tagesetappen durch die schönsten Gebiete des Vogtlandes führt.

Wir stellen Ihnen mit den folgenden Zeilen einige ausgewählte Teilgebiete des Vogtlandes vor, die keinesfalls vollständig sind. Jedes prägt ein unverwechselbarer und besonderer Charakter, der die Vielseitigkeit des Vogtlandes ausmacht. Beginnen wir unsere kleine Rundreise im Musikwinkel. 350 Jahre ist die Tradition des Musikinstrumentenbaus im Vogtland tief verwurzelt. Bis heute werden hier alle Arten von Streich-, Zupf-, Holz- und Metallblasinstrumenten sowie Hand- und Mundharmonikas gebaut. In den Orten Klingenthal, Markneukirchen, Schöneck und Erlbach arbeiten über 100 meisterhafte Musikinstrumentenbauer, die sich bei der Entstehung der klingenden Kostbarkeiten gerne über die Schulter schauen lassen. Viele der familienbetriebenen Werkstätten arbeiten bereits in 5. und 6. Generation. Das Vogtland ist nicht nur Zentrum des deutschen Orchesterinstrumentenbaus, hier kann man auch hochkarätige Veranstaltungen, Internationale Musikwettbewerbe, Konzerte und Festivals mit einzigartigem Flair erleben. Ein besonders Erlebnis ist das Musikinstrumenten Museum in Markneukirchen. Die ca. 1.500 ausgestellten Instrumente entführen in klangvolle Welten der einheimischen Musikindustrie aber auch fremder Kulturen.

Die Stadt Klingenthal ist musikalisch durch den Harmonika- und Akkordeonbau bekannt. Als Musik- und Wintersportstadt ist sie ein interessantes Ausflugsziel. Zahlreiche internationale Spitzensportler begannen hier ihre sportliche Laufbahn. Mit der 36 km langen Kammloipe inmitten des Naturparks Erzgebirge/Vogtland besitzt das Vogtland eine der schönsten und schneesichersten Loipen Deutschlands. Ideale Bedingungen für Langlauf, Ski-Alpin und Snowboard machen auch die Region um Schöneck bei Wintersportlern sehr beliebt. Die neue Skiwelt Schöneck bietet modernste Sportanlagen für alle Anhänger des „weißen Sportes".

Unweit des Musikwinkels befinden sich die traditionsreichen sächsischen Staatsbäder Bad Elster und Bad Brambach. Insgesamt elf Mineralquellen und das heilende Naturmoor finden im königlichen Ambiente ihre Anwendung. Dabei werden medizinische Kompetenz und die Qualität der Angebote groß geschrieben. Bad Elster ist eine Kultur- und Festspielstadt mit royalem Flair und großem Kulturangebot. Exklusive Wellnessangebote, moderne Badelandschaften und sehr gastfreundliche Menschen sind ein unübertrefflicher Rahmen zum Wohlfühlen und Entspannen. Verträumt und idyllisch gibt sich das bekannte Radonbad Bad Brambach. Ein Geheimtipp

The Vogtland region is located in the most southerly part of the Free State of Saxony at the point where the states of Saxony, Bavaria, Thuringia and the Czech Republic meet. In earlier times it was governed by the medieval reeves (Vögte), hence the name. Geographically the Vogtland region is located between the Fichtel Mountains, the Ore Mountains and the Thuringian Slate Mountains. The names of more than 70 Vogtland villages include the word "grün" (green). Different geological formations with rolling hills, romantic valleys with streams and valleys, extensive forests and meadows with colourful flowers make the Vogtland region a popular and varied holiday destination. There is a wide selection of unique cultural events and many new tourist attractions have been created. The Vogtland Arena in Klingenthal with the most modern ski-jumping facilities in Europe (more on this on page 212), the new German Space Exhibition in Morgenröthe-Rautenkranz or the Schöneck Skiing World are just three examples of this. A secret not known to many people is the 220 kilometre long Vogtland Panorama Weg® (Path), which is divided up into 12 daily stages and takes people through the most beautiful areas of the Vogtland region.

We would like to write a few lines to introduce you to some of the parts of the Vogtland region, but this is not the whole story by any means. Each of them has a unique and special character, which helps to make up the variety of the Vogtland region. Let us start with a small tour of Musicon Valley. The tradition of making musical instruments in the Vogtland region has deep roots going back 350 years. All kinds of stringed, plucking, woodwind and brass instruments, accordions and mouth organs are still made here today. More than 100 master instru-

(Fotos/Photos by Tourismusverband Vogtland e.V., Text/Text by Archiv Tourismusverband Vogtland e.V., Silke Weidlich, Egelmann, J. Hesse, Thomas Harbig, Sächsische Staatsbäder GmbH)

Touristische Höhepunkte / Tourist Highlights

ment makers, who are happy to let people watch over their shoulders as they create their masterpieces, work in Klingenthal, Markneukirchen, Schöneck and Erlbach. Many of the family-run workshops are still working with fifth or sixth generation family members. The Vogtland region is not only a centre of orchestral instrument making in Germany, but it is also home to high-quality events, international music competitions, concerts and festivals with a unique flair. The Musical Instrument Museum in Markneukirchen is a special experience. The 1500 hundred instruments or so on display carry people away to musical worlds created by the local musical industry and also foreign cultures.

The town of Klingenthal is well-known in musical circles for its mouth organs and accordions. It is an interesting destination for music and winter sports. Many international top athletes began their sporting career here. The Vogtland region has one of the most attractive cross-country ski routes in Germany in the shape of the 36 km long ridge track at the heart of the Ore Mountains/Vogtland National Park – and snow is almost guaranteed. Ideal conditions for cross-country skiing, downhill skiing and snowboarding make the Schöneck area very popular with winter sports enthusiasts. The new Skiing World in Schöneck provides the latest skiing equipment for any enthusiast of snow sports.

The traditional spa towns of Bad Elster and Bad Brambach are located not far from Musicon Valley. A total of eleven mineral springs and the therapeutic natural moor mud are used in a royal atmosphere. Great importance is attached to medical expertise and the quality of the facilities. Bad Elster is a cultural and festival town with royal flair and a wide selection of culture. Exclusive wellness facilities, modern swimming pools and very hospitable people create an outstanding framework for people to feel at home and relax. The well-known radon spa at Bad Brambach is located in a dreamy and idyllic setting. This is a really exciting destination for all those who love romantic walks, the twittering of birds and a variety of natural surroundings.

Our journey takes us to the central Vogtland region, first to Adorf, the "gateway to the Upper Vogtland region". There is plenty to admire here: a unique collection on the history of river pearl oysters, a miniature exhibition of the Vogtland area ("Klein Vogtland") and the magnificent botanical gardens with their wealth of different plants. Not far from here is the "Sperken town of Oelsnitz", once Germany's biggest centre of carpet manufacturing. By the way, "Sperken" is the Vogtland expression for sparrows, as the residents of Oelsnitz are affectionately known. The recreation area at Pirk reservoir is situated very close to Oelsnitz.
Our journey continues to the sleepy villages of the Burgstein area. The peace and tranquillity of the former West German-East German border area is simply magical. The glistening white of St Clara's Chapel in Heinersgrün can be seen from a great distance. There is a certain mysticism about the village of Krebes with its picturesque castle ruins. The unique landscape, which inspired the local painter Hermann Vogel, has been attracting nature lovers, artists and people on outings for a long time.

Plauen is the largest city in the Vogtland region with approx. 70,000 inhabitants and it is also the business and cultural capital of the area. The city gained international fame

---

für alle, die romantische Spaziergänge, Vogelzwitschern und die Natur von Ihrer schönsten Seite lieben.

Die Reiseroute führt uns Richtung mittleres Vogtland, zunächst nach Adorf „dem Tor zum Oberen Vogtland". Eine einmalige Sammlung zur Geschichte der Flussperlmuschel, das Vogtland en miniature im „Klein Vogtland" und der herrliche artenreiche botanische Garten, können hier bewundert werden. Nicht weit entfernt befindet sich die „Sperkenstadt Oelsnitz", einst größter Teppichproduzent Deutschlands. Als „Sperken", wie die Einwohner von Oelsnitz liebevoll genannt werden, bezeichnet man im Vogtland übrigens Spatzen. Vor den Toren von Oelsnitz befindet sich das Naherholungszentrum Talsperre Pirk.
Weiter geht's in die verträumten Orte des Burgsteingebietes. Die Ruhe und Beschaulichkeit im ehemaligen deutsch-deutschen Grenzgebiet ist einfach bezaubernd. In hellem Weiß strahlt schon von weitem die Kapelle St. Klara in Heinersgrün. Dem Dörfchen Krebes mit den malerischen Burgsteinruinen, haftet eine gewisse Mystik an. Die einmalige Landschaft, die den Heimatmaler Herrmann Vogel inspirierte, zieht seit langer Zeit Ausflügler, Naturfreunde und Künstler an.

Mit ca. 70.000 Einwohnern ist Plauen die größte Stadt im Vogtland und zugleich wirtschaftliches und kulturelles Zentrum. Weltbekannt wurde die Stadt durch die „Plauener Spitze", welche 1900 auf der Weltausstellung in Paris mit einem Grand Prix ausgezeichnet wurde. Plauen ist eine lebendige Stadt voller Originalität und mit einladender Atmosphäre. Auch im Plauener Umland gibt es Sagenhaftes zu

Touristische Höhepunkte / Tourist Highlights

Tourismusverband Vogtland e.V.
Friedrich-Ebert-Str. 21 a
D-08209 Auerbach
Telefon + 49 (0) 3744 18886-0
Telefax + 49 (0) 3744 18886-59
info@vogtlandtourist.de
www.vogtlandtourist.de

entdecken. Hier lebt in Sachsens einziger Tropfsteinhöhle in Syrau der legendäre Drache Justus. Und selbst „der Mittelpunkt der Erde" ist nicht weit. Wer das nicht glaubt fährt nach Pausa. Im Rathaus des Ortes darf man die Erdachse bestaunen und diese unter Aufsicht der ehrenswerten „Erdachsendeckelschanierschmiernippelkommission" sogar schmieren.

Erfrischend und angesagt ist die Region um die Talsperre Pöhl. Aufgrund der herrlichen Natur um die tief eingeschnittenen Täler der Weißen Elster und der Trieb, wird das Gebiet auch „Vogtländische Schweiz" genannt. Über klassische Rundfahrten mit den Fahrgastschiffen „Pöhl" und „Plauen" bis hin zu Klettertouren in atemberaubender Höhe im Kletterwald Pöhl, zeigt sich hier nicht nur der Sommer von seiner sonnigsten Seite. Beliebtes Ausflugsziel für Wanderer und Radfreunde ist die landschaftlich reizvolle Umgebung um das Trieb- und Elstertal mit der berühmten Elstertalbrücke.

Östlich von Plauen durchzieht der Flusslauf der Göltzsch das Vogtland. In Netzschkau überspannt die größte Ziegelsteinbrücke der Welt – die Göltzschtalbrücke – das Flüsschen. Das phänomenale Bauwerk wurde 1846 – 1851 aus 26 Millionen Ziegeln erbaut und zählt bis heute als wahre technische Meisterleistung. Sie dient, ebenso wie die Elstertalbrücke, als Eisenbahnverbindung von Norden nach Süden. Nördliches Tor des Vogtlandes und Geburtsort der Theaterreformatorin Friederike Caroline Neuber ist die Stadt Reichenbach, die größte Stadt des Vogtlandkreises. Übrigens ist Reichenbach 2009 Gastgeber der Landesgartenschau in Sachsen. Märchenhafte Geschichten erzählt der Freizeitpark Plohn mit lustigen Attraktionen wie einer Wildwasserbahn, der Achterbahn „Silver Mine" oder Deutschlands verrücktestem Baumhaus.

Immer eine Reise wert ist das östliche Vogtland mit den Städten Auerbach, Rodewisch und Falkenstein. Der Schlossturm aus dem 12. Jahrhundert sowie die Türme der Stadtkirche „St. Laurentius" und der Katholischen Kirche „Zum Heiligen Kreuz" verhalfen Auerbach zum Beinamen „Drei-Türme- Stadt". Eingebettet in die Täler zwischen Göltzsch und Wernesbach liegt Rodewisch. Mittelpunkt der Stadt ist die Schlosshalbinsel mit Renaissanceschlösschen. Besonders beliebt bei Schulklassen, Vereinen und Gruppen ist der Waldpark Grünheide eine Freizeitwelt für Körper, Geist und Seele inmitten herrlicher Natur.

Im „Waldgebiet" endet unsere kleine Rundreise. Hier befindet sich Europas einziger Topasfelsen – der Schneckenstein. Die edlen Steine schmücken sogar die Krone der englischen Königin. Im Vogtländisch-Böhmischen Mineralogiezentrum sind interessante Ausstellungsstücke zu bestaunen und im Besucherbergwerk „Grube Tannenberg" erlebt man mit einem Schuss Bergmannshumor die Arbeit eines Gangerzbergwerkes des 20. Jahrhunderts. Und noch ein Tipp! Viel Wissenswertes über den Weltraum vermittelt auf anschauliche Weise die neue Deutsche Raumfahrtausstellung in Morgenröthe Rautenkranz

Das Vogtland ist eine vielseitige, interessante und zu jeder Jahreszeit reizvolle Urlaubsregion. Rund 10.000 Gästebetten stehen in familiären Pensionen, Ferienwohnungen und modernen Hotels mit sehr gutem Service bereit.

through "Plauen lace", which was awarded a "grand prix" at the World Fair in Paris in 1900. Plauen is a lively town with plenty of originality and it has an appealing atmosphere. There are also many legends to discover in the area round Plauen. The legendary dragon Justus lives in Saxony's only cave with stalactites and stalagmites in Syrau. And the "central point on earth" is not far away either. If you do not believe this, then go to Pausa. You can admire the earth's axis in the town hall here and even grease it under the supervision of the "Earth Axis Cover Hinge Greasing Nipple Commission"!

The area around Pöhl reservoir is refreshing and popular. It is also known as "Vogtland Switzerland" because of the magnificent natural surroundings with the deep valleys created by the White Elster and Trieb rivers. Summer is not the only time when visitors can enjoy the area on board the "Pöhl" or "Plauen" pleasure steamers or on a climbing expedition at a breath-taking height at the Pöhl Climbing Forest. The beautiful surrounding area near the Trieb and Elster valleys with the famous Elster Valley Bridge is a favourite destination for hikers and cyclists.

The river Göltzsch winds its way through the Vogtland region east of Plauen. The largest brick bridge in the world – the Göltzsch Valley Bridge – crosses the river in Netzschkau. This phenomenal construction was built during the period 1846 – 1851 and consists of 26 million bricks. It is one of the technical wonders of the world today. It is used by the railway line running north-south, just like the Elster Valley Bridge. The town of Reichenbach, the largest town in the Vogtland district, is the northern gateway to the Vogtland region and is the birthplace of the theatre reformer Friedericke Caroline Neuber. By the way, Reichenbach is hosting the National Horticultural Show in Saxony in 2009. Plohn Leisure Park, with its many fun attractions like a log flume, the "Silver Mine" roller coaster or Germany's craziest tree house, also illustrates many a fairy tale.

The eastern part of the Vogtland district with the towns of Auerbach, Rodewisch and Falkenstein is also worth a visit. The castle town dating from the 12th century and the towers of the St. Laurentius Church and the "Holy Cross" Catholic Church have given Auerbach the nickname the "three towers town". Rodewisch is embedded in the valleys between the rivers Göltzsch and Wernesbach. The central focus in the town is the Renaissance castle almost surrounded by water. Grünheide Forest Park is particularly popular with school classes, associations and other groups. It is a leisure park for body, soul and spirit set in magnificent scenery.

Our little journey ends in a forest. Here we find Europe's only topaz rock called the Schneckenstein. These precious stones even adorn the crown worn by the English queen. Visitors can admire interesting exhibits at the Vogtland-Bohemian Mineralogy Centre and they can gain some insight into the life of an ore miner in the 20th century at "Tannenberg Mine" with a touch of underground humour. And here is another tip! The new German Space Exhibition in Morgenröthe-Rautenkranz provides visitors with a great deal of information about the world of space in a very descriptive manner.

The Vogtland region is a varied, interesting and charming holiday region at any time of the year. Some 10,000 beds in family guest houses, holiday apartments and modern hotels with very good service are available to welcome visitors.

(Foto/Photo by Engelmann - Tourismusverband Vogtland e.V.)

(Übersetzung/Translated by David Strauss)

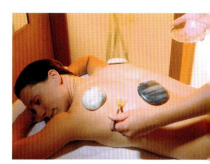

Tourist Highlights — 253

BAD ELSTER / BAD BRAMBACH — Wellness, Kuren, Kultur & Sport

Bad Elster and Bad Brambach – Wellness, Spas, Culture & Sports

Die sächsischen Staatsbäder Bad Elster und Bad Brambach, gelegen in der südlichsten Region des Vogtlandes, bilden ein Kompetenz-Zentrum für Wellness, Kuren, Kultur und Sport. Die Wirkung der vorhandenen natürlichen Heilmittel Moor und Mineralwasser hat Bad Elster seit mehr als 150 Jahren zu einem der traditionsreichsten Moor- und Mineralheilbäder Deutschlands werden lassen. Das benachbarte Bad Brambach ist für seine weltweit stärkste Radonquelle bekannt. Bereits die Sächsische Königsfamilie wusste die natürlichen Heilkräfte dieser Region zu schätzen und errichtete glanzvolle Bäderbauten, die einen nostalgischen Charme ausstrahlen.

Noch heute kann man dieses zauberhafte historische Ambiente genießen und dabei alles erleben, was man für Gesundheit und Wohlbefinden braucht. Neben klassischen Gesundheitsanwendungen mit Moor, Mineralwasser und Massagen findet man eine Vielzahl individueller Verwöhnprogramme, die bestens dafür geeignet sind, sich entspannt aus dem Alltag tragen zu lassen. Körper und Sinne werden in exklusiven Wellnessbereichen und im wohlfühlwarmen Wasser der Bade- und Saunalandschaften „Elsterado" und „Aquadon" umschmeichelt.

Beide Heilbäder bieten gemeinsam eine Vielzahl an Pauschalangeboten, die als Tages- und Mehrtagesangebote sowie als ein- und mehrwöchige Arrangements gebucht werden können. Vitalurlaub, Prävention und Klassische Kuren stehen dabei ebenso im Vordergrund wie Wellness sowie Kunst- und Kulturgenuss in einer der zahlreichen Veranstaltungsstätten.
Bisher einzigartig in Deutschland sind die in den Sächsischen Staatsbädern gebotenen berufsspezifischen JobFit®-Kuren, die nach den speziellen Bedürfnissen ausgewählter Berufsgruppen, zum Beispiel Lehrkräfte, Kraftfahrer, Bäcker, Floristen, Winzer oder Journalisten, ausgerichtet sind.

The Saxon State Spas at Bad Elster and Bad Brambach, located in the most southerly part of the Vogtland district, form a centre of expertise for wellness, spas, culture and sports. The effectiveness of the natural remedies in the shape of moor mud and mineral water has made Bad Elster one of the moor mud and mineral spas in Germany with the greatest traditions for more than 150 years. Neighbouring Bad Brambach is well-known for having the world's strongest radon spring. The Saxon royal family knew how to appreciate the natural healing powers of this region and built splendid spa buildings, which emit nostalgic charm.

This magical historical atmosphere can still be enjoyed today. People can experience everything they need to be healthy and feel at ease. The spas not only offer classical health applications with moor mud, mineral water and massages, but also a variety of individual programmes to spoil people; they are ideally suited to ensure that people can leave their everyday cares behind them. The body and senses are pampered in exclusive wellness areas and in the warm water of the "Elsterado" and "Aquadon" swimming baths and saunas.

Both spas jointly offer a variety of all-inclusive deals, which can be booked for a single day or several days or there are one-week or two-week arrangements. A break providing vitality or prevention and classical spa treatments are just as much part of the focus as wellness and the enjoyment of the arts and culture in one of the many cultural centres. The JobFit® spa treatments offered to specific professional groups at the Saxon State Spas are unique in Germany. They are directed at the special needs of particular professional groups – for example, teachers, drivers, bakers, florists, wine growers or journalists.

Infos & Buchungen/ Information & bookings:
Sächsische Staatsbäder GmbH
Bad Elster - Bad Brambach
Badstraße 6 · 08645 Bad Elster
Telefon + 49 (0) 37437 71111
Telefax + 49 (0) 37437 71222
info@saechsische-staatsbaeder.de
www.saechsische-staatsbaeder.de

(Fotos/Photos by Uwe Tölle Berlin, Text/Text by Sächsische Staatsbäder GmbH, Übersetzung/Translated by David Strauss)

Kultur- und Festspielstadt Bad Elster
The Cultural and Festival Town of Bad Elster

Kultur- und Festspielstadt Bad Elster: Das sind Kultur-Erlebnisse mit der besonderen Note! Nachdem Bad Elster 1324 erstmals urkundlich Erwähnung fand, wurde hier 1669 die erste Quelle medizinisch untersucht und dem damaligen Landesherren Herzog Moritz von Sachsen-Zeitz gewidmet. Diese Heilquelle und das Naturmoor wusste 1795 auch Johann Wolfgang von Goethe in seinem Epos „Herrmann und Dorothea" zu würdigen. Der Bade- und Kurbetrieb und damit der Publikumsverkehr begann in Bad Elster zu Beginn des 19. Jahrhunderts: So wurde bereits 1817 die heutige Chursächsische Philharmonie gegründet und schon 1818 die ersten „Curen" angeboten. Im Jahr 1848 wurde Bad Elster dann zum „Königlich Sächsischen Staatsbad" erhoben und zählt seitdem zu den traditionsreichsten und renommiertesten Heilbädern Deutschlands.

Aufbauend auf dieser Tradition hat sich das Sächsische Staatsbad Bad Elster in den letzten Jahren erfolgreich zu einer Kultur- und Festspielstadt mit internationalem Flair entwickelt. Grundlage dieser Entwicklung und der großen Publikumsresonanz ist seit Königszeiten das herausragende, qualitative Veranstaltungsangebot in dem historisch gewachsenen „königlichen" Ambiente Bad Elsters. Besonders die sieben, in Parklandschaften gelegenen historischen Veranstaltungsstätten („Festspielmeile der kurzen Wege"), wie das berühmte König Albert Theater, das herrlich im Wald gelegene NaturTheater, das repräsentative Königliche Kurhaus, die KunstWandelhalle und die drei Musikpavillons bieten dem Publikum einen speziellen, einzigartigen Rahmen für kulturelle Erlebnisse mit dem gewissen Etwas.

The cultural and festival town of Bad Elster: cultural events of a special quality are available here! After Bad Elster was first mentioned in official documents in 1324, the first spring was checked medically in 1669 and was dedicated to the ruler of the area at the time, Duke Moritz of Saxony-Zeitz. Johann Wolfgang von Goethe knew how to appreciated this therapeutic spring and the natural moor mud in his epic "Herrmann and Dorothea" written in 1795. The swimming and spa business and therefore public operations began in Bad Elster at the start of the 19th century. Today's Chursächsisch Philharmonic was founded in 1817 and had offered its first "cures" in 1818. Bad Elster was then elevated to a "Royal Saxon State Spa" in 1848 and has been one of the most renowned spas in German with the greatest traditions.

Based on this tradition, the Saxon State Spa at Bad Elster has successfully developed into a cultural and festival town with international flair over the past few years. The basis of this development and the huge response from the public are the outstanding, high-quality events in the historically developed "royal" atmosphere of Bad Elster. The seven historical event centres surrounded by parks ("the festival mile with everything on the spot") like the famous King Albert Theatre, the open-air theatre in magnificent surroundings in the woods, the representative Royal Spa House, the KunstWandel Hall and the three music pavillons offer the public a special and unique framework for cultural events with a certain extra.

(Fotos/Photos by Chursächsische Veranstaltungs GmbH, Text/Text by Chursächsische Veranstaltungs GmbH, Übersetzung/Translated by David Strauss)

Touristische Höhepunkte / Tourist Highlights

Die Churs ächsische Veranstaltungsgesellschaft führt hier mit hoher Besucherresonanz jährlich über 1.000 (Kultur-) Veranstaltungen aller Genres mit berühmten Künstlern, Ensembles und internationalen Stars durch. Das umfassende Angebot reicht dabei von Konzerten der hier beheimateten Churs ächsischen Philharmonie, Oper, Operette, Ballett und Schauspiel u. a. der Frauenkirche und Semperoper Dresden, des Staatsschauspiels Dresden sowie der Landesbühnen Sachsen bis hin zu Entertainment, Kabarett, Galas, Bällen, Kunstausstellungen, Präsentationen, Kongressen und Sportveranstaltungen.

„Königlich genießen" kann das Publikum insbesondere bei den etablierten Veranstaltungsreihen wie den „Churs ächsischen Mozartwochen" (März), dem „Churs ächsischen Sommer – Sächsisch|Böhmisches Kulturfestival" (Mai – Oktober), den „Internationalen Jazztagen" (August), den „Churs ächsischen Festspielen" (September) und den „Churs ächsischen Winterträumen – Ein Fest für alle Sinne" (Dezember) sowie bei ausgewählten Spitzenveranstaltungen. Abgerundet wird das Angebot im dem renommierten Moorheilbad mit den passenden Verwöhnangeboten aus Wellness und Kulinarium. Damit ist Bad Elster ganzjährig ein lohnenswertes Reiseziel!

The Churs ächsisch Event Organisation Company puts on more than 1,000 (cultural) events of all kinds featuring famous artists, ensembles and international stars – and they are hugely popular with visitors. The extensive programme ranges from concerts given by the Churs ächsisch Philharmonic, opera, operetta, ballet and drama etc performed by the Church of Our Lady and the Semper Opera House in Dresden, the State Theatre in Dresden and state theatres in Saxony and even includes entertainment, cabaret, galas, balls, art exhibitions, presentations, congresses and sports events.

The public can particularly "enjoy a royal occasion" at the established series of events like the "Churs ächsisch Mozart Weeks" (March), the "Churs ächsisch Summer – Saxon|Bohemian Culture Festival" (May – October), the "International Jazz Days" (August), the "Churs ächsisch Festival" (September) and the "Churs ächsisch Winter Dreams – a Festival for all the Senses" (December) as well as selected top events. The range of events is rounded off by suitable pampering in the wellness and culinary departments. So Bad Elster is worth visiting all year round!

Alle Informationen über Bad Elster und die Region sowie zu den Veranstaltungen erhalten Sie über: **Ticketshop Bad Elster** Servicecenter der Churs ächsischen Veranstaltungs GmbH im Königlichen Kurhaus Bad Elster

You can obtain any information about Bad Elster, the region and the events from: **Ticketshop Bad Elster** the service centre of the Churs ächsisch Event Organisation Company in the Royal Spa Centre in Bad Elster

Telefon +49 (0) 37437 53 900
Telefax +49 (0) 37437 53 90 54
ticket@chursaechsische.de
www.chursaechsische.de

Öffnungszeiten: täglich
Opening times, daily:
10.00 bis 12.00 Uhr u. 14.00 bis 18.00 Uhr
10 a.m. – noon and 2 p.m. – 6 p.m.

IFA-Schöneck Hotel & Ferienpark

So machen Ferien Spaß
How to Enjoy your Holiday!

Herzlich willkommen im IFA-Schöneck Hotel & Ferienpark. In 800 Meter Höhe, auf dem »Balkon des Vogtlandes«, genießen Sie einen imposanten Panoramablick über das Vierländereck Sachsen, Bayern, Thüringen und Böhmen. Besonders beliebt ist der Ferienpark bei Wanderern, Rad- und Wintersportlern, weil sich unmittelbar an das Gelände anschließend Wander- und Radwege, Loipeneinstiege, Skipisten und Lifte befinden. Im Hotel lädt ein großes Gastronomie-, Freizeit- und Erlebnisangebot zu unvergesslichen Ferientagen ein.

Während Ihres erlebnisreichen Urlaubs wohnen Sie in komfortablen Hotelzimmern und Ferienwohnungen mit behaglicher Atmosphäre und moderner Ausstattung: Satelliten-TV mit hauseigenem Info-Kanal, Telefon, Dusche/WC und in den Ferienwohnungen zusätzlich Elektroherd, Kühlschrank, Kaffeemaschine und Spüle in der Küchenzeile.

365 Tage im Jahr Badespaß pur bietet das tropische Erlebnis-Badeparadies. Tauchen Sie ein ins Lagunenbecken oder erleben Sie Riesengaudi im Wellenbecken, auf der Riesen- oder Wildwasserrutsche. In der warmen Jahreszeit erfrischen Sie sich beim Schwimmen im Freibad. Entspannung pur finden Sie im Whirlpool in der Badelandschaft, in der Saunalandschaft mit vier verschiedenen Saunen oder in der Wellness-Oase bei Massage, Fango-Packung oder Entspannungsbad.

Spiel, Sport und gute Laune gehören zum Urlaub. Die Angebote im IFA-Ferienpark reichen von Tennis und Squash, über Beachvolleyball verschiedenen Kinderspielplätzen, dem Fitness-Center, Bowling- und Kegelbahn bis hin zu einem Kletter- und Seilbahnwald. Im Playcenter spielen Sie Tischtennis, Dart oder Billard. Einzigartig in Deutschland: die Space-Station, eine fantastische Welt aus Dschungel-Abenteuer und atemberaubendem Weltraumflug.

Kulinarische Genüsse erleben Sie in den Restaurants und Bars. Besonders beliebt ist das PPS – Pizza-Pasta-Steak-Restaurant. In den Panorama-Restaurants Pfau und Bella Vista wählen Sie aus vogtländischen und internationalen Gerichten. Der idyllische Wintergarten ist ein Cocktail-Paradies und im Sommer können Sie das alles auch auf der Terrasse genießen. Stimmungsvoll klingen Ihre Urlaubstage im Beer- & Whisky-Kontor mit urigem Pub-Ambiente aus, das auch zu Disco- und Tanzabenden einlädt.

Mit fünf Seminarräumen in separater Tagungslandschaft (33 bis 240 m²) und Bankettsälen bis 350 Personen ist der IFA-Schöneck Hotel & Ferienpark auch ein etabliertes Seminar- und Tagungshotel. Für Clubs, Vereine und Busunternehmen (ab 20 Personen) werden außerdem umfangreiche, attraktive Pauschalprogramme angeboten. Fordern Sie deshalb den Tagungs- bzw. Gruppenreisen-Prospekt an.

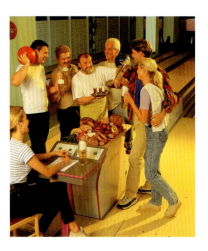

(Fotos/Photos by IFA-Schöneck Hotel & Ferienpark)

IFA-Schöneck Hotel & Ferienpark

» *Die Komfort-Ferienanlage mit dem großen Freizeit- und Erlebnisangebot!.* «

» *The comfort holiday centre with a huge variety of leisure and adventure facilities!* «

A warm welcome to the IFA-Schöneck Hotel & Holiday Park. Situated 800 metres above sea level on what is known as the "Vogtland Balcony", you can enjoy an impressive panoramic view over the German states of Saxony, Bavaria and Thuringia and the Czech Republic. The holiday park is particularly popular with hikers, cyclists and winter sports enthusiasts, because there are hiking and cycle paths, cross-country ski tracks, ski slopes and lifts right next to the holiday park grounds. A huge variety of catering, leisure and adventure facilities in the hotel mean guests will spend an unforgettable holiday here.

During your exciting holiday here, you will stay in comfortable hotel rooms and holiday flats with a cosy atmosphere and modern facilities: satellite TV with an in-house information channel, telephone, shower/WC and the holiday flats also have an electric cooker, a fridge, a coffee machine and a sink in the kitchenette.

The tropical adventure pool provides fun for swimmers 365 days a year. Dive into a lagoon pool or enjoy the fun in the wave pool or on the large or white water slides. If the weather is warm, you can cool down by swimming in the outdoor pool. You will find pure relaxation in the whirlpool in the swimming pool, the sauna area with its four different kinds of sauna or in the wellness oasis enjoying a massage, a fango pack or a relaxing bath.

Games, sport and a good atmosphere are part and parcel of a holiday. The facilities at the IFA Holiday Park range from tennis and squash to beach volleyball and different children's playgrounds, the fitness centre, a ten-pin bowling alley and even a climbing and ropeway adventure area in the woods. You can also play table tennis, darts or billiards in the games centre. And this is something here that is unique in Germany: the space station, a fantastic world of jungle adventures and breath-taking space flights.

There are plenty of culinary delights to be savoured in the restaurants and bars. The PPS – Pizza-Pasta-Steak – restaurant is particularly popular. And you can choose from Vogtland and international dishes in the Pfau and Bella Vista panoramic restaurants.

The idyllic conservatory is a cocktail paradise and in summer you can enjoy all this on the outside patio. You can spend your holiday evenings in the beer and whisky bar with its original pub atmosphere and there are disco and dance evenings to enjoy here too.

With its five seminar rooms in a separate conference area (33 – 240 m²) and banqueting halls catering for up to 350 persons, the IFA-Schöneck Hotel & Holiday Park is also an established seminar and conference hotel. Comprehensive, attractive, all-inclusive programmes are also available for clubs, associations and bus companies (for at least 20 people). So just ask for the conference or group travel brochures.

IFA-Schöneck Hotel & Ferienpark
Hohe Reuth 5
D-08261 Schöneck/Vogtland
Telefon +49 (0) 37464 30
Telefax +49 (0) 37464 31000
info@ifahotels.com
www.ifahotels.com
www.lopesanhotels.com

So schön ist Schöneck – und das zu jeder Jahreszeit
Schöneck is Beautiful – at Any Time of the Year

Schöneck, der höchstgelegene Ort im Vogtland ist staatlich anerkannter Erholungsort und wird auch als „Balkon des Vogtlandes" bezeichnet. Der idyllische Ort bietet eine moderne touristische Infrastruktur, welche den Erholungssuchenden genauso anspricht wie den sportlich orientierten Urlauber. 120 Kilometer markierte Wanderwege und 130 Kilometer Bike-Wege laden zur Bewegung in der Natur ein. Und all das bei immer wieder sich bietenden herrlichen Panoramausblicken. Nicht umsonst lautet unser Slogan: „Schöneck – Ferien mit Panoramablick".

Vielfältige Möglichkeiten findet der sportlich orientierte, aktive Gast. Das Erlebnisbad Aquaworld, Tennishalle und -plätze, Squash, Bowling und vieles mehr sorgen für einen erlebnisreichen Urlaub auf dem „Balkon des Vogtlandes".

Das gut markierte Wanderwegnetz lädt zum Erkunden der Umgebung mit zahlreichen Sehenswürdigkeiten ein. Auch ausgewiesenen Nordic-Walking-Strecken stehen zur Verfügung.

Auch aktive Radfahrer kommen in und um Schöneck auf ihre Kosten. 130 Kilometer lang ist das Mountainbike-Netz von Schöneck, welches sowohl leichte Rundtouren für Familien wie auch anspruchsvolle Trails für Mountainbiker bietet. Schöneck ist Etappenort der CRAFT BIKE Trans Germany, dem ersten Mountainbike-Etappenrennen quer durch die schönsten deutschen Mittelgebirge. 500 Teams nehmen an diesem Mountainbike-Spektakel teil. Auf der langen Zielgeraden in Schöneck wird ihnen natürlich ein gebührender Empfang bereitet.

Für Abwechslung gesorgt ist in Schöneck natürlich auch im Winter. Die „Skiwelt Schöneck" mit mehreren Pisten, Loipen und anderen Winterangeboten ist nicht nur bei Urlaubern sehr beliebt, sondern auch bevorzugtes Ziel vieler Tagesgäste, die das umfassende Angebot in Schöneck schätzen. Attraktion der Skiwelt ist die Skischaukel im neu erschlossenen Skigebiet Hohe Reuth/Streugrün. Ebenso auf ihre Kosten kommen die Freunde des Langlaufs. Ein 40 Kilometer langes Loi-

Schöneck, the highest town in the Vogtland region, is a recognised holiday centre and is also called the "balcony of the Vogtland region". The idyllic town provide modern tourist facilities, which appeal to holiday-makers wanting to rest and relax or those who want plenty of sporting action. 120 kilometres of marked footpaths and 130 kilometres of cycling paths are available for people to enjoy the natural surroundings. And then there are the magnificent views from many locations. It is no accident that our motto is: "Schöneck – Holidays with a Panoramic View".

Active holiday-makers will find plenty to do here. The Aquaworld swimming baths, indoor and outdoor tennis facilities, squash, bowling and a great deal more ensure that people will have something to write home about during their holiday at the "balcony of the Vogtland region".

The well marked network of footpaths encourages people to discover the region with its many sights. Nordic walking routes are also marked.

Active cyclists will also get their money's worth in and around Schöneck. The town's mountain bike network is 130 kilometres long and provides both easy circular trips for families and challenging trails for mountain bikers. Schöneck is a stage finishing point for CRAFT BIKE Trans Germany, the first mountain bike stage race right through the most attractive central uplands in the country. 500 teams participate in this mountain bike spectacle. A worthy reception awaits them on the long straight finishes in the town.

Schöneck also has plenty to offer guests who come in winter. The "Schöneck Skiing World" with several pistes, cross-country skiing tracks and other winter sports is not only popular with holiday-makers, but also with people on day trips. They fully appreciate the facilities in the town. The cable car on the skiing area just opened at Hohe Reuth/Streugrün is one of the attractions of the Skiing World. But fans of cross-country skiing do not lose out either. The cross-country skiing network is 40 kilometres long and machines create the tracks, so

(Fotos/Photos by Silke Weidlich, Text/Text by Touristinformation Schöneck, Stadtverwaltung Schöneck, Übersetzung/Translated by David Strauss)

Schöneck – Balkon des Vogtlandes

CRAFT BIKE Trans Germany: Eine Etappe der Tour führte die Mountainbiker durch Schöneck. Im Bild die Erstplatzierten auf der Schönecker Hauptstraße. (Foto: Harald Sulski)

pennetz, das maschinell gespurt wird, ermöglicht herrliche Touren durch den zauberhaften Winterwald. Zudem ist Schöneck Ausgangsort der bekannten 36 Kilometer langen Kammloipe nach Johanngeorgenstadt – eine der schönsten und schneesichersten Loipen Deutschlands.

Nach der sportlichen Betätigung locken zahlreiche Wellnessangebote in den Ferienpark Schöneck. In der Badelandschaft, der Sauna oder bei einer wohltuenden Massage findet man Ruhe und Entspannung und tankt Energie für die nächsten Aktivitäten.

Die vogtländische Gastlichkeit können Urlauber in einer der zahlreichen Gaststätten genießen. Bei einem Besuch im Schönecker Heimat- und Zigarrenmuseum ist viel Interessantes aus der Schönecker Ortsgeschichte zu erfahren.

Auch die Schönecker Ortsteile haben sich in den vergangenen Jahren verstärkt auf den Tourismus eingestellt. In Schilbach beispielsweise wurde mit dem Ausbau des ehemaligen Rittergutes und mit der Neugestaltung des sehenswerten Schlossparkes ein Kleinod geschaffen, das einen Besuch lohnt.

Bei einem Rundgang durch Schöneck werden Sie feststellen, was sich in den vergangenen Jahren alles entwickelt hat. Die höchstgelegene Stadt des Vogtlandes zeigt sich in schmuckem Kleid. Der Albertplatz mit dem Sagenbrunnen, die neu gestaltete Hauptstraße oder der Burgenspielplatz sind Beispiele für die gelungene Gestaltung der Stadt.

Die weitere Entwicklung Schönecks wird sich in besonderem Maße einem Thema widmen: Kneipp. Schöneck möchte sich in Zukunft als Kneipp-Kurort profilieren. Entsprechende Angebote können bereits genutzt werden. Dazu gehören das Terrainkurwegenetz, die ausgewiesenen Nordic-Walking-Strecken oder der Kneippgarten an der Schule mit Kräutern und Wassertretbecken. Weitere Gesundheitsangebote werden folgen.

Willkommen in Schöneck, auf dem Balkon des Vogtlandes! Verbringen Sie bei vielfältigen Möglichkeiten Ferien mit Panoramablick! Im Tourismusbüro erhalten Sie Informationen für Ihren Urlaub in Schöneck.

that people can enjoy magnificent trips through the magical winter forests. Schöneck is also the starting point for the well-known ridge track to Johanngeorgenstadt – which is 36 kilometres long and one of the most attractive in Germany, where snow is almost guaranteed.

After all these sports activities there are plenty of wellness facilities at the holiday park in Schöneck. Visitors can rest or relax at the swimming pool, the sauna or during a refreshing massage – and recharge their batteries for the next activities.

Holiday-makers can enjoy Vogtland hospitality in one of the many restaurants. And there is plenty to discover about Schöneck's past during a visit to the Schöneck Local History and Cigar Museum. The various districts of Schöneck have also increasingly responded to tourism over the past few years. The redevelopment of the former manor house and the newly designed Castle Park have made Schilbach a jewel that is really worth seeing.

During a stroll through Schöneck you will discover what has been accomplished over the past few years. The highest town in the Vogtland region has spruced itself up. Albert Square with its Legend Well, the newly designed high street or the Castle playground are just a few examples of the successful renovation work completed in the town.

Schöneck is also devoting a great deal of time and energy to developing its Kneipp facilities. Schöneck would like to advertise itself at a Kneipp spa centre in future. Some of the facilities can already be used. They include the network of spa footpaths, the Nordic walking routes or the Kneipp garden at the school with its herbs and paddling pool. Other health facilities will follow.

Welcome to Schöneck on the balcony of the Vogtland region! Spend your holidays enjoying a variety of facilities with a panoramic view! You can obtain information about your holiday in Schöneck from the tourist office.

Kontakt/Contact:
Tourismusbüro Schöneck
Bauhofstraße 1
D-08261 Schöneck
Telefon +49 (0) 37464 330011
Schneetelefon
Snow phone + 49 (0) 37464 82000
Telefax +49 (0) 37464 330013
info@schoeneck.eu
www.schoeneck.eu

Der Himmel auf Erden – Deutsche Raumfahrtausstellung
Heaven on Earth – The German Space Travel Exhibition

So dusselig kann Hein Blöd doch gar nicht sein. Wie sonst hätte die knuddelige Plüsch-Ratte ausgerechnet den Weltraum erobern können? Kosmonaut Reinhold Ewald hatte 1997 bei seinem Weltraumflug mit Sojus TM-25 den tapsigen Leichtmatrosen aus der bekannten Kindersendung „Käpt'n Blaubär" als Maskottchen mit an Bord genommen. Und Hein Blöd ist nicht die einzige Fernseh-Trickfigur mit realer Weltraumerfahrung. Bereits 1978 begleitete das mittlerweile gesamtdeutsche Sandmännchen den Vogtländer Dr. Sigmund Jähn, den ersten deutschen Kosmonauten, bei seinem Start mit Sojus 31. Die beiden Kosmos geprüften Puppenfiguren sind heute Bestandteil der rund 1000 Exponate umfassenden neuen Deutschen Raumfahrtausstellung in Morgenröthe-Rautenkranz. Ende März 2007 eröffnet, hat sie sich zu einem wahren Besuchermagnet entwickelt. Denn bereits fünf Monate später konnte die europaweit einzigartige Exposition über Raumfahrt und Weltraumforschung den 50.000 Besucher begrüßen. „Das hat unsere kühnsten Erwartungen weit übertroffen", freut sich Museumsleiterin Romy Mothes über die große Resonanz.

1979, ein Jahr nach dem Weltraumflug von Sigmund Jähn, war im alten Bahnhof seines Heimatortes eine ständige Ausstellung zum ersten gemeinsamen Kosmosflug DDR-UdSSR eröffnet worden. Nach der Wende wurde die Exposition zu einer gesamtdeutschen Ausstellung erweitert. Seither ist Morgenröthe-Rautenkranz das Mekka für alle Raumfahrtfans. Dazu trug vor allem auch die Gründung des Betreiber-Vereins „Deutsche Raumfahrtausstellung" bei, der 1992 unter Schirmherrschaft der Gemeinde aus der Taufe gehoben wurde. Heute engagieren sich weit

Hein Blöd, a puppet and star of a German children's programme, cannot really be as foolish as he seems on the TV show. Or how else could the cuddly rat have been able to conquer space? Cosmonaut Reinhold Ewald took the clumsy seaman from the famous children's show "Käpt'n Blaubär" as a mascot on board his Soyuz TM-25 rocket for a space flight in 1997. And Hein Blöd is not the only TV cartoon star with real space experience. The Sandman, which is now a character known to children across Germany, accompanied Sigmund Jähn, the first German cosmonaut, who was born in the Vogtland region, when he lifted off on his Soyuz 31 mission back in 1978. The two puppets with space experience are now part of the new German Space Travel Exhibition in Morgenröthe-Rautenkranz, which has about 1,000 exhibits. Opened in March 2007, it has now become a real magnet for visitors. Only 5 months after its opening, the only exhibition on space travel and space exploration in Europe was able to welcome its 50,000th visitor. "This has exceeded our highest expectations," says museum director Romy Mothes commenting on the response.

One year after Sigmund Jähn's space flight in 1979, a permanent exhibition to commemorate the first joint flight in space between East Germany and the Soviet Union was opened at the old station in his home town. After German reunification, the exhibition was extended to cover the whole of the country. Ever since then, Morgenröthe-Rautenkranz has become the Mecca of all space travel fans. One of the reasons for this success was the creation of the German Space Travel

(Fotos/Photos by Igor Pastierovic, Text/Text by Ekkehard Glaß, Übersetzung/Translated by David Strauss)

Deutsche Raumfahrtausstellung

über 200 nationale und internationale Mitglieder in diesem Verein und nahezu alle deutschen Astronauten und Kosmonauten sind Mitglied.

Die seit 1997 jährlich stattfindenden „Raumfahrttage" des Vereins finden weltweit Beachtung.

Mit der Zeit wurden die Ausstellungsräume im alten Bahnhof viel zu klein. „Schon seit Anfang der 90er Jahre gab es die Vision von einem neuen Standort für unsere Ausstellung", blickt Romy Mothes zurück. 2007 dann sollte der Traum Wirklichkeit werden. Dank eines rührigen Gemeinderates mit seinem Bürgermeister Konrad Stahl an der Spitze, des Engagements der Vereinsmitglieder und einer komplexen, finanziellen Förderung durch die EU, den Freistaat Sachsen, den Vogtlandkreis und den Kulturraum Vogtland ist unweit des alten Standortes auf 1000 Quadratmetern für rund 2,1 Millionen Euro die neue „Deutsche Raumfahrtausstellung" entstanden. An der Grundkonzeption, den Nutzen der Weltraumforschung einer breiten Öffentlichkeit nahe zu bringen, hat sich nichts geändert. Schwerpunkte sind die Darstellung der Geschichte der Raumfahrt von den Anfängen bis zur Gegenwart, die unbemannte und bemannte Raumfahrt sowie vor allem die Missionen mit deutscher Beteiligung. „Aber die neue Ausstellung ist mehr denn je eine Schau für die gesamte Familie - für alle Altersklassen eben", macht die Museumsleiterin aufmerksam. Hier wird Raumfahrt im wahrsten Wortsinn „populärwissenschaftlich" erlebbar gemacht. So können jetzt zum Beispiel weiterführende Ausstellungs-Informationen von PC-Terminals abgerufen werden. Für die Jüngsten gibt's Spiele und Quizrunden zum Thema. Per Mausklick kann die aktuelle Wettersituation über Europa dargestellt werden, direkt vom Satelliten aus

Exhibition Association in 1992 with the backing of the town authorities. Today more than 200 national and international members support this association and almost every German astronaut and cosmonaut is a member.

The annual "Space Travel Days" held by the society have attracted global attention since 1997.

In the course of time the exhibition rooms in the old station building proved to be far too small. "We had a vision of a new location for our exhibition back in the 1990s," Romy Mothes recalls. This dream would finally become reality in 2007. Thanks to the commitment of the town council and mayor Konrad Stahl, the efforts made by the association's members and a complicated funding programme provided by the European Union, the Free State of Saxony, the Vogtland District and the Vogtland Cultural Region, the new building for the "German Space Travel Exhibition" has been constructed. It was built on an area measuring 1000 m² close to the former location and cost approximately € 2.1 million. The initial concept of bringing space travel and exploration closer to a broader public has not changed. The main emphasis is still on the history of space travel from its beginnings to the present day, manned and un-manned space flights and the space missions involving German personnel. "But the new exhibition is much more a show for the whole family – for any age group," the museum director stresses. Space travel is turned into popular science here in the true sense of the word. Additional information on the exhibits can now be accessed on computer terminals, for example. There are games and quizzes on this theme for young visitors. The current weather

Deutsche Raumfahrtausstellung

» *Natürlich hat auch Sigmund Jähn seine ganz spezielle Erinnerungsecke in der Ausstellung – mit Sandmann, versteht sich.* «

» *Obviously Sigmund Jähn has his very own corner in the exhibition, full of memorabilia, including the Sandman.* «

dem All eingespeist. Als absoluter Renner hat sich das Raumfahrtkino erwiesen, wo interessante Filmbeiträge zum Thema laufen. Zwei digitale Waagen zeigen Besuchern ihr spezifisches Gewicht an, das sie auf dem Mond oder dem Mars hätten und welches um ein Vielfaches leichter ist, als auf der Erde. „Besonders Damen nutzen die Waagen gern", plaudert Frau Mothes aus dem Nähkästchen.

Die Ausstellung lebt von den vielen neuen Exponaten: zum Beispiel Originalnachbildungen der Raumfahrtanzüge von Juri Gagarin, von John Glenn oder Neil Armstrong, aber auch eine Vielzahl an Modellen vom Sputnik 1 über das Space Shuttle bis hin zu den europäischen Arianeträgerraketen, von denen eine sechs Meter hohe Nachbildung ein echter Hingucker ist. Aktuell wird der Stand des Ausbaus der Internationalen Raumstation ISS im Modell dokumentiert. Bis 2010 soll die ISS fertiggestellt sein - im All, wie im Museum. Natürlich hat auch Sigmund Jähn seine ganz spezielle Erinnerungsecke in der Ausstellung – mit Sandmann, versteht sich. Und im Freigelände bietet der Planetenpark Gelegenheit, sich über Größenverhältnisse und Entfernungen in unserem Planetensystem anschaulich zu informieren. Glanzstück der Ausstellung aber ist das Original des Basisblocks des MIR-Trainingsmoduls, der erlebbar und nachvollziehbar macht, wie eng und begrenzt die Arbeits- und Lebenswelt eines Kosmonauten im All ist.

Auch wenn die neue „Deutsche Raumfahrtausstellung" wahrhaft noch neu ist, fertig ist sie nicht. „Denn wie sich die Raumfahrt weiter entwickelt, so muss natürlich auch unsere Ausstellung immer weiter entwickelt werden", blickt Romy Mothes voraus und verweist auf große Holzkisten, die nur noch aufs Auspacken warten. Ein kürzlich angeliefertes Ingenieurmodell des 1. deutschen Satelliten namens „Azur" harrt seiner Aufstellung. Und dann muss natürlich auch noch der für Ende 2007 geplante Flug des deutschen Astronauten Hans Wilhelm Schlegel zur ISS museal aufgearbeitet und dokumentiert werden. Ob Schlegel wohl auch ein Maskottchen mit nach „Oben" nimmt?

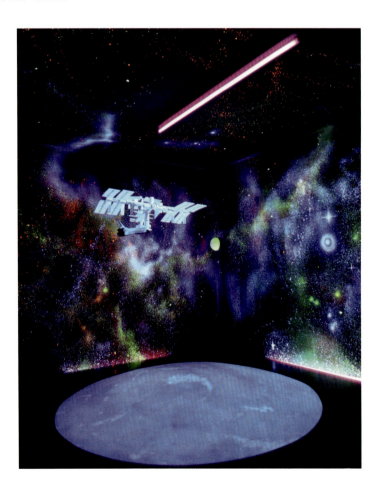

situation over Europe can be shown with data coming directly from the satellite – all at the click of a mouse. The space travel cinema showing interesting films about this subject is a real hit. There are also two pairs of scales which show visitors how much they would weigh on the moon or on Mars – far less than on earth. "Women in particular like these scales," Mrs Mothes comments.

The exhibition comes alive with its many new exhibits; these include original reproductions of the space suits worn by Yuri Gagarin, John Glenn or Neil Armstrong. But a vast number of models from Sputnik I to the Space Shuttle or the European Ariane rockets, one of them over 6 metres high, also catch people's attention. There is a model reconstructing the current state of the work on the International Space Station or ISS. The ISS is due to have been completed by 2010 – in space and at the museum. Obviously Sigmund Jähn has his very own corner in the exhibition, full of memorabilia, including the Sandman. And the open-air site at the museum in the planet park gives visitors the chance of experiencing the different proportions and distances in our planetary system in a vivid manner. However, the highlight of the exhibition is the original base unit of the MIR training module. This clearly shows visitors how small the working and living space is for a cosmonaut in space.

Even though the new "German Space Travel Exhibition" is still new, it is far from complete. "As space exploration evolves, our exhibition will also have to continue to develop," explains Romy Mothes and points at a wooden box that is waiting to be unpacked: A recently delivered engineering model of the first German satellite "Azur" is still waiting to go on display at the exhibition. And then there is also the flight by German astronaut Hans Wilhelm Schlegel to the ISS, scheduled for the end of 2007. This will have to be documented and recorded in the museum. Who knows whether Schlegel may also take a mascot with him "up there"?

Blick in die Unterwelt
Glimpse into the Underworld

Das Vogtland ist reich an unterirdischen Sehenswürdigkeiten, die in den letzten Jahren zunehmend für den Tourismus erschlossen wurden.

Im idyllischen Göltzschtal befindet sich die **Tropfsteingrotte Alaunwerk Mühlwand**. Eine halbe Stunde dauert der Rundgang durch das im September 2001 eröffnete Besucherbergwerk. Zwischen 1691 und 1827 existierte an dieser Stelle ein Alaunwerk, von dem die heute noch vorhandene unterirdische Anlage sowie Überreste einer Röstbühne, alte Fundamente, ein Mundloch und eine Halde künden. Eine Gruppe Naturfreunde erforschte in den Jahren 1957-1960 das unterirdische Stollen- und Höhlensystem. Es wurden verschüttete Gänge freigelegt und entwässert. Die entdeckten Höhlen, farbigen Tropfsteine und bunten, sinterhaltigen Gesteine waren von einzigartiger Schönheit. Nach Bodenproben und unter Beachtung der bestehenden Sicherheitsvorschriften öffnete man einige Eingänge wieder. Aufgrund eines zum damaligen Zeitpunkt geplanten Talsperrenbaus mussten die Arbeiten eingestellt werden. Dem ehrenamtlichen Engagement des 1998 gegründeten Fördervereins sowie der engagierten Arbeit von ABM-Kräften ist es zu danken, dass die Anlage heute öffentlich begangen werden kann.

Alaun ist ein Salz der Schwefelsäure, das zum Blutstillen, als Gerb- und Holzschutzmittel, zum Färben, Beizen und Leimen und für viele andere Zwecke benutzt wurde. Sachzeugen dieses alten Gewerbes sind heute rar.
www.alaunwerk.de

The Vogtland region is rich in underworld attractions and they have increasingly been opened up for tourism over the last few years.

The **Mühlwand Alum Mine stalactite** cave is located in the idyllic Göltzsch valley. The tour of the mine, which was opened to visitors in September 2001, takes half an hour. There was an alum mine here between 1691 and 1827; evidence of this can be found in the shape of the underground mining equipment and remains of a charcoal-like pile, old foundations, an entrance hole and a waste heap. A group of nature lovers explored the underground system of galleries and caves from 1957 to 1960. Blocked gangways were uncovered and drained. They discovered caves, multi-coloured stalactites and colourful rocks containing sinter of extraordinary beauty. After taking samples of the soil and paying attention to the safety regulations, some of the entrances were reopened. But this work had to be halted on account of the plans that existed at that time to build a reservoir here. Thanks to the voluntary commitment of the development association set up in 1998 and the excellent work carried out by people on job creation schemes, visitors can now come to the site.

Alum is a sulphuric acid salt; it was used to stanch blood, colour, stain and glue substances, it was used as a tannery and wood preservative and for many other purposes. There are few people who know about this art today.

Öffnungszeiten/Service
Tropfsteingrotte Alaunwerk Mühlwand (direkt an der historischen Bergstrecke zwischen Reichenbach/Rotschau und Buchwald/Mühlwand im Mittleren Göltzschtal)
Regelmäßige Führungen: Sonnabends und sonntags von 13 bis 16 Uhr, im Juli/August täglich.
Außerhalb der Öffnungszeiten nach Anmeldung unter Telefon (03765) 521898, 13986 und 0162 1774538, post@alaunwerk.de

(Fotos/Photos by Verein Tropfsteingrotte Alaunwerk Mühlwand/Reichenbach e.V., Igor Pastierovic, Vogtland-Kultur GmbH, Drachenhöhle Syrau, Text/Text by Petra Steps, Übersetzung/Translated by David Strauss)

Ausflugstipps

(1)

(2)

(3)

Das Vogtland hat jedoch noch ein zweites Beispiel parat: Das **Alaunbergwerk „Ewiges Leben" in Plauen (1)**. Eine Stunde dauert die Führung, an der sogar Rollstuhlfahrer teilnehmen können. Bei konstanten 9 Grad Celsius und 92 Prozent Luftfeuchte werden begehbare Teile auf 650 Metern vorgestellt. Der weitere Ausbau läuft. Um die Besucher kümmert sich der Vogtländische Bergknappenverein zu Plauen. Gemeinsam haben die Kumpels das Alaunbergwerk auf Vordermann gebracht, einen Luftschutzkeller ausgebaut und einen historischen Zollkeller mitten im Herzen von Plauen hergerichtet. Die drei Sehenswürdigkeiten haben maßgeblichen Anteil daran, dass Plauen 2005 den ersten Platz und damit 30.000 Euro beim Innenstadtwettbewerb „Ab in die Mitte – Die Cityoffensive Sachsen 2005" gewann, mit dem Projekt „Plauen entdecken – über und unter Tage".
www.alaunbergwerk-plauen.de

Das bekannteste **Besucherbergwerk** im Vogtland ist die **„Grube Tannenberg" (2)**. Ihre Geschichte hängt eng mit dem Zinnbergbau zusammen. Im Mittelalter wurde das Zinn über Tage abgebaut. Erst im 18. Jahrhundert entstand der Stollen, der seit 1996 begangen werden kann. Während der einstündigen Führungen erfahren die Gäste allerhand Wissenswertes zum Thema Bergbau in der Region. Höhepunkt ist die Besichtigung eines riesigen Hohlraumes mit 50 Metern Höhe, 30 Metern Breite und einer Länge von 60 Metern, in dem sich noch ein See mit bis zu 70 Metern Tiefe befindet. Er gilt als einer der größten durch Bergbau entstandenen Hohlräume Sachsens.
www.schneckenstein.de
www.vogtland-kultur.de

Sagenhaft geht es in der **Drachenhöhle Syrau (3)** zu. Sie wurde 1928 ganz zufällig bei Arbeiten im Steinbruch entdeckt – durch das Verschwinden eines Meißels in der Tiefe. Die Gemeinderäte reagierten blitzschnell und beschlossen innerhalb einer Woche den Ausbau der Touristenattraktion, nach reichlich sechs Monaten wurde die Freigabe gefeiert. Die Drachenhöhle Syrau ist die einzige Schauhöhle Sachsens und gilt als eine der schönsten Tropfsteinhöhlen Deutschlands. Justus, der Drache erwartet ganzjährig seine Gäste, lediglich im Dezember und Januar gibt es einige Schließtage. 2008 ist ein ganz besonderes Jahr für die Höhle, denn gleich zwei Jubiläen stehen an: der 80. Jahrestag der Entdeckung und der Eröffnung. Übrigens kann man in der Drachenhöhle auch heiraten. Etwas für das Auge hält die Laser-Show bereit, die jedoch nur zu bestimmten Zeiten angeboten wird.
www.drachenhoehle.de

(1)

But the Vogtland region has a second example of this historic process: the **"Eternal Life" alum mine in Plauen.** The guided tour lasts one hour and is even accessible to people in wheelchairs. 650 metres of the mine can be accessed; the temperature is a constant 9 degrees Celsius with 92% humidity. Efforts are being made to open up more of the mine. The Vogtland Miners Association in Plauen looks after visitors. The miners have tidied up the alum mine, expanded an air-raid shelter and an historic underground bonded cellar right at the heart of Plauen. The three places of interest played a major role in Plauen gaining first place and € 30,000 in the inner-city competition entitled "The 2005 Saxon City Offensive – To the Centre of Town" with its project called "Discovering Plauen Above and Below Ground".

The best known **exhibition mine** in the Vogtland region is the **"Tannenberg Mine"**. Its history is closely linked to tin mining. Tin was extracted at open-cast mines in the Middle Ages. An underground gallery was not built until the 18th century and people have been able to enter this again since 1996. Visitors discover all kinds of information about the mining activities in the region during the guided tour that lasts one hour. The highlight is a visit to a huge cavern, which is 50 metres high, 30 metres wide and 60 metres long. It contains a lake that is 70 metres deep in places. It is one of the largest caverns created by mining work in Saxony.

The **Dragon's Cave at Syrau** is shrouded in legend. It was discovered by chance by workers in the quarry in 1928 – when a chisel disappeared into the depths. The town council reacted very quickly and decided to develop the tourist attraction within one week; it was opened to the public six months later. The Dragon's Cave at Syrau is the only one in Saxony that can be visited and it is one of Germany's most attractive underground caves with stalactites and stalagmites. Justus the dragon receives his guests all year round – but the cave is closed for a few days in December and January. 2008 is a very special year for the cave with two jubilees coming up: the 80th anniversary of its discovery and opening. It is also possible for couples to get married in the dragon's cave. The laser show is also a wonderful sight, but can only be seen at special times.

Außenansicht Hans-Gerber-Haus

Ein besonderes Handwerk hautnah erleben
Experiencing Special Skills Close Up

Am 23. Februar 2008 jährt sich zum 125. Mal der Tag, an dem der Gewerbeschullehrer Paul Apian-Bennewitz zur Gründung eines Gewerbemuseums in Markneukirchen aufrief. Das Sammeln von Musikinstrumenten aller Zeiten und Völker sah er neben dem Anschaffen von Rohmaterialien, Werkzeugen und einer Fachbibliothek als bedeutungsvoll für die Stadt an, die seiner Meinung nach durch den Instrumentenbau einzigartig ist, aber allein durch die geografische Lage viele Nachteile hat. Ihm war von Anfang an bewusst, dass die Sammlung sowohl für die einheimischen Instrumentenbauer als auch für Besucher der Stadt von großem Interesse sein wird.

3,5 Millionen Gäste aus aller Welt haben das Museum seit seiner Unterbringung im „Paulus-Schlössel" im Jahr 1942 besucht. Die Sammlung wächst ständig und umfasst zurzeit über 4.000 Exponate, darunter 3.200 Musikinstrumente sämtlicher Kontinente. Im vergangenen Jahr konnte die Ausstellung um ein originales Handelskontor einer 1834 in Markneukirchen gegründeten Exportfirma und Instrumentenbauwerkstätten (Zupfinstrumenten- und Bogenbau) erweitert werden. Mehrmals im Jahr finden hier Vorführungen der heute tätigen Instrumentenbaumeister statt.

Was die Ausstellung so sehr interessant macht, ist ihre Vielseitigkeit. Neben den allgemein bekannten Musikinstrumenten findet man in jeder Abteilung Unikate und Kuriositäten. Einmalig ist die gestreckte Tuba, die mit einem Schallstückdurchmesser von über einem Meter jeden Besucher im Foyer begrüßt. Das Riesen-Piano-Akkordeon, das 1938 im benachbarten Zwota für die Artistengruppe Doorlay gebaut wurde, ist ebenfalls eine einzigartige Meisterleistung. Von den kleinsten Geigen von nur 56 mm Größe bis zum extragroßen Kontrabass, von den üblichen Materialien wie Holz und Messing bis hin zu Plexiglas, von den zartklingendsten Instrumenten bis hin zur Straßenorgel ist fast alles vertreten, was die Welt der Musikinstrumente so bunt und für den Laien ebenso interessant macht wie für den Kenner.

The 125th anniversary of the day when the vocational training college teacher Paul Apian-Bennewitz called for the founding of an industrial museum in Markneukirchen is on 23 February 2008. He believed that it was important to create a collection of musical instruments from every age and people and acquire raw materials and tools and set up a specialist library for the town, which is unique on account of its instrument making, but suffers many disadvantages simply from its geographical location. He was aware from the outset that the collections would be of great interest to local instrument makers and visitors to the town.

3.5 million people from all over the world have visited the museum since it moved to the "Paulus Schlössel" in 1942. The collection of exhibits is growing all the time and now numbers more than 4,000, including 3,200 musical instruments from every continent on the planet. The exhibition was expanded in 2006 by the addition of an original trading room from an export company and musical instrument workshops set up in 1834 (plucking instruments and bow making). Guided tours by current master instrument makers take place here several times a year.

The variety of the exhibition is what makes it so interesting. Visitors not only see familiar musical instruments, but they discover unique objects and items. There is the unique stretched tuba, which welcomes each visitor in the foyer with a bell that measures more than one metre in diameter. The huge piano accordion, which was made in neighbouring Zwota for the artists' group called Doorlay in 1938, is also a unique masterpiece. Visitors will find almost everything here from the smallest violins measuring just 56 mm to the extra large double bass, from normal materials like wood or brass to perspex, from instruments that sound so delicate to a barrel organ – and this makes the world of musical instruments so colourful and interesting for lay people and connoisseurs alike.

Gefördert durch den Kulturraum Vogtland als regional bedeutsame Einrichtung

Musikinstrumenten Museum
der Musikstadt Markneukirchen
Bienengarten 2
D-08528 Markneukirchen
Telefon   +49 (0) 37422 2018
Telefax   +49 (0) 37422 6023
info@museum-markneukirchen.d
www.museum-markneukirchen.de

(Fotos/Photos by Frank Fickelscherer-Faßl, Text/Text by Heidrun Eichler, Übersetzung/Translated by David Strauss)

Goldmuseum
The Vogtland Gold Museum in Buchwald – A True El Dorado

Das Vogtländische Goldmuseum Buchwald – Ein Eldorado Einen Kindheitstraum hat sich Sven Kreher gemeinsam mit seiner Frau Tabea im Wohnhaus der Familie in Buchwald erfüllt: Im Sommer 2006 eröffneten beide das Vogtländische Goldmuseum & Naturalienkabinett, das sich über das Treppenhaus, eine ehemalige Wohnung und einen Teil des Außengeländes erstreckt. Inspiriert wurde der Initiator durch eine alte Karte mit Goldfundstellen im Vogtland, die er im Alter von zwölf Jahren im Museum der Mylauer Burg gesehen hatte. Wenn es früher hier Gold gab, dann müssen auch heute noch Spuren davon zu finden sein, dachte sich Sven Kreher und ging vor etwa zehn Jahren in vogtländischen und thüringischen Bächen auf die Suche. Schon ein Jahr später fand er ein Prachtstück: den größten existierenden Naturgoldnugget von sächsischem Boden. Er wiegt 2,263 Gramm und ist gemessen an üblichen Funden von etwa 0,4 Milligramm ein echter Riese.

Die Pläne zum Einrichten des Museums reiften, als in der Wohnung der Krehers alle Vitrinen aus den Nähten platzten und die Funde sowie Ankäufe ein Schattendasein in Kartons fristen mussten. Außer Goldwäscher ist Sven Kreher auch Fossiliensammler und hat im Laufe von etwa 30 Jahren eine ganze Menge an Raritäten und Kuriositäten angehäuft.

Die Museumsführung beginnt vor dem Haus. Dort wird in großen Bottichen Gold gewaschen. Die Gäste dürfen auch selbst an die flachen Goldwaschpfannen. Anschließend können die Objekte unter dem Mikroskop angeschaut werden. Mit Goldwaschrinnen wird demonstriert, wie es einst beim Goldrausch am Klondike River zugegangen sein muss.

Im Mittelpunkt der Sammlung stehen natürlich Goldfunde. Dazu kommen mineralogische, naturkundliche und kulturgeschichtliche Exponate, zum Beispiel Fossilien von Dinosauriern und Mammuts, Meteoriten, eine Insektensammlung oder Mikroskop-Präparate. Besonders für Schulklassen und kleine Gäste gibt es einiges zum Anfassen, wie Bärenknochen, versteinertes Holz oder ein Haifischgebiss. Ein hervorragendes Anschauungsmaterial ist eine Sammlung des Periodensystems der chemischen Elemente mit 87 von derzeit nachgewiesenen 111 verschiedenen „Vertretern".
www.vogtlandgold.de

Sven Kreher has fulfilled his childhood dream with his wife Tabea in their family residence in Buchwald: they opened the Vogtland Museum of Gold and Natural History in the summer of 2006. The museum is located in the stairway, a former apartment and part of the outside of their house. The founder of the museum was inspired by an old map with the sites where gold was found in the Vogtland region, which he saw in the museum at Mylau Castle at the age of 12. Sven Kreher thought that if gold had been there in the past, it must have left traces that can still be seen now. So he started his search for gold in streams in the Vogtland region and the state of Thuringia about ten years ago. Only one year later he found a real beauty: the largest existing natural gold nugget found in Saxony. It weighs 2.263 grams and, compared to the usual findings that weigh about 0.4 milligrams, it is a real giant.

The idea of opening a museum originated when all the display cabinets in the Kreher's apartment were bursting at the seams and any finds and acquisitions had to wile their time away in cardboard boxes. Besides being a gold prospector, Sven Kreher also collects fossils and he has accumulated quite a collection of rare and strange items over the past 30 years.

The tour of the museum starts in front of the house. Visitors can watch gold panning in tubs and can use the flat gold pans themselves. Afterwards what has been found can be examined under a microscope. Gold panning channels illustrate what life must have been like during the Gold Rush along the Klondike River. The exhibition concentrates on discoveries of gold. But it also has exhibits that are important for mineralogy or natural and art history, such as fossils of dinosaurs and mammoths, meteorites, an insect collection or microscope slides. There are a lot of exhibits that school children or younger guests can touch: the bones of a bear, petrified wood or a set of shark's teeth. Another superb exhibit is a collection of the Periodic Table of Elements with 87 of the 111 chemical elements that have been proven to exist.

(Fotos/Photos by Petra Steps, Text/Text by Petra Steps, Übersetzung/Translated by David Strauss)

Bergbaumuseum – Bergbau hautnah
Mining Museum – Mining from Close Up

Der Bergbautechnik im Osten Deutschlands hat sich Michael Straub aus Netzschkau verschrieben. Jahrelang sammelte, sägte und hämmerte der Hobbybergmann, bis er 2002 mit seiner Idee in die Öffentlichkeit ging. 2004 wurde das private Museum offiziell eröffnet. Seitdem geben sich vor allem Schulklassen, Neugierige und Leute vom Fach die Klinke in die Hand.

Im Museum wurden die Räume ähnlich wie in einem Bergwerk gestaltet, nur dass alles viel kleiner und sauberer ist. Die Führung beginnt in der Kaue, dem Umkleideraum der Bergleute, in dem die Kleidungsstücke originalgetreu an der Decke hängen. Auf Wunsch ist hier das Umkleiden möglich. Weiter geht es in die nachgebaute Lampenstube. Ein weiterer Teil ist der Grubenwehr gewidmet. Dort befinden sich Rettungsgeräte der Grubenwehr wie zum Beispiel Atemgeräte und ein Schleifkorb, mit dem verletzte Bergleute aus der Gefahrenzone gebracht wurden. In einem Selbstretterregal stehen die Atemmasken der Kumpel für den Notfall. Weiterhin ist eine Hängebank mit Förderkorb dargestellt. Über diesen Weg gelangten die Bergleute mit ihren Arbeitsmaterialien und Gerätschaften untertage und die geförderten Erze aus der Grube heraus. Eine Grundstrecke des Bergwerks, das Unter-Tage-Magazin mit Werkzeugausgabe und Materiallager werden ebenfalls gezeigt. Für allgemeine Belustigung, manchmal auch Verblüffung, sorgt die so genannte Kübelstation, in der eine Bergmann-Puppe gerade ihr „Geschäft" verrichtet. Über eine Leiter geht es direkt „vor Ort", also zum Arbeitsplatz der Bergleute. Eine Schrapperbahn sorgt für die Beförderung des gesprengten Haufwerkes. Die gemütliche Steigerstube bietet Platz für etwa 25 Personen, aber auch für zahlreiche Ausstellungstücke.

Ehemaligen Wismut-Kumpeln steht manchmal das Wasser in den Augen, wenn sie die vielen Zeitzeugen sehen, die sie einst bei ihrer schweren Tätigkeit unter Tage begleiteten. Manch einer kommt dann noch einmal nach Netzschkau und bringt Dokumente, Fotos oder Ausrüstungsgegenstände mit, weil er sie bei Michael Straub gut aufgehoben weiß. So vergrößert sich die Sammlung nach und nach, genau so, wie das Museum immer weiter wächst. Demnächst werden weitere Räume im Keller dazukommen.
www.vogtlaendisches-bergbaumuseum.de
(Führungen nur nach Voranmeldung)

Michael Straub from Netzschkau has devoted his energy to mining techniques in Eastern Germany. The amateur miner collected, sawed and hammered for years until he went public with his idea in 2002. The private museum was officially opened in 2004. Since then school groups, inquisitive people and experts in this field enjoy opening the door.

The rooms in the museum have been designed as if they were in a mine – but everything is much smaller and cleaner. The guided tour starts in the locker room, the miners' changing room, where original clothes still hang from the ceiling. People can change here if they wish. Then visitors continue into the lamp room. Another part of the museum is devoted to the mine rescue brigade. There people will find rescue equipment – breathing apparatus and rescue basket used to remove injured miners from the danger zone. The miners' breathing masks for emergencies are on a self-rescue shelf. There is also a pit head with a suspended basket for taking people down the mine. The miners and their working equipment and tools were taken underground in this way and the mined ore was brought out of the mine. A bottom road in a mine, the underground store house where tools were issued and materials were stored, is also on display. The so-called bucket station, where a miner's puppet is doing its "business" also causes general laughter and sometimes even amazement. A ladder leads straight to where the miners are working. A conveying system moves the broken material that has been blasted out. The cosy pit deputy's room has space for about 25 people, but also many exhibits. Tears sometimes come to the eyes of former Wismut miners when they see the many items that once accompanied them during their heavy work underground. Some of them then come back to Netzschkau and bring documents, photos or items of equipment because they know that they will be well cared for by Michael Straub. In this way the collection is gradually expanding, just as the museum is growing. More rooms in the cellar will be added to it soon.

(Fotos/Photos by Petra Steps, Text/Text by Petra Steps, Übersetzung/Translated by David Strauss)

Schloss Schönberg – ein Besuch lohnt sich
Schönberg Castle – Worth a Visit

„Was du ererbt von deinen Vätern hast, erwirb es, um es zu besitzen. Was man nicht nützt, ist eine schwere Last ...", heißt es in Goethes Faust. Wie das mit dem historischen Erbe und seiner Nutzung ist, davon kann Familie Rubner in Schönberg ein Lied singen – eins, das nicht nur nach „Jauchzet, frohlocket" klingt. Im Jahr 2000 kauften sie das Schloss in einem Zustand, der die Bezeichnung katastrophal rechtfertigt.

Wer das Kleinod heute besichtigt, der trifft auf eine liebevoll restaurierte Gebäudehülle, ein Schloss-Café und ein Trauzimmer mit wiederhergestellten Wandmalereien nach Originalbefunden sowie familiär gestaltete Führungen durch die Schlossherrn. Die Geschichte des Schlosses geht bis ins 13. Jahrhundert zurück. Aus dieser Zeit stammt der Turm, der vermutlich zur Überwachung des Handelsweges von Norden bis Genua diente. 1563 wurde um das Bauwerk herum ein Schloss gebaut, das ursprünglich von einem Wassergraben umgeben war. Der Turm dient heute als dekoratives Treppenhaus. Im oberen Geschoss befindet sich ein Turmzimmer mit wunderschöner Aussicht bis weit ins Böhmische.

Ab 1484 gehörte das Rittergut Schönberg der Familie von Reitzenstein. Die letzte Besitzerin, Pia Magyari von Reitzenstein (1876 – 1945/46) wurde nach Rügen deportiert. Das Inventar ging unwiederbringlich verloren. Durch das beherzte Eingreifen eines Kreisfunktionärs wurde wenigstens der bereits geplante Abriss des Schlosses verhindert. Zu DDR-Zeiten reichte die Nutzung von Wohnung, Gemeindeamt, Post, Arztzimmer bis zu Schule oder Kinderferienlager. Die neuen Besitzer sind froh, dass sie den hochbetagten und inzwischen verstorbenen Sohn der Baronin noch kennenlernen durften, denn er konnte viele Geschichten erzählen.

Günther Rubner stammt aus Schönberg und kehrte gemeinsam mit seiner Frau Hildegard aus Würzburg in die frühere Heimat zurück. Gemeinsam mit Restauratoren und der Denkmalbehörde bemühen sich die Eigentümer ständig um Kompromisse zwischen historischen Befunden, neuzeitlichen Vorschriften und Nutzungskonzepten. Es lohnt sich, von Zeit zu Zeit nach dem Baufortschritt zu schauen, denn im Schloss warten noch mehrere Räume auf ihre Restaurierung und ein großer Nachlass mit wertvollen Möbeln, Gemälden und Einrichtungsgegenständen auf die dauerhafte Ausstellung. Außerdem ist das 2006 eröffnete Café ein echter Geheimtipp.

www.schloss-schoenberg.info

"What you have inherited from your forefathers, acquire and take possession of it. What you do not use is a heavy burden ..." is a quotation from Goethe's Faust. The Rubner family in Schönberg could sing a song about their historical inheritance and its use – but it would not be one that just has a message of joy and happiness. They bought the castle in 2000 in a condition, which justifies the use of the term "catastrophic".

Anybody who sees the jewel today will find a lovingly restored shell of a building, a castle café and a marriage room with restored wall paintings matching the originals found here and informal guided tours given by the lord of the castle. The history of the castle goes back to the 13th century. The tower stems from this period – it was presumably used to guard the trade route from the north to Genoa. A castle, which was originally surrounded by a moat, was built around the structure in 1563. The tower now serves as a decorative stairway. There is a tower room on the upper floor with a wonderful view right into the Czech Republic.

Schönberg Manor belonged to the von Reitzenstein family from 1484 onwards. The last owner, Pia Magyari von Reitzenstein (1876-1945/6) was deported to Rügen. All the fixtures were lost for ever. At least one plucky district official in East German times intervened and prevented the demolition of the castle, for which plans had been drawn up. In East German days, the building was used as an apartment, the municipal office, the post office, a doctor's surgery and even a school or children's holiday centre. The new owners are delighted that they were able to get to know the baron's son, who was very old and has now died. He was able to tell them many stories.

Günther Rubner comes from Schönberg and returned to his former home with his wife Hildegard from Würzburg. The owners are constantly seeking to find compromises with restorers and the listed buildings authority regarding historical finds, new regulations and plans for using the building. It is worth while going to see how the work is progressing from time to time, because many rooms in the castle still have to be restored and there is a huge estate with valuable furniture, paintings and fixtures that is waiting to be exhibited. A visit to the café, which was opened in 2006, is highly recommended.

(Fotos/Photos by Petra Steps, Text/Text by Petra Steps, Übersetzung/Translated by David Strauss)

Das kleinste der Welt
The Smallest in the World

Kennen sie das kleinste Musikinstrumenten-Museum der Welt? Es steht im Vogtland. Genauer gesagt, in Mehltheuer bei Familie Karl-Heinz und Regina Teuschler in der Hohe Straße 9.

Auf 32 Quadratmetern im ausgebauten Keller des Wohnhauses werden über 270 historische Instrumente gezeigt. Das älteste ist ein Jagdhorn aus dem Jahre 1662, das kleinste eine Mundharmonika in Größe eines Lippenstiftes. Zu den Besonderheiten der Ausstellung zählen auch ein original Edison-Phonograph und ein Walkman aus dem Jahres 1913. Historische Musikliteratur, Poster und Requisiten vervollständigen die nostalgische Musiklandschaft. Während der einstündigen Führung können Sie auch die Schauwerkstätte besuchen, in der Zupf-, Streich- und Zungeninstrumente hergestellt werden können. Ab und an veranstalten Teuschlers Schellackabende, bei denen die Besucher in Erinnerungen schwelgen können.

2007 feierte das Musikinstrumentenmuseum sein zehnjähriges Bestehen. Karl-Heinz Teuschler, der bis zum Neubau der Kolonnaden auf der Plauener Bahnhofstraße sein Musikgeschäft führte, hat das Museum mit etwa 80 historischen Instrumenten eröffnet. Heute zählt seine Sammlung fast 200 Raritäten mehr. Jüngste Errungenschaften des gelernten Akkordeonbauers sind beispielsweise ein vierchöriges Akkordeon aus dem Jahre 1880, eine Harmonette, 1850 in Italien gebaut, und eine Zither, 80 Jahre alt und mit Intarsien versehen.

Das kleinste Museum dieser Art wurde 2001 ins Guinessbuch der Rekorde aufgenommen. Seither hat den Teuschlers diesen Eintrag niemand streitig gemacht. Karl-Heinz Teuschler führt jeden Besucher gern durch seine Ausstellung. Jedoch ist eine telefonische Anmeldung angeraten: 037431/4159

Have you heard of the smallest Musical Instrument Museum in the world? It is in the Vogtland region – to be exact, in Mehltheuer, Hohe Strasse 9, where Karl-Heinz and Regina Teuschler live.

There are 270 historical instruments on display in the cellar that measures 32 square metres. The oldest is a hunting horn dating from 1662; the smallest a mouth organ the size of lipstick. The museum's unique exhibits include an original Edison phonograph and a walkman from 1913. Historical musical literature, posters and requisites make up the nostalgic musical collection. During the hour-long tour of the museum, you can visit the exhibition workshop where plucking, stringed and reed instruments would be made. Now and again, the Teuschlers organise gramophone record evenings when visitors can reminisce about the past.

This year, the museum celebrated its tenth birthday. Karl-Heinz Teuschler, who had a music shop until the Colonnade Shopping Centre was rebuilt in Plauen's Bahnhofstrasse, opened the museum with about 80 historical instruments. Another 200 rare items have now been added to the collection. The trained accordion maker's most recent acquisitions include a four voice accordion dating from 1880, a harmonette small busker's organ built in Italy in 1850 and a zither which is 80 years old and inlaid with intarsia.

The smallest museum of its kind was included in the Guinness Book of Records in 2001. So far nobody has challenged the entry. Mr Teuschler enjoys taking visitors round the exhibition. But it is best to make an appointment in advance. The telephone number is 037431/4159.

(Fotos/Photos by Igor Pastierovic, Text/Text by B. Kempe-Winkelmann, Übersetzung/Translated by David Strauss)

Ein Mal im Jahr „Piepshow"

"Peepshow" Once a Year

Natur- und Jagdausstellung im Schloss Leubnitz

Das 1796 im frühklassizistischen Stil erbaute Schloss mit seinem reizvollen Landschaftspark in Leubnitz ist auch für Naturfreunde einen Ausflug wert. Seit dem Jahr 2000 schuf man in acht Räumen eine ständige Ausstellung mit dem Ziel, dem Besucher Jagd und Naturschutz als eine Einheit näher zu bringen. Das Zimmer mit dem Thema „Natur erleben mit allen Sinnen" besitzt besondere Anziehungskraft – nicht nur für Kinder. In spielerischer Form kann man sich an mehreren Stationen über unsere heimische Tier- und Pflanzenwelt Wissen aneignen. Seit dem Frühjahr 2007 können Besucher ein Mal jährlich in der „Leubnitzer Piepshow" die gefiederten Bewohner des Schlosses bei ihrem Nist- und Brutverhalten beobachten. Außerdem gibt es seit dem Sommer 2007 das Modell eines Teichbiotopes zu betrachten und eine Tafel, an welcher man mit Hilfe von Magnetbildern die Vögel unserer Heimat ihrem natürlichen Lebensraum zuordnen kann. In anderen Räumen werden Trophäen aus Spanien, Sibirien, der Mongolei und Nordamerika sowie Großantilopen und andere Tiere Afrikas und Australiens gezeigt. Kombiniert wird das Ganze mit einer Gemäldegalerie bekannter vogtländischer Tiermaler. Im „Weißen Saal" des Schlosses finden klassische Konzerte statt. Das Schloss wird von einem 12 Hektar großen Landschaftspark umgeben, welcher 1890 angelegt wurde. Überwiegend einheimische Gehölze, gut ausgebaute Wege und zwei Teiche laden zum Verweilen ein.

Öffnungszeiten der Ausstellung:
Montag + Donnerstag
09.00 – 13.00 Uhr
Dienstag + Mittwoch
09.00 – 16.00 Uhr
Samstag
13.00 – 16.00 Uhr

Nature and Hunting Exhibition at Leubnitz Castle

The castle built in early Classicist style in 1796 with its beautiful landscaped park in Leubnitz is a great outing for anyone who loves nature. An exhibition has been on display in eight rooms since 2000 with the aim of showing visitors how hunting and nature conservation go hand in hand. The room with the title "Experiencing Nature with All Your Senses" is particularly popular – and not just for children. People can acquire some knowledge about our local animals and plants at several points in an entertaining way. Since the spring of 2007, visitors have been able to enjoy the "Leubnitz peepshow" once a year when they watch the feathered residents of the castle nest and breed. Since the summer of 2007, there has been a model of the pond biotope and a board, on which you can arrange the birds found in the region in their natural habitat using magnets. Other rooms display hunting trophies from Spain, Siberia, Mongolia and North America and large antelopes and other animals from Africa and Australia. The whole presentation is combined with a picture gallery of well-known Vogtland animal painters. Classical concerts are held in the "White Room" at the castle. The castle is surrounded by a landscaped garden measuring 12 hectares, which was designed in 1890. Woods mainly consisting of local trees, well marked footpaths and two ponds encourage people to enjoy the surroundings.

Opening times for the exhibition:
Mondays + Thursdays
9 a.m. – 1 p.m.
Tuesdays + Wednesdays
9 a.m. – 4 p.m.
Saturdays
1 p.m. – 4 p.m.

(Fotos/Photos by B. Kempe-Winkelmann, Text/Text by B. Kempe-Winkelmann, Übersetzung/Translated by David Strauss)

Müllerburschenweg von Mühle zu Mühle
Miller's Apprentice Path from Mill to Mill

Wanderweg im Vogtländischen Mühlenviertel

In der Wanderregion Vogtland gehört der Müllerburschenweg zu den jüngsten. Natürlich konnte man die Routen schon immer unter die Füße nehmen, aber 2006 hat Heike Preuß vom Fremdenverkehrsverein Rosenbach im „Vogtländischen Mühlenviertel" den Namen kreiert, die Geschichten der Mühlen aufgeschrieben, Flyer herausgebracht. Wer es wissen möchte, erfährt nun, dass der Müllerburschenweg etwa 50 Kilometer lang ist und im nordwestlichen Teil des Vogtlandkreises verläuft, nämlich im „Vogtländischen Mühlenviertel". Dort, um die Orte Leubnitz, Syrau, Pausa, Mühltroff und Mehltheuer, standen einst viele Mühlen, größtenteils Wassermühlen, aber auch einige Windmühlen. Wenige sind erhalten geblieben, werden heute anderweitig genutzt oder sind liebevoll restauriert und zu Gaststätten oder Museen umgebaut worden.

Natürlich kann man vom Müllerburschenweg auch nur Teilabschnitte bewältigen. Wo man beginnt, ist egal. Ob man in Mühltroff startet oder in Pausa, in Syrau oder in Rodau, man trifft auf erhalten gebliebene Mühlen und auf Spuren des einst so regen Gewerbes – der Müllerei. Ziele sind die Lippoldsmühle, die Wallengrüner Mühle, die Zebaothsmühle, Oertelsmühle, der Standort der abgerissenen Stadtmühle Pausa, die Hasenmühle und die Reste der Oberpirker Windmühle, die wohl bekannteste Syrauer Windmühle und die heutige Gaststätte Teichmühle, die Forstmühle, die Papiermühle (Connys Bauernstube), die Rößnitzer Mühle und die Gaststätte Weißmühle, Hahnmühle, Obermühle und Herrenmühle. Informationstafeln gibt es an allen Standorten. Im Flyer wird auf Öffnungszeiten von Einkehrstätten ebenso aufmerksam gemacht wie auf Möglichkeiten, ein Stück des Wegs mit Bahn oder Bus zurückzulegen.

Hiking Path in the Vogtland Mill Area

The Miller's Apprentice Path is one of the newest in the Vogtland hiking region. Of course, people have been able to walk here for centuries, but it was only in 2006 that Heike Preuss from the Rosenbach tourist association in the "Vogtland Mill District" created the path's name, wrote down the stories of the mills and published leaflets about it. For those who would like to know, the Miller's Apprentice Path is about 50 kilometres long and passes through the "Vogtland Mill District" in the north-west of the Vogtland rural district. There were once many mills here, most of them water-mills, but there are a few windmills too near Leubnitz, Syrau, Pausa, Mühltroff and Mehltheuer. Some of them have been preserved but are used for other purposes nowadays or have been lovingly restored and turned into restaurants or museums.

Of course, people can also just cover individual sections of the Miller's Apprentice Path. It is irrelevant where you start. Regardless of where you set off – in Mühltroff or Pausa, in Syrau or Rodau – you will find preserved mills and traces of a business that was once so important here – the milling industry. You can walk to Lippoldsmühle, Wallengrün mill, Zebaothsmühle, Oertelsmühle, the site of where the town mill was demolished in Pausa, the Hasenmühle and the remains of the Oberpirk windmill, the Syrau windmill – probably the best known – or the Teichmühle restaurant, the Forstmühle, the Papiermühle (Connys Bauernstube), the Rössnitz mill or the Weissmühle restaurant, the Hahnmühle, Obermühle or Herrenmühle. There are information boards at all the mill sites. Leaflets describe when eating places are open or inform people how they can cover part of the path by train or by bus.

(Fotos/Photos by Gemeinde Syrau, Text/Text by B. Kempe-Winkelmann, Übersetzung/Translated by David Strauss)

Impressum/Imprint

Das Beste aus dem Vogtland Band II
Leistung trifft auf Leidenschaft
The Very Best of Vogtland Volume II
Performance meets Passion

Herausgeber/Published by

Realisation/Production
Dieses Projekt wurde realisiert unter Mitarbeit des Landratsamtes des Vogtlandkreises, zahlreicher Autoren, Stadt- und Gemeindeverwaltungen des Vogtlandes, Vereinen, Verbänden und portraitierten Unternehmen./This project has been produced with the help of the District Administrator's Office of the Vogtland district, many authors, town and village local government offices in the Vogtland region, clubs, associations and the companies, which have been featured.

Bildnachweis/Picture credits
benannte Bildautoren, portraitierte Unternehmen, Städte und Gemeindeverwaltungen, Vereine und Verbände
Named sources, featured companies, town and village local government offices, clubs and associations
Fotos Titelseite/Photos on the title page by:
Igor Pastierovic [6], Harald Sulski [3]

Übersetzungen/Translated by
David Strauss, M.,A., englischer Muttersprachler und öffentlich bestellter und allgemein beeidigter Übersetzer für die englische Sprache;
portraitierte Unternehmen/Overall production responsibility

Gesamtherstellung/Collect-run Production
briese © vogtlandwerbung Inh. Hartmut Briese
Grünbacher Straße 12, D-08223 Falkenstein
Telefon +49 (0) 3745 71727, Telefax +49 (0) 3745 751239
www.briesewerbung.de

Druck/Printers by
Süddruck Neumann GmbH & Co. KG, Plauen
Druck im November 2007

Vervielfältigung und Nachdruck/Reproduction and reprints
Alle Rechte vorbehalten. **briese © vogtlandwerbung**
Kein Teil des Buches darf ohne die schriftliche Genehmigung der Vogtlandwerbung Briese vervielfältigt oder verarbeitet werden. Verstöße werden rechtlich verfolgt./All rights reserved. No part of this book may be duplicated or used in any other way without permission in writing from Vogtlandwerbung Briese. Any violations of this will be prosecuted in the courts.

Empfohlener Verkaufspreis 24,90 EUR

ISBN 978-3-00-022807-0

Mit freundlicher Unterstützung der Sparkasse Vogtland